COMPARATIVE
ORGANIZATIONS

COMPARATIVE
ORGANIZATIONS

the results
of empirical research

edited by
WOLF V. HEYDEBRAND
Washington University

PRENTICE-HALL, INC., ENGLEWOOD CLIFFS, NEW JERSEY

Library of Congress Cataloging in Publication Data

HEYDEBRAND, WOLF V.   comp.
   Comparative organizations.

   Includes bibliographical references.
1. Organization—Addresses, essays, lectures.
2. Management—Addresses, essays, lectures.
I. Title
HM131.H45   338.7'08   72-7321
ISBN   0-13-153932-9

10 9 8 7 6 5 4 3 2 1

PRINTED IN THE UNITED STATES OF AMERICA

Prentice-Hall International, Inc., London
Prentice-Hall of Australia, Pty. Ltd., Sydney
Prentice-Hall of Canada, Ltd., Toronto
Prentice-Hall of India Private Limited, New Delhi
Prentice-Hall of Japan, Inc., Tokyo

CONTENTS

PREFACE

The idea for this book emerged from my courses and seminars on comparative organizational research and from the frustration of teaching "comparative organizations" without an adequate text or reader. There are, of course, many summary analytic discussions of *the comparative study of organizations,* such as those by Peter Blau, Tom Burns, Amitai Etzioni, Henry Landsberger, Charles Perrow, and Stanley Udy.[1] But these discussions tend to be in the context of conceptual schemes in which the relevant empirical work is either simply reviewed or where it remains implicit. There are also numerous texts and readers on organizations, some of which claim to have a "comparative" approach or perspective. Indeed, comparative analysis is now almost a *sine qua non* of empirical and theoretical work on organizations. Yet there is, to my knowledge, not a single collection of *comparative studies of organizations* in which empirical comparative analysis is itself the *criterion of selection.* In many current and previous readers, field research, laboratory experiments, quantitative studies, and case-studies of organizations are simply juxtaposed, but the actual comparative task is left to the reader, frequently with no analytic guidance as to how such comparisons can be done. Moreover, the typical textbook-reader, in an attempt to satisfy a wide variety of didactic and intellectual needs, includes the usual assortment of selections from Weber, Barnard, and Parsons without making judgments as to the empirical utility of such an eclectic pluralism.

It is one of the main points of this book to avoid theoretical pluralism, to use a significant methodological principle—comparative analysis—as the main

[1] Peter M. Blau, "The comparative study of organizations," *Industrial and Labor Relations Review,* 18, 1965:323–38; T. Burns, "The comparative study of organizations," in V. H. Vroom, ed., *Methods of Organizational Research* (Pittsburgh: University of Pittsburgh Press, 1967), pp. 113–70; Amitai Etzioni, *A Comparative Analysis of Complex Organizations* (Glencoe: Free Press, 1961); Henry Landsberger," A Framework for the Cross-cultural Analysis of Formal Organizations," in Henry A. Landsberger, ed., *Comparative Perspectives on Formal Organizations,* (Boston: Little, Brown and Co., 1970) pp. 1–16; Charles Perrow, "A Framework for the Comparative Analysis of Organizations," *American Sociological Review,* 32 (April 1967), 194–208; and Stanley H. Udy, Jr., "The comparative analysis of organizations," in J. G. March, ed., *Handbook of Organizations* (Chicago: Rand McNally, 1964), pp. 678–709.

criterion of selection, and to provide a reasonably comprehensive and unified conceptual framework within which empirical studies can be logically and meaningfully located (see Chart I). It is no accident, therefore, that there is a high degree of conceptual, terminological interrelation and of theoretical continuity among the studies included here even though they deal with many different types of organizations and were written by authors with widely different backgrounds.

The theoretical continuity of these studies is important for another reason. There has been much talk of *interorganizational analysis* as distinct from *intraorganizational analysis* as if we were dealing with two separate disciplines. The relevant studies included here, and the basic conceptual dimensions they share, should easily dispel the notion that inter- and intra-organizational analysis are fundamentally different approaches to the study of organizations. Obviously, studies may differ in their relative emphasis on external as over against internal organizational parameters, as is demonstrated by some of the work represented in this book. But—as is equally well demonstrated—a large number of studies use intra- and interorganizational analysis within a holistic framework, transcending the questions of boundaries, linkages, and interdependence, and working with images of organizations as both products and producers of external social change. Thus, the *psychology* and *social psychology of organizations* —the study of their internal structure and their interaction with each other— is increasingly augmented by a *sociology of organizations*—the study of chains, networks, and systems of organizations.

Studying the development and structure of such multiorganizational systems —within the framework of a genetic or *historical structuralism*, as it were— means to treat organizational and interorganizational processes as integral parts of the political economy and of the totality of cultural and macro-social phenomena. Clearly, if organizational boundaries become elements—rather than limits—of organizational analysis, it then becomes also somewhat artificial to quibble over the disciplinary boundaries of that analysis which has, in any case, straddled a wide variety of academic and practical fields.

Four of the studies included here have not been previously published. They deal with universities (Boland), hospitals (Heydebrand), private welfare agencies (Heydebrand and Noell), and interprofessional relationships in state and local public health and mental health agencies (Kriesberg). Other studies deal with various types of business organizations, professional organizations (including hospitals, accounting firms, and public personnel agencies), governmental units (such as finance and employment departments and divisions), and voluntary associations. In sum, I hope that besides the methodological and theoretical aspects of this book, the contribution of all of the individual studies to the substantive and practical understanding of specific types of modern organizations will be enhanced.

WOLF HEYDEBRAND

ACKNOWLEDGEMENTS

There are always many people who, in a direct or indirect way, influence one's intellectual career. The development of my own interest in organizations is no exception. It would be impossible to acknowledge adequately my debt to friends, students, colleagues, and teachers. However, for their particular efforts that contributed to the making of this volume, I want to thank Alvin Gouldner, Jay Noell, Margaret Park, John Richards, Neil Smelser, and especially Al Lesure of Prentice-Hall. A special note of thanks is also due to the graduate students who have participated in my Seminar on Comparative Organizational Analysis at Washington University. I gratefully acknowledge the support provided by the Medical Care Research Center, and its Executive Director, Rodney Coe.

Finally, I want to thank Isabel Blase for helping with the preparation of the manuscript, and David Carpenter, former chairman of the Department of Sociology at Washington University, for generously providing two indispensable ingredients of scholarly work: time and peace.

COMPARATIVE
ORGANIZATIONS

GENERAL INTRODUCTION

This book represents the first inventory of a relatively recent tradition of research: the systematic, quantitative-comparative analysis of large-scale, complex, formal organizations. The unique common feature of the empirical studies brought together here lies in their comparative character which permits the exploration and analysis of several organizational dimensions at once. These studies, therefore, represent a significant step beyond the case-study approach in which comparisons are typically either internal or implicit, or altogether absent. Theoretically, the studies are unified by their focus on a set of basic, general characteristics of organizations, and on the patterns of relationships among these characteristics. In addition, each study contributes to the substantive understanding of modern organizations, based on empirical research rather than on mere conceptual analysis or the exposition of principles of organizations.

The book is, then, intended as a contribution to the substantive knowledge about organizations, to the methodology of organizational analysis, and to the advancement of organizational theory. Taken together, these three intended contributions provide the criteria of selection of the studies, and constitute a significant departure from previous and current treatments of the subject of organizations and bureaucracy. Let me briefly spell out the implications of these claims.

First, the studies brought together here seek to say something about organizations as substantive phenomena in their own right, rather than using organizations as contexts and environments for the behavior of groups or individuals. Moreover, the studies deal with organizations as natural, historically concrete units rather than as products of ad hoc experimentation and of the laboratory.

With few exceptions, the studies are based on organizations as the unit of analysis; in some studies, departments or subunits are used as "cases"; in others, the unit is a supra-organizational structure, an interorganizational network, an association of organizations (a "roof" organization), an industry or a conglomerate. In those studies in which aggregate data on organizations are used, e.g., with industries as the unit of analysis, inferences about organizational structure are based on the analysis of structural relationships and patterns regardless of the unit under investigation.

Second, the studies collected here illustrate a method of organizational analysis which seeks to produce explanations of structural differences among organizations on the basis of quantitative comparisons. The comparative method itself is, of course, well-established; what is new is the application of the method to rather complex phenomena, and the possibility of comparing widely divergent organizational patterns and thousands of concrete organizations in such a way as to make meaningful statements about their similarities and differences. The major thrust of this methodology is toward generating empirical and ultimately theoretical generalizations about organizational structures and their environments, rather than describing cases or developing typologies. This is not to disparage the contributions of case studies to organizational analysis and to the conceptualization and exploration of important organizational dimensions. But the method of quantitative comparisons addresses itself to a different order of phenomena, namely classes, species, groups, and systems of organizations, rather than specific types and cases. It is in this sense that the expansion of the scope and application of quantitative comparisons constitutes a breakthrough not only *qua* methodology, but as a crucial vehicle for further theoretical development.

Third, it is this element of theoretical development which is perhaps the most significant aspect of the studies selected for this volume, and one that is designed to put into perspective such notions as "organizational revolution" and "organizational society."[1] Weber's ideal-type construct of legal-rational bureaucracy, the classical and neoclassical organization theorists, systems theory, and even "modern organization theory"—all of these theoretical perspectives are rich in suggestive leads but somewhat underdeveloped in terms of a hard empirical basis. Textbooks and readers on organizations tend to give a well-rounded, pluralistic view of organization theories, emphasizing the need for integration and synthesis, but in the end fail to integrate data, method, and theory into a coherent, meaningful whole. Unless social scientists deny the existence of an objective organizational reality which increasingly determines our lives and therefore must be understood and transcended, they must constantly seek to overthrow particularistic perspectives in the interest of more comprehensive and universalistic ones. If organization theory is to develop a "paradigm" it must begin to relate organizational research and theory, as well as theory and organizational practice.[2]

While this book does not provide such a unified theoretical framework, its

[1] Kenneth Boulding, *The Organizational Revolution* (New York: Harper & Row, 1953); R. V. Presthus, *The Organizational Society* (New York: Knopf, 1962).
[2] Thomas S. Kuhn, *The Structure of Scientific Revolutions* (Chicago: University of Chicago Press, 1962).

organizing principle—namely, to understand the dynamics of structural variation and change—is based on the assumption that theoretical development and systematic empirical research are interdependent. A naive empiricist, purely inductive, or "grounded" approach to complex phenomena such as organizations is ultimately just as powerless to "explain" as is a highly abstract, axiomatic-conceptual scheme from which certain invariant processes are deduced and then categorically "applied" to concrete cases so as to "account," after the fact, for differences and variations among them. Significant theoretical development is dependent on the possibility of generalizations, and generalizations must ultimately be grounded in systematic comparisons, however simple the comparative process may be. The conceptual overlap among organizational-theoretical perspectives is already great and is increasing, as this book demonstrates. It is hoped that the results of research brought together here will provide further impetus to theoretical development in organizational studies.

WHAT KINDS OF ORGANIZATIONS?

Selections such as this one necessarily deal with studies of specific types of organizations. The range of functional types—business, government, voluntary, professional—included here is therefore not exhaustive of the universe of organizations. But the range of variation of functional types is much broader than that of structural patterns. The extent of structural variation, in turn, is greater than the range of definitions of what an organization is and what its boundaries are. While a number of studies focus on the variation among functional types, the majority of studies are concerned with the nature and extent of structural variation within functional types.

Both kinds of comparisons—those between different types and those within a given type—have characteristic advantages and disadvantages. An analysis dealing with one type of organization—e.g., hospitals—is implicitly limited to the "case" of hospitals. Such an analysis represents a methodological "retrogression" to the case study since it can generalize only to one type, viz., hospitals. But it has the advantage of dealing with a fairly well-defined, functionally homogeneous universe for which a number of assumptions can be held in common and for which many extraneous or "error" variables can be considered constant. Moreover, the lack of functional variety can be offset by systematically controlling for basic general dimensions of organizations—e.g., size or complexity—within the functional type, especially when the number of cases is large.

On the other hand, an analysis involving many different types of organizations simultaneously—e.g., business organizations, government agencies, hospitals, welfare agencies, and voluntary associations—can deal with the question of structural variation across functional types in a more general way. Nevertheless, the distinction between functional types still does not solve the problem of generalizations on the basis of theoretically relevant categories and dimensions. Thus, although dealing with a greater range of types, it is still necessary to articulate or hold constant those organizational parameters which distinguish between types, should structural variation be observed. The ideal lies, of course, in the use of both within-group and between-group analysis by using an adequate number of cases for each. Since this book focuses on structural variation among organizations, the question of functional types and of boundaries is somewhat subordinated to the question of structure. The sections of this book are organized according to the structural problems dealt with in the different studies. Thus, different functional types will be the subject matter of studies appearing in the same sections because the respective studies illustrate similar structural problems and variables. While the majority of studies focuses on a comparative analysis based on the variation within functional types, some studies include a wide range of functional types.

The definition of "organization" used here is that of a concrete social structure formally established (incorporated, chartered) for the purpose of achieving specific objectives. This definition is intended to distinguish organizations from other concrete social structures which have grown informally, "naturally," and in an unplanned manner such as a gang, a community, or a historically developed nation-state. Clearly, insofar as such structures are established, planned, chartered, or enacted, they may be viewed as "organizations."

The definition used here also distinguishes an organization from an "institution," a term which technically refers to a sociocultural complex of norms, roles, and behavior patterns, but which is often used synonymously with organization. For example, schools are sometimes referred to as educational institutions, jails as correctional institutions, psychiatric hospitals as mental institutions. In order not to confuse normative patterns of behavior and concrete social structures, I have tried to avoid the term "institution" as much as possible.

As to the question of the boundaries of an organization, an attempt was made to select only studies which deal with relatively clearly delimited, independently established organizations, the prototype of which is probably the business organization, or the hospital. Some studies, however, deal either with departments or other kinds of subunits of independently established organizations (e.g., departments of state governments). Still others use aggregate census data on industries to make inferences about organizational structure. The criterion of using only studies involving autonomous organizations as the unit of analysis has therefore not been followed rigorously because the latter types of studies deal with important structural dimensions whose interrelations and effects can be generalized to the actual organizations constituting the basic units for data collection.

The distribution of functional types in these studies represents both the preponderance of certain types of research on organizations as well as my own interests and biases. The following are the broad areas covered by the thirty selections:

FUNCTIONAL TYPE USED	NUMBER OF STUDIES
One Functional Type Used	25
Business organizations	8
Professional & Service (Total)	11
Health	(4)
Welfare	(3)
Education	(2)
Accounting & Public Personnel	(2)
Governmental organizations	2
Voluntary associations	4
Several Functional Types Used	5

No typology is intended by classifying organizations in terms of these four broad areas, although it is probably not accidental that the criteria for assessing effectiveness, quality, and efficiency differ radically in each of the four major areas. Thus, productivity and profit are clearly of paramount importance in business organizations, while quality of service is the main concern of professional organizations. In voluntary associations, the quality of social interaction and of the interpersonal social and political climate is perhaps as important as the achievement of certain objectives and targets, while governmental organizations must define effectiveness in terms of political criteria, which may or may not include standards of technical quality.

There are as yet few studies, however, that use effectiveness or quality as their ultimate "dependent variable," i.e., as that aspect of the organization's activity that needs to be explained and evaluated.

THE PROBLEM OF METHOD

The multitude and diversity of organizational types, as indicated above, raises questions of comparability. This includes the question of the possibility as well as the wisdom of even attempting to compare different organizations to each other, or comparing them with a more or less abstract definition or model.

Various approaches to this problem are possible. The case historians occupy one extreme, where each case is seen as a separate, complex, unique phenomenon that does not permit comparisons and generalizations. Much of the "inside view" perspective of early ethnography and the emphasis on "natural logic" and "common sense" in ethnomethodology and phenomenology seem to exemplify this approach.[3]

Closely related in their position are the ideal-type constructionists who are

---

[3] Robert Redfield, *The Little Community* (Chicago: University of Chicago Press, 1957); Benjamin L. Whorf, "Science and Linguistics," *In* Theodore M. Newcomb and Eugene Hartley (eds.), *Readings in Social Psychology* (New York: Holt Rinehart & Winston, 1947), pp. 210–18; Maurice Natanson (ed.), *Philosophy of the Social Sciences* (New York: Random House, 1963).

interested in generating type-cases by conceptualizing certain salient characteristics of their cases in terms of more analytical dimensions. By putting these dimensions together into a more or less complex property-space, they are able to construct models of a fairly complex nature. Such models do not correspond to one specific organizational reality, but they represent a whole range of "similar," hence comparable, realities: the ideal-type.

The ideal-type method is uniquely suited to grasp complex social phenomena and makes them amenable to "understanding" and even to simple forms of measurement. Yet, as a method it remains essentially a device for "intellectual comparisons," for conceptual rather than empirical testing, and for the establishment of comparative histories and etiologies. Weber's historical and structural conception of bureaucracy is, of course, the classical example.

The other extreme of approaching the complexity of modern organizations consists in reducing complexity and variation to a few, general, a priori categories of analysis. A favorite method here is the identification and definition of organizations in terms of system characteristics, e.g., basic input-output processes, adaptation, homeostasis, negative feedback, integration, and goal attainment. Since broad analytical schemes such as system models are by definition applicable to almost all "cases," they tend to lose some of their explanatory power. Such general schemes of analytical variables may result from the search for "functions" and their corresponding "structures" or institutional forms, or from the general treatment of organizations as social systems characterized by a dominant orientation toward the attainment of specific goals.[4]

One may, of course, compare social units in terms of general analogies such as stages of development or levels of institutionalization, as, for example, in Parsons's recurrent analytical distinction between technical, managerial, and institutional levels in all organizations.[5] In this approach, structure is reified and fixed, and only the functions and goals are held to vary slightly, as, e.g., among the four basic system problems of adaptation, goal attainment, integration, and pattern maintenance. The comparison is, therefore, already built into the very application of the scheme, and tends to miss genuine differences, distinctive historical developments, and the whole question of organizational transformation and change. Rather than providing a crucial method of a causal explanation of the differences between organizational structures, it locates them in a conceptual property-space. Differences are accounted for by differences in definition, not explained by empirically testable propositions.

The result of using comparisons as an analytical, taxonomic procedure is that the application of a general conceptual scheme always reflects the same social and organizational reality to which the concepts have reference, espe-

---

[4] Walter Goldschmidt, *Comparative Functionalism* (Berkeley: University of California Press, 1966), pp. 57–117; Talcott Parsons, *Structure and Process in Modern Societies* (New York: Free Press, 1960), pp. 16–96.
[5] Parsons, *Structure and Process.*

cially when they are defined on a very high level of abstraction. The conceptual model thus has the same meaning from one comparative case to another. While the model has a high degree of generality and scope and thus encompasses virtually all "cases," it tends to lose the power to explain variation and change. Change itself is often redefined in terms of "recurrent changes," i.e., in terms of process. Organizational reality becomes a set of constants. One way of dealing with organizational constants, in turn, is in terms of "principles of organization."[6]

What are the criteria for establishing a methodological bridge between the case study and the system model? In the first place, it would be necessary to define a set of empirically given organizations on the basis of various attributes "relevant" to the investigator and his theoretical perspective. Second, these attributes should be conceptually precise and specific, but empirically variable. In other words, the attributes—as variables—should be capable of distinguishing between differences in concrete instances, i.e., between organizations. Yet as part of the overall conceptual and theoretical framework, they must also be capable of explaining these differences. This is, of course, nothing more or less than elementary "scientific method." However, an important option of this method is its relative "openness" in finding a solution to the two problems of explanation: ex post facto accounting, and tautology. A wide open approach, if it is more than description, usually tries "to make sense" of the findings once they are reported. In contrast, a "closed" scientific system imposed on reality involves analytical variables which, in the case of extreme operationalism, identifies the system of analysis with the object of analysis, resulting in the renowned "objectification" and "demystification" of the world.

In sum, a flexible approach to organizational analysis must retain the *power to encompass* differences between concrete instances, yet also have the *power to explain* these differences, rather than "accounting" for them after the fact. Essentially, then, such an approach must resolve the fundamental contradiction in all scientific endeavor between theoretical scope (the problem of generality) and conceptual-operational precision (the problem of testability).[7]

---

[6] See, e.g., Herbert Simon's critique of the "principles of administration" in his *Administrative Behavior* (New York: Macmillan, 2nd ed., 1957), pp. 20–44.

[7] Johan Galtung, *Theory and Methods of Social Research* (New York: Columbia University Press, 1967), pp. 315–39, 458–65. It is instructive, in the context of this discussion of comparative analysis, to recall the methodological self-consciousness and even agony that characterized Marx's attempt to present his exceedingly complex subject matter in a reasonably palatable, yet scientifically adequate form. In considering how to proceed from the concrete historical given to simplified, but abstract conceptions, and from there back to an integral whole "as a rich aggregate of many conceptions and relations," Marx writes: "The concrete is concrete, because it is a combination of many objects with different destinations, i.e., a unity of diverse elements. In our thought it therefore appears as a process of synthesis, as a result, and not as a starting point, although it is the real starting point and, therefore also the starting point of observation and conception." Karl Marx, *A Contribution to the Critique of Political Economy* (Chicago: Kerr, 1904), p. 293.

A comparative organizational analysis, then, that avoids the "Scylla" of confinement to historically unique cases and the "Charybdis" of general analytical schemes without explanatory content, appears to require three main elements or criteria: (1) a large number of separate, concrete organizational units in which (2) there is a significant amount of variation in the observed variables and which (3) contain theoretically significant and empirically measurable dimensions which can be said to explain the observed variation. As I have indicated elsewhere, this procedure essentially amounts to the quantification of the comparative method.[8] Having said all this, I must emphatically state a *caveat* concerning comparative analysis, in general, and quantitative comparisons, in particular.

THE "FETISHISM" OF COMPARISONS: A CRITICAL NOTE

It is perhaps no overstatement to say that everything "comparative" and "quantitative" has become quite fashionable in the social sciences today. In the hands of Marx, Weber, and Durkheim, the comparative method tended to have a holistic quality, even though it is true that the ideal type approach generates the comparisons of cases, but rarely of distributions.[9] Today, the comparative-quantitative concern reflects perhaps not only the influence of computer technology, but also a general reaction against the excessive emphasis on case studies, type cases, and qualitative typologies.[10]

However, the thrust of my *caveat* is not against ideal-type constructs or case studies, but the tendency for comparisons to become ends in themselves, to isolate the units to be compared from their sociohistorical context, and to generate an endless number of small-scale and middle-range theories which bypass, and frequently obscure, a view of the whole. Therefore, a fourth criterion for comparative organizational analysis needs to be stressed, in addition to the three criteria previously mentioned. If comparative analysis is to contribute to a theory of organizations, it must do so within the framework of a general—and perhaps critical—theory of society. This criterion requires that organizations be studied in their larger context, in relation to each other, in relation to the limits imposed on them by the characteristics of modern nation-states, and in relation to the international order, or world society.

The point can best be illustrated with reference to cross-national compari-

---

[8] Wolf Heydebrand, "The Study of Organizations," *Social Science Information*, 6 (Oct. 1967), 59–86, at p. 65.
[9] cf. John C. McKinney, *Constructive Typology and Social Theory* (New York: Appleton-Century-Crofts, 1966), pp. 20–34.
[10] cf. Richard L. Merritt and Stein Rokkan (eds.), *Comparing Nations: The Use of Quantitative Data in Cross-National Research* (New Haven: Yale University Press, 1966), especially the paper by Karl Deutsch, "The Theoretical Basis of Data Programs," pp. 27–56.

sons and to the self-imposed limitation of recent macrosociology, namely to focus on the nation-state rather than on world society.[11]

In the perspective of a world sociology, cross-national comparisons constitute a form of misplaced concreteness. The national units are relatively meaningless when seen in isolation; they become relevant in their interrelation with each other and with larger wholes such as regional, economic and political groupings, and ultimately, world society. Thus, what happens in the social and political boundaries of American society must ultimately be related to what happens in the rest of the world, unless we pretend that "understanding" can be achieved only by imposing certain theoretical cutting points on social reality. Clearly, the selective inattention of social theory seems to be a virtue from the point of view of a value free social science and of middle-range theories; but it is a vice from the perspective of the urgent need for comprehensive, more universalistic understanding and explanation. There are few social phenomena today that are not affected by the contemporary historical scene and by the "big" social, economic, and political variables which originate and operate at the national and international level.

What I have argued for the nation-state, then, I am arguing for organizations as more or less neatly packaged units of analysis. This is not only a question of "international" organizations as legitimate units of analysis, organizations that cut across national and political boundaries. It is the question whether and to what extent national and international policies in different institutional spheres affect and determine the organizational structures located in and emerging from these spheres. To what extent are hospitals, schools, and welfare agencies affected by the health, education, and welfare policies of their respective nation-states, and to what extent do these policies, in turn, reflect world-wide changes in the social, political, and economic structure of the advanced industrial nations, and in their relation to the rest of the world? To what extent do the armies of underdeveloped countries "modernize" in the light of models provided by those superpowers in whose political and military orbits they find themselves? To what extent are methods of business organization and management, indeed, methods of industrial development, diffused, exported, or imposed on primitive economies by the more developed ones? It seems that organizational models in every conceivable sector of society can be viewed as commodities which can be bought and sold, exported, imposed, and suppressed. Therefore, the assumption that organizations can be studied *in statu nascendi*, in isolated "natural" habitats, or as expressions of universal societal forces and processes must be radically questioned. While it is true that

---

[11] Wilbert Moore's proposal for a "global sociology" is an important step in the direction of what I have in mind, although he conceives of it more as a specialty within sociology rather than as a framework for studying world society as a specific historical phenomenon; see Wilbert Moore, "Global Sociology: The World as a Singular System," *American Journal of Sociology*, 71 (Mar. 1966), 475–82.

the thrust of scientific analysis is toward theoretical generalizations, it is also true that such generalizations must be historically informed.

There seem to be two reasons why the theoretical generalizations and the historical relatedness of organizational analysis need not contradict each other.

First, organizations constitute a special class of social structures with unusually well-defined boundaries. They are, therefore, also especially convenient and manageable as units of analysis. Their very structure facilitates analytical simplification; as abstractions, they respond easily to the social scientist's quest for pattern and order. Insofar as it is possible to "bracket," or hold constant, the larger contextual and historical influences on certain types of organizations at a certain point in time, they are ideally suited for the analysis of structural patterns, regularities, and uniformities.

Secondly, the comparative-quantitative study of organizations may be viewed as a necessary phase of development in the social sciences, linking the earlier focus on case studies and on the behavior of individuals-in-organizations with the emerging perspective on organizations as integral parts of larger wholes. Such larger environments may be interorganizational networks, community organizational systems, or the organizational structure of nation-states. Organizations thus may be viewed as structural and historical links in a chain of events which extends between the individual, on the one hand, and the world-society that appears to take shape, on the other.

In this sense, the development of organizational analysis is not unlike that which characterized the development of the social sciences, in general. This is especially true of the transition from psychology to social psychology and sociology, with the individual—rather than the organization—being the initial unit of analysis. Of course, much of social analysis today continues to view the individual as the crucial unit of analysis, a view that is essentially that of psychology. The emergence of the systematic analysis of interpersonal relations, social networks, and small groups led to the development of a social psychology, just as interorganizational analysis tends to focus on the "behavior" of organizations, and on the influence of the larger context on their orientation, action, creativity, adaptation, and survival.[12]

But a sociology of organizations must deal with the conditions of organizational formation, persistence, and transformation. It is the variability and continuity of organizational structures themselves that must now be explained. Such a perspective necessarily focuses not only on networks and systems of organizations, but on a wide variety of contextual variables and events which determine and structure organizational environments themselves and transform them into new units of analysis in their own right. It is at this point where organizational analysis, political sociology, economic sociology, and compara-

---

[12] Daniel Katz and Robert L. Kahn, *The Social Psychology of Organizations* (New York: John Wiley, 1966); James D. Thompson, *Organizations in Action*, (New York: McGraw-Hill, 1967); Gary Steiner, *The Creative Organization* (Chicago: University of Chicago Press, 1965).

tive historical analysis cease to be separate disciplines and merge into a larger, more comprehensive framework of analysis.

In order to articulate the direction in which I believe an informed comparative perspective might lead, I have organized the studies selected here in terms of their emphasis on the relation between organization and the larger context, starting out with a focus on environmental complexity, autonomy, and change, and concluding with studies of the internal structure of organizations. The variables and dimensions used for this purpose do not, at this point, constitute a coherent system of organizational analysis. But taken together, they provide a link between the internal structure and the external environment of organizations, and in that sense serve to mediate between the various levels of a multi-dimensional theoretical universe. It is to the exposition and discussion of these major dimensions that I want to turn to next.

BASIC DIMENSIONS OF ORGANIZATIONAL ANALYSIS

While developing a common language and a conceptual framework for the comparative analysis of organizations, I have found it useful to distinguish among several clusters of variables. These clusters also serve, in a rough way, to organize the studies selected for this volume around common themes.

The first cluster deals with the nature and complexity of the organizational environment and with the problem of organizational autonomy. A second set of variables is related to the organizational goal and task structure, a complex sometimes referred to as "charter." In the current framework, this set of variables includes the number and diversity of major objectives, geographical dispersion, the variability of tasks, and organizational size as well as the dimensions of effectiveness and change. A third set of variables deals with the internal structural differentiation of organizations, that is, internal division of labor, technological complexity, and skill structure. Finally, there is a cluster of variables which refers to the dimensions of organizational coordination and control. Of particular theoretical and practical interest in modern organizations are the nonbureaucratic modes of coordination, such as professionalization, in addition to those involving bureaucratic forms of administration and decision making.

These four major clusters, environment and autonomy, goal and task structure, division of labor, and coordination constitute a framework within which the broad, external variables may be seen as progressively determining the more internal structural characteristics of organizations. This progressive influence on internal by external variables is not to be understood as a simple causal chain, but rather as a network of paths connecting the internal clusters and blocks of variables to those characterizing the larger organizational context. It should be obvious from the start that these clusters of variables are in reality closely interconnected, even though some of them constitute conceptually relatively homogeneous blocks, e.g., the task structure variables, or technology and division of labor, or the modes of coordination. Indeed, it is the *relations* between these clusters of variables that provide a framework for the formulation of hypotheses and the analysis of causal relationships.

Thus, while the conceptual framework itself suggests a number of analytical distinctions, most of the studies actually cut across the major clusters and examine certain empirical relationships between them. Moreover, the causal assumptions underlying organizational analysis must not be confused with the broader theoretical concern of what organizations do and how they do it. Thus, the causal imagery of external variables determining internal ones should not obscure the equally important imagery of "organizations in action," i.e., of what organizations do, how they achieve their goals and tasks, and what effect they have on their environment.

In order to present an overall view of how and to what extent the various studies deal with the external-internal continuum, I have matched the studies and the variables they use in the form of a matrix. Chart I provides such an overview of these studies in terms of twenty-four variables.[13] This matrix may serve as a rough guide to the theoretical concerns and the relative emphasis of each of the studies. It also provides an index of the concepts and variables common to different types of studies, the degree of overlap between them, and the distribution of variables among them. In the following, I will briefly define the variables involved, discuss their demonstrated or potential usefulness in a comparative approach to the study of organizations, and suggest how an analysis of the empirical interrelations may contribute to a theory of organizations.

ORGANIZATIONAL ENVIRONMENT AND AUTONOMY

As indicated above, the first major cluster of variables focuses on the interaction between organization and environment. This cluster includes therefore the degree of complexity of the organizational environment, organizational age, and the question of the nature and extent of organizational autonomy.

Complexity of the Organizational Environment. The characteristics of an organization's environment constitute, at the same time, contextual attributes of the organization itself. Such attributes typically have a twofold conceptual status. As characteristics of a given environment, they *define* its relevant

---

[13] The first selection in this volume (Heydebrand) is excluded from the chart since it is a programmatic essay rather than an empirical study. The first two rows of the chart show the number of units used by each study, as well as the number of variables. However, the number of variables indicated does not in all cases correspond to those shown in the chart. The reason is that some studies use multiple indicators for the same variable, or that a given author distinguishes between different aspects of a given variable. In all these cases, an entry was made in the last column labeled "Other."

CHART 1. CROSS-TABULATION OF 24 ORGANIZATIONAL VARIABLES AND 29 EMPIRICAL STUDIES

Variable	2. Pugh, Hickson, Hinings, Turner	3. Udy	4. Dill	5. Fouraker and Stopford	6. Elling and Halebsky	7. Heydebrand	8. Simpson and Gulley	9. Kriesberg (1)	10. Litwak and Hylton	11. Kriesberg (2)	12. Aiken and Hage	13. Heydebrand and Noell	14. Liebetson and Allen	15. Tsouderos	16. McWhinney	17. Kochen and Deutsch	18. Terrien and Mills	19. Anderson and Warkov	20. Rushing	21. Pondy	22. Boland	23. Pugh, Hickson, Hinings, Turner	24. Stinchcombe	25. Hall	26. Indik	27. Blau, Heydebrand, Stauffer	28. Montagna	29. Blau	30. Bell
Number of Units or Cases	15	30	2	170	126	6825	211	1470	2	123	16	122	6341	10	150	1	428	49	41	45	115	52	13	27	116	156	12	254	30
Number of Variables	15	7	6	10	6	10	7	9	4	7	11	7	4	6	6	6	2	3	5	5	6	11	5	8	2	6	5	8	5
1. Environment: Aggregate Characteristics	X	X	X	X	X	X	X	X	X	X		X	X																
2. Environment: Relational and Structural Characteristics	X	X	X		X										X														
3. Organizational Age	X			X	X			X	X	X	X																		
4. Legal and Political Autonomy	X	X	X	X	X	X	X		X	X	X	X	X	X										X					
5. Functional and Economic Autonomy	X	X	X	X	X	X				X	X	X																	
6. Diversity of Objectives	X	X		X		X	X						X																
7. Number of Objectives	X										X		X					X		X		X							
8. Geographical Dispersion	X																												X
9. Variability of Tasks	X		X			X	X	X			X																		
10. Organizational Size (T=Task, R=Resourc., P=Pers., M=Memb.)	P			R	T	P,T	M	M,P			X	P	P	M	M,P	T	T	T	P	P	P,T	P	P		P,M	P	P	P	
11. Organizational Change				X											X	X													
12. Organizational Effectiveness					X	X	X				X	X		X	X	X			X	X	X	X		X		X			
13. Functional Specialization	X	X		X	X	X	X			X	X	X										X		X				X	
14. Departmental Specialization		X		X	X	X	X		X		X											X						X	
15. Technological Complexity	X					X		X			X	X										X							
16. Skill Structure, Professionalization	X	X	X			X	X	X		X	X	X	X	X					X		X	X	X	X	X	X	X	X	X
17. Committees							X	X																					
18. Incentives (M=Material, S=Social, N=Normative)		M					M,S,N																						
19. Formalization, Written Rules	X	X	X	X	X	X	X		X	X	X	X	X	X	X						X	X	X	X	X	X	X	X	
20. Hierarchical Levels	X					X					X				X		C					X		X	X	X	X	X	
21. Span of Control; Manager Ratios		X				X	X	X	X										X		X							X	X
22. Administrative Staff and Communic. (C=Clerical; S=C+other)		X				S	X				S	S		S	S		C	S	C,S'	S		C	C			C	C	X	X
23. Decision making	X	X	X				X		X												X	C	X		X	X	X	X	X
24. Other				X							X	X		X		X								X					X

dimensions from the point of view of one constituent element: the organization or class of organizations under study. In particular, organizations in the same general category may constitute part of the environment for each other.

But as contextual variables, environmental characteristics also imply a causal relationship between organization and environment. For example, communities and their characteristics may constitute an organizational environment for a certain class of organizations, such as colleges. For these colleges, the characteristics of the communities constitute contextual variables, including, for example, the size and demographic composition of the community, its economic profile and vitality, its political structure and its cultural "atmosphere." Moreover, a particularly important contextual variable would be the number of other colleges in each community since that simple fact can be assumed to influence competition and exchange in the local academic marketplace, the quality and supply of faculty and students, the availability and distribution of financial resources, and styles of educational organization and administration.[14]

Of course, the environmental unit may not only be communities, but states, regions, nation-states, as well as "networks" of organizations such as markets, community welfare systems, "roof" organizations, and conglomerates.

In sum, there appear to be two general elements in the complexity of the organizational environment: first, the differentiation and heterogeneity of its *aggregate* characteristics, e.g., degree of industrial diversification, or different types and degrees of social differentiation and stratification, such as median educational attainment, percentage of white collar of the labor force, percentage in manufacturing, median family income, ethnic and religious differentiation.

The second general element in the complexity of the organizational environment is the number of other (similar or dissimilar) organizations with whom a given organization can potentially interact. This second *relational* characteristic leads to the consideration of the next two variables in this cluster, namely, organizational age and organizational autonomy.

Organizational Age. One may consider the age of an organization as a variable specifying organization-environment relationships. Aside from the possible association between age and size, or growth, as well as the various possible

---

[14] See, e.g., Warren Bennis, "The Effect on Academic Goods of Their Market," *In* James D. Thomson et al., (eds.), *Comparative Studies in Administration* (Pittsburgh: University of Pittsburgh Press, 1959), pp. 71–79; for a description of external effects in the case of hospitals, see Ivan Belknap and John G. Steinle, *The Community and its Hospitals* (Syracuse: Syracuse University Press, 1963); also Paul R. Lawrence and Jay W. Lorsch, *Organization and Environment: Managing Differentiation and Integration* (Cambridge: Harvard University Press, 1967); James D. Thompson, *Organizations in Action.* For useful recent reviews and codifications of the relevant literature, see Shirley Terreberry, "The Evolution of Organizational Environments," *Administrative Science Quarterly,* 12 (Mar. 1968), 590–613, and Roland L. Warren, "The Interorganizational Field as a Focus for Investigation," *Administrative Science Quarterly,* 12 (Dec. 1967), 396–419.

stages of organizational development, age is also relevant in a broader ecological sense. Thus, when considering a given class of organizations such as certain kinds of industrial enterprises, welfare organizations, or voluntary associations, age is an indicator of when and where, in a given environmental context of existing organizations, a new organization enters the stage.[15]

Presumably, older organizations are internally more differentiated and complex than younger ones; older ones should be more stable and have firmer roots in the external environment, especially since they are surviving compared to organizations which dropped out of the life cycle at an earlier point, and are therefore typically excluded from the comparison. On the whole, organizational age—apart from specific historical determinants—can be seen as an intervening variable which helps to determine the external conditions surrounding organizational change.

Organizational Autonomy. There are at least two ways in which it is useful to conceptualize the nature of organizational autonomy. First, there is the legal status and political independence of an organization, usually associated with ownership and control. Second, there is the functional autonomy and economic independence of an organization, usually associated with its financial resources and its functional position within the division of labor among organizations,[16] its relative dominance or dependence within a market system of suppliers and customers, its salience and influence within a service system comprising clients, professionally defined quality standards, and public policies, or simply its relative numerical weight within the aggregate of other similar organizations, i.e., whether the organization is the only one of its kind or whether it is one out of two, ten, fifty, or a thousand.[17]

One may view the legal-political aspect as the normative, de jure, upward or vertical dimension of the concept of autonomy, and the functional-economic aspect as its relational, de facto, or horizontal dimension.

While the empirical and dynamic relation between these two aspects of organizational autonomy is of deep theoretical and political interest, insofar as each can, under certain conditions, be seen as limiting or influencing the other, I believe it is useful to maintain the analytical distinction between them. For example, organizations may be economically relatively independent although

---

[15] The best treatment of the relation between the age of organizations and their environments is by Arthur L. Stinchcombe, "Social Structure and Organizations," *In* James G. March (ed.), *Handbook of Organizations* (Skokie, Ill.: Rand McNally, 1965), pp. 153–69.
[16] Stanley Lieberson, "The Division of Labor in Banking," *American Journal of Sociology*, 66 (March 1961), 491–96.
[17] For a study of the influence of environmental complexity on the structure of Canadian hospitals, measured in terms of the number of other hospitals present in a given community, see Wolf Heydebrand, Peter Galloway, John DeRoche, and Dennis Magill, "Task Structure, Technological Complexity, and Bureaucratic Organization," presented at the *Annual Meetings of the Canadian Sociology and Anthropology Association*, Winnipeg, Canada, May 29, 1970; see also Ray Elling and Sandor Halebsky, "Organizational Differentiation and Support," selection 6 in this volume.

they are legally and politically nonautonomous. Certain politically safe and routinely fully-budgeted government agencies such as the CIA and FBI would come under this heading[18] or subsidiary business organizations which are part of larger parent organizations.[19]

Conversely, certain private professional organizations or voluntary associations may be de jure, i.e., legally and politically autonomous, but de facto, i.e., economically highly dependent. This latter phenomenon sometimes takes the form of "the right to be poor," or of having class and status, but no power.

Operationally, one may define organizational autonomy in terms of the degree of control over policies (low external bureaucratization),[20] or the degree of control over resources and budget, the unstated assumption being that organizations always strive to maximize their autonomy on both scores. Specific indicators would be the relative independence of decision making within various functional sectors, e.g., independence in critical decisions to expand, diversify, merge, appoint top personnel, allocate resources or, generally, commit the organization to certain long-term objectives or courses of action.

For certain purposes, the distinction between public and private control may be sufficient as a rough indicator of organizational autonomy. However, that particular dichotomy tends to obscure the potential independent variation of the political and economic dimensions of autonomy.

COMPLEXITY OF GOAL AND TASK STRUCTURE

Among the major elements of the organizational goal and task structure are the number and diversity of objectives, the variability of goals and tasks, the extent of geographical dispersion, organizational size, organizational growth and other aspects of change, and the criteria of effectiveness, including output and productivity, efficiency, quality, and adaptability. While there is no immediate justification of putting these seemingly diverse elements under one conceptual roof, there is also no convincing way of separating the question of goals from that of change or effectiveness. The analytical distinction between these elements becomes all the more important, as many studies using these variables demonstrate.

One of the most important characteristics of the task structure of an organization seems to be that it may serve as an indicator of the underlying goal structure.

Thus, while it is difficult, if not impossible, to define the goals of an organi-

[18] See, e.g., Harold Wilensky, *Organizational Intelligence* (New York: Basic Books, 1967), pp. 9, 58–67, 135n, 137.

[19] See, e.g., Lawrence E. Fouraker and J. M. Stopford, "Organizational Structure and Multinational Strategy," selection 5 in this volume.

[20] See, e.g., Reinhard Bendix, *Work and Authority in Industry* (New York: Harper Torchbooks, 1963), pp. 239–44.

zation at any one point in time, it is comparatively easy to identify the actual programs and activities, tasks and priorities in terms of which organizational objectives manifest themselves, and which define the organization as a going concern. The difference between stated goals and manifest conduct is similar to that between a person's statement of purpose and his subsequent actual behavior. Both may coincide; but if they do not coincide, the actual conduct is clearly the more valuable information, for most practical purposes, particularly since stated goals tend to be redefined so as to be consistent with the actual behavior.

The task structure of an organization, i.e., the nature of its objectives, and its charter, may of course still be far removed from its actual conduct. A task can be viewed as a program of action in which the objectives are more or less clearly defined. The clarity and specificity of the objectives are thus factors in the complexity of the task.

Diversity and Number of Objectives. Defining the complexity of the organizational task structure, one may begin with a basic element such as the different types of objectives as well as the number of objectives within each type. For example, an industrial conglomerate may manufacture a variety of products for two or three different markets, the number of different markets being a rough measure of the organization's degree of diversification. But, in addition, for each market a number of distinct products may be identified. Similarly, the diversity of objectives of a university may be found in its differential emphasis on undergraduate, graduate, and professional education as well as in research, as manifested in various institutes and affiliated organizations. But *within* graduate education, for example, the number of academic or "subject matter" departments constitutes a further aspect of the complexity of the task structure, subject to considerable empirical variation.

Geographical Dispersion. Another aspect of the complexity of the task structure is the geographical location and dispersion of the organization's physical and structural units, i.e., the number and quality of input and output locations. Among the various implications of the number and quality of locations are distance and accessibility, since they will affect not only the speed and routinizability of communication and transportation, but quite generally the cost of delivering services, as well as the cost of coordination.[21]

While the ecological and geographical dimension links the task structure with the complexity of the organizational environment, the variability or routinization of tasks links the task structure with the technology used by the organization, as well as with the whole complex of goal attainment and organizational change.

Variability of Tasks. A crucial aspect of the complexity of the task structure is the variability introduced by nonroutine tasks and by variations in the

[21] See Manfred Kochen and Karl Deutsch, "Toward a Rational Theory of Decentralization," selection 17 in this volume.

task structure, even if they are predictable, hence routinizable. However, such variations are clearly distinct from unpredictable or "poorly" predictable (emergent) types of variability and change. Examples in the former category are variable work loads, seasonal variations, the effects of geographical location and dispersion, or certain types of unsolved problems. But only the second type of variability generates a measure of *uncertainty* in the organizational task environment, and hence raises the question of the viability and realizability of objectives, in contrast to their operational specificity and problems arising from implementation. The difference between nonroutine tasks and routine changes in task structure is, of course, one of levels of generality in the problem encountered. Nonroutine tasks, such as, for example, a surgical operation or a police search, may be performed without changes in the higher level task structure of the respective organizations. It is only when nonroutine tasks repeatedly *cannot* be performed that a change in the task structure is called for. But even such changes can often be planned for and routinized to a considerable extent.[22]

Organizational Size. Another aspect of the task structure is the volume or size of the task, e.g., the number of output units per product during a given time period, or the volume of service as measured by the number of people served, cured, referred, graduated, rehabilitated, etc., as the case may be.

Insofar as the task size is part and parcel of the organization's objectives, it is plausible to assume that provisions are made to match the size of the task by comparable resources, both financial and in terms of personnel. Organizational size can, therefore, be measured in terms of either task size, budget or resource size, or size of labor force or membership. But even though these measures will tend to be highly correlated in most organizations, they are independently variable. Moreover, the ratio of personnel resources to task size is one of the more sensitive measures of organizational analysis, especially when the intervening effect of technology (e.g., type of production process or investment in plant and equipment) is taken into account.[23] A high ratio of personnel to task size may serve as a measure of effectiveness or quality in professional and service organizations. However, in manufacturing organizations, a high ratio may imply low capital intensity, and therefore possibly a lower level of productivity for a given organization.

Organizational Change. In the present context, organizational change refers to changes in and of the goal and task structure. This includes changes in the number or diversity of objectives, e.g., product changes as well as diversification, and changes in size, e.g., organizational growth. In contrast to mere variability of the task structure which can eventually be routinized, organiza-

[22] Charles Perrow, "A Framework for the Comparative Analysis of Organizations," *American Sociological Review*, 32 (Apr. 1967), 194–208.
[23] See, e.g., James D. Thompson and Frederick L. Bates, "Technology, Organization, and Administration," *Administrative Science Quarterly*, 2 (Dec. 1957), 325–43.

tional change refers to a major restructuring and transformation of an organization. Such transformations often occur in response to unpredictable changes in the organizational environment, such as changes in the market structure, or in resources and technology, or in the number and type of clientele. Thus, growth, diversification, and innovation can be conceptualized as organizational change, although there are doubtless many other forms of change.

In general, it appears that the extent to which organizational goals underlying the task structure are realizable is an important contingency that affects the task structure itself. Thus, the degree of specificity of goals and tasks relates not only to the definition of organizational change, but also to the definition of organizational effectiveness.

Organizational Effectiveness. Organizational effectiveness will be defined here in terms of quality, volume, and efficiency of goal attainment, as well as in terms of adaptability. All of these elements of effectiveness are closely tied to the specificity and complexity of the goals, objectives, and tasks of an organization. Effectiveness in performing a series of tasks as defined by certain objectives involves the consideration of the means relative to the ends, the "realistic" assessment of "operational goals,"[24] and the definition of the quality of problem solving in terms of optimal, "satisficing" solutions, rather than maximizing ones.

It may be useful in this context to distinguish explicitly between adaptation and innovation. Adaptation to changing conditions and external contingencies occurs in the interest of maintaining a given task structure and charter. Innovation and invention are forms of organizational transformation and involve an element of new design, a change in the overall task structure of the organization. The effectiveness of organizations can, therefore, not be evaluated from the perspective of the organization alone, nor from a single case. The determination, explanation, and evaluation of effectiveness appear to depend on a broad understanding of the class or category of organizations under consideration, on the nature of the organizational environment, and on the specific historical dimensions of social and organizational change as it affects the baseline for evaluating effectiveness. Changes in organizational size and complexity can conceivably be viewed in terms of adaptability and effectiveness. But it should be clear that it depends on the broader theoretical framework one uses whether growth or diversification are seen as quantitative increments *within* a given task structure, or as qualitative changes *of* that very structure.

If the evaluation of effectiveness is based on organizational variables more limited in scope than the goal and task structure, or if it is based on one case, then it tends to focus on problems of efficiency and integration, on internal problem solving in relation to productivity and the implementation of opera-

[24] James G. March and H. A. Simon, *Organizations* (New York: John Wiley, 1958), pp. 154–58.

tional goals, on cost-benefit ratios, and on goal attainment as successful pattern maintenance.[25]

In sum, the complexity of an organization's goal and task structure is seen in terms of a whole cluster of variables: the multiplicity and diversity of objectives, the ecological-geographical dispersion or concentration of the organization, the specificity and variability of tasks, the size of the task and of the requisite resources in terms of budget or personnel, the extent of organizational change as reflected in changes in and of the task structure and, finally, the criteria of effectiveness, including quality, output, productivity, and adaptability. It is especially from the perspective of effectiveness that an analysis of the task structure of an organization tells something about the nature of the underlying goal structure, without actually revealing it.

INTERNAL STRUCTURAL DIFFERENTIATION

Within this cluster of variables, I want to emphasize three related but analytically distinct elements: the division of labor within an organization, the nature and complexity of the technology used, and the nature of the skill structure.

Division of Labor. A central element in the notion of work division is the number of different functions which must be performed—sequentially or simultaneously—so as to accomplish a given task or set of tasks.

Since the terms "functions" and "functional" are fairly nonspecific, it is useful to distinguish between functions in the sense of specific occupationally defined work activities, in contrast to groups or categories of activities which empirically may appear in work groups, teams, departments, divisions, and other organized subunits. I will refer to the former in terms of *functional specialization*, and to the latter in terms of *departmental specialization*, fully aware that these designations are arbitrary and relative, and that their usage in the literature is highly inconsistent.

As to *functional specialization*, measures involving the number of different job titles in an organization provide rough indicators of the degree to which functions basic to the operations of the organization are specialized relative to each other and differentiated from each other. Such indicators of overall differentiation are based on the assumption that work *activities* can be inferred

---

[25] See, e.g., Ephraim Yuchtman and Stanley E. Seashore, "System Resource Approach to Organizational Effectiveness," *American Sociological Review*, 32 (Dec. 1967), 891–903. The general social systems approach is exemplified by Talcott Parsons, *Structure and Process;* for a context oriented approach to effectiveness, although couched in social-psychological terms, see James D. Thompson and William J. McEwen, "Organizational Goals and Environment: Goal-Setting as an Interaction Process," *American Sociological Review*, 23 (Feb. 1958), 23–31; for a consideration of the broader linkage between bureaucracy and political sociology, see Nicos P. Mouzelis, *Organization and Bureaucracy* (Chicago: Aldine-Atherton, 1968), pp. 7–37.

from roles and job titles, i.e., from *prescriptions* and formal definitions, an assumption that may not hold in small, rapidly changing, or otherwise underformalized or "flexible" organizations. Nevertheless, for large classes of organizations, measures of functional specialization can be assumed to gauge the total *amount* or *extent* of division of labor within an organization.

Since the number of functions present may vary from one organization to the next, even within very homogeneous classes of organizations, it is sometimes useful to establish a baseline of functions which standardizes the range of work functions for a given class of organizations. The degree of functional specialization can then be measured by the proportion of job titles actually occupied by personnel.

In contrast to functional specialization, the idea of *departmental specialization* involves the number and relative size of specialized and differentiated subunits of an organization.[26] An important advantage of such a measure of internal differentiation is that it can be defined in terms of both a priori as well as empirically grounded categories of subunits (e.g., production, sales, research and development, maintenance, and administration). Another advantage is that such a measure gives differential weight to the various subunits according to their size. Finally, the concept of departmental specialization permits the analytical separation between functional and hierarchical (horizontal and vertical) role differentiation since it usually involves the major subunits at the organizational level. In perfectly pyramidal hierarchical organizations, (e.g., certain governmental departments) the number of subunits tends to correspond to the executive's span of control. In other types of organizations, e.g., medium-sized business organizations or professional service organizations, departmental specialization tends to involve the major elements or phases of the work flow. It thus becomes an important determinant of "functional" interdependence, a phenomenon which, in turn, is closely related to the problem of organizational coordination.

Whatever specific measure is finally adopted, the idea of departmental specialization is theoretically relevant to measuring basic structural characteristics of organizations, both within specific types of organizations as well as across different types.

Technology. It is obvious that the internal division of labor of an organization is intimately linked with both the nature and degree of technological complexity, as well as with the total skill structure of the organization. In the present framework, an attempt is made to deal with division of labor, technology, and skill levels as separate problem areas. Consequently, technology is not seen as an overriding independent determinant of internal structure as

[26] For specific uses of such measures, see, e.g., Wolf Heydebrand, "Autonomy, Complexity, and Non Bureaucratic Coordination in Professional Organizations," selection 7 in this volume; William A. Rushing, "The Effects of Industry Size and Division of Labor on Administration," selection 20 in this volume; D. A. Pugh et al., "Dimensions of Organizational Structure," selection 23 in this volume.

is often true of conceptions of organizations as sociotechnical systems.[27] Rather, I am using a relatively specific conception of technology, namely the extent and nature of the use of machines, i.e., the degree of mechanization and automation of the work process. This specific use of the term corresponds most closely to the notion of operations technology, in contrast to materials technology and knowledge technology.

Such a narrow conception of technology makes it possible to treat sociotechnical systems, where they exist, as socially defined structures, rather than as falling within the domain of an impersonal "technological imperative."[28] A narrower use also enables one to avoid the pitfalls of a simple technological determinism[29] and to deal with technology—as well as the skill structure—as a factor influenced by the autonomy, the goals, and the task structure of an organization. Technical devices—just like specialized skills—may or may not be used in the performance of certain tasks. Therefore, the decision to use an advanced or an intermediate technology for certain purposes is, and perhaps should be, a function of social definitions and political choices, and should be based on a consideration of the costs and consequences of technology for social structure. That such choices and decisions may temporarily interdict the performance of certain tasks (such as landing on the moon) or the production of certain commodities (such as supersonic transport planes), is a question of public policy. Although such questions are deeply relevant to the autonomy and task structure of organizations, they need not be further considered here.

Skill Structure. The skill structure of an organization is closely related to its internal division of labor and to technology. However, there are certain dimensions which warrant separate consideration in a comparative organizational analysis.

One dimension is the distinction between *generalists* who perform many, or even all, specialized functions in a given work process, and *specialists* whose work is limited to one particular—although potentially complex—function.

Crosscutting this dimension is a second one, namely the distinction between *professional, technical or subprofessional, and nonprofessional* workers. The latter two categories may also be subdivided into skilled, semi-skilled, and unskilled categories.

Adding to the professional/nonprofessional dimension such categories as

---

[27] Thompson, *Organizations in Action;* Perrow, "A Framework for Comparative Analysis"; Edward Harvey, "Technology and the Structure of Organizations," *American Sociological Review*, 31 (Apr. 1968), 247–64; Joan Woodward, *Industrial Organization: Theory and Practice* (London: Oxford University Press, 1965); and William L. Zwerman, *New Perspectives on Organization Theory* (Westport, Conn.: Greenwood, 1970). For an excellent recent review of technological typologies, see David J. Hickson et al., "Operations Technology and Organization Structure: An Empirical Reappraisal," *Administrative Science Quarterly*, 14 (Sept. 1969), 378–97.
[28] See, e.g., Emery L. Trist et al., *Organizational Choice* (London: Tavistock, 1963).
[29] See, in this connection, the critique voiced by Louis Pondy, "Effects of Size, Complexity, and Ownership on Administrative Intensity," selection 21 in this volume.

"managerial," "white collar," and "blue collar" yields a third dimension, namely the implicit *stratification system* of an organization, linking it with the stratification system of the environment.

Finally, corresponding to—and reinforcing—the stratification system is the *authority structure* of the organization. The stratification system and the authority structure are not coterminous. But insofar as there is a single basis of legitimacy and hierarchy within the organization, social status and hierarchical authority functions will tend to converge. Conversely, the greater the complexity of the task structure and thus the likelihood of multiple hierarchies, the more will status and hierarchical differentiation tend to be independent of each other.

In the present framework, I want to deal only with the first two dimensions of the skill structure: technical specialization and professionalization. Thus, in order to avoid confusing skill, social status, and authority, I will discuss the authority system in relation to the question of control and coordination. Organizational stratification systems, on the other hand, may be discussed as specific pathological aspects of the control structure of organizations and of their relation to the larger society.[30]

A consideration of the skill structure as separate from the division of labor requires the distinction between the specialization of workers in contrast to the specialization of jobs or functions. Highly specialized, but routinized, functions may be performed by persons who are not highly trained as workers, and who may in fact be relatively unskilled. Conversely, the performance of complex, general, nonroutine functions will almost always require the services of highly trained experts, and sometimes the knowledge, judgment, and specific client-orientation characteristic of the general professional practitioner.

The availability and use of technical experts and professionals in organizations is, therefore, of considerable consequence, not the least because the two dimensions of job specialization and person specialization may be seriously mismatched.

The importance of technical expertise and competence (or the proportion of technical experts) as an organizational variable derives from the obvious fact that certain complex work functions must be, or tend to be, performed by persons with special knowledge and skills. Moreover, highly trained experts, especially professional practitioners, coordinate and integrate the various elements of their work themselves on the basis of internalized work norms and rules. It may also be useful here to recall the distinctions between professionals and scientists, on the one hand, and technicians, on the other. Professionals apply knowledge and use judgment in relation to clients, whereas scientists

---

[30] For a sensitive, early discussion of some of these relationships, see Chester I. Barnard, "Functions and Pathology of Status Systems in Formal Organizations," *In* William F. Whyte (ed.), *Industry and Society* (New York: McGraw-Hill, 1946), pp. 46–83; see also Ralf Dahrendorf, *Class and Class Conflict in Industrial Society* (Stanford: Stanford University Press, 1959).

produce knowledge for the "scientific community." The technician, like the professional, does not produce knowledge, but he applies it to more or less well-defined situations and "cases," rather than to undefined and undiagnosed ones.

Professionals share an element of "charisma" with entrepreneurs and politicians because of their "generalist" use of discretion and judgment. Members of all three of these occupational types tend to be concerned with the broad specification of goals, objectives, and results, but are opposed to the detailed specification of bureaucratic procedures. Scientists, especially applied scientists as well as technicians, may work very well within an organizational or bureaucratic framework since their job specialization and their person specialization tend to coincide. That coincidence is, of course, proverbial for Weber's legal-bureaucratic expert who is a specialist but rarely a professional practitioner.

Lining up these various categories of "experts" in ideal typical fashion along the generalist-specialist dimension, one may well find the following distribution, ranging from the professional generalists to the organizational specialist: general professional practitioner (independent professional), basic research scientist, specialist professional, applied scientist, new professional and semiprofessionals, technicians, bureaucrat-experts (e.g., civil service officials). Thus, for the general professional practitioner, organizational goals and orientations are separated from, and possibly even in contradiction with, professional ones. But for the bureaucratic technical expert, professional and organizational concerns tend to be closely integrated. Specialists and especially "new" professionals such as engineers, teachers, social workers, and nurses are frequently an integral part of a system of division of labor and of organizational hierarchies. In professional organizations, such hierarchies are themselves made up of professionals, experts, and specialists. A confusing and often outright misleading element in many studies of the relation between professionals and their organizations is the fact that all of these "experts" tend to be combined under the term "professional." Examples of studies in which these distinctions between professional practitioner and technical expert are *not* made and which therefore lead to inconsistencies and "surprises" are Blau, Heydebrand, and Stauffer.[31] An example of a study which *does* recognize the need for an analytical distinction is Montagna's study of accounting firms.[32]

In sum, there are two important aspects of the skill structure of an organization: the number or proportion of specialists, seen along a dimension of varying degrees of person specialization, and the degree of professionalization of different components of the labor force, especially of the "production" component. It should be clear from the preceding discussion that technical

[31] "The Structure of Small Bureaucracies," selection 27 in this volume; Peter M. Blau, "The Hierarchy of Authority in Organizations," selection 29 in this volume.
[32] Paul D. Montagna, "Professionalization and Bureaucratization in Large Professional Organizations," selection 28 in this volume.

specialization and professionalization are used here as structural attributes of the organization as a whole, not as attributes of individuals, careers, or occupations.[33]

This last major cluster of variables comprises two aspects of the control structure of organizations: the nonbureaucratic modes of coordination (e.g., professionalization, committees, incentives), and the "classical" elements of legal-bureaucratic administration (e.g., formal, written rules, hierarchical levels of authority, the span of control, the administrative and clerical staff as well as the communication structure, and, generally, the centralization of authority and decision making).

Nonbureaucratic Modes of Coordination. In modern organizations, one may observe a variety of forms of nonbureaucratic coordination of specialized work activities. Such nonbureaucratic forms can be characterized in terms of certain basic elements of social interaction and of processes of communication: cooperation and its various manifestations such as bargaining and negotiation, coalition formation, cooptation,[34] various forms of competition and conflict resolution, the transformation of power relations into exchange relations, and the strategic use of different types of incentives.[35]

Specifically, in work organizations the nature of work activities of professionals, craftsmen, and technical specialists constitute a form of work integration and coordination. Similarly, the functional and technical interdependence among specialized activities, insofar as it is present within the work flow, will tend to generate lateral communication and "horizontal" forms of coordination.[36]

The effects of professionalization on coordination can, therefore, be viewed

[33] For a discussion of these latter attributes in relation to the former, see Richard H. Hall, "Professionalization and Bureaucratization," selection 25 in this volume.

[34] Thompson and McEwen, "Organizational Goals and Environments."

[35] Peter B. Clark and James Q. Wilson, "Incentive Systems," *Administrative Science Quarterly*, 6 (Sept. 1961), 129–66; on organizational conflict, see Louis Pondy, "Organizational Conflict: Concepts and Models," *Administrative Science Quarterly*, 12 (Sept. 1967), 296–320; on the transformation of power relations into exchange relations, see Richard M. Emerson, "Power-Dependence Relations," *American Sociological Review*, 27 (Feb. 1962), 31–41; for the opposite argument, viz., the transformation of inequality in the control of resources into super- and subordination, see Peter M. Blau, *Exchange and Power in Social Life* (New York: John Wiley, 1964), pp. 118–25.

[36] Richard L. Simpson, "Vertical and Horizontal Communication in Formal Organizations," *Administrative Science Quarterly*, 4 (Sept. 1959), 188–96; Henry A. Landsberger, "The Horizontal Dimension in Bureaucracy," *Administrative Science Quarterly*, 6 (Dec. 1961), 299–332. As Landsberger has emphasized again recently, the idea of organizations as open, nonbureaucratic and nonhierarchical systems based on lateral communication and interaction among equals is closely related to Barnard's conception or formal organizations as "cooperative systems;" see Henry A. Landsberger (ed.), *Comparative Perspectives on Formal Oganizations* (Boston: Little Brown, 1970), pp. 1–2.

as intervening between task complexity and internal bureaucratization, just like the consequences of functional interdependence for coordination. Both professionalization and functional interdependence may thus be interpreted as co-determinants of bureaucratic processes since they condition the effect of task complexity on administration. For example, certain forms of prestructuring of the work process, such as functional and geographic decentralization in delivering highly valued services, contain a built-in element of coordination. As a consequence, normative and hierarchical modes of coordination and control can be reduced or altogether dispensed with.[37] The "administration of things" supplants the "administration of people."

Committees play a central role among structural devices for controlling and channeling lateral consultation, negotiation, representation, and participation in decision making. The size of committees tends to vary with their primary function—e.g., large, representative committees for purposes of discussion and participation, medium size for bargaining and compromise, and small for highly technical and executive decision making. However, a common element is their capacity to handle "political" problems within otherwise administrative-bureaucratic structures. Committees and other nonbureaucratic structures facilitating lateral coordination will tend to be particularly important, frequent, and highly developed in organizations with multiple bases of legitimacy and with multiple and separate hierarchies of authority.

Incentive systems constitute another set of nonbureaucratic modes of coordination. Clark and Wilson distinguish between material, solidary, and purposive incentives based, respectively, on material monetary, status and sociability-related, and normative-ideological rewards. These distinctions lead to a corresponding typology of utilitarian, solidary, and purposive organizations.[38] The incentive typology is similar to Etzioni's analytical typology which differentiates organizations on the basis of compliance relations, where "incentives" are replaced by different types of "involvement" of "lower participants."[39] Two of Etzioni's major organizational types, utilitarian and normative organizations, correspond closely to Clark and Wilson's utilitarian and purposive organizations, i.e., business organizations and voluntary associations.

The view of incentives and types of involvement as nonbureaucratic modes of organizational coordination is justified only insofar as it is feasible to assume, within organizations, the existence of internal symbolic states, as well as goal-directed behavior which responds more or less to external conditions. Of course, fear of punishment and compliance in anticipation of coercion (Etzioni's third type) points to external agencies of control, i.e., the enforcement of conformity to rules. The relationship between external rules and the

[37] Kochen and Deutsch, selection 17, this volume.

[38] Clark and Wilson, "Incentive Systems."

[39] Amitai Etzioni, *A Comparative Analysis of Complex Organizations* (Glencoe: Free Press, 1961), pp. 12–20. As Etzioni points out, the most frequent types of compliance relations are, of course, those where the power-involvement categories are congruent, viz., remunerative-calculative, normative-moral, and coercive-alienative compliance.

potentially punitive structure of enforcement is widely recognized as a central feature of bureaucratic control structures where participants develop an alienative orientation to coercive power and to "punishment-centered" bureaucracy.[40]

Bureaucratic Modes of Coordination. Among structural measures of bureaucratization, the number of hierarchical levels, the managerial ratio (or, conversely, the average span of control), and the relative size of the administrative-clerical staff have been most prominent. By contrast, more normative approaches to the concept of bureaucracy tend to emphasize rules, procedures, impersonality, formalization, as well as various orientations to, and perceptions of, hierarchical differentiation and distance.[41] However, these normative elements, and in particular, rules, can be shown to have pervasive consequences for other aspects of bureaucratic structure, depending on the structural conditions from which they emerge and within which they operate.

Rules, as normative prescriptions or proscriptions regulating behavior, may be viewed as articulating the distinction between nonbureaucratic and bureaucratic modes of coordination. It is useful in this connection to recall two aspects of the nature of rules. One dimension of rules governing work activities refers to the *degree of externality*, i.e., whether the rules are specific, written prescriptions for behavior which specify procedures in detail and consequently require detailed, step by step, "close" supervision. The immediate enforcement of conformity to specific procedures and rules is typically provided by the hierarchical line structure of an organization. The nature and externality of rules can therefore be seen as an important determinant of the shape of the hierarchy, in general, and the number of hierarchical levels, in particular.

Conversely, if all rules and norms governing work activities are internalized, then external supervision, enforcement, and coercion are unnecessary. Indeed, external and close supervision would generate opposition and would be dysfunctional and counterproductive.

While the internalized rules may be viewed as nonbureaucratic mechanisms of coordination typically associated with technical expertise and professional practice, external, "written" rules and regulations, together with the requisite hierarchical structure and enforcement apparatus, are typical characteristics of "bureaucratic" structures.

The second aspect of rules I want to emphasize here refers to the fact that rules may apply to specialized work operations, or they may apply to the regulation and coordination of such specialized work operations. The former type, *"operative" rules*, is usually an integral part of job descriptions, blueprints for specific technical operations (e.g., how to assemble a certain machine, or check its performance, etc.), and generally of functionally special-

---

[40] Alvin W. Gouldner, *Patterns of Industrial Bureaucracy* (New York: Free Press, 1954).
[41] Hall, selection 25, this volume.

ized activities within a larger system of division of labor. Such rules are typically imbedded already in the nature of the production process, that is, in the task structure. The second type, *"regulative" rules* (sometimes seen as the core element of bureaucratic red tape), refers to the highly formalized procedures of legal-bureaucratic administration. Regulative rules are thus explicitly part of the organizational control structure. While few writers referring to rules and formalization make this distinction, it has become commonplace to observe that a craftsman or professional practitioner may have internalized highly specific operative rules as well as standards of workmanship and quality without engaging in "bureaucratic" behavior. Similarly, the "professional" administrator may have enough discretion and decision-making autonomy to be "flexible" about the legalistic application of regulative rules.

The point is that by defining *operative and regulative rules as variable aspects of organizational structures,* one can directly compare a relatively wide range of organizational phenomena without being confined by ideal-type constructs and rigid analytical typologies. Once standardization and formalization are specified in terms of at least these two types of rules, other aspects of bureaucratic structure follow.

Thus, hierarchical levels, the span of control, supervision vs. audits (i.e., direct vs. post hoc control), frequency of review as a function of discretion and responsibility,[42] the nature of the communication structure, and centralization or decentralization behavior—all of these can be seen as causally related to the nature, specification, and externality of rules.

I have argued that professionals coordinate their own work through internalized work norms. But the specification of goals—rather than of procedures —may also apply to teams, departments, or whole organizations, where it can then be dealt with in terms of decentralization or organizational autonomy.

The complexity and variability of the structure of activities in modern organizations are often seen as factors which militate against the "implicit" rules of the informal organization and against "muddling through."[43]

The uncertainty of prediction and control associated with a complex and variable task structure tends to generate strong interests in instituting "public" (i.e., external) guidelines, norms, and rules. This process of reducing uncertainty and unpredictability, in turn, leads to the "routinization of emergencies," and to the development of explicit agreements and conventions.[44]

---

[42] E. Jaques, *The Measurement of Responsibility* (Cambridge: Harvard University Press, 1956).

[43] Charles Lindblom, "The Science of Muddling Through," *Public Administration Review,* 19 (Spring, 1959), 79–88; for a critique of Lindblom's concept of "muddling through," see Yehezkel Dror, "Muddling Through—Science or Inertia," *Public Administration Review,* 24 (Sept. 1964), 154–56; and my review of Dror and Lindblom, Wolf V. Heydebrand, "Administration of Social Change," *Public Administration Review,* 24 (Sept. 1964), 163–65.

[44] See Michel Crozier, *The Bureaucratic Phenomenon* (London: Tavistock, 1964); also relevant here is Anselm Strauss, "The Hospital and its Negotiated Order," in Eliot Freidson (ed.), *The Hospital in Modern Society* (New York: Free Press, 1963), pp. 147–69.

Most writers concerned with the transition from traditional or simple forms of social organization to modern-rational and more complex ones have pointed to the rise of "public" and civil law, as well as of regulative legal norms, with an increasingly complex apparatus of litigation, mediation, and adjudication. Similarly, in modern organizations, the rise of internal bureaucratization, that is, the increase in the size and complexity of the communication structure and of various "staff" categories (administrative, clerical, legal, public relations, personnel, "supportive," etc.) can be seen as a direct consequence of changes in the complexity of the task structure, as well as of changes in the nature and extent of organizational autonomy.

Insofar as modern organizations are made up of competing groups with frequently divergent and conflicting interests,[45] we can view them as pluralistic structures in which both political and administrative questions are constantly raised in terms of each other. To the extent, then, that modern complex organizations are *not* dominated by what Mannheim has called "bureaucratic conservatism," they will be capable of dealing with both types of questions simultaneously and in their own right, rather than compulsively turning "problems of politics into problems of administration."[46]

SUMMARY

I have presented a general perspective on the development of organizational analysis. In particular, I have made certain claims as to the threefold contribution of recent empirical research to this development: an increase of basic, substantive knowledge of modern organizations, an advancement of the methodology of organizational analysis in terms of systematic, quantitative comparisons, and a sharpening of the conceptual focus as well as an extension of the theoretical scope of organizational analysis. To what extent these claims are justified will ultimately be judged by future organizational researchers and practitioners and, more concretely, by the degree to which people can control organizations and use them as instruments of human purposes.

Among the functional types of organizations dealt with in the various studies are business organizations, professional organizations, government agencies, and voluntary associations. Most of the studies included here are concerned with the nature and extent of structural variation within a given functional type, with a few studies focusing on the variation among several functional types. I have described the advantages and disadvantages of comparisons within types as over against those between types, and I have discussed the problem of organizational boundaries and of defining organizations in relation to their environment.

---

[45] See, e.g., R. M. Cyert and J. G. March, *A Behavioral Theory of the Firm* (Englewood Cliffs: Prentice-Hall, 1963).
[46] Karl Mannheim, *Ideology and Utopia* (New York: Harvest Books, 1936), p. 118.

Methodologically, the studies brought together here exemplify a new approach to organizational analysis. I have described the characteristics of this new approach as an extension and systematic application of the comparative method to the multivariate phenomena of complex organizational structures, based on samples or total populations of organizations. In contrasting the "systems" approach and the multivariate, comparative approach, I have argued in favor of the latter on the grounds that it is more flexible and encompassing as a research instrument, more open to the historical determinants of organizations, and more adequate for purposes of meaningful description, comparison, and explanation.

Finally, I have critically discussed the "fetishism of comparisons" by showing the need for a less reified and more holistic approach to organizational studies. Such an approach takes into account macro-social variables by showing how the structural context of organizations has developed historically, and how it affects the organizational units that are to be compared. While macrovariables can at times be bracketed, there appear to be cogent historical and theoretical reasons why such bracketing and selective inattention becomes today more and more artificial, narrowly scientistic, and therefore scientifically indefensible.

In developing a conceptual framework for general comparative purposes, as well as for the purpose of organizing the empirical studies included here, I have distinguished between a number of basic dimensions of organizational analysis. These dimensions are shown in Chart I which relates them, in the form of a matrix, to the respective empirical studies. Taken together, the dimensions describe a hypothetical continuum of variables connecting the internal characteristics of organizations to the external environment. This hypothetical continuum is conceptualized in terms of four major clusters of variables: (1) the nature and complexity of the organizational environment and the extent of organizational autonomy within that environment; (2) the degree of complexity of the organizational goal and task structure; (3) the degree of internal structural differentiation, notably division of labor, technology, and skill structure; and (4) the bureaucratic and nonbureaucratic modes of coordination and control.

These four clusters, as well as the specific variables included in each, provide a conceptual framework which is capable of expansion and refinement in both the internal and the external directions. The studies themselves, however, tend to deal with relationships between the clusters, thus developing various theoretical and causal linkages between the elements of the conceptual framework. Hopefully, both the studies and the conceptual framework will stimulate the further interaction between theory and research, and contribute to an informed and socially responsive organizational praxis.

1. THE STUDY OF ORGANIZATIONS

Wolf V. Heydebrand

The study of large, complex, formal organizations has changed in recent years from an esoteric social science specialty to a major field of investigation. There are two outstanding reasons for this change: a concern with the "testing of ideas" in the wake of increasing theoretical and methodological sophistication in the social sciences, and a pragmatic orientation toward problem-solving within, and through, organizations. Both of these concerns have contributed greatly to the development of systematic research on organizations, and to the formulation of empirical and theoretical generalizations about the nature of bureaucratic and organizational structures.

In this paper, it is my purpose to examine the recent advances in organizational research in terms of the sociological study of organizations. In particular, I will focus on the methodological implications of a number of empirical studies for a new approach to organizational analysis. More specifically, I want to spell out

Reprinted by permission of the publisher, the International Social Science Council, from *Social Science Information*, Vol. 6 (October 1967), pp. 59–86.

some of the elements of a quantitative approach to the study of organizations. I will illustrate this approach by describing the main features of the organizational research program in which I have been engaged. Finally, I will attempt to formulate some general criteria that appear to be useful for the future development of the study of organizations.

THE EMPIRICAL STUDY OF ORGANIZATIONS

In sociological research involving organizations two sources provide the dominant theoretical perspectives: Weber's historical and structural conceptions of bureaucracy, and Barnard's and Simon's neo-classical approach to the social and rational dimensions of human behavior and decision-making in organizations.[1]

[1] M. Weber, *The Theory of Social and Economic Organization*. Transl. by A. M. Henderson and T. Parsons. T. Parsons (ed.), (New York: Oxford University Press, 1947), p. 324–406; C. I. Barnard, *The Functions of the Executive* (Cambridge: Harvard University Press, 1938); H. A. Simon, *Administrative Behavior*, 2nd ed. (New York: Macmillan, 1957); H. A. Simon, *Models of Man* (New York, John Wiley, 1957).

While these two traditions have different philosophical and cultural roots and therefore have often been considered antithetical, they share a number of theoretical elements. Perhaps the most important common element in these approaches is a rationalistic conception of organizations as unitary systems of collective action. Such systems are assumed to maintain continuity, integration, and identity either in terms of the nature of legitimacy as a shared system of definitions, or in terms of the logic of the goal-attainment process, i.e., the nexus between means and ends. A logical variant of the goal-attainment emphasis is the conception of organizations as social systems.[2] However, there are indications that these system models may ultimately be capable of theoretical rapprochement or integration, whether they are considered as normative, mechanistic, organic, servo-mechanistic, natural, or even pluralistic.[3]

More importantly, the various theoretical perspectives have remained relevant to the practical questions of rational planning, democratic regulation, and effective coordination in government, industry, and various other sectors of society. At the same time, these perspectives have provided significant guidelines for empirical research.[4] Moreover, empirical studies have increasingly focused on the "goodness of fit" between individual and organization, on the consequences of organizational coordination and control for productivity and performance, and on the relative cost in human and social terms of the cult of efficiency.[5] In other words, research in this area has tended to approach the same basic questions of substantive as over against formal or functional rationality, but primarily in terms of "human relations" within, rather than in terms of the structural characteristics of, organizations. This all too brief sketch of the theoretical and substantive questions underlying empirical research on organizations must suffice to indicate the broad range of problems and issues that have become part of this new field of investigation. The main

---

[2] T. Parsons, *Structure and Process in Modern Societies* (Glencoe, Ill.: Free Press, 1960), pp. 16–96.

[3] See, e.g., A. W. Gouldner, "Organizational analysis," *In*: R. K. Merton et al. (eds.), *Sociology Today* (New York: Basic Books, 1959), p. 400–29; T. K. Hopkins "Bureaucratic authority: The convergence of Weber and Barnard," *In* A. Etzioni (ed.), *Complex Organizations* (New York: Holt, Rinehart & Winston, 1961), pp. 82–98; E. Litwak, "Models of bureaucracy which permit conflict," *American Journal of Sociology* 67, 1961:177–84; E. W. Bakke, *Bonds of Organizations* (New York: Harper & Row, 1950); cf. also T. Burns and G. M. Stalker, *The Management of Innovation* (London: Tavistock, 1961); and M. Crozier, *The Bureaucratic Phenomenon* (London: Tavistock, 1964).

[4] P. Selznick, *TVA and the Grassroots* (Berkeley: University of California Press, 1953); A. W. Gouldner, *Patterns of Industrial Bureaucracy* (Glencoe, Ill.: Free Press, 1954).

[5] F. J. Roethlisberger and W. J. Dickson, *Management and the Worker* (Cambridge: Harvard University Press, 1939); W. F. Whyte, *Money and Motivation* (New York: Harper & Row, 1955); C. Argyris, *Personality and Organization* (New York: Harper & Row, 1957); R. Likert, *New Patterns of Management* (New York: McGraw-Hill, 1961); K. Mannheim, *Man and Society in an Age of Reconstruction* (London: Routlege and Kegan Paul, 1940), pp. 39–78, 239–381; D. Bell, "Work and its discontents: The cult of efficiency in America," in his *The End of Ideology*, rev. ed. (New York: Free Press, 1965), pp. 227–72.

question that concerns us in this paper is the nature of the research strategy and methods which have been adopted to explore, test, and refine knowledge about organizations.

The differences between theoretical perspectives in terms of which organizational studies have approached their common subject matter have been paralleled in more or less unsystematic fashion by a great diversity of methods. They range from participant observation and small groups experiments to field research on whole organizations, and from case and typological studies to the sample survey.

Two basic methodological problems stand out in this diversity. One of these is the question: what is considered as the object of analysis, and what relationships are selected as most important? The other question is: to what extent is it possible to generalize from the findings? As to the object of analysis, a large number of organization studies are based on the investigation of the behavior of individuals (and status-role incumbents) or of work groups.[6] Here, bureaucracy or a specific organization provides merely the setting, and the dependent variable is the behavior of *individuals* and the *informal*

organization, i.e., the network of interpersonal relationships and the nature of unofficial norms. In such studies, the independent variables range from "atmosphere," morale, style of supervision and leadership to organizational size, type of organization, technology, and stability of environment.

Recent studies, however, contrast with this approach insofar as they use as the dependent variable the structural characteristics of organizations themselves. Moreover, there is now an increasing emphasis on interorganizational relationships and systems of organizations, i.e., on macroorganizational phenomena, in addition to the continued concern with internal structure and individual behavior.[7]

As to the question of generalization, one is faced with somewhat of a paradox: as organizational research has moved closer to considering the whole organization as the

---

[6] See, e.g., L. SAYLES, *The Behavior of Industrial Work Groups* (New York: John Wiley, 1958); A. S. Tannenbaum and R. L. Kahn, "Organizational control structure," *Human Relations* 10, 1957:127–40; H. Wilensky, *Intellectuals in Labor Unions* (Glencoe, Ill., Free Press, 1956); A. H. Stanton and M. F. Schwartz, *The Mental Hospital* (New York, Basic Books, 1954). For a comprehensive review and bibliography of these and many similar studies, see J. G. March and H. A. Simon, *Organizations* (New York: John Wiley, 1958).

[7] S. H. Udy, Jr., "The comparative analysis of organizations," *In* J. G. March, (ed.), *Handbook of Organizations* (Chicago: Rand McNally, 1965), pp. 678–709; A. L. Stinchcombe, "Social structure and organizations," In March, (ed.), *Handbook*, p. 142–83; J. D. Thompson and W. J. McEwen, "Organizational goals and environment: Goal setting as an interaction process," *American Sociological Review* 23, 1958:23–31; J. D. Thompson et al. (eds.), *Comparative Studies in Administration* (Pittsburgh: University of Pittsburgh Press, 1959); F. Heady and S. L. Stokes (eds.), *Papers in Comparative Public Administration* (Ann Arbor: University of Michigan, Institute of Public Administration, 1962); W. Bennis, *Changing Organizations* (New York: McGraw-Hill, 1966); A. Etzioni, *Political Unification* (New York: Holt, Rinehart and Winston, 1965); Crozier, *Bureaucratic Phenomenon*; T. Burns, "The comparative study of organizations," *In* V. H. Vroom (ed.), *Methods of Organizational Research* (Pittsburgh, University of Pittsburgh Press, 1967), pp. 113–70.

unit of analysis, rather than the behavior of individuals, groups, or departments, it has, nevertheless, relied almost exclusively on the case-study approach.[8]

Case studies of the internal structure and the external relations of organizations have provided important insights on the basis of which certain generalizations about more or less invariant aspects of organizational structure and process could be formulated. Although such studies tend to be limited to a descriptive analysis of particular types of organizations, such as corporations, unions, or government agencies, it must not be overlooked that case studies may, at times, generate sensitizing concepts and analytical variables which, of course, have to be tested by broader comparative, systematic, and quantitative investigations.

Certain organizational case studies have used a form of analysis which makes it possible to extrapolate or generalize from *internal comparisons* of organizational subunits to the larger organization. This device is useful especially if data on many similar types of organizations are not readily available. One of the first studies making use of this kind of internal comparison is Gouldner's analysis of a gypsum factory.[9] The work organization of surface operations is compared with that of the gypsum mine proper. From this comparison, Gouldner develops a typology of bureaucratic structure based on the distinction between different styles of supervision in the enforcement of rules. The major types are conceptualized as "representative" and "punishment-centered" bureaucracy.

A type of case study which uses both internal and external comparisons is Blau's study of interpersonal relations in two government agencies.[10] The contrast between the two agencies is supplemented by an internal analysis of the formal and informal organization of two departments in one of the agencies. Following in part Barnard's and Roethlisberger and Dickson's distinctions, Blau characterizes and compares the two departments in terms of the determinants and consequences of cooperative as over against competitive practices.

A third example of a study making use of this kind of internal comparison is that of the International Typographical Union.[11] Structural characteristics such as size and composition of locals, chapels and shops in the union are held constant, thus enabling the researchers to investigate the differential effect of these characteristics on other variables, for example, on the degree of political activity, or the extent of democratic practices within the subunits of the larger organization.

Finally, two recent examples of comparative case studies are of unusual interest because of their conceptual differentiation, richness in detail, and theoretical sophistication.[12] Burns and Stalker's study of

[8] Selznick, *TVA*; Gouldner, *Patterns*; P. M. Blau, *The Dynamics of Bureaucracy* (Chicago: University of Chicago Press, 1955); S. M. Lipset, M. A. Trow and J. S. Coleman, *Union Democracy* (Glencoe, Ill.: Free Press, 1956).

[9] Gouldner, *Patterns*.

[10] Blau, *Dynamics*.

[11] Lipset et al.

[12] Burns and Stalker, *Management*; Crozier, *Bureaucratic Phenomenon*.

twenty British firms uses both the organization of work and the managerial system in a broad explanatory framework concerning the nature of innovation and change in production organizations. One of the results of the study is the development of a typological distinction between mechanistic and organic systems of management, conceived as differential responses to conditions of external instability and change.

Crozier's study is a comparative analysis of a "clerical agency" and an "industrial monopoly," the latter being a government-owned production organization with over thirty subunits or plants, three of which are studied intensively, and twenty more extensively.

Although Crozier refrains from developing an explicit typology of organizations, his and the British studies share a number of theoretical and methodological elements. Both succeed in extracting from their interview and case-study material significant analytical variables which play an important role in subsequent theoretical generalizations; both focus on the influence of the external environment—be it the market system or the larger cultural context—on organizational processes, and both studies develop new theoretical ideas concerning power relationships and organizational change from their respective analyses of the effects of uncertainty.

The strategic use of empirical data in all of these studies enables the respective researchers to develop hypotheses of more general theoretical interest and to formulate generalizations toward greater understanding of organizations. The method of internal comparison is probably best suited for the study of organizational subunits where the larger organizations have not been, or cannot be, sampled, yet theoretically relevant structural differences can be systematically controlled.

The study of a small number of comparable subunits within an organization will ordinarily permit a more detailed investigation of each unit and its members. However, in order to develop and test general propositions about organizations, their subunits and system-subsystem relationships, it is necessary to go beyond the case-study approach. Thus, an important step toward systematic, quantitative research is the definition of the whole organization as the unit of analysis, and the sampling of such units from more or less homogeneous universes of organizations.

The ideal research strategy would, consequently, be based on samples of organizations classified or stratified according to a variety of theoretical criteria. Examples of such criteria are size, type of tasks, complexity of goal structure, degree of autonomy, type of technology, type of clientele and members, types of contextual characteristics (political, economic, demographic, etc.) and many others.

The great variety of organizations in modern societies has led many investigators to develop a corresponding variety of criteria of classification which, in turn, has stimulated the proliferation of numerous typologies. However, most typologies based on *substantive* distinctions between types of organizations (e.g., business vs. government vs. welfare organizations) do not really order the variety of organizational phenomena; they either reflect that variety or else they tend to impose an unwarranted or at best useless conceptual scheme which oversimplifies the multidimensional universe of organizations.[13] Moreover, typologies tend to combine various analytical dimensions for the purpose of organizing a complex subject matter, but often do so at the expense of analytical clarity and precision. The problem here is that ideal-type constructs and typologies are essentially limited to *comparison of individual cases*. Comparative studies based on substantive typologies are therefore inherently tied to the case-study approach and do not really transcend its methodological limitations. Conversely, comparative studies based on two or a few cases tend to resolve the methodological dilemma by developing ideal-types and typologies. But at the same time they create the new dilemma of overdetermined models where the number of variables exceeds the number of cases or observations.

Typologies of organizations and the selection of "comparable" facts and cases represent a transitional phase in the study of organizations. In anthropology, political science, history, or clinical psychology the comparative method is based on the analysis of two or a few type-cases, comparable in some respects but not in others. But here as well as in organization research the next step would be to *sample* the units of analysis statistically. It becomes possible now to select a relatively large number of organizational variables for systematic comparison and for the analysis of covariation.[14]

In sum, the identification and description of patterns of structural relationships in different types of organizations and the discovery of structural similarities are obviously of central concern to the comparative approach to organizations, whether the comparison be qualitative or quantitative. However, quantification as such is hardly an end in itself. All too often, it leads only to a meaningless compilation of data. The comparative method must, ultimately, be related to statements of *causal relationships*, i.e., to systematic explanations and theoretical generalizations. Comparing partially different organizational phenomena is but a game if the intellectual process involved is not aiming at an explanatory subsumption or synthesis that is finally to result in a new coordinate system or paradigm in which the original comparative types are simply discrete points on a dimension.

APPROXIMATING ORGANIZATIONAL SURVEY ANALYSIS

For organizational research, the above considerations imply the use of multivariate statistical analysis based on probability samples of organizations. Initially, this method entails the classification of a given sample of organizations into subgroups and the use of partial correlation based on quantitative variables.[15] The subgroups usually represent dichotomous

---

[13] Two notable exceptions are P. M. Blau and W. R. Scott, *Formal Organizations; A Comparative Approach* (San Francisco: Chandler, 1962), and A. Etzioni, *A Comparative Analysis of Complex Organizations* (Glencoe, Ill.: Free Press, 1961).

[14] For an example of such a multivariate description of groups, see H. C. Selvin and W. O. Hagstrom, "The empirical classification of formal groups," *American Sociological Review* 28, 1963:399–411.

[15] Cf. S. A. Stouffer, *Social Research to Test Ideas* (Glencoe, Ill., Free Press, 1962), p. 265.

attributes or a few discrete categories on a nominal or ordinal scale, and they may tie in with "empirical types." As soon as the discrete categories defining the subgroups can be quantified, the group-by-group comparisons are superseded by a new level of analysis and the subgroup design is incorporated into the statistical techniques of multivariate analysis.[16] Essentially, this procedure amounts to the quantification of the comparative method.

If typologies, ideal types, and the comparison of "representative" cases are phases in social science research which mark the transition from the case study to quantitative research, the question of the measurement of organizational attributes appears in a new light. Several organizational studies are characteristic of an attempt to apply quantitative techniques and survey research methods to the analysis of social structure. Among these studies, it is possible to distinguish those that assess organizational characteristics indirectly from those that use direct methods. The use of individual perceptions and responses about organizational properties and the use of aggregate statistical data can be said to constitute indirect methods. The use of analytical and structural properties and the

survey of organizations constitute direct methods. In the following, these distinctions will be spelled out in somewhat more detail.

INDIVIDUALS' RESPONSES ABOUT ORGANIZATIONAL PROPERTIES

This type of study determines organizational properties by using as measures the responses of individuals about their organizational environment. This method is potentially useful if adequate techniques of sampling individuals from different subunits of a given organization or from a sample of organizations can be employed.

Two variants of this method are of particular interest. One of these is the characterization of the organizational climate or atmosphere in terms of the proportion of individuals who have a particular opinion or attitude concerning, for example, the extent of discretion permitted in each job or the amount of cooperation prevailing in the organization. By pooling the individual responses, it is possible to compare organizations and their subunits in terms of the proportion who believe they have much freedom in their jobs or who perceive others around them as cooperative rather than competitive.[17]

---

[16] See also P. F. Lazarsfeld, "Interpretation of statistical relations as a research operation," *In* P. F. Lazarsfeld and M. Rosenberg (eds.), *The Language of Social Research* (Glencoe, Ill., Free Press, 1955), pp. 115–25; P. F. Lazarsfeld and H. Menzel, "On the relation between individual and collective properties," *In* Etzioni, (ed.), *Complex Organizations*, pp. 422–40; see also Selvin and Hagstrom, "Empirical Classification," p. 404, on the successive transformation of integral into aggregative variables as higher levels of group structure are characterized in terms of the attributes of lower ones.

[17] One example of this approach is a study of the problem of coordination of patient care using the responses of 1058 employees in ten hospitals; cf. B. S. Georgopoulos and F. C. Mann, *The Community General Hospital* (New York: Macmillan, 1962). However, since supervisory and nonsupervisory employees are involved in the measures of perception of influence, style of supervision, and coordination, there is the problem of stability and consistency of perception across organizational levels as well as between different categories of personnel. On this general problem, see A. F. Wessen, "Hospital ideology and communication between ward personnel," *In* G. E. Jaco (ed.),

The systematic use of such proportions or "analytical" properties of collectivities is particularly important in research problems where sociologically dissimilar organizations are involved, or where the collective responses of individuals, as the constituent units, are used as the only basis of comparison.[18]

The second major variant of the method using individual responses about organizational properties is a modification of the time-honored anthropological technique of interviewing "key informants." While early ethnography and anthropology used such interviews on the assumption that certain key individuals—or sometimes just any informant—are "representative" of their culture and its modal characteristics, the assumption in organizational research would be that key informants have special knowledge as well as access to certain kinds of information by virtue of their position in the organization. It is important here to distinguish the *judgment* of key informants from the *factual knowledge* they can provide. In the first case, one may be interested in an opinion or policy stated by someone "in authority," just like in an elite interview. In the second case, the key informant would provide factual knowledge on the basis

of his specialized function and competence.[19] While the use of resource persons may provide information for the measurement of analytical and structural properties, the subjective responses of key informants, e.g., an executive director or board president, may yield information on global properties insofar as they have relevance or objective consequences for the organization as a whole.

In sum, the use of individuals' responses about organizational properties is potentially an adequate tool of organizational research. This is true, in particular, if questions are limited to objective and independently ascertainable data, and if the key informant's responses are restricted to his area of competence and jurisdiction. Of course, as soon as attitudinal data are involved, the question of adequate sampling of both organizations and individuals within organizations becomes of utmost importance.[20]

THE USE OF AGGREGATE STATISTICS

A second type of indirect measurement of organizational properties consists in the use of aggregate statistical data such as census data. While analytical or "aggregative" properties of organizations, e.g., the proportion of production workers in manufacturing establishments, constitute the original data, they are recorded and

---

Patients, Physicians, and Illness (Glencoe, Ill., Free Press, 1958), pp. 478–91, and M. Patchen, "Alternative questionnaire approaches to the measurement of influence in organizations," *American Journal of Sociology* 69, 1963:41–52.—The classical example for the general approach described here is still, of course, S. A. Stouffer et al., *The American Soldier* (Princeton, Princeton University Press, 1949).
[18] On the latter problem, see, e.g., R.H. Hall, "The concept of bureaucracy: An empirical assessment," *American Journal of Sociology* 69, 1963:32–40.

[19] For an interesting example of a study using high-ranking union officials in 65 local unions as sources for factual information, see E. E. Raphael, "Power structure and membership dispersion in unions," *American Journal of Sociology* 71, 1965:274–83.
[20] An excellent example here is P.F. Lazarsfeld and W. Thielens, Jr., *The Academic Mind* (Glencoe, Ill.: Free Press, 1958).

available only in the form of averages and other measures characterizing classes of organizations. Thus, Bendix uses the ratio of administrative employees to production workers (A/P ratio) in selected industries and countries. He also shows that technical specialization increases with size of establishment while internal bureaucratization does not.[21] Methodologically quite similar is Stinchcombe's comparative study of the building industries and selected mass manufacturing industries.[22] Stinchcombe shows that the proportion of clerks among administrative personnel is lower in craft production than in mass production, and that the opposite is true of personnel in professional authority positions. On the basis of this study Stinchcombe concludes that the professionalization of the labor force constitutes an alternative to bureaucratic administration, and that both professional and bureaucratic administration can be conceived as forms of rational administration. Although this study lacks controls for the effects of such variables as size, task complexity, or internal division of labor, Stinchcombe's conclusions have been of far-reaching importance in stimulating discussion and research efforts in this area.

[21] R. Bendix, *Work and Authority in Industry* (New York: Harper Torchbooks, 1963), p. 221–22. Bendix' findings are essentially confirmed in a similar study of manufacturing establishments based on United States Census data; cf. O. D. Duncan, "Size and structure of organizations: Manufacturing establishments," University of Chicago, 1961 (unpublished manuscript).
[22] A. L. Stinchcombe, "Bureaucratic and craft administration of production: A comparative study," *Administrative Science Quarterly* 4, 1959:168–87.

COLLECTIVE PROPERTIES OF
ORGANIZATIONS

Among the direct methods of studying organizational characteristics, the use of structural variables is of great interest because of their quantitative character and because their construction is based on detailed and comprehensive information on organizational subunits as well as on the number and distribution of organizational statuses. Such information may be available in the form of published or otherwise accessible census data or administrative statistics recorded and collected as a matter of routine.

An important example of the possibilities of this approach is Anderson and Warkov's study of forty-nine Veterans' Administration hospitals.[23] The study focuses on three structural variables which are important in organizational theory: organizational size, functional complexity, and the degree of internal bureaucratization. Size is measured by the average daily patient load, with hospitals being grouped into three size categories. Functional complexity is used as a dichotomous attribute, where thirty general medical-surgical hospitals represent high complexity, and nineteen tuberculosis hospitals represent low complexity. The degree of internal bureaucratization is measured by the proportion of personnel in administrative and clerical positions in each hospital.

The purpose of the study is to investigate the relationship between

[23] T. R. Anderson and S. Warkov, "Organizational size and functional complexity: A study of administration in hospitals," *American Sociological Review* 26, 1961: 23–28.

organizational size and the relative size of the administrative staff (internal bureaucratization) by controlling for the effect of functional complexity. This problem is, of course, of great interest from the point of view of testing one of Parkinson's famous laws. The major conclusion is that functional complexity, rather than size as such, is a crucial determinant of the degree of internal bureaucratization.

Another example of the use of structural variables for purposes of quantitative organizational analysis is a study of about 7000 American hospitals which I conducted in 1962-1963.[24] The major objectives of this project were to develop a theoretical framework for the analysis of organizations, to further elaborate quantitative methodological procedures applicable to organizations as the unit of analysis, and to test the usefulness of both the theoretical framework and the methodological procedures by applying them to data on U.S. hospitals. The raw data were collected by the American Hospital Association as part of a routine survey of their 7000 member hospitals in 1959, with a response rate of over ninety percent.

Among the structural variables derived from the raw data are the three used by Anderson and Warkov, namely, organizational size, the relative size of the administrative-clerical staff (internal bureaucratization), and

[24] For a preliminary report, see W. V. Heydebrand, "Differential modes of coordination in formal organizations," Los Angeles, 1963 (paper read at the Annual Meeting of the American Sociological Association); see also my *Hospital Bureaucracy: A Comparative Study of Organizations* (New York: Dunellen-Univ. Press of Cambridge, 1972).

the degree of complexity, represented here by a distinction between psychiatric hospitals (low complexity) and general hospitals (high complexity). In addition, a number of variables are constructed which serve as indicators of important dimensions of organizational structure. Thus, the complexity of the goal structure is further measured in terms of the diversification of major objectives expressed through the dichotomy of teaching versus nonteaching hospitals. Organizational autonomy, or external bureaucratization, is assessed in terms of types of ownership and external control. The internal hierarchical structure is measured in terms of the managerial-supervisory personnel ratio expressed here as the proportion of professional nurses in administrative-supervisory positions, which excludes administrative-clerical staff.

Further, the internal division of labor of the organization is conceptualized in terms of two related but independently measured variables. One of these, the degree of functional specialization, is indicated by the percent of occupational titles actually filled in a given hospital. The other aspect of the division of labor is the degree of departmental specialization. Theoretically, this measure refers to the number and relative size of the basic departments and personnel categories in a hospital, such as medical staff, professional nurses, technical staff, maintenance personnel, administrative staff, and so on. In the present study, the Gini coefficient of concentration is used to measure the evenness of distribution of the total personnel among seven basic departments and personnel categories.

Finally, the degree of professionalization is measured by the proportion of graduate professional nurses. The assumption underlying this measure is that the total patient care process is significantly determined by the extent to which graduate professional nurses are involved in its implementation and coordination, rather than aides, attendants, and other auxiliary personnel. One might wonder why the measure of professionalization is based on the nursing staff and not on the medical staff. However, in the organizational context of the hospital, physicians initiate and direct the "work process" but do not, as a rule, contribute to its implementation. For most of these variables, several operational measures are constructed with the aim of exploring the significance of the diverse conceptual components describing the various organizational characteristics.

Perhaps the most important single conclusion from this study is that an understanding of organizational structure cannot be obtained from the correlation of any two characteristics alone. While the relationships between size, complexity, division of labor, professionalization, bureaucratization, and other variables have been studied before, it is the complex pattern of their interrelations which constitute the "new reality" of organizational studies.

Substantively, the results demonstrate the critical importance of *nonbureaucratic* modes of coordination, as over against bureaucratic ones. Nonbureaucratic modes of coordination based on professionalization and interdependence among specialized departments become crucial particularly with increasing structural complexity of modern work organizations. For example, in types of hospitals with a relatively simple goal structure, the relative size of the administrative staff (internal bureaucratization) becomes larger as a result of increasing internal complexity, but is independent of, or negatively related to, professionalization. However, in structurally more complex types, where the goal structure is diverse, the opposite occurs. The administrative staff increases as a result of a higher degree of professionalization, but not any longer as a result of increasing structural differentiation or internal complexity.

One may conclude from these findings that in a highly differentiated organizational context, professional work assumes a "specialist" rather than a "generalist" character; furthermore, interdependence among specialized departments leads to forms of "structural coordination," i.e., mechanisms of conflict resolution, mutual regulation, and lateral communication and coordination.

As to the hierarchical structure of authority, the findings show that professionalization as well as the relative diversity of organizational goals contribute to the dispersion of authority.

To summarize, the development of nonbureaucratic modes of coordination, such as professionalization and lateral communication and coordination, tends to change the structure of bureaucratic authority and to affect the overall patterns of organizational coordination and control in complex organizations.

Methodologically, the significance of this study lies in its systematic framework designed for quantitative comparisons among the structural patterns of a relatively large number of formal organizations in terms of sociologically relevant variables, however crudely they are measured. Moreover, the use of multivariate statistical techniques makes it possible to explore a great variety of interrelations and interactions among organizational attributes and to test specific hypotheses suggested by sociological and organizational theory.

THE DIRECT SURVEY OF
ORGANIZATIONS

From the point of view of comparative, quantitative research of organizations, this type of approach is the most comprehensive and promising. It requires systematic sampling of different types of organizations as well as a combination of the methods described above.

An early example of this approach is Udy's pioneering study of 426 primitive production organizations sampled from 150 different socio-cultural environments on the basis of data from the Human Relations Area File.[25] Starting out with seven different types of production organizations, Udy constructs an index of technological complexity in terms of which organizational types can be quantitatively distinguished and ranked.

He then proceeds to test some sixty-four hypotheses on various aspects of organizational structure and its relation to the environment. Of particular interest are his findings on the determinants of bureaucratic characteristics in primitive work organizations, given the context of predominantly ascriptive societies.

Most of Udy's analysis is based on dichotomous variables and two-by-

two classifications without the use of multivariate techniques. Another more implicit difficulty is the fact that the organizational data represent 150 different societies and cultures, coded from a variety of sources, a fact which can be assumed to hide a considerable amount of unaccountable variation.

Udy's conclusions are based on findings involving the covariation among such areas as technological process, production organization, reward system, and social setting. Thus, Udy's work is of considerable scope and significance for the construction of a broad comparative framework.[26] Another example of the direct survey of organizations using a variety of methods is a recently published study of 100 British firms.[27] This study, which was begun as early as 1953, makes use of statistical material for the construction of analytical and structural variables, and it also involves interview data, case studies, and documentary material. The results are, in many respects, similar to those of Udy's study in that technological aspects of production organization are found to be major determinants of the hierarchial and administrative structure of the organization.

In sum, it must be recognized that on the whole only a few studies of organizations have been guided by a systematic effort to test theoretical generalizations about bureaucracy and organizational structure. With the deliberate use of a comparative and quantitative research strategy, it

---

[25] S. H. Udy, Jr., *Organization of Work*, New Haven, Human Relations Area File Press, 1959; see also his "Administrative rationality, social setting, and organizational development," *American Journal of Sociology* 68, 1962:299–308.

[26] See also Udy's recent elaboration of this framework, *In* J. G. March (ed.), *Handbook*.
[27] J. Woodward, *Industrial Organization: Theory and Practice* (London: Oxford University Press, 1965).

has become more feasible to test specific hypotheses. More researchers have, therefore, engaged in organizational analysis not only to describe certain types of organizations or to deal with topical questions, but to study basic organizational characteristics and processes with a view towards generalization, reconceptualization, and theoretical refinement.

A COMPARATIVE ORGANIZATION RESEARCH PROGRAM

The study of U.S. hospitals described earlier (see footnote 24) had demonstrated the feasibility of using data on the collective properties of organizations, such as hospitals, for the purpose of testing general, theoretically relevant hypotheses about organizational structure. The original plan for that study included a two-step strategy whereby new questions and avenues of investigation emerging from the analysis of the published data were to become the focus of a more detailed investigation of a sample of the organizations on the basis of interviews with key informants, e.g., the hospital administrator, the director of nursing, the chief of the medical staff, etc. In this way, it was hoped to maximize the gains of the quantitative analysis and to supplement it by a more qualitative and focused inquiry into the processes of decision-making and innovation.

In addition, the substantive results and theoretical implications drawn from the general approach developed in the hospital study seemed to warrant the consideration and planning of a series of studies focusing on different types of organizations within a common theoretical and compara-tive framework. In the summer of 1964, the National Science Foundation provided funds for the establishment of a comprehensive research program to be conducted at the University of Chicago under the direction of Peter M. Blau and myself.[28]

OBJECTIVES AND METHOD

The major organizational variables used in this research program are those that proved to be of particular theoretical interest in the earlier study of hospitals, such as complexity of goal structure (e.g., number and types of major objectives), organizational size, functional specialization, departmentalization, professionalization, and internal bureaucratization (hierarchical structure and administrative staff), also ownership and external control (organizational autonomy), size of community, and, generally, differentiation of the organizational environment. The objectives of the program include the refinement of a number of operational measures used in previous research on organizations as well as the construction of new ones, the measurement of generalized organizational variables in different types of organizations, the testing of specific hypotheses and the formulation of new generalizations. The data are obtained from published sources, through mail questionnaires, through interviews with key informants in samples of organizations, and from

[28] Cf. Comparative Organization Research Program (CORP), University of Chicago, Department of Sociology, National Science Foundation Grant GS-553, P.M. Blau and W. V. Heydebrand, Principal Investigators; see also P. M. Blau, "The comparative study of organizations," *Industrial and Labor Relations Review* 18, 1965:323–38.

the records of these organizations. Organizations on which data have been obtained so far include teaching hospitals and hospitals affiliated with medical schools (subsamples from the above-mentioned hospital study), state and local government finance agencies, metropolitan school systems, state and local employment security agencies, and private welfare agencies.

A PILOT PROJECT

One of the first projects to be conducted within the framework of the Comparative Organization Research Program (CORP) was a study of Public Personnel Agencies.[29] This study of about 150 executive agencies of the Civil Service Commission in most of the states and large cities in the United States and Canada is based on data collected by the Public Personnel Association and published in a special report. As a pilot study by CORP, it was intended to test the feasibility of doing comparative organizational research on the basis of relatively limited but easily available published data. Moreover, the project permitted evaluation of the applicability of a broadly conceived conceptual framework to organizations other than hospitals.

The design of this project was patterned after the earlier empirical studies of Bendix, Udy, Stinchcombe, Anderson and Warkov, and Heydebrand (see footnotes 21-25). In turn, the study has informed the design and

[29] For detailed reports, see P. M. Blau, W. V. Heydebrand and R. E. Stauffer, "The structure of small bureaucracies," *American Sociological Review* 31, 1966:179–91; and R. E. Stauffer, P. M. Blau and W. V. Heydebrand, "Organizational complexities of public personnel agencies," *Public Personnel Review* 25, 1966:82–87.

procedure of many of the subsequent projects of CORP. For example, a large number of contextual and environmental variables (not used in the published analysis cited above, however) are included in subsequent projects. Similarly, some of the crude operational measures that had to be used here as well as in the earlier hospital study provoked search for more refined techniques.

Several substantive conclusions can be drawn from the study of Public Personnel Agencies. For example, the findings suggest that the centralization of managerial authority and professionalization constitute alternative modes of coordination; that an advanced division of labor tends to facilitate centralization or professionalization, but not necessarily both at the same time; that the complexities introduced by increasing division of labor and professionalization increase costs, but that a sufficiently large administrative staff facilitates communication and coordination in the more complex organizations and thus helps to reduce costs.

These conclusions, however, must be considered tentative. The main reason for this qualification is that the measure of centralization used in this study is ambiguous in two respects. First, a high ratio of managerial personnel is interpreted as decentralization. But it is not clear whether the measure refers to the concentration or dispersion of decision-making authority, or simply to the supervisory span of control. Secondly, even if decision making and supervision are assumed to be coterminous, the fact remains that the the use of a ratio as a measure of hierarchial structure imposes the concept of a two-level hierarchy on an organization which may, in fact, have more than two levels. Thus, a large number of managers could be associated with the proliferation of hierarchial levels. Furthermore, given a certain number of managerial personnel, their formal authority will be delegated and thus dispersed to the extent that it extends over many hierarchical levels of authority. Of course, as the hospital study had already shown, one of the major intervening factors in the determination of the authority structure of an organization is the complexity of the division of labor and the degree of professionalization. Thus, a high degree of internal functional differentiation as well as of professionalization is likely to increase the number of levels and will hence facilitate the delegation and decentralization of authority. Centralization of authority, on the other hand, will tend to prevail under conditions of routinization of work and a low degree of professionalization.

This study of Public Personnel Agencies has been described in some detail because it is one of the first self-contained projects of CORP. The other studies follow a similar design and pattern of analysis, although there is some variation in the method of data collection. Since it was not entirely clear at the outset of the overall research program as to whether it is feasible to collect systematic data on the characteristics of several hundred organizations by questioning a few key informants in each, it may be useful to say a few words about the field work experience.

INTERVIEWS AND MAIL
QUESTIONNAIRES

In two of the projects data were obtained through personal interviews

with key informants, using somewhat different procedures in each. The fieldwork for the study of government finance agencies was conducted by the field staff of the National Opinion Research Center. The data for the study of Employment Security agencies were collected by three of CORP's research assistants who traveled to all state agencies in the United States (except Alaska and Hawaii from where data were collected by mail) where they obtained data not only on the organization of the state agencies, but also on that of the 2000 local offices which are their constituent units.

Both interviewing procedures provided satisfactory information at a high response rate, notably after some follow-up by mail and phone to obtain duplicates of organizational records originally promised, and to clarify obscure points.

Mail questionnaires appear to be suitable for collecting information on organizational characteristics provided they are sponsored by an association of the organizations under study. The experience at CORP indicates that the successful administration of mail questionnaires depends both on the type of organization and on the availability of "official" sponsorship or endorsement of the study.

For example, the annual routine questionnaire surveys of the member hospitals of the American Hospital Association have comparatively high reliability and a response rate of over ninety percent. They have, in the past, yielded valuable raw data which proved useful for the construction of a wide variety of organizational variables (see footnote 24). A questionnaire survey conducted by the National Federation of Settlements and Neighborhood Centers furnished extremely detailed data on these private welfare agencies, although the response rate was low (about forty-five percent), partly due to the fact that this survey was one of the first more detailed ones in their history. Finally, a mail questionnaire provided some important data on hospitals affiliated with medical schools to supplement those available from the main annual surveys, from a special hospital survey conducted by the American Hospital Association for the U.S. Public Health Service in connection with the introduction of Medicare in 1966, and from other published sources.[30]

However, the experience with mail questionnaires sent to the smaller public finance agencies was less encouraging. These questionnaires were sent out to complement the interview data obtained in the large finance agencies. This mail survey yielded a relatively low return rate (sixty percent) and many inadequate responses. It may well be, however, that satisfactory mail questionnaires can be used for organizational research in the future as more experience is gained in the proper wording of questions and instructions to elicit the appropriate data on administrative structure.[31]

SPECIFIC RESEARCH PROJECTS

As to the specific projects in which CORP was involved, I have already indicated that a variety of organizations and of organizational problems were being studied. For example, the study of 1250 U.S. *teaching hospitals* represents a follow-up investigation of a subsample of a highly complex and professionalized type of organization. The main objectives of this study are to examine in more detail the influence on the hospital structure of the degree of organizational complexity (multiple goals and diversified and specialized tasks) as indicated by the number of different residency programs as well as the extent of involvement of the hospital in various other aspects of medical and paramedical education.[32]

Another objective of this study is to investigate organizational change, specifically the effect of the organization's age, and of change in technological complexity and in the pattern of external relations between 1950 and 1960 on managerial succession and the bureaucratic and nonbureaucratic modes of coordination. One aspect of this study is the further investigation of a subsample of 240 of the above hospitals, i.e., those that are affiliated with *medical schools* and are thus directly involved in the training of medical students, not merely of interns and residents. An important focus of this study is the relationship between the organization of a collegial body—the medical staff —and that of a semibureaucratic

---

[30] See, for example, the publications of the American Medical Association, the American Association of Medical Colleges, the American College of Hospital Administrators, and the U.S. Public Health Service.

[31] For an interesting description of the use of mail questionnaires for international comparative studies conducted at the Columbia University Bureau of Applied Social Research, see W. A. Glaser, "International mail surveys of informants," *Human Organization* 25, 1966:78–86.

[32] I am indebted to Professor Jack Feldman, formerly of NORC, for first suggesting to me the idea of using the number of residency programs as well as the types of internships available at a given teaching hospital as indicators of medical and organizational complexity.

structure—the hospital administration. Still another concern is the connection between the hospital and its immediate environment as articulated by emergency room practice.

The study of *finance departments* of all state governments, municipal governments of large cities (over 50,000), and those of large counties (over 100,000) in the United States includes over 250 cases based on personal interviews conducted by the field staff of the National Opinion Research Center, and about 150 usable cases of smaller departments based on mail questionnaires. Of central concern in this investigation is the nature of the hierarchical authority structure, the various structural characteristics of the organization that influence it and the question of how, in turn, it influences decision-making and operating procedures. A number of other problems are being investigated in this project, such as the impact of mechanization (the use of computers) on the organization, and various aspects of decision making and change.

Another study of CORP involves the investigation of organizational patterns in the 132 largest *school systems* in the United States, based on data published by the National Education Association. One of the problems studied here is the significance of the administrative and managerial components for the organization of the teaching staff. A school system is a highly professionalized organization, with all states requiring at least some college preparation for teachers. There are, however, differences in the degree of professionalization of school systems, and this project will explore the interrelation between such organizational attributes as professionalization, centralization of authority, and administrative specialization.

The study of the *Organization of Employment Security* in the United States, consisting of 53 independent state and approximately 2000 local agencies, is based on data collected in the field by CORP staff, as previously described. Is is supplemented by data from a variety of published and unpublished sources. Thus, information on the activities, productivity, and personnel of these organizations was collected by the U.S. Department of Labor, and data on Employment Security interviewing personnel was collected and made available to CORP by the U.S. Department of Health, Education, and Welfare. This study includes both of the major components of Employment Security, the public employment service and the unemployment insurance program, which are under the same overall organizational authority in most states, although they constitute two distinct agencies in a few. The large amount of data on different organizational levels (state and local) available in this project makes it possible to investigate the entire gamut of problems and hypotheses considered in CORP. For example, it is possible to study intensively the interrelations between the complexity of the organization's overall responsibility, the differentiation of tasks, the extent of departmentalization, the degree of professionalization of the staff, the structure of hierarchical authority, the administrative-clerical staff, the use of mechanized equipment, the formalization of operating procedures and personnel policies as indicated by the relative proliferation of written rules covering these areas, and the degree of centralization of authority in various areas of decision making, such as policy, budget, procedures, personnel, and others. It will also be possible to study how variations in these organizational characteristics, holding constant the qualifications of professional personnel, affect operating costs and effective performance and to trace the significance of changes in both administrative structure and operating procedures.

An extensive coding scheme for reducing highly complex organizational charts to data suitable for quantitative analysis has been developed for the purposes of this analysis. A special feature of this project is that the structure of about 1500 local agencies (excluding the 500 smallest ones) can be analyzed within the context of the "roof organization"— the state agency—of which they are a part, i.e., the characteristics of the state agencies can be used as contextual variables for the analysis of the local agencies.

The study of *private welfare agencies*—settlement houses and neighborhood and community centers—is based on mail questionnaires administered under the sponsorship of the National Federation of these centers. Data on organizational structure and personnel are being analyzed for 122 agencies, with about one-fifth having two or more metropolitan-wide, geographically dispersed branches. These relatively small and loosely structured organizations confront special problems created by changing social conditions in metropolitan America, by the fact of competition for services, funds, and clientele with the public welfare establishment and with other private welfare and community organizations, and by the pressures to conform to federally supported programs such as those connected with the "war on poverty." The study

focuses on the effect of the diversity of group and neighborhood programs, the complexity of educational and welfare services offered, and the research and development programs conducted on such internal structural variables as the division of labor, the formalization of departments around occupational and professional specialities, professionalization, the hierarchical authority structure, standardization of procedures, and financial operations. This study, obviously, has great potential significance for contributing to our understanding of the interrelation between organizations and their environment.

A few independent smaller studies are being conducted under the general auspices of CORP, largely entailing Ph. D. dissertations by graduate students in sociology. One of them is a study of a sample of *local industrial unions* which focuses particularly on the conditions of leadership turnover and oligarchy in these unions. Another study extends the approach of CORP to a very different type of organization, namely *religious communities* of women (Roman Catholic orders of nuns). This investigation seeks to examine the influence of the hierarchical structure and the distribution of duties on the occurrence of certain aspects of change in these religious orders on the basis of quantitative data collected from a sample of them.

PLANS FOR AN ORGANIZATIONAL
DATA ARCHIVE

Finally, CORP included plans for a comparative organization research file, i.e., an inventory of materials and the coding of organizational case studies similar to the idea of the Human Relations Area File. The inventory of materials to be assembled will initially be confined mainly to two types of items, namely source-books on organizations and their associations, and an accumulation of data cards, tapes, and codebooks from CORP's studies, appropriately indexed, to make these data easily accessible for comparative analyses across different organizational types, and for future use by other research-ers. Later on, materials and data from other organizational studies may be incorporated into the File, which would ultimately develop into a *data archive* for organizational research. A scheme for coding information from published case studies of organiza-tions has been developed, and its use-fulness has been tested by applying it to a few such studies of single organi-zations.

ORGANIZATION OF RESEARCH AT CORP

It should be mentioned here that the research staff of CORP was drawn predominantly from among graduate students in the Department of Soci-ology at the University of Chicago. The students were serving as project directors and research assistants on specific CORP projects while working on their respective Master's and Doc-tor's dissertations. While such a peonage system harbors certain in-justices, one may say in its defense that students interested in this type of research may derive partial or complete financial support from re-search activities which are potentially useful for their dissertations. The projects and their staffs, including coders, computer programmers, and clerical personnel, were coordinated by a research associate and directed by the two principal investigators. Although this organization chart sug-gests a functional and clear-cut orga-nizational hierarchy, it should be noted that CORP itself provides the datum for an important conclusion to the contrary: hierarchical distinc-tions do not necessarily grow out of the need for coordination among specialized projects, especially in the area of professional activities and scientific research where teamwork is of great significance. Quite the opposite seems to hold: hierarchical distinctions are frequently imposed from without so as to maintain or justify extra-organizational status ar-rangements; or else they obscure or simply impede a rational division of labor which is rooted in the com-plexity of the task and in the separate requirements of individual projects and research teams. In this sense, the organization of research in CORP was no exception to most of the organi-zational phenomena which were its object of analysis.

SOME CRITERIA FOR THE FUTURE DEVELOMENT OF ORGANIZATIONAL RESEARCH

It may be useful, by way of sum-mary, to formulate some of the meth-odological and theoretical criteria which would seem to play an impor-tant role in the future development of quantitative-comparative research on organizations.

The first three criteria involve, respectively, the problem of the unit of analysis, the quantification of structural characteristics of organiza-tions and the question of sampling.

ORGANIZATIONS AS THE UNIT OF ANALYSIS

Knowledge about organizations and, more importantly, about the making of effective organizations will be significantly advanced if *whole organizations*, not their subunits, are considered the unit of analysis in organizational research. Such a focus draws attention to the economic, political, and socio-cultural determinants of organizational phenomena as well as to the ongoing processes of interaction and interdependence among organizations and among classes, groups, and systems of organizations.

THE QUANTIFICATION OF STRUCTUAL CHARACTERISTICS

A methodological consequence of this view is the need to construct operational measures referring to *group characteristics*, rather than to attributes of individuals-in-organizations. Among the collective properties of organizations are, in ascending order of importance, global (integral), analytical (aggregative, compositional), systemic (internal-structural, relational) and contextual (external-structural) properties (see footnote 16).

The practice of sampling individuals or subunits from within organizations so as to obtain a "representative" picture of the organizations under study is a poor substitute for the adequate measurement of organizational characteristics as long as sampling methods cannot be perfected to get at structural properties. Organizations are not aggregates of individuals or subunits; they are structured and "organized," however loose, temporary, or merely prescriptive the formal structure may be. It is, therefore, important to be aware of the problem of direct sampling of individuals-in-organizations and its underlying assumption of random distribution, to limit the use of analytical, aggregative, compositional

variables to the broadly descriptive role in which they may be useful, and to maximize the analysis of organizations in terms of truly structural, relational, and systemic variables.

By the same token, global characteristics tend to be nominal and dichotomous; at best, they represent an ordinal scale from "low" to "medium" and "high." It seems important to transform global into continuous-structural variables with true zero points as soon as the techniques of data collection and measurement permit. It is fashionable, for example, to talk about organizations as "large-scale," "complex," and "formal." However, all three of these global characteristics can be quantified. Thus, size, complexity, and formalization, rather than remaining dichotomous attributes, become continuous variables in terms of which degree or quantity of these properties can be measured. Similarly, in my original study of hospitals, I distinguished between psychiatric and general hospitals, i.e., comparisons were based on global-dichotomous properties of hospitals. In the same way, a distinction between teaching and nonteaching hospitals was made. Later, both of these dimensions were quantified: the organizational complexity of hospitals can be described in terms of the number of medical specialties present, ranging from psychiatry at one end of the continuum to up to thirty different specialties, at the other, i.e., ranging up to the most "general" of general hospitals. Moreover, the degree of "teachingness" of a hospital can be measured by the number of intern and resident positions offered or actually filled (the latter could also be used as a quality indicator). Alternatively, one could use the number of medical students, or the number of medical schools with which the hospital is affiliated, or an index composed of all of these multiple indicators.

The variety of research strategies in organizational studies will be maximized if the collection of data is based on a *large number of units* (N), preferably random samples of organizations, and if it is oriented toward obtaining a *large number of variables* (n) *on each unit organization*. Obviously, N should be larger than n so as to avoid over-determination of the system of variables. Both of these conditions, N's and n's, jointly constitute a close approximation to an experimental design. In this sense, quantitative organizational research and modern sample survey research involving individual respondents share similar operating assumptions—and the same limitations.

While these first three sets of criteria are relatively obvious in their methodological implications, the next points are theoretically relevant as well. They deal with the problems of choice among alternative theoretical models, the continuity between organizations and their environment and the definition of organizational boundaries, the influence of macro-sociological and cultural systems on organizations, the study of organizational change and the comparative analysis of trends, and the problem of organizational effectiveness.

ALTERNATIVE THEORETICAL MODELS

Alternative definitions of what an organization is have consequences for research strategies, questions asked, problems investigated, and "findings" and conclusions derived from the analysis of the data. It would, therefore, seem important that organizational analysis is sensitive to the implications of alternative theoretical perspectives. For example, organizations may be viewed as single-purpose systems, or as more or less integrated, pluralistic clusters of structured activities directed toward multiple ends.

The *system approach* typically entails a conception of organizations as pursuing a specific objective or goal, or a system of goals, with the differentiated subsystems organized around specialized subgoals.[33] Such an organizational system is conceived as integrated in terms of one set of symbols of legitimacy, a set of consistent perceptual, cognitive and normative constructs shared by all participants, a unitary hierarchy of authority, and a pattern of growth and change operating according to principles of structural differentiation, boundary maintenance, and homeostasis. There are many unifunctional, relatively simple organizations which can usefully be analyzed in terms of a system model.

Alternatively, the *"cluster"* approach involves the recognition of a goal structure with a plurality of goals, diversified objectives, multiple and possibly incompatible definitions of goals and objectives, dual or multiple bases of legitimacy, and multiple hierarchies.[34] Such organizational structures are not, as a rule, mono-

---

[33] See, for example, T. Parsons, *Structure and Process*, pp. 17–44.

[34] See also Burns and Stalker, *Management and Innovation*. Preface to the second edition (London: Social Science Paperbacks, 1966), pp. vii–xxii; and Burns, in Vroom (ed.), *Methods*.

cratic, although they may be auto-cephalous (i.e., having their own single head). The image emerging here is that of a loosely structured cluster of heterogeneous and semi-autonomous units representing different interests and claims to power. Such organizational phenomena as General Motors, IBM, or the "multi-versity" are difficult to apprehend with a system model. They are aptly called "conglomerations" by some economists. Insofar as they possess stability and continuity it tends to be based on integrating forces other than shared goals and unity of command. Comparative research would simply fail to grasp the nature of such pluralistic organizations, if they were approached in terms of the categories of "monocratic bureaucracy" or of the classical notion of "formal organization." This may be true even of modern government bureaucracies, as our research shows. The paradigm underlying the idea of a stable, integrated social system tends to blind rather than alert the researcher to the complexities of the task and goal structure of such organizations, the power struggle and other relational problems between subunits and the different and precarious modes of coordination.[35] One may, of course, redefine the non-fitting elements and dysfunctions as functional for some larger system, a procedure which amounts to the resolution of empirical questions by definitional fiat.

THE CONTINUITY BETWEEN ORGANIZATION AND ENVIRONMENT

The analysis of the interrelation between organizations and their ex-

ternal environment poses the same problem dealt with in the previous section, but in a slightly different light. The definition of what an organization is will determine, in part, the definition of the organizational environment. It raises the question of how their interrelation is to be conceptualized.[36]

For purposes of illustration, let us take the case of the state finance agencies from our research experience (see the description of CORP, above). These agencies are departments of state governments which perform highly specialized functions within the context of a larger organization. From this perspective, the finance agencies are not autonomous organizations, but departments or, at best, subsystems of a larger unitary organization, namely, the state government. Thus, the unit of analysis turns out to be located on a particular *level* in a larger organization. This fact immediately raises the question of the *degree of autonomy* of the unit under study. The problem of organizational autonomy has at least two dimensions in this case. One is the vertical relation of the finance department to the higher level in the same organization, the other is the horizontal relation to the other departments. The vertical relationship in this case is dealt with in terms of the degree of *external bureaucratization*. The horizontal relationships might be dealt with in terms of *functional interdependence* if a system model is adopted; or else, in terms of various other types of relationships, such

---

[35] Cf. also Crozier, *Bureaucratic Phenomenon*.

[36] For a perceptive discussion of this problem, see E. W. Bakke, "Concept of the social organization," in M. Haire (ed.), *Modern Organization Theory* (New York: John Wiley, 1959), pp. 16–75.

as cooperation, bargaining and exchange, competition, opposition and conflict, coalition formation, cooperation, integration, as well as simple coexistence.[37]

While these questions must remain open in the case of the finance agencies, since data on the lateral relationships with other specialized departments are not available, it will be possible to investigate the generic problem of the effect of a given organizational level on lower level units in the study of the employment agencies (see CORP, above), because data were deliberately collected on the state agencies as well as on their constituent subunits, the local offices.

However, to return to the larger question of the characterization of the environment, it is clear that the same types of relationships *within* organizations may exist also *between* organizations. Thus finance departments may interact in various ways with other organizations in the community, such as business firms and other revenue producing organizations, the political structure of the

community in which they are located, and many more. Once again, the question of the unit of analysis becomes of paramount importance, since it is an integral part of the problem of defining the *boundaries* of organizations. Another aspect, therefore, of the problem of continuity between organization and environment is the need for new categories of organizational classification. Typologies of organizations tend to be of limited applicability insofar as they depend on the identification of primary (i.e., single) functions and goals. It will be necessary in future comparative research to develop *formal typologies* capable of discriminating between organizational structures independently of their substantive goals. For example, different types of social, economic, political, and ecological relationships between organizational units and their larger context might be used to define boundaries, concentration of functions, internal structure, and relative autonomy or dominance of organizations, much like the ecologist's delimitation of a metropolis vis-à-vis its hinterland and other cities in the region.

In general, it is proposed here to use various forms of affiliation and degrees of association between organizational units, i.e., *relational categories* as criteria of organizational classification. For example, the number of different relationships, the relative looseness or closeness of affiliation, and other aspects of the nature of the association, and the number of contacts or transactions per time unit could be used as criteria for determining organizational units of analysis. Specific examples of such relationally defined organizational structures and systems of organiza-

---

[37] It should be noted that many of these relational terms referring to *processes of interaction* have been dealt with in terms of the perspective and the categories of formal sociology. Cf. especially K. H. Wolff, transl. and ed., *The Sociology of Georg Simmel* (Glencoe, Ill.: Free Press, 1950). See also W. M. Evan, "The organization-set: Toward a theory of interorganizational relations," in J. D. Thompson (ed.), *Approaches to Organizational Design* (Pittsburgh: University of Pittsburgh Press, 1966), pp. 173–91; H. Guetzkow, "Relations among organizations," in R. V. Bowers (ed.), *Studies on Behavior in Organizations* (Athens, Ga.: University of Georgia Press, 1966), pp. 13–44; E. Litwak and L. F. Hylton, "Inter-organizational analysis: A hypothesis on coordinating agencies," *Administrative Science Quarterly* 6, 1962:395–426.

tions can be suggested very briefly.

Considering a public school system, a set of chain stores, a large custodial mental hospital, the Veterans Administration, or the Internal Revenue Service, we find a characteristic segmentation and repetition of essentially similar units. Structurally quite similar are "roof organizations," i.e., associations and federations of similar kinds of organizations. While both of these structural types are similar with respect to *homogeneity of units,* the *delegation of authority* may be *downward* in the case of public schools or chain stores. Associations of organizations, on the other hand, tend to be formed by a process of *upward delegation of authority* (see, for example my earlier references to the American Hospital Association or the National Federation of Settlements).

In the case of *heterogeneity of units,* one may distinguish between those that are structurally differentiated and interrelated by functional interdependence, as over against those types of organizations where such interrelation is more tenuous or absent. For example, a general hospital or an automobile manufacturing firm are multifunctional organizations with heterogeneous, functionally differentiated and interdependent subunits. Another example would be a department store or a liberal arts college, where most subunits are functionally differentiated, but structually similar. Still another example can be found in diversified organizations representing multiple and heterogeneous objectives which may not be functional for each other, but happen to co-exist by virtue of being part of one corporation or being under one "authority" such as federal, state, and city governments. Another example is the "multiversity" with its teaching departments, research institutes, professional schools, foundations, hospitals and clinics, real estate interests, and many other types of units. Finally, an example of particular interest from the point of view of community structure are the chains and clusters of economically interdependent organizations, such as Du Pont or IBM or American Telephone and Telegraph, ranging from trusts which have monopolistic control over different phases of a production-distribution system to more or less "open" market structures, where organizations are nevertheless bound together by a *modus vivendi* of exchange and interdependence, regulated mainly by impersonal price mechanisms. The associational and organizational network of modern communities falls somewhere in between these two extremes of closed and open systems.

It is partly an empirical question, partly one of theoretical interest to determine at what point seemingly unitary, integrated organizations can be treated as clusters or chains of smaller units which stand in some relation of cooperation, competition, or conflict to each other or, generally, in a relation of interdependence. If the need for redefining organizational structures in inter-organizational, relational terms involves the concerns of formal sociology, it also requires the systematic development of *categories of social process* for the analysis of internal coordination as well as external relationships. In short, intra-and inter-organizational analysis may be viewed as part of the same continuous framework of inquiry.

THE INFLUENCE OF
MARCO-SOCIOLOGICAL AND
CULTURAL SYSTEMS

The conception of organizations as continuous with their environment, i.e., with other organizations as well as with social organization in general, precludes the necessity of making a special case for comparative analysis in the conventional sense, i.e., for *cross-cultural organizational analysis.* The comparative study of the interrelation between communities and organizational structures, and of the influence of cultural patterns, macroeconomic and macro-political systems on specific organizational arrangements is, therefore, a more or less natural extension of organizational analysis, in general, and does not require a special theoretical or methodological *raison d'être.*

It seems that such an analysis should fulfill three minimum requirements. First, it should spell out the *relative significance* of specific types of organizations in different communities and cultures, i.e., in different macro-systems. Second, such analysis should bring out the degree of *structural variation* insofar as it is independent of cultural and other influences. Third, the problems of organization due to *cultural variation* and other macro-level influences should be isolated. This procedure is likely to contribute to an empirical assessment of the way in which different cultures and national societies handle basic functional problems, such as production, distribution, law enforcement, defense, education, health, welfare, and so on. In other words, such an analysis would focus on the *systemic properties of cultures,* by using organizations as the primary manifestations of institutional structure.[38]

ORGANIZATIONAL TREND ANALYSIS

There is an increasing need for the analysis of organizational processes over time. Specifically, comparative trend research might profitably focus on the historical dimensions of structural change, i.e., on the transformation of organizations as well as of their contexts. This focus is particularly important in the case of "clusters" and associations of organizations, as well as for the question of the effect of change in size and complexity, technology and professionalization on the modes of coordination and control; especially the emergence of nonbureaucratic modes of coordination as supplementing and superseding bureaucratic modes must be studied in terms of historical and structural change.

The routine collection of organizational data over time, preferably by an agency such as the Bureau of the Census is, of course, a basic requirement for the establishment of data archives on organizational statistics, routine comparative trend analysis, and social forecasting.

ORGANIZATIONAL EFFECTIVENESS

Finally, a contextual approach in comparative organizational research must take into account not only the *determinants* of organizations, but also their *effects* and *consequences.* Thus, we come back full circle to the question of the objectives and

[38] See also Crozier, *Bureaucratic Phenomenon,* Part IV.

goals, and with that to the thorny problem of goal attainment, quality, and, generally, *organizational effectiveness*. The analysis of inter organizational relationships can potentially contribute much to the question of "output," since the extent and nature of such relationships frequently constitute an integral part of effectiveness. Specific examples are total number of sales per time unit, proportion of clients served (both individuals and organizations), number of referrals made, proportion of inventions produced or innovations accepted, and so on. While there are, admittedly, many problems remaining in this area of research, such as the definition of quality of output, the determination of input of resources in relation to output, i.e., the problems of efficiency, productivity, and cost, the basic question is one of measurement and as such is not insurmountable.

In general, it will be a significant part of future organizational research to examine the role of organizations in social change. It is here that we encounter the question of organizational effectiveness in its most generalized form. An important example is the process of modernization, i.e., the interaction of social, economic, and political innovations. This process is hardly conceivable without the idea of social, economic, and political power generated by organizations, be they public bureaucracies or private associations. In this sense, organizations share an element with all forms of social organization, namely, the mobilization of resources both for the attainment of established goals and for the definition and realization of new ones.

part one

ORGANIZATIONAL ENVIRONMENT
AND AUTONOMY

INTRODUCTION

The eight studies in this section focus on the interaction between the environment of organizations and their autonomy, as well as on the influence of both environment and autonomy on other structural characteristics. A brilliant example of both of these concerns is the study by Pugh and his associates. Moreover, this study uniquely demonstrates the power and potential of comparative-quantitative organizational analysis.[1]

The present paper by Pugh and his associates delineates a series of environmental variables, conceptualized as determinants of internal structure. The authors define "organizational context" in terms of origin and history, ownership and control (legal autonomy), dependence on other organizations (functional and economic autonomy), size, location and charter (goal and task structure), and technology. The authors then use multivariate analysis to show the effect of the environmental variables on three dimensions of internal organizational structure. The three internal structural factors are obtained by means of factor analysis and are labeled "structuring of activities," "concentration of authority," and "line control of workflow."

The analysis shows that the structuring of activities is strongly influenced by size and technology, that the concentration of authority is significantly determined by dependence and location, and that the line control of workflow varies directly with certain aspects of the charter, specifically with the operating variability.

Size, functional autonomy, and task structure thus emerge as major determinants of organizational structure, a conclusion which is highly consonant

---

[1] A second key report from the former Aston research group deals with details of the internal structure of the fifty-two British manufacturing organizations investigated, as well as with the methodological procedures employed. It is reprinted here in Part III, selection 23.

with the results of other studies, including those of professional and service organizations.

Methodologically, the results of this research project argue most persuasively for a multivariate approach to the study of organizations. This approach has become a major way of systematically gauging the joint effect of external and internal factors on organizational processes and outcomes. It is studies of this kind that constitute the most significant advance over the organizational case studies of the 1950s, and promise to contribute to a general theory of organizations.

One of the earliest and most influential comparative studies of organizations is Udy's analysis of preindustrial production organizations. Udy develops a causal model of the dynamics of organizational structure. He relates technical complexity (a composite index based on the number, sequentiality, and integration of specialized activities) to external community involvement, on the one hand, and to the internal authority and reward structure, on the other. Udy's thirty preindustrial work organizations represent thirty different sociocultural contexts. The unit of analysis is therefore, strictly speaking, the *institutional form* of work organization, rather than specific work organizations, since the ethnographic approach relies on "representative" cases or, alternatively, constructs an ideal type from the observation of a number of specific cases of organizations. A crucial question raised by Udy's study is the relationship between the cultural and the structural-technical variation of organizational forms. While the limitation of the data, i.e., one case from each of thirty sociocultural settings, prevents a systematic answer to this question, the attempt to construct a causal model of organizational structure constitutes an important step in this direction. Udy shows by means of a series of eight propositions that technical complexity is a powerful determinant of the authority structure, that social involvement leads to an expansion of the authority structure over and above that which can be expected on technical grounds, and that the scope of the reward system is directly related to the degree of specialization and rationality. The findings hold especially for the technically complex work organizations.

Dill's study of two Norwegian business organizations is an early attempt to use environmental variables within a comparative framework. The three major sets of "external" variables employed are the aggregate characteristics of the surrounding community and market, some relational characteristics of the organizational context (e.g., affiliations with other organizations), and certain aspects of functional autonomy which Dill locates in the organizational "task environment." It should be stressed that managerial autonomy of decision making is the dependent variable in this study, whereas the task environment (including functional autonomy) is one of the independent variables. Thus Dill's concept of autonomy refers to an "internal" organizational characteristic, as well as to interpersonal relations among top managers. But the concept is applicable and, indeed, relevant to the more "external" dimensions of organizational autonomy of the two business firms studied, especially if one considers the crucial distinction between what Dill calls "upward" and "horizontal" autonomy.

Dill's study is methodologically at the lower limit of the logic of comparative analysis, thus lending itself to the conceptualization of each of the two firms as "ideal types," reminiscent of Burns and Stalker's "mechanistic" (Alpha) and "organic" (Beta) organizational types.[2] As a consequence, such factors as interpersonal relationships, accessibility, perception, and interpretation of information, administrative styles, and even personality variables are more visible and important in this type of analysis than in any of the other studies. The characteristics of the administrator and his staff are treated simultaneously as personal, interpersonal (relational), and organizational (structural) variables. Such a technique is applicable especially when it can be assumed that the executive effectively "speaks for" the organization. In such cases, organizations can be characterized by the type of administrator they have or tend to attract, by administrative styles, or by organizational-structural characteristics which may reflect, for example, a history of democratic-decentralized or autocratic-centralized styles of administration.

Of particular interest here is Dill's analysis of the role of committees in each of the two companies. Although still informed by a social-psychological interest in the interaction patterns of small, problem solving groups, Dill anticipates here the structural importance of committees for organizational coordination, a topic dealt with also by Kriesberg (9) and Aiken and Hage (12).[3]

Fouraker and Stopford focus on the effect of the complexity of the task structure, especially diversification, on expansion into foreign markets as well as on internal structural differentiation and coordination among 170 American business corporations in 1964/65. The authors take their lead from A. D. Chandler's influential *Strategy and Structure*, a study of the seventy largest U.S. corporations in 1959. Fouraker and Stopford's study is essentially designed to test and specify Chandler's structural typology, with Type I representing the classical owner-dominated, entrepreneurial business organization, Type II the vertically integrated and functionally coordinated one-product domestic enterprise, and Type III the diversified and fairly decentralized multinational corporation. Among the variables considered by this study are environmental (market) factors, organizational age, ownership patterns, number and diversity of products (using Gort's index of diversification), organizational size (assets), departmental specialization, and ability to compete (effectiveness). Fouraker and Stopford confirm Chandler's typology, especially with respect to Types II and III, by showing that the diversified Type III organizations tend to develop a multinational strategy and a leading position in foreign investments.

[2] Tom Burns and G. M. Stalker, *The Management of Innovation* (London: Tavistock, 1961), pp. 96–125.
[3] Numbers refer to selections in this volume.

Elling and Halebsky's study of 126 upstate New York hospitals focuses on the interrelation between different aspects of organizational autonomy, and on the effect of community stratification systems on the provision of hospital-based health care. Using types of hospital ownership and control (voluntary vs. local governmental) as indicators of sponsorship and autonomy, the authors find that voluntary, nondemoninational hospitals receive relatively more community support (funds, patients, community participation) than local governmental hospitals, unless there is only one such hospital in the community. The problem of low support for governmental hospitals is interpreted in terms of organizational differentiation and adaptation, suggesting a social class role of government in the sense that the political system serves to balance and correct the inequities of social stratification within communities. While the authors tend to interpret the data along the lines of a functionalist theory of stratification, one may suggest, alternatively, that governmental sponsorship of hospital-based health care serves to maintain and protect the community class structure since it permits and encourages the "upper elements" to develop and control segregated community organizations.

Heydebrand's study of almost 7000 American hospitals deals with the effects of ownership patterns (legal autonomy) and the complexity of the task structure on internal structural differentiation and coordination. The study focuses particularly on certain nonbureaucratic modes of coordination, such as professionalization of the labor force and the phenomenon of structural balance. In addition to the two types of hospital ownership and control (voluntary and local governmental) used in the preceding study by Elling and Halebsky (6), federal (Veterans Administration) hospitals are investigated, i.e., the ownership type underlying the Anderson-Warkov study (19). The distinction between teaching and nonteaching hospitals, and between general and psychiatric hospitals makes it possible to develop separate operational definitions of the complexity of the task structure and of the internal structural complexity typically associated with the division of labor.

The study shows that organizational autonomy has a strong effect on the level and variability of internal structural complexity, as well as on the relative size of the administrative-clerical staff. Diversified and internally complex organizations such as teaching general hospitals tend to have flexible, open boundaries, whereas unifunctional organizations such as large state mental hospitals operate more like closed systems. The study suggests that a high level of departmental specialization can be interpreted as structural balance and becomes itself a factor of coordination, thus specifying the relationship between the task structure and the modes of coordination. Finally, it is suggested that the nature of professional work in hospitals is contingent on the degree of internal complexity. With increasing departmental specialization, professional work is transformed from the "generalist" form into a more task-specific, differentiated, "specialist" form.

Focusing on the effect of aggregate community characteristics on the goal structure of 211 voluntary associations, Simpson and Gulley show that centralization, membership involvement, and the extent of internal communication are influenced by the multiplicity of goals and by the degree of community support. Both goal structure and community involvement are reconceptualized in terms of environmental pressures. Voluntary associations with high environmental pressure, i.e., multiple goals and extensive community involvement, tend to be decentralized, have a high degree of membership involvement, and a high level of internal communication. The study thus leads a long list of others[4] showing that the complexity of the goal and task structure has a debureaucratizing and democratizing effect on organizations and associations. These findings thus imply a modification of the Weberian, administrative science, and functionalist traditions which hold that increasing task complexity requires bureaucratic modes of coordination and, especially, a centralized, hierarchical form of organization.

Kriesberg's study deals with another type of voluntary association, namely international nongovernmental organizations. The study seeks to determine in what way and to what extent joint American and Soviet representation affect the membership, structure, and activities of international nongovernmental organizations.

Based on an analysis of data on 1470 such organizations, drawn from the 1962/63 *Yearbook of International Organizations*, the author reaches several conclusions relevant to the dynamics of voluntary associations. Thus, joint American and Soviet representation occurs most often in organizations engaged in high consensus activities, such as science or health, as contrasted with low consensus areas such as economic and social issues. In organizations engaged in high consensus activities, the member associations from the two countries are seen as having many like, complementary, and common interests, and few conflicting ones. However, regardless of area, joint representation leads to the proliferation of committees, a structural device which provides a nonbureaucratic mode of coordination. Thus, committees appear to be more important for dealing with potential conflict than the bureaucratic devices of hierarchical differentiation and a larger administrative staff.

---

[4] See, e.g., the studies by Udy (3), Dill (4), Fouraker and Stopford (5), Heydebrand (7), Kriesberg (9), Stinchcombe (24), and Bell (30).

2. THE CONTEXT OF ORGANIZATION STRUCTURES

D. S. Pugh, D. J. Hickson, C. R. Hinings, and C. Turner

The structure of an organization is closely related to the context within which it functions, and much of the variation in organization structures might be explained by contextual factors. Many such factors, including size, technology, organizational charter or social function, and interdependence with other organizations, have been suggested as being of primary importance in influencing the structure and functioning of an organization.[1]

There have been few attempts, however, to relate these factors in a comparative systematic way to the characteristic aspects of structure, for such studies would require a multivariate factorial approach in both context and structure. The limitations of a unitary approach to organizational structure have been elaborated elsewhere (Hinings et al,. 1967), but

Reprinted by permission from *Administrative Science Quarterly*, March 1969, pp. 91–114.

[1] This work was conducted when the authors were members of the Industrial Administration Research Unit, the University of Aston in Birmingham, England. Research conducted by that Unit is jointly supported by the Social Science Research Council and the University.

its deficiencies in the study of contextual factors are no less clear. Theorists in this area seem to have proceeded on the assumption that one particular contextual feature is the major determinant of structure, with the implication that they considered the others less important. Many writers from Weber onwards have mentioned size as being one of the most important causes of differences between structures, and large size has even been considered as characteristic of bureaucratic structure (Presthus, 1958). Others argue for the pre-emptive importance of the technology of production or service in determining structure and functioning (Dubin, 1958; Perrow, 1967; Woodward, 1965; Trist et al., 1963). Parsons (1956) and Selznick (1949) have attempted to show in some detail that the structure and functioning of the organization follow from its social function, goals, or "charter." Eisenstadt (1959) emphasized the importance of the dependence of the organization on its social setting, particularly its, dependence on external resources and power, in influencing structural characteristics and activities. Clearly all of these contextual factors, as well as others,

TABLE 1 CONCEPTUAL SCHEME FOR EMPIRICAL STUDY
OF WORK ORGANIZATIONS

Contextual Variables	*Structural Variables*†
Origin and history	STRUCTURING OF ACTIVITIES
Ownership and control	
Size	Functional specialization
Charter	Role specialization
Technology	Standardization (overall)
Location	Formalization (overall)
Resources	
Dependence	CONCENTRATION OF AUTHORITY
Activity Variables*	Centralization of decision making
	Autonomy of the organization
Identification	Standardization of procedures for
(charter, image)	selection and advancement
Perpetuation	
(thoughtways,	LINE CONTROL OF WORKFLOW
finance,	Subordinate ratio
personnel services)	Formalization of role performance
Workflow	recording
(production,	Percentage of workflow superordinates
distribution)	
Control	RELATIVE SIZE OF SUPPORTIVE COMPONENT
(direction,	Percentage of clerks
motivation,	Percentage of nonworkflow personnel
evaluation,	Vertical span (height)
communication)	*Performance Variables*
Homeostasis	Efficiency
(fusion,	(profitability,
leadership,	productivity,
problem solving,	market standing)
legitimization)	Adaptability
	Morale

* Bakke (1959).
† Pugh *et al.* (1968).

are relevant; but without a multivariate approach, it is not possible to assess their relative importance.

A previous paper described the conceptual framework upon which the present multivariate analysis is based (Pugh *et al.*, 1963), and a subsequent paper its empirical development (Pugh *et al.*, 1968). It is not a model of organization in an environment, but a separation of variables of structure and of organizational performance from other variables commonly hypothesized to be related to them, which are called "contextual" in the sense that they can be regarded as a setting within which structure is developed. Table 1 summarizes the framework and also includes a classification of activities useful in the analysis of organization functioning (Bakke, 1959).

The design of the study reported in the present paper treats the contextual variables as independent and the structural variables as dependent. The structural variables are (i) *structuring of activities*; that is, the degree to which the intended behavior of employees is overtly defined by task specialization, standard routines, and formal paper work; (ii) *concentration*

TABLE 2 ELEMENTS OF ORGANIZATION CONTEXT

Elements of Context	Product-Moment Correlation with Structural Factors		
	Structuring of Activities	*Concentration of Authority*	*Line Control of Workflow*
ORIGIN AND HISTORY (3)*			
Impersonality of origin	−0.04	0.64	0.63
Age	0.09	−0.38	−0.02
Historical changes	0.17	−0.45	−0.03
OWNERSHIP AND CONTROL (7)			
Public accountability	−0.10	0.64	0.47
Concentration of ownership with control	−0.15	−0.29	−0.21
SIZE (3)			
Size of organization†	0.69	−0.10	−0.15
Size of parent organization†	0.39	0.39	−0.07
CHARTER (7)			
Operating variability	0.15	−0.22	−0.57
Operating diversity	0.26	−0.30	−0.04
TECHNOLOGY (6)			
Workflow integration	0.34	−0.30	−0.46
Labor costs	−0.25	0.43	0.32
LOCATION (1)			
Number of operating sites	−0.26	0.39	0.39
DEPENDENCE (10)			
Dependence	−0.05	0.66	0.13
Recognition of trade unions	0.51	0.08	−0.35

*Numbers in parentheses indicate number of primary scales.
† Logarithm of number of employees.

of authority; that is, the degree to which authority for decisions rests in controlling units outside the organization and is centralized at the higher hierarchical levels within it; and (iii) *line control of workflow*; that is, the degree to which control is exercised by line personnel instead of through impersonal procedures. The eight contextual variables were translated into operational definitions and scales were constructed for each of them. These were then used in a multivariate regression analysis to predict the structural dimensions found.

This factorial study using cross-sectional data does not in itself test hypotheses about *processes* (e.g., how changes in size interact with variations in structuring of activities), but it affords a basis for generating such hypotheses.

SAMPLE AND METHODS

Data were collected on fifty-two work organizations, forty-six of which were a random sample stratified by size and product or purpose. The sample and methods have been described in detail in a previous paper, (Pugh *et al.*, 1968). For scaling purposes, data on the whole group were used, but for correlational analyses relating scales to each other, and for prediction analyses relating contextual variables to structural ones, only data on the sample of forty-six organizations were used. None of the data was attitudinal.

The data were analyzed under the heading of the conceptual scheme. To define the variables operationally, scales were constructed that measured the degree of a particular characteristic. The scales varied widely. Inkson *et al.* (1967) discussed the variety of scaling procedures used. Some were simple dichotomies (such as impersonality of origin) or counts (such as number of operating sites); some were ordered category scales, locating an organization at one point along a postulated dimension (such as closeness of link with customers of clients). Some were stable, ordered scales established by linking together a large number or items exhibiting the characteristic on the basis of cumulative scaling procedures, such as workflow rigidity, an aspect of technology. Some were summary scales extracted by principal-components analysis to summarize a whole dimension, such as operating variability, an aspect of charter. In this way, forty primary scales of context were constructed and then reduced to fourteen empirically distinct elements, which are listed in Table 2 together with their correlations with the main structural variables as defined in Table 1. Table 3 gives their intercorrelations. The methodological implications of this analysis are discussed in Levy and Pugh (1969).

The study of contextual aspects of organizations will inevitably produce a much more heterogeneous set of scales than the comparable study of the structural aspects; for the scales are selected, not from a common conceptual base, but for their postulated links with structure. One of the objectives of using the multivariate approach described here would be to test the relationship between disparate aspects of context, and to attempt a conceptual clarification of those aspects demonstrated to be salient in relation to organizational structure.

It was not possible to investigate the variable "resources" adequately. For human and ideational resources, the wide-ranging interviews within a comparatively short time span made it impossible to obtain adequate data. Material and capital resources were found to reduce to aspects of size, and the relative disposition of these resources (e.g., capital versus labor) was found to be better regarded as an aspect of technology.

CONTEXTUAL VARIABLES

ORIGIN AND HISTORY

An organization may have grown from a one-man business over a long period of time, or it may have been set up as a branch of an already existing organization and so develop rapidly. During its development it may have undergone many or few radical changes in purpose, ownership, and other contextual aspects. An adequate study of the impact of these factors on organizational structure must be conducted on a comparative longitudinal basis (Chandler, 1962); but even in a cross-sectional study such as this, it is possible to define and make operational three aspects of this concept.

TABLE 3 INTERCORRELATIONS OF CONTEXTUAL VARIABLES (PRODUCT-MOMENT COEFFICIENTS, $N = 46$)

Scale Title	Impersonality of Origin	Age	Historical Changes	Public Accountability	Concentration of Ownership with Control*	Size of Organization†	Size of Parent Organization†	Operating Variability	Operating Diversity	Workflow Integration	Labor Costs	No. of Operating Sites	Dependence	Trade Unions
Impersonality of origin	−													
Age	−0.20	−												
Historical changes	−0.34	0.50	−											
Public accountability	0.66	0.00	−0.25	−										
Concentration of ownership with control*	−0.40	−0.03	0.02	−0.50	−									
Size of organization†	0.07	0.16	0.29	0.00	−0.21	−								
Size of parent organization†	0.45	−0.12	−0.10	0.51	−0.55	0.43	−							
Operating variability	−0.26	−0.24	−0.16	−0.34	0.29	−0.24	−0.19	−						
Operating diversity	−0.23	0.00	0.13	−0.14	0.00	0.26	−0.10	0.02	−					
Workflow integration	−0.24	0.07	0.05	−0.35	0.10	0.07	−0.09	0.57	0.33	−				
Labor Costs	0.41	−0.24	−0.31	0.34	−0.09	−0.28	0.08	−0.27	0.01	−0.50	−			
No. of operating sites	0.14	−0.07	−0.08	0.34	−0.20	0.14	0.16	−0.56	−0.05	−0.58	0.16	−		
Dependence	0.53	−0.32	−0.38	0.53	−0.50	−0.17	0.63	0.05	−0.19	−0.05	0.26	0.05	−	
Recognition of trade unions	0.04	−0.04	−0.11	0.17	−0.21	0.36	0.37	0.19	0.01	0.20	−0.15	−0.12	0.22	−

* $N = 42$ for all correlations with this variable.
† Logarithm of number of employees.

Impersonality of Origin. This variable distinguishes between entrepreneurial organizations, personally founded, and bureaucratic ones founded by an existing organization. Impersonally founded organizations might be expected to have a higher level of structuring of activities, whereas personally founded organizations would have a higher degree of concentration of authority. The data on the present sample, however, show no relationship between impersonality of origin and structuring of activities ($r = -0.04$), but a strong relationship between impersonality of origin and concentration of authority ($r = 0.64$). (With $N = 46$, all correlations 0.29 and above are at or beyond the ninety-five percent level of confidence.) To a considerable extent this relationship is due to the fact that government-owned, and therefore impersonally founded, organizations tend to be highly centralized. Such organizations tend to be line controlled in their workflow, thus contributing to the relationship ($r = 0.36$) between impersonality of origin and line control of workflow. The lack of relationship with structuring of activities, which is common to all three scales of this dimension, underlines the need to examine present contextual aspects in relation to this factor rather than historical ones.

Age. The age of the organization was taken from the time at which the field work was carried out. The range in the sample varied from an established metal goods manufacturing organization, founded over 170 years previously, in 1794, to a government inspection department, which began activities in the area as a separate operating unit 29 years previously. No clear relationship was found between age and impersonality of origin ($r = -0.20$). Stinchcombe (1965) has argued that no relationship should be expected between the age of an organization and its structure but rather between the structure of an organization and the date that its industry was founded. The present data support this conclusion in that no relationship is found between age and structuring of activities ($r = 0.09$) or line control of workflow ($r = 0.02$). Age was related to concentration of authority ($r = -0.38$), older organizations having a tendency to be more decentralized and to have more autonomy.

Historical Changes. The organizations in this sample did not have adequate historical information on the extent of contextual changes for use in a cross-sectional investigation; but it was possible to obtain limited information as to whether particular changes had occurred, and thus to develop a scale for the *types* of contextual changes that had occurred, namely whether at least one change had occurred (i) in the location of the organization, (ii) in the product or service range offered, and (iii) in the pattern of ownership. Item analysis carried out using the Brogden-Clemens coefficient (Brogden, 1949) gave a mean item-analysis value of 0.85, suggesting that it was possible to produce a scale of historical changes by summing the items. The organizations were distributed along the scale from no changes to all three types of changes. As expected, there was a strong correlation of this scale with age ($r = 0.51$), older organizations tending to have experienced more types of change. There was also a strong relationship, perhaps mediated by age, between historical changes and concentration of authority ($r = -0.45$), such changes being associated with dispersion of authority.

OWNERSHIP AND CONTROL

The differences in structure between a department of the government and a private business will be due to some extent to the different ownership and control patterns. Two aspects of this concept, public accountability and the relationship of the ownership to the management of the organization were investigated. For wholly owned subsidiary companies, branch factories, local government departments, etc. this form of analysis had to be applied to the parent institution exercising owning rights, in some cases through more than one intermediate institution (e.g., committees of the corporation, area boards, parent operating companies, which were themselves owned by holding companies, etc.). The ultimate owning unit is referred to as the "parent organization."

Public Accountability. This was a three–point category scale concerned with the degree to which the parent organization, (which could, of course, be the organizational unit itself, as it was in eight cases) was subject to public scrutiny in the conduct of its affairs. Least publicly accountable would be a company not quoted on the stock exchange; next, organizations that raised money publicly by having equity capital quoted on the stock exchange, also public cooperative societies; and most publicly accountable were the departments of the local and central government. On the basis of the classical literature on bureaucracy as a societal phenome-

non, it might be hypothesized that organizations with the greatest exposure to public accountability would have a higher degree of structuring of activities, and a greater concentration of authority. The data on the present sample show relationships more complicated than this, however.

First, it must be emphasized that although this sample included eight government departments, all the organizations had a nonadministrative purpose, which could be identified as a workflow, Pugh et al. (1968) Table 1. This is not surprising in this provincial sample, since purely administrative units of the requisite size (i.e., employing more than 250 people) are few outside the capital. The relationships between public accountability and structure must be interpreted in the light of this particular sample.

No relationship was found between public accountability and structuring of activities ($r = -0.10$). This structuring factor applies to the workflow as well as administrative activities of the organization, and it appears that government organizations with a workflow are not differentiated from nongovernment organizations on this basis. On the other hand there was a positive relationship between public accountability and concentration of authority ($r = 0.63$) standardization of procedures for selection and advancement ($r = 0.56$) and line control of workflow ($r = 0.47$). These all point to centralized but line-controlled government workflow organizations (Pugh et al., 1969). The scale of standardization was a bipolar one, and a high score meant that the organization standardized its procedures for personnel selection and advancement, and also that it did *not* standardize its procedures for workflow. The relationship between public ac-

TABLE 4 OWNERSHIP AND CONTROL (*N* = 42)

Scale Number and Title		Range %	Mean	S.D.
12.01	Concentration of voteholdings (Percentage of equity owned by top twenty shareholders)	0–100	38.47	32.37
12.03	Voteholdings of individuals (Percentage of individuals among top twenty shareholders)	0–100	17.19	26.89
12.04	Directors among top twenty voteholders (Percentage of directors among top twenty shareholders)	0–100	20.69	29.39
12.05	Directors' voteholding (Percentage of equity owned by all directors combined)	0–99.9	9.40	19.61
12.06	Percentage of directors who are executives	0–100	46.11	32.73
12.09	Interlocking directorships (Percentage of directors with other directorships beyond owning organization)	0–100	45.22	33.73

countability and this standardization scale suggests that the government workflow organizations standardize their personnel procedures, but rely on professional line superodinates for workflow control.

Relationship of Ownership to Management. The concepts of Sargent Florence (1961) were found most fruitful in studying this aspect of ownership and control, but the method used was the selection of variables for a correlational approach, rather than classification on the basis of percentages. Florence studied the relationships of shareholders, directors, and executives. Where these groups were completely separate there was full separation of ownership, control, and management; where they were the same, then ownership, control and management coalesced. Between these two extremes, the scales were designed in the present study to measure the degree of separation. Company records and public records were examined and five scales developed for the patterns of shareholding and the relationships between the ownership and the management of the orga-

nization. For the four foreign-owned organizations in the sample, this information was not available in England; the analysis was therefore based on *n* = 42 (Table 4). A sixth scale was developed for interlocking directorships; that is, the percentage of directors who held other directorships outside the owning group. The intercorrelation matrix of these six variables suggested that factor analysis would be helpful in summarizing an extensive analysis of ownership (Table 5). A principal-components analysis was thus applied to the matrix, and a large first factor accounting for 56 percent of the variance was extracted, which was heavily loaded on all variables except interlocking directorships and was therefore termed "concentration of ownership with control."

As would be expected, there was a negative relationship between public accountability and concentration of ownership with control ($r = -0.51$); the more publicly accountable the ownership, the less concentrated it was, with central and local government ownership epitomizing diffuse ownership by the voting public.

TABLE 5 OWNERSHIP AND CONTROL: INTERCORRELATION MATRIX
PRODUCT-MOMENT COEFFICIENTS ($N = 42$)

	Concentration of Voteholdings	Voteholdings of Individuals	Directors Among Top Twenty Voteholders	Directors' Voteholdings	Percentage of Directors Who are Executives	Interlocking Directorships
Concentration of voteholdings	–					
Voteholdings of individuals	0.62	–				
Director among top twenty voteholders	0.54	0.87	–			
Directors' voteholdings	0.55	0.90	0.78	–		
Percentage of directors who are executives	0.26	0.30	0.37	0.20	–	
Interlocking directorships	0.32	0.03	0.04	0.09	0.33	–

The discussion about the effects of differing patterns of personal ownership on organizations and society originated with Marx, and has since polarized into what Dahrendorf (1959) has called the "radical" and "conservative" positions. It is generally agreed that there has been a progressive dispersion of share ownership following the rise of the corporation, but there is little agreement, or systematic evidence, on the effects of this. The radicals (Burnham, 1962; Berle and Means, 1937) argue that present ownership patterns have produced a shift in control away from the entrepreneur to managers, who become important because of their control over the means of production and the organization of men, materials, and equipment. The result then of dispersion of ownership is likely to be dispersion of authority. However, the conservatives (Mills, 1956; Aaronovitch, 1961) argue that the dispersion of capital ownership makes possible the concentration of

economic power in fewer hands, because of the inability of the mass of shareholders to act, resulting in a concentration of authority.

The results obtained with this sample support neither of these positions. The correlation given in Table 2 of concentration of ownership with control with concentration of authority ($r = -0.29$) might suggest that concentration of ownership is associated with dispersion of authority; but it must be remembered that this correlation is obtained for the whole sample, which includes government-owned organizations, whereas the discussion of the effects of ownership patterns has been concerned entirely with private ownership. When the government organizations were extracted from the sample, the correlation disappeared ($r = -0.08$ for $N = 34$). No relationships were found between the structure of an organization and the ownership pattern of its parent organization. This lack of relationship is quite striking, particularly in view of the extent of the correlation found with other contextual variables. Since ownership and control seemed to have its impact through the degree of public accountability, and the other variables did not have an additional effect, there seemed to be grounds for not proceeding with them in a multivariate analysis.

SIZE

There has been much work relating size to group and individual variables, such as morale and job satisfaction, with not very consistent results (Porter and Lawler, 1965). With few exceptions, empirical studies relating size to variables of organization structure have confined themselves to those broad aspects of the role structure which are here termed "configuration" (Starbuck, 1965). Hall and Tittle (1966), using a Guttman scale of the overall degree of perceived bureaucratization obtained by combining scores on six dimensions of Weberian characteristics of bureaucracy in study of twenty-five different work organizations, found a small relation between their measurement of perceived bureaucratization and organization size ($\tau = 0.252$ at the 6 percent level of confidence).

In this study the aspects of size studied were number of employees, net assets utilized, and number of employees in the parent organizations.

Number of employees and net assets. It was intended that the sample be taken from the population of work organizations in the region employing more than 250 people, but the sample ranges from an insurance company employing 241 people to a vehicle manufacturing company employing 25,052 (mean 3,370; standard deviation 5,313). In view of this distribution, it was felt that a better estimate of the correlation between size and other variables would be obtained by taking the logarithm of the number of employees (mean 3.12; standard deviation 0.57).

"Net assets employed by the organization" was also used, because financial size might expose some interesting relationships with organization structure that would not appear when only personnel size was considered. The sample ranged from under £100,000—an estimate for the government inspection agency whose equipment was provided by its clients—to a confectionery manufacturing firm with £38 million. The attempt to differentiate between these two aspects of size proved unsuccessful, however, as the high correlation between them ($r = 0.78$) shows. Taking the logarithm of the two variables raised the correlation ($r = 0.81$). For this sample, therefore, a large organization was big both in number of employees and in financial assets. The logarithm of the number of employees was therefore taken to represent both these aspects of size.

The correlation between the logarithm of size and structuring of activities ($r = 0.69$) lends strong support to descriptive studies of the effects of size on bureaucratization. (This correlation may be compared with that between actual size and structuring of activities, $r = 0.56$, to demonstrate the effects of the logarithmic transformation). Larger organizations tend to have more specialization, more standardization, and more formalization than smaller organizations. The *lack* of relationship between size and the remaining structural dimensions, i.e., concentration of authority ($r = -0.10$) and line control of workflow ($r = -0.15$) was equally striking. This clear differential relationship of organization size to the various structural dimensions underlines the necessity of a multivariate approach to context and structure if oversimplifications are to be avoided.

Indeed, closer examination of the relationship of size to the main structural variables underlying the dimension of concentration of authority (Pugh *et al.*, 1968: Table 4) points up a limitation in the present approach, which seeks to establish basic dimensions by means of factor analysis. As was explained in that paper, the structural factors represent an attempt to summarize a large amount of data on a large number of variables to make possible empirically based comparisons. But the cost is that the factor may obscure particular relationships with the source variables which it summarizes. For some purposes therefore, it may be interesting to examine particular relationships. The lack of relationship between size and concentration of authority, for example, summarizes (and therefore conceals) two small but distinct relationships with two of the component variables. There is no relationship between size and autonomy ($r = 0.09$), but there is a negative relationship between size and centralization ($r = -0.39$), and a positive one between size and standardization of procedures for selection and advancement ($r = 0.31$). The relationship with centralization has clear implications for the concept of bureaucracy. Centralization correlates *negatively* with all scales of structuring of activities except one: the more specialized, standardized, and for-

malized the organization, the *less* it is centralized. Therefore on the basis of these scales, there can be no unitary bureaucracy, for an organization that develops specialist offices and associated routines is decentralized. Perhaps when the responsibilities of specialized roles are narrowly defined, and activities are regulated by standardized procedures and are formalized in records, then authority can safely be decentralized. Pugh *et al.* (1969) discuss the interrelationship of the structural variables in particular types of organization.

Size of Parent Organization. This is the number of employees of any larger organization to which the unit belongs. The literature on bureaucracy often implies that it is the size of the larger parent organization that influences the structure of the subunit. The important factor about a small government agency may not be its own size, but that of the large ministry of state of which it is a part. Similarly, the structure of a subsidiary company may be more related to the size of its holding company. The number of employees in the parent organizations ranged from 460 to 358,000 employees. The size of the parent organization correlated positively (after logarithmic transformation) with structuring ($r = 0.39$) and concentration of authority ($r = 0.39$) but not with line control of workflow ($r = -0.07$). The classical concept of bureaucracy would lead to the hypothesis that the size of the parent organization would be highly correlated with structuring of activities and concentration of authority, therefore the support from this sample was relatively modest. The correlation with structuring ($r = 0.39$ is much lower than the correlation of *organi-*

TABLE 6 CHARTER

Distribution N = 46	Score	Scale Number and Title
		Scale No. 14.02
		Multiplicity of outputs
19	1	Single output with standard variations
8	2	Single output with variations to customer specification
19	3	Two or more outputs
		Scale No. 14.03
		Type of output
14	1	Service (nonmanufacturing)
32	2	Manufacturing (new physical outputs in solid, liquid or gaseous form)
		Scale No. 14.04
		Type of output
16	1	Consumer (outputs disposed of to the general public or individuals)
7	2	Consumer and producer
23	3	Producer (outputs disposed of to other organizations which use them for, or as part of, other outputs)
		Scale No. 14.06
		Customer orientation
11	1	Standard output(s)
7	2	Standard output(s) with standard modifications
6	3	Standard output(s) with modification to customer specification
22	4	Output to customer specification
		Scale No. 14.07
		Self-image
24	1	Image emphasizes qualities of the *organization itself*
6	2	Image emphasizes both the organization and the output
16	3	Image emphasizes qualities of the *output* of the organization
		Scale No. 14.08
		Policy on outputs multiplicity
5	1	Contracting the range of outputs
26	2	Maintaining the range
15	3	Expanding the range
		Scale No. 14.09
		Ideology: client selection
28	1	No selection, any clients supplied
14	2	Some selection of clients
4	3	Clients specified by parent organization

zation size and structuring ($r = 0.69$). The impact of the size of an organization is thus considerably greater than the size of the parent organization on specialization, standardization, formalization, etc. But a relationship with concentration of authority is not found with organization size ($r = -0.10$). Thus large groups have a small but definite tendency to have more centralized subunits with less autonomy. This relationship would be partly due to the government-owned organizations, inevitably part of large groups, which were at the concentrated end of this factor.

TABLE 7 INTERCORRELATION MATRIX (PRODUCT-MOMENT
COEFFICIENTS, $N = 46$)

	Multi-plicity of Outputs	Service-Manu-factur-ing	Con-sumer-Producer	Cus-tomer Orien-tation	Self-Image	Client Selection	Expan-sion-Contrac-tion of Range
Multiplicity of outputs	–						
Service-manufacturing	0.15	–					
Consumer-producer	0.05	0.37	–				
Customer orientation	0.38	0.18	0.59	–			
Self-image	−0.05	−0.17	−0.33	−0.13	–		
Client selection	−0.14	−0.02	0.28	−0.04	−0.18	–	
Expansion-contraction of range	0.07	−0.14	−0.09	0.07	0.10	−0.09	–

TABLE 8 CHARTER: PRINCIPAL-COMPONENTS ANALYSIS

	Factor Loadings	
Scales	*Operating Variability**	*Operating Diversity†*
Consumer-producer output	0.85	0.16
Customer orientation of outputs	0.74	−0.41
Type of output (service-manufacturing)	0.57	0.00
Self-image	−0.52	−0.34
Multiplicity of outputs	0.37	−0.66
Client selection	0.23	0.66
Expansion-contraction of range	−0.15	−0.48

* Percentage of variance = 30%
† Percentage of variance = 20%

CHARTER

Scales. Institutional analysts have demonstrated the importance of the charter of an organization; that is, its social function, goals, ideology, and value systems, in influencing structure and functioning (Parsons, 1965; Selznick, 1949). To transform concepts which had been treated only descriptively into a quantitative form that would make them comparable to other contextual aspects, seven ordered category scales were devised. Four of them characterized the purpose or goal of the organization in terms of its "output," the term being taken as equally applicable to products or services: (i) multiplicity of outputs—ranging from a single standard output to two or more outputs; (ii) type of output—a manufacturing–service dichotomy, (iii) consumer or producer outputs or a mixture of both, and (iv) customer orientation of outputs—ranging from completely standard outputs to outputs designed entirely to customer or client specification. Three scales were devised for ideological aspects of charter: (v) self–image—whether the ideology of the organization as indicated by slogans used and image sought emphasized the qualities of its outputs; (vi) policy on multiple outputs—whether the policy was to expand, maintain, or contract its range of outputs; and (vii) client selection—

whether any, some, or no selectivity was shown in the range of customers or clients served by the organization. Table 6 gives the details of the seven scales and Table 7 the intercorrelation matrix between them. This suggested that factor analysis would be helpful in summarizing the data, and a principal components analysis applied to the matrix gave the results shown in Table 8.

Operating Variability. This factor, accounting for 30 percent of the variance, was highly loaded on the variables, consumer or producer outputs, customer orientation of outputs, and type of output. It was therefore conceptualized as being concerned with manufacturing nonstandard producer goods as against providing standard consumer service. The manufacturing producer end of the scale was linked with an organizational emphasis on self–image, whereas the consumer service end emphasized outputs. The scale was therefore constructed by a weighted summing of the scores on all these variables (the weighting being necessary to equate the standard deviations) and then standardizing the sums to a mean of 50 and a standard deviation of 15. This produced the range of scores on the scale given in Table 9. The lower scores distinguished organizations giving only a standard service (e.g., teaching, transport, retailing), from organizations (with high scores) producing nonstandard producer outputs to customer specification (metal goods firm, engineering repair unit, packaging manufacturer, etc.), with those organizations having a standard output range in the middle.

Operating Diversity. This factor of charter, accounting for 20 percent

of the variance, emphasized multiplicity of outputs, policy on whether to expand the range of kinds of outputs, client selection, and self-image. The more diversely operating organizations were a glass manufacturer, a metal manufacturer, and a brewery; the more restricted were a motor component manufacturer, a domestic appliance manufacturer, and a scientific inspection agency.

Eisenstadt (1959), Parsons (1956), Selznick (1949, 1957), Wilson (1962), and Clark (1956) have discussed the effects of the goals of an organization on its structure, but there has been almost no detailed empirical work on the actual relationship between goals and structure. Selznick (1949) showed how the goal of democracy led to decentralization in the TVA, and also suggested that the role structure of an organization is the institutional embodiment of its purpose. Wilson (1962) suggested a relationship between goals and methods of recruitment and means of selection. Clark (1956) as well as Thompson and Bates (1967) emphasized both the marginality and the degree of concreteness of the goal as a determinant of the direction of organizational adaptation. Blau and Scott (1962) made one of the few attempts to classify organizations by their goals, suggesting that internal democracy goes with mutual benefit goals, efficiency with business goals, a professional structure with service goals and bureaucratic structure with commonweal goals.

Scales of organizational charter were related to structure, and operating variability was shown to be strongly associated with line control of workflow ($r = -0.57$). Thus the more an organization is concerned with manufacturing nonstandard pro-

TABLE 9 OPERATING VARIABILITY

Number of Organizations N = 46	*Score*	*Type of Organization*
1	48	Component manufacturer
6	45	Two metal goods manufacturers Component manufacturer Abrasives manufacturer Packaging manufacturer Glass manufacturer
2	43	Printer Repairs for government department
4	42	Two component manufacturers Motor component manufacturer Metal motor component manufacturer
2	41	Vehicle manufacturer Engineering tool manufacturer
1	40	Component manufacturer
3	37	Civil engineering firm Carriage manufacturer Metal goods manufacturer
3	36	Vehicle maunfacturer Confectionery manufacturer Local authority water department
2	35	Motor–tire manufacturer Commercial vehicle manufacturer
4	34	Motor component manufacturer Non ferrous metal manufacturer Research division Food manufacturer
3	33	Engineering component manufacturer Domestic appliances manufacturer Local authority civil engineering department
1	32	Component manufacturer
2	31	Government inspection department Toy manufacturer
3	30	Brewery Insurance company Food manufacturer
1	27	Local authority transport department
6	25	Local authority baths department Co–operative chain of retail stores Chain of retail stores Savings bank Chain of shoe repair stores Department store
1	23	Omnibus company
1	21	Local authority education department

ducer goods, the more it relies upon impersonal control of workflow; the more it is providing a standard consumer service, the more it uses line control of its workflow through the supervisory hierarchy. Organizations showing operating diversity, however, tended to be more structured in activities ($r = 0.26$) and more dispersed in authority ($r = -0.30$).

TECHNOLOGY

Scales. Technology has come to be considered increasingly important as a determinant of organizational structure and functioning, although comparative empirical studies of its effects on structure are few, mainly case studies on the effects on the operator's job and attitudes (Walker, 1962). Thompson and Bates (1957), however, compared a hospital, a university, a manufacturing organization, and a mine for the effects of their technologies on the setting of objectives, the management of resources, and the execution of policy. The main work on the classification of technology in relation to organization structure has been that of Woodward (1965). She related mainly "configuration" aspects of the structure of manufacturing organization (e.g., number of levels of authority, width of spans of control to a classification of their production systems according to the "controlability and predictability" of the process.

In the present study the need to develop suitable measurements of overall organizational technology made the level of generality achieved by the Woodward classification desirable; but the need to develop concepts of technology that applied to all the organizations in the sample precluded the direct adoption of that

scale. A full account of the development of scales of technology and their relationship to organization structure is given in Hickson *et al.* (1969). Only the scales included in the present analysis are described here.

Technology is here defined as the sequence of physical techniques used upon the workflow of the organization, even if the physical techniques involve only pen, ink, and paper. The concept covers both the pattern of operations and the equipment used, and all the scales developed are applicable to service as well as to manufacturnig organizations. Five scales of related aspects of technology were developed.

Thompson and Bates (1957) defined the "adaptability" of the technology as "the extent to which the appropriate mechanics, knowledge, skills and raw materials can be used for other products" and, it may be added, services. An attempt to operationalize some aspects of this definition is given in Table 10, which shows a scale of *workflow rigidity*. This consists of eight biserial items concerned with the adaptability in the patterns of operations; for example, whether the equipment was predominantly multi-purpose or single-purpose, whether rerouting of work was possible, etc. Since this was a scale of composite items, item analysis was used to test the scaleability. The mean item-analysis value of 0.84 indicates that it is legitimate to add the scores on these items to form a workflow rigidity score for an organization.

Two other scales of technology utilized the concepts outlined by Amber and Amber (1962). They postulated that "the more human attributes performed by a machine,

TABLE 10 SCALE OF WORKFLOW RIGIDITY

Item	Number of Organizations (N = 52)[+]	Item Analysis Value*
No waiting time possible (versus waiting time)	8	0.82
Single-purpose equipment (versus multi-purpose)	13	0.78
Production or service line (versus no set line)	42	1.00
No buffer stocks and no delays possible (versus buffer stocks and delays)	8	0.71
Single-source input (versus multisource input)	12	0.67
No rerouting of work possible (versus rerouting possible)	15	0.80
Breakdown stops all workflow immediately (versus not all workflow stops)	6	0.97
Breakdown stops some or all workflow immediately (versus no workflow stops)	35	0.95

* Mean item analysis value = 0.84.

[+] Since this is a test of internal consistency and scaleability, the whole group of 52 organizations was used. (D. S. Pugh *et al.*, 1968.)

the higher its automaticity" and compiled a scale of automaticity together with clear operational definitions, which could be applied to any piece of equipment from a pencil to a computer, and which categorized each into one of six classes. The two scales based on these concepts were: the *automaticity mode*, i.e., the level of automaticity of the bulk of the equipment of the organization; and the *automaticity range*; i.e., the highest-scoring piece of equipment an organization used, since every organization also scored the lowest possible by using hand tools and manual machines.

The fourth scale, *interdependence of workflow segments*, was a scale of the degree of linkage between the segments of an organization; a segment being defined as those parts into which the workflow hierarchy was divided at the first point of division beneath the chief executive. The three points on the scale were: (i) segments duplicated in different locations, all having the same final outputs; (ii) segments having different final outputs, which are not inputs of other segments; (iii) segments having outputs which become inputs of other segments. The final scale, *specificity of criteria of quality evaluation*, was a first attempt to classify the precision with which the output was compared to an acceptable standard. The three points on the scale were: (i) personal evaluation only; (ii) partial measurements, of some aspect(s) of the output(s); (iii) measurements used over virtually the whole output, to compare against precise specification (the "blueprint" concept).

Correlations. As expected, these measures tend to be highly intercorrelated. A principal components analysis extracted a large first factor accounting for 58 percent of the variance, with loadings of over 0.6 on all scales, and of over 0.8 on three of them. A scale of *workflow integration* was therefore constructed by summing the scores on the component scales. Among organizations scoring high, with very integrated, automated, and rather rigid technologies, were an automobile factory, a food manufacturer, and a swimming baths department. Among those scoring low, with diverse, non-automated, flexible technologies, were retail stores, an education department, and a building firm.

There were no clear relationships between workflow integration and the variables of size, origin and history, or concentration of ownership with control and negative relationship with public accountability ($r = -0.35$), largely because the government-owned organizations in the sample were predominantly service and therefore at the diverse end of the workflow integration scale. The correlation between workflow integration and operating variability ($r = 0.57$) and diversity ($r = 0.33$) reflect the close relationship between the ends of the organization and the means it employs to attain them.

Workflow integration showed modest but distinct correlations with all the three structural factors, the only contextual variables to do so, as can be seen from Table 2. The relationships of technology are therefore much more general than is the case with size, for example, which has a greater but more specific effect. The positive correlation between workflow integration and structuring of activities ($r = 0.34$) would be expected since highly integrated and therefore more rigid technologies would be associated with a greater structuring of activities and proce-

dures. Similarly, the correlation with concentration of authority ($r = -0.30$) suggests that because of the increasing control resulting directly from the workflow itself in an integrated technology, decisions tend to become more routine and can be decentralized. But the fact that the correlations are not higher than this emphasizes that structuring may be related to other contextual factors, such as size. The relationship of technology to line control of workflow, however, was very clear ($r = 0.46$); the more integrated the technology, the more the reliance on impersonal control. It must be emphasized, however, that these relationships were found on the whole sample of manufacturing and service organizations. When manufacturing organizations only were considered, some of the relationships showed considerable change (Hickson *et al.*, 1969).

Labor Costs. This is a second related, but conceptually distinct, aspect of the technology of the workflow and is expressed as a percentage of total costs. The range in the sample was from 5 to 70 percent, with engineering organizations scoring low and public services high. The scale correlated with workflow integration ($r = -0.50$), high integration being associated with reduced labor costs. Its correlations with the structural factors are comparable with those for technology (after adjusting the signs).

LOCATION

The geographical, cultural, and community setting can influence the organization markedly (Blau and Scott, 1962). This study controls for some of these effects in a gross way,

TABLE 11 DEPENDENCE

Distribution N = 46	Score	Scale Number and Title
		Scale No. 18.07
		*Relative Size**
		Range = 0–100 Mean = 37.4 S.D. = 37.3
		Scale No. 12.10
		Status of Organization Unit
16	1	Branch
4	2	Head branch (headquarters on same location)
18	3	Subsidiary (legal identity)
8	4	Principal unit
		Scale No. 12.11
		Organizational representation on policy-making bodies†
19	1	Organization not represented on top policy-making body
4	2	Organization represented on local policy-making body but not on top policy-making body
23	3	Organization represented on policy-making body
		Scale No. 18.06
		Number of specializations contracted out‡
		Range = 1–16 Mean = 7.2 S.D. = 4.0
		Scale No. 18.17
		Vertical integration§
		Range = 1–16 Mean = 7.7 S.D. = 3.5
		Scale No. 18.03
		Integration with suppliers
4	1	No ownership ties and single orders
7	2	No ownership and single contracts or tenders
8	3	No ownership and short-term contracts, schedule and call-off
6	4	No ownership and yearly contracts, standing orders
7	5	Ownership and contractual ties
14	6	Ownership and tied supply
		Scale No. 18.05
		Response in outputs volume to customer influence
12	1	Outputs for stock
5	2	Outputs for stock and to customer order
21	3	Outputs to customer order
2	4	Outputs to customer order and to schedule and call-off
6	5	Outputs to schedule and call-off
		Scale No. 18.08
		Integration with customers: type of link with customers
24	1	Single orders
9	2	Regular contracts
10	3	Long-term contracts (over two years)
3	4	Ownership
		Scale No. 18.09
		Integration with customers: dependence of organization on its largest customer
30	1	Minor outlet (less than 10% of output)
10	2	Medium outlet (over 10% of output)
3	3	Major outlet (over 50% of output)
3	4	Sole outlet

TABLE 11 *Continued*

Distribution N = 46	Score	Scale Number and Title
		Scale No. 18.10
		Integration with customers: dependence of largest customer on Organization
11	1	Minor supplier (less than 10% of particular item)
5	2	Medium supplier (over 10% of particular item)
21	3	Major supplier (over 50% of particular item)
9	4	Sole supplier with exclusive franchise

* Size of unit as a percentage of size of parent organization.
† Internal and parent organizations.
‡ The specializations are those of functional specialization (D. S. Pugh *et al.*, 1968: Appendix A). Scores are out of a possible 16.
§ This scale is formed by the total of the scores on the 18 items representing the following five scales: 18.03, 18.05, 18.08, 18.09, 18.10.

for all organizations of the sample were located in the same large industrial conurbation, and the community and its influence on the organizations located there were taken as given (Duncan *et al.*, 1963). Compared with the national distribution, the sample was overrepresented in the engineering and metal industries, and unrepresented in mining, shipbuilding, oil refining and other industries. Because of the location, however, regional cultural differences of the sort found by Thomas (1959) as to role conceptions, were avoided.

One aspect of location which discriminated between organizations in the sample, was *number of operating sites*. The range formed a Poisson distribution, with 47 percent of the sample having one site; but six organizations had over a hundred sites, and two over a thousand. This distribution did not appear to be a function of size ($r = 0.14$) but of the operating variability aspect of charter ($r = -0.56$). Manufacturing organizations were concentrated in a small number of sites (the largest number being nine), whereas services range across the scale. The number of

operating sites was therefore correlated with the workflow integration scale of technology ($r = -0.58$), and with public accountability ($r = 0.34$), this last correlation reflecting the predominantly service function of the group of government-owned organizations.

This pattern of inter-relationships among the contextual variables led to the expectation of relationships between number of operating sites and the structural dimensions which would be congruent with those of operating variability and workflow integration. The correlations of number of operating sites with structuring of activities ($r = -0.26$), concentration of authority ($r = 0.39$) and line control of workflow ($r = 0.39$) confirm the relationships with charter and technology, and suggest a *charter-technology-location* nexus of interrelated contextual variables having a combined effect on structure.

DEPENDENCE

The dependence of an organization reflects its relationships with other organizations in its social environment, such as suppliers, customers, competitors, labor unions, management organizations, and political and social organizations.

Dependence on Parent Organization. The most important relationship would be the dependence of the organization on its parent organization. The *relative size* of the organization in relation to the parent organization was calculated as a percentage of the number of employees. This ranged from under one percent in two cases—a branch factory of the central government, and a small subsidiary company of one of the largest British private corporations in the country—to 100 percent in eight independent organizations. The distribution was Poisson in form with a mean and standard deviation of 37 percent. The next scale was a four-point category scale concerned with the *status* of the organization in relation to the parent organization: (i) principal units (8 organizations)

where the organization was independent of any larger group although it might itself have had subsidiaries or branches; (ii) subsidiary units (18 organizations) which, although part of a larger group, had their own legal identity with, for example, their own boards of directors; (iii) head branch units (4 organizations) which did not have separate legal identity although they were the major operating components of the parent organization and the head office of the parent organization was on the same site; (iv) branch units (16 organizations) operating parts of a parent organization which did not satisfy the preceding criteria.

The third aspect of the relation between the organization and the parent organization was given by the degree of *organizational representation on policy-making bodies.* This three-point scale ranged from the organization being represented on the policy-making body of the parent organization (e.g., board of directors, city council), through the organiza-

TABLE 12 DEPENDENCE: INTERCORRELATION MATRIX
(PRODUCT-MOMENT COEFFICIENT $N = 46$)

	Relative Size	Status of Organization Unit	Organizational Representation on Policy-Making Body	Specializations Contracted Out	Vertical Integration	Trade Union
Relative size	–					
Status of organization unit	0.68	–				
Organizational representation on policy-making body	0.50	0.65	–			
Specializations contracted out	−0.60	−0.51	−0.52	–		
Vertical integration	−0.40	−0.34	−0.36	0.45	–	
Trade unions	−0.09	−0.16	−0.25	0.19	0.28	–

tion being represented on an intermediate policy-making body (e.g., board of directors of an operating company but not of the ultimate owning holding company, committee of the city council), to the organization having no representative on any policy-making body of the parent organization. As would be expected, these three variables were highly correlated (Tables 11, 12).

A related variable was the number of *specializations contracted out* by the organization. In many cases these would be available as services of the parent organization to the organization, although account was also taken of the various specialist services (e.g., consultants) used outside the parent organization. The specializations were as defined in the structural scale of functional specialization (Pugh *et al.*, 1968; Appendix A), and ranged from one specialization contracted out (two engineering works, a printer, and a builder) to no less than fifteen of the sixteen specializations contracted out (an abrasives manufacturer and a packaging manufacturer) with a mean 7.2 and standard deviation 4.0.

Dependence on Other Organizations. The suppliers and customers or clients of the organization must also be considered. The operating function of the organization can be regarded as being the processing of inputs and outputs between supplier and client, and the degree to which the organization is integrated into the processual chain by links at either end can be measured. Five category scales were developed to elucidate this concept with details given in Table 11. They were concerned with the integration with suppliers and clients, and response in the output volume to

client influence, etc. To establish a single dimension measuring the degree to which the organization was integrated into this system, the five scales were transformed into biserial form. Item analysis was carried out on the 18-item scale generated and yielded a mean item analysis value of 0.70, which seemed to justify the addition of the items into a total scale, *vertical integration*. At one extreme was a confectionery manufacturer and an engineering components firm supplying goods from stock with a large number of customers after obtaining their supplies from a large variety of sources; at the other extreme were organizations (vehicle components, civil engineering, scientific research) obtaining their resources from a small number of suppliers and supplying their product or service to a small number of clients (often the owning group only) who had a marked effect upon their workflow scheduling.

For *trade unions*, a scale of five ordered categories was developed of the extent to which unions were accepted as relevant to the activities of the organization. The scale was (*i*) no recognition given; (*ii*) only partial recognition given (i.e., discussions for certain purposes, but not negotiations); (*iii*) full recognition given to negotiate on wages and conditions of service on behalf of their members; (*iv*) full recognition given plus facilities for union meetings to be held regularly on the time and premises of the organization; (*v*) as in the preceding plus the recognition of a works convenor to act on behalf of all unions with members in the organization. Organizations in the sample were located in all the categories, with the modal position being full recognition; but five organizations did not recognize unions, and eleven

TABLE 13 DEPENDENCE

	Concentration of Ownership with Control	Size	Size of Parent Organization	Operating Variability	Workflow Integration	Size of Organization	Structuring of Activities	Concentration of Authority	Line Control of Workflow
Status of organization unit	0.45	0.11	−0.27	0.01	0.05	0.17	0.13	−0.63	−0.07
Organizational representation on policy-making bodies	0.41	0.15	−0.19	−0.01	0.19	0.20	0.14	−0.63	−0.18
Number of specializations contracted out	−0.32	0.14	0.40	0.11	0.09	0.01	0.18	0.53	0.00
Relative size	0.47	0.06	−0.38	−0.08	−0.03	0.16	0.03	−0.40	−0.13
Vertical integration	−0.15	−0.01	0.39	0.21	−0.12	−0.06	0.06	0.29	−0.04
Trade unions*	−0.21	0.26	0.25	0.19	0.21	0.36	0.51	0.08	−0.35
Impersonality of origin	−0.40	0.13	0.36	−0.27	−0.25	0.07	−0.04	0.64	0.36
Public accountability of parent organization	−0.51	0.04	0.45	−0.35	−0.35	0.01	−0.10	0.64	0.47
Dependence	−0.49	−0.06	0.37	0.05	−0.05	−0.17	−0.05	0.66	0.13

*This variable was not included in the scale of dependence.

gave the maximum recognition including a works convenor.

Examination of the intercorrelations between these six variables of dependence (Table 12) and of their correlations with other important aspects of context (Table 13) shows considerably higher correlations with size of parent organization than with size of organization, and considerably higher correlations with concentration of ownership with control (a variable applied to the parent organization) than with operating variability or workflow integration (variables applied to the operations of the individual organizations themselves). This pattern lends support to the view that these measures are tapping aspects of the dependence of the organization, particularly its dependence on external resources and power as in Eisenstadt's (1959) formulation. The one exception was the variable of recognition of trade unions, which had its largest contextual correlation with organization size, and is therefore concerned with a different aspect of interdependence. Impersonality of origin (from origin and history) and public accountability (from ownership and control) show the same pattern of higher correlation with the parent organization than with the unit, indicating that impersonally founded organizations are likely to be more dependent on their founding organizations; and that more publicly accountable organizations are more likely to be dependent on outside power with government–owned organizations being the extreme case.

These relationships suggested the application of factor analysis to a correlation matrix containing the seven variables. A principal–component analysis applied to the matrix produced a large first factor *dependence*[2] accounting for 55 percent of the variance, which was heavily loaded on all seven scales (on six of the seven, the loadings were above 0.7; the remaining loading on vertical integration was 0.58). The scores for dependence were obtained by an algebraic weighted sum of the scores on the four most highly loaded component scales, the weightings being obtained by a multiple regression analysis of the component scales on the factor. A high score characterized organizations with a high degree of dependence, which tended to be impersonally founded, publicly accountable, vertically integrated, with a large number of specializations contracted out, small in size relative to their parent organization, low in status, and not represented at the policy-making level in the parent organization (e.g., branch units in packaging, civil engineering, and food manufacture, a central government repair department, and a local government baths department). Organizations with low dependence were independent organizations characterized by personal foundation, low public accountability, little vertical integration, few specializations contracted out, and where the parent organization was the organization itself (e.g., a printing firm, the very old metal goods firm, a chain of shoe repair stores, and an engineering component manufacturer).

The correlation of dependence with the structural factors was focused largely on concentration of

[2] We are grateful to our colleague Diana C. Pheysey for suggesting this formulation and for much valuable critical comment on an earlier draft of this paper.

TABLE 14 SALIENT ELEMENTS OF CONTEXT (PRODUCT-MOMENT
CORRELATIONS WITH STRUCTURAL FACTORS)*

Elements of Context	Structuring of Activities	Concentration of Authority	Line Control of Workflow
Age	–	−0.38	–
Size of organization†	0.69	–	–
Size of parent organization†	0.39	0.39	–
Operating variability	–	–	−0.57
Operating diversity	–	−0.30	–
Workflow integration	0.34	−0.30	−0.46
Number of operating sites	–	0.39	0.39
Dependence	–	0.66	–

* With $N = 46$, correlations of 0.29 are at the 5% level of confidence, and correlations of 0.38 are at the 1% level of confidence.
† Logarithm of number of employees.

authority ($r = 0.66$), in every case, for dependence and its component scales the correlation being much greater than with the other factors, as Table 13 shows. Indeed, apart from the correlations with impersonality of origin and public accountability, none of the other correlations reached the 5 percent level of confidence. Dependent organizations have a more centralized authority structure and less autonomy in decision making; independent organizations have more autonomy and decentralize decisions down the hierarchy.

The relationships between dependence and the component scales of concentration of authority vary. Centralization, as defined and measured in this study, is concerned only with the level in the organization which has the necessary authority to take particular decisions (Pugh et al., 1968: 76); the higher the necessary level, the greater the centralization. No account was taken of the degree of participation or consultation in decision-making as in Hage and Aiken's (1967) formulation of the concept. These were regarded as aspects for study at the group level of analysis. Neither is it possible for

such a statement as the following to hold: "The decisions were centralized on the foreman since neither the superintendent nor the departmental manager had the necessary experience." In the present formulation this would be regarded as relative decentralization. Autonomy was measured by the proportion of decisions that could be taken within the organization as distinct from those which had to be taken at the level above it. Thus independent organizations of necessity had more autonomy, since there was no level above the chief executive, and the correlation between dependence and this component of concentration of authority was $r = −0.72$. The relation of centralization (which is concerned with the whole range of levels in the hierarchy) with dependence is less, but still high ($r = 0.57$). Dependent organizations also have a distinct tendency to standardize the procedures for selection and advancement ($r = 0.40$), a major component of concentration of authority. So dependent units have the apparatus of recruitment routines, selection panels, formal establishment figures, etc., of their parent organizations.

In this investigation of the relationship of organization structure to aspects of the context in which the organization functions, the use of scaling and factor analytic techniques has made possible the condensation of data and reorganization of concepts and has established eight distinctive scales of elements of context. These scales, shown in Table 14 together with their correlations with the structural dimensions, denote the variables that are salient among those which have been thought to affect structure. Relationships between structure and age, size, charter (operating variability, operating diversity), technology (workflow integration) location (number of operating sites) and dependence on other organizations are exposed by the correlations. At the same time the correlations raise questions about the relationship between ownership pattern and administrative structure.

THE MULTIVARIATE PREDICTION OF STRUCTURE FROM CONTEXT

From inspection of Table 14 and of the intercorrelation matrix in Table 3, certain elements of context can now be identified. The variables in Table 14 are now used as independent variables in a prediction analysis of the structural dimensions. The pattern of these correlations, that is, that where they are high they are specific, and where they are low, they are diffused, indicates that the predictions should be attempted on a multivariate basis. In this case consideration had to be given to choosing not only predictors with high correlations with the criterion, but also having low intercorrelations among themselves. If high intercorrelations among the predictors were allowed, then, since the high correlations with the criterion would be aspects of the same relationship, the multiple correlation would not be increased to any extent. If the intercorrelations between the predictors were low, then each would make its distinct contribution to the multiple correlation.

These problems can be illustrated from the attempt to obtain a multiple prediction of structuring of activities from the three contextual variables correlated with it (Table 14). Size is clearly the first predictor, with a correlation of $r = 0.69$, and the question is whether taking account of size of parent organization and workflow integration will increase predictive accuracy. In spite of its greater correlation with the criterion, the size of the parent organization would be expected to make a smaller contribution to the prediction than workflow integration, since it has a strong correlation with the first predictor ($r = 0.43$); whereas the technology measure is not correlated with organization size ($r = 0.08$). This is in fact the case as shown in the first section of Table 15, which gives the multiple prediction analyses for the three structural factors.

Table 15 shows for each predictor variable, the single correlation with the criterion, the multiple correlation obtained by adding this predictor to the preceding ones, the F ratio corresponding to the increase obtained on the addition of this predictor, the degrees of freedom corresponding to the F ratio when $N = 46$, and the level of confidence at which the in-

TABLE 15 MULTIPLE PREDICTION ANALYSIS OF STRUCTURAL FACTORS

Contextual predictors of structural factors	Single Correlation	Multiple Correlation	F Ratio	Degrees of Freedom	Level of Confidence
STRUCTURING OF ACTIVITIES					
Size	0.69	0.69	39.6	1 : 44	> 99%
Workflow integration	0.34	0.75	8.2	1 : 43	> 99%
Size of parent organization	0.39	0.76	1.9	1 : 42	NS
CONCENTRATION OF AUTHORITY					
Dependence	0.66	0.66	34.2	1 : 44	> 99%
Location (number of operating sites)	0.39	0.75	12.5	1 : 43	> 99%
Age of organization	−0.38	0.77	2.5	1 : 42	NS
Operating diversity	−0.30	0.78	3.0	1 : 41	NS
Workflow integration	−0.30	0.78	0.0	1 : 40	NS
Size of parent organization	0.39	0.79	0.4	1 : 39	NS
LINE CONTROL OF WORKFLOW					
Operating variability	−0.57	0.57	20.7	1 : 44	> 99%
Workflow integration	−0.46	0.59	1.7	1 : 43	NS
Number of sites	0.39	0.59	0.1	1 : 42	NS

crease due to this predictor can be quoted. It will be seen from the first section of Table 15 that the correlation 0.69, between size and structuring of activities, is increased to a multiple correlation of 0.75 when workflow integration is added as a predictor. But the multiple correlation shows no noticeable increase when size of parent organization is added as a third predictor; that is, its predictive power has already been tapped by the two previous variables.

It must be emphasized that this procedure assesses only the predictive power of the contextual variables, not their relative importance in any more general sense. It cannot be concluded that the relationship of size of parent organization to structuring of activities is less important than that of workflow integration, because it adds less to the multiple correlation. Indeed the original higher correlation shows that this is not the case. Because of the interaction of the variables, the effects of organizational size and size of parent organi-

zation are confounded, in this study, as the correlation between them shows. A full examination of their relative effects would require a sample in which they were not correlated, as is the case with the technology measure.

The same argument applies to the multiple prediction of concentration of authority (Table 15). Here again there is a clear first predictor, dependence, with a correlation of 0.66 but then a choice of intercorrelated variables. The selection was made in order to get as high a multiple correlation as possible with as few predictors as possible, but the fact that the later predictors add nothing to the multiple correlation does not mean that they have no impact, only that predictive power has been exhausted by previous related variables. The existence of the charter-technology-location nexus referred to above is supported by the fact that when any one of these variables is used as a predictor, the remaining two do not add to the multiple correlation. Table

15 shows the multiple correlation of 0.75 obtained by using the location measure together with dependence as predictors. When the technology scale of workflow integration is substituted as the second predictor, the multiple correlation is 0.71; when the operating diversity scale of charter is used, the multiple correlation is 0.70.

The prediction of line control of workflow shows this same phenomenon, where the addition of predictors, because of their interrelationships, does not improve on the original single correlation of operating variability with the criterion.

The size of the multiple correlations obtained with the first two factors, each 0.75 with two predictors, together with the small number of predictors needed, strongly supports the view that in relation to organization structure as defined and measured in this study, salient elements of context have been identified. Thus a knowledge of the score of an organization on a small number of contextual variables makes it possible to predict within relatively close limits, its structural profile. Given information about how many employees an organization has, and an outline of its technology in terms of how integrated and automated the work process is, its structuring of activities can be estimated within fairly close limits. Since in turn the score of the organization on structuring of activities summarizes an extensive description of broad aspects of bureaucratization, the organization is thereby concisely portrayed in terms of this and similar concepts. Likewise, knowing the dependence of an organization on other organizations and its geographical dispersion over sites tells a great deal about the likely concentration of authority in its struc-

ture. *Size, technology, dependence and location* (number of sites) are critical in the prediction of the two major dimensions (structuring of activities, concentration of authority) of the structures of work organizations.

Multiple predictions of the order of magnitude obtained are as high as can be expected with this level of analysis. Higher values would imply that there were no important deviant cases, and that differences as to policies and procedures among the members of an organization have no effect on its structure. And this is obviously not so. The multiple predictions discussed here are applicable only to this sample. When the regression equations obtained are applied to another similar sample for prediction purposes, there is likely to be a reduction in the multiple correlations. The extent of this reduction can be strictly gauged only by investigating another similar sample of organizations. This cross-validation study is at present being undertaken, but a first attempt to estimate the likely amount of reduction was made by splitting the sample into two subsamples of 23 organizations, each stratified in the same way as the whole sample. Table 16 gives the multiple regressions on structuring of activities and concentration of authority for the whole sample and for the two subsamples separately. The multiple correlations and the weightings are of the same order of magnitude. A "robust" prediction on the basis of simple weightings was also calculated. These correlations should be less subject to shrinkage. The stability of the correlation of 0.57 between operating variability and line control of workflow is indicated by correlations on the two subsamples of 0.50 and 0.65.

TABLE 16 MULTIPLE REGRESSION ON STRUCTURAL FACTORS

Structural Factors	Whole Sample	Subsamples		"Robust" Weightings
		1	2	
STRUCTURING OF ACTIVITIES				
Weightings of predictors				
Size	0.67	0.72	0.60	2
Workflow Integration	0.29	0.14	0.43	1
Multiple correlation	0.75	0.73	0.79	0.74
CONCENTRATION OF AUTHORITY				
Weightings of predictors				
Dependence	0.64	0.50	0.77	2
Location	0.36	0.40	0.33	1
Multiple correlation	0.75	0.66	0.84	0.75

SUMMARY AND DISCUSSION

This study has demonstrated the possibilities of a multivariate approach to the analysis of the relationships between the structure of an organization and the context in which it functions. Starting from a framework as outlined in the conceptual scheme summarized in Table 1, aspects of the context and structure of the organization were sampled in order to establish scales which discriminated among organizations in a large number of aspects. From this sampling 103 primary scales of structure and context were developed as a basis for the analysis of the interrelationships among them.

By scaling and factor analytic techniques, these were then summarized to form three basic dimensions of structure and eight salient elements of context (Table 14). The analogy with the psychological test constructor who samples behavior in order to establish dimensions of personality is clear, and the same limitations apply. Thus while a claim can be made for the internal consistency and scaleability of these measures,

no claim can be made as to the comprehensiveness with which they cover the field. This is particularly clear in the attempt to elucidate aspects of context, a concept which, although in some respects narrower than that of environment, is still very wide. Emphasis was therefore placed on those aspects of context that had been held to be relevant to structure on the basis of previous writings. The size of the multiple correlations obtained indicates that at least some of the salient aspects of context were tapped.

The predicability of the structural dimensions from contextual elements serves as external validating evidence for the structural concepts themselves. It has now been shown that besides being internally consistent and scaleable, as previously demonstrated, they can also be related in a meaningful way to external referents. Indeed the size of the correlations inevitably raises the question of causal implications. It is tempting to argue that these clear relationships are causal—in particular, that *size, dependence, and the charter-technology-location nexus largely determine structure.*

It can be hypothesized that size causes structuring through its effect on intervening variables such as the frequency of decisions and social control. An increased scale of operation increases the frequency of recurrent events and the repetition of decisions, which are then standardized and formalized (Haas and Collen, 1963). Once the number of positions and people grows beyond control by personal interaction, the organization must be more explicitly structured. Insofar as structuring includes the concept of bureaucracy, Weber's observation that "the increasing bureaucratic organization of all genuine mass parties offers the most striking example of the role of sheer quantity as a leverage for the bureaucratization of a social structure" is pertinent (Gerth and Mills, 1948).

Dependence causes concentration of authority at the apex of publicly owned organizations because pressure for public accountability requires the approval of central committees for many decisions. The similar position of small units in large privately owned groups is demonstrated by the effect that a merger may have upon authority. After a merger, a manager of the smaller unit "may no longer be able to take a certain decision and act upon it independently. He may have to refer matters to people who were complete strangers to him a few months earlier" (Stewart *et al.*, 1963).

Integrated technology may be hypothesized to cause an organization to move towards the impersonal control end of the line-control dimension. Line control is adequate in shops or in municipal schools or building maintenance gangs, where the technology of the tasks is not mechanized and each line supervisor and primary work group is independent of all the others. But as workflow integration reaches the production line or automated stages, where large numbers of tasks are interdependent, more control is needed than can be exercised by the line of command alone. Udy (1965) summarizes this in his proposition, "The more complex the technology . . . , the greater the emphasis on administration."

The causal argument need not run only one way. It can be suggested that a policy of specializing roles and standardizing procedures, that is, of structuring, would require more people, that is, growth in size. Concentration of decisions in the hands of an owning group is likely to result in more economic integration among the subsidiaries concerned, that is, more dependence; while the production control, inspection, and work-study procedures of staff control might raise the level of workflow integration in the technology.

But a cross-sectional study such as this can only establish relationships. Causes should be inferred from a theory that generates a dynamic model about changes over time. The contribution of the present study is to establish a framework of operationally defined and empirically validated concepts, which will enable processual and dynamic studies to be carried out on a much more rigorous and comparative basis than has been done previously. The framework is also seen as a means of controlling for organizational factors when individual and group level variables are being studied. Such studies must now be conducted with reference not only to differences in size, but also in dependence, operating function, workflow integration, etc., and with reference to the demonstrated relationship between these aspects of context and organization structure.

REFERENCES

AARONOVITCH, S. 1961. *The Ruling Class.* London: Lawrence and Wishart.

AMBER, G. H. and P. S. AMBER. 1962. *Anatomy of Automation.* Englewood Cliffs, N.J.: Prentice–Hall.

BAKKE, E. W. 1959. "Concepts of the social organization." *In* M. Haire (ed.), *Modern Organization Theory.* New York: John Wiley.

BERLE, A. A. and G. MEANS. 1937. *The Modern Corporation and Private Property.* New York: Macmillan.

BLAU, P. and W. R. SCOTT. 1962. *Formal Organizations.* San Francisco: Chandler.

BROGDEN, H. E. 1949. "A new coefficient: application to biserial correlation and to estimation of selective efficiency." *Psychometrika,* 14: 169–82.

BURNHAM, J. 1962. *The Managerial Revolution.* London: Penguin.

CHANDLER, A. D. 1962. *Strategy and Structure.* Cambridge, Mass.: M. I. T. Press.

CLARK, B. R. 1956. "Organizational adaptation and precarious values." *American Sociological Review,* 21: 327–36.

DAHRENDORF, R. 1959. *Class and Conflict in Industrial Society.* Stanford, California: Stanford University Press.

DUBIN, R. 1958. *The World of Work.* Englewood Cliffs, N.J.: Prentice-Hall.

DUNCAN, O. D., W. R. SCOTT, S. LIEBERSON, B. DUNCAN and H. WINSBOROUGH. 1963. *Metropolis and Region.* Baltimore, Md.: Johns Hopkins University Press.

EISENSTADT, S. N. 1959. "Bureaucracy, bureaucratization and debureaucratization." *Administrative Science Quarterly,* 4: 302–20.

FLORENCE, P. S. 1961. *Ownership, Control and Success of Large Companies.* London: Sweet and Maxwell.

GERTH, H. H., and C. WRIGHT MILLS (eds.), 1948. *From Max Weber: Essays in Sociology.* London: Routledge and Kegan Paul.

HAAS, E. and L. COLLEN. 1963. "Administrative practices in university departments." *Administrative Science Quarterly,* 8: 44–60.

HAGE, J. and M. AIKEN. 1967. "Relationship of centralization to other structural properties." *Administrative Science Quarterly,* 12 (June): 72–92.

HALL, R. H. and C. R. TITTLE. 1966. "A note on bureaucracy and its correlates." *American Journal of Sociology,* 72: 267–72.

HICKSON, D. J., D. S. PUGH and D. C. PHEYSEY. 1969. "Operations technology and formal organization: an empirical reappraisal." *Administrative Science Quarterly* (to appear).

HININGS, C. R., D. S. PUGH, D. J. HICKSON and C. TURNER. 1967. "An approach to the study of bureaucracy." *Sociology,* 1 (January): 62–72.

INKSON, J. H. K., R. L. PAYNE and D. S. PUGH. 1967. "Extending the occupational environment: the measurement of organizations." *Occupational Psychology,* 41: 33–47.

LEVY, P. and D. S. PUGH. 1969. "Scaling and multivariate analyses in the study of organizational variables." *Sociology,* 3 (to appear).

MILLS, C. WRIGHT. 1956. *The Power Elite.* London: Oxford University Press.

PARSONS, T. 1956. "Suggestions for a sociological approach to the theory of organizations, I and II." *Administrative Science Quarterly,* 1 (June and September): 63–85, 225–39.

PERROW, C. 1967. "A framework for the comparative analysis of organizations." *American Sociological Review,* 32 (April): 194–208.

PORTER, L. W. and E. E. LAWLER III. 1965. "Properties of organization structure in relation to job attitudes and job behavior." *Psychological Bulletin*, 64: 25–51.

PRESTHUS, R. V. 1958. "Towards a theory of organizational behavior." *Administrative Science Quarterly*, 3: 48–72.

PUGH, D. S., D. J. HICKSON and C. R. HININGS. 1969. "An empirical taxonomy of work organization structures." *Administrative Science Quarterly*, 14 (to appear).

PUGH, D. S., D. J. HICKSON, C. R. HININGS, K. M. MACDONALD, C. TURNER and T. LUPTON. 1963. "A conceptual scheme for organizational analysis." *Administrative Science Quarterly*, 8: 289–315.

PUGH, D. S., D. J. HICKSON, C. R. HININGS and C. TURNER. 1968. "Dimensions of organization structure." *Administrative Science Quarterly*, 13: 65–105.

SELZNICK, P. 1949. *T.V.A. and the Grass Roots*. Berkeley, Calif.: University of California Press.

SELZNICK, P. 1957. *Leadership in Administration*. New York: Harper & Row.

STARBUCK, W. H. 1965. "Organizational growth and development." *In* J. G. MARCH (ed.), *Handbook of Organi-zations*. Chicago: Rand McNally.

STEWART, R., P. WINGATE and R. SMITH. 1963. *Mergers: The Impact on Managers*. London: Acton Society Trust.

STINCHCOMBE, A. L. 1965. "Social structure and organization." *In* J. G. March (ed.), *Handbook of Organizations*. Chicago: Rand McNally.

THOMAS, E. J. 1959. "Role conceptions and organizational size." *American Sociological Review*, 24: 30–37.

THOMPSON, J. D. and F. E. BATES. 1957. "Technology, organization and administration." *Administrative Science Quarterly*, 2: 323–43.

TRIST, E. L., G. W. HIGGIN, H. MURRAY and A. B. POLLOCK. 1963. *Organizational Choice*. London: Tavistock.

UDY, S. H. 1965. "The comparative analysis of organizations." *In* J. G. March (ed.), *Handbook of Organizations*. Chicago: Rand McNally.

WALKER, C. R. 1962. *Modern Technology and Civilization*. New York: McGraw–Hill.

WILSON, B. R. 1962. "Analytical studies of social institutions." *In* A. T. Welford *et al.* (eds.), *Society: Problems and Methods of Study*. London: Routledge and Kegan Paul.

WOODWARD, J. 1965. *Industrial Organization, Theory and Practice*. London: Oxford University.

3. TECHNICAL AND INSTITUTIONAL FACTORS IN PRODUCTION ORGANIZATION: A PRELIMINARY MODEL

Stanley H. Udy, Jr.

While it is true that administrative structure is likely to be strongly influenced by technical exigencies as well as by the institutional setting, at the same time, existing systematic models of organization are largely restricted to variations in the internal workings of administrative structures.[1] For many purposes this is indeed quite appropriate, but often the absence of explicit technical and institutional variables from organizational models is severely felt.

Two fairly common examples may be cited: The first is the frequent necessity, *faute de mieux*, of using the essentially residual concept "informal organization" as an explanatory variable where institutional conditions are actually involved. The second, on the technical side, is the difficulty in accounting for—if not the fre-

quent lack of recognition of—differences in patterns of job satisfaction among workers engaged in different types of technical activity.[2] Both instances, and others like them, point to the need for systematic organizational models which explicitly introduce technical and institutional variables as influencing administration. It is the purpose of this paper to develop and test a preliminary model of this type.

Specifically, the unit to be described is the *production organization*; that is, any social group manifestly (though not necessarily exclusively) engaged in producing material goods from raw materials. Since any such organization is carrying on a technological process in a social setting, it will be oriented not only to an *administrative system* (a system of role expectations defining interactive relationships among members), but also to a *technical system* (a system of activities performed on raw materials by members), and an *institutional system* (a system of norms and roles through which participation and motivation

Reprinted by permission of the author and publisher, The University of Chicago Press, from *The American Journal of Sociology*, Vol. 67 (Nov. 1961), 247–54.

[1] See, however, James G. March and Herbert A. Simon, *Organizations* (New York: John Wiley & Sons, 1958); Talcott Parsons, *Structure and Process in Modern Societies* (Glencoe, Ill.: Free Press, 1960), pp. 16–96.

[2] Robert Blauner, "Work Satisfaction and Industrial Trends in Modern Society," *In* W. Galenson and S. M. Lipset (eds.), *Labor and Trade Unionism* (New York: John Wiley & Sons, 1960), pp. 339–60.

to work are institutionalized and carried out).[3] Our model, essentially, attempts to show how certain aspects of administrative structure are shaped by certain technical and institutional influences, in the course of production. The model in no sense purports to be exhaustive; the purpose here, rather, is to demonstrate the feasibility of the method with a view toward further work on a more complete version. The empirical basis of the analysis is a sample of thirty production organizations in thirty different societies, using data drawn from the Human Relations Area Files, supplemented by additional ethnographic materials.[4]

DEFINITIONS

The particular aspect of the technical system which will concern us is the *flow of production*; that is, the pattern of spatial and/or temporal division of labor among work positions differentiated in the same process.[5] Three principal dimensions of

the flow of production are: *specialization* (the differentiation of activities performed simultaneously); *specification* (the differentiation of sequential sets of specialized activities over time); and *combined effort* (the manifest rhythmic integration of simultaneous activity).[6] For the thirty cases studied it proved possible to construct process charts from the ethnographic descriptions. The degree of specialization could thus be measured in each case by the maximum number of specialized activities ever performed at once in the process; the degree of specification, by the number of sets of such activities temporally differentiated in the process; and the degree of combined effort, by its presence at any point (1) or its absence at all points (0). The total *technical complexity* of any flow of production is defined as the arithmetic sum of these three quantities.

We shall consider two dimensions of administrative systems: *authority* (institutionalized power over the actions of others); and *rationality* (in this context, role expectations based on planning for the announced objectives of the organization). Organization charts were reconstructed from the descriptions of the cases, and the amount of authority was measured in each case by counting the number of hierarchical levels. Similarly, the

---

[3] Parsons, *Structure and Process*, pp. 60–65.
[4] This sample represents all those cases employed in an earlier comparative study of work organization on which adequate data were available for present purposes. The following societies are represented here: Aleut, Andamanese, Atayal, Azande, Bemba, Betsileo, Buka, Cambodian, Central Chinese, Crow, Dahomean, Haitian, Hopi, Jukun, Kabyle, Karen, Kikuyu, Li, Lobi, Maanyan, Malekulan, Mam, Mbundu, Navaho, Ojibwa, Paiute, Sanpoil, Siriono, Sotho, Tibetan (for details on methods of selection and bibliography see Stanley H. Udy, Jr., *Organization of Work: A Comparative Analysis of Production among Nonindustrial Peoples* [New Haven: HRAF Press, 1959]).
[5] Arnold S. Feldman and Wilbert E. Moore, "The Work Place," *In* W. E. Moore and A. S. Feldman (eds.), *Labor Commitment and Social Change in Developing*

Areas (New York: Social Science Research Council, 1960), p. 27.
[6] Max Weber, *The Theory of Social and Economic Organization,* trans. A. M. Henderson and T. Parsons (New York: Oxford University Press, 1947), pp. 225–26; Karl Bücher, *Die Entstehung der Volkswirtschaft* (Tübingen: J. C. B. Mohr, 1920–21), Vol. 1, chap. viii–ix; W. G. Ireson and E. L. Grant, *Handbook of Industrial Engineering and Management* (Englewood Cliffs, New Jersey: Prentice-Hall, 1955), pp. 291–92.

data permitted classification of the organizations studied into three ranks of increasing rationality, depending on whether none, one, or both of the following characteristics were reported present: (*a*) limited objectives (announced objectives limited to production); (*b*) segmental participation based on any kind of mutual limited agreement.

On the institutional level we shall be concerned with two dimensions of production organization: social involvement and the scope of the reward. Any production organization is socially involved to the degree that participation and motivation are institutionalized through expectations and obligations existing independently of the production situation. The organizations studied were ranked into six categories of presumed increasing social involvement, as follows:

1. Participation of all members voluntary, in the sense of no socially prescribed sanctions attached to nonparticipation.
2. Agreement to participate voluntary for all members, but participation obligatory in terms of an agreement, once such agreement is made.
3. Participation of a permanent core of members required on the basis of kinship and/or political obligations, but not continuously for each separate occasion; participation of temporary auxiliary members the same as category 2 above.
4. Participation of all members as in the permanent core of category 3.
5. Participation of a permanent core of members as in the permanent core of category 3; participation of temporary auxiliary members based on institutionalized reciprocity, without option to refuse.
6. Participation of all members required on the basis of kinship and/or political obligations, continuously required on each separate occasion and sanc-

tioned legitimately by force if necessary.

The above rank order was devised by asking: "To what extent do members or potential members have the option to refuse to participate?" Category 1 is clearly the "most voluntary" from this standpoint. Initial membership is also voluntary for category 2, but members must remain members once they have agreed to participate. In categories 2 through 6, on the other hand, all or a major part of the membership is ascriptive; one may not refuse to participate. Category 3 is ranked below category 4 because it contains an element of option; category 5 is ranked above category 4 because it involves compulsory reciprocity in addition to kinship and/or political criteria. Category 6 is ranked above categories 3, 4, and 5 because participation is continuously (rather than just usually) required and may be compelled by force.

One might reasonably dispute the relative ranking of categories 4 and 5, on the ground that kinship and political ties are stronger than the convention of reciprocity. Inversion of these two categories in the analysis produced no change in the over-all results beyond a slight lowering of a few τ values. (It is hoped that any other possible alterations in the ordering appear as unreasonable to the reader as they do to the author, for when they are made the outcome is severely disrupted.)

The institutionalization of participation and motivation may also (or alternatively) center on some type of reward system, a reward being any material object accruing to some party as a consequence of production by a given production organization and a reward system being the pat-

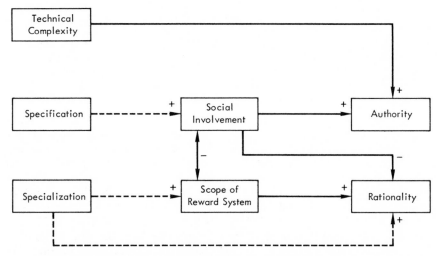

FIG. 1 INTERRELATIONS AMONG TECHNICAL, INSTITUTIONAL, AND AD-
MINISTRATIVE FACTORS IN PRODUCTION ORGANIZATIONS

tern of allocation of rewards relative to the membership of the organization. The scope of the system of any production organization will be deemed broad or narrow to the degree that motivation to participate and work is or is not, respectively, expected on the basis of rewards received by the organizational membership. A rough ranking could be achieved of the organizations studied, on the basis of the number of different aspects of participation of members which entered into determination of the type or quantity of rewards. The following situations were counted, and the organizations ranked in presumed order of increasing scope of reward system, according to the number of the situations: differential allocation of rewards on the basis of proprietorship (control over possession of the means of production); differential rewards in the office by organization; differential rewards according to performance (quantity and/or quality of work done); allocation of rewards to members doing physical work on raw material; absence of contributions by members lower in the hierarchy to those of higher authority.

THE MODEL: PROPOSITIONS AND FINDINGS

Figure 1 illustrates the proposed model schematically. The boxes represent variables already defined, with lines and arrows indicating causal patterns and alleged causal direction. Plus and minus signs denote positive and negative relationships, respectively; dotted lines indicate relationships which apply only to complex organizations, as that concept is defined below.

TECHNICAL COMPLEXITY AND AUTHORITY

The relationship between technical complexity and authority is contextual, relative to the other relationship in the model. In an earlier paper I discussed in some detail two as-

TABLE 1

	Authority ≥ 3	Authority < 3
Technical complexity ≥ 5 ...	9	1
Technical complexity < 5 ...	1	19

$$Q = +.98 \quad x^2 + 18.01 \quad p < .001$$

sumptions.[7] From these assumptions —(1) that technical complexity plus one is a valid measure of the number of items to which administrative attention must be given in order to assure production flow, and (2) that five such items is the maximum effective limit of the human span of attention—it follows that:

1. Organizations having a technical complexity of five or more tend to possess at least three levels of authority.

The results in Table 1 confirm this hypothesis; a similar result was reported in the earlier paper.

The argument maintains only that technical complexity determines a minimum amount of authority consistent with gross effectiveness. Presumably, other circumstances may have the effect of increasing the number of levels of authority beyond the technical minimum and also, conceivably, of decreasing the number of levels, presumably at the expense of effectiveness. Overall technical complexity thus emerges as essentially a base line relative to which other effects alleged by the model must be observed. It is not, however, continuous in its effects; it serves, rather, to differentiate organizations into types. Accordingly, in the re-

mainder of the analysis, we shall distinguish between simple organizations (where technical complexity is less than five) and complex organizations (where technical complexity is five or greater). The findings appear not only to justify the establishment of different base lines but also to indicate that other qualitative distinctions are involved as well.

As Figure 1 suggests, not only does total technical complexity have this effect on the structure of authority, but two components of technical complexity—specification and specialization—are alleged to have in and of themselves separate effects on other aspects of organization. The implied formal properties of the system demand some clarification. Technical complexity requires administrative attention, which, in turn, "generates" a minimal structure of authority. For present purposes it is assumed that it makes no difference whether the attention required results from specification, specialization, or, for that matter, combined effort—insofar as the direct relationship with authority is concerned. However, specification in itself is alleged to affect social involvement through a different, essentially ecological and adaptive mechanism quite independent of its generation of a need for integrative administrative attention. Similarly, specialization per se is alleged to affect rationality and the scope of rewards through a mechanism which is different from its contribution to

[7] Stanley H. Udy, Jr., "The Structure of Authority in Nonindustrial Production Organizations," *American Journal of Sociology*, 64 (May, 1959), 582–84.

the required level of overall administrative attention. It thus would appear proper to treat technical complexity, specification, and specialization as three separate variables, provided one bears in mind that from a purely formal standpoint (1) a high level of technical complexity implies as a minimum a high level of either specification or specialization, with attendant consequences, and (2) a low level of technical complexity severely restricts the possible ranges of variation of both specification and specialization.

SPECIFICATION, SOCIAL INVOLVEMENT, AND AUTHORITY

One would expect specification to have organizational consequences quite independent of its effect as a component of technical complexity, on the basis of ecological reasoning. For specification per se involves (1) redefinition of proximate organizational objectives, and (2) reallocation of personnel and resources. It is in the social setting of the organization that objectives are ultimately evaluated and personnel and resources procured. Consequently one would expect specification in particular to involve adaptive problems vis-à-vis the external environment. Therefore:

2. The more specification, the more social involvement.

As alleged in the model, social involvement in turn tends to lead to an expansion in the number of levels of authority beyond the technical minimum. Any organization is faced with the problem of legitimating the authority system. In a socially involved administrative system, general differences in societal status are carried over into the organization and act as a basis for such institutionalization; differences in authority are perceived as legitimate on external social grounds. When legitimation of authority occurs in this way, however, the social selection of the status system is presumably governed by the conditions of proposition 1. The number of levels differentiated in the external system must be at least as great as the technically required minimum; otherwise the organization will not be effective. There is, however, no technical reason why the external status system cannot distinguish more levels than the minimum requirement. If it does, under conditions of social involvement, such "extra" levels will presumably also be carried over into the administrative system. Under the assumption that a one-to-one correspondence between minimum technical requirements and number of levels of status in any available external system is unlikely, one therefore infers that:

3. The more social involvement, the more levels of authority, over and above the technical minimum.

Table 2 shows the results of a rank correlation test of propositions 2 and 3. The results are generally consistent with the hypotheses but indicate that social involvement is affected by specification only under conditions of complexity. In part, this would have to be true on purely formal grounds, inasmuch as specification cannot by definition vary greatly in simple organizations. Such variation as it does exhibit, however, appears to have little or no relationship to social involvement; furthermore, simple organizations are just as socially involved as complex ones (the average rank is 3.3 for each type). The implication is that speci-

TABLE 2 SPECIFICATION, SOCIAL INVOLVEMENT, AND AUTHORITY
(ZERO-ORDER VALUES OF KENDALL'S τ)

	Entire Sample (N = 30)	Simple Organizations (N = 20)	Complex Organizations (N = 10)
Specification/Social involvement	+.31	+.10	+.90
Social involvement/ Authority	+.28	+.41	+.81

fication controls social involvement under conditions of complexity; whereas social involvement can vary independently under conditions of simplicity. Evidently simple organizations are indeed so simple from a technical viewpoint that operations can be carried on effectively regardless of the mode of institutionalization. Maintenance of a given pattern of interdependence among substructures is essentially not a problem.

As regards social involvement and authority, the fact that the correlations appear higher for both simple and complex organizations separately than for the entire sample lends support to the alleged status of overall technical complexity as a variable of the context. It also appears that the correlation is higher for complex than for simple organizations. This again may be interpreted as indicating that complexity increases the salience of organizational solidarity; where operations are relatively simple, organization can be quite loosely knit and still be adequate to the task at hand. But as complexity increases, the degree of interdependence among substructures becomes greater. Such broad interpretations can, of course, hardly rest on these findings alone. They are mentioned at this point, however, because they are also suggested by findings elsewhere in the model.

SPECIALIZATION, SCOPE OF REWARDS, AND RATIONALITY

Like specification, specialization also has organizational consequences of its own which are independent of its effects as a component of over-all technical complexity. For a large number of specialized activities implies an emphasis on specificity of administrative roles if structural cooperation is to occur. This suggests explicit agreement in the organization as to what the members are supposed to be doing. Therefore:

4. The more specialization, the more rationality.

As the number of specialized activities increases, furthermore, the problem of differentiating the persons performing them becomes increasingly acute. Presumably this could be done by means of social involvement. Indeed, certain social criteria of assignment of roles are well known to be universal, such as division of labor on the basis of sex. Unlike the case of specification, however, there is no mechanism involved in specialization per se which would tend to bring the organization into contact with its external setting and hence actually produce more social involvement as specialization increases (the actual τ value is −.11). If social involvement is already present for some other reason, it presumably can provide a

TABLE 3 SPECIALIZATION, RATIONALITY, AND SCOPE OF REWARD
SYSTEM (ZERO-ORDER VALUES OF KENDALL'S τ)

	Entire Sample ($N = 30$)	*Simple Organizations* ($N = 20$)	*Complex Organizations* ($N = 10$)
Specialization/ Rationality	+.23	+.05	+.39
Specialization/Scope	+.21	+.07	+.41
Scope/Rationality	+.44	+.41	+.33

TABLE 4 SOCIAL INVOLVEMENT, SCOPE OF REWARD SYSTEM,
AND RATIONALITY (ZERO-ORDER VALUES OF KENDALL'S τ)

	Entire Sample ($N = 30$)	*Simple Organizations* ($N = 20$)	*Complex Organizations* ($N = 10$)
Social involvement/ Scope	−.34	−.36	−.61
Social involvement/ Rationality	−.89	−.87	−.94

basis for differentiation and assignment of roles, but if not, there is no reason to believe that it will be produced by anything inherent in specialization. An alternative mode of differentiation, internal to the organization and hence subject to the effects of specialization, is the attachment of differential rewards to positions and activities. Hence, assuming the model to be exhaustive:

5. The greater the degree of specialization, the greater the scope of the system of rewards.

A reward system which is broad in scope links organizational activity directly to personal motivation and hence supports incentives to organized planning. Therefore:

6. The more extensive the system of rewards, the more rationality.

These hypotheses were likewise tested by rank correlation, with the results shown in Table 3. Again, the results are generally consistent with the hypotheses, but with the suggestion again that administration is not a technical problem in simple organizations. Also, the relationships appear less pronounced than in the previous series, suggesting that possibly the model is open to more question at these points.

SOCIAL INVOLVEMENT, SCOPE OF REWARDS, AND RATIONALITY

Social involvement and a system of rewards emerge as potentially competing ways of institutionalizing administrative activity. It appears that under some circumstances social involvement overrides rewards or renders them superfluous, while under others the opposite is true. Rewards, for example, can be removed by forcible action and work still compelled, if enough social involvement is present. It is also conceivable that social involvement can be adequate to differentiate roles, thus rendering differentiation by rewards unnecessary, at least on cognitive grounds. On the other hand, a broadening scope of rewards can undermine a traditional system of obligations, as for example in the case of the introduction of general media of exchange in folk society. Thus, apparently for a variety of reasons:

7. Social involvement and scope of the system of rewards vary inversely in a reciprocal causal relationship.

Social involvement by definition implies the introduction of ascriptive elements into recruitment and assignment. Therefore:

8. The more social involvement, the less rationality.

Rank correlation of the variables in propositions 7 and 8 yields the results shown in Table 4. Again the relationships seem more marked in the case of complex organization, particularly as regards social involvement and scope of rewards. The inverse relationship between social involvement and rationality on the other hand seems ubiquitous. Complex organizations appear to be neither more or less socially involved nor more or less rational than do simple organizations. The average rank of social involvement for both types is 3.3, and the average rank of rationality, 1.8. However, complex organizations appear possibly to possess systems of rewards of somewhat broader scope than do simple ones (the average ranks are 3.8 and 3.1, respectively). This may indicate that rewards do not begin to interact with social involvement until they reach some minimal threshold of importance.

The results by and large sustain the realistic character of the model proposed, particularly in the case of complex organizations. In simple organizations, certain of the proposed relationships are attenuated or disappear entirely. This might be because (1) the technical system is so simple that virtually any administrative form can adapt to it; (2) organizational solidarity becomes more important as complexity increases; and (3) the scope of rewards is too narrow in simple organizations to be felt in terms of social involvement.

Alternative explanations, equally consistent with the empirical findings, are of course possible. One could, for example, maintain that rational planning can rid the organization of social involvement, that social involvement produces specification, and so forth. We have alleged those which seem most plausible in view of existing theory and research. For example, in view of the fact that social involvement stems from the setting within which rationality takes place, it seems plausible that it influences rationality, rather than the other way around, at least most of the time. This contention is also in accord with most findings on human relations. It is easier to explain the differences in specification and social involvement between simple and complex organizations if one assumes the explanation of cause and effect posited in the model, although it may well be true that under certain conditions socially involved organizations "invent" extra specified tasks to fill idle time if the system is already complex. As regards the including of additional arrows in the model, given the present data, one must again rely largely on verbal theoretical reasoning. The presence of tied ranks, as well as the numbers of cases, ruled out the possibility of partial correlation; the fact that the data could not defensibly be converted to interval ordinal scales unfortunately ruled out causal analysis of the type proposed by Simon and Blalock—a method of analysis which otherwise would seem particularly appropriate.[8] It should, however, perhaps be noted that when all variables are correlated, the τ values for relationships not alleged by the model are in all instances lower than those where direct causal relationships are alleged.

This rough model illustrates the relevance of technical and institutional features to certain aspects of administrative structure. Furthermore, if the relationships alleged are correct, they suggest the existence of certain endemic organizational problems and tensions, and also indicate further research possibilities. The interplay of social involvement, rationality, and scope of reward system would appear to be of particular interest, especially if some measure of the efficiency of performance could be added to the model. Assuming that rationality "produces" efficiency, organizations involving a great diversity of specified tasks which are also highly specialized would be expected to face rather severe difficulties. It is possible that such difficulties are minimized through certain systems of rewards. Similarly, the technical complexity–authority–social involvement–rationality set of interrelations seems of particular relevance to problems of "human relations."[9] In any event, it is hoped that the model proposed may prove useful in ordering data in cases where technical and institutional conditions have a bearing upon administration.

[8] Herbert A. Simon, *Models of Man* (New York: John Wiley & Sons, 1957), pp. 37–49; H. M. Blalock, Jr., "Correlation and Causality: The Multivariate Case," *Social Forces*, 39 (March, 1961), 246–51; also see Blalock's *Social Statistics* (New York: McGraw-Hill Book Co., 1960), chap. xix.

[9] Stanley H. Udy, Jr., " 'Bureaucracy' and 'Rationality' in Weber's Organization Theory: An Empirical Study," *American Sociological Review*, 24 (December, 1959), 791–95.

4. ENVIRONMENT AS AN INFLUENCE ON MANAGERIAL AUTONOMY

William R. Dill

Administrative science needs propositions about the ways in which environmental factors constrain the structure of organizations and the behavior of organizational participants. Until we can identify relevant environmental variables and can predict their impact on behavior, we cannot know how findings about behavior in one situation must be modified if they are to serve as prescriptions for behavior in other situations where groups are subject to different environmental "demands."

This paper reports an exploratory study of environmental influences on the top-management groups in two Norwegian business firms, each with 250–300 employees.[1] One, which I shall call Alpha, manufactured a varied line of clothing and sold it to wholesalers and retailers throughout Norway. The second, Beta, was a sales, engineering, and contracting firm. It sold, installed, and serviced a wide variety of supplies and machinery for state, industrial, and private users. Both Alpha and Beta were among the larger, older firms in their industries.

The two firms differed sharply in the degree to which the department heads and top staff men thought and acted autonomously, both with respect to their peers and with respect to their superior, the owner-manager. This paper reports differences between Alpha and Beta in top-management autonomy, and it contrasts the environments in which the two

Reprinted by permission from *Administrative Science Quarterly* (March 1958), pp. 409–43.

[1] This research was begun in Norway. Thanks are due to the Norwegian Fulbright Committee for financial aid and for permission to depart from the usual academic program and to the owners and employees of Alpha and Beta for cooperating on all phases of the study. Rolf Waaler, Harriet Gullvåg, and Sverre Lysgaard generously took time from their own work to criticize plans for gathering data. Analysis of the data was carried out, in part, under a Ford Foundation grant to the Graduate School of Industrial Administration for research on decision making in organizations. During the analysis Melvin Anshen, Harold Guetzkow, Allen Newell, H. A. Simon, and Donald Trow offered valuable criticisms and suggestions. A more detailed report of the study and of the findings is available in my thesis, "An Analysis of Task Environment and Personal Autonomy in Two Management Organizations" (unpublished doctor's dissertation, Carnegie Institute of Technology, 1956).

management groups worked. The final section proposes relationships between environmental variables and autonomy.

BASIC CONCEPTS AND A FRAME OF REFERENCE

TASK VARIABLES

Each management group planned action on the basis of information it received about environmental events. I have denoted that part of the total environment of management which was potentially relevant to goal setting and goal attainment as the task environment.[2]

The task environment of management consisted of inputs of information from external sources. These inputs did not represent "tasks" for the organization; by *task* I mean a cognitive formulation consisting of a goal and usually also of constraints on behaviors appropriate for reaching the goal. When we study the task environment, we are focusing on the stimuli to which an organization is exposed; but when we study tasks,

we are studying the organization's interpretations of what environmental inputs mean for behavior. These interpretations are subject to errors of perception and to the bias of past experience.[3]

The task environment, as information inputs, as tasks, as cognitive formulations to guide action, need further to be distinguished from task-fulfilling activities, the actual behavior or men in organizations. In many studies where task variables have been considered,[4] clear distinctions have not been made among things that the organization does (*activities*), things that the organization sets itself to do (*tasks*), or stimuli that the organization might respond to (*task environment*). There are many relevant inputs of information which organizations do not attend to as well as

[2] Clear delineation of the boundaries of task environment requires more information than I gathered on the goals of management. C. J. Haberstroh proposes a scheme for the systematic mapping of organizational goal structures in "Processes of Internal Control in Firms" (Ph.D. thesis, University of Minnesota, 1958). He starts with the statements that executives make in research interviews, in conversations with co-workers, and in written documents. He codes separately each sentence or part of a sentence that identifies a goal or that identifies means-ends relationships. This analysis yields matrices of means-ends relationships among goals, subgoals, and tasks. From these matrices a number of important dimensions of organizational goal structures can be identified.

[3] *Task environment* may not seem to be a useful concept, since we can gain access to the environment only through our perceptions of it. In complex situations, however, it seems important to distinguish the environmental "demands" presented to a person from the person's interpretation of the demands and formulation of them into "tasks." The power of this distinction in laboratory experiments is shown in papers such as R. F. Bales, "The Equilibrium Problem in Small Groups," in T. Parsons, R. F. Bales, and E. A. Shils (eds.), *Working Papers in the Theory of Action* (Glencoe, Ill., 1953), pp. 111–61; H. Guetzkow and H. A. Simon, "The Impact of Certain Communication Nets upon Organization and Performance in Task-oriented Groups," *Management Science*, 1 (1955), 233–50; and H. Guetzkow and W. R. Dill, "Factors in the Organizational Development of Task-oriented Groups," *Sociometry*, 20 (1957), 175–204.

[4] For example, T. Burns, "The Direction of Activity and Communications in a Departmental Executive Group," *Human Relations*, 7 (1954), 73–97; S. Carlson, *Executive Behaviour* (Stockholm, 1950); C. L. Shartle, *Executive Performance and Leadership* (Englewood Cliffs, N.J., 1956).

many tasks which they formulate but never act upon.

AUTONOMY

The dependent variable for this study was *autonomy*, or freedom from influence. A department head or top staff man was judged autonomous with respect to peers or to the president to the extent that he and his subordinates were independent in formulating tasks or in carrying through courses of action.

The measures I have used are varied. They include statements by members of management about their relations with colleagues as well as reports and observations of specific samples of behavior. The measures represent primarily short-run freedom from influence. The study, which spanned four months, was too short for analyzing long-term interpersonal influence. Over the long run, moreover, much of the instruction and suggestion that a man receives tends to get internalized so that the man, in acting, feels that he is responding to internal choice rather than to external pressure.

In reporting data on autonomy, I shall make a distinction between *upward* and *horizontal* autonomy. The former is the freedom that first-rank subordinates had with respect to the owner-manager, their common superior; the latter, the freedom that they had with respect to one another or to one another's subordinates.

INFLUENCE OF TASK ENVIRONMENT ON AUTONOMY

The relationships between environment and autonomy in Alpha and Beta were not simple.

We can assume that the behavior of each management group was a function of the inputs that were, or that had been, accessible from the environment. But even in short time intervals, vast numbers of inputs became accessible. Of these, only a small proportion could be—and were —attended to.

Most inputs were simply statements about the condition of the organization or of parts of the environment. Some inputs took the form of goals suggested or specified for management. Only rarely, however, were inputs complete task formulations that included both goals to be attained and detailed specifications for courses of action. Even where environmental inputs specified courses of action, they rarely specified in any direct way the degree of autonomy that was to prevail in management relationships.[5]

Thus to understand the degree of autonomy that a leader showed in Alpha and Beta, we must look beyond the environmental inputs to which he was exposed. We must ask which inputs he was cognizant of, how he grouped inputs and elaborated their meaning for the organization, how he ascribed such properties as urgency or complexity to the tasks they suggested, and how he mapped actual courses of action. We must ask how the thoughts and actions of different men in the same firm, each exposed to the environment in a different way, mesh or conflict. Our problem, briefly, is to explore the task environment as it impinged on management and to search for characteristics of the environment that

---

[5] Even in laboratory experiments the relationship of the experimenter's instructions to the tasks which subjects set for themselves may frequently not be as direct as the experimenter assumes them to be.

might have influenced one key aspect, the autonomy, of management behavior.

SOURCES OF DATA

The analysis which follows is based mainly on interviews with management people in Alpha and Beta and on observations of them interacting with one another and with the environment. Before the intensive study began, the manager and his immediate subordinates in each firm were interviewed as part of a more general survey of patterns of autonomy in Norwegian management. Then over a four-month period these men were interviewed again, and additional interviews were held with all higher-level supervisors, with most foremen and foreladies, and with most specialists—salesmen, engineers, designers, technicians, accountants, and other office service personnel. Only a few clerical and hourly employees were interviewed.

These interviews were intended to elicit information about each man's career with the firm, about his job activities, and about his relationships with others in the firm. The interviews were supplemented by informal conversations with employees about jobs they were then doing and by observations of management at work. Two questionnaires were used to get additional data about what members of management did, how they worked together, and what they thought of their positions.

To gain perspective I explored the history of the two firms and interviewed men in other organizations about their relationships to Alpha and Beta. I have also drawn extensively on sources of general information about Norwegian society and the Norwegian economy.[6]

The data are far from complete, and little of what was learned deals directly with information from and about the environment *as it became accessible* to the two management groups during the study. The data, however, are rich enough to delineate major differences between Alpha and Beta and to suggest hypotheses for more carefully controlled research.

BACKGROUND INFORMATION ABOUT THE TWO FIRMS

GENERAL BACKGROUND

Before going further with the analysis, let us look briefly at Alpha and Beta and at the men who led them. Alpha was founded before the turn of the century; Beta, shortly after. By the time of the study Alpha was one of the largest and most diversified firms in its branch of the Norwegian clothing and textile industry. The only son of one founder was the president, and sons of another founder still served on the board of directors. These men controlled the firm.

Beta began as a very small specialty contracting firm for products and facilities that were undergoing rapid technological change. Its most rapid growth occurred after the twenties, when the founder withdrew in favor of the present owner-manager. Functions of the firm at the time of the study included importing foreign

---

[6] These sources included Norwegian newspapers and periodicals, regular and special publications of the Central Bureau of Statistics, and a variety of professional and partisan commentaries on the Norwegian economy and on Norwegian society.

manufactures for resale, some assembly and manufacturing work, and a wide variety of engineering, installation, and maintenance services.

Men in Alpha recognized four major sequences of activity within the organization. Each sequence, to a large extent, involved unique processes, required special personnel, and led to outputs that were clearly differentiable from the outputs of other sequences. Men in Beta clearly recognized thirteen such sequences of activity.

Over the years the volume of business for both firms had increased greatly, but the nature of products and services provided changed much more radically in Beta than Alpha. From a staff of ten to twelve men in

TABLE 1 ALPHA: TOP-MANAGEMENT INVOLVEMENT
IN WORK GROUPS AND JOB SEQUENCES

Major Work Groups	Group Size Rank*	Directly Affiliated Members of Top Management†	Extent of Management Involvement in Major Routine Job Sequences‡			
			No. 1	No. 2	No. 3	No. 4
Board of Directors	*	President (M)				
Top executive	*	President (L)	P	P	P	P
Mail committee	*	Pres. (L); Office mgr., Sales mgr., Scheduling mgr., Production leaders 1 & 2 (M).				
		ADMINISTRATIVE GROUPS				
		OPERATING AND SERVICE GROUPS				
Sales	13	Sales manager (D)	P	P	P	P
Services	10	Office manager (L)	P	P	P	P
Scheduling	11	Scheduling manager (L)	P	P	P	S
Production–H	3	Production leader 1 (L)	P	–	–	–
Production–S } Production–U	2	Production leader 2 (L)	–	P	P	–
Production–O } Production–Y	8	Production leader 3 (L)	S	S	P	S
Production–Sp	7	Production leader 4 (D)	–	–	–	P
Production–D	12	Production leader 5 (L)	S	S	S	S
Fashion	15	Stylist (L)	P	P	P	P
Industrial eng.	14	Industrial engineer (D)	P	P	P	P

*Groups in *both* firms have been ranked *together*, from largest to smallest, by the number of employees in them at the time of the study. The actual group sizes ranged from 125 to 1 (the stylist in Alpha had no subordinates). Administrative groups were not included in the ranking.

† The letter to the right of each man's title in this column indicates his primary role in the work group: *D*, if he had led the group since its inception as a separate unit in the firm; *L*, if he was the group leader at the time of the study (but not the original leader); *M*, if he was a subordinate member.

‡ For each numbered job sequence, the expected (formal) involvement of every member of top management is indicated by one of the following symbols: *P*, involvement as frequent participant in routine activities and decisions; *S*, involvement only as supervisor or evaluator; *A*, occasional involvement as planner or adviser on matters which required coordination among two or more job sequences; *dash*, substantially no involvement. *P* represents the highest degree of involvement in a job sequence; *dash*, the least.

1910, Beta had grown to a firm of nearly three hundred at the time of the study. Over the same period the number of employees at Alpha had decreased, dropping from more than five hundred to about two hundred and fifty.

MAJOR WORK GROUPS

Each of the two firms was composed of a number of distinct work groups. Tables 1 and 2 identify these groups and suggest the extent of their involvement in the major work sequences.

Certain groups were administrative; that is, they sponsored and con-trolled activities for the firm as a whole, and they were regarded inside and outside the firm as loci of ultimate responsibility for decisions and actions of the firm. The top administrative group in Alpha was a relatively passive board of directors composed of major stockholders. Only one director, the firm's president, concerned himself with day-to-day operating problems; the others met bimonthly to review accounting statements. The president of Beta had established a policy committee, composed of himself and five top subordinates, which had legal power to perform many of the functions of a corporate board. This committee met

TABLE 2 BETA: TOP-MANAGEMENT INVOLVEMENT IN WORK
GROUPS AND JOB SEQUENCES

Major Work Groups	Group Size Rank*	Directly Affiliated Members of Top Management†	Extent of Management Involvement in Major Routine Job Sequences†												
			1	2	3	4	5	6	7	8	9	10	11	12	13
Owners	*	President (L)													
Policy committee	*	President (D); Office mgr., Division mgrs. 1, 2, 3, & 4 (M)													
Top executive	*	President (L)	S	S	S	S	S	S	S	S	S	S	S	S	S
Mail committee	*	Pres. (D); Office mgr., Division mgrs. 1, 2, & 3 (M)													
ADMINISTRATIVE GROUPS															
OPERATING AND SERVICE GROUPS															
Services	6	Office manager (D)	S	S	S	S	S	S	S	S	S	S	S	S	S
Consumer contracting	1	Division manager 1 (D)	P	S	S	A	–	–	–	–	–	A	A	–	–
Producer contracting / Equipment sales	4	Division manager 2 (D)	A	–	A	S	S	S	S	S	S	A	A	A	A
Manufacturing / Retail sales	5	Division manager 3 (D)	–	A	A	–	–	–	–	–	A	P	S	A	A
Specialty contracting	9	Division manager 4 (L)	–	–	–	–	–	–	–	–	A	–	A	P	P

* See notes to Table 1.

at least once a month to review accounts and to discuss operating problems.

The presidents at Alpha and Beta took active personal leadership of operations, but both relied for assistance on mail committees, made up of key members of top management. These committees met daily to review incoming mail and to discuss other problems which committee members wanted to raise.

The operating and service groups were organized differently in the two firms. At Alpha most of the groups had been in existence for a long time, and most did work associated with two or more of the firm's major programs. No group did work associated with a program in which no other group was involved. At Beta the histories of operating and service groups varied more widely. The groups were frequently responsible for more than one program apiece, and in Beta some groups had sole responsibility for their programs.

TOP MANAGEMENT

In each firm one could distinguish several people who had perceptibly higher status as "management" than others in the organization. These included the two presidents and those of their immediate subordinates who had significant professional or supervisory responsibilities.[7] These subordinates will be known in this study as *key men.*

Top management in Alpha differed from top management in Beta in the following ways:

[7] The groups of "leading subordinates" do not include all employees who reported directly to the two presidents. Personal secretaries and a few special assistants are omitted.

1. The group at Alpha, defined by a criterion of apparent status, was larger (the president and ten subordinates *vs.* the president and five subordinates at Beta).
2. The group at Alpha was younger (median age, Alpha, 38 years; Beta, 50 years) and had fewer years of service with the firm (median service, Alpha, 7 years; Beta, 30 years).
3. All but three of the men at Alpha held jobs that had been established and developed by predecessors. All five subordinates at Beta, however, had had the task of creating and developing the positions that they held.
4. The men at Alpha had had less formal education. Two of the eleven (*vs.* three of the six at Beta) had had full university training.
5. The job titles and salary rates of the men at Alpha were less likely to earn high status in the business and social community outside the firm than those at Beta.

It is the two groups of key men —ten in Alpha and five in Beta— which will receive our attention in the pages which follow.

AUTONOMY IN THE TWO GROUPS OF SUBORDINATE LEADERS

By almost every measure that was tried, the five key men at Beta seemed more autonomous with respect to one another and with respect to their common superior, the president, than the ten key men at Alpha. The major evidence is summarized below.

PERCEIVED AUTONOMY

The key men from Beta perceived for themselves a greater degree of autonomy than the key men from Alpha. This was inferred from: (1) the proportions of each group who, in interviews and conversations, *spontaneously* mentioned autonomy or lack of autonomy as a prominent characteristic of their jobs; (2) the frequencies and types of working contacts men in each firm reported with their peers and with the president; and (3) the men's responses to eight questions (in a list of forty-five) which probed the degree of autonomy that they enjoyed.*[8]

OBSERVATIONS OF CONFERENCE BEHAVIOR

The perceptual evidence is supported by behavioral evidence. In Alpha the president and five of his key men met nearly every morning as the mail committee, chiefly to review incoming mail but also to discuss other problems. The president and four key men formed a similar committee at Beta. In Beta, too, all six members of top management met eight to twelve times a year as the policy committee to review company performance, to approve major departmental decisions, and to plan for the organization as a whole.

Upward Autonomy. Observations of the committees in session corroborate the proposition that key men in Alpha functioned less autonomously with respect to the president than did key men in Beta. The president at Alpha determined every day when the meeting would start, and he con-

[8] The measures which have been starred (*), as here, yielded differences between the two groups that were larger than one could reasonably attribute to chance variation. I have starred only differences (1) which I had an appropriate statistical test for, (2) which, when tested by a strong statistical criterion, proved significant at the 5 per cent level or better, and (3) which were not likely, on the basis of other information, to be overvalued by the statistical test.

trolled the length of the meeting and most of the agenda for it. He was the first to see the incoming mail. The mail committee did not meet in his absence; and when a meeting was called all members on the premises were expected to attend.

Subordinate committee members at Beta were the first to receive correspondence, and they generally decided whether it should be discussed with the president. The president seldom arrived less than half an hour after the meetings began, and meetings were held daily whether or not he was expected to attend. Attendance was voluntary, and two of the four key men came only two or three times a week. The office manager, who had routine information to report, was the only subordinate who regularly stayed at the meetings until the president arrived.

These overall impressions that the president at Alpha controlled conference activities more than did the president at Beta are supported by data on interaction within meetings.[9]

[9] To code interaction I broke the conversation into *units*. The main boundary between units was signaled by change of speaker or, rarely, within one man's speech, by major shifts of topic or addressee. For each unit I recorded the speaker, the apparent addressee, and the function of the unit in the discussion as apparently intended by the speaker. Six functions were distinguished: (1) giving information, (2) questioning, (3) offering suggestions, proposals, opinions, (4) stating decisions or rules of policy, (5) giving orders, requesting action, and (6) talking socially. Functions 1 and 2 were classed as "low influence" and 4 and 5 as "high influence." The conversation was episoded by topic discussed, and the nature of each topic was noted briefly. I coded seven mail-committee meetings in Alpha (560 units, 140 minutes of conversation) and three in Beta (368 units, 130 minutes), as well as one policy-committee meeting in Beta.

TABLE 3 ROLES OF THE PRESIDENTS IN CONFERENCES WITH SUBORDINATES

Measure of Role	President Alpha 7 Mail-Committee Meetings	President Beta 3 Mail-Committee Meetings	President Beta 1 Policy-Committee Meeting
Number of topics he initiated as a percentage of:			
Number of topics taken up when he was present	83	29*	30*
Number of topics taken up during entire meetings	83	12*	30*
Number of conversation units in which he was speaker or direct addressee as a percentage of:			
Number of units spoken when he was present	92	12*	72*
Number of units spoken during entire meetings	92	40*	72*
Number of low-influence units he contributed as a percentage of all his units	45	42	58*
Number of high-influence units he contributed as a percentage of:			
All his units	18	8	8
Number of high-influence units contributed by all members of committee	98	100	47*

* The starred (*) Beta percentages are significantly different from the corresponding Alpha percentages by the criteria outlined in footnote 8.

Table 3 shows that the president at Alpha was more active than the president at Beta as an initiator of topics for discussion, as a direct participant (speaker or addressee) in the conversation, and as a contributor of high-influence acts (for example, "stating decisions or policy" and "giving orders, requesting action"). Most of the differences become significant, by the criteria described in footnote 8, if we take into consideration the interaction which occurred at Beta while the president was not present.[10]

Horizontal Autonomy. Evidence from the meetings also indicates that the subordinate committee members had less autonomy with respect to one another in Alpha than in Beta.

Attendance at mail committee meetings in Beta was sporadic. Members generally did not stay through the entire meeting; they entered and left the meeting room at will. Silence was common in the period before the president arrived. Several minutes might pass while men read mail without a word being said. The average rate of interaction (number of con-

[10] The one inconsistent finding in Table 1 is that the president at Alpha (in contrast to the manager at Beta) had a greater percentage of contributions to conversation in the low-influence categories of "giving information" or "asking questions." This is probably an artifact of the former's role as the man who summarized the contents of

incoming mail to the group as he distributed it. At Beta this function was performed by clerks, who sorted the mail before meeting and prepared a summary list of its contents for circulation to members of top management later the same day.

versation units recorded per minute) was 2.4 for 85 minutes when the president was not present. This contrasts with rates of 3.6 for 45 minutes when the president was present and of 4.0 for 140 minutes of interaction (with the president in attendance) at Alpha.[11]

Social conversation in mail committee meetings amounted to 4 per cent of the recorded units at Alpha; to 15 per cent of the recorded units at Beta.* Most of the social interchanges at Beta occurred among subordinate members before the manager arrived.

As further evidence that key men in Alpha used meeting time more intensively to counsel and influence each other, let us look at variations in individuals' participation in the discussion of different topics. In both firms the topics taken up varied greatly in their relevance to different individuals. If we assume equal variability in the two firms, evidence that men in Beta keyed their participation more closely than men in Alpha to the topics under discussion can be interpreted as evidence of greater autonomy in Beta.

A simple, strong measure of topic-to-topic variability in participation rates is the frequency with which each subordinate committee member "withdrew," or remained silent, when topics were discussed. On the average, each man was silent during 16 per cent of the major topics discussed at Alpha, and for 27 per cent at Beta.[12] At Beta, though, the two men

who were least often silent were also the two who spent least time at the meetings. If we define "withdrawal" to include voluntary absence, the mean frequency of withdrawal for Alpha does not change, but the mean frequency for Beta rises to 45 per cent.*

RECOLLECTIONS OF BEHAVIOR ON "MOST IMPORTANT" TASKS

To get a sample of behavior outside scheduled meetings, I used management reports of activities. For at least two weeks every member of top management was asked to describe each day the "most important matter" he had handled that day and to answer questions about his involvement in activity on the task. The number of usable responses from key men ranged from three to twelve per man, with a median of seven. Each task reported required, in the median, two hours of the respondent's time during the day.

Although the data summarized below are subordinates' recollections of involvement in task performance, the data—as recollections—should be subject to a minimum of error. In most cases the questionnaires were filled out on the day when the behavior reported occurred, and the questions asked about behavior were specific.[13]

---

[11] A critical variable for this comparison, the average length of time spanned by each conversation unit, was not measured, but it was roughly comparable in the two firms.
[12] The calculations omitted minor topics (1) which were discussed with only two

committee members present and (2) for which the total number of units contributed by subordinate members was less than twice the number of subordinates present.
[13] For data confirming the importance of getting information about people's activities soon after the activities have occurred, see T. Burns, *Human Relations*, 7, and R. M. Stogdill and C. L. Shartle, *Methods in the Study of Administrative Leadership* (Columbus, O., 1955), pp. 27–30.

1. *Upward Autonomy.* The "most important" task data confirm our other evidence about differences in upward autonomy between Alpha and Beta.

The president was more often reported as initiator of activity by key men in Alpha than by key men in Beta. Six of nine respondents in Alpha named the president as initiator at least once. He was named as initiator of action on eleven (14 per cent) of 77 reported tasks. None of the five key men in Beta named the president as initiator of action on *any* task that he reported.*

The president at Alpha was also more frequently involved as a participant in task performance. He was named as a co-worker on eighteen (23 per cent) of 77 reported tasks. Each key man named him as a co-worker at least once. At Beta, in contrast, the president was named as a co-worker on only six (15 per cent) of 39 tasks.* All six namings were made by three of the five respondents. It is worth noting that in all cases the president at Beta participated at the invitation of a subordinate, but that the president at Alpha initiated half the tasks on which he was named as a co-worker.

Data from a very small sample of cases suggest that, when working with the president, key men at Alpha made decisions less often than the subordinates at Beta and that the actions of subordinates in Alpha were often restricted to the low-influence roles of "collecting information" and "preparing proposals."

2. *Horizontal Autonomy.* The data about handling of "most important" tasks also support the judgment that key men in Alpha had less freedom with respect to one another than had

key men in Beta. The more independent they were, for example, the less one would expect them to agree with one another in their choice of one task as "most important" for a particular day. In Alpha two men agreed in their choices in eight of a possible 165 instances. The fraction is small; but in Beta no coincident choices occurred in thirty possible pairings.*[14]

In addition, key men reported more cross-departmental initiation of tasks by peers at Alpha (26 per cent of 77 tasks) than at Beta (8 per cent of 39 tasks).* In naming co-workers on tasks, key men in Alpha reported interaction with peers and with subordinates of peers from more departments, and reported such interaction more frequently, than key men in Beta.*

SUMMARY

A variety of measures, then, give consistent support to the generalization that the key men at Alpha had less autonomy than the key men at Beta, both with respect to their direct superiors and with respect to one another.[15]

---

[14] The number of possible pairings for each firm is small relative to the number of men and to the number of responses because not all men filed responses for the same dates.

[15] Were autonomy the main focus of this paper, we might explore more fully the relationship of upward to horizontal autonomy. Both types were lower in Alpha than in Beta. But there is evidence that this need not be the case—that under certain conditions low upward autonomy may lead to high horizontal autonomy. See C. Argyris, *Executive Leadership* (New York, 1953), pp. 62–86.

THE TASK ENVIRONMENTS OF
TOP MANAGEMENT

Can the differences in autonomy be attributed to differences in the task environments with which the top-management groups of Alpha and Beta dealt? To answer this question, we first require a description of environmental characteristics.

COMPOSITION OF THE TASK
ENVIRONMENT

For both firms the "elements" of task environment that had greatest impact on goal attainment included *customers* (both distributors and users), *suppliers* (of materials, labor, equipment, capital, and work space), *competitors* (for both markets and resources), and *regulatory groups* (government agencies, unions, and interfirm associations). The people and institutions who had active or potential interest in the outputs of Alpha and Beta were mostly Norwegian. Neither firm exported goods or services extensively. Organization-customer relations were important to both firms because in the short run they had to adapt to customers' demands and patterns of behavior. Only in the long run could either firm significantly influence consumer preferences and market structure.

Alpha and Beta were especially alert to the markets at the time of the study. For nearly a decade they had enjoyed a sellers' market, but now because of increased domestic competition and relaxation of import restrictions some departments in both firms were running at a loss. For the first time in fourteen years the government had removed or substantially relaxed price controls; and, increasingly, Norwegian companies were reluctant to honor voluntary private agreements on pricing and marketing practices.

Increased competition for markets made relations with suppliers crucial, too. Some resources—notably foreign currencies and new plant or office facilities—were extremely scarce and still formally rationed. (The government controlled not only new construction but also renovation of old facilities.) Even resources that were routinely in demand were difficult or expensive to obtain. Skilled workers, particularly, were scarce because industry around Oslo had grown faster than men had been trained or than housing for migrants from other districts had been provided. Skilled personnel, particularly at management levels, were sometimes recruited from abroad.

Since most materials, production equipment, or goods bought for resale came directly or indirectly from other countries, fluctuations in international political and economic conditions complicated the arrangement of purchases.

Competitors did not have the direct influence that suppliers and customers had in specifying goals for Alpha and Beta. But competitors, working toward their own objectives, could thwart or limit the attainment of goals by Alpha or Beta, and they could introduce a large measure of uncertainty into the two firms' operations. Information about competitors gave management in Alpha and Beta criteria for setting goals and for evaluating performance. Dissatisfaction with performance at Alpha, for example, stemmed partly from knowledge that other mills were increasing sales while Alpha was losing customers.

The fourth significant part of the

task environments of the two firms comprised regulatory agencies, organizations with powers of sanction that restricted the operation of market mechanisms.

At the time of the study labor unions were committed to win from Norwegian employers a new general contract covering all industries, as well as specific contracts for different industries and for individual firms. Their demands included a general wage increase, guarantees of minimum earnings, pay for holidays, assurances of job security, and adjustments in incentive rates. The unions had a strong bargaining position. For many demands they had at least tacit backing from the government, and because good workers were scarce and competition was keen few firms felt they could afford a disgruntled work force.

The government, controlled by the Labor party for two decades, exercised strong controls over (1) the rate and direction of investment; (2) the use of capital in foreign trade; (3) prices and marketing practices; and (4) the pay-off on operations, through taxes and dividend restrictions. These controls had delayed the expansion of manufacturing activities in Beta for several years.

Two federations of interfirm organizations had important regulatory roles, even though their existence depended on the consent of firms like Alpha and Beta. The Employer's Association (NAF) was organized at the turn of the century to deal collectively with labor, which had previously formed a national organization. The Federation of Industries (NIF) was founded to represent firms in dealing with the government, the public, and foreign groups. Both were national federations of regional and industrial branch organizations. As institutions with wide membership and long history, NAF and NIF had acquired full-time administrative staffs and had developed programs which member firms could not easily alter. Even on questions decided by vote of the membership, Alpha and Beta were bound by the will of the majority. The majority, in turn, was reluctant to accept any program that might induce any of the largest members, or groups of members, to withdraw.

COMPARISON OF THE TASK
ENVIRONMENTS

What were the important differences between the task environments of top management in Alpha and Beta? From a host of specific differences we can abstract some major points of contrast between the two task environments. These will be analyzed in some detail.

1. *Degree of Unity and Homogeneity.* For each member of top management (and for his work groups), certain sectors of the firm's total task environment were of more interest than others. To what extent were the leaders concerned with the same environment? Where they dealt with sectors that did not overlap, were the sectors similar in nature and in their relation to the firm?

As individuals, the leaders at Alpha dealt with sectors of the task environment that were less differentiated than those with which the leaders at Beta dealt; where they were differentiated, the sectors dealt with by the Alpha leaders were more homogeneous.

Key men at Alpha were more often involved with the same environmental groups than key men at Beta. Most of the wholesalers and retailers who bought from Alpha ordered from all four product lines. The main purchases for all products were made twice a year at the same time. Contracts with Alpha on discounts and deliveries were seldom specific with regard to particular products or work groups. Even Norwegian families, the ultimate consumers of Alpha's output, generally purchased every year some of each major type of clothing that the firm manufactured.

At Beta the leaders were generally concerned with different, quite distinct markets. Some work groups subcontracted work for shipyards and building contractors, and most of their inquiries came from customers in the vicinity of Oslo. Others sold to specialized wholesalers all over Norway. Still another, in contrast to all other work groups, sold to individual consumers through a retail shop in Oslo. Two groups were the only ones concerned with the food-processing and storage industries and the only ones that regularly sold a major part of their output in north Norway. Even where groups shared customers, the nature of demands were quite different. Take two, for example, that served public and private industrial firms. One supplied material for maintenance and for routine inventories on a continuing basis. The other supplied major equipment and provided engineering services that a firm might need only once in twenty years.

The different leaders in Alpha worried about the same competitors, by and large, and dealt with the same union. The firm was associated with only one affiliate each of NAF and NIF. On the other hand, since Beta was not organized to fit traditional industry patterns, its leaders were concerned with different competitors. Most groups competed against other specialty contracting and engineering firms; but some groups that imported goods for resale to industrial users or to wholesalers competed with Norwegian manufacturers of similar goods. One competed against similar retail shops in Oslo, as well as against a broader class of suppliers of luxury goods to private consumers.

Not only were different groups at Beta concerned with different groups of competitors, but these competitors propounded distinct problems to each group. Some faced most difficulty in obtaining customers and in counteracting the prices of other firms. Two other groups which had customers could not supply the customers' demands; the foreign manufacturers on which the two groups depended were finding it more advantageous to sell in countries other than Norway.

Similarly, in contacts with regulatory groups, Beta had workers in each of three unions. Not all departments in the firm were affiliated with the same branches of NAF and NIF. Government regulations that applied to one work group frequently did not apply to other groups in the firm.

Other examples could be given, but the difference between the two task environments should be clear. At Alpha leaders of different work groups were more often concerned with the same customers, suppliers, competitors, and regulatory groups. Where the leaders dealt with different individuals or groups, these individuals still tended to be homogeneous in their role in the economy, in their geographical dispersion around Europe, and in the content and timing of demands that they made on Alpha. At Beta, in contrast, the leaders of various work groups were more distinctly concerned with different sub-portions of a highly differentiated, heterogeneous task environment.

2. *Degree of Stability.* The environment of an organization, like the organization itself, is continually changing. What were the important differences between the task environments of Alpha and Beta in the manners in which they were changing?

The long-term stability of environmental systems and environmental demands was greater, and would probably continue to be greater, for Alpha than for Beta; but at the time of the study important sectors of the task environment were less stable at Alpha. Fewer abrupt, short-run changes were occurring in Beta's environment.

A few examples will illustrate the long-run difference. The market that Alpha served had changed relatively little in fifty years. Its size had increased: population had risen by 50 per cent, distant customers were easier to supply, and less clothing was made at home. Yet the Norwegian family remained the only important customer; products and means of distribution were basically the same. Demand for only one really new type of clothing had developed. Since the twenties, at least, families had not been using increments in real income to buy more clothing.[16] For Beta, however, markets that had existed when the firm was founded had grown in some cases, disappeared in others. Only two of the major work programs continued operations initiated before

World War I; the other eleven had resulted from the growth (approximately tenfold) and diversification of the industries which used Beta's services, from rapid technological development of the equipment and processes Beta specialized in, and from increases in the real prosperity of the Norwegian consumer. Beta profited from increments in real income, since these were spent in large measure for durable and semidurable goods sold by shops like Beta's or produced by firms which Beta served.

At the time of the study Alpha had recently installed new, more automatic production equipment, but they had not begun to work extensively with any of the new synthetic fibers. Beta was under continual pressure to expand the scope of its operations from suppliers who wanted to market new products and from customers who wanted more complete service.

The prospects for future expansion of markets were small at Alpha, large at Beta. For the first time Alpha and its competitors had capacity to meet domestic demand, limited prospects for export sales, and no expectations of radically new products. Beta, however, was confronted with a large, unfilled domestic demand in many of its lines of activity and with the expectation of an accelerated rate of technological change within the industry. Within six years the government planned a 75 per cent increase in the country's capacity to generate electric power. Beta would benefit from this and from the new industries that would follow.

Yet at the time of the study, somewhat paradoxically, the short-run changes occurring in Alpha's task environment were greater than those occurring in Beta's. New synthetic fibers of many types were becom-

---

[16] This is an example of inferences based on data gathered outside Alpha and Beta. The source here is Statistiske Sentralbyrå, *Husholdningsregnskaper, oktober 1951–september 1952* (N.O.S. XI. 128: Oslo, 1953), pp. 29–34, 40–44.

ing available to Norwegian manufacturers. There were strong pressures to revise marketing practices to conform with American ideas. And most important, of course, was the sudden change from an industry with too little to one with too much production capacity. During the study, import restrictions on foreign textiles were relaxed; price controls, already superfluous, were removed; and many firms were threatening to break voluntary agreements about marketing practices. At the same time sales were falling, costs were rising. Alpha, which had to pay premium wages because of its location, was more concerned than competitors about union demands for higher pay.

3. *Disruptiveness of Environmental Inputs.* Inputs to an organization can vary a great deal in the directness with which they serve as checks, or feedback, on company operations. At the time of the study Alpha was more subject than was Beta to inputs that indicated the firm was not doing well. Salesmen reported resistance to pricing policies. Customers complained directly about delays in delivery of orders. Information about the progress of certain competitors contrasted unfavorably with data about Alpha's own performance. Two "outsiders," a new sales manager and a recently hired consultant, were using their knowledge of other firms to make critical observations about current policies and practices in Alpha.

Except for one or two major work programs at Beta, instances of unfavorable feedback were either less frequent or less obvious to the responsible members of management.

4. *Demands for Direct Personal Interaction.* Top management at Alpha had fewer demands for, and were subject to fewer inducements to, direct interaction with individuals or groups in the task environment than top management at Beta. In Alpha's case more transactions with the environment were routine, and more messages could be coded for transmission in brief, standard form. When a customer ordered clothing or when a leader in Alpha ordered raw materials, a few symbols on paper sufficed to initiate the production and delivery of the order. In most transactions with customers and suppliers there was little room for bargaining about prices or specifications; and since most commitments were of relatively short duration, there was little need for flexibility to change terms of an agreement.

Most customers of Beta, however, were not ordering standard products. They were frequently not expert enough fully to determine their own needs. They depended on leaders in Beta for technical advice, and they expected to bargain on terms of a bid or contract. For large projects, which sometimes lasted three or four years and which involved cooperation of Beta with customers, suppliers, and other contractors at the same time, details of Beta's role could not be planned completely in advance. Customers established direct contact with key men in Beta to facilitate adjustments in their demands as the project progressed.

The instability of relationships with customers and with suppliers at Beta also contributed to the greater pressures for direct personal interaction. Alpha had a steady group of potential customers, retailers and wholesalers, who restocked at least twice a year and who shopped regularly among different manufacturers to find styles that they could sell. Beta had a constant need to find new customers. Changing technology made new products and new markets available at a rapid rate, and purchasers of capital goods did not restock twice each year. Customers expected Beta in part to anticipate their needs and to suggest other transactions they might make.

In other respects, contacts with outsiders were likely to be more attractive to leaders in Beta than to those in Alpha. Such contacts were easier to make since much of Beta's work was done on customers' or on suppliers' premises. More frequently the Beta leaders who had contacts with customers or suppliers dealt with equals or superiors in education and social rank (transactions at Beta generally were more complex and involved larger commitments of resources). For leaders in Beta, too, there were fewer causes for tension and mistrust in relations with men from other firms. The industries with which Beta was affiliated were further than the clothing industry from a period of zero profits, empty prospects for new business, and intense competition. The clothing industry, in contrast, was split by threats of individual firms to abandon long-honored agreements on pricing and marketing practices. Finally, Beta had greater need for two resources, funds for foreign trade and space for expansion, that the government controlled. Personal contact with the groups that rationed these resources was essential for bargaining and persuasion.

5. *Routing of Inputs.* Inputs from the task environment were routed less directly to the leaders they concerned in Alpha than they were to the leaders in Beta. Information from customers of Alpha, for example, did not come directly to the sales manager or to the production foremen. Salesmen relayed routine orders and inquiries about delivery to the sales manager or to the scheduling chief. They reported suggestions about styles to the president as often as to the fashion designer. The stylist received inputs that were more relevant to the sales personnel, and important information about consumer preferences came from the chief industrial engineer. The production supervisors, bound to tasks within the plant, had few contacts with outside groups.

At Beta, in contrast, almost all information about the market environment of any department was received or gathered either by the department head or by his subordinates. Little came through the president or through other departments. These department heads were more exposed to market inputs than the leaders in Alpha because much more of their work was done on customers' premises.

Suppliers to Alpha were conditioned by previous contacts with the firm to make first contacts with the president or with the office manager in most cases, but suppliers to Beta made more contacts with individual department leaders. Beta's multiple affiliations with competitors, unions, and branches of NAF and NIF also gave its subordinate leaders more exposure to external union and employer groups. At Alpha such contacts were usually made through the managing director.

6. *Complexity of Inputs.* The order of skills required for transactions with the environment was less in Alpha than in Beta. The transactions in which Beta was involved were distinguished by their complexity in

comparison with the ones in which Alpha was involved. First, the technological training and experience necessary to prepare a bid or to plan a purchase from suppliers was greater at Beta. Second, while operations in Alpha generally had a planning horizon of a few days to six months, it was not infrequent for Beta to become involved in activities with planning horizons of several years. Third, while Alpha had major problems of internal coordination of activities, the leaders there were able to deal rather independently with various external groups. The nature of Beta's relationships with external groups were such that Beta's leaders frequently could not deal with a customer, for example, without dealing at the same time with suppliers and with other groups involved in the same project. Fourth, while most of the external groups that Alpha dealt with directly were Norwegian, Beta had important direct connections with groups—particularly with suppliers—in other parts of Europe. Men in Beta had greater need for mastery of languages other than Norwegian.

INTERNAL CONSTRAINTS ON TOP MANAGEMENT

Not only did the two top-management groups confront the external task environments we have discussed above but they also were constrained by features of the organization which they led. These "internal" constraints may be regarded in one sense as part of the task environment of management, for in the short run they were outside management's control. The dimensions along which we find differences between Alpha and Beta in this area include:

1. *Stress of Formal Rules and Procedures on Autonomy in the Management Relationship.* An examination was made of job instructions, policy statements to employees, accounting routines, and rules for the preparation and signing of correspondence. In Alpha all these stressed the dependence of subordinate leaders on the president and on one another. In Beta they stressed autonomy as a major goal of top-management organization and specified fewer, weaker dependencies among members of top management.

2. *Department Independence in Routine Work.* At Alpha nearly all members of top management (or their subordinates) were involved at some phase in each of the four major routine work programs. The programs required, for execution, close interdepartmental coordination in the parallel or sequential performance of tasks. At Beta most of the thirteen major work programs were executed by subordinates of a single top leader, and usually subgroups of his subordinates handled individual programs semiautonomously. There were few instances where groups under two leaders were required to work in parallel effort or in sequence.

3. *Top-Management Involvement in Routine Activities.* More often in Alpha than in Beta top management was routinely involved as participants rather than as supervisors in major work programs. The president of Alpha, for example, made most purchasing decisions himself, and he and the sales manager set prices. At Beta the president had no direct role in routine activities, and no members of top management were involved regularly as participants in six of the thirteen major work programs. Even

their supervisory roles in the six programs were quite limited.

4. *Competition for Scarce Resources.* Although at both firms there was frequent competition among work programs for such resources as labor, capital, and assistance from specialists in the firm, cases of simultaneous demand seldom involved as many departments or recurred as frequently in Beta as in Alpha.

5. *Barriers to Management Interaction.* There were fewer hindrances to interaction among members of top management at Alpha than at Beta. Communications were facilitated at Alpha since all but one member of top management and all but one small group of employees worked in the same building. The leaders crossed paths often because the subordinates of each were scattered in many locations. Only three leaders had closed offices, and only the president had a secretary to screen visitors. A spacious lunchroom provided facilities for informal, private conferences. A loudspeaker system could be used to summon men who could not be reached by telephone.

Work groups at Beta were dispersed among four major and several minor locations. While all but one member of top management had offices in one building, major groups of subordinates to three of the five key men worked at locations five minutes to a half hour (of walking) away. All but one leader had a closed office, and there were no facilities for the men to meet regularly for lunch. The network of telephones was more extensive but less useful than the network at Alpha. Telephone contacts were difficult to make because the leaders spent a lot of time outside their offices and off the firm's premises.

6. *Number of Employees Under Leaders.* Only two key men in Alpha had more men working under them than the median key man in Beta; and six of the ten in Alpha had fewer than thirteen, the lowest total for any key man in Beta.

7. *Barriers to Identification with Subordinates.* Differences in sex, education, and status in Alpha formed stronger barriers to close identification by key men with their subordinates. While all but one of the key "men" in Alpha were male, most subordinates were women. Beta employed few women, even in clerical jobs. Fewer subordinates in Alpha (36 percent *vs.* 89 percent) in the next lower echelons had more than an elementary or tradeschool education. Of the next lower subordinates, too, the majority in Alpha were "workers" or "functionaries." The majority in Beta were themselves supervisors or specialists. None of the subordinates in Alpha were likely to be promoted into top management, but at Beta many were. All but one member of top management at Beta had among their subordinates (a) older men who functioned as close assistants and understudies or (b) younger men who were being trained as candidates for future openings in top management.

INTERPRETATIONS OF THE DATA

We have now summarized some differences between Alpha and Beta in the task environments of top management and in the degree of autonomy that members of top management displayed. What hypotheses do these findings suggest?

CONSIDERATIONS IN FORMULATING HYPOTHESES

Before hypotheses are offered, some of my major assumptions deserve review:

1. *Long-Run* vs. *Short-Run Phenomena.* The kind of theory we build depends greatly on the time span we deal with. In the short run, for example, behavior can be regarded as the outcome of the two "constants," personality and environment. Over a longer period personality and environment vary as functions of each other. Personality changes as men internalize attitudes and patterns of behavior that are consistent with their circumstances. In the case of organizations environment influences the "personality" of leaders by determining what kind of men stay with certain kinds of jobs. Shortly after my study one man in Alpha left its management because he lacked autonomy; in Beta, earlier, a middle-level manager was fired because of his failure to maintain effective relations with others in and outside the firm.

2. *Differential Roles in Organizations.* Hypotheses about the impact of environment on individual autonomy need to be framed with respect to role differences among individuals in their organizations. For example, in considering access to information as a factor in autonomy, we need to know not only how many members of management had access but also how those that had access could use the information.

3. *Indirectness of Environmental Impact.* There was little evidence from either firm that task environment *prescribed* the measure of autonomy observed in management behavior. Formal rules that governed management action appeared to prescribe; but in fact these were only effective where they reflected stable, informally derived patterns of behavior. In making demands on the firms the environment usually prescribed outcomes rather than the means by which outcomes were to be achieved.

It is more reasonable to assume that environmental factors constrained behavior by cueing management's attention to associations between current events and situations with which they had programs to deal, as well as by making some courses of action appear more attractive than others. It was probably true that management had more ways to achieve desired outcomes than they generally realized.

4. *Automaticity of Response.* In both Alpha and Beta leaders seldom talked explicitly about how they would act, and their implicit choices of courses of action were made quickly. The uniformity of response to similar inputs suggests that management acted to a large extent on the basis of "programs" it had developed and adopted for dealing with different classes of inputs.[17]

[17] The concept of a "program" will be familiar to readers who have worked with electronic data-processing machines or who have read recent papers by H. A. Simon and Allen Newell that apply programming concepts to theories of problem solving. See, for example, "The Logic Theory Machine," *Proceedings 1956 Joint Symposium on Information Theory*, Institute of Radio Engineers, Cambridge, Mass., Sept. 10–12, 1956.

A NEGATIVE FINDING: TASK
IMPORTANCE, TASK ROUTINENESS,
AND AUTONOMY

A frequent hypothesis in the folklore of organization asserts that low autonomy is more likely the greater the importance of a task to the organization and the less its routineness— that unfamiliar tasks or tasks where "the stakes are high" are least likely to be handled by a single individual.[18]

Data from the "most important" task questionnaire[19] provide a crude test, since for each task they described respondents were asked to rate: (1) implications of the task for conservation of resources (as "payoff," "cost," or "risk"); (2) the quantity of money associated with the task; (3) the number of groups in the firm perceived as having a stake in action on the task; (4) the length of time for which action on the task was likely to commit the firm; and (5) the similarity of the task to previous tasks.

Table 4 shows first, that members of management were frequently unable to estimate significant aspects of task "importance," and, second, that the reported behavior of individual leaders showed no significant links between importance or routineness and autonomy. Interview data confirm the finding that leaders had difficulty evaluating the consequences of tasks for their firms.

TENTATIVE INFERENCES

Examination of observation and interview data on a number of action

sequences in the two firms crudely supports a hypothesis that the amount of autonomy in leaders' behavior was a function of four factors: (1) the ease of formulating independent task assignments for different work groups in the firm; (2) leaders' estimates of the probability that action on tasks would lead to unpleasant personal consequences by producing unwanted results for the organization or by producing conflict with other activities in the firm, especially in other work groups; (3) the exclusiveness of each leader's control over information about tasks or activities he was formally responsible for; and (4) leaders' estimates of the costs and gains associated with attempts to seek or to give advice.

These factors seem to account for behavior differences on similar tasks between the firms and on different tasks within the firms. Let us consider each factor briefly in relation to our observations about the task environments of management in Alpha and Beta.

1. *Ease of Formulating Independent Tasks.* The descriptions of tasks that key men gave were more likely in Alpha than in Beta to imply the involvement of not just one work group but of many. Several characteristics of Alpha's task environment may have contributed to this difference. Because the environment of management at Alpha was less differentiated, more inputs were addressed to the firm as a whole. If they did not demand uniform action from different work groups, they frequently made it difficult to avoid coordinated action. A single customer's order might request simultaneous delivery of several products; a union complaint about incentive rates would

---

[18] This hypothesis is implicit, for example, in recent work that E. Jaques has done to compare the discretion men can exercise at different organizational levels. See his *Measurement of Responsibility* (London, 1956).
[19] See p. 113 above.

TABLE 4 REPORTED TASK CHARACTERISTICS VS. AUTONOMY*

Task Characteristic	Percentage of Tasks Where Respondent Did Not Estimate the Value of the Task Characteristic	Percentage of Leaders Whose Behavior Confirmed Hypothesis (14 Leaders)
Implication for resources of firm	38	14
Quantity of money involved	44	21
Number of people concerned with consequences	0	36
Duration of commitments involved	20	36
Similarity to previous tasks	9	50

* Data from Alpha and Beta have been combined. Results in the two firms did not differ significantly.

For a particular characteristic certain values could be defined as indicating high or low importance (or routineness). With respect to any characteristic an individual leader's behavior was judged to confirm the hypothesis on page 124 if for tasks where he reported a value, the frequency with which he named others as initiators of action or as co-workers varied directly with estimates of task importance (or inversely with estimates of task routineness).

require adjustments in all departments. Receiving inputs from common sources thus accented interdepartmental dependence and probably in the long run contributed to the development of programs of perceiving inputs that reinforced the interdependence.

At Beta a highly differentiated and heterogeneous task environment, whose elements seldom addressed themselves to the firm as a whole, reinforced tendencies of work groups to see their tasks as distinct from the tasks of other groups in the firm. The differences in language and other skills required by various groups for transactions with customers and suppliers also tended to obscure interrelationships among tasks.

At Beta, too, most environmental inputs were routed directly to the relevant key man or to one of his subordinates. There was less chance than at Alpha that the content of inputs would be distorted in transmission. At Alpha, for example, the production leaders had direct access to

few parts of the environment. Most information they received came from the president, the sales manager, or the scheduling chief. The content of inputs was frequently distorted by the interpretations of the relayers.

2. *Estimates of Undesirable Consequences.* Within action sequences, autonomy seemed to decrease whenever environmental inputs were perceived as evidence of impending conflict or of impending personal failure if individuals acted alone. One can assume, for example, that the two presidents would be most likely to intervene where they saw a need to protect their investment or their reputation with outside groups, or that key men would seek advice from peers or superiors where they feared failure or interference from others in the firm.

We noted in our analysis of task environment that abrupt changes had occurred in Alpha's relation to customers and competitors and that most environmental feedback on Alpha's performance was negative. These changes meant that programs Alpha had used for many years no longer sufficed. A great deal of the management interaction I observed at Alpha was directed toward rebuilding sales and competitive position.

Similar conditions prevailed in two major work programs at Beta. These were the two on which the president was spending time; the others he left almost completely to subordinates. Although the environment of management at Beta was unstable, the key men had grown accustomed to the instability and could anticipate many of the changes that would occur. They had more evidence than men at Alpha of program success, less of program failure.

A second undesired consequence of action was conflict within the organization. The leaders at Alpha were confronted more frequently with situations that would lead them to expect their actions to interfere with the freedom of others to plan and act. Execution of customer orders or adjustments in labor practices, for example, raised more demands for parallel or sequential coordination of activities. Simultaneous claims on scarce resources were more frequent and more widespread. Attempts to develop new patterns of action and to meet changes in the task environment also gave rise to expectations of conflict. More than at Beta new policies or relationships with the environment suggested by one group interfered with the plans or commitments of others.

3. *Control Over Access to Information.* Even where a key man expected conflict or feared failure, he was in a stronger position to act autonomously if he and his subordinates

alone had access to inputs that indicated the results of his action. In general, the key man who had most exclusive access to environmental inputs that pertained to his work groups and their activities was in the strongest position to avoid unsolicited advice.

Key men at Alpha had less exclusive access to information than key men at Beta. The indirect routing of inputs—and particularly the routing of all correspondence through the president—kept most leaders in Alpha well posted on matters of concern to departments other than their own. At Beta each key man and his subordinates had direct and exclusive access to large segments of their environments, and thus they could limit the flow of information to their peers or to the president. (I have already noted a higher incidence in Beta than in Alpha of subordinate initiation of action involving several leaders.)

Because the task environment of management at Alpha was relatively undifferentiated and homogeneous, we might expect the key men there to have less exclusive control of information. Since the men knew that others in management had, in the past, been exposed to similar sets of inputs, they would be more disposed to seek or to offer advice. In contrast, the heterogeneity and the instability of Beta's environment had probably prevented key men from developing ability to anticipate information that others had received.

Finally, there were environmental influences that led to more informal interaction among key men, and thus greater "leakage" of information, in Alpha than in Beta. By the nature of the firm's operations most key men in Alpha were under strong constraints to spend their working days on company premises. Their paths crossed often as each supervised his scattered work groups. Lunchtable groups usually included men who had only marginal responsibility for many of the topics the groups discussed. Unplanned interaction, then, was quite frequent at Alpha. It was less frequent at Beta, where environmental pressures led members of management to spend large amounts of time away from company premises, where the on-premise work locations of key men were isolated from one another, and where adequate facilities did not exist for staging *ad hoc* conferences.

Over the long run, as we shall see in the next section, the high level of informal interaction in Alpha and the low level in Beta were probably self-perpetuating.

4. *Estimates of Interaction Cost.* Interaction among leaders was not all accidental; some was planned specifically for the handling of certain tasks. But in both firms, because task loads were high, the cost of meetings (in time consumed and in other jobs not done) was regarded as high. Leaders' estimates of the worth of interaction were higher at Alpha than at Beta. This is the result of both short- and long-run environmental influences.

Interaction was probably more attractive at Alpha because of the perceived interdependence of tasks, because of the inevitable sharing of information, and because of the risks inherent in independent action. But it was also more attractive at Alpha because it was easier to arrange and because it yielded more satisfying results. Most leaders (excepting the sales manager and the president, who left the premises frequently) could be

found for a conversation at nearly any time of day. Familiarity with a common environment enabled the men to talk a common language, and common access to recent inputs enabled them to begin deliberations without extensive briefing sessions. The relative simplicity and stability of the environments the men dealt with made it possible for them, even where their environments differed, to become experts, over time, in one another's work.

At Beta, leaders frequently could not contact one another at will. Where telephone conversations would not suffice, face-to-face meetings required at least one member of the group of leaders to come from a distant work location. Because the leaders did not have common access to one another's information flows, the discussion of many problems had to be preceded by periods of briefing. Incomplete knowledge of one another's work and the barriers to attainment of such knowledge combined to make fruitless many attempts at collaboration.

Over the years short-run decisions for or against interaction combined to strengthen interdependence in Alpha and autonomy in Beta. For by interacting frequently in Alpha, the leaders were doing a great deal to establish the common frame of reference and the type of organizational adjustments that would make continued interaction attractive. The leaders in Beta, in contrast, were not disregarding constraints against interaction often enough to develop the familiarity with one another's work that would make meetings seem worth while. At the time of the study an attempt was made at Beta to initiate two series of meetings among subgroups in middle management.

Both groups served many customers in common, but they were accustomed to working independently. Neither attempt appeared likely to succeed, and there were complaints in both cases that the interaction was simply a waste of time.

CONCLUSION

An understanding of the factors which limit or facilitate autonomy in organizations has both scientific and practical significance. Upward autonomy is a key variable in the centralization-decentralization controversy.[20] More generally, autonomy has been linked to the success of executive training, to the efficiency of managerial control, to employees' feelings of frustration and conflict, to the costs of making decisions, to the flexibility of company response to new tasks, and to other important aspects of organizational performance.[21]

Such relationships have usually been stated as if they were applicable in many different organizational settings, and where they have not been so stated they have too frequently been so interpreted by organizational planners.[22] The investigation of environmental influences that are relevant to organizational planning is very important.

The essential argument of this paper has been threefold. First, the investigation of the impact of environmental factors on behavior in organizations is one of the most important tasks for organization theorists. Second, by conceptualizing the environment as a flow of information to participants in an organization (and as a body of accessible information), it is possible to make systematic and meaningful comparisons of the environments of different organizations. Finally, intensive field and laboratory observation of organizations in action are a necessary step to the fuller understanding of organizational processes. These observation studies (as well as interview studies and attempts at historical reconstruction of organizational action) should put explicit emphasis on the cognitive activities of organizational participants as a link between environmental "stimuli" and the participants' overt "responses."

---

[20] See, for example, H. Baker and R. France, *Centralization and Decentralization in Industrial Relations* (Princeton, 1954); H. A. Simon et al., *Centralization vs. Decentralization in Organizing the Controller's Department* (New York, 1954); and P. Stryker, "The Subtleties of Delegation," *Fortune*, 51 (March 1955); 94–97.

[21] The role of opportunity for autonomy as a motivational factor is discussed by C. Argyris, "The Individual and Organization: Some Problems of Mutual Adjustment," *Administrative Science Quarterly*, 2 (June 1957), 1–24. A more general review of the effects of opportunity for autonomy on employee motivation and on organizational performance is included in the forthcoming book by J. G. March and H. A. Simon, *Organizations*. In the latter work

the generality of some hypotheses about autonomy under varying environmental conditions is considered.

[22] H. A. Simon discusses the ambiguity of traditional propositions about centralization and decentralization, for example, in *Administrative Behavior* (New York, 1957), pp. 234–40.

5. ORGANIZATIONAL STRUCTURE AND THE MULTINATIONAL STRATEGY

Lawrence E. Fouraker and John M. Stopford

One of the landmark studies in the field of business administration is *Strategy and Structure* by A. D. Chandler, Jr. A central proposition in Chandler's book is that the strategy of diversification led to organizational problems and eventually to the emergence of a new corporate structure. The purpose of this article is to see if Chandler's proposition is useful in examining recent organizational changes in the international field.[1]

International business activity is a form of diversification that has become increasingly important for many large American companies in the last two decades. In some sense, this development may be considered a replication against which Chandler's thesis may be tested. That is, this new form of diversification should be dominated by firms with experi-

Reprinted by permission from *Administrative Science Quarterly* (June 1968), pp. 47–64.

[1] A. D. Chandler, Jr., *Strategy and Structure* (Garden City, N. Y.: Anchor, 1966). We have received, and greatly appreciate, the help of J. Berman, C. R. Christensen, J. H. McArthur, B. R. Scott, and R. Vernon. This research was financed by a grant from the Ford Foundation for the study of the multinational corporation.

ence in managing diversified activities. Furthermore, the new diversification should lead to new problems of organization and, finally, to different structural accommodations.

MODEL

Chandler states: "Historically, the executives administering American industrial enterprises have followed a recognizable pattern in the acquisition and use of resources."[2] This process consists of a developmental transition through several distinct phases: "Thus four phases or chapters can be discerned in the history of the large American industrial enterprise: the initial expansion and accumulation of resources; the rationalization of the use of resources; the expansion into new markets and lines to help assure the continuing full use of resources; and finally the development of a new structure to make possible continuing effective mobilization of resources to meet both changing short-term market demands and long-term market trends."[3] These four

[2] *Ibid.*, p. 478.
[3] *Ibid.*, p. 479.

phases produced three fairly distinct organizational structures:

Type I. The organization is an extension of the interests, abilities, and limitations of its chief executive, who is often the creator and owner of the organization. This structure is generally limited to a single product line and often emphasizes one function (e.g., production) more than others. It is also constrained by the sequential decision-making pattern that characterizes a single problem solver. This is the entrepreneurial business organization, which serves as a building block for most economic models.

Type II. This is the vertically integrated, functionally coordinated enterprise. Generally such an organization continues to be limited to one or a few related product lines. The emphasis is on rational use of resources, efficiency, and coordination of functional activities.

Yet the dominant centralized structure had one basic weakness. A very few men were still entrusted with a great number of complex decisions. The executives in the central office were usually the president with one or two assistants, sometimes the chairman of the board, and the vice presidents who headed the various departments. The latter were often too busy with the administration of the particular function to devote much time to the affairs of the enterprise as a whole. Their training proved a still more serious defect. Because these administrators had spent most of their business careers within a single functional activity, they had little experience or interest in understanding the needs and problems of other departments or of the corporation as a whole.[4]

The type II structure might be enormously efficient in the production of some classes of products, but did not produce professional management.

Type III. The accumulation of resources by a successful type II firm often led to diversification of product lines, (1) to avoid risk, (2) to ensure continuation of the organization after the major product had completed its life cycle, or (3) to sell outside the company by some divisions due to integrated production requiring plant facilities of varying capacities at different stages.

The strategy of product diversification caused many administrative problems. The functional approach of the type II firm required that the senior marketing executive coordinate the marketing activities for all the organization's products, even though they might utilize different forms of distribution, advertising, and sales effort. The senior production officer was confronted with similar complexity. These functional responsibilities could be delegated to subordinates, most appropriately on the basis of product assignments; but profit contribution of functional specialists could not be measured against performance, so control and comparison became even more difficult. The unavoidable problems of conflict and coordination at the lowest levels of the organization would frequently have to be passed up to the highest functional levels for adjudication. And some operating issues could not be settled there, but would have to reach the office of the chief executive.

Attempts to add product lines in such an environment could lead to organizational stasis because of the limited ability of the chief executive's office to cope with the new demands on its decision-making capacity. Man-

[4] *Ibid.,* p. 50.

agement would then be confronted with a choice: either abandon the strategy of product diversification, or abandon the functional form of organization.

Many organizations chose structural reorganization. This reorganization took the form of a multidivisional product structure with many functional responsibilities delegated to the division general managers. The divisions were separated on a product basis and were relatively autonomous. Generally, each division served as a profit center for control purposes; coordination and control from the central office was concentrated on finance and some general staff functions such as planning and research.

"Besides allocating decision making more effectively and assuring more precise communication and control, the new structure proved to have another advantage over the functionally departmentalized organization. It provided a place to train and test general executives."[5] This ability to produce general managers allowed the type III organization to operate successfully in unrelated product areas.

With great diversity of products, staff, technologies, and managerial talents, the type III decentralized organization could move simultaneously to exploit opportunities in a variety of independent areas. The management innovation of moving from a type II structure to type III began, in the United States, in the 1920s. As is often the case,[6] the type III structure developed independently in several organizations; du Pont,

General Motors, Standard Oil, and Sears are given special attention by Chandler. Many other organizations imitated these pioneers, with most of the transitions being delayed by the depression of the 1930s and World War II, so that many companies undertook the transition in both strategy and structure in the 1950s and 1960s.

In the type III organization, new products can be added, or old ones dropped, with only marginal effect on the organization. Indeed, given the prospect of finite life expectancy for any commercial product, the management is committed to a strategy of research and development as a means of ensuring the continued life of the organization. This sort of activity is compatible with the diversity and independence of parts in a type III organization. "In fact, the systematizing of strategic decisions through the building of a general office and the routinizing of product development by the formation of a research department have, in a sense, institutionalized this strategy of diversification."[7]

Since the type III organization makes it possible to manage a variety of heterogeneous activities, it also makes it feasible for research and development activity to be incorporated in the structure. Burns and Stalker, in a study of electronic firms in England and Scotland, found that certain types of business organizations did not develop research and development departments; such activity could not normally be absorbed by their "mechanistic" structures, which closely resembled Chandler's type II organizations.[8] The organiza-

---

[5] *Ibid.*, p. 385.
[6] A. L. Kroeber, *Anthropology: Race, Language, Culture, Psychology, Prehistory* (Rev. ed.; New York: Harcourt Brace Jovanovich, 1948), pp. 445–72.

[7] Chandler, *Strategy and Structure*, p. 490.
[8] T. Burns and G. M. Stalker, *The Management of Innovation* (London: Tavistock, 1961).

tions that were successful in establishing research and development departments ("organic" structures) were described in terms that seem characteristic of Chandler's type III. These results are reinforced by the field work of Lawrence and Lorsch.[9]

This connection between research and development, product innovation, and organizational structure is important for the thesis of this paper, because the innovative capacity may be an important source of competitive advantage in foreign markets. Vernon and others have argued that the United States tends to export products developed for the U.S. market that are not being produced abroad, and this monopoly position in world markets offsets high labor costs in the U.S.[10] Furthermore, at some point the organization will invest in plant and equipment abroad in order to protect its export market, particularly if that market has grown to a size that is consistent with the most efficient current productive techniques.

The result of this chain of arguments is that type III organizations can be expected to dominate foreign direct investment. The initial structural response to this strategy of diversifying direct investment around the world is to establish an international division in the type III organization. Such a division reports to

one man. This focuses responsibility and control for foreign operations and economizes on the need for general managers with broad international experience (who are inevitably in short supply when the organization first expands its foreign operations).

The international division is at the same organizational level, and will tend to receive the same general treatment, as the product divisions. This same general treatment tends to create stresses that will make the international division a transient form. It is not a product division, but is rather less autonomous, for it depends more on the cooperation and assistance of the product divisions than they typically depend on each other. As a result, the product division manager is subjected to stresses and conflicts that are not always in the best interests of the organization. The product division manager, who is judged against domestic measures of performance, is therefore somewhat motivated to (*1*) fill his domestic orders before extending assistance to foreign markets; (*2*) assign his best employees to domestic tasks and shunt the others to the international division; and (*3*) argue for a larger domestic share of the capital budget.

These are natural responses that may be quite costly if foreign markets are growing faster than domestic markets, which has often been the case in the postwar period. In many organizations, top management has responded to these lost opportunities in several ways. First, it has given product and functional managers more international experience and eventually more responsibility. Second, it has replaced the international division with some new organizational structure; for example, world-

[9] P. R. Lawrence and J. W. Lorsch, *Organization and Environment* (Boston, Mass.: Division of Research, Harvard Business School, 1967).

[10] R. Vernon, "International Investment and International Trade in the Product Cycle," *Quart. J. Econ.*, 80 (May 1966), 190–207; C. P. Kindleberger, *The Dollar Shortage* (New York: John Wiley, 1950); Staffan Burenstam-Linder, *An Essay on Trade and Transformation* (Uppsala, Sweden: Almqvist & Wicksell, 1961).

wide product divisions, world-partitioning geographic divisions, or some combination of these, perhaps retaining an international division for some purposes, or setting up a separate international company. Indeed some companies moved directly to these new structures, avoiding the problem of a conflict of interests between product divisions and the international division, and the possibility of a coalition of product divisions against the international division. This is most common where the vehicle for growth abroad has been merger with other organizations whose foreign interests are in different product lines.

Each of the possible alternative forms of the organization of international activities has distinct characteristics. The international division is the sole profit center for foreign operations, requiring only one general manager with international expertise. The manager of the international division and his staff become the repository of all the organization's international experience, causing problems of capital allocation, transfer pricing, and especially communication.

The world-wide product division structure avoids many of these problems by containing the areas of potential conflict within each division. The division manager is responsible for the profit performance of his product line throughout the world. This structure requires at least as many international general managers as there are product divisions operating abroad.

The geographic divisions partitioning the world also require an increased number of international general managers. The predominant characteristic is that the area divisions (of which the U.S.A. or North America is one) are headed by general managers of equal status in the structure. Each has the profit responsibility for an area, regardless of the product lines involved. Typically, this structure is associated with those organizations that have mature, standardized product lines for which marketing, rather than production or technology, is the critical variable.

The mixed structural form is a combination of two or all of the above forms, adapted to the particular needs of a firm. A food company diversifying into chemicals might retain its international division for all the food products and establish the chemical division with world-wide responsibilities.

The separate international company is usually a response to lack of success abroad or to an unwillingness on the part of top management to become more involved abroad. Typically, this move precedes the sale of all or part of the foreign operations. It should be noted that this response does not necessarily include the incorporation of the international division as a separate subsidiary, since such incorporation is normally used as a method of reducing taxes.

The structures that have been adopted to replace the international division may not be stable. As the foreign business grows and diversifies, further structural changes may be required. Operations within the U.S. require a balance between product and functional management, with area requirements relatively unimportant. However, once the organization operates abroad to a significant degree the benefits to be gained from both regional and product line control or coordination may become large. This has led a few organizations to adopt a "grid" structure, where product, area, and functional responsibilities are linked in what may be viewed as a three-dimensional organization structure. There are serious problems associated with this form, but the ability of an organization to learn to operate within such a structure may be the key to the maintenance of the flexibility of administration necessary for continued growth and prosperity abroad.

DATA

Chandler classifies the 70 largest American industrial companies in 1959 into three categories: (*1*) industries consisting of companies that tended to remain as type II organizations: steel and nonferrous metal; (*2*) industries partially accepting the type III structure: agricultural processing, oil, rubber, and mass merchandising; and (*3*) industries consisting of firms that had generally adopted the type III structure: electrical, automobile (transportation), power machinery, and chemicals.

The last four industries have clearly played a prominent role in the economic processes that we have been discussing. They are quite diversified, supporting Chandler's thesis that diversification leads to the adoption of the type III structure.[11] They are leaders in research and development activity, supporting the Burns and Stalker propositions.[12] They are the source of most of the U.S. export strength, as indicated by Gruber and others.[13] And they are among the

leaders in foreign direct investment in plant and equipment.

A crude measure of aggregate diversification is the number of manufacturing employees outside the primary industrial activity in which the firm has been classified. Of the 17 manufacturing industries of interest,[14] the five leaders are shown in Table 1. It should be noted that this is a measure of domestic diversification, and that Chandler's four industries are among the five leaders.

Table 1 also shows an aggregate measure of research and development activity provided by total employment figures for people placed in these categories by their employers. Chandler's type III industries dominate the research and development activity of U.S. manufacturing establishments. The leading manufacturing contributors to the U.S. trade balance are also identified. Eight of the seventeen manufacturing industries had export surpluses on an industry basis; nine had deficits. Chandler's four represented 96.4 percent of the total export surplus by industry category of the U.S. in 1964. This is consistent

---

[11] Chandler, *Strategy and Structure*, pp. 16, 17.

[12] Burns and Stalker, *Management of Innovation*.

[13] W. Gruber, D. Mehta, and R. Vernon, "The R&D Factor in International Trade and International Investment of United States Industries," *J. Pol. Econ.*, 25 (Feb. 1967), 20–37.

[14] There are 21 two-digit Standard Industrial Classification (SIC) manufacturing industries. However, the Department of Commerce presents data for foreign direct investment on a combined basis for primary and fabricated metals industries (SIC numbers 33 and 34), excludes petroleum from manufacturing, and provides foreign trade data that omit petroleum and furniture. We have comparable data for 17 two-digit industries. These are: 20 (food), 21 (tobacco), 22 (textiles), 23 (apparel), 24 (wood products), 26 (paper), 27 (printing), 28 (chemicals), 30 (rubber), 31 (leather), 32 (stone, clay, and glass), 33–34 (primary and fabricated metal), 35 (machinery), 36 (electrical), 37 (transportation), 38 (scientific and similar instruments), 39 (misc.).

TABLE 1 EMPLOYMENT OUTSIDE PRIMARY INDUSTRY AND IN RESEARCH
AND DEVELOPMENT; EXPORT SURPLUS AND DIRECT
FOREIGN INVESTMENT FOR MAJOR INDUSTRIES

	Number of Employees		Export Surplus 1958–1964 (Millions of Dollars)[2]	Direct Foreign Investments 1959–1966 (Millions of Dollars)[3]
Industry (and SIC Number)	Outside Primary Industry 1958[1]	For Research and Development 1958[1]		
Transportation (37)	474,095	27,094	+493.6	4,870
Primary and fabricated metals (33–34)	342,284	–	–	1,962
Electrical (36)	265,473	36,305	+486.3	1,401
Machinery (35)	254,160	4,526	+2,063.0	2,698
Chemicals (28)	170,875	14,667	+752.7	4,130

[1] U.S. Bureau of the Census, *Enterprise Statistics 1958* (Washington, D.C.: Government Printing Office, 1963).

[2] Trade Relations Council of the U.S., *Employment, Output, and Foreign Trade of U.S. Manufacturing Industries, 1958–1964/65,* (New York, 1966).

[3] U.S. Department of Commerce, *Survey of Current Business* (Washington, D.C.: Government Printing Office, various dates).

with the Vernon position, as is the evidence that these same industries tend to follow their trade advantage with direct foreign investment as shown in Table 1.[15]

The evidence is summarized in Table 2, which relates the four industries Chandler identified as having generally accepted the type II structure and the four activities under discussion. The numbers in the body of the table indicate the rank of the organizations in these activities among the 17 industries.

From these two tables, it seems evident that the American manufacturing company with extensive international interests is likely to be: (*1*) diversified in its domestic business activities; (*2*) type III in organizational structure; (*3*) a leader in research and development; and (*4*) a major exporter from the U.S. These propositions can be investigated in greater detail by using relative measures and data on individual companies.

Chandler distributed the 70 largest industrial companies (1959) in his three categories. Joan Curhan,[16] under the direction of Raymond Vernon, compiled a list of 170 companies that were in the 1964 or the 1965 *Fortune*[17] classifications and that had manufacturing subsidiaries in six or more foreign countries at the end of 1963 where the parent company owned 25 percent or more of the subsidiaries. The Curhan list represents most of the American-controlled manufacturing activity abroad.

Comparison of the Chandler and the Curhan lists shows that only 35 percent of Chandler's first group (predominantly type II organizations) were also on the Curhan list. The only steel company on both lists was

[15] Vernon, "International Investment."

[16] J. Curhan, private communication.
[17] *Fortune*, The 500 Largest U. S. Industrial Corporations, (June 1965 and June 1966).

TABLE 2 Rank of Chandler-type III Industries (out of 17) as to Diversification, Research and Development, Export Surplus, and Foreign Investment

	Chemical	Machinery	Electrical	Transportation
Diversification	5	4	3	1
Research and development	3	4	1	2
Export surplus	2	1	4	3
Foreign investment	2	3	5	1

the most decentralized of the steel companies. In Chandler's mixed second group, 45 percent of the companies were also on the Curhan list, (54 percent if merchandising was excluded from Chandler's group, as it was from the Curhan list). Chandler's third group of companies were all on the Curhan list except for one company which had gone out of existence through merger.

The mechanism by which this relationship is maintained was examined in more detail. The 170 companies of the Curhan list were sorted into the following categories: (*1*) Type II organizations, (*2*) Type III with an international division, and (*3*) Type III with the other forms of organized international activity that were described earlier. This sorting was done on the basis of annual reports, interviews, and secondary sources.[18] The large sample size made it inevitable that most of the information was gathered from published material. As a result, the classification reflects the formal structure and ignores possible discrepancies between the formal structure and informal control. No discrepancies were found between the analyses from published materials and the evidence gained from the interviews with a limited number of the companies. Therefore, the classification may be considered to be sufficiently accurate for the purposes of this paper. The main possible source of error is for those companies in transition between the categories, since the formal organization may often lead or lag behind actual administrative practices. This, however, was not considered a serious source of error.

The classification of each company on the basis of only a few structural forms was aimed at recording the central tendency of the structure observed. Various rules were developed to allow for the many possible minor variations in the control procedures. The most important of these rules were:

1. Foreign mining, agricultural, or service operations were not considered to be part of the manufacturing activities and were therefore ignored for the purposes of the structural classification.
2. Given an international division, the presence of one or two foreign joint-ventures reporting directly to a product division and accounting for an insignificant volume of the foreign business did not constitute a "mixed" form.
3. The international division did not have to control exports from the U. S.
4. Canadian subsidiaries were classified as part of the U. S. operations.

[18] For example, E. B. Lovell, *The Changing Role of the International Executive* (New York: National Industrial Conference Board, 1966).

TABLE 3 STRUCTURAL CLASSIFICATION OF COMPANIES BY INDUSTRY

Industry SIC Number	Number of Companies in Sample	Structure		
		Stage II	Stage III with International Division	Stage III with Other Forms of International Structure
20	28	5	16	7
21	1	–	1	–
22	2	–	2	–
25	1	–	1	–
26	5	1	3	1
27	1	–	1	–
28	41	1	21	19
29	8	–	2	6
30	5	–	5	. –
31	1	–	1	–
32	7	1	5	1
33	8	4	2	2
34	8	1	4	3
35	19	4	9	6
36	17	1	8	8
37	11	–	4	7
38	5	–	4	1
39	2	–	1	1
Total	170	18	90	62

Each company was also classified by the two-digit Standard Industrial Classification number of its largest product line.[19] The result of these classifications is summarized in Table 3 which shows that only 18 of the 170 companies in the sample have type II structures. This finding immediately suggests that foreign investment is dominated by type III organizations, which is the thesis of this paper.

From Table 3 a structural index for eight industries was calculated as follows:

1. A ratio of the number of type II companies to all type III companies was calculated and normalized by as-

signing the value 1.00 to the industry with the largest proportion of type II companies.
2. A ratio of the number of type III companies with an international division to all type III companies was calculated and normalized, with a value of 1.00 assigned to the industry with the highest ratio.
3. The two normalized ratios were summed to form the index which is shown in Table 4. Low values of this index indicate the predominance of type III structures, particularly type III with some relatively complex form of organized international activity. Low values of the index therefore indicate the relative abundance of both general management in the United States and international general management.

This method of calculating a structural index is purely arbitrary. It is clear from Table 3, however, that any index reflecting the proportions of the

[19] The source of this classification was the Securities Exchange Commission, *1965 Directory of Companies Filing Annual Reports with the Securities Exchange Commission* (New York, 1966).

TABLE 4 STRUCTURE AND DIVERSIFICATION; FOREIGN INVESTMENT,
EMPLOYMENT IN RESEARCH AND DEVELOPMENT, AND
EXPORT/IMPORT RATIO IN MAJOR INDUSTRIES

Industry (and SIC Number)	Index of Structure	Gort's Index of Diversification[1]	1959–1966 Direct Foreign Investment Relative to Domestic[2]	Research and Development Employees as Percentage of Central Administrative Employment[3]	Export/ Import Ratio 1958– 1960[4]
Food (20)	1.175	.933	13.2%	3.10	.79
Paper (26)	1.300	.893	16.7	2.21	.31
Chemicals (28)	0.580	.752	27.7	22.49	2.79
Rubber (30)	1.000	.697	41.3	16.46	1.19
Primary and fabricated metals (33–34)	1.545	.810	20.3	6.37	.67
Machinery (35)	1.188	.807	21.8	12.56	6.37
Electrical (36)	0.638	.667	23.7	47.00	3.85
Transportation (37)	0.364	.728	35.3	34.32	1.49

[1] Michael Gort, *Diversification and Integration in American Industry* (Princeton, N.J.: Princeton University, 1962), Table 8, p. 33.

[2] U.S. Department of Commerce, *Survey of Current Business* (Washington, D.C.: Government Printing Office, various dates).

[3] U.S. Bureau of the Census, *Enterprise Statistics: 1958* (Washington, D.C.: Government Printing Office, 1963).

[4] Trade Relations Council of the U.S., *Employment, Output, and Foreign Trade of U.S. Manufacturing Industries, 1958–1964/65* (New York, 1966).

structures of the sample of companies within an industry will provide approximately the same ranking as that shown in Table 4.

Also to be found in Table 4 is an index of diversification as calculated by Michael Gort.[20] Gort's index is derived from a sample of 111 large manufacturing companies, drawn from the 200 largest companies in 1954. This particular index (Gort does present other measures of diversification) represents the ratio of domestic employment in the primary two-digit SIC industry divided by total domestic employment, adjusted for employment associated with vertical integration.[21] These relationships

tend to be stable over time, so that they should retain some relevance for the present problem; also the time difference is in the direction required for Chandler's thesis. The eight industries in Table 4 are those for which data are available on foreign direct investment. This implies that they are the leading manufacturing industries in this respect, since the others have too little foreign direct investment to be reported separately. Gort's diversification index for SIC 33–34 is an average of his figures for those two industries, weighted by their respective employment sizes and representation on his sample.

Table 4 discloses some relationships immediately; that is, the four

[20] M. Gort, *Diversification and Integration in American Industry* (Princeton, N. J.: Princeton Univ. Press 1962).

[21] Gort's index is based on data in U. S. Bureau of Census, *Company Statistics:*

1954 Census of Business, Manufacturing, Mineral Industries (Washington, D. C.: Government Printing Office, 1958), Table 2.

most diversified industries are four industries with the lowest structural index: chemicals, rubber, electrical machinery, and transportation. The four least diversified industries are four industries with the highest structural index: food, paper, primary and fabricated metals, and machinery. The Spearman coefficient of rank correlation between diversification and structure is 0.64. This result provides additional support for Chandler's thesis that there is a relationship between diversification and structure.

Table 4 also shows the importance of foreign direct investment in plant and equipment relative to domestic direct investment in plant and equipment, for the period 1959–1966. Again a relationship is apparent; that is, the four industries with the greatest relative direct foreign investment are the four most diversified (also with lowest structural index): chemicals, rubber, electrical machinery, and transportation. The four industries with the least foreign investment are the four least diversified (also with the highest structural index): machinery, primary and fabricated metal, food, paper. The coefficient of rank correlation between the relative direct investment measure and Gort's diversification index is .86; between the relative direct investment measure and the structural index it is 0.69.[22]

A relative measure of research and development activity is shown in Table 4 for 1958. The four leading research and development industries are those that are the most diversified, have the lowest structural indexes, and are the most international

in their investment practices. The coefficient of rank correlation between research and structure is 0.81; between research and diversification it is .90. The relationship between research and diversification is also apparent when the analysis is made at the more detailed three-digit SIC industry level. The median specialization ratio for organizations with research and development employees is .814 in 1958, and .939 for organizations without research and development employees. The specialization ratio measures the number of manufacturing employees classified in a primary three-digit SIC industry divided by total manufacturing employment in that industry.[23]

The export/import ratio for 1958–1960 is also shown in Table 4. Here the four leading industries are the same as in the case of the trade balance (rubber ranks fifth and is replaced by machinery among the leading four). The coefficient of rank correlation between the export/import ratio and structure is 0.52. The correlation between the research and development measure and the export/import balance is .71, which is consistent with the findings of Gruber and associates.[24]

CONCLUSION

It may now begin to appear that the evidence would support *any* hypothesis about the industry characteristics of the organizations that have led the movement abroad, simply because those industries are outstand-

---

[22] The structural and diversification indexes were ranked from the lowest to the highest values, so that the "most diversified" industry was given first rank on that scale.

[23] U. S. Bureau of the Census, *Enterprise Statistics: 1958* (Washington, D. C.: Government Printing Office, 1963).
[24] Gruber et al., "The R&D Factor in International Trade."

ing on all relevant scales for measuring business performance. This is not the case, however. Consider the not unusual statements that it is the largest, most capital intensive and most integrated organizations that dominate foreign activity. If size is measured by assets per organization, this view is not supported by census data.[25] The rank correlation between assets per organization and the structural index is .40; between assets per organization and relative importance of foreign direct investment the correlation is .33. Gort also found that there was little association between size and diversification, as measured by the ratio of primary to nonprimary employment.[26] The correlation between the measure of size used here and Gort's diversification index is .29.

The measure of integration, taken from Gort, has a *negative* correlation with foreign activity, diversification (which agrees with his results), and decentralization for the eight internationally important industries.

Finally, the ratio of capital per production worker is negatively correlated with relative foreign activity (−.14). There is also a negative correlation between capital per production worker and the export/import ratio (−.40), as first suggested by Leontief.[27] The negative relationships carry over to the measures of structure (−.21) and diversification (−.36) used here. U.S. strength in international competition is concentrated in

products with a relatively large labor content—probably the highly skilled technical labor required for product innovation and development, according to Vernon.[28]

The organizations that are left at home may be among the largest, most integrated, most capital intensive, and most profitable firms in the economy. Furthermore, they are not as likely to have problems of organization, management recruitment and training, staff-line conflicts or of identifying what business the organization is really engaged in, or should be engaged in.

So, in the end, the question of the characteristics of the organization is a question of management's choice between sets of problems. Some business leaders have decided to make their organizations more cohesive by making them more integrated, capital intensive, and often more profitable. They have retained type II structures, and have tended to concentrate on domestic markets. Other business leaders have undertaken the difficult task of transforming an institution, of moving from a type II to a III structure. Many problems arise in this transition; for example, new systems of evaluation, reward, and control must be constructed. A critical aspect of the transition is teaching men to accept new roles—in this case roles as general managers. Once the organization had developed this educational capability, it could continue to diversify in an effective and efficient manner. It may be that the same pattern is being repeated in the international field: when the company has small foreign interests, it economizes on competent international management by having one

[25] *Enterprise Statistics.*
[26] Gort, *Diversification and Integration,* p. 74.
[27] W. Leontief, "Domestic Production and Foreign Trade: The American Capital Position Re-examined," *Proceedings of the American Philosophical Society* 97 (Sept. 1953), pp. 332–49.
[28] Vernon, "International Investment."

man coordinate foreign activities. The growth of foreign markets and opportunities requires diversification, reorganization, and the training of many more general international managers. The organizations that have been most successful in meet- ing this new challenge have been those type III organizations that had already developed the ability to produce general managers capable of controlling and guiding a heterogeneous, diverse enterprise.

6. ORGANIZATIONAL DIFFERENTIATION AND SUPPORT: A CONCEPTUAL FRAMEWORK

Ray H. Elling and Sandor Halebsky[1]

In 1958, of the twenty-one million admissions to nonfederal, short-term general hospitals in the United States, almost one-fifth—approximately four million—were to city or county hospitals.[2] Codes of medical ethics as well as general values of our society lead us to expect that patients handled in these hospitals will have in general as good treatment and facilities as those cared for in other institutions. Yet if a hospital does not receive adequate support, it is not as likely to achieve its goals as the well-supported hospital. Thus patients in such a hospital would be handicapped because of social elements not directly related to their illness.[3]

It is interesting but hardly accidental that social science research has only very recently developed an interest in the problem of hospital support.[4] Medical care expenditures

Reprinted by permission from *Administrative Science Quarterly* (Sept. 1961), pp. 185–209.

[1] This research is supported by N.I.H. Grant W-127. The authors gratefully acknowledge the assistance they have received from others associated with the project, particularly Professors Milton I. Roemer, Rodney F. White, and Vaughn Blankenship.
[2] Estimate made from *Hospitals*, 33 (Guide issue; Aug. 1, 1959), Part 2.

[3] Differential treatment according to social characteristics rather than diagnosis has been documented elsewhere. Cf. A. B. Hollingshead and F. C. Redlich, *Social Class and Mental Illness* (New York, 1958).
[4] Sol Levine and Paul E. White, "Exchange as a Conceptual Framework for the Study of Interorganizational Relationships," *Administrative Science Quarterly*, 5 (1961), 583–601. A study of hospital-community relations has begun at the University of Michigan. A study in Mississippi used judges to rate community relations of hos-

in general and expenditures for hospital care in particular have risen significantly in recent years both in this country[5] and abroad.[6] Added to these personal expenditures have been the large outlays for hospital plant and facilities which in turn require large sums for maintenance once they are established. Increased spending for health services and facilities has occurred for a number of reasons—increased specialization of medicine, rapid change in technology and need for hospital improvements, increasing costs of equipment, rising staffing ratios, higher salaries, and so on.[7] In capital expenditures alone, with population expansion, rising demand for hospital care, and costs per hospital bed ranging around twenty thousand dollars, the investment of almost ten billion dollars between 1945 and 1959 for new hospitals has been insufficient to keep up with the needs.[8]

But increasing expenditures, though important, are not the only reason for current concern with the problem of hospital support. Over the last century, the hospital has changed from a segmental institution, serving only those who could not provide adequate facilities at home, to a community institution used and valued by almost all segments of the community. Coupled with this development of greater contact between hospital and community, however, has been a gradual depersonalization of treatment relationships attendant upon increased specialization and complexity. Thus while the hospital is more recognized and valued for its potentialities, it may incur resentment because of its cost and impersonality. Public criticism is reflected in numerous popular articles and opinion polls.[9] It has become a practical question of some import, then, to discover the types of hospitals and kinds of settings which have been associated with the hospital's receiving support under our relatively unregulated system of hospital care.

Many factors may affect the ability of an organization to achieve its goals. Internally there may be a lack of harmony; members of the institution[10] may be unclear as to goals; there may be conflicts between goals;

---

pitals in general, but did not consider explicitly the receipt of support. See J. V. D. Saunders and J. H. Bruening, "Hospital-Community Relations in Mississippi," *Rural Sociology*, 24 (1959), 48–51.

[5] Health Information Foundation, "Our Increased Spending for Health," *Progress in Health Service*, 9 (Feb. 1960).

[6] T. E. Chester, "Health and Hospital Services in the United States, A Comparative Analysis," *The Hospital*, 56 (Sept.–Oct., 1960), 15.

[7] Henry N. Pratt, "Factors Affecting Hospital Costs," *New York State Journal of Medicine*, 60 (1960), 369 ff.

[8] *Principles for Planning the Future Hospital System* (U.S. Department of Health, Education and Welfare, Public Health Service Publication No. 721; Washington, D.C.: U.S. Government Printing Office), Table 3, p. 216; Edward T. Chase, "Revolution in Hospitals," *Architectural Forum*, 111 (Aug., 1959), 127 ff.

[9] For example, see special supplement, "The Crisis in American Medicine," *Harpers*, 221 (October, 1960), 121–68; and E. L. Koos, " 'Metropolis'—What City People Think of Their Medical Services," *In* E. G. Jaco (ed.), *Patients, Physicians and Illness* (Glencoe, 1958), pp. 113–19.

[10] The terms "institution" and "organization" are used interchangeably here to mean a group of persons organized in a division of labor into a hierarchy of social roles to achieve certain purposes and having at their disposal shared vocabulary and some physical setting and materials. See Everett C. Hughes, "The Study of Institutions," *Social Forces*, 20 (1942), 307–11, for the distinction between the use of the word "institution" in this sense and its use in the sense of a practice such as "marriage" or "property."

or there may be other internal factors familiar to students of organizational theory.[11] On the other hand, environmental conditions may also influence effectiveness. Competition with other organizations,[12] changing societal definitions of goals,[13] shifts in the legitimacy granted to an institution,[14] and general economic and cultural conditions[15] can influence the organization's attainment of objectives directly[16] or through their influence on support.

In view of the importance of relations between an organization and its environment, it is curious that social scientists have been preoccupied in their empirical researches with human relations within organizations.[17] There are a number of exceptions,[18]

[11] James G. March and Herbert A. Simon, *Organizations* (New York, 1958).

[12] Walter B. Miller, "Inter-Institutional Conflict as a Major Impediment to Delinquency Prevention," *Human Organization*, 17 (1958), 20–23; also, Marshall E. Dimock, "Expanding Jurisdictions: A Case Study in Bureaucratic Conflict," *In* R. K. Merton, *et al.* (eds.), *Reader in Bureaucracy* (Glencoe, 1952).

[13] James D. Thompson and William McEwen, "Organizational Goals and Environment: Goal Setting as an Interaction Process," *American Sociological Review*, 20 (1955), 206–10; Burton R. Clark, "Organizational Adaptation and Precarious Values," *American Sociological Review*, 21 (1956), 327–36.

[14] Clark, "Organizational Adaptation"; Christopher Sower *et al.*, "The Death of the Health Council," *In Community Involvement* (Glencoe, 1957), ch. xi.

[15] Sheldon L. Messinger, "Organizational Transformation: A Case Study of a Declining Social Movement," *American Sociological Review*, 20 (1955), 3–10. The organization facing a new cultural environment may have to incorporate a new role, that of the intermediary; see John Adair, "The Indian Health Worker in the Cornell-Navaho Project," *Human Organization*, 19 (1960), 59–63.

[16] A comparative study revealed that good patient care is achieved in Swedish hospitals with fewer personnel per patient than in American hospitals. There is evidence that more than one of the conditions we have mentioned may be operating directly on goal attainment. For example, the author suggests that efficiency may be greater because of the presence of full-time physicians, thereby avoiding the duplication and

likely confusion. On the other hand, a general cultural emphasis on hard work and cooperation may help explain the findings. Cf. Paul A. Lembcke, "Hospital Efficiency —A Lesson from Sweden," *Hospitals*, 33 (1959), 34–38.

[17] William F. Whyte, *Man and Organization*, (Homewood, Ill., 1959), Part I; Amitai Etzioni, "New Directions in the Study of Organizations and Society," *Social Research*, 27 (1960), 223–28.

[18] Philip Selznick, *TVA and the Grass Roots* (Berkeley, 1949), and those works already noted. Also, William R. Dill, "Environment as an Influence on Managerial Autonomy," *Administrative Science Quarterly*, 2 (1958), 409–43; Amitai Etzioni, "Interpersonal and Structural Factors in the Study of Mental Hospitals," *Psychiatry: Journal for the Study of Interpersonal Processes*, 23 (Feb., 1960), 13–22; John M. Gaus, *Public Administration and the U.S. Department of Agriculture* (Chicago, 1949); Neal Gross, "Some Contributions of Sociology to the Field of Education," *Harvard Educational Review*, 29 (1959), 275–87; Morris Janowitz *et al.*, *Public Administration and the Public* (Ann Arbor, 1958); Charles Perrow, "Organizational Prestige: Some Functions and Disfunctions," *American Journal of Sociology*, 66 (1961), 335–91; Robert V. Presthus, "Social Bases of Bureaucratic Organization," *Social Forces*, 38 (1959), 103–109; Robert Somer, "The Mental Hospital in the Small Community," *Mental Hygiene*, 42 (1958), 487–96; James D. Thompson *et al.* (eds.), *Comparative Studies in Administration* (Pittsburgh, 1959). For earlier works with implications for the study of organization and environment, see O. D. Duncan, "Urbanization and Retail Specialization," *Social Forces*, 30 (1951), 267–71; A. B. Hollingshead, *Elmtown's Youth* (New York, 1949); Everett C. Hughes, "The Ecological Aspect of Institutions," *American Sociological Review*, 1 (1936), 180–88. Many studies of the operation of political parties in different settings are also relevant, of course. For a work that treats the environment as the

but, generally, external relations and particularly problems of gaining support have been underemphasized.[19]

Some attention has been given to support, in the minimal sense of elements necessary for group existence and maintenance. Georg Simmel, for example, gave attention to such essential elements as a name, banner, or other identifying symbols. He also pointed up the importance of numbers of individuals both in the formation of certain types of groups and in lending continuity to groups.[20] Malinowsky has clarified other essential elements of an institution—a system of social roles reflecting a division of labor, material facilities, and a statement of purpose.[21] Only recently,

however, has support, beyond conditions of mere group existence and maintenance, come into focus.[22]

This research set out to discover the aspects of the hospital and its environment that are related to the hospital receiving some of the elements it needs in order to give good patient care.[23] We suggest a framework to study the relations between internal and external variables or attributes of an organization and the support it receives from its environment. This paper will report our findings with respect to one internal attribute, namely sponsorship.[24] As used in this framework, support refers to an institution receiving from its environment those elements it needs to

---

major motive force in human development, consult H. T. Buckle, *History of Civilization in England* (New York, 1913), especially Vol. I, pt. I.

[19] Generally, when an organization's relationship to its environment is studied, it is primarily in terms of its attempts to maximize its power or influence. Thus there is consideration of the activities of interest groups in general, as in David Truman's *The Governmental Process* (New York, 1951); or of particular interest groups, as for example Wesley McCune's *The Farm Bloc* (New York, 1943); Grant McConnell's work on the American Farm Bureau Federation, *The Decline of Agrarian Democracy* (Los Angeles, 1953); or Oliver Garceau's study of the American Medical Association, *The Political Life of the American Medical Association* (Cambridge, Mass., 1941). There is little direct attention given, however, to an institution's external relationships as these center upon the particular problem of its obtaining support from the environment.

[20] *The Sociology of Georg Simmel*, Kurt H. Wolff, trans. and ed., (Glencoe, 1950).

[21] *A Scientific Theory of Culture* (Chapel Hill, 1944). He uses the notion of the charter to exemplify the goal statement of an institution. This implies an excessively formal and explicit statement, however, which is inappropriate for the study of many informal organizations.

[22] Levine and White, "Exchange as a Conceptual Framework." This paper conceptualizes exchanges between health organizations. The definition given to exchange admits of negative interactions such as insults, impediments, or more serious signs of conflict, but the authors' development of this concept seems to include only positive interactions between organizations, that is, those which would aid in the attainment of goals. Thus, the use of exchange by these investigators is equivalent to our notion of support.

[23] An early statement of the research plan and suggestions from exploratory studies is given in Milton I. Roemer and Rodney F. White, "Community Attitudes toward the Hospital," *Hospital Management*, 89 (Jan.–Feb., 1960). A research note on variation in types of support appears in Ray H. Elling, "What Do We Mean by Hospital Support?," *Modern Hospital*, 96 (Jan., 1961), 84.

[24] The term sponsorship designates the nature of the controlling and administrative body legally responsible for a hospital. Four types of sponsorship are common: a voluntary, nondenominational corporation; a governmental body—either city, county, state, or federal; a religious organization; or a private individual or corporation. In this paper, local governmental (city and county) hospitals are compared with voluntary, nondenominational hospitals.

achieve its goals. Without support an organization cannot be effective. As used here, support is held to be both an independent variable determining various internal aspects of hospital effectiveness and also a dependent variable determined by various internal aspects of the hospital and by external characteristics of the hospital community. In the study reported here, the external characteristic of particular importance is the stratification system. It is held that the research findings support the interpretation that hospital sponsorship is important in determining the elements in the community stratification system with which the hospital will be associated. Different sponsorship leads to different associations. This in turn influences the degree of support forthcoming from the community to the hospital.

Many comparisons of extreme differences in support might be made from those examined. To take one, there is the county hospital in an urban center which closed its doors just as the study was starting. It was a short-term general hospital like all the others in the study. The community, according to a Community Chest report, needed more beds, but this hospital was located in a converted jail and its facilities had not been renovated. This example might be compared with two voluntary hospitals in the same city which merged and obtained enough money from a fund drive and Hill-Burton (federal) aid to build a new plant. The county hospital had lost in its relative proportion of admissions over the years and the other two had gained. The county hospital had an insignificant staff of volunteer workers associated with it while the other two, especially after their merger and the construction of the new building, had a very active staff of volunteers. These women not only worked in the hospital but made articles in their homes for the hospital gift center and sought subscriptions for new equipment, art works for the lobby, and contributions for patient-library facilities. The new hospital, as compared to the county hospital, had considerably more funds, patients, and volunteers.

These are important elements of support but they are not the only ones. A hospital also needs a qualified and devoted staff, active board members, a generally favorable climate of attitudes, and other help as well. The elements of support required for any particular type of institution depend upon its needs with respect to achieving its goals. In the case of a friendship group, support may be determined simply by conditions affecting the frequency of members' interaction and the extent of their identification with the group. In the case of a complex organization like an industrial concern or a hospital, the elements of support will be manifold.

We could compare the county hospital with the merged voluntary hospital in many respects. As Talcott Parsons points out, any system may be regarded in its "internal" and "external" aspects.[25] We might point up

[25] "General Theory in Sociology," *in* R. K. Merton *et al.* (eds.), *Sociology Today* (New York, 1959), p. 5. Parsons' treatment of "external" and "internal" follows Homans' development of these concepts. This approach treats the external elements of an organization as those which mediate between the particular organization and its environment, whereas internal elements are those relationships which are concerned with the integration of the elements which compose the organization. While our research employs these distinctions, we also use these terms to distinguish between characteristics or components of the hospital (for example, number of personnel per patient) and those of its surrounding com-

differences in size, qualifications of medical staff, equipment, number of services, socioeconomic characteristics of patients, death rates, and other "internal" characteristics. On the other hand, we could also discuss differences between these hospitals in their relations to the environment. Although the hospitals discussed here are in the same community and therefore differences in the overall environment cannot operate to influence support, as they might in the case of a cross-community comparison, it is clear that there may be differential ties to the community which help to explain the differences we noted in support. Doctors of the merged voluntary hospitals may tend to belong to *the* country club while doctors in the county hospital may be general practitioners with relatively low incomes who play golf at the municipal golf links. The patients may come from different social-class levels and living areas. The board members of the voluntary hospitals may come from top prestige and influential levels while the county hospital may have mainly the less influential lawyers or businessmen on its board.

The community stratification system within which the hospital must function and seek support is an external feature to which it has to adjust. Any given system of vertical stratification tends to order the institutions, associations, individuals, behaviors and ideologies in a community into a hierarchy of prestige groups with certain associated values. Of particular importance of this research is the fact that institutions may become identified with given

elements of the stratification system. Such identification may be in part a matter of intent and in part a matter of latent operation of the stratification system.

The hospitals within a community may be regarded as players in a game who seek to differentiate themselves, as would members of any social system, both with respect to their internal characteristics and with respect to their ties to the environment.[26] This may be a conscious process, as when the administrator of one hospital tries to establish ties to a medical school before administrators in other hospitals are able to do so. Much of this differentiation seems to occur in a latent way with little deliberate action or awareness of how the system operates. The importance of institutional differentiation for our problem is that it may influence a hospital's relative ability to draw support from its environment.

The sponsorship of the hospital was one of the internal characteristics which we felt would be related to environmental support. From the point of view of the surrounding community, knowledge of the controlling body of an organization is essential in determining whom the institution represents. Within a system of stratification, in other words, the nature of the sponsoring group is important in differentiating an institution from others in terms of its class character and consequently, it was felt, might result in the organization's being associated with different sources having varying amounts of support to offer.

---

munity environment (for example, per capita expendable income). Thus our use of "external" may refer to external relations as well as characteristics of the context.

[26] Everett C. Hughes, in a personal communication regarding an earlier draft of this paper, has reminded us of this important point. See further Norton Long, "The Local Community as an Ecology of Games," *American Journal of Sociology*, 64 (1958), 251–61.

METHODS AND PROCEDURES

The data-gathering procedures of this research were carried out in two phases. The first, from which the findings of this paper are taken, consisted essentially of gathering from a number of sources data on support, internal characteristics, and community characteristics for all (136) upstate New York short-term general nonproprietary hospitals. Of this group, 90 were voluntary and nondenominational; 23 were local governmental hospitals. This phase of the study was intended (1) to permit a check on hypothesized relationships between internal and environmental characteristics and community support by securing information on enough cases to allow cross tabulations to be made and (2) to permit the selection of high-low support pairs for detailed comparison during the field-study phase of the research. In this second phase, two hospitals of similar size and sponsorship in single-hospital towns provided one comparison. Other comparisons were made between two well-supported hospitals and two poorly supported hospitals in the same urban center. One objective of the field study was to gather data on internal hospital characteristics. Visits were made to each, using observation, interviewing, and questionnaire techniques. Another purpose of the field study was to examine the relationships between the selected hospitals and their communities. Consequently, data on these relationships and the social organization of the communities were gathered through interviews with key informants and through interviews and questionnaires administered to three categories of persons —community leaders, practicing physicians, and the general public. This data should contribute significantly toward further clarifying the relationship suggested here between sponsorship, social stratification, and support. Analysis of data from the field-study phase is in process. The present paper is based on the first phase in which data were collected from the census of hospitals.

Like any other type of organization one might study, the hospital shades off into other institutions. There are, for example, nursing homes and sanatoriums, which one would hesitate to exclude from the category of hospitals. On the other hand, there are some organizations called hospitals which hardly fit the usual pattern. Thus it was decided somewhat arbitrarily to include only those institutions listed in the 1959 American Hospital Association's annual guide issue of *Hospitals*. This resulted in the exclusion of eleven institutions that have the word "hospital" in their names but are not listed in the guide because they do not meet certain minimal criteria. The study sample further excluded proprietary hospitals, long-term hospitals (those with an average length of stay of 30 days or more), special hospitals (those treating one disease such as tuberculosis or mental illness), and those in or near the New York metropolitan area. It was thought that the remaining 136 could be regarded as relatively homogeneous with respect to goals,[27] disease range, and length of

---

[27] As Levine and White indicate, "Exchange as a Conceptual Framework," the objectives of an organization are important determinants of what it receives from and sends to other organizations. There is variation among the hospitals in our sample as to their emphasis on teaching and research. There is also variation in the diseases treated, since some may receive a higher proportion of serious cases or more cases of a particular type such as maternity or

stay, but would still allow variation in important internal and external characteristics without involving the complexities of the metropolitan environment.

Since it would be difficult to study the degree to which a complex institution receives every element it needs to fulfill its goals, we limited our examination to three important types of support which could be measured relatively easily.

Feeling that a hospital needs sufficient funds for expansion to meet the increasing utilization of hospitals and for improvements to adjust to a rapidly changing technology, we constructed a monetary support index from information about donations, fund drives, increase in permanent endowment, bond issues, Hill-Burton aid, and other governmental appropriations. Income from patients was excluded since there is considerable

evidence that hospitals in our system need and desire as much external income as they can obtain, even to balance their budget in current operations, to say nothing of making capital improvements.[28] Dollar amounts were obtained for a ten-year period, 1949–1958, from several sources[29] and were totaled. Results were expressed in terms of dollars per 100 beds in order to control for size of hospital. Since great reliance could not be placed on the exact dollar amount obtained by totaling figures from several sources, it was decided to place the distribution into broad categories of high, medium, and low.

Aside from the financial support it gains from patients, the hospital obviously must have patients in order to fulfill its goals. Also, if a hospital gains significantly in admissions, the administrator is able to make a good case that it should expand. The guide issue from 1949 to 1958 of *Hospitals* provided information on admissions

---

operative. These are ways in which hospitals are differentiated from one another and may influence the support received by the institution. Some variation in these respects is desired, however, in order that their effects can be examined. But it is felt that relative homogeneity as to goals exists. The goal of profit has been more or less excluded by omitting proprietary hospitals. And it is probably true that almost all hospitals mix teaching and research in some degree with patient care. In any case, it is relatively safe to assume that good patient care is the dominant goal in all our hospitals, for it is the goal by which the hospital gains legitimacy and it is the rallying point around which disputes as to hospital organization are usually settled. In this connection, see the exchange between a medical administrator and a representative of the American Board of Radiology; Albert W. Snoke, "Financial Relationships between Radiologists and Hospitals," *Hospitals*, 34 (Jan. 16, and Feb. 1, 1960), 38–42, 43–45 ff.; also Paul R. Hawley, "Responsibility of the Hospital to the Community," *Hospital Progress*, 37 (May, 1957), 86–88 ff.

[28] "The chronic difficulties, however, which many (administrators) even among the bigger American hospitals experience, their uncertain recourse to flag days, charities and community chests for making up existing deficits are a wholesale reminder that perhaps we (in Britain) have made some progress since the war!" Chester, *The Hospital*, 56, p. 13.

[29] The New York State Joint Hospital Survey and Planning Commission provided information on Hill-Burton funds. Information on money received from fund drives, bond issues, and other governmental funds was obtained from a mail questionnaire. Annual reports made by all hospitals to the New York State Department of Social Welfare yielded data on donations from community chests and other sources for current operations and gave information on increases in permanent endowment funds; these reports also yielded information for validating monetary support since we were able to calculate increase in plant value.

which served as an index of patient channeling.[30]

The third type of support examined was community participation in the hospital. Measures of volunteer activity and personnel turnover were used to reflect this type of support.[31]

In order to facilitate some aspects of the analysis, a general index of support was constructed on the basis of each hospital's position with respect to funds, patients, and community participation.[32] It should be noted that while we refer to this as a "general index" it is not an index

of *general support*, which would have to include many more types of support.

Information was obtained from numerous sources on internal hospital characteristics such as number of physicians on the staff, range of services, personnel-patient ratio, death rate, characteristics of the administrator, and other aspects. Information on various characteristics of the hospital's locality[33] were obtained through the census or similar sources.[34] Data for these localities include an estimate of population increase, industrial composition, effective buying income per capita, educational level, and other aspects of the hospital's environment.

One source of primary data employed in the first phase of the research was a 14-page questionnaire which was mailed to the administrators of all the hospitals included in our study. Relatively complete returns were received from 126 (92 percent). This was very encouraging in view of the numerous questionnaires which administrators receive. In part, the result was attributed to follow-up with letters, phone calls, and in numerous cases personal visits. It is probable that the investigators' association with Cornell and the

[30] An attempt to use rate of occupancy as the index of patient channeling failed because it can increase as a result of decreasing the number of beds and reporting habits were found to vary considerably. The term "patient channeling" is used instead of "patient choice" in recognition of the factors other than patient election (such as doctor's preference) that determine which hospital a patient goes to. A hospital's relative position on patient channeling was determined by (1) the gain or loss it showed in its proportion of admissions to all hospitals in the study over the ten-year period, 1949–1958, and (2) the percentage gain or loss it showed in its own admissions between 1949 and 1958.

[31] A mail questionnaire sent to administrators yielded the data to calculate number of volunteers per 100 beds and number of volunteer hours per 100 beds in 1957 and 1958. Personnel turnover was determined by information on the number of employees leaving during these years and information from *Hospitals*, guide issues, for these years on number of employees. Each hospital was assigned to a high- or low-community-participation position on the basis of its position relative to other hospitals on the distributions above. Equal weight was given to each measure. Since there are two measures of volunteer activity and only one of personnel turnover, the former contribute most to the index of community participation.

[32] Detailed information on the procedures followed in the construction of this index as well as other indices used in the study will be supplied on request.

[33] The named place in which a hospital is located served to determine the boundary of its community. The problem of delineating a hospital's community by any other means (such as its service area) seems to be an insurmountable one if a number of hospitals are to be compared and data obtained on the characteristics of the surrounding areas thus determined.

[34] *Sales Management*, 83 (July, 1959), current survey of industrial buying power; U.S. Bureau of the Census, *Census of Population: 1950*, Vol. 2, Part 32 (Washington, D.C., 1952); State of New York, Department of Commerce, *Business Fact Book*, (Albany, 1957).

TABLE 1 SPONSORSHIP AND MONETARY SUPPORT

Sponsorship	Low		Medium		High		Total	
	No.	%	No.	%	No.	%	No.	%
Voluntary	22	(25)	31	(35)	35	(40)	88	(100)*
Governmental	12	(57)	6	(29)	3	(14)	12	(100)*

*Information was insufficient on two voluntary and two governmental hospitals.

Sloan Institute of Hospital Administration also contributed to this good response.

In this paper, we give major emphasis to the hospital's sponsorship. Sponsorship classifications indicated in *Hospitals*, guide issue, 1959, were used. The support received by city and county hospitals sponsored by local government is compared with the support received by hospitals sponsored by voluntary, nondenominational organizations. The position of church-sponsored hospitals will be discussed in future publications. Since we are dealing with the census of hospitals in the upstate area, no significance tests are applied in the tables which follow.

RESULTS

The local government hospitals studied received considerably less monetary support in general than did the voluntary, nondenominational hospitals. Table 1 shows that whereas 40 percent of the voluntary hospitals were in the top category in the monetary index, only 14 percent of governmental hospitals were in this category. In the lowest category, we find 57 percent of the governmental and only 25 percent of the voluntary hospitals.

This finding is valid with respect to particular kinds of monetary support, such as money received from fund drives and contributions. One might object that this is to be expected, for even though there is no prohibition against their receiving money in this way, local governmental hospitals generally obtain additional funds through bond issues or governmental grants. While the governmental hospitals in our study show some gain through these channels, it is not enough to make up for the greater amount received by voluntary hospitals from legacies, donations, and fund drives. Even with respect to Hill-Burton aid, which is presumably open to all hospitals in areas with demonstrated needs and is administered by a quasi-governmental state agency, Table 2 shows that whereas slightly more than half (51 percent) of the voluntary hospitals received this support, little more than one-third (35 percent) of the governmental hospitals received this support.

This tendency for the governmental hospital to receive less monetary and material support is true with respect to a general measure of plant growth, that is, increase in plant value.[35] Lo-

[35] Information on this item was obtained from annual reports to the New York State Department of Social Welfare. It seemed useful to check our results on the monetary index by examining increases in plant value because on occasion hospitals receive gifts of buildings and land rather

TABLE 2 SPONSORSHIP AND HILL-BURTON AID

	Hill-Burton Aid					
	None		Some		Total	
Sponsorship	*No.*	*%*	*No.*	*%*	*No.*	*%*
Voluntary	44	(49)	46	(51)	90	(100)
Governmental	15	(65)	8	(35)	23	(100)

TABLE 3 SPONSORSHIP AND GAIN IN PATIENT ADMISSIONS
OVER A TEN-YEAR PERIOD
(IN LOCALITIES HAVING MORE THAN ONE HOSPITAL)

	Gain in Admissions					
	Low		Medium-High		Total	
Sponsorship	*No.*	*%*	*No.*	*%*	*No.*	*%*
Voluntary	13	(41)	19	(59)	32	(100)*
Governmental	6	(86)	1	(14)	7	(100)

* Two voluntary hospitals are new since 1949 and are not included here.

cal governmental hospitals have more often declined in value or but slightly increased while voluntary hospital plants have more often greatly increased in value. Impressions gained from visits to most of the localities in our sample suggest that city and county hospitals are more often in old, inadequate buildings, while most voluntary hospitals are not.

Turning to patient channeling as a measure of support, we find the trend less sharp but still in the same direction. Whereas about three-fifths (61 percent) of the voluntary hospitals in the study were in the "high" category of our index of patient channeling, only about half (52 percent) of the governmental hospitals were in this position. When we examine only those hospitals within localities where two or more hospitals exist, the rela-

tionship is thrown into high relief. In Table 3 we see that in centers with more than one hospital, nearly three-fifths (59 percent) of voluntary hospitals showed moderate to high gains while only one of seven governmental hospitals in these settings (14 percent) escaped the "low" category. Noting the trend toward lower occupancy figures in municipal hospitals, one investigator attributed the change in the use of the hospital to health insurance.[36] While insurance may play a role in patient channeling, there is generally no formal arrangement which prevents the insured patient from using the local governmental hospital. Yet they have tended to go to voluntary hospitals, and this movement, as we shall see, is consonant with the generally lower support received by governmental hospitals.

With respect to community participation in the hospital, the distinction

than money and this item could be expected to reflect over-all plant growth. Since information for a number of hospitals was missing on this item, it can only be used as a partial validation of our results on funds.

[36] E. Ginsberg, *A Pattern for Hospital Care, Final Report of the New York State Hospital Study* (New York, 1947), pp. 149–70.

TABLE 4 SPONSORSHIP AND POSITION ON A GENERAL INDEX OF SUPPORT

| | Support | | | | | | | |
| | Low | | Medium | | High | | Total | |
Sponsorship	No.	%	No.	%	No.	%	No.	%
Voluntary	29	(33)	36	(40)	24	(27)	89	(100)*
Governmental	13	(59)	4	(18)	5	(23)	22	(100)*

* Included here are all cases for which information was available on at least two of the three areas—funds, patients, and community participation. Therefore the totals in this table are larger than in some of the previous ones. A blank in one area of support simply meant that it was not counted in arriving at an average score. There was insufficient information on one voluntary and one governmental hospital.

between voluntary and governmental sponsorship is least clear. Local governmental hospitals seem to do almost as well as voluntary hospitals in obtaining volunteers, and there is only a slight tendency for governmental hospitals to have a higher rate of personnel turnover. Still, when we examine the number of hours contributed by volunteers per 100 beds, we find that of those providing complete information[37] 53 percent of the voluntary hospitals in contrast to 7 percent of the governmental hospitals were above the median on this measure. While the governmental hospital may be at some disadvantage in the area of community participation, it is apparently not quite as handicapped with respect to this type of support as it is in other areas. It would be interesting to compare the composition of the volunteer groups associated with governmental and voluntary hospitals in terms of social class and other variables. Unfortunately, our study does not include this information.

When the indices for funds, patients, and community participation

[37] Fourteen voluntary and four governmental hospitals did not return questionnaires or gave incomplete responses on this point.

are combined in a general index of support which gives equal weight to each type of support, the picture of differences between voluntary and governmental hospitals is considerably sharpened. Table 4 indicates that only around a third (33 percent) of the voluntary hospitals fell in the low-support category while approximately three fifths (59 percent) of the governmental cases received low support.

This general position of local governmental hospitals is exemplified in the following quotation from a local newspaper concerning recent efforts of a poorly supported city hospital to improve its position:

(Hospital Switchboard): "Good morning. General Hospital."
(Caller): "Oh, I'm sorry. I must have the wrong number."
(Switchboard): "No, this is City Hospital, but the name has been officially changed to General Hospital."
(Caller): "Oh, sure, I DID read something about that. . . ."

With a flourish of his pen, Gov. Nelson A. Rockefeller last Friday signed a bill changing the name, but the actual transformation of a practical public image and elimination of the "City Hospital" reflex will take a bit more doing.

Wonder why anyone would go to such trouble to change the name of a hospital? The hospital's board of managers felt the name "City Hospital" tended to stigmatize the institution as one primarily interested in serving welfare patients, as is the case with some municipally operated hospitals elsewhere. City . . . oops, General . . . Hospital, however, counts only 15 to 20 percent of its patients as welfare recipients.[38]

Perhaps other factors explain the relationship we have found between sponsorship and support. The news story suggests that a hospital is stigmatized by having a high proportion of welfare patients. It is true that the local governmental hospitals in our study tend to have a higher proportion of welfare patients. When this factor is controlled,[39] however, it does not significantly alter the tendency for the governmental hospitals to receive less support. When there is a low proportion of welfare patients, the governmental hospital tends to receive about the same support as the voluntary hospital. When there is a medium or high proportion of welfare patients, however, the voluntary hospital receives more support than the governmental hospital.

[38] The source is not cited here for reasons of identity. Actually, the figure given for the proportion of welfare patients places this hospital in the upper 13 percent of the distribution of all hospitals in our study on this characteristic. The median for welfare patients was between 7.5 percent and 9.0 percent.

[39] Controls were applied in terms of broad categories such as high, medium, and low. Thus within the group of hospitals having a high proportion of welfare patients, the voluntary hospitals tend to receive more support than do the governmental cases. It should be noted, however, that when such controls are applied the number of expected cases in any category becomes so small that these findings can only be taken as suggestive.

Perhaps when other internal factors are held constant the relationship disappears. Perhaps there would be no relationship between sponsorship and support if we held constant (one at a time) the following factors: size of the hospital, range of services offered, number of house and paid staff per 100 patients, number of active and associate physicians on the staff, number of other personnel per 100 patients, interest in research as indicated by number of papers published by the medical staff, affiliation with a medical school, presence of an outpatient department, length of time administrator has been in the field, occupational composition of the board, or the death ratio. While some of these variables appear to weaken the relationship between sponsorship and support when they are held constant, the tendency for cases to fall in the expected direction remains.

The same holds true for the external variables which we examined. Whether one holds constant the estimated percentage change in population between 1950 and 1958, the size of the locality in terms of estimated population in 1958, the number of firms employing 500 or more persons, the effective buying income per capita, educational level, or other characteristics of the locality on which we have data, the relationship between sponsorship and support does not disappear. Again by controlling variables, the relationship becomes less marked, but the tendency remains. As an example of this type of analysis, if we hold the number of hospitals in the locality constant, we find, as indicated in Table 5, that the general index of support remains related to sponsorship whether we examine the relationship within localities having a single hospital or

TABLE 5 SPONSORSHIP AND GENERAL INDEX OF SUPPORT BY
NUMBER OF HOSPITALS IN THE LOCALITY

No. of Hospitals	Sponsorship	Support					
		Low		High		Total	
		No.	%	No.	%	No.	%
One	Voluntary	15	(27)	41	(73)	56	(100)
	Governmental	7	(47)	8	(53)	15	(100)*
More than one	Voluntary	14	(42)	19	(58)	33	(100)*
	Governmental	6	(86)	1	(14)	7	(100)

* Information is lacking from one voluntary and one governmental hospital on more than one of the three components of this index—i.e., funds, patients, and community participation.

several hospitals. A close inspection of Table 5, however, suggests that the relationship is clearer in localities with more than one hospital. In other words, the governmental hospital tends to receive more support when it is the only hospital than it does when there are other hospitals in the community.

While it appears that the relationship between sponsorship and support stands in spite of controlling other variables on which we have data, holding sponsorship constant does not destroy the relationship of certain other variables to support. These are not discussed here since the object of this paper is not to explore exhaustively the factors influencing the support received by an institution, but rather to present a framework and employ it in an empirical example.

DISCUSSION

Two questions arise here. First, what are the implications of our findings with respect to sponsorship for a theory of support? And second, how is local governmental sponsorship as compared to voluntary sponsorship related to support? These are

interrelated questions. By examining the second, we may also arrive at some answer to the first.

Although the relative position of governmental as compared to voluntary institutions in the health field is of great interest, the position of governmental institutions in our society is a much broader problem. The whole civil service movement may be regarded as an effort to upgrade the quality and prestige of persons employed in governmental organizations. The pioneering studies of Leonard D. White[40] determined that the public's attitudes toward public employment were not as favorable as those held toward corresponding private positions. He also reported that the lowest prestige was attached to employment by a municipality. And although state and national employees carried more prestige, they did not attain the level of prestige accorded employees of private enterprise. A more recent study by Janowitz, Wright, and Delany suggests that there has been an improvement in the prestige level of governmental

[40] "The Prestige Value of Public Employment," *American Political Science Review*, 26 (1932), 910–14, and *The Prestige Value of Municipal Employment in Chicago* (Chicago, 1929).

as compared to private employment in recent years. But this investigation still reports that 53 percent of the respondents would grant greater prestige to a doctor on the staff of a voluntary hospital while only 25 percent would attribute greater prestige to the doctor attached to a city hospital.[41] Furthermore, these investigators found that contrary to the general tendency of persons to rate the prestige of their own positions above the level granted them by others, governmental employees and their families tended to rate governmental employment lower than others did. The lack of respect for government regulations and the feeling that the government is somehow a thing apart from the community are often encountered. Pedestrian, dirty tasks like sewage disposal and street cleaning are left to government while various voluntary citizens' groups of "middle-class" and "upper-middle-class" character undertake the glamorous, challenging endeavors of public service.

Does our study of support offer any explanation of the position of governmental hospitals and perhaps shed some light on the position of governmental institutions in our society?

It does not seem entirely adequate to explain the low support of local governmental hospitals solely in terms of their serving a higher proportion of welfare and other low-prestige patients, although this undoubtedly is a

factor. Such patients have been shown to receive less adequate care in other settings.[42] An example is given by a physician in one of the communities studied who pointed up the use of the county hospital as a medical "dumping ground," when he asked, "When they close the county hospital, where will I send my crocks?" But as we have seen, controlling the factor of proportion of welfare patients does not destroy the relationship between sponsorship and support. Furthermore, the problem of low support remains in any case, since one may go beyond the association between welfare patients and other low-prestige patients and governmental hospitals to ask, "Why should these patients be channeled to these hospitals?" Perhaps part of the explanation of low support is circular. The fact that local governmental hospitals tend to be in less adequate buildings and in some ways receive less acceptable personnel[43] may deter patients and doctors from using them and work against interest and support. Again, these explanations only point up the problem.

The city or county general hospital is similar in most respects to the voluntary general hospital. Medically, it is similar in offering a wide range of services—emergency, medical, surgical, maternity, pediatric, and so on. Organizationally, it has board, staff, and administrative relationships similar to those of the voluntary hospital. There is a pronounced *social* difference, however. Until the modern hospital movement

[41] M. Janowitz *et al., Public Administration and the Public—Perspectives toward Government in a Metropolitan Community* (Michigan Governmental Studies No. 36; Ann Arbor, 1958), p. 64. It should be noted, however, that since a *particular* city hospital was named in their questions, this result may be influenced by other characteristics of the institution.

[42] Hollingshead and Redlich, *Social Class and Mental Illness.*

[43] The Hospital Council of Greater New York, "Foreign-Trained Interns and Residents in New York City Hospitals," *The Bulletin,* 14 (1959), 1–6.

developed in the latter part of the nineteenth century with the advent and practice of bacteriology and aseptic surgery, all hospitals, as Edward D. Churchill points out, were institutions providing last comforts to the sick poor.[44] There was no problem of various strata of society associating with one another in the same institution. But with improved medical technology, hospitals became places to go for cure rather than places to die. "The best" in .nedical care moved from the home and the doctor's office into the hospital. As the hospital became a treatment center positively valued by all classes, but especially the "middle" and "upper" classes, a certain amount of specialization in type of patient developed and preserved thereby the stratification of the community. Voluntary hospitals have drawn business, industrial and society leaders to their boards and have not left any channel of formal control open to the broader public. City and county hospitals, on the other hand, while they may have similar persons on their boards,[45]

have remained "the people's" hospitals in the sense that popular control and identification has been partially retained through the election of local governmental officials.

It is suggested that as a consequence of the class character of their control, voluntary and governmental hospitals experience differentials in support consistent with the general differential distribution of rewards in society according to class position. Perhaps the relatively higher support received by the governmental hospital when it is the sole community hospital is due to there being less of a division of labor along social-class lines in such a setting than there is when the community's support must be divided among several hospitals.

While other investigators have offered evidence for the low position of governmental institutions, the comparison of local governmental hospitals with voluntary hospitals suggests an explanation. The political system is the major means of control of governmental institutions. In a democratic society, the political system, far from being the power instrument of the capitalist ruling class, as Marx maintained, has often been a major means of control and representation available to ordinary citizens. As changes in medical technology have encouraged the use of the hospital by all elements of society, "upper" elements have preserved the class structure of the community by organizing their own facilities outside of control of the masses and to some extent beyond their participation. As Peter H. Rossi states:

Historically, the development of voluntary civic associations may be interpreted as the reaction to the loss of political power on the local scene by high

---

[44] "The Development of the Hospital," *In* N. Faxon (ed.), *The Hospital in Contemporary Life* (Cambridge, Mass., 1949), pp. 33–34.

[45] While local governmental hospitals may have some of the same types of business and industrial leaders on their boards, the findings of our study suggest that the proportions differ. Information on occupations of board members was gathered and classified with high reliability according to categories which included one for "top economic and production people." Whereas 28 percent of voluntary hospitals had more than 30 percent of the board members in this category, none of the governmental hospitals had more than 30 percent of their boards composed of this type of person. See further C. Covert, "No 'Common Man' on Hospital Boards," *Syracuse Herald-Journal*, Oct. 20, 1959.

status groups who built a set of community organizations which they could control, being out of reach of the mass vote of lower class groups.[46]

To us it appears that it is the role played by governmental institutions in our society in general which has led to the low support of governmental hospitals. We are not employing the usual argument of the popular critic of government that it is inherently bad or incapable. Our findings are, rather, a comment on the position of governmental organizations in American society in general. It should be noted, however, that our findings may be limited to local governmental institutions. Perhaps at the state and national levels, control of government is distant enough from the ordinary person to minimize class differences between private and governmental spheres.

Our study raises the question of the social-class role of government. What is this role at the local, state, and national levels within our own society? What relationship has government had to different classes in different societies and different historical periods? For example, could the exercise of power in the political sphere have been regarded as "dirty" or crude when the king and his court ruled and "the public" had less control than is the case in a democracy?

Sponsorship has theoretical significance from two points of view. To the administrator and other role-players in the organization, it indicates the segment of the community with which the institution is associated both in terms of control and in terms of support. And to the community and the wider society, it appears to serve as one way of differentiating institutions and dividing resources among them. The processes involved in the governmental organization receiving less support and other factors important in these processes remain as questions for further exploration. There is a further point of theoretical interest. Even though we have examined the relationship between an "internal" characteristic of an organization and the support it receives, we had to discover the meaning of the internal factor in the broader social environment before we could understand its implications for support. This is the case since support must come from the environment. Internal factors will only have significance for support insofar as they have meaning in the social environment of an organization.

SUMMARY

By way of exemplifying a framework and its use in an empirical investigation, the problem of support was examined in 136 upstate New York short-term general hospitals. The literature relative to the problem of support was discussed. Support was defined as the receipt by an organization of the elements it needs in order to achieve its goals. Voluntary, nondenominational hospitals were compared as to their receipt of funds, patients, and community participation. Although differences were not great as to receipt of patients, volunteers, and turnover, they were marked in the area of funds. A combined index of support clearly indicated the disadvantaged position of

---

[46] "A Theory of Community Structure," paper delivered at the annual meeting of the American Sociological Association, Chicago, Sept. 4, 1959.

governmental hospitals. While certain other variables included in the study weakened this relationship when they were held constant, the small number of cases available for such analysis tend to fall in the expected direction in spite of applying such controls. This result is interpreted in terms of the social-class role of governmental institutions in our society, and it is suggested that sponsorship differentiates between organizations so as to associate them with elements of the community which have varying ability to channel support to the organization.

7. AUTONOMY, COMPLEXITY, AND NON-BUREAUCRATIC COORDINATION IN PROFESSIONAL ORGANIZATIONS

Wolf V. Heydebrand

The purpose of this paper is to examine the effects of organizational autonomy and complexity on the modes of coordination in professional organizations.* The general functional type chosen to represent professional organizations are contemporary American hospitals. The analysis will focus especially on nonbureaucratic modes of coordination such as those deriving from a high degree of professionalization of the organizational labor force, as well as from the "structural balance" associated with a high degree of departmental specialization.

* I am grateful to Robert Crain, Louis Pondy, Arthur Stinchcombe, and Harrison White who commented on an earlier version of this paper entitled "Division of Labor and Coordination in Organizations."

THEORETICAL BACKGROUND

In discussing the assumptions and the theoretical background of this study, let me first define what I mean by professional organizations and professionalization. I will then take up the question of organizational autonomy and, finally, spell out my assumptions about the relationship between complexity and coordination in organizations.

PROFESSIONAL ORGANIZATIONS AND PROFESSIONALIZATION

In contrast to professional associations, professional organizations are defined here as work organizations in which professionals constitute the production component as well as the administrative line structure of the organization. In the case of hospitals, professional nurses are seen as constituting the production component as well as staffing the administrative line structure, except for the position of the hospital administrator who may or may not be a professional nurse. Physicians typically initiate and direct the process of medical care, but do not, as a rule, implement it. The implementation of medical care and of the wider process of comprehensive patient care is the responsibility of the professional nurse. Therefore, the proportion of professional nurses will be used as an indicator of the degree of professionalization in hospitals.

An important point to be kept in mind here is the distinction between the *degree* as over against the *kind of professionalization*. The *degree* of professionalization, in the present context, refers to the extent to which the organizational labor force consists of professionals. The *kind* of professionalization, on the other hand, may differ, depending on whether professional work takes more the form of "general practice" or whether it approaches more the form exemplified by the professional and technical "specialists." In this paper, only the *degree* of professionalization will be empirically measured, whereas the question of the *kind* of professionalization is treated as problematic. In the second part of this paper, therefore, certain theoretical generalizations will be suggested concerning the kind of professionalization in simple as over against complex types of hospital organization. These generalizations will, of course, require further systematic investigation.

However, psychiatric hospitals appear to conform more closely to a classical or generic conception of "professional organization," with the psychiatric medical and nursing staff providing a relatively homogeneous, unitary line structure. General hospitals, on the other hand, are less clearcut in their status as "professional" organizations, since there are not only different "professions" present, but each is also technically more specialized as well as internally differentiated.

OWNERSHIP AND CONTROL AS INDICATORS OF ORGANIZATIONAL AUTONOMY

For hospitals, the type of ownership and control may be used as an indicator of organizational autonomy. According to Weber, "autonomy means that the order governing the organization has been established by its own members on their own authority, regardless of how it has taken place in other respects. In the case of heteronomy, it has been imposed by an outside agency."[1]

Voluntary "private," non-profit hospitals may be said to be relatively autonomous in contrast to "public" state and local governmental hospitals as well as federal hospitals. In this study, the degree of organizational autonomy will be controlled by systematically distinguishing between these three main types of hospital ownership and control. As will be shown, the main effect of holding organizational autonomy constant is

---

[1] Max Weber, *Economy and Society*, G. Roth and C. Wittich (eds.) (New York: Bedminster Press, 1968, Vol. 1), 49–50. Recent studies which have used Weber's distinction are W. Richard Scott, "Reactions to Supervision in a Heteronomous Professional Organization," *Administrative Science Quarterly*, 10, (June 1965), 65–81; and Richard Hall, "Professionalization and Bureaucratization," *American Sociological Review*, 33 (Feb. 1968), 92–104.

reflected in the difference between federal and non-federal rather than public (governmental) as over against private (voluntary) hospitals.

COMPLEXITY AND COORDINATION

Complexity in modern organizations is problematic because of the interaction of two dimensions of organizational complexity: the degree of complexity of the goal and task structure of the organization, and the degree of complexity of the internal division of labor, that is, of the internal structure. In this paper I am suggesting a way of relating these two aspects of complexity. I will attempt to show that, on both counts, increasing complexity generates not hierarchical but lateral modes of coordination through horizontal communication and interaction between subunits. In short, the more complex organizations become, both internally and in their goal and task structure, the more likely will nonhierarchical modes of coordination predominate, and the less likely will bureaucratic-hierarchical modes of coordination be prevalent.

In addition to bureaucratic modes of coordination such as hierarchical differentiation and a specialized administrative-clerical staff, there are many nonbureaucratic, more horizontal forms of coordination in modern organizations. On the whole, such nonbureaucratic forms have received relatively little attention in organizational studies. Examples of nonbureaucratic modes of coordination are the various mechanisms of representation, negotiation, and participatory decision making such as committees, and various structures of mediation and arbitration designed to deal with the consequences of inter-dependence and conflict.[2] However, I will focus only on two types of nonbureaucratic coordination—first, on that deriving from the departmental specialization of, and the consequent functional interdependence between, subunits within organizations, and, second, on professionalization and its role in providing "coordination by feedback."[3]

Specifically, I will argue that the functional interdependence between specialized departments and subunits can be viewed as giving rise to lateral modes of coordination, and that the internal structural complexity of organizations both generates problems of coordination and at the same time contributes to their resolution.

For the kind of analysis attempted here, it is important to distinguish be-

[2] For a discussion of some of these non-bureaucratic modes of coordination, see, e.g., Tom Burns and G. M. Stalker, *Management for Innovation* (London: Tavistock, 1961); E. W. Bakke, *Bonds of Organization* (New York: Harper & Row, 1950); Louis Pondy, Issue Editor, "Conflict Within and Between Organizations," *Administrative Science Quarterly*, 14 (Dec. 1969), 499–607; Richard E. Walton and Robert B. McKersie, *A Behavioral Theory of Labor Negotiations* (New York: McGraw-Hill, 1965); Henry A. Landsberger, "The Horizontal Dimension in Bureaucracy," *Administrative Science Quarterly*, 6 (Dec. 1961), 299–332; Richard L. Simpson, "Vertical and Horizontal Communication in Formal Organizations," *Administrative Science Quarterly* 4 (Sept. 1959), 188–96. On the coordinative role of committees, see Louis Kriesberg, "U. S. and U.S.S.R. Participation in International Non-Governmental Organizations," *In* Louis Kriesberg (ed.), *Social Processes in International Relations* (New York: John Wiley, 1968), pp. 466–87; and Franz Schurmann, *Ideology and Organization in Communist China* (Berkeley: University of California Press, 2nd. ed., 1968), pp. 55–57, 89–90.

[3] James March and Herbert Simon, *Organizations* (New York: John Wiley, 1958), pp. 160–61.

tween the *level* or degree of complexity of an organization at a given point in time, and the *pattern* of internal structural relationships that obtains at that point. For example, among hospitals the differences between *levels* of complexity reflect their organizational history in terms of the development of task structure, technology, and various environmental influences. Thus, the distinction between "simple" organizations (e.g., large state mental hospitals which are structurally relatively undifferentiated although they may be fairly segmented) and "complex" organizations (e.g., private general teaching hospitals which tend to be internally highly differentiated) may serve to exemplify, in a relatively crude way, a method of distinguishing between *levels* of complexity. I will show that this distinction can be made qualitatively, i.e., in terms of degrees of complexity of the task structure, as well as quantitatively, i.e., in terms of the degree of internal structural complexity.

By contrast, the *pattern* of internal structural relationships may vary, depending on the level of complexity of an organization. For example, professionalization may be positively influenced by departmental specialization at a low level of complexity, but negatively at a high level of complexity. Such a variation in the structural pattern may not be detected unless the level of complexity is controlled. Whether the structural pattern in "simple" organizations differs from that of "complex" organizations is an empirical question and must therefore be taken as problematic.

I will deal with both the pattern of structural relationships, in general, and the problem of pattern variation in the light of different levels of complexity.

Accordingly, I will first examine the general pattern of interrelations among the structural variables, as well as the joint effect of autonomy (ownership and control) and of the complexity of the task structure (teaching and service) on the internal structural complexity of hospitals, holding size constant. Second, I will demonstrate the extent of pattern variation in the relation between size, functional specialization, and the relative size of the administrative-clerical staff, holding autonomy and task structure constant. Third, I will examine the joint effect of two non-bureaucratic modes of coordination, departmental specialization and professionalization, on two bureaucratic modes, the relative size of the administrative-clerical staff and hierarchical differentiation (the supervisory ratio). Thus, by holding constant the level of complexity both in terms of task structure and in terms of departmental specialization, I will be examining one particular structural pattern, namely the relationship between bureaucratic and nonbureaucratic modes of coordination. In doing so, I will deal with some of the implications of my research for the work of Anderson and Warkov, as well as that of Stinchcombe.[4]

DATA AND METHOD

The present study represents one of the first large-scale, systematic

[4] Theodore R. Anderson and Seymour Warkov, "Organizational Size and Functional Complexity: A Study of Administration in Hospitals," *American Sociological Review*, 26 (Feb. 1961), 23–28; Arthur L. Stinchcombe, "Bureaucratic and Craft Administration of Production: A Comparative Study," *Administrative Science Quarterly* 4 (Sept. 1959), 168–87.

applications of the method of comparative-quantitative organizational analysis.[5] It is assumed here that a crucial condition for exploring theoretically expected relationships is the systematic, quantitative analysis of data on a large number of units, in this case, organizations. This approach implies not only the use of structural characteristics of organizations as variables, but also the extension of the comparative method to samples or total populations of organizations.[6]

A unique possibility to study structural patterns in a large number of organizations occurred when almost 7000 U.S. hospitals returned a detailed questionnaire in a survey ad-

ministered by the American Hospital Association to its member hospitals in 1959.[7]

The analysis of the data obtained from the questionnaires involves the conceptualization and operationalization of two major types of organizational characteristics: "discrete" characteristics, referring to organizational autonomy and the complexity of the task structure, and "continuous" variables, referring to organizational size, the degree of specialization on the departmental and on the job (or "functional") level, the degree of professionalization of the organizational labor force, and the degree of bureaucratization, represented here by the supervisory ratio and the relative size of the administrative-clerical staff. The following is a summary of the operational definitions of these variables.

Organizational autonomy. Based on the assumption that differences in ownership and control of hospitals reflect differences in the degree of external control over policies and resources, three types of ownership and control were chosen to represent different degrees of autonomy: (1) federal hospitals, specifically the hospitals under the control of the Veterans Administration, (2) local governmental (state, county, municipal, etc.) hospitals, and (3) voluntary non-profit, non-church related ("community") hospitals. The underlying dimension of organizational autonomy is indicated by the two extremes,

---

[5] This paper is based on a larger comparative study of organizations which was initially formulated in two papers, "A Theoretical Framework for the Comparative Study of Organizations," read at the *Annual Meetings of the Society for Social Research*, University of Chicago, 1962; and "Differential Modes of Coordination in Formal Organizations," read at the *Annual Meetings of the American Sociological Association*, Los Angeles, 1963. The establishment of the Comparative Organization Research Program at the University of Chicago (with Peter M. Blau) in 1964 subsequently led to the expansion of this type of comparative research on organizations. Cf. also Peter M. Blau, Wolf V. Heydebrand, Robert E. Stauffer, "The Structure of Small Bureaucracies," *American Sociological Review*, 31 (1966), 179–91, and Wolf V. Heydebrand, "The Study of Organizations," *Social Science Information*, 6 (Oct. 1967), 59–86.

[6] Paul F. Lazarsfeld, "Interpretation of Statistical Relations as a Research Operation," in Paul F. Lazarsfeld and Morris Rosenberg (eds.), *The Language of Social Research* (New York: Free Press, 1955), pp. 115–25; Paul F. Lazarsfeld and Herbert Menzel, "On the Relation Between Individual and Collective Properties," in Amitai Etzioni (ed.), *Complex Organizations* (New York: Holt, Rinehart, and Winston, 1961), pp. 422–40.

[7] I am grateful to the American Hospital Association and its former Director of Research, Dr. Paul Feldstein, for making these data available to me. I would also like to acknowledge the support provided by George Bugbee and Odin Anderson, Center for Health Administration Studies (formerly Health Information Foundation), University of Chicago, between 1962 and 1964.

with federal hospitals assumed to be least autonomous, and voluntary non-profit hospitals being most autonomous. The local governmental hospitals are assumed to occupy an intermediate position. Since the "distances" or intervals between these three positions on the autonomy dimension are not known, we are dealing here at best with an ordinal scale.

Complexity of Task Structure. Two dimensions are used to indicate the degree of complexity of the task structure: (1) the diversity of major objectives, indicated by the distinction between teaching and non-teaching hospitals, and (2) the number of medical services, indicated by the distinction between psychiatric and general hospitals. The combination of both dichotomies yields different degrees of complexity of the task structure. Thus, the non-teaching psychiatric hospital represents a single-goal, specialized organization with a relatively simple task structure; the general teaching hospital represents a multigoal organization with diverse objectives (medical education in addition to medical service) and a relatively complex task structure.[8]

Organizational Size. Size is measured here by the average daily inpatient census. This measure is highly correlated in the total hospital population with two alternative measures of size: the number of beds ($r = .98$), and the total number of full-time equivalent personnel ($r = .90$).

Functional Specialization. The degree of functional specialization refers to the total amount of internal division of labor and is indicated by the proportion of job titles actually occupied out of a maximum total of 39 distinct titles

which were used as a standard base line across all hospitals. The measure ranges from 0.0 to 1.0.

Departmental Specialization. The degree of departmental specialization is indicated by the Gini coefficient of concentration,[9] based on seven major organizational components or departments: *medical* (salaried physicians, residents, and interns), *professional nursing* (graduate professional nurses), *nonprofessional nursing* (auxiliary nursing personnel), *technical personnel* (medical technologists, X-ray technicians, occupational and physical therapists, pharmacists, etc.), *maintenance* (maintenance, kitchen, housekeeping, and laundry personnel), *administrative-clerical* (business and clerical personnel, including the hospital administrator and his staff), and *other* (a residual category consisting mainly of special technical personnel). The measure ranges from 0.0 to 1.0, with 1.0 indicating a high degree of departmental specialization where the total labor force is evenly distributed

---

[8] The teaching status of a hospital is defined in terms of its affiliation with a medical school and the presence of a program for medical residents and/or interns approved by the American Medical Association.

[9] The Gini coefficient measures the evenness of distribution of the organizational labor force among a number of departments or categories of personnel. Specifically, it measures the deviation from a theoretical distribution in which all categories are of equal size, i.e., it measures the differentiation among categories relative to each other, independent of an arbitrary origin. In order to avoid spurious index correlation between the Gini index and the professional and administrative components, respectively, the Gini coefficient was computed several times, each time with the respective component removed. For a more detailed technical discussion, see Maurice G. Kendall, *The Advanced Theory of Statistics* (London: Griffin, 1943) 1, pp. 43–47. For a substantive discussion and interpretation of the Gini index as a measure of certain structural characteristics of organizations, see my "The Logic of the Gini Index," in Wolf Heydebrand, *Hospital Bureaucracy: A Comparative Study of Organizations* (New York: Dunellen-University Press of Cambridge, 1972), Chap. 10.

among all seven categories or departments, and 0.0 indicating a low degree of departmental specialization where the labor force is concentrated in only one of the seven categories. The measure is highly correlated ($r = .95$) with a similar index of "division of labor" adapted from Gibbs and Martin and computed for all hospitals.[10]

Professionalization. This variable refers to the proportion of graduate professional nurses of the total personnel. Thus, professionalization is an organizational characteristic and does *not* refer to the degree to which nursing, as an occupation, is professionalized.[11]

Hierarchy. The degree of hierarchical differentiation is measured by the proportion of graduate professional nurses

---

[10] Jack P. Gibbs and Walter T. Martin, "Urbanization, Technology, and the Division of Labor," *American Sociological Review*, 27 (1962), 667–77. See also, Jack P. Gibbs and Harley L. Browning, "The Division of Labor, Technology, and the Organization of Production in Twelve Countries," *American Sociological Review*, 31 (1966), 81–92.

[11] The choice of nursing, rather than medicine, as the basis of this measure is justified by the position of each in the organizational division of labor of hospitals. While physicians initiate and direct the patient care process, nurses are responsible for its continuous implementation. Thus, nurses are seen here as the "production component" of the hospital labor force; cf. Everett C. Hughes, *Men and Their Work* (New York: Free Press, 1958), pp. 73–74; Robert W. Habenstein and Edwin A. Christ, *Professionalizer, Traditionalizer, Utilizer* (Columbia: University of Missouri Press, 1955); Hans O. Mauksch, "The Organizational Context of Nursing Practice," in Fred Davis (ed.), *The Nursing Profession* (New York: John Wiley, 1966), pp. 109–37. Significantly, the Joint Commission on Accreditation of Hospitals requires an accredited hospital to have a professional nurse on duty at all times, but not a licensed physician; cf. *Hospital Accreditation References* (Chicago: American Hospital Association, 1961), pp. x–xi.

who occupy administrative and supervisory positions.[12]

Administrative-clerical Staff. The relative size of the administrative-clerical staff refers to the proportion of personnel in business and clerical positions, *including* the hospital administrator and his immediate staff, but *excluding* department heads as well as nurses in administrative and supervisory positions.[13]

Table 1 gives the means of the six quantitative variables[14] for all

---

[12] This measure of hierarchical differentiation is equivalent to, although not identical with the *supervisory ratio* within the main administrative line structure of hospitals. In hospitals, this line structure extends from the hospital administrator through the director of Nursing Service to assistant directors, supervisors, headnurses, and staff nurses. In calculating this measure, supervisors were counted as "administrative-supervisory" personnel, whereas headnurses were counted as nonadministrative personnel, together with staff nurses. The rationale for this procedure was derived from Habenstein and Christ, *Professionalizer, Traditionalizer, Utilizer.* It should be noted that the larger the proportion, the greater is the degree of hierarchical differentiation. This relationship assumes an increase in the number of levels as the proportion of administrative-supervisory personnel increases. It implies, therefore, a certain constancy in the supervisory span of control from level to level, rather than assuming that a small proportion of supervisors implies centralization of decision making and control at the top level.

[13] This measure is, of course, similar to the well-known A/P ratio, but it excludes technical, salaried, maintenance, and other "supportive" personnel categories. Cf. Reinhard Bendix, *Work and Authority in Industry* (New York: Harper Torchbooks, 1963), pp. 216–17.

[14] Most of the technical operations involved in the preparation of the data and in the analysis were carried out by computer. A special program was written to transform the raw data into the required variables on each of the 6825 hospitals. I am indebted to Sanford Abrams for writing this program and for helping to prepare the data

TABLE 1 Means of Six Variables

	ALL U.S. HOSPITALS	ALL 12 GROUPS	Voluntary Non-Profit				State & Local Governmental				Federal: Veterans Administration			
			NON-TEACH		TEACH		NON-TEACH		TEACH		NON-TEACH		TEACH	
			PSY (1)	GEN (2)	PSY (3)	GEN (4)	PSY (5)	GEN (6)	PSY (7)	GEN (8)	PSY (9)	GEN (10)	PSY (11)	GEN (12)
N =	6,825	3,544	30	1507	13	467	139	956	91	185	23	56	17	60
1. Size (Average Daily Patient Census)	193	253	80	58	195	249	1812	49	2326	385	1161	281	1595	611
2. Functional Specialization (% Job Titles Occupied)	51	54	37	49	58	75	53	43	67	72	67	65	74	75
3. Departmental Specialization (Gini coefficient)	.53	.54	.52	.52	.61	.63	.43	.50	.51	.63	.56	.65	.58	.72
4. Professionalization (% Professional Graduate Nurses)	22	23	13	27	12	23	5	22	8	18	8	15	8	14
5. Hierarchy (% Administrative Nurses: "Supervisory Ratio")	30	27	45	27	45	13	44	33	27	18	15	13	12	10
6. Administrative Staff (% Business Clerical Personnel)	8	8	8	8	8	9	6	8	6	8	12	18	11	17

U.S. hospitals (N = 6825), for the combined twelve subgroups resulting from the three-way classification in terms of ownership and control, teaching status, and type of medical service (N = 3544), and for each of the twelve subgroups. For each of these twelve groups, the number of cases is identical with, or approximates closely, the actual number of cases in the total hospital population in 1959.

The main points to be noted about the variables given in Table 1 are as follows. Psychiatric hospitals tend to be larger than general hospitals, and teaching hospitals tend to be larger than non-teaching hospitals. Federal and local governmental hospitals tend to be larger than voluntary non-profit

hospitals. In terms of functional and departmental specialization, general and teaching hospitals are internally more differentiated than psychiatric and non-teaching hospitals. Federal hospitals tend to have a higher level of internal structural complexity than either of the other two categories of ownership and control. General hospitals are more professionalized than psychiatric hospitals. Since professionalization is inversely related to size, the larger hospitals in all categories appear to have a lower level of professionalization, a relationship which disappears when size is controlled. A similar effect may be observed with respect to the relative size of the administrative-clerical staff as well as hierarchy. Therefore, the differences between the twelve subgroup means of professionalization and the two measures of bureaucratization reflect the hidden influence of size, in addition to the influence of autonomy and task structure. However, it is worth noting that the relative size of the administrative-clerical staff is significantly larger in the V.A. hospitals than in hospitals under other types of ownership and control. This observation, suggesting the presence of the proverbial "red tape" of government agencies, i.e., of nonautonomous organizations, needs to be tempered by the fact that the V.A. hospitals have a consistently higher level of internal structural complexity than other types. Since V.A. hospitals are also relatively large, the question of the relative effect of size, complexity, and autonomy on the relative size of the administrative staff appears in a new light and suggests the need to investigate these relationships *within* different categories of ownership and control, as well as of task structure. However, we may already con-

for computer input, to David Kleinman for his generous advice on various phases of data processing, and to Allen Herzog for making available his program version for the multivariate analysis of variance (MANOVA). The analysis of structural differences between the twelve hospital types was done by means of an analysis of variance and covariance; the analysis of structural relationships within types was based on multiple regression and correlation. The analysis was performed at the University of Chicago Computation Center whose support under grants from the National Institutes of Health (USPHS Grant FR 00013 from the Division of Research, Facilities and Resources) and from the National Science Foundation is gratefully acknowledged. In the respective statistical analyses, transformations of the actual variables were used. The logarithmic scale was used for the size variable (average daily census) since it ranged from six to over 8000. The arcs in transformation was used for the Gini coefficient and the proportions; cf. Helen Walker and Joseph Lev, *Statistical Inference* (New York: Holt, Rinehart & Winston, 1953), pp. 423–24. Table I gives the means for each of the variables *before* transformation so as to retain their descriptive character.

TABLE 2 INTERCORRELATIONS AMONG SIX VARIABLES ($N = 6825$)

Variables	1	2	3	4	5
1. Size	–				
2. Functional Specialization	.75	–			
3. Departmental Specialization	.29	.59	–		
4. Professionalization	−.33	−.03	.01	–	
5. Hierarchy	−.34	−.49	−.37	−.32	–
6. Administrative-Clerical Staff	−.13	−.04	.09	.06	−.03

clude at this point that the differences in *levels of internal structural complexity*, independent of the task structure variables, point to important differences between the V.A. system, the state and locally controlled hospitals, and the "private" community hospitals.[15]

In line with the question raised in the preceding paragraph, I will now turn to a more detailed analysis of the effect of autonomy and task structure on the internal division of labor as well as on the internal bureaucratization of hospitals.

THE EFFECTS OF AUTONOMY AND TASK STRUCTURE ON INTERNAL DIVISION OF LABOR AND BUREAUCRATIZATION

In hospitals, the general pattern of interrelationships among structural variables illustrates the theoretical expectations one might have concerning the structural properties of work organizations, in general, and of professional organizations, in particular. Thus, size has a positive effect on functional and departmental specialization, but a negative effect on professionalization (see Table 2). That

size should have a negative effect on bureaucratization may contradict Parkinsonian expectations, but fits with the notion of "economy of scale" as well as a host of empirical studies of work organizations in which such a negative effect has been observed.[16] To classical organization theorists it may also come as a surprise that functional and departmental specialization, both indicators of internal structural complexity, should be negatively related to hierarchical differentiation, and almost not at all related to the relative size of the administrative-clerical staff. However, proponents of a normative conception of professionalism should be encouraged by the negative correlation between hierarchy and professionalization.

While these relationships may tell us something about certain regularities in the variability of structural patterns, they clearly do not permit us to generalize about the structure of professional organizations, let alone the structure of all organizations. Simple correlations between different dimensions of "organization" or "bureaucracy," if taken at face value, imply a simplistic, additive conception of organizations,

---

[15] Cf. James A. Hamilton, *Patterns of Hospital Ownership and Control* (Minneapolis: University of Minnesota Press, 1961), pp. 25–66.

[16] Louis R. Pondy, "Effects of Size, Complexity, and Ownership on Administrative Intensity," *Administrative Science Quarterly,* 14 (March 1969) 47–61.

rather than one in which different dimensions are seen as potentially contradictory, functionally interdependent, or as interacting with each other as, for example, when size and functional specialization are controlled in relation to bureaucratization. Moreover, simple correlations do not reveal the variability of structural patterns which is due to the variation in basic organizational parameters such as environmental complexity, autonomy, and task complexity.

Let me, therefore, first examine the effect of autonomy and task structure on size and on the two indicators of internal structural complexity, viz., functional specialization and departmental specialization.

First of all, it is clear that organizational autonomy (the three types of ownership and control) has a strong effect on size and internal structure (Table 3, col. 1, rows 1, 2, and 3).[17] This effect remains relatively strong and stable when size and functional specialization are introduced as control variables (Table 3, col. 1, rows 4, 5, and 6). Organizational autonomy can therefore be viewed as an important determinant of size and internal structure, even though auton-

omy "interacts" to some extent with task structure (Table 3, cols. 4–7).

It is interesting to recall in this connection that the V.A. hospitals have a fairly high and constant level of functional specialization, while range and variability is greater among the voluntary hospitals, despite the fact that in this group the size differences are smaller. This suggests that especially voluntary hospitals vary in their staffing policies, while the V.A. hospitals have a more uniform procedure of listing and filling positions. This finding is in line with the widely shared notion that federal hospitals are more "planned" as organizations than other types.

The smaller differences in functional specialization among the V.A. hospitals, in spite of considerable size differences, suggest also that functional specialization varies directly with size only up to a certain maximum. Once a certain size limit is reached, the increase in functional specialization levels off.

In general, we can say that although the effect of autonomy is largely mediated by the complexity of the structure (see the significant interaction effects involving autonomy, Table 3), it nevertheless reaches into the internal structure of hospitals and helps to determine the level of the division of labor.

As to the main effects of task structure variables (teaching and service) on size, it is obvious that they are extremely strong and that, for all practical purposes, size can be considered as one aspect of the complexity of the task structure in that it articulates the volume of the task. With respect to functional specialization, the difference between teaching and non-teaching hospitals also generates an unusually high F-value,

---

[17] Table 3 gives the results of an analysis of variance describing and summarizing the differences between cell means in Table 1, rows 1, 2, and 3, hospital types 1 through 12. In Table 1—in contrast to Table 3—the "main effects" can be directly inspected by comparing the relevant groups of cells, e.g., the size differences between psychiatric and general hospitals, and among the three types of ownership and control. In Table 3, the interaction effects between autonomy and task structure variables are above the level of significance, indicating that the main effects are *not* independent of each other. However, it will be noted that the interaction is reduced when size and functional specialization are used as controls.

TABLE 3 THE EFFECTS OF OWNERSHIP AND CONTROL, TEACHING STATUS, AND SERVICE ON SIZE, FUNCTIONAL AND DEPARTMENTAL SPECIALIZATION, ALONE AND WITH SIZE (AND FUNCTIONAL SPECIALIZATION) CONTROLLED

F-Ratios*

| | MAIN EFFECTS | | | INTERACTIONS | | | |
| | Autonomy: | Complexity of Task Structure: | | First Order | | | Second Order |
Dependent Variables Alone:	Ownership and Control	Teaching	Service	Autonomy × Teaching	Autonomy × Service	Teaching × Service	
1. Size	404.00	2149.85	1834.87	14.15	215.37	153.12	15.29
2. Functional Specialization	136.92	1320.91	10.54	20.96	30.43	27.54	5.25
3. Departmental Specialization	325.02	1106.31	317.90	12.95	25.16	10.54	.27
With Controls:							
4. Functional Specialization with Size Controlled	281.94	7.71	1119.49	7.22	58.99	29.94	1.00
5. Departmental Specialization with Size Controlled	261.62	342.70	520.48	7.95	61.54	.23	.58
6. Departmental Specialization with Size and Functional Specialization Controlled	222.58	371.60	58.71	3.54	34.35	10.59	.13
$df_1 =$	2	1	1	2	2	1	2

*F-Ratios needed for significance at the .01 level:
4.60 ($df_1 = 2$), 6.64 ($df_1 = 1$); $df_2 = 3532$ (for all effects).

169

TABLE 4 SIMPLE CORRELATION COEFFICIENTS (r), PARTIAL REGRESSION COEFFICIENTS (b*) AND MULTIPLE CORRELATION COEFFICIENTS (R) FOR SIZE, FUNCTIONAL SPECIALIZATION, AND ADMINISTRATIVE STAFF BY OWNERSHIP AND CONTROL, TEACHING STATUS, AND SERVICE

| | U.S. HOSPITALS | ALL 12 GROUPS | Voluntary Non-Profit | | | | State & Local Governmental | | | | Federal: Veterans Administration | | | |
| | | | NON-TEACH | | TEACH | | NON-TEACH | | TEACH | | NON-TEACH | | TEACH | |
			(1) PSY	(2) GEN	(3) PSY	(4) GEN	(5) PSY	(6) GEN	(7) PSY	(8) GEN	(9) PSY	(10) GEN	(11) PSY	(12) GEN
$N=$	6,825	3,544	30	1,507	13	467	139	956	91	185	23	56	17	60
Simple Correlation Coefficients (r)														
1. Size and Administrative Staff	−.13	−.01	.05	.01	−.63	−.10	−.33	.00	−.66	−.24	−.27	−.14	−.18	−.08
2. Functional Specialization and Administrative Staff	−.04	.12	−.32	.07	−.73	−.12	.01	.05	−.49	−.17	.14	−.09	−.32	−.15
3. Size and Functional Specialization	.75	.74	.61	.79	.83	.82	.51	.17	.67	.83	.39	.79	.01	.54
Partial Regression Coefficients (b)*														
4. Size on Administrative Staff	−.22*	−.22*	.39	−.11*	−.08	−.02	−.45*	−.07	−.60*	−.33*	−.39	−.18	−.18	.00
5. Functional Specialization on Administrative Staff	.12*	.28*	−.55*	.16*	−.66	−.11	.23*	.10*	−.09	.10	.29	.05	−.32	−.15
Multiple Correlation Coefficients (R) and Coefficients of Determination (R²)														
6. Multiple R	.15	.19	.44	.10	.73	.12	.39	.07	.66	.25	.38	.14	.37	.15
7. Coefficients of Determination (R²)	.023	.036	.194	.010	.533	.014	.152	.005	.436	.063	.144	.020	.137	.023

* Indicates that the value for b* is at least twice its error.

while the effect of service is barely significant (Table 3, row 2). For departmental specialization, both teaching and service effects are highly significant (Table 3, row 3). However, since we have already observed the influence of size on both functional and departmental specialization (see Table 2) as well as the strong association between size and task structure (Table 3, row 1), we must take the presence of the significant size differences between psychiatric and general, as well as between teaching and non-teaching hospitals into account. When size is used as a control variable, the results are rather striking (Table 3, rows 4 and 5). Compared to the situation where functional specialization is analyzed alone, the effects of teaching and service are completely reversed (Table 3, row 2 vs. row 4).

As to the influence of service (general versus psychiatric hospitals) on functional specialization, the data lend strong support to the hypothesis that when size is held constant, specialized unifunctional organizations are internally less differentiated than complex multifunctional organizations. These results provide empirical confirmation for our initial assumption that the distinction between psychiatric and general hospitals yields a meaningful dimension of task complexity, and that the complexity of the goal and task structure is reflected in the internal structural complexity of the organization.[18]

The effects of teaching and service on departmental specialization operate essentially in the same way as those on functional specialization. When size is controlled (Table 3, row 5), the effect of teaching is reduced, while the effect of service increases.

Finally, when both size and functional specialization are used as control variables, the F-ratio for the service effect drops, while that of the teaching effect increases slightly (Table 3, row 6). It is of some interest that the difference between teaching and nonteaching hospitals should become greater when size and functional specialization are held constant. It suggests that the complexity introduced by diversification (i.e., teaching in addition to service) is of a different nature than that distinguishing unifunctional organizations (e.g., psychiatric hospitals) from multifunctional ones (e.g., general hospitals). Put in very simple terms, one could say that a minimum *number of jobs*, i.e., some minimum of functional specialization, must be present in a given organization before any *relationship among the different jobs* or, essentially, departmental specialization can develop. In other words, functional specialization is a necessary condition for departmental specialization.[19]

---

[18] By implication, these findings confirm the validity of the distinction between general and TB hospitals in terms of functional complexity which Anderson and Warkov used as the basis of their study. For Anderson and Warkov it was important to control for size because the V.A. general hospitals are larger, on the average, than the TB hospitals. In the present case, size has to be controlled because the less complex psychiatric hospitals are the larger ones; while the general hospitals are smaller. The only exception occurs among the voluntary teaching hospitals, where the general hospitals are somewhat larger than the psychiatric ones. Cf. Anderson and Warkov, "Organizational Size and Functional Complexity."

[19] This relationship between the two aspects of the internal division of labor is all the more important as both are independent

Further, from the perspective of the organizational level, one may say that a number of specialized activities (as, e.g., in a general hospital) must be present before diversification (e.g., teaching) can develop in an organization.

AUTONOMY, TASK STRUCTURE AND INTERNAL BUREAUCRATIZATION

To illustrate the effects of autonomy and task structure on internal structural elements in still another way, let us briefly look at the much debated set of relationships between size, functional specialization and the relative size of the administrative-clerical staff *within* each of the twelve subgroups (Table 4, rows 1, 2, and 3), as well as the separate and joint effects of size and functional specialization on this measure of bureaucratization (Table 4, rows 4, 5, and 6).

First of all, as expected, the variations in organizational autonomy, as indicated by the three types of ownership and control, as well as the variations in the degree of the complexity of the task structure (teaching vs nonteaching, psychiatric vs general hospitals) generate a considerable amount of variation in the relationship between size and the relative size of the administrative-clerical staff (Table 4, row 1). The generally negative relationship tends to be stronger in the structurally simpler psychiatric hospitals, and more moderate—but also somewhat less variable—among the structurally more complex federal hospitals.

---

measures, the former being based on the proportion of specialized functions, the latter on the relation among categorically defined organizational components.

Secondly, the relationship between functional specialization and the relative size of the administrative-clerical staff is relatively unstable. Nevertheless, eight out of twelve hospital types show an unexpected negative relationship, with psychiatric teaching hospitals ranking highest in this respect (Table 4, row 2, types 3, 7, and 11).

Finally, the strong positive relationship between size and functional specialization remains strong for almost all types, although definite variations due to autonomy and task structure can be observed (Table 4, row 3). Because of these variations, it is of some interest to examine the separate and joint effects of size and functional specialization on the relative size of the administrative-clerical staff.

In the multiple regression of size and functional specialization on the relative size of the administrative-clerical staff, the relationship of each of the two independent variables to the dependent variable is sharpened and articulated (Table 4, rows 4 and 5). The effect of size becomes generally more negative, whereas the effect of functional specialization becomes more clearly patterned than in the zero-order relationship.

The general result of controlling for the joint influence of size and functional specialization on bureaucratization is to exhibit a pattern in which the negative effect of size tends to be complemented by a positive contribution of functional specialization. But here again, as in Table 3, there is evidence of some degree of interaction between size and functional specialization.

Our findings suggest that a positive relationship between functional specialization and administrative staff obtains particularly for intermediate levels of functional specialization, i.e., in the non-teaching general hospitals (types 2, 6, and 10). In these types, specialization and differentiation are neither frozen on a relatively low level due to technological factors or budgetary limitations, nor have they reached a ceiling or plateau due to standardization or to limits of expansion imposed by external control. These observations hold also for two of the three non-teaching psychiatric hospital types (types 5 and 9).

By contrast, in the teaching hospitals the joint control of size and functional specialization tends to produce a reduction of the generally negative effect of size on the administrative staff, and the appearance of a negative effect of functional specialization. Moreover, in the internally more complex general hospitals, joint control of both variables leads to their convergence toward zero, and to a consequent reduction of their joint explanatory value for the relative size of the administrative-clerical staff, as reflected in the low multiple correlation coefficient (R) or its square (Table 4, rows 6 and 7).

Substantively, a negative effect of functional specialization on bureaucratization may be interpreted in terms of a dialectical conception of the division of labor. Functional specialization measures the amount of the overall division of labor, i.e., the specialization among work functions formally defined by job titles and job descriptions. Any change in the number of functions necessary for the performance of given tasks will have distinct consequences for the total organization of work, especially if it is made up of interdependent work processes. For example, an increase in functional specialization, starting from a relatively low level, may at first require an increase in size (i.e., personnel and volume of service) which in turn manifests itself in role differentiation and the delegation of functions. Further specialization requires a larger administrative staff, but also generates new skill levels, particularly professional ones which reduce the need for procedural communications and thus tend to cancel the positive effect of specialization on the administrative staff. However, still further increases in functional specialization (due to a more complex technology, or changes in the organizational goal structure, or volume of service, or simply administrative decree) produce a reorganization of the work processes such that additional skill levels and intermediate structural levels, e.g., departments, must be instituted.

These structural changes create complex problems for overall organizational coordination that would lead one to expect a sharp increase in the relative size of the administrative-clerical staff. Instead, however, the structural changes create new interdependencies, especially among those subunits that tend toward equal size and power. Consequently, the subunits develop a capacity to absorb the relative overload of friction and lateral communication. For this reason it is held that further increases in functional specialization from an already high level generate new modes of coordination which are nonbureaucratic while at the same time impeding, or at least not pressing, the further expansion of the administrative staff.

The two apparent exceptions (types 1 and 8) to the general pattern observed in Table 4 are not inconsistent with this interpretation. Thus, in the voluntary non-teaching psychiatric hospitals (type 1) functional specialization is negatively related to the administrative staff. In these psychiatric hospitals, the level of functional specialization is exceedingly low ($\overline{X}$ = 37%, see Table 1). They also tend to be very small as compared to the other psychiatric types. In these hospitals, unlike any of the other twelve types, the partial effect of size on the relative size of the administrative-clerical staff is positive (b* = .39, Table 4, row 4). It may be suggested that the overriding organizational problem of these private psychiatric non-teaching hospitals is to increase their size and volume of service (including, of course, their occupancy rate which generally tends to increase with size). At the same time, changes in the internal division of labor may occur at a much lower rate due to budgetary limitations or poor planning, thus producing a fairly strong negative relationship between functional specialization and the administrative staff (b* = −.55, Table 4, row 5).

On the other hand, in the general teaching hospitals controlled by state and local governments (type 8), the effect of size is negative while functional specialization has a slightly positive effect on the administrative staff. This deviates somewhat from the pattern observed in the other two general teaching types (types 4 and 12) both of which are internally more complex. However, the possibility should not be ruled out that here the type of external control (viz., state and local governments) generates, for once, a mild Parkinsonian syndrome, namely, the proliferation and symbiosis of functional and administrative roles, including the provision of patronage jobs.

In sum, functional specialization as well as the implicit structural differentiation that goes with it appear to be dependent on the *absolute level* as well as *relative changes* in size, but not completely so. I am arguing here that there are lower and upper limits in the degree to which functions are subdivided in a hospital of a given size and under given technological condition. Organizational growth and expansion produces internal as well as external ramifications. Thus, an increase in size has definite consequences for the internal elaboration of the division of labor such as the establishment of a clerical pool, a personnel department and other subunits.

However, if new objectives, products or tasks are added due to external pressures and diversification (e.g., adding teaching to service) it is likely that the causal direction between size and functional specialization is reversed so that there will be a further increase in size and facilities to accommodate the increased complexity, and to justify it economically and financially. Furthermore, the analysis presented in Table 4 suggests that the effects of the complexity of the task structure and of functional specialization on bureaucratization are not simply additive, i.e., an increase in functional specialization within the more complex hospital types does not imply a proportional increase in the administrative staff. On the contrary, the higher the *level* of functional specialization within a given type, the less will a *further increase* in functional specialization have a *positive* effect on the administrative staff. In fact, on a comparatively high level of functional specialization, any further increase will have a negative effect on the relative size of the administrative-clerical staff.

Considering the joint, interactive effect of size and functional specialization on internal bureaucratization, we may conclude that the negative feedback observed here is due to the fact that the relative size of the administrative staff increases at a decreasing rate as a degree of internal structural differentiation of an organization increases. In part, this is due to the fact that the degree of functional specialization itself increases at a decreasing rate as the size of the organization increases. However, it is also due to the fact that increasing functional specialization gives rise to departmental specialization, i.e., to the elaboration of the internal division of labor in terms of subunits and the development of new structural levels.

I have interpreted these findings in terms of certain contradictory effects of the division of labor. If an organization changes in its internal division of labor towards a higher level of structural differentiation and greater complexity, nonbureaucratic modes of coordination emerging at intermediate levels of the organization tend to reduce the need for overall administrative coordination. The specific effect of these new structural elements, viz., departmental specialization and professionalization, will be discussed in the next section of this paper.

However, before turning to this discussion, I want to draw attention to a theoretically related point concerning the joint effect of size and functional specialization on the administrative staff. The multiple correlation coefficients (R) in Table 4 are consistently larger for the psychiatric as compared to the general

hospitals. This pattern holds throughout, i.e., when other variables not shown in this table are considered. While an explanation of these differences cannot be attempted on the basis of the effects of size and functional specialization alone, there is reason to suggest that specialized professional organizations such as psychiatric hospitals operate more like closed systems which have rigid organizational boundaries as well as a more integrated, unitary structure due to the greater homogeneity of the professional staff. In fact, system models of organizations appear to be more applicable to these types of professional organizations than to their more complex and diffuse counterparts. Thus, if changes in the basic organizational variables such as size or functional specialization occur they tend to have strong repercussions throughout the internal structure.

By contrast, the multifunctional and more diversified general hospitals appear to have permeable, flexible boundaries and a more open and diffuse structure which is more responsive and adaptive to changes in the external environment.[20] Such com-

---

[20] Similar observations have been reported for other kinds of organizations which have undergone technological and structural change from simple unifunctional forms to more complex, multifunctional ones, as for example, universities, medical schools, research organizations, business corporations, welfare agencies, and the military establishment. Cf. Clark Kerr's conception of the "multiversity," Clark Kerr, *The Uses of the University* (Cambridge: Harvard University Press, 1962); A. H. Halsey, "The Changing Functions of Universities in Advanced Industrial Societies," *Harvard Educational Review*, 30 (1960), pp. 118–27; Robert K. Merton, George Reader, Patricia L. Kendall (eds.), *The Student-Physician* (Cambridge: Harvard University Press, 1957); Peter H. Rossi, "Researchers,

plex organizations are less likely to operate as integrated systems. Since they are more amorphous and pluralistic, if not more chaotic, than structurally simpler organizations, they cannot be as easily analyzed in terms of system models of formal organizations. At best, they may be seen to operate as "open systems."[21]

A partial test of this hypothesis

consists in examining the effect of the external environment such as the degree of urbanization and the relation between the hospital and other organizations on the internal structure. As to the effect of the complexity of the external environment, e.g., urbanization, on the mutability and plasticity of the internal structure, our data tend to support this interpretation.[22]

NONBUREAUCRATIC COORDINATION: DEPARTMENTAL SPECIALIZATION AND PROFESSIONALIZATION

The preceding analysis of the internal structural variation among hospitals suggests that departmental specialization, as measured by the Gini coefficient of concentration, may be viewed as a theoretically and empirically powerful indicator of the internal division of labor, i.e., of internal structural complexity.[23] Departmental specialization was shown to reach its highest level in those hospitals which have the most complex task structure, viz., general teaching hospitals. Since these hospitals are also among the most professionalized, as

Scholars, and Policymakers: The Politics of Large Scale Research," *Daedalus*, 93 (1964), pp. 1142–61; Warren G. Bennis, *Changing Organizations* (New York: McGraw-Hill), pp. 3–78; Edward S. Mason (ed.), *The Corporation in Modern Society* (Cambridge: Harvard University Press, 1959); Wilbert E. Moore, *The Conduct of the Corporation* (New York: Random House, 1962), pp. 180–276; Kenneth E. Boulding, "Alienation and Economic Development: The Larger Background of the Settlement Movement," in *Neighborhood Goals in a Rapidly Changing World* (New York: National Federation of Settlements and Neighborhood Centers, 1958), pp. 61–69; and his *The Organizational Revolution* (New York: Harper and Row, 1953); Wolf V. Heydebrand, "On the Process of Organizational Association in Welfare Organizations" (unpublished manuscript, University of Chicago, 1966); Morris Janowitz, *The Professional Soldier* (New York: Free Press, 1960). In an earlier study Janowitz writes: "The complexity of the machinery of warfare and the requirements of research, development, and technical maintenance tend to weaken the organizational boundary between the military and the nonmilitary. . . ." Morris Janowitz, *Sociology and the Military Establishment* (New York: Russell Sage Foundation, 1959), pp. 16–17.

[21] Daniel Katz and Robert L. Kahn, *The Social Psychology of Organizations* (New York: John Wiley, 1966), pp. 14–29; James D. Thompson, *Organizations in Action* (New York: McGraw-Hill, 1967); for a recent discussion of "social chaos" in terms of Durkheim's notion of "anomie," see Philip M. Hauser, "The Chaotic Society: Product of the Social Morphological Revolution," *American Sociological Review*, 34 (Feb. 1969), 1–19.

[22] When the size of the Standard Metropolitan Statistical Area in which the hospital is located is used as a measure of the degree of urbanization and differentiation of the hospital environment, it is in fact more highly correlated with the various measures of internal structure in general hospitals than in psychiatric hospitals.

[23] For a recent application of the closely related Gibbs-Martin index of division of labor, see William A. Rushing, "The Effects of Industry Size and Division of Labor on Administration," *Administrative Science Quarterly*, 12 (Sept. 1967), 273–95.

TABLE 5 Correlations Between Departmental Specialization and 1. Professionalization, 2. The Relative Size of the Administrative-Clerical Staff, and 3. The Supervisory Ratio, by Service, Teaching Status, and Ownership and Control

	U.S. Hospitals	All 12 Groups	Voluntary				State and Local Government				Federal (V.A.)				Within-Group Homogeneity*
			Non-teach		Teach		Non-teach		Teach		Non-teach		Teach		
			(1)	(2)	(3)	(4)	(5)	(6)	(7)	(8)	(9)	(10)	(11)	(12)	
			PSY	GEN	PSY	GEN	PSY	GEN	PSY	GEN	PSY	GEN	PSY	GEN	
N =	6,825	3,544	30	1,507	13	467	139	956	91	185	23	56	17	60	
1. Professionalization	.01	.03	.26	.15	−.04	−.17	.24	.16	.63	−.20	.58	−.35	.36	.18	0
2. Administrative-Clerical Staff	.09	.21	.11	.06	.04	−.10	.23	.06	.55	−.20	.24	−.13	−.60	−.16	8
3. Supervisory Ratio	−.37	−.37	−.07	−.25	−.31	−.27	−.28	−.22	−.21	−.44	−.14	−.18	.04	−.16	11

*Number of groups with a correlation coefficient lower (in absolute numbers) than that of the combined 12 groups (Col. 2).

well as among those with the relatively largest administrative-clerical staff and the smallest supervisory ratio, the question arises as to the intervening effect of departmental specialization and professionalization on both of these aspects of bureaucratization. Presumably, departmental specialization should serve to increase both bureaucratization and professionalization, but professionalization is assumed to have a negative effect on bureaucratization. Let us look at the data in question.

The simple (zero-order) correlations between departmental specialization and professionalization as well as bureaucratization give a foretaste of the nature of this fairly complex set of relationships (Table 5). First of all, we see that professionalization is not directly related to departmental specialization if we look at all U.S. hospitals or the combined twelve groups (Table 5, row 1, columns 1 and 2). But among the twelve groups, there are certain significant variations in this relationship.[24] Thus, in

psychiatric hospitals, professionalization tends to be positively related to departmental specialization, but the correlation tends to be lower or even negative in general hospitals.

Similarly, the relative size of the administrative-clerical staff tends to be positively related to departmental specialization in the psychiatric hospitals, but the relationship becomes negative in the more complex teaching general hospitals and in most of the V.A. hospitals (Table 5, row 2).

Clearly, the relationship between professionalization and bureaucratization, on the one hand, and internal structural complexity on the other, appears to depend on the *level* of internal complexity at which this relationship is being considered. Thus, whether we use as indicators of the complexity level the degree of complexity of the task structure, or the degree of functional or departmental specialization, both professionalization and the relative size of the administrative-clerical staff tend to be negatively related to departmental specialization in those hospitals where the level of complexity is relatively high.[25]

The relationship between hierar-

[24] Note that the within-group homogeneity is low, as shown by the fact that all within-group correlations are higher than that for the combined total of the 12 groups ($N = 3544$). This "index" is useful to the extent that it shows whether the correlations observed in the ungrouped total of 3544 hospitals tend to be higher, to remain substantially the same, or to be lower when they are computed *within* the twelve "cells" generated by the three-way classification of hospitals. The overall relationship between any two variables can be assumed to be the result of greater within-group variance if this index approaches zero; or the result of greater between-group variance (or within-group homogeneity) if the index approaches "12," provided that the correlation coefficients do not have values close to the one observed in the ungrouped total. If this latter condition should occur we would conclude that the dimensions of sub-classification do not elaborate, specify, or

explain the observed overall relationship. For a description and application of this technique, see Leo F. Schnore, "The Statistical Measurement of Urbanization and Economic Development," *Land Economics,* 37 (1961), 239; on the general idea of multivariate analysis involved here, see Paul F. Lazarsfeld, "Interpretation of Statistical Relations as a Research Operation," *In* Paul F. Lazarsfeld and Morris Rosenberg (eds.), *The Language of Social Research* (New York: Free Press, 1955), pp. 115–23.

[25] Note that in these correlations the respective structural components used (% professional nurses, % administrative-clerical staff) are removed from the Gini index so as to avoid spurious correlation.

chical coordination (the supervisory ratio) and departmental specialization presents a somewhat different picture (Table 5, row 3). First of all, the relationship in the hospital universe and the combined twelve groups is moderately negative. Secondly, most of the correlations within the groups, while also negative, are lower.

The generally negative character of the relationship between the supervisory ratio and departmental specialization suggests that the extent of hierarchical coordination decreases as a result of departmental specialization. The greater the internal structural complexity of hospitals, the smaller the supervisory ratio.

Let us now turn to a multivariate analysis of this relationship, using the relative size of the administrative-clerical staff and the supervisory ratio as dependent variables, respectively, with departmental specialization, professionalization, and size as the independent variables. (Table 6).

The results of this analysis generally clarify and strengthen the findings based on the simple correlations, as shown above in Table 5 as well as those discussed earlier (Tables 2 and 4).

The upper panel of Table 6 (Panel A) shows the joint effect of departmental specialization, professionalization and size on the relative size of the administrative-clerical staff.

First, we note the fact that the relationship between departmental specialization and the administrative staff changes from moderately positive to zero and moderately negative as the internal complexity of the organizational types increases. The state mental hospitals are among the least complex, but it is here where an increasing degree of departmental specialization contributes most to an increase in the relative size of a specialized administrative staff. And again, it is among voluntary psychiatric teaching and especially the V.A. hospitals that the inverse relationships between departmental specialization and bureaucratization becomes most pronounced.

Corresponding to this change from a positive to a negative relationship is an almost perfectly "parallel" but opposite change in the relation between professionalization and bureaucratization as we move from the less to the more internally differentiated organizational structures, especially among psychiatric hospitals (from types 5 and 7 to 1, 3, 9, and 11). Thus, it is in the voluntary psychiatric teaching and the V.A. psychiatric hospitals that the positive relationship between professionalization and bureaucratization most visibly complements the negative one between departmental specialization and bureaucratization.

The pattern observed here holds particularly for psychiatric hospitals, but not as clearly for general hospitals. As I have already suggested, psychiatric hospitals appear to conform more closely to the idea of a "professional organization" integrated by a relatively homogeneous professional staff. An increase in internal differentiation and complexity can therefore be expected to have particularly salient ramifications for both kind and degree of professionalization in such hospitals. In general hospitals, on the other hand, "professionalization" refers to a greater diversity of task-specific nursing functions, thus making the concept and its empirical referent more diffuse, and blurring the relationship between professionalization and bureaucratization. It should be obvious that this

TABLE 6 THE JOINT EFFECT OF DEPARTMENTAL SPECIALIZATION, PROFESSIONALIZATION, AND SIZE ON TWO MEASURES OF BUREAUCRATIZATION: REGRESSION COEFFICIENTS (b*) AND MULTIPLE R^2'S FOR THE RELATIVE SIZE OF THE ADMINISTRATIVE-CLERICAL STAFF (UPPER PANEL) AND THE SUPERVISORY RATIO (LOWER PANEL) AS DEPENDENT VARIABLES, RESPECTIVELY, AND DEPARTMENTAL SPECIALIZATION, PROFESSIONALIZATION, AND SIZE AS INDEPENDENT VARIABLES, BY SERVICE, TEACHING STATUS, AND OWNERSHIP AND CONTROL

	U.S. HOSPITALS	ALL 12 GROUPS	Voluntary				State and Local Governmental				Federal (V.A.)			
			NON-TEACH		TEACH		NON-TEACH		TEACH		NON-TEACH		TEACH	
			(1)	(2)	(3)	(4)	(5)	(6)	(7)	(8)	(9)	(10)	(11)	(12)
			PSY	GEN	PSY	GEN	PSY	GEN	PSY	GEN	PSY	GEN	PSY	GEN
$N =$	6,825	3,544	30	1,507	13	467	139	956	91	185	23	56	17	60
						A. Administrative-Clerical Staff as Dependent Variable								
1. Departmental Specialization	.14	.23	.12	.06	−.09	−.08	.31	.06	.22	−.09	−.25	−.16	−.86	−.17
2. Professionalization	−.01	−.03	.00	−.09	.12	−.04	−.27	−.01	−.14	.00	.63	−.22	.14	−.03
3. Size	−.16	−.09	.07	.00	−.60	−.07	−.37	−.01	−.58	−.19	−.12	−.20	−.46	−.11
4. Multiple R^2	.03	.05	.02	.01	.42	.02	.19	.00	.45	.06	.29	.08	.58	.04
						B. Supervisory Ratio as Dependent Variable								
5. Departmental Specialization	−.19	−.18	−.09	−.08	−.36	−.14	−.11	−.09	−.11	−.21	.27	−.15	−.03	−.12
6. Professionalization	−.46	−.47	−.10	−.34	−.55	−.33	−.47	−.36	−.47	−.44	−.23	−.20	−.52	−.30
7. Size	−.42	−.42	−.18	−.34	−.20	−.42	−.32	−.28	−.33	−.58	−.15	−.41	−.74	−.34
8. Multiple R^2	.36	.32	.03	.28	.33	.30	.26	.22	.17	.51	.08	.18	.44	.16

interpretation needs to be tested on the basis of separate measures referring to two different "kinds" of professionalization, namely the more "generalist" type, as well as the one involving a higher degree of "specialist," task-specific, technically based job specialization and a correspondingly lower level of person specialization.

As to the lower half of Table 6 (Panel B), the moderate negative relationship between the supervisory ratio and departmental specialization, especially in the more complex teaching hospitals, lends support to the hypothesis that hierarchical coordination is not a result of increasing internal structural complexity, but rather of the homogeneity and routinization of work processes. These findings suggest a specification of Weber's assumption of hierarchical, monocratic authority as essential for the effective discharge of complex administrative tasks. Where complex problem solving is capable of routinization, standardization, and "seriability," hierarchical administrative patterns may, indeed, be more effective and therefore more prevalent, as for example, in large mental hospitals. However, where the task complexity is generated by multiple and diverse objectives and services, as is the case in general teaching hospitals or, for example, in preindustrial work organizations with diffuse, multiple objectives,[26] nonbureaucratic, "associational" forms of administration involving lateral coordination will predominate. Weber, of course, has dealt with these alternative forms of administration in terms of his concept of "democratic administration" and the "principle of collegiality." This principle limits or modifies monocratic authority insofar as it involves the separation of powers, consultation and cooperation among a plurality of individuals or advisory collegial bodies, mutual veto powers, and voting.[27]

In general, the empirical findings derived from the analysis of hospital structure force us to reconsider the implications of a complex division of labor for specific modes of coordination as well as for overall organizational coordination. We can assume that in the organization of patient care in modern hospitals the specialization of functions and especially of departments implies a high degree of interdependence.

Interdependence provides a basis for coordination insofar as work functions represent phases or elements of an interdependent work flow. Interdependence among people, among specific activities, and among specialized departments raises countless problems of coordination and mutual adjustment. *Structuring the resolution of these problems on the interpersonal and subunit level implies coordination on the organizational level insofar as the organization is a "going concern."*[28]

---

[26] Stanley H. Udy, *Organization of Work* (New Haven: Human Relations Area File Press, 1959), p. 40.

[27] Weber, *Economy and Society*. Vol. III, 948–52.

[28] This phenomenon is, of course, what Durkheim refers to as "organic solidarity." The more rationally oriented theory of March and Simon refers to it as "coordination by plan" based on process specialization, while Coleman has described it in terms of the mitigating effects of social structure on community conflict and Gouldner has dealt with it in terms of the need for functional autonomy. Emile Durkheim, *The Division of Labor in Society*, trans. George Simpson (New York:

DISCUSSION AND IMPLICATIONS

I will now turn briefly to a discussion of my findings, and especially of their implications for the seeming contradiction between the Anderson-Warkov hypothesis (viz., "bureaucratization is directly related to complexity") and Stinchcombe's hypothesis (viz., "bureaucratization is inversely related to professionalization"). Thus, the following question may be raised. If, on the one hand, the degree of *both* bureaucratization and professionalization increases with increasing internal structural complexity and if, on the other hand, professionalization counteracts—or provides an alternative for—bureaucratization, how can these contradictory consequences of complexity and professionalization for bureaucratization be interpreted and theoretically reconciled?

We have seen that professionalization tends to increase with depart-

Free Press, 1947), pp. 219–29; James G. March and Herbert A. Simon, *Organizations* (New York: John Wiley, 1958), pp. 113–71; James S. Coleman, *Community Conflict* (Glencoe: The Free Press, 1957), pp. 21–23. See also Luther Gulick and L. Urwick (eds.), *Papers on the Science of Administration* (New York: Institute of Public Administration, 1937), pp. 3–45, 159–69; Henry C. Metcalf and L. Urwick (eds.), *Dynamic Administration: The Collected Papers of Mary Parker Follet* (New York: Harper and Row, 1940), pp. 30–49, 71–117; Chester I. Barnard, *The Functions of the Executive* (Cambridge: Harvard University Press, 1962), pp. 82–95, 127–38; Alvin W. Gouldner, "Reciprocity and Autonomy in Functional Theory," in Lewellyn Gross (ed.), *Symposium on Sociological Theory* (Evanston: Row, Peterson, 1959), pp. 241–70; Louis R. Pondy, "Organizational Conflict: Concepts and Models," *Administrative Science Quarterly*, 12 (1967), 296–320.

mental specialization in the psychiatric hospitals, but that in general hospitals this relationship was either zero or negative (Table 5). Interpreted in terms of *levels* this means that both departmental specialization and professionalization are dependent on each other as long as they appear on a comparatively low level, as is true especially in state psychiatric hospitals. As the internal division of labor becomes more complex, professionalization also reaches a higher level, but at the same time it becomes more independent of the division of labor or even counteracts it. One could say that job specialization and person specialization are more likely in conflict with each other at higher levels of specialization, but not when both are in a rudimentary form or at an incipient stage of development.[29]

The interaction between departmental specialization and professionalization is particularly salient with respect to the administrative-clerical staff, as shown in Table 6, Panel A. Both variables affect this aspect of bureaucratization in opposite directions, depending on the *level* of departmental specialization, i.e., on the degree of internal structural complexity. This finding, then, is of particular importance for the conclusions of both the Anderson-Warkov and Stinchcombe studies.

The Anderson-Warkov hypothesis suggests that the crucial intervening variable between size and bureaucratization is "functional complexity" or the degree of role specialization,

[29] The evolutionary-developmental analogy implied in these statements must at the present relatively modest "level" or general theoretical development in the social sciences be treated as largely heuristic, i.e., as a conceptual crutch rather than as an explanatory device.

a concept combining both task complexity and division of labor.

The Stinchcombe hypothesis, on the other hand, focuses on the inverse relationship between professionalization and bureaucratization by considering two different production settings: mass production (high job specialization and routinization) and the building industry involving craft-type subcontractors (high worker specialization and nonroutinization, including seasonal variation).

By considering the *joint effect* of departmental specialization and professionalization *under conditions of high and low structural complexity* (departmental specialization), it is possible to evaluate the Stinchcombe and Anderson-Warkov models simultaneously.

By way of summarizing these complex relationships, let me suggest a theoretical interpretation which is based on variations in the *level* of internal structural complexity (departmental specialization) as well as on the distinction between generalist and specialist variants of professionalization.[30]

If a given hospital has a high level of compositional homogeneity and task routinization, and generally, a low level of internal structural com-

plexity, this pattern is characterized by inverse relationships between professionalization and hierarchical coordination, on the one hand, and the relative size of the administrative-clerical staff, on the other. For this "simple" structural pattern, then, one may accept Stinchcombe's hypothesis that a ("generalist") professionalized labor force constitutes an alternative to bureaucratic administration.[31]

The "simple" structural pattern also shows the positive effect of departmental specialization on the relative size of the administrative-clerical staff, suggesting a confirmation of the Anderson-Warkov hypothesis. Thus, with respect to the administrative-clerical staff, both the Anderson-Warkov and the Stinchcombe hypotheses are compatible and hold jointly under conditions of low internal structural complexity.[32]

---

[30] As indicated before, the ideal-typical distinction between generalist and specialist professionalization can be no more than a heuristic device at this point since there was no clearcut measure available for either. But it should be noted that these two forms of professionalization are not necessarily at opposite poles of one continuum, but two separate variables. In other words, even though a high value for one will *tend* to be associated with a low value for the other, it is conceivable that organizations have, e.g., high levels of *both* generalist and specialist professionalization at the same time.

[31] On the basis of similar findings by other students of organizations, one could further generalize that this alternative becomes relevant primarily under conditions of internal structural change, instability, and uncertainty. Thus, bureaucratic coordination may be required for the accomplishment of routine tasks under stable conditions, while novel, emergent situations might either provoke charismatic leadership or demand reliance on generalist professional judgment. The innovative leadership, spirit of inquiry, or creativity of professionals can, of course, also be viewed as a "charismatic" element.

[32] It may be suggested that under these conditions, division of labor does not necessarily imply a high degree of functional specificity so that generalist professionals are likely to share at least some functions with others resulting in some overlap of tasks, i.e., in a more diffuse content of the division of labor. This overlap, in turn, makes it more likely for professionals to be oriented toward the needs and problems of the larger organization, i.e., it implies the "local" orientation of the home guard among professionals.

By contrast, in hospital types with a more complex internal structure, the opposite of the Stinchcombe and Anderson-Warkov hypotheses holds. The administrative-clerical staff tends to be inversely related to departmental specialization, but positively to professionalization.

We can interpret this reversal as the result of the interaction between division of labor and professionalization. As the internal division of labor becomes more complex, the nature of professional work is transformed by becoming more task specific, differentiated, and specialized. Professional work becomes an integral part of the division of labor and thus contributes to the very complexity which it helps to integrate and coordinate under conditions of lower structural complexity.[33]

Since professional work itself becomes functionally more specific, it contributes relatively less to organizational coordination. This two-fold loss of coordination, therefore, increases the need for the regulation of specialists, i.e., for a larger administrative-clerical staff. Once this process has advanced to the point where professionals are highly specialized, departmental development based on the new professional specialities may, once again, be expected to reduce the

need for bureaucratic-administrative forms of coordination.[34]

In short, the interpretation advanced here suggests a differentiation of the concept of professionalization in at least two directions. First, specialist professional work is more narrowly task specific than its generalist ancestor. While the latter involves the notion of a total work process in which the product is completed by, and visible to, the worker, specialist work is much more fragmented, if not truncated. It approximates job specialization rather than person specialization, although the latter is at a relatively high level.

Second, general practice, apart from its independent economic base and the elements of entrepreneurship, is "free" in the sense that it provides its own communication system and hierarchy of work rules, rather than

---

[33] Hughes has pointed out that an organizational setting provides both context and impetus for the increased specialization of professionals. Rossi has described the same phenomenon in relation to research organizations. Everett C. Hughes, "Professions," *Daedalus*, XCII (1963), 663; Peter H. Rossi, "Researchers, Scholars, and Policy-Makers: The Politics of Large-Scale Research" *Daedalus*, XCIII (1964), 1151–53; see also Franz Schurmann's discussion of the distinction between generalists and specialists, Schurmann, *Ideology and Organization in Communist China*, p. 100.

[34] In his earlier as well as his recent concern with professionalization and new types and forms of professionalism, Wilensky, too, suggests that professional and bureaucratic (organizational) elements tend to mix and interpenetrate. Although I question the utility of Wilensky's ideal-typical conception of professions and would rather assume a continuum of rationalization of special knowledge, I concur strongly with his view of newly emerging structural forms which combine elements from both the professional and bureaucratic models and which represent mixed forms of organizational control. Harold L. Wilensky, "The Professionalization of Everyone?" *American Journal of Sociology*, LXX (1964), 137–58; see also his *Intellectuals in Labor Unions: Organizational Pressure on Professional Roles* (New York: Free Press, 1956), pp. 196–208. This conclusion is essentially shared by Louis C. Goldberg and his associates, in their article "Local-Cosmopolitan: Unidimensional or Multidimensional?," *American Journal of Sociology*, 70 (1965), 704–10; see also Warren G. Bennis' conception of future organizations, in his *Changing Organizations* (New York: McGraw-Hill, 1966), pp. 7–14.

requiring external rules and controls. Of course, every skilled task performance involves a measure of autonomy and discretion. But the scope of specialist practice—unless it is conducted as a "private practice"—is considerably more narrow, its decision making more routinized, its definition of the product more dependent on the definition and participation of others in the work process. Professional specialists are therefore also more dependent on administrative services which provide communication, coordination, and regulation, not to mention protection from the potential encroachment of others on their power and status privileges.

The necessity to coordinate specialists gives rise to administrative-clerical services more likely than to a bureaucratic hierarchy. Conversely, the bureaucratization of professionals —where it occurs to any degree— does not by definition, nor in all organizational contexts, imply hierarchical coordination; it also contains elements of administrative-clerical specialization.[35]

From this perspective, the increasing bureaucratization of professionals implies closer ties between their administrative tasks and their specialized work functions. This process parallels the transformation of professional work from the specification of goals to the specification of procedures, i.e., to a form of technical specialization. This means that the frame of reference of professional work ceases to be the occupational structure or the larger social system, as Parsons has suggested, and becomes, instead, an organization or a class of organizations.[36] Such a transformation implies further that professional behavior in the sense of self-regulation through reference group membership is shifting toward a type of collectivity orientation in which organizational and personal-professional loyalties tend to coincide.[37] This does not mean that cosmopolitans would become locals, but that the distinction is superseded by new forms and combinations, especially in those highly complex organizations which are able to combine professionally-specialized and organizational-administrative concerns. Such a development would restrict the usefulness and control of professional reference and peer groups, reducing them to mere interest groups. In modern professional organizations, this would also imply a new post-Weberian form of integration of professional-technical expertise and organizational position, if not rank.[38]

---

[35] If the administrative and the supervisory functions of bureaucratic professionals were measured independently, it could probably be shown that only the hierarchical element decreases with increasing departmental and professionalization, but not the administrative functions of professionals, at least not to the same extent. Only highly valued professionals might be able to delegate most administrative functions to others, while they themselves become increasingly involved in consultation and policy-making.

[36] See Parsons' conception of professions in terms of functional specificity relative to the larger social system; Talcott Parsons, "The Professions and Social Structure," in *Essays on Sociological Theory* (New York: Free Press, 1949), pp. 198–99.

[37] See also Goldberg et al., "Local-Cosmopolitan."

[38] For critical discussions of the consequences of such technocracies, see e.g., Robert Boguslaw, *The New Utopians: A Study of System Design and Social Change* (Englewood Cliffs: Prentice-Hall, 1965); Jacques Ellul, *The Technological Society* (New York: Vintage Books), 1967. A more "tolerant" view is expressed in John K.

In spite of the similarity, there are certain differences between this modern form of bureaucratic professionalism and Weber's concept of legal-bureaucratic administration. First, one may expect a greater degree of role specialization among such modern professionals, a difference which is comparable to that between professional specialists and technicians. Secondly, one would expect the elaboration of a stratification system among professionals, as well as the formation of professional elites, operating within, and on the basis of, correspondingly stratified organizational systems. Third, while the scope of any given organizational system may be smaller than the large, monolithic, public bureaucracy envisaged by Weber, it is now possible to discern a wide variety of organizations and occupational groups, which constitute an organizational market structure as well as a system of stratification within certain classes and types of organizations.[39]

These considerations certainly apply to the most advanced and complex types of hospitals where hierarchical and "purely" professional types of coordination are giving way to structural and administrative-regulative modes, i.e., where professional specialization becomes part of the overall specialization of functions and of the generally more differentiated and diversified organization of work. The development suggested here for hospitals and other professional organizations has certain implications for a new "democratic" conception of organizations, which I have elaborated elsewhere.[40]

CONCLUSION

I have presented the results of a comparative-quantitative analysis of professional organizations. Based on data collected from almost all American hospitals in 1959, it has been shown that organizational autonomy as well as the nature and complexity of the organizational task structure have a pervasive influence on internal structural complexity, in general, and on different modes of coordination, in particular.

Organizational autonomy was operationalized in terms of three types of ownership and control, with federal ⸱(V.A.) hospitals exhibiting strikingly different characteristics as compared to local governmental and voluntary non-profit hospitals. On the whole, federal hospitals conform more closely to the conception of "planned," formally established organizations than the other two types, that is, the variability of structural characteristics *within* this category of ownership and control tends to be much smaller than that within the other two categories. The generalization suggested here is that the lower the degree of organizational autonomy (or the higher the degree of external control), the lower the degree of

---

Galbraith, *The New Industrial State* (New York: Signet Books), 1967.

[39] For example, some of these phenomena have been documented for colleges and universities: Paul F. Lazarsfeld and Wagner Thielens, *The Academic Mind* (New York: Free Press, 1958); Theodore Caplow and Reece McGee, *The Academic Marketplace* (New York: Basic Books, 1958); James A. Davis, *Great Aspirations* (Chicago: Aldine-Atherton 1964); Albert Somit and Joseph Tanenhaus, *American Political Science, A Profile of a Discipline* (New York: Atherton Press, 1964).

[40] Heydebrand, *Hospital Bureaucracy,* Chap. 11.

structural variation. More generally, this suggests that the variability of structural characteristics is directly related to the degree of organizational autonomy, and inversely to the degree of external control.

In addition to having a lower level of structural variation, federal hospitals are also internally more complex and have a significantly larger administrative apparatus than nonfederal hospitals. This effect of autonomy, however, is not entirely independent of the second major organizational parameter used in this study, the degree of complexity of the task structure. Thus, the teaching status of hospitals as well as the type of medical service were also shown to have a profound effect on internal complexity and coordination. Together with size and autonomy, task structure variables such as the number and the diversity of major objectives account for a significant amount of variation in the level of internal structural complexity, as well as for significant differences between patterns of structural relationships.

An examination of one such pattern, the relationship between size, functional specialization, and the relative size of the administrative-clerical staff, revealed that in relation to the latter, size tends to have a negative effect especially in structurally simple organizations, whereas functional specialization tends to have a negative effect in structurally more complex organizations. These findings were interpreted in terms of a dialectical conception of the division of labor. Thus, the relative size of the administrative-clerical staff increases at a decreasing rate as the degree of functional specialization in an organization increases. This relationship, in turn, is dependent on the fact that the degree of functional specialization itself increases at a decreasing rate as organizational size increases. Furthermore, as organizations become internally more complex, they appear to operate less as "closed systems." Rather, they appear to approach a more open, pluralistic, and "democratic" structural pattern in that they develop subunits of increasingly equal size and become more interdependent with their environment.

In order to explore and test the idea that increasing structural complexity changes the nature of coordination in professional organizations, departmental specialization and professionalization were reconceptualized as "nonbureaucratic" modes of coordination, in contrast to the two bureaucratic modes, viz., hierarchical differentiation and the relative size of the administrative-clerical staff.

In organizational studies, it is generally taken for granted that complexity, i.e., the multiplicity and diversity of elements and relations, generates the need for coordination insofar as the organization is viewed as an entity and as a "going concern." But what kind of coordination, or how much coordination is needed are open, empirical questions. This study has mainly been concerned with the kinds of coordination associated with certain kinds of structure, rather than with the question of "how much" coordination. To answer the latter question requires the use of definite criteria of operating efficiency and effectiveness in relation to coordination. Since organizations may be over- or under-coordinated, it would be necessary to determine adequate levels of coordination. For hospitals, such criteria are difficult to establish short of a comprehensive analysis of community health systems.

But it is possible to answer the question of "what kind" of coordination, especially if we analyze hospitals as special cases of complex, formal, professionalized work organizations. For the purposes of that analysis, I have found the distinction between bureaucratic and nonbureaucratic modes of coordination relevant and useful. The assumption that bureaucratic modes of coordination are the most prevalent form of integration of the elements of a complex division of labor has not only been challenged, but can be modified by isolating various aspects of bureaucratization. Thus, I have shown that the complexity of the task structure in hospitals favors the development of an administrative-clerical staff, but not that of a bureaucratic hierarchy.

I have further shown that both departmental specialization and professionalization can be seen as intervening between the task structure and the bureaucratic modes of coordination. Thus, a high level of departmental specialization becomes itself a factor of coordination. Administrative and bureaucratic-hierarchical modes of coordination are gradually shifted from the organizational level to subunit levels, a phenomenon typical of processes of delegation and decentralization. A high level of departmental specialization will not only increase the interdependence among subunits, but will also generate new modes of lateral communication and interaction. It is likely that lateral transactions include such processes as competition, conflict, as well as various forms of cooperation.

The nature and rate of such transactions, of course, needs to be observed and confirmed empirically. Here, I have confined myself to spelling out the logical implications of a high level of departmental specialization for lateral coordination. The Gini coefficient of concentration and similar indexes of structural characteristics are particularly well suited for studying the internal structural complexity of organizations within a comparative-quantitative framework.

The second nonbureaucratic mode of coordination intervening between task structure and bureaucratization is professionalization. I have shown that the degree of professionalization and of departmental specialization interact in conditioning the relation between structural complexity and bureaucratic-administrative coordination. Thus, Stinchcombe's hypothesis concerning the coordinating function of professionalization of the labor force appears to hold under conditions of relatively low internal structural complexity. I have suggested that under these conditions, division of labor does not imply a high degree of functional specificity so that professionals will tend to act as generalists and are likely to share at least some functions with others, with the result of some overlap of tasks. The "generalist" definition of professionalization is consistent with Stinchcombe's use of the term.

However, in organizations with a more complex internal structure—due to a more complex task structure and technology—the coordinating effect of professionalization disappears. The professionalization of the labor force is accompanied by an increasing specificity of functions, contributing to an increasing need for the administrative-regulatory coordination of professional specialists. This finding is inconsistent with Stinchcombe's hypothesis because of the changed nature and meaning of professionalization. Our data suggest, in general, that the nature of professional work is contingent on the organizational context, i.e., on the type and degree of division of labor. Under conditions of high departmental specialization, the nature of professional work is transformed by becoming itself more task-specific, differentiated and specialized. Obviously, this idea can be proposed only in the form of a hypothesis which needs to be tested on the basis of specific operational distinctions between generalist and specialist forms of professionalization.

8. GOALS, ENVIRONMENTAL PRESSURES, AND ORGANIZATIONAL CHARACTERISTICS*

Richard L. Simpson and William H. Gulley

Writers have often noted that the purposes for which an organization exists, and the environment in which it operates, will have effects on its internal structure and operating practices. Blau and others in the Weberian tradition, for example, have

Reprinted by permission of the American Sociological Association from *American Sociological Review*, 27 (June 1962), 344–51.

* This research was supported by a grant from Nationwide Insurance Companies to the Institute for Research in Social Science, University of North Carolina. Bert N. Adams did most of the IBM work and made many useful suggestions in connection with analysis methods. We are also indebted to W. Dwight Weed of Nationwide Insurance Companies for facilitating the research, to Donald M. Freeman and Donald D. Smith for work in data collection and preliminary analysis, and to Ruth E. Searles, Ida Harper Simpson, and Harry S. Upshaw for advice.

pointed out that a primarily "instrumental" organization designed to accomplish specific ends must place its main emphasis on efficiency, and hence is likely to be organized bureaucratically rather than democratically.[1] Lipset, Trow, and Coleman hypothesize that the most thoroughly centralized and undemocratic organizations will be those with narrowly defined instrumental goals; the broader the range of goals, the more likely the members are to desire some measure of control over policies.[2] Homans' concept of the "external system" emphasizes the shaping of the organization by its goals and en-

[1] See, for example, Peter M. Blau, *Bureaucracy in Modern Society* (New York: Random House, 1956), pp. 22–23.
[2] Seymour Martin Lipset, Martin Trow, and James S. Coleman, *Union Democracy* (Glencoe, Ill.: The Free Press, 1956), pp. 407, 415–16.

vironment.[3] These writings exemplify a growing recognition that the purposes and environmental situation of an organization will influence its structure and behavior. However, little research except case studies of single organizations has been done to specify how these influences operate.[4]

In this paper we attempt to show some ways in which goals and environmental situations can influence the internal characteristics of one kind of organization, national voluntary associations. The general hypothesis is that organizations which must adapt to a wide range of pressures will differ in internal characteristics from those which face a narrower range of pressures. It is assumed that voluntary associations which pursue numerous goals, and which must satisfy demands made by the general community as well as by their own members, confront a more complex variety of pressures than associations which have few goals and little or no need to satisfy community expectations. Since they are exposed to pressures which are greater in number and different in kind, we would expect them to be organized differently. For example, we might expect that an association which has many goals and must satisfy an external constituency will be relatively decentralized, with initiation of activity concentrated at the local level and with a strong concern for grass-roots membership involvement and internal communication. With this kind of organization the leadership can respond to local community demands and to the changing desires of a membership which has diverse goals.

Following this kind of reasoning, we will present a typology of voluntary associations and a test of three specific hypotheses. Associations are classified as *focused* or *diffuse*, depending on the number of goals they pursue, and as *internal* or *external*, depending on whether they must satisfy their members alone, or both their members and the outside community. By these criteria, *focused internal associations* face the fewest pressures and *diffuse external associations* the most. The hypotheses are: (1) Focused internal associations will tend to be centralized in authority structure and action-initiation, diffuse external associations decentralized, and the other two types of associations (focused external, diffuse

[3] George C. Homans, *The Human Group* (New York: Harcourt, Brace, 1950), pp. 90–94. For a treatment of a somewhat related problem, see also James D. Thompson and William D. McEwen, "Organizational Goals and Environment: Goal-setting as an Interaction Process," *American Sociological Review*, 23 (February, 1958), 23–31.

[4] Case studies showing relationships between goals and environmental circumstances and the internal features of single organizations are numerous. Examples include studies of government agencies, such as Philip Selznick, *TVA and the Grass Roots* (Berkeley and Los Angeles: University of California Press, 1949); studies of voluntary associations, such as David L. Sills, *The Volunteers* (Glencoe, Ill.: The Free Press, 1957); "industry and community" studies, such as W. Lloyd Warner and J. O. Low, *The Social System of the Modern Factory* (New Haven: Yale University Press, 1947); and studies of political machines, such as Harold F. Gosnell, *Machine Politics: Chicago Model* (Chicago: University of Chicago Press, 1937). Theoretical discussions of this topic are found in Selznick, *TVA*, pp. 250–59, reprinted in part as "A Theory of Organizational Commitments," *In* Robert K. Merton, Ailsa P. Gray, Barbara Hockey, and Hanan C. Selvin, (eds.), *Reader in Bureaucracy* (Glencoe, Ill.: Free Press, 1952), pp. 194–202; and in Chester I. Barnard, *The Functions of the Executive* (Cambridge, Mass.: Harvard University Press, 1938), pp. 194–99.

internal) intermediate in degree of centralization. (2) Diffuse external associations will tend to stress loyal, active involvement of rank-and-file members in their activities, focused internal associations will tend not to stress membership involvement, and the other two types of associations will be intermediate in this respect. (3) Diffuse external associations will tend to emphasize internal communication, focused internal associations will tend not to emphasize internal communication, and other associations will be intermediate in this respect.

METHOD AND SAMPLE

The method used was the sample survey by mail questionnaire, with national voluntary associations as the units of analysis. Associations were chosen from the *Encyclopedia of American Associations* and *World Convention Dates*.[5] Coverage of a wide variety of types and sizes, rather than simple randomness, was the criterion for sampling. Even if randomness had been desired, it would have been impossible, since the available listings of voluntary associations are not complete. An original mailing asked officials of national associations to return questionnaires and to send us lists of local chapters, individual members, or both; these lists were used for subsequent mailing of questionnaires to local officials and rank-and-file members. In all, 1010 questionnaires were mailed out, and of

these, 546 or 54 percent were returned.[6] Of the 546 respondents, 485 representing 211 different organizations answered both questions used in establishing the typology of associations and were thus eligible for inclusion in the sample. So that no organization would appear more than once in the sample, one respondent was selected randomly from each organization having more than one respondent or, if respondents disagreed in answering the questions used to establish the typology, one was selected randomly from those giving the modal answer.[7]

[6] A more detailed description of the survey procedure appears in William H. Gulley, "Relative Effectiveness in Voluntary Associations," unpublished doctoral dissertation, University of North Carolina, 1961.

[7] An exception to this procedure was made in the case of 15 associations each represented by two respondents who disagreed as to typological classification. In these instances respondents were chosen purposively to equate the four types of associations as nearly as possible in the percentages of respondents in the sample who were national officials, local officials, and rank-and-file members. This departure from randomness seemed desirable since preliminary tabulations had shown that these three basic levels of respondents differed in their perception of organizational characteristics. These differential perceptions do not materially affect the findings of this paper since the proportional representation of the three levels is almost entirely controlled in the analysis sample, as is shown in Table 1. While the absolute scores on the three indexes differed, with officials assigning slightly higher scores than members on all three indexes, the comparative positions of the four types of organizations on the three indexes were generally the same when the associations whose respondents were national officials, local officials, and members were analyzed separately. Specifically, on the centralization index, all three levels of respondents placed the focused internal and diffuse external associations at the predicted extremes except that local officials placed diffuse external

[5] *Encyclopedia of American Associations,* 2nd ed. (Detroit: Gale Research Co.), 1959. F. A. Duzette, editor, *World Convention Dates,* (Hempstead, N. Y.: Hendrickson Publishing Co.), published monthly. Several 1959 issues were used.

TYPOLOGY OF ASSOCIATIONS

To form a typology of voluntary associations, we have classified them by two criteria. The first, *focused or diffuse*, refers to the number of goals an organization pursues. Associations are classified as focused or diffuse in goals on the basis of response to a question which asked, "How much better off do you feel that your members are then they would be if they did not belong to your organization, with respect to each of the following things?" (1, their income, financial condition, etc.; 2, their prestige or status in the community; 3, their feeling of contribution to society or community; 4, their knowledge of world or community problems; 5, their social lives, friends, etc.; 6, their cultural or artistic lives; 7, their ability to express points of view, have their ideas put into practice, etc.). With respect to each of these seven items representing organizational goals, respondents could indicate that mem-

bership led to a person's being "much better off," "somewhat better off," or "no better off," or that the item was "not relevant to the goals of our organization." If a respondent indicated that members were much better off or somewhat better off with respect to an item, this was taken to mean that he regarded the item as a goal of the organization.[8] The 112 associations whose sample respondents cited from one of four goals were defined as having focused goals; the 99 whose sample respondents cited from five to seven goals were defined as having diffuse goals.[9]

---

associations in the position next to the predicted extreme; the same was true of the membership involvement index except that national and local officials placed focused internal associations in the position next to the predicted extreme; and on internal communication, national officials and members placed both focused internal and diffuse external associations at the predicted extremes but local officials placed neither type at the predicted extreme. Thus out of nine tabulations controlling level of respondent, in only one (local officials' responses concerning internal communication) were the relationships not essentially as predicted, despite the fact that many of the categories of levels of respondents within associational types had very small frequencies ranging from six to ten respondents. The nine tabulations just discussed are not shown in this paper; they are similar in logic and format to the tabulations for organizational size classes shown in Table 2, below.

[8] A critic has suggested that this method of ascertaining goals may have led us to classify associations as diffuse in goals, not because the organizations actually had numerous goals, but because these were associations which happened to be represented in our sample by enthusiastic respondents whose enthusiasm caused them to say that membership made a person "better off" in numerous ways. If this were so, it would point to a serious weakness in our method of classification, but there are three principal reasons for doubting that it is so. First, most respondents in all four associational types were officials, and one can probably assume that officials of all four types tended to be enthusiastic supporters of their organizations. Second, when we asked each respondent to rate his association on an eleven-point scale from full achievement of its goals (10) to no achievement at all (0), with 5 being "reasonable achievement," the ratings by respondents from focused and diffuse associations were very similar. The medians were 6.67 for focused and 6.77 for diffuse associations, and the means were 6.40 for focused and 6.53 for diffuse associations, suggesting that the two sets of respondents differed very little in enthusiasm. The third reason is the check on the reliability of the classification described in footnote 11.

[9] The thirteen associations whose respondents cited no goals at all were eliminated along with four whose respondents did not answer, and these associations are not among the 211 in the sample used for analysis.

TABLE 1 SAMPLE OF ASSOCIATIONS BY TYPE
AND LEVEL OF RESPONDENT

| | Percent of Each Type's Respondents Who Were: | | |
Type of Association	National Officials	Local Officials	Members
Focused internal ($N = 70$)	60.0	20.0	20.0
Focused external ($N = 42$)	64.3	19.0	16.7
Diffuse internal ($N = 48$)	62.4	18.8	18.8
Diffuse external ($N = 51$)	60.8	19.6	19.6

The second criterion by which associations are classified, *internal or external*, refers to the absence or presence of involvement with the community. An internally oriented association must satisfy its members but is not expected to satisfy any demands from the general community, while an externally oriented association faces demands from both the general community and its own members. To classify associations as internal or external in orientation, the following question is used: "Some organizations need more support from the general community than others need. Check the one statement below which comes closest to describing your situation." (1, We could never accomplish anything without strong community support. 2, Community support is important to us but not absolutely essential for everything we do. 3, Community support is desirable, but not really a major factor in our success. 4, It does not really matter whether the community supports our program or not. 5, We hope to accomplish our goals despite opposition from a major element of the community.) The 93 associations whose respondents checked the first or second alternative, indicating need for community support, were classified as externally oriented; the remaining 118 were classified as internally oriented.[10]

By these procedures we arrived at the sample described in Table 1.[11]

[10] No sample respondent checked the fifth alternative, indicating community opposition.

[11] It will be recalled that when an association had more than one respondent, one giving the modal responses was selected for inclusion in the sample, and that respondents from the same association sometimes disagreed in their answers to the questions used for classifying it. As a check on the reliability of the classification, we compared the classification each association would have been given if the classification had been based on the mean of all its respondents' answers to the two classification questions, with the classification it actually received on the basis of answers by its one respondent included in the sample. The means were based on the number of goals cited, for the focused-vs-diffuse question, and on the code numbers used in the text of this paper to identify the five possible responses ranging from extreme community involvement to extreme lack of involvement, for the internal-vs-external question. If we define the classification based on the means as the "proper" classification for the purpose of this reliability check, then 23 associations or 11 percent of the 211 were improperly classified in the sample used for analysis. When we regard the focused internal and diffuse external associations as extreme types in the range of pressures they face, only two of 211 associations were classified in the analysis sample at the wrong extreme.

The representation of different organizational levels among the respondents is shown in order to indicate that this variable, which might have affected the results, has been largely controlled. When this typology is used to indicate the range of pressures to which voluntary associations are exposed, the polar types are the focused internal associations, facing the fewest pressures, and the diffuse external, subjected to the widest variety of pressures. (Note that "external" really means "external plus internal," since nothing in our data suggests that they face fewer internal pressures than the organizations we have called "internal"; the difference is that they additionally face external pressures.) For present purposes the focused external and diffuse internal associations may be regarded simply as intermediate types, although they are intermediate for different reasons and may very well differ from each other in ways not revealed by our data.[12]

[12] Other typologies of voluntary associations are given in George A. Lundberg, Mirra Komarovsky, and Mary Alice McInerny, *Leisure: A Suburban Study* (New York: Columbia University Press, 1934), pp. 129–69; Arnold M. Rose, *Theory and Method in the Social Sciences* (Minneapolis: University of Minnesota Press, 1954), p. 52; and C. Wayne Gordon and Nicholas Babchuk, "A Typology of Voluntary Associations," *American Sociological Review*, 24 (Feb. 1959), 22–29. Our typology is analytic and not based on the manifest functions of the organizations, and organizations of numerous kinds were classified in all four analytic types. Occupational organizations including academic, scientific, and professional societies, trade associations, and labor unions made up 43 of 70 focused internal, 12 of 42 focused external, 29 of 48 diffuse internal, and 25 of 51 diffuse external associations. Nonoccupational organizations included recreational, social, and hobby associations, interest and pressure groups working to advance nonoccupational goals (e.g., a veterans'

FINDINGS

Table 2 tests the three hypotheses given earlier. It shows, for each associational type, the medians for three indexes composed of responses to questions in which respondents were asked to describe various characteristics of their organizations. Each index relates to one of the three hypotheses.

Centralization. Hypothesis 1 was that focused internal associations would tend to be the most centralized in authority structure and action-initiation, and diffuse external associations the least. Three items went into the centralization index: (1) "Where would you say the main activity of your organization is carried out?" (National level is scored 1; regional, state, or local level is scored 0.) (2) "When changes have taken place in your ... programs ... from where has the initiative for the change usually come?" (National officials is scored 1; lesser officials or individual members is scored 0.) (3) "Please check the one statement below which most nearly describes the top leadership structure of your national organization." (Decisions made by national leaders alone is scored 1; decisions made by local officials or members, or by national leaders only after consultation with local officials or members, is scored 0.)

organization) or benefit some nonoccupational group (e.g., a religious pressure group), and charitable or philanthropic organizations. When we classified associations into eight types based on their principal manifest functions—four occupational and four non-occupational types—organizations of all eight functional types were found in all four of our analytic types, except that no recreational society or trade association was classified as diffuse external.

TABLE 2 MEDIAN CENTRALIZATION, MEMBERSHIP INVOLVEMENT,
AND INTERNAL COMMUNICATION SCORES BY
SIZE AND TYPE OF ASSOCIATION

Index and Size of Association	Focused Internal Median (N)		Focused External Median (N)		Diffuse Internal Median (N)		Diffuse External Median (N)	
Centralization								
All associations	2.14	(55)	1.54	(39)	1.80	(45)	1.37	(44)
Small only	2.29	(23)	1.75	(9)	2.30	(14)	1.83	(8)
Medium only	2.00	(21)	1.63	(13)	1.70	(18)	1.58	(13)
Large only	1.75	(11)	1.43	(17)	1.33	(13)	1.00	(23)
Membership Involvement								
All associations	1.42	(56)	1.67	(39)	1.97	(46)	3.03	(46)
Small only	1.31	(25)	0.88	(9)	1.92	(13)	1.75	(9)
Medium only	1.75	(23)	2.00	(13)	1.79	(20)	3.00	(14)
Large only	0.50	(8)	1.87	(17)	2.38	(13)	3.27	(23)
Internal Communication								
All associations	1.80	(60)	2.33	(38)	2.27	(47)	2.67	(48)
Small only	1.88	(25)	2.33	(9)	2.10	(14)	1.83	(8)
Medium only	1.71	(23)	1.60	(13)	2.31	(19)	2.86	(14)
Large only	1.50	(12)	2.77	(16)	2.50	(14)	2.69	(26)

On this three-item index, median scores ranged from a high of 2.14 for the focused internal associations to a low of 1.37 for the diffuse external associations. The direction of relationships supports the hypothesis.[13]

Membership Involvement. Hypothesis 2 was that diffuse external associations would show the greatest concern with involving rank-and-file members in their activities and main-

[13] The findings were not tested for significance, since the sample was not a random one of any known universe, for the reason mentioned earlier. Writers on both sides of the recent controversy over the use of tests of significance seem to agree that such tests are hard to interpret, if not wholly meaningless, when random sampling procedures have not been followed. See Hanan C. Selvin, "A Critique of Tests of Significance in Survey Research," *American Sociological Review*, 22 (Oct. 1957), 519–27; and James M. Beshers, "On 'A Critique of Tests of Significance in Survey Research,'" *American Sociological Review*, 23 (Apr. 1958), 199.

taining membership loyalty, and focused internal associations the least. Membership involvement was measured with an index of four items. The responses which received scores of 1, paraphrased here to save space, were: (1) That members take an active part in the work of the organization is very important. (2) The members would feel a terrible loss if the organization did not exist. (3) Promoting cooperation among members is very important. (4) Recruiting members is very important.

As predicted, diffuse external associations scored highest in membership involvement, with a median of 3.03, and focused internal associations scored lowest, with a median of 1.42.

Internal Communication. Hypothesis 3 was that diffuse external associations would place the greatest emphasis on maintaining channels of internal communication, and focused internal associations the least. Emphasis on internal communication was measured with a three-item index. Responses which received scores of 1, slightly paraphrased, were: (1) Educating members as to the objectives of the organization is very important. (2) Keeping members informed of the organization's activities is very important. (3) That members keep leaders informed of their opinions is absolutely essential or very important.

Again, the results are in the direction predicted by the hypothesis. Diffuse external associations showed the greatest emphasis on internal communication, with a median of 2.67, and focused internal associations showed the least, with a median of 1.80.

These findings thus tend to support all three hypotheses. Moreover, on all 10 separate items which went into the three indexes, the types of associations we have defined as lowest and highest in the range of pressures to which they are exposed—focused internal and diffuse external—were at the predicted extremes in the response distributions. In addition, if we compare the focused and diffuse associations within the internal and external categories considered separately, and the internal and external associations within the focused and diffuse categories considered separately, their relative scores on all three indexes are what we would predict: the associations facing more pressures scored lower in centralization, higher in membership involvement, and higher in internal communication.

Organizational Size as a Control Variable. A number of studies have shown that the size of organizations is related to their organizational char-

acteristics, as one would expect from bureaucratic theory.[14] Since the associations of our four types differed in average size, it seemed advisable to find out whether the differences we found in their organizational characteristics would hold up when the size of associations was controlled. To control size, we divided the associations into three size classes, from data on size of membership given in the *Encyclopedia of American Associations*.[15] Associations with 2499 or fewer members were defined as small, those with from 2500 to 24,999 members were defined as medium, and those with 25,000 or more members were defined as large.

Table 2 shows median centralization, membership involvement, and internal communication scores for

[14] Some examples include William Foote Whyte, *Human Relations in the Restaurant Industry* (New York: McGraw-Hill, 1948), pp. 17–30; Frederic W. Terrien and Donald L. Mills, "The Effect of Changing Size upon the Internal Structure of Organizations," *American Sociological Review*, 20 (Feb. 1955), 11–14; Lipset, Trow, and Coleman, *Union Democracy*, pp. 150–54, 163–71; Theodore Caplow, "Organization Size," *Administrative Science Quarterly*, 1 (Mar. 1957), 484–505; Edwin J. Thomas, "Role Conceptions and Organizational Size," *American Sociological Review*, 24 (Feb. 1959), 30–38; Amitai Etzioni, "The Functional Differentiation of Elites in the Kibbutz," *American Journal of Sociology*, 64 (Mar. 1959), 476–87; Sergio Talacchi, "Organization Size, Individual Attitudes and Behavior," *Administrative Science Quarterly*, 5 (Dec. 1960), 398–420; R. W. Revans, "Industrial Morale and Size of Unit," *In* Walter Galenson and Seymour Martin Lipset (eds.), *Labor and Trade Unionism* (New York: Wiley, 1960), pp. 295–300; and Theodore R. Anderson and Seymour Warkov, "Organizational Size and Functional Complexity: A Study of Administration in Hospitals," *American Sociological Review*, 26 (Feb. 1961), 23–28.

[15] *Encyclopedia of American Associations.*

small, medium, and large associations in each of the four typological categories. Most of the hypothesized relationships held up among the medium and large associations, especially those regarding centralization and membership involvement. For example, focused internal associations were always at the predicted extreme of the response distribution except that medium sized associations of this type were next to the predicted extreme in internal communication. Similarly, diffuse external associations were at the predicted extreme except that large associations of this type were next to the predicted extreme in internal communication. The small associations, however, deviated from the general pattern. Among these, the focused internal associations were next to the predicted extreme on all three indexes, while the diffuse external associations were next to the predicted extreme twice and at the "wrong" extreme in internal communication.

These findings seem to support the conclusion that the range of pressures to which an organization is exposed, as indicated by our typology, is related to organizational characteristics in medium-sized and large associations, though perhaps not in small ones. One could feel safer in drawing this conclusion if the frequencies in the subcategories were larger, but by the same token it is noteworthy that the predicted relationships generally hold up despite the smallness of some frequencies.

DISCUSSION

In interpreting the findings one should bear in mind that they did not hold up within organizations having fewer than 2500 members, that the differences were smaller and the relationships slightly less consistent with respect to internal communication than with respect to the other two indexes, and that the analysis assumes that officials and members can accurately perceive the characteristics of their organizations. However, the over-all consistency of the findings seems to lend support to the general hypothesis and the three sub-hypotheses.

It can be plausibly argued that the organizational features most frequently found in the different types of voluntary associations represent characteristically different modes of adaptation to their diverse situations. Consider the focused internal associations, with their tendencies toward minimal concern over membership involvement, lack of interest in maintaining internal communication channels, and centralized authority structure. In comparison with other associations, these are organizations which seek limited sets of goals and do not need the support of outsiders. Given this situation, it is understandable if their officials do not concern themselves deeply with recruiting, motivating, and keeping in touch with their members. The members do not need to act as ambassadors to the outside world, and therefore a high degree of membership loyalty and activity is not necessary. The members join for limited purposes, and as long as the officials stick to these purposes, the members do not have to be persuaded to support activity aimed at other goals. If the goals are limited, the chances are that the officials understand what the members want; therefore upward communication from members to officials need not be emphasized. Conversely, from the member's standpoint, neither frequent communication nor a democratic voice in policy-making would seem crucially important, so long as the officials deliver the rather well-defined goods they are expected to deliver.[16]

The situation of the diffuse external associations is somewhat the reverse. Nevertheless, the finding that these organizations, which must operate under a complicated set of pressures, tend to be relatively decentralized and democratic, might seem inconsistent with the ancient observation that "a tight situation makes for a tight authority structure." It has been said, for example, that the reason why military organizations must be authoritarian is that they need to move fast in exceedingly demanding situations.[17] The demands placed on organizations may differ, however, in nature as well as in complexity or urgency. In the case of diffuse external voluntary associations, the difficulty of their situation stems specifically from their need to satisfy both members and outsiders who have varied and possibly conflicting expectations. Therefore their mode of adaptation consists of trying to guarantee that the various pressures will be communicated to the

leadership so that it can plan accordingly, and that the leadership's plans will be communicated to the members, on the local level, where the basic activities in these organizations tend to occur. The more decentralized authority structure, coupled with greater emphasis on membership involvement and communication, enables the leaders to keep in touch with local activities and the members to make their varied wishes known.

On a more general level, the findings seem to support the proposition that the characteristics of organizations will be systematically related to their goals and to the environmental circumstances in which they operate. It also seems clear that the relationships are amenable to statistical survey techniques using organizations as the units of analysis, along with other methods more commonly used in the past for studying complex organizations, such as individual case study.[18]

---

[16] Lipset has made this same point in his discussion of internal union politics: Seymour Martin Lipset, *Political Man: The Social Bases of Politics* (Garden City, N. Y.: Doubleday, 1960), p. 390. A similar statement also appears in Lipset, Trow, and Coleman, *Union Democracy*, p. 407.

[17] See, for example, George C. Homans, *The Human Group*, p. 432; and Homans, "The Small Warship," *American Sociological Review*, 11 (June, 1946), 300.

[18] Survey analysis with organizations as the statistical units is analogous to some of the research which uses cultures or societies as the units and examines relationships among their attributes; for example: Leonard T. Hobhouse, G. C. Wheeler, and Morris Ginsberg, *The Material Culture and Social Institutions of the Simpler Peoples* (London: Chapman and Hall, 1915); George Peter Murdock, *Social Structure* (New York: Macmillan, 1949); Linton C. Freeman and Robert F. Winch, "Societal Complexity: An Empirical Test of a Typology of Societies," *American Journal of Sociology*, 62 (Mar. 1957), 461–66; Stanley H. Udy, Jr., *The Organization of Work* (New Haven: HRAF Press, 1959); and M. F. Nimkoff and Russell Middleton, "Types of Family and Types of Economy," *American Journal of Sociology*, 66 (Nov. 1960), 215–25.

9. U.S. AND U.S.S.R. PARTICIPATION IN INTERNATIONAL NON-GOVERNMENTAL ORGANIZATIONS

Louis Kriesberg

The study of international nongovernmental organizations can be useful for the understanding of the conditions for international peace[1,2] and

for the sociology of organizations. International nongovernmental organizations, hereafter called NGO's, typically are associations of voluntary organizations from several nations. At present, there are about 1,500 NGO's in existence.[3] The names of

Reprinted by permission of the author and publisher from Louis Kriesberg (ed.), *Social Processes in International Relations.* New York: John Wiley & Sons, Inc. ©1968, pp. 466–87.

[1] The research reported upon here was made possible by a grant from the Syracuse University International Organization Research Program, funded by the Ford Foundation. Alphonse J. Sallett assisted in the coding of the necessary information. An abridged version of this paper was presented at the American Sociological Association meetings, 1966.

[2] For example, see William M. Evan, "Transnational Forums for Peace," in Quincy Wright, William M. Evan, and Morton Deutsch (eds.), *Preventing World War III: Some Proposals* (New York: Simon and Schuster, 1962); Lyman C. White, *International Non-Governmental Organizations* (New Brunswick, N. J.: Rutgers University Press, 1951); Ernst B. Haas, *The Uniting of Europe* (Stanford: University of California Press, 1958); Louis Kriesberg, "German Businessmen and Union Leaders and the Schuman Plan," *Social Science,* 34 (April, 1960), pp. 114–21; Peter H. Rohn, *Relations Between the Council of Europe and International Non-Governmental Organizations* (Brussels: Union of International Associations, 1957);

J. J. Lador-Lederer, *International Non-Governmental Organizations and Economic Entities* (Leyden, Netherlands: A. W. Sythoff-Leyden, 1962). Also see G. P. Speeckaert, *Select Bibliography on International Organization 1885–1964* (Bruxelles: Union of International Associations, 1965).

[3] In the 1962–1963 edition of the *Yearbook of International Organizations,* published by the Union of International Associations, Brussels, Belgium, more than 1700 international organizations are listed and over 1500 are non-governmental. In order to be listed, the organization must (1) have members (with voting powers and who are active) from at least three countries; (2) be nonprofit; (3) be active within the preceding two years; and (4) derive financial support from more than one country.

Certain types of organizations are excluded: movements without any definite structure, international institutes whose activities are primarily limited to teaching or training, fan clubs, fraternity and university clubs, and trusts or foundations. In addition, if there is insufficient information, the organization is not listed. (From personal communication by A. Judge, Research Secretary, and G. P. Speeckaert, some of the NGO's indicate their diversity: the International Chamber of Commerce, the International Confederation of Free Trade Unions, the Women's International Cycling Association, the Scandinavian Society of Anesthesiologists, and the International Union of Health Education.

Analyses of NGO's can indicate the extent to which a world society exists and cast light upon the actual and potential role of NGO's in the development of a world society. NGO's may contribute to the conditions that underlie world political institutions and their effective functioning in several ways. Members of NGO's may develop perspectives that are broader than national ones.[4] NGO activities may ameliorate the material and social conditions that underlie certain international conflicts. They may foster the development of international interest groups which cross-cut national boundaries. Formulas for

___

Secretary General, Union of International Associations, June 8, 1964).

For purposes of the analysis reported upon here, other international non-governmental organizations were excluded: NGO's which are confederations of other NGO's, or sections of other NGO's, or whose membership consists only of exile groups. The number of NGO's remaining is 1470. Furthermore, NGO's for which information about the nations which participate is not given are exclude from much of the analysis reported in this paper.

[4] For an analysis of the consequences of interaction within international governmental organizations, see Chadwick F. Alger, "Personal Contact in Intergovernmental Organizations," in Herbert C. Kelman (ed.), *International Behavior* (New York: Holt, Rinehart and Winston, 1965), pp. 523–47; for a discussion of the contributions of international non-governmental sociological associations, see Paul F. Lazarsfeld and Ruth Leeds, "International Sociology as a Sociological Problem," *American Sociological Review*, 27 (Oct. 1962), pp. 732–41.

settling international conflicts may be developed in NGO's and then used in governmental organizations or international law. NGO's may develop structural arrangements for handling conflicts among their own members that can be utilized by governmental organizations. On the other hand, NGO's may simply reflect and reinforce international divisions as they are expressed in regional and other alliances and political groupings. More fundamentally, NGO's may be essentially trivial, transitory, epiphenomena with little impact upon the conditions relevant for the effective operation of world organizations. Or they may simply reflect the governmental conditions and have little independent effect upon the governmental order or the social conditions underlying the political structure.

In any case, the study of NGO's can be useful for the understanding of the conditions related to international peace. In addition, since NGO's are voluntary organizations which differ in many ways from national voluntary organizations, their inclusion in the realm of sociological analysis can aid our understanding of voluntary associations and formal organizations in general. A comprehensive analysis of NGO's would require an immense research effort. Nevertheless, considerable information about NGO's has been collected by the Union of International Associations and is published in the *Yearbook of International Organizations*. The data for the present analysis has been drawn largely from the 1962–1963 edition of the *Yearbook*.

THE QUESTION AND SOME HYPOTHESES

In this paper I will consider one important question pertaining to

NGO's and the world community. To what extent do particular national differences affect the membership, structure, and activities of NGO's? The answer to the question will suggest some of the limits of the role which NGO's can play in fostering a world community.

Several ideas from the study of voluntary associations are pertinent in seeking an answer to the question. We may begin with the premise that among potential members of an organization, it is those whose common, like, or complementary interests overweigh their conflicting interests who will join together in an organization.[5]

[5] This premise is consistent with the point of view of MacIver and Page, when they write: "An association is likely to be formed wherever people recognize a like, complementary, or common interest sufficiently enduring and sufficiently distinct to be capable of more effective promotion through collective action, provided their differences outside the field of this interest are not so strong as to prevent the partial agreement involved in its formation." Robert MacIver and Charles H. Page, *Society* (New York: Holt, Rinehart and Winston, 1949), p. 437.

Like interests exist when persons have similar goals and the attainment of those goals by some persons does not necessarily diminish their attainment by others. *Common* interests exist when persons have goals whose attainment is shared so that some persons cannot approach that goal without the others doing so. *Complementary* interests exist when two or more persons each have resources which the other values sufficiently to make possible a mutually satisfactory exchange. *Conflicting* interests exist when two or more persons have goals such that as one attains his, the other's attainment is diminished. This may be the case if they have the same or different goals. What is critical is that one or both parties is unable to exchange compensating resources with the other party or is unwilling and finds it unnecessary to do so. My use of these terms is similar to that of MacIver and Page, *Society*, p. 440.

For an important discussion of the ambi-

On the basis of that premise, we would expect that nations which have few like, common, or complementary interests and have many conflicting interests are least likely to be represented in many of the same organizations. Furthermore, the organizations in which they do participate will be those which involve like, common, or complementary interests rather than conflicting ones.

Actually, of course, nations are not members of NGO's. Since national associations or even individuals may be members, the selection may not be representative of the nation. Particular religious, political, or economic groups join together because they perceive certain common or complementary interests with similarly situated or oriented persons in other nations. An analysis of national differences in terms of the nationality of members of the NGO's therefore is a crude indicator of actual national differences in interests among members. Nevertheless, most NGO's are concerned with activities that have relevance for occupational roles.[6]

guities in the relationship between national similarities and differences as a basis for the formation of international organizations, see Amitai Etzioni, *Political Unification,* (New York: Holt, Rinehart and Winston, 1965), esp. pp. 19–27.

[6] Within the United States, voluntary associations are even more overwhelmingly organized in relationship to occupational activities. The distribution of types of organizations at the national level, since they in large measure constitute the market of potential members in NGO's, sets some limit to the distribution of types of NGO's. For data on types of voluntary associations in the United States, see *Encyclopedia of American Associations* (Detroit, Michigan: Gale Research Company) and Sherwood Dean Fox, "Voluntary Associations and Social Structure," unpublished Ph.D. dissertation, Department of Social Relations, Harvard University, 1952. An accurate

This sets some limits to the self-selection of national members and makes economic differences among nations a relevant national characteristic. Significantly, too, the fact that most NGO's are formed in terms of members' occupational roles indicates that such roles involve experiences and interests which can be shared and even collectively aided across national boundaries. These ties are among the most fundamental in the development of a world community.

The interests of the members are only one side of the equation. Membership depends upon the characteristics of the organization as well as upon the interests of potential members. We must consider what it is that participation in the organization requires of its members and what benefits they may derive. Several plausible hypotheses about the consequences of different balances of interests among members upon organizational structure and activities can be suggested. First, it may be hypothesized that if members have many conflicting as well as some like, common, or complementary interests and yet are members of the same organization, the organization will operate in a fashion which minimizes demands upon the members even if this means that little is received by the members. On the other hand, it may be hypothesized that participation for such members must yield a great deal of benefits to them, making membership attractive, even if this

entails making relatively high demands. A third hypothesis is that special structural arrangements will be developed to insulate possible conflict while maximizing possible benefits. Finally, one may hypothesize that organizational requirements are so dominant that if members with many conflicting interests do share membership, this will have little effect upon the structure and activities of the organization. Since the balance of interests may differ in different types of organizations testing these hypotheses among different types of NGO's will permit further specification of the hypotheses.

THE FINDINGS

Membership of associations from the United States and from the Union of Soviet Socialist Republics in the same NGO's is used to indicate a high ratio of conflicting interests to common, like, or complementary ones.[7] The use of this indicator has particular political significance, but in the context of the present analysis, it is the set of like, common, complementary, and conflicting interests that is important. Thus the differences in the organization of the economies of the two societies limit the similar-

___

comparison of the types of national and of international associations is impossible without a common set of categories and coding of the associations. Nevertheless, the rank order of the percentage of various types of organizations in the U.S. and among the NGO's is probably similar.

[7] A more precise measure of the balance of interests among members would require information about the associations which actually belong to the NGO's. Such a measure, however, would obviate the possible significance arising from national differences in general. Even using national representation as a measure could be variously done. Instead of the joint participation of two particular nations, nations could be grouped in terms of many different criteria and the relative proportion of each type of nation represented in the NGO could be used as a measure.

ity and commonness of interests in the economic sphere. The similarities in scientific activities, on the other hand, make probable some like and complementary interests, if not common ones. Differences in political ideologies and international power positions entail conflicting interests; the extent to which this colors other spheres of potential NGO members' interests is problematical. In general, it would seem that common interests are not as probable as are like or complementary ones. This is indicated by the stated objectives of NGO's with and without joint U.S. and U.S.S.R. representation. One NGO objective is the promotion of social or material status of the members or representing the members in relations with other organizations. Among NGO's in which the U.S. and U.S.S.R. both participate, only 7 percent claim this objective; among NGO's in which the U.S. but not the U.S.S.R. participates, 20 percent make this claim; among NGO's in which the U.S.S.R. but not the U.S. is represented, 54 percent state this objective; and among NGO's in which neither the U.S. nor the U.S.S.R. participate, 37 percent state this objective.

The first expectation we will examine concerns the likelihood that the U.S. and the U.S.S.R. will tend not to participate in the same NGO's. Among the NGO's for which information is available, about one-third restrict membership to some geographic area. Among the remaining NGO's, 21 percent have members from both the U.S. and U.S.S.R., 50 percent from the U.S. but not the U.S.S.R., 3 percent from the U.S.S.R. but not the U.S., and 26 percent have members who are from neither the U.S. nor the U.S.S.R. This does not support the first expectation. It is true that only one out of five of the organizations which are not regionally restricted have U.S. and U.S.S.R. members and that the U.S. is more often represented in NGO's without the U.S.S.R. than ones with U.S.S.R. members.[8] But if the generally high U.S. level of participation in NGO's and the very low U.S.S.R. level are considered, the U.S. and U.S.S.R. are each more likely to be in NGO's with the other country than in NGO's in which the other is not represented.

These findings can be interpreted in several ways. First, the relative proliferation of associations in the United States must be considered. The number and variety of American associations means that there are more potential members of NGO's in the U.S. than in the U.S.S.R. Furthermore, the relative freedom of association in the U.S. facilitates the self-selective quality of membership which in turn facilitates associational membership in NGO's.[9] Moreover, in addition to the fact that there are fewer Soviet associations, their international participation is affected by

[8] The People's Republic of China (Communist China) is represented in very few NGO's, probably about 3 percent of those which are not regionally restricted. This probably reflects the Chinese government's policy, but also the level of associational proliferation and contact with voluntary associations in other countries.

[9] Recent disclosures of support for international activities by the Central Intelligence Agency of the United States testifies to the importance of NGO's. Such financial aid also indicates that in many cases it is difficult to make a perfectly clear distinction between governmental and non-governmental organizations, even in the United States. See, for example, Sol Stern, "A Short Account of International Student Politics and the Cold War With Particular Reference to the NSA, CIA, etc.," *Ramparts*, 5 (March, 1967), pp. 29–38.

Soviet governmental policy.[10] Furthermore, potential members within the Soviet bloc are fewer than in the non-Soviet bloc. Nevertheless, these findings suggest that even if there are conflicting interests among potential Soviet and American members, at least in certain spheres of activity, there are also common, like, and complementary interests. Indeed, they suggest that for potential Soviet members, membership with American associations offers particular attractions.[11]

---

[10] For example, before World War II, Soviet international sport participation was limited to the Red Sport International. Only after the war did the Soviet policy change and participation in sport activities with "bourgeois" sporting organizations begin. By 1952, the Soviet Union had joined practically every international sport federation. See Henry W. Morton, *Soviet Sport* (New York: Collier Books, Crowell-Collier Macmillan, 1963), pp. 65–102. Changes in Soviet and foreign policy after Stalin have probably led to an increased Soviet participation in NGO's. Soviet participation in the United Nations Specialized Agencies, especially UNESCO, is an indicator of these changes and probably was accompanied and followed by representation in various NGO's. For an account of Soviet policy in regard to sociology and the initial participation of Soviet sociologists at meetings of the International Sociological Association, see "The Social Sciences in the U.S.S.R." *Soviet Survey*, No. 10 (November, 1956), pp. 1–19.

[11] An explanation of this attraction is suggested by Johan Galtung, "East-West Interaction Patterns," *Journal of Peace Research*, 2 (1966), pp. 146–76. He reasons that interaction between the top levels of two interacting social systems is more frequent than is interaction between the lower levels of the two groups or between the top level of one group and the lower levels of the other group. Smoker's analysis of international non-governmental organizations lends support to this hypothesis. See Paul Smoker, "A Preliminary Study of an International Integrative Subsystem," *International Associations*, 17 (June, 1965), pp.

The issue is clarified when we consider the types of NGO's in which the U.S. and U.S.S.R. are represented. Joint membership varies with the type of organization. One can compare the proportion a given type of organization constitutes in the various categories of national representation. For example, NGO's which are made up of workers, as in trade union organizations, are a major type of NGO. There are few such NGO's, however, in which both the U.S. and the U.S.S.R. are represented.[12] Professional and trade union organizations constitute about 10 percent of the NGO's in which the U.S. but not the U.S.S.R. is represented, 14 percent of the ones in which the U.S.S.R. but not the U.S. participates, and 17 percent of the NGO's in which neither the U.S. nor the U.S.S.R. is represented; but such NGO's constitute only 1 percent of all the NGO's in which both the U.S. and the U.S.S.R. participate. The pattern for NGO's in the area of commerce and industry is similar: 11, 4, 18, and 2 percent, respectively. On the other hand, in science and scientific research, the

---

638–46. The data in this paper have not been organized to test the above-stated hypothesis. Nevertheless, the reasoning and evidence of Galtung and Smoker help account for the finding reported here. The U.S. and U.S.S.R., as leaders of their respective blocs, have an interest in interacting with each other, *if* there is to be *any* interaction between the two blocs. As leaders, they have some like interests.

[12] From 1945 to 1948, many Communist and non-Communist trade unions belonged to the World Federation of Trade Unions. In 1949, the International Confederation of Free Trade Unions was founded without Communist trade unions. For an account of the international labor movement, see Lewis L. Lorwin, *The International Labor Movement* (New York: Harper and Row, 1953).

percentages are quite different: 4, 0, 2 and 18 percent, respectively.

On the basis of the framework outlined earlier and in order to permit detailed analysis, the NGO's were divided into three types in terms of their potentiality for consensus. The types are intended to reflect varying degrees to which the international community, and particularly the U.S. and U.S.S.R., share goals and beliefs about the means to reach the goals. Thus Type 1 includes NGO's concerned with technology, science, medicine, or sports; consensus is presumably relatively high in these areas. Type 2 consists of the social or economic NGO's such as employer or profession, trade union, commerce and industry, social and political science, law and administration, or bibliographic NGO's; in these, consensus is presumably moderate. Type 3 includes NGO's dealing with matters about which consensus is presumably low; NGO's concerned with philosophy or religion, international relations, social welfare, education and youth, and the arts are included. In classifying NGO's, their categorization in the *Yearbook of International Organizations* was utilized; see note 2 of Table 1.

It is likely that in areas in which consensus is high, issues are viewed as technical matters. Where consensus is low, value differences are likely to be prominent. In the latter case, the mode of handling the issues is likely to involve bargaining, logrolling, and other political methods rather than the means used in technical matters. Nevertheless, as will be discussed later in the paper, the extent to which an issue is viewed as a technical or as a value matter is not inherent in the issue. It depends, in part, upon the context and han-

dling of the issue. Organizational arrangements may affect the context and style of handling issues; they may even be structured so that the issues are viewed as relatively technical matters. This mode of adaptation may be used particularly in organizations which have members with many conflicting interests relative to like, complementary or common interests. Consequently, the level of consensus and the degree to which organizations deal with technical or value issues, although empirically related, may be analytically distinguished.

One of the previously mentioned features of NGO's can mitigate the significance of an area of interest having low consensus. National representation in an NGO can consist of self-selected associations or associations with specially selected individuals. This is particularly likely in organizations involved in highly value-related activities. In the case of Types 1 and 2 NGO's, however, comprehensive national associations are likely to pre-date and be formed independently of the NGO so that such self-selection is less likely.[13] Never-

[13] The distinction between NGO's formed by the confederation of pre-existing national units or by the establishment of national units by a parent organization is an important one. In many organizations, some combination of both sequences can be found. The consequences for the structure and authority system in these organizations are likely to differ. For analyses of the consequences of such differences within national voluntary associations, see, for example, Seymour M. Lipset, "The Political Process in Trade Unions: A Theoretical Statement," in Morroe Berger, Theodore Abel, and Charles H. Page (eds.), *Freedom and Control in Modern Society* (New York: D. Van Nostrand Co., 1954), pp. 82–124; and David L. Sills, *The Volunteers* (New York: The Free Press, 1957), esp. pp. 2–8.

theless, even in such NGO's self-selection of various kinds can occur. For example, during the immediate post World War II period when the World Federation of Trade Unions included Communist and non-Communist trade unions, the American Federation of Labor was not a member; the Congress of Industrial Organizations, however, was a member. Even within NGO's without Communist representation, self-selection of membership can occur which reduces potential dissensus and conflict among members. Thus the U.S. Farm Bureau withdrew from the International Federation of Agricultural Producers, largely because of policy differences over the role of governments in agriculture; other U.S. farm organizations remained members.[14] In the case of the International Chamber of Commerce, instead of the U.S. Chamber of Commerce, the American

---

Even when the national components predate the establishment of the NGO, another process may facilitate more consensus at the international level than an analysis of the characteristics of each national organization would lead one to expect. In the case of organizations established to meet the needs of the national members, the international activities may be peripheral to the concerns of the rank-and-file members and even of the organizations' leadership. In some such cases, at least, the staff persons or officials involved in international organization relations may have considerable freedom of action and be selected or self-selected because of their concern with international relations in general or because of their compatibility with the style and direction of the NGO.

Furthermore, leaders may share concerns and develop common understanding with leaders of other organizations which are not shared with their own rank and file members. See Louis Kriesberg, "Societal Coordination by Occupational Leaders," *PROD*, III (Sept. 1959), pp. 34–36.

[14] *New York Times*, March 26, 1959.

member is the U.S. Council of the International Chamber of Commerce. The U.S. Council was established at the close of World War II and consists of members who are heavily involved in international trade.

On the whole, the findings presented in Table 1 are consistent with the expectation that the U.S. and U.S.S.R. are most likely to be represented in organizations concerned with matters of presumably high consensus. About half of the NGO's in which they both participate are in the science, health, etc., category, while among the organizations in which they both do not participate, only about one-fifth are concerned with such matters. The lack of any real difference in the participation of American and Soviet associations in NGO's of presumably low consensus compared to those of moderate consensus may be due to the self-selective factor discussed above. In any case, it does appear that joint U.S. and U.S.S.R. representation is most likely in NGO's engaged in areas of activity in which American and Soviet associations are particularly likely to share similar goals and beliefs about reaching them. In such organizations, representatives of the U.S. and U.S.S.R. would tend to have like, complementary, and even common interests, while conflicting interests would be relatively few.

The second set of issues to be explored in this paper is the possible effect of joint U.S. and U.S.S.R. participation upon the structure and activities of NGO's. Actually, these issues are not independent of the likelihood of both the U.S. and U.S.S.R. being represented in the same organizations. Certain organizational arrangements or levels of activity may be conducive to Amer-

TABLE 1   TYPE OF NGO BY TYPE OF NATIONAL PARTICIPATION[1]

	Type of National Participation			
Type of NGO[2]	U.S. AND U.S.S.R.	U.S. BUT NOT U.S.S.R.	U.S.S.R. BUT NOT U.S.	NEITHER U.S. NOR U.S.S.R.
Science, health, etc.	53	22	18	18
Economic, social, etc.	28	41	43	56
Religion, art, international relations, etc.	19	36	39	26
Total (%)	100	99	100	100
(*N*)	(192)	(451)	(28)	(241)

[1] In this table, and in all the following tables, NGO's which restrict membership to any geographic area are excluded.

[2] The science, health, etc., type includes NGO's classified in the *Yearbook of International Organizations* under: technology; science, scientific research; medicine and health; sport, touring, recreation. In the economic, social, etc., type are included NGO's classified in the following fields of activity: employers, professions; trade unions; commerce and industry; economics and finance; agriculture; transport; communications; law and administration; social and political sciences; and bibliography, press. In the religion, art, international relations, etc., type are NGO's classified in the following categories: philosophy, religion; international relations; politics; social welfare; education and youth; and arts, literature, cinema.

ican and Soviet joint representation. As a matter of fact, it is true that Type 1 NGO's, compared to other types, are less likely to have their own paid staff or a large staff, to have more than two levels in the organizational structure, or to have frequent meetings of the general membership. Do these characteristics of Type 1 organizations contribute to the attractiveness of such organizations for joint U.S. and U.S.S.R. representation? Or does the joint participation of the U.S. and U.S.S.R. induce such modifications in NGO's and the concentration of U.S. and U.S.S.R. membership in Type 1 organizations help account for such characteristics of Type 1 NGO's?

First we will examine the kind of activities which the organizations report conducting. Nearly all organizations report the facilitation of the members' activities as an organizational aim. We coded several ways in which this was reported to be done. One way is the exchange of informa-

tion and establishment of personal relations through congresses, institutes, and exchange visits. Since nearly all organizations report these activities, they are of little relevance to our purposes here. Three other kinds of activities are of more pertinence: (1) engaging in joint efforts such as coordinating research or other work of members, (2) providing services for members such as libraries, abstracting services, and training programs, and (3) developing common standards or agreements about nomenclature and uniform codes. Obviously, these activities vary in frequency among the different types of organizations. But more pertinent to our present interest, within each type of NGO, those in which both the U.S. and the U.S.S.R. are represented are more likely to report such activities than are organizations in which either or both countries are not represented (see Table 2). However, among the Type 1 organizations, there is no difference in reports

TABLE 2 PERCENT OF NGO'S REPORTED TO ENGAGE IN SPECIFIED
ACTIVITIES BY TYPE OF NATIONAL PARTICIPATION,
AND BY TYPE OF NGO

Activity	Science, Health, etc.		Economic, Social, etc.		Religion, Art, International Relations, etc.	
	U.S. AND U.S.S.R.	NOT U.S. AND U.S.S.R.	U.S. AND U.S.S.R.	NOT U.S. AND U.S.S.R.	U.S. AND U.S.S.R.	NOT U.S. AND U.S.S.R.
Engage in joint efforts	46	44	72	58	56	38
Provide services for members	14	16	42	25	47	27
Develop common standards or agreements	40	22	34	23	12	4
(N)	(101)	(147)	(53)	(328)	(34)	(233)

of joint efforts of service to members between NGO's with both U.S. and U.S.S.R. participation and NGO's in which either or both countries are not represented. Presumably, the organizational requirements are more important for these matters than whether or not the U.S. and U.S.S.R. are both represented in the same Type 1 organization. Since the organizations in which the U.S. and U.S.S.R. are both represented tend to be ones with a large number of members and such organizations tend to report engaging in these activities more than do NGO's with few nations represented, it is necessary to control for number of nations represented. Holding constant the number of nations represented, we find that in some kinds of activities, among the small organizations, there is no longer any difference between NGO's with and without joint participation of the U.S. and U.S.S.R. Nevertheless, on the whole, it appears that their joint participation is not accompanied by a lessening of activity, but often by a higher level of activity.

Other information from the *Yearbook of International Organizations*

can be used to test this inference. The level of organizational activity is in part indicated by the size of the organization's staff and this is reflected in the size of the budget. The size of the staff in voluntary associations has significance in addition to the level of organizational activity. A large staff is likely to mean that staff persons or the executive secretary of the organization has relatively great power in the organization's policy formation.[15] The delegation of such power to staff persons is not likely in organizations which have few common and many conflicting interests. Therefore it is to be expected that in NGO's with both the U.S. and U.S.S.R. participating, the staff and budget will tend to be small or nonexistent. On the other hand, we have already noted some evidence that NGO's with both the U.S. and US.S.R. represented tend to have higher levels of organizational

[15] Sills, *The Volunteers*, Lipset, *In Freedom and Control*, and Bernard Barber, "Participation and Mass Apathy in Associations," in Alvin W. Gouldner, *Studies in Leadership* (New York: Harper and Row, 1950), esp. pp. 492–93.

activity than other NGO's—or at least no lower levels. Consequently, we have discrepant expectations about the relationships between national representation in NGO's and the size of the organizations' budget and staffs.

Budgetary information is lacking for many NGO's. Among the NGO's for which information is available, NGO's with and without joint representation of the U.S. and U.S.S.R. do not appear to differ in the size of their budgets. If we hold constant the number of nations represented in the organizations, a suggestive difference is revealed. The comparison can only be made among the larger NGO's because of the small number of cases for which information is available among the smaller NGO's. Among the large NGO's there is a tendency for those with joint U.S. and U.S.S.R. representation to have medium-sized budgets (between $10,000 and $49,000) rather than very large or very small budgets. The pattern for staff size is similar. Overall, staff size also does not differ markedly among NGO's with and without U.S. and U.S.S.R. participation. When the number of nations represented in the NGO's is held constant, however, some suggestive differences are again revealed (see Table 3). Among the NGO's of presumably high or moderate consensus, those with joint U.S. and U.S.S.R. representation are slightly less likely than other NGO's to have very large staffs. Among the large NGO's with presumably low consensus, those with or without joint U.S. and U.S.S.R. representation are equally likely to have large staffs. First of all, it is clear that the sphere of organizational activity would affect the size of the staff: staffs are relatively small in NGO's concerned with science, health, etc. Whether or not there is joint U.S. and U.S.S.R. representation is not a major determinant. This may be due to what are in this context conflicting implications of staff size: a high level of activity and delegation of decision-making. Before making any concluding references, it is necessary to examine other findings.

The preceding discussion was based upon the supposition that NGO's with joint U.S. and U.S.S.R. participation will not have centralized decision-making. One indicator of this characteristic available from the *Yearbook* is the number of levels in the organization. Presumably, the larger the number of levels, the more centralized is decision-making and the greater is the delegation of authority by the members. In the case of voluntary associations, the argument is that rank and file direct participation in decision-making is less where several levels exist than where few exist, except that a general membership and only an executive committee may also indicate relatively high delegation of authority by the rank and file members.[16]

Within each type of NGO, organizations with or without U.S. and U.S.S.R. joint representation are

[16] In a bureaucratic organization, with authority flowing from the top down, a large number of levels may be considered to indicate decentralization rather than centralization. Many levels, holding the size of staff constant, would indicate dispersion of decision making. As Peter Blau has pointed out to me in a personal communication, this conceptualization underlies the treatment of a low ratio of managers to non-supervisory officials as an indication of centralization in the paper, Peter M. Blau, Wolf V. Heydebrand, and Robert E. Stauffer, "The Structure of Small Bureaucracies," *American Sociological Review*, 31 (April, 1966), pp. 179–91.

TABLE 3 SIZE OF NGO STAFF BY NUMBER OF NATIONS IN NGO, BY TYPE OF NATIONAL PARTICIPATION, AND BY TYPE OF NGO

Size of Staff	Twenty-Five or More Nations Represented						Twenty-Four or Fewer Nations Represented					
	Science, Health, etc.		Economic, Social, etc.		Religion, Art, International Relations, etc.		Science, Health, etc.		Economic, Social, etc.		Religion, Art, International Relations, etc.	
	U.S. AND U.S.S.R.	NOT U.S. AND U.S.S.R.	U.S. AND U.S.S.R.	NOT U.S. AND U.S.S.R.	U.S. AND U.S.S.R.	NOT U.S. AND U.S.S.R.	U.S. AND U.S.S.R.	NOT U.S. AND U.S.S.R.	U.S. AND U.S.S.R.	NOT U.S. AND U.S.S.R.	U.S. AND U.S.S.R.	NOT U.S. AND U.S.S.R.
None	59	46	27	31	31	35	67	61	56	47	–	45
Volunteers or use other organizations'	13	20	20	8	19	8	13	21	22	15	–	24
1–2	17	22	20	15	9	11	20	7	11	19	–	15
3–9	9	8	18	16	19	19	0	4	11	9	–	9
10 or more	0	3	9	24	22	21	0	2	0	4	–	3
Some, but number not given	1	1	5	6	0	6	0	5	0	6	–	5
Totals (%)	99	100	99	100	100	100	100	100	100	99	–	101
(N)	(86)	(65)	(44)	(93)	(32)	(105)	(15)	(84)	(9)	(235)	(4)	(129)

TABLE 4 NUMBER OF LEVELS IN ORGANIZATION BY TYPE OF
NATIONAL PARTICIPATION, AND BY TYPE OF NGO

Number of Levels	Science, Health, etc.		Economic, Social, etc.		Religion, Art, International Relations, etc.	
	U.S. AND U.S.S.R.	NOT U.S. AND U.S.S.R.	U.S. AND U.S.S.R.	NOT U.S. AND U.S.S.R.	U.S. AND U.S.S.R.	NOT U.S. AND U.S.S.R.
Only general membership	7	7	0	6	3	5
2 levels	67	62	65	61	60	57
3 levels	20	25	35	27	37	30
4 or more levels	3	1	0	2	0	3
Executive committee only	3	5	0	4	0	6
Totals (%)	100	100	100	100	100	101
(N)	(99)	(146)	(52)	(325)	(35)	(233)

equally likely to have three or more levels (see Table 4). Holding the number of nations constant, there is still no difference except among small Type 2 NGO's and large Type 3 NGO's; in these types, NGO's with U.S. and U.S.S.R. participation tend to have only one or two levels (there are too few cases to permit comparison among small Type 3 NGO's). There is a slight tendency, moreover, for NGO's without both the U.S. and U.S.S.R. as participants to have four levels or to have only an executive committee, except among NGO's with potentially high consensus.

If delegation of authority is somewhat less likely in NGO's with both U.S. and U.S.S.R. participation, then general membership meetings might be expected to be substituted. Yet frequent general membership meetings may be relatively difficult if the members have few common, like, or complementary interests and many conflicting ones. As a matter of fact, we find that NGO's with both the U.S. and U.S.S.R. represented have less frequent general membership meetings than do other NGO's (see

Table 5). Among the NGO's with potentially low consensus, surprisingly, this pattern does not hold. Presumably, the self-selection of constituent organizations is an important factor here. Among these NGO's, those with U.S. and U.S.S.R. participation are particularly likely to either have few or many general membership meetings. Holding constant the size of the NGO's does not alter these relationships.

The findings thus far, taken together, have some puzzling inconsistencies. Joint U.S. and U.S.S.R. participation does not seem to decrease the activities conducted, but the development of a large staff to implement the activities may be inhibited. In part, this may be due to the avoidance of delegating authority to a staff and a secretary-general. Similarly, an elaborated number of organizational levels may be inhibited; but frequent general membership meetings are not substituted to compensate for this structural arrangement. These inconsistencies in the findings are partially resolved when we consider one other organizational characteristic: the

TABLE 5 FREQUENCY OF GENERAL MEMBERSHIP MEETINGS BY TYPE
OF NATIONAL PARTICIPATION, AND BY TYPE OF NGO

Frequency of General Membership Meeting	Science, Health, etc.		Economic, Social, etc.		Religion, Art, International Relations, etc.	
	U.S. AND U.S.S.R.	NOT U.S. AND U.S.S.R.	U.S. AND U.S.S.R.	NOT U.S. AND U.S.S.R.	U.S. AND U.S.S.R.	NOT U.S. AND U.S.S.R.
No general meetings	5	8	0	5	3	6
1 every 5 years or less often	3	4	14	5	18	6
1 every 4 years	23	11	14	5	12	10
1 every 3 years	24	20	23	17	3	19
1 every 2 years	20	20	27	21	26	23
1 a year or more often	24	37	22	46	38	35
Totals (%)	99	100	100	99	100	99
(*N*)	(95)	(143)	(49)	(131)	(34)	(217)

number of committees in the NGO's.

Despite the jokes and satire about committees and their proliferation, committees can be a useful device for organizations. In the context of the present analysis, an important utility lies in the possibility than they tend to transform problems from issues to be decided by political bargaining and negotiation to technical matters to be decided by consensus among experts. This can be made clearer if we consider what the differences are between technical and nontechnical issues. As noted earlier in the discussion of consensus and dissensus, the distinction, in large measure, depends upon the persons trying to solve the issue and how they try to handle it. The distinction is not inherent in the issue or content area. If the mode of reaching a decision involves log-rolling and bargaining and the style of the discussion involves polemical debate, the issue will be seen as nontechnical and political in a fundamental sense. Certain conditions make such elements more or less prominent. If the participants have clear constituencies who can hear the discussion, if there

are many constituencies represented, and if the issues are phrased in such broad terms that, at least for the participants, basic value differences are connected to the substantive issue, then the issue is not likely to be viewed as a technical one.

The establishment of committees can affect these conditions. Thus committees meet in relative privacy and all phases of the discussion are not heard by the constituents. Members of a committee may be selected because of their specialized knowledge—their "expert" qualities; this enhances the likelihood that they will discuss the issue in technical terms and feel independent of a definite constituency. A small committee limits the number of constituencies involved in the discussion. Handing problems to a committee usually means first dividing the problem into some of its components and this makes each component seem relatively technical. Most fundamentally, the processes in a committee meeting regularly can help transform an issue. A few persons, meeting regularly and frequently, can develop rules of discussion

TABLE 6 NUMBER OF NGO COMMITTEES BY TYPE OF NATIONAL
PARTICIPATION, AND BY TYPE OF NGO

Number of Committees	Science, Health, etc.		Economic, Social, etc.		Religion, Art, International Relations, etc.	
	U.S. AND U.S.S.R.	NOT U.S. AND U.S.S.R.	U.S. AND U.S.S.R.	NOT U.S. AND U.S.S.R.	U.S. AND U.S.S.R.	NOT U.S. AND U.S.S.R.
None	52	75	47	64	50	69
1–6	14	5	9	10	11	8
7–10	7	1	4	4	3	2
11 or more	9	1	11	3	6	2
Some, but number not given	18	18	28	19	31	19
Totals (%)	100	100	99	100	101	100
(N)	(101)	(148)	(53)	(328)	(36)	(237)

and common understanding. The shared understandings diminish value differences.[17]

The number of committees NGO's have is highly associated with whether or not the U.S. and the U.S.S.R. both participate in them. Within each type of NGO, if the U.S. and U.S.S.R. both participate, the NGO is much more likely to have committees and many of them compared to other NGO's (see Table 6). Furthermore, it should be noted, this organizational characteristic does not vary among the different types of organizations; it is true that large NGO's tend to have committees and more of them than do small NGO's. Nevertheless, even holding constant the size of the NGO, those with joint U.S. and U.S.S.R. participation tend to have

[17] Haas analyzes the role of committees in the formation of consensus in an international governmental organization with a legislative structure. He also points out some of the limitations of the resulting consensus. Ernst B. Haas, *Consensus Formation in the Council of Europe* (Berkeley: University of California Press, 1960). Also see Theodore Caplow, *Principles of Organization* (New York: Harcourt Brace Jovanovich, 1964), pp. 248–49.

committees and many of them. The establishment and proliferation of committees, then, may be an important organizational device to minimize and channel potentially disruptive consequences of joint U.S. and U.S.S.R. participation in NGO's.

CONCLUSIONS

The political and economic characteristics of a nation affect the extent to which its voluntary associations join the same NGO's as do associations from particular other nations. In the cases examined in this paper, the similarities and differences between the U.S. and the U.S.S.R. do seem to have affected the type of NGO in which they both are represented. NGO's pertaining to substantive issues about which members of the two countries are likely to have consensus are most likely to have joint representation. Even in NGO's concerned with issues of relatively low consensus, the self-selection which freedom of association makes possible presumably facilitates joint participation. In addition, complementarity of interests may be of great significance in joint representation when consensus is low.

The NGO's concerned with science, technology, medicine, and sports are considered to deal with matters about which the U.S. and U.S.S.R. have relatively high consensus. Significantly these NGO's tend to have a lower level of activity and less centralized decision-making than do NGO's concerned with social or economic or with moral or political matters. Effectiveness in the latter spheres would seem to require more concerted action than in the former spheres. Such requirements may be an additional factor encouraging joint U.S. and U.S.S.R. participation. These findings indicate some of the limits which national differences set to the role that NGO's can play in the development of a world community.

On the other hand, these same findings have another meaning. For many aspects of the organizations under study, whether or not the U.S. and the U.S.S.R. are both represented in the same NGO has relatively little consequence. Any given aspect of characteristic of an organization is affected by, and itself affects, a multitude of other organizational characteristics and environmental conditions. Herein, of course, lie some of the hopes attached to the joint participation of associations from different nations. If organizational processes unrelated to the conflicting interests of sets of organization members have relatively great importance, then the possibility of forming stable and effective organizations cross-cutting national political boundaries is increased.

In this paper, the analysis has focused upon the consequences of joint U.S. and U.S.S.R. participation in NGO's. We noted that such joint participation seems to be associated with an increased probability of NGO's reporting engaging in a variety of activities. The inference was drawn that in order for members with many conflicting interests relative to common, like, or complementary interests to participate in the same NGO, the NGO must provide attractive benefits. This inference is supported by the indication that among NGO's concerned with issues about which the U.S. and U.S.S.R. are most likely to have consensus, whether or not the U.S. and U.S.S.R. jointly participate has the least consequence.

In order for an organization, at least a voluntary association, to provide many benefits to the members, the members must make high contributions to the organization. One such contribution may be delegation of authority to the leadership or staff of the organization. Presumably, if both the U.S. and U.S.S.R. are represented in the same NGO, there would be some reluctance to do this. Indeed, we found some evidence of this in regard to the number of levels in the organization, size of staff, and size of budget.

The implied inconsistencies in the above findings were resolved by the findings in regard to the structural elaboration of NGO's. The implementation of activities does not seem to be accomplished by an increased frequency of general membership meetings which might compensate for limiting staff size or hierarchal differentation. This form of adaptation, indeed, may be the source of additional strains with both the U.S. and U.S.S.R. represented. The analysis revealed that joint U.S. and U.S.S.R. representation is usually associated with infrequent general membership

TABLE 7 PERCENT OF NGO's HAVING COMMITTEES BY ENGAGING
IN JOINT ACTIVITIES, BY TYPE OF NATIONAL
PARTICIPATION, AND BY TYPE OF NGO

Type of NGO	Engage in Joint Activities		Do Not Engage in Joint Activities	
	U.S. AND U.S.S.R.	NOT U.S. AND U.S.S.R.	U.S. AND U.S.S.R.	NOT U.S. AND U.S.S.R.
Science, health, etc.	89	52	16	5
	(44)	(63)	(51)	(77)
Economic, social, etc.	68	50	13	17
	(38)	(189)	(15)	(138)
Religion, art, international relations, etc.	78	53	25	19
	(18)	(87)	(16)	(144)

meetings. The proliferation of committees appears to be an important organizational arrangement which resolves many of the inconsistencies and dilemmas discussed. Committees can help de-politicize issues and help transform them into technical matters. Committees can also provide a basis for organizational integration different from hierarchal differentiation, federalism, or collective union of sentimental attachments or like interests. The proliferation of committees can be a kind of *functional differentiation.* Just as many NGO's embody a functional differentiation within the world community, cross-cutting national boundaries, so can divisions based upon particular sets of problems within an organization cross-cut national differences among the membership. This kind of differentiation provides an alternative basis for organizational integration.

These findings have implications for the study of organizations in general and of the role of NGO's in the building of world community. Attention to organizational arrangements such as functional differentiation points to the ways in which organizations can be integrated and maintain their activities to some ex-

tent independently of the characteristics of individual members of the organization. The empirical findings also indicate that the international exchange which participation in NGO's can provide may be limited by some of the adaptive arrangements that may help to preserve and perhaps promote the life and effectiveness of NGO's.

In short, characteristics of potential members of an NGO affect whether or not they will belong to an NGO and whether or not they belong is affected by certain characteristics of the NGO. Some of the organizational characteristics, moreover, are affected by the composition of the organization's membership. The impact of the membership composition upon the NGO, in turn, is also dependent upon many other aspects of the NGO and its environment. Some of these mutual relationships are further illustrated in Table 7. Clearly, in each type of NGO, those which report engaging in some joint activities by the members are much more likely to have committees that are other NGO's. Furthermore, among NGO's engaging in joint membership activities, those with both the U.S. and U.S.S.R. represented are more likely than other NGO's to have committees. This pattern is particularly marked among NGO's concerned with science, health, etc. Committees, then, do seem to be a way of getting organizational tasks done. This way is particularly appropriate when members have many conflicting interests relative to common, like, and complementary ones. This adaptive arrangement is particularly likely in organizations in which members tend to view issues as technical matters.

Despite the crudity of the measures used, some clear findings have emerged from the analysis. The implications of the findings, both for the study of organizations and for the role of NGO's in a world community appear significant enough to warrant further research. Such additional research is needed to specify and test the findings and interpretations presented in this paper.

part two

INTERORGANIZATIONAL NETWORKS, TASK STRUCTURE, AND CHANGE

INTRODUCTION

Once organizations are treated as the unit of analysis, it is only a small further step to deal with the relationships among such units. The study of interorganizational relationships and networks of organizations is a significant advance in the direction of a sociology of organizations. However, empirical studies of interorganizational relations are still rare, and tend to be theoretically explorative and methodologically limited.

Theoretically, one problem is to conceptualize and operationalize the great variety of possible relations and transactions that may occur among different organizations and among different parts and levels of complex service delivery systems. Another theoretical problem is, of course, to relate whole networks and systems of organizations to the macrosocial and political variables operating within the larger environment of such organizational systems.[1]

[1] Early attempts to provide a unitary conceptual framework are Philip Selznick, *TVA and the Grass Roots* (Berkeley: University of California Press, 1953), stressing the concept of "cooptation"; Sol Levine and Paul E. White, "Exchange as a Conceptual Framework for the Study of Inter-Organizational Relations," *Administrative Science Quarterly*, 5, (Mar. 1961), pp. 583–601; and James D. Thompson and William J. McEwen, "Organizational Goals and Environment: Goal-Setting as an Interaction Process," *American Sociological Review*, 23, (Feb. 1958), pp. 23–31, subsuming cooptation, exchange, and coalition under the concept of cooperation. More recent conceptual schemes are Harold Guetzkow, "Relations among Organizations," in Raymond V. Bowers (ed.), *Studies on Behavior in Organizations* (Athens: University of Georgia Press, 1966), pp. 13–44; William M. Evan, "The Organization-Set: Toward a Theory of Interorganizational Relations," in James D. Thompson (ed.), *Approaches to Organizational Design* (Pittsburgh: University of Pittsburgh Press, 1966), pp. 173–92; James D. Thompson, *Organizations in Action* (New York: McGraw-Hill, 1967); and Roland Warren, "The Interorganizational Field as a Focus for Investigation," *Administrative Science Quarterly*, 11, (Dec. 1967), pp. 396–419. F. E. Emery and E. L. Trist, "The Causal Texture of Organizational Environments," *Human Relations*, 18 (1965), 21–31; Shirley Terreberry, "The Evolution of Organizational Environments, *Administrative Science Quarterly*, 12 (March 1968), 590–613; Herman Turk, "Interorganizational Networks in Urban Society: Initial Perspective and Comparative Research, *American Sociological Review*, 35 (Feb. 1970), 1–19; and

Methodologically, the problem is how to deal with the new units of analysis, e.g., with "organization-sets,"[2] interorganizational networks, community organizational systems,[3] and state, national, and international organizational structures.[4]

The eight studies in this section all make a unique contribution to the understanding of such larger organizational entities. At the same time, they invariably demonstrate the close connection between task structure and organizational change, especially when the task structure is imbedded in an interorganizational context.

Litwak and Hylton's statement of the nature of interorganizational analysis —in contradistinction to intraorganizational analysis—is based on a comparative-historical analysis of two types of organizations coordinating other organizations within community welfare systems. The two types of coordinating agencies are Community Chests and Social Service Exchanges. The authors identify nine typical problems of such coordinating agencies and propose to "account" for them in terms of a general hypothesis: the development and continued existence of coordinating agencies is a function of organizational interdependence, the level of organizational awareness, the standardization of organizational activities, and the number of organizations involved. This general hypothesis—while bordering on a definition of the concept of "coordinating agency"—nevertheless links the four major interorganizational variables employed in this study. While the analysis is more in the nature of an illustration than an explanatory study, the authors show that the different problem areas can, indeed, be accounted for in terms of the variation of the four interorganizational variables.

Kriesberg's study, published here for the first time, focuses on the way in which organizational arrangements facilitate or constrain cooperation among different types of professionals. Based on interviews with key informants at state (50 states) and local levels (123 communities), the author seeks to determine those organizational factors which condition the relations between public health and mental health professionals working within the context of various public health or mental health programs. Among the environmental and structural characteristics of the programs considered are the structural "location"

Cora B. Marrett, "On the Specification of Interorganizational Dimensions," *Sociology and Social Research*, 56 (Oct. 1971), 83–99.

[2] Evan, "The Organization Set."

[3] Charles M. Bonjean, Terry N. Clark, Robert L. Lineberry (eds.), *Community Politics: A Behavioral Approach* (New York: Free Press, 1971); see also Terry N. Clark (ed.), *Community Structure and Decision-Making: Comparative Analyses* (San Francisco: Chandler, 1968).

[4] see, e.g., James J. Noell, "Government and Society: An Empirical Analysis of Bureaucracy and Budget Allocations in the American States," unpublished Ph.D. dissertation, Department of Sociology, Washington University, St. Louis, 1971; see also Robert T. Holt and John E. Turner (eds.), *The Methodology of Comparative Research* (New York: Free Press, 1970) and Ivan Vallier (ed.), *Comparative Methods in Sociology* (Berkeley: Univ. of California Press, 1971).

of the respective units, their degree of autonomy, their age, and the type of community in which they are located, the number of objectives (subprograms), the degree of departmental specialization, and certain aspects of the skill structure, such as status and hierarchical dimensions among different types of professionals. One of Kriesberg's main conclusions is that interprofessional cooperation is facilitated by joint administration of different programs, but that hierarchical and status subordination among professionals hinders cooperation.

Whereas Kriesberg's study focuses on interprofessional cooperation as an outcome of joint program administration, Aiken and Hage look at the number of joint programs in terms of their effect on the intraorganizational characteristics of sixteen health and welfare agencies in one community. Following the lead of Litwak and Hylton (10), Elling and Halebsky (6), Dill (4), Simpson and Gulley (8), and others, the authors formulate five hypotheses linking such variables as interdependence (number of joint programs), internal structural complexity, organizational innovation (number of new programs), internal communication (including number of committees), centralization of authority, and formalization. Most of the variables are based on indexes constructed from the scaled responses of individuals about the organization in which they work. Methodologically, the study shares, therefore, some of the advantages and disadvantages with others using such indexes, for example, the studies by Hall (25) and Bell (30). While the advantages of this technique lies in conceptualizing organizational dimensions in terms of participants' perceptions, some of the disadvantages are related to the inevitable reductionist assumptions made, the problem of sampling respondents, and the problem of relating individual to group data, i.e., problems relating to the unit of analysis.[5] A provocative observation of the study is the interaction between internal complexity, decentralization, innovativeness, and integration with the external environment, a syndrome already observed in relation to complex general teaching hospitals (7).

Heydebrand and Noell's study of 122 private welfare agencies focuses on organizational innovativeness as the main dependent variable. Moreover, the emphasis is on the relationship between innovativeness and the complexity of the task structure, on the one hand, and the nature of the skill and control structure, on the other. Innovativeness (number of research and demonstration projects) is favored by a complex task structure (especially geographical dispersion, measured here by the number of branches), and by the degree of professionalization of an agency. However, bureaucratization (number of levels) and size have a moderately negative effect on innovativeness. Advancing a

---

[5] see, e.g., Etzioni's conception of "lower participants" vs. "elites," in Amitai Etzioni, *A Comparative Analysis of Complex Organizations* (New York: Free Press, 1961), pp. 89–126. For a critique of Hall's approach, see David Gold, "A Criticism of an Empirical Assessment of the Concept of Bureaucracy on Conceptual Independence and Empirical Independence," *American Journal of Sociology*, 70 (Sept. 1964), pp. 223–26, and Wolf V. Heydebrand, "The Study of Organizations," *Social Science Information*, 6 (Oct. 1967), pp. 66–67 (selection 1 in this volume).

structural interpretation of professionalization, the authors argue that "new" professions tend to become more rationalized in terms of their knowledge base, rather than more professionalized in the sense of assuming the characteristics of the "old" established professions. However, the innovative character of R & D programs appears to be linked to the "generalist" professional aspects of diversified and geographically dispersed social work agencies, rather than to their more "specialist," rationalized, and bureaucratic characteristics.

In general, the total amount of variation in innovativeness accounted for by variations in task complexity and professionalization is relatively low. For a more adequate explanation of the number of R & D projects in private welfare agencies one must, therefore, look to the larger historical, economic, and political context of social welfare in American cities in the 1960s.

The next two studies deal with the interrelation between the task structure of voluntary associations and the larger interorganizational and environmental context. Lieberson and Allen, in an "ecological approach" to organizations, examine the effect of various external factors on the location of national headquarters of voluntary associations. The study, based on over 6000 voluntary associations in the United States, considers such factors as the social, economic, and political characteristics of cities, the nature and diversity of the associations' objectives and major functions, and the geographical dispersion of the membership. The authors argue that the administrative centers of voluntary associations tend to be located in a way which enables them to relate their members to various relevant political, financial, industrial, and other specialized centers of activity and power. The authors draw on additional historical and case materials to substantiate their argument.

Tsouderos' study of growth and change patterns in voluntary associations is an attempt to link increasing formalization, standardization, and bureaucratization to changes in membership size. Following F. Stuart Chapin's theory of cyclical institutional change, the author shows that there are certain regularities of social process which seem to correspond to a logistic curve. While the original study draws on a random sample of 119 voluntary associations, the present paper is limited to an intensive analysis of ten selected cases. The variables considered in this study are membership, income, administrative expenditures, number of administrative staff, and amount of property held. The increase of administrative staff with increasing size in the first cycle of growth is conceivably due to the fact that the author uses absolute numbers rather than the relative size of the administrative staff. However, a positive correlation has also been observed for another type of voluntary association, namely unions.[6] Thus, the generally observed negative relationship between

---

[6] The Anderson-Warkov hypotheses have been tested by Raphael in a study of sixty-five local unions. (Edna Raphael, "The Anderson-Warkov Hypotheses in Local Unions: A Comparative Study," *American Sociological Review*, 32 (Dec. 1967), 768–776.) Contrary to expectations the author finds that the relative size of the administrative staff *increases* with size, and *decreases* as the number of work places increases. This double inversion in the relationship of administration to size and complexity (occupational diver-

size and proportion of administrative personnel may hold for work organizations, but not for voluntary associations. Theoretically, however, it is interesting to note that the formalization cycle appears to be very similar to the dialectical relationship between managerial succession and bureaucratic rules observed by Gouldner.[7] The organization is assumed to cope with certain problems by means of formalization (rules, etc.), then loses membership (or loyalty) as a result of the increasing formalization which generates opposition, and finally responds to the new threat to continuity by still further formalization.

The greater the potential theoretical content of a study, the stronger seems to be the critical response. McWhinney's paper takes issue with two influential "model" approaches to organizations: Chapin's geometric model on which the previous study by Tsouderos is based, and Mason Haire's biological model of organizational growth. McWhinney thus makes a significant and rare contribution to the critical analysis of certain popular elements of organization theory, and points to important limitations of these two models of organizational change. His critique of Haire, particularly, goes far beyond the immediate problem of the relation between "internal" and "external" organizational functions, since it tackles the a priori notion of a homeostatic equilibrium central to biological analogies.

The last paper in this section presents a mathematical model of functional decentralization in organizational service and delivery systems. Kochen and Deutsch construct their model by considering total service cost as a function of the fixed cost per service facility, number of facilities, distance between facilities (geographical dispersion), work load or volume of service (task size), and costs associated with the amount and speed of information and transportation. Optimal increases in the dependability and speed of services, and decreases in overall cost are formulated as the result of decentralization, i.e., an increase in the number of duplicated facilities. The authors start out with a simple version of the model, and then introduce successively more demanding conditions.

Kochen and Deutsch believe that economic and technological development

---

sity) is attributed to the differences in the control structure and the nature of social constraints in voluntary associations (e.g., unions), as over against service organizations (e.g., hospitals, school districts) or business organizations. Raphael suggests that in voluntary associations formal control is located at the base of the hierarchical pyramid, but at the top in business and service organizations. The author suggests further that these differences, together with the differential geographical dispersion of the respective organizations, account for the negative findings in terms of the Anderson-Warkov hypotheses. One may add that Raphael's findings are partly limited by the fact that in voluntary associations such as unions, geographical dispersion represents a form of *segmentation of membership* rather than a *differentiation of places* at which the work of the association itself is performed. The negative correlation of "dispersion" (segmentation) with the administrative component is therefore not really surprising, nor is the positive correlation of dispersion with size and the negative one of dispersion with diversity.

[7] Alvin Gouldner, *Patterns of Industrial Bureaucracy* (New York: Free Press, 1954).

both demand and facilitate an increase in functional decentralization. An increasing demand in volume and precision of services is seen as a "rational" consequence of relatively lower costs being associated with a greater number of multiple service facilities. It is easy to imagine the practical application of such a model to health delivery systems, food distribution centers, self-service gas stations, and a host of other futuristic service systems. The authors' underlying cost-benefit perspective is no doubt highly realistic in the context of modern society. Moreover, it links capitalist technology and the utopian-socialist "administration-of-things-instead-of-people," and suggests a convergence of the regulated market economy and state-capitalist (or state-socialist) planning. Nevertheless, one wonders who plans the planners of such highly efficient service delivery systems, and who decides on the values and priorities implied, i.e., on the nature and quality of goods and services. Functional decentralization in the delivery of services is undoubtedly an extremely attractive organizational equivalent of a fool's paradise (*Schlaraffenland*). But it remains to be seen whether it is, indeed, an image of a future of ever increasing control of people over things, or rather of things over people.

10. INTERORGANIZATIONAL ANALYSIS: A HYPOTHESIS ON COORDINATING AGENCIES

Eugene Litwak and Lydia F. Hylton

One major lacuna in current sociological study is research on interorganizational relations—studies which use organizations as their unit of analysis.[1] There are some investigations, which bear tangentially on this problem, such as studies on community disasters and community power,[2] and the study of Gross and others on the school superintendency.[3] There are some explicit formulations of general rules of interorganizational analysis among some of the sociological classics of the past, such as Durkheim's discussion of organic society and, in a tangential way, Marx's analysis of class.[4] But little

has been done in current sociological work to follow up the general problems of interorganizational analysis as compared to the problems of intraorganizational analysis, that is studies in bureaucracy.[5]

DIFFERENCES BETWEEN INTERORGANIZATIONAL AND INTRAORGANIZATIONAL ANALYSIS

One of the major sociological functions of organizational independence

Reprinted by permission from *Administrative Science Quarterly* (March 1962), pp. 395–420.

[1] We are indebted to Henry J. Meyer for helpful comments on this paper.
[2] William H. Form and Sigmund Nosow, *Community in Disaster* (New York, 1958), pp. 243–44; Floyd Hunter, *Community and Power Structure* (Chapel Hill, N. C. 1953).
[3] Neal Gross, W. S. Mason, and A. W. McEachern, *Exploration in Role Analysis: Studies of the School Superintendency Role* (New York, 1958).
[4] Emile Durkheim, *The Division of Labor in Society* (Glencoe, Ill., 1947). If the concept of organization is used very broadly, it could be argued that Marx provided in

his theory of class conflict a view of interorganizational analysis which, according to him, explains all social behavior.
[5] The systematic study of *intra*organizational analysis has proceeded at a rapid pace since the 1940s as indicated by the many studies in bureaucracy as well as the development of industrial sociology. For a review of some of this literature, see Peter M. Blau, *Bureaucracy in Modern Society* (New York, 1956). Interorganizational analysis has received no such systematic attention. This contrasts somewhat with related social sciences, where interorganizational analysis has been a major concern. For some illustrations in economics see John K. Galbraith, *American Capitalism: The Concept of Countervailing Power* (Boston, 1952), pp. 117–57; Friedrich A. Hayek, *The Road to Serfdom* (Chicago, 1944), pp.

is to promote autonomy. This is important when there is a conflict of values and the values in conflict are both desired. For instance, a society might stress both freedom and physical safety. These two values may conflict in many areas of life; yet the society seeks to maximize each. One way of assuring that each will be retained, despite the conflict, is to put them under separate organizational structures; i.e., have the police force guard physical safety and the newspapers guard freedom of the press. If both safety and freedom were the concern of a single organization, it is likely that when conflict arose, one of the values would be suppressed, as, for example, where the police have control over the press.

This conflict between organizations is taken as a given in interorganizational analysis, which starts out with the assumption that there is a situation of partial conflict and investigates the forms of social interaction designed for interaction under such conditions. From this point of view the elimination of conflict is a deviant instance and likely to lead to the disruption of interorganizational relations (i.e., organizational mergers and the like). By contrast, intraorganizational analysis assumes that conflicting values lead to a breakdown in organizational structure. Thus Weber's model of bureaucracy assumed that the organization had a homogeneous policy.[6] Blau's modification of Weber's analysis (i.e., the individual must internalize the policies of

the organization) assumes that the organization has a single consistent system.[7] Selznick has pointed out that deficiencies in the Tennessee Valley Authority centered around the problem of conflicting values.[8]

By distinguishing between interorganizational and intraorganizational analysis, the investigator is sensitized to the organizational correlates of value conflict and value consistency. Without such a distinction he might concentrate on showing that value conflicts lead to organizational breakdown without appreciating that interorganizational relations permit and encourage conflict without destruction of the over-all societal relations.

Organizational independence for autonomy is functional not only in value conflict but in most forms of social conflict. For instance, values may be theoretically consistent, but limited resources force individuals to choose between them without completely rejecting either choice. (This is one of the classic problems of economics.) Or it may be that a given task requires several specialties, i.e., a division of labor, and limited resources at times of crisis force a choice between them, although all are desirable (for example, the conflicts between the various military services). In such cases organizational independence might be given to the specialties to preserve their essential core despite competition.

A second point follows from the preceding discussion. Interorganizational analysis stresses the study of social behavior under conditions of

---

56–127; K. William Kapp, *The Social Costs of Private Enterprise* (Cambridge, Mass., 1950); E. F. M. Durbin, *Problems of Economic Planning* (London, 1949).
[6] H. H. Gerth and C. Wright Mills (eds.), tr., *From Max Weber: Essays in Sociology* (New York, 1946), pp. 196–203.

[7] *Bureaucracy in Modern Society*, pp. 57–68.
[8] Philip Selznick, *TVA and the Grass Roots: A Study in the Sociology of Formal Organization* (Berkeley, Calif., 1949).

unstructured authority. International relations between nations is the polar model for interorganizational behavior,[9] a modicum of coordination is necessary to preserve each nation, yet there is no formal authority which can impose cooperation. By contrast, most intraorganizational analysis is made under the assumption of a fairly well-defined authority structure. As a consequence, formal authority plays a larger role in explaining behavior within the organization than it does in interorganizational analysis with exceptions, of course, as where the society has a strong monolithic power structure and is very stable. Because of this difference, interorganizational analysis will frequently use, as explanatory variables, elements that are disregarded or minimized in intraorganizational studies.

In summary, interorganizational analyses suggest two important facets of analysis which differ somewhat from intraorganizational analysis: (1) the operation of social behavior under conditions of partial conflict and (2) the stress on factors which derive equally from all units of interaction rather than being differentially weighted by authority structure.

To point out that multiple organizations are effective in situations of partial conflict is not to suggest that they necessarily arise from such situations or that conflict is the only reason for their persistence. Multiple organizations might be the consequence of social growth. Thus in one city, there may be twenty family agencies, with no rational basis for separation except that their growth was an unplanned consequence of immediate social pressure. They might, indeed, be in the process of consolidation. Yet at any given time in a changing society, the investigator must expect to find multiple organizations because the processes of centralization and decentralization are slow. Culture values also condition the development of multiple organizations. In the field of business enterprise there is a tendency to argue that a competitive situation is a good per se; even where a monopoly is more efficient, society might reject it. Within the welfare field, family agencies may be separated by religious beliefs. In short, where there is a situation of partial conflict (which all societies must have because of limited resources for maximizing all values simultaneously), where a society is constantly changing, and where cultural values dictate it, the problem of multiple organizations will be an important one. Consequently there is a need for theories dealing with interorganizational analysis—situations involving partial conflict and interactions without a structure of formal authority.

THE PROBLEM OF CO-ORDINATION

One strategic problem in interorganizational analysis concerns coordination, a somewhat specialized coordination, since there is both conflict and cooperation and formal

[9] Current relations between the United States and Russia are a case in point. These two nations do not recognize any authority superior to them. Because of the potential destructive power of atomic warfare and the interrelated character of international relations they are interdependent, i.e., each can destroy the other or each must take the other into account in order to achieve its national goals. At the same time they have conflicting ideologies, which lead them to seek to maintain regions of legitimized conflict, i.e., national sovereignty.

authority structure is lacking. If the conflict were complete, the issue could be settled by complete lack of interaction or by some analogue to war. Where the conflict overlaps with areas of support, however, the question arises: What procedures ensure the individual organizations their autonomy in areas of conflict while at the same time permitting their united effort in areas of agreement?

One such mechanism is the coordinating agency—formal organizations whose major purpose is to order behavior between two or more other formal organizations by communicating pertinent information (social service exchange and hospital agencies), by adjudicating areas of dispute (Federal Communications Commission), by providing standards of behavior (school accrediting organizations), by promoting areas of common interest (business associations, such as the National Association of Manufacturers, restaurant associations, grocery store associations), and so forth. What characterizes all these organizations is that they coordinate the behavior between two or more organizations. Furthermore, the organizations being coordinated are independent, because they have conflicting values or because the demands of efficiency suggest organizational specialization, yet share some common goal which demands cooperation.

From this reasoning we can advance the following hypothesis: Coordinating agencies will develop and continue in existence if formal organizations are partly interdependent; agencies are aware of this interdependence, and it can be defined in standardized units of action. What characterizes the three variables in this hypothesis (interdependence, aware-

ness, and standardization of the units to be coordinated) is the extent to which they are tied to the organizations to be coordinated. By contrast, if this were an intraorganizational analysis, the development of coordinating mechanisms might be accounted for by authority structure with little concern for the awareness of the units to be coordinated, without standardization, and without significant variations in interdependence. For instance, the leadership might institute coordinating mechanisms because they are aware of interdependence where the units to be coordinated are unaware of this; or they might introduce coordinating mechanisms not to increase efficiency of the organization but to perpetuate their own authority structure; or they might introduce coordinating mechanisms despite lack of standardization because they feel this might speed up the process of standardization. In other words, authority structure is important in understanding intraorganizational behavior, while the variables suggested here for understanding interorganizational analysis may be insignificant.[10]

---

[10] Some of the current studies in industrial organization also suggest the need to consider localized discretion and the decentralization of authority. Seymour Melman's *Decision-Making and Productivity* (Oxford, 1958), pp. 3–23, is a case in point. It is not always easy to know when a situation fits the intraorganizational or interorganizational model. Concerns such as General Electric are nominally one organization but at times resemble a series of independent ones in coalition, while the steel industry consists of formally separated groups which for many purposes tend to act as a unit (in labor bargaining, on pricing of goods, and against political pressure groups).

STUDY DESIGN AND DEFINITION OF TERMS

In order to provide a limited test of this hypothesis, specific attention is directed to two types of coordinating agencies—community chests and social service exchanges. The following nine "traditional" problems of community chest and social service exchanges will be used to show how they can be accounted for by the general hypothesis about coordinating agencies:

1. The emergence and continuing growth of community chest programs.
2. The fluctuations in financial campaigns of community chest programs.
3. The resistance of national agencies such as the American Cancer Society to participating in the local community chest.
4. The ability of some agencies to exclude others from the chest—Catholic agencies exclude planned-parenthood agencies.
5. The development of dual campaigns —Jewish agencies and the Red Cross participate in local community chests as well as run independent national campaigns.
6. The decline of the social service exchange.
7. The fact that community chest agencies have adjudication functions while social service exchanges do not.
8. Principles of growth of new coordinating agencies.
9. The increasing encroachment of community chest agencies on member agencies' budget decisions.

If, in fact, it can be demonstrated that these diverse problems are all variations on a common theme (specified by our hypothesis), then we shall feel that our hypothesis has had initial confirmation. If nothing more,

it has met the test of Ockham's razor.

To simplify the presentation, each element of the hypothesis will be examined separately. Although normally all are simultaneously involved, there are certain forms of coordination which more clearly represent the influence of one of these variables rather than another. In the concluding discussion, systematic consideration will be given to the simultaneous interaction among all three variables as well as alternative mechanisms of coordination (aside from the formal coordinating agency).

First it seems appropriate to define the three terms of the hypothesis —interdependence, awareness, and standardization. By interdependence is meant that two or more organizations must take each other into account if they are to accomplish their goals.[11] The definition of this term has been formally developed by Thomas who points out that there are several kinds of interdependency. The initial discussion here will concentrate on competitive interdependence (where one agency can maximize its goals only at the expense of another), while the later discussion will introduce and relate facilitative interdependence (where two or more agencies can simultaneously maximize their goals). By awareness we mean that the agency, as a matter of public policy, recognizes that a state of interdependency exists. By standardized

---

[11] For a more formal definition and discussion of interdependence see Edwin J. Thomas, "Effects of Facilitative Role Interdependence on Group Functioning," *Human Relations*, 19 (1957), 347–66. In the definition used here the phrase "take into account" is meant in a very immediate sense for in a broad sense all organizations must take each other into account.

actions we mean behavior which is reliably ascertained and repetitive in character, e.g., requests for funds, information on whether the client is served by another agency, price of goods, cost of living index, and the like.[12]

THE EVIDENCE ON INTERDEPENDENCY

HISTORICAL EMERGENCE AND CONTINUED GROWTH OF COMMUNITY CHESTS

If the factors accounting for the origin of community chest programs[13] are examined, one explanation which appears repeatedly is the complaints of donors and fund raisers that they were being confronted with too many requests for assistance and that fund raising was both time-consuming and economically wasteful.[14] It was at the urging of these donors and fund raisers that many of the community chest programs had their beginnings.

It is argued here that these complaints of the donors and their consequent demands for centralized fund raising were manifestations of the increasing interdependence of welfare agencies in the community, for what in effect had occurred was an increase in the number of agencies drawing on a limited local community fund. This meant that any given agency which drew from this common fund was depriving some other agency of a source of money, and that the same donor received many requests for funds. How much the donors' feelings of waste were a consequence of agencies' increasing interdependence on a limited and common pool of funds can be seen if one envisions the situation of few agencies and much money. In such cases no two agencies need go to the same donor. The donor as a consequence, would not feel plagued by many requests and thus become aware of the inefficiency of many agencies carrying on independent fund raising activities.

Community chest programs have continued to grow partly because financial dependence has grown— agencies' demands for funds have grown at the same or a faster rate than national income.[15]

FLUCTUATIONS IN FINANCIAL CAMPAIGNS OF COMMUNITY CHEST PROGRAMS

If the development of coordinating agencies is a function of interdependency, then any fluctuation in interdependency should lead to a fluctuation in coordination. If the pool of resources in the community is suddenly decreased while the number of

---

[12] In contrast to these illustrations the diagnosis and treatment of mental illness is nonstandardized and not public in character.

[13] For a detailed account of the beginnings of the federation movement see: John R. Seely *et al., Community Chest* (Toronto, 1957), pp. 13–29; Frank J. Bruno, *Trends in Social Work: 1874–1956* (New York, 1957), pp. 199–206; and William J. Norton, *The Cooperative Movement in Social Work* (New York, 1927), pp. 8 ff., 112 ff.

[14] Norton, *Cooperative Movement in Social Work*, pp. 50 ff., 68 ff., 113 ff.

[15] An indirect measure of this is that for 1940–1955, where comparable figures were available, the amount collected by united funds (including Red Cross) increased at the same or slightly higher rate than disposable personal income. See *Trends in Giving, 1955* (New York, 1956), p. 3. The rate of increase of gross national product and united community funds is roughly similar between the period 1948 to 1958. See *Trends in Giving, 1958* (New York, 1959), p. 2.

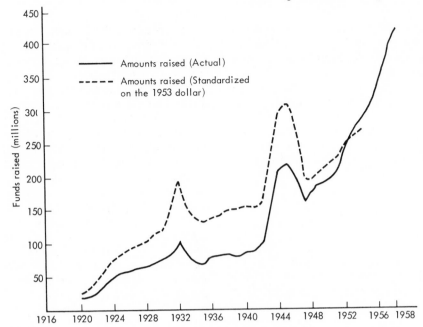

FIG. 1 FEDERATED FUND RAISING

agencies remains the same or increases, then the agencies' competition for funds should increase and their interdependency increase accordingly. Such limitations of community funds occur during periods of crisis—natural catastrophies, depressions, or wars. In one major historical instance, in Cincinnati, the community chest program arose not as a result of donor pressures but was formed as a consequence of a disastrous flood.[16] The same point is made in the study of a modern catastrophe by Form and Nosow, who say, "Hence [inter]organizational integration is the most crucial dimension in disaster."[17]

[16] Norton, *Cooperative Movement in Social Work*, pp. 96 ff., 133 ff.
[17] "While in everyday affairs organizations implicitly are dependent on one another to meet routine problems, they are rarely called out in force to function effectively

Coordination should grow both in periods of prosperity (World War II) and depression, since greater interdependency can be expected in both these periods. Figure 1 indicates that the funds raised by community chest programs rose sharply during the early thirties (prior to governmental intervention in public relief) and again during the war years of the 1940s.[18] These are peak years as

together as one unit. Yet this is precisely what is required in a disaster—the full mobilization and cooperation of interdependent organizations, which normally operate autonomously. Hence organizational integration is the most crucial dimension in disaster" (Form and Nosow, *Community in Disaster*, pp. 243–44).
[18] Sources of data: J. Frederic Dewhurst *et al.*, *America's Needs and Resources* (New York, 1955), p. 437; Russel H. Kurtz, *Social Work Yearbook, 1957* (New York, 1957), p. 175; *Trends in Giving, 1957, 1958, 1959* (New York, *1958, 1959, 1960*). The

compared to the years immediately preceding and following. These data suggest that the coordinating agencies were strengthened during these periods and that interdependency, not the level of income, was an important factor. In summary, instead of three *ad hoc* explanations, i.e., war, depression, and catastrophe, we offer one which provides a general explanation for all three.[19]

RESISTANCE OF NATIONAL AGENCIES
TO LOCAL COMMUNITY CHESTS—
FIXED MARKETS

Interdependency should also be able to account for the fact that certain agencies are able to resist efforts to include them in the coordination process. The answer to such resistance should lie in part in the limited dependence of these agencies on

other agencies in the community; i.e., they can raise money regardless of what other agencies in the community do. When examined, such agencies are seen to have "fixed markets" as far as fund raising is concerned. For instance, the American Cancer Society knows that in any open competition with other agencies, it will receive more funds than most other organizations, because of the public's tremendous concern with, and awareness of, the injurious effects of cancer.[20] The Red Cross is another agency which can resist, to ˙some extent, local community chest involvement because its historic tradition has created a following among donors which amounts to a "fixed market." Fixed markets in fund raising are also enjoyed by religious agencies in cities where their members form a large element in the local community. Such agencies can generally count on receiving priority in any competition for funds. In other words, where an agency, by virtue of cultural norms (religious), historical tradition (Red Cross), or through current interest (American Cancer Society), is able to establish a "fixed money market," it is less dependent on other agencies in the community and can resist efforts at incorporation into community chest programs.

The problem of resistance to community chest programs is a variation on the same basic theme which explains the historical emergence and

---

amount of funds raised is affected by short-term crises and is therefore a more sensitive measure of organizational strength than number of organizations, which do not reflect short-term declines because of career and job commitments. Also, when the dollar value was stabilized by computing all figures on the basis of the 1953 dollar, no significant change in the character of the fluctuations occurred.

[19] The reader can note from Fig. 1 that there is a continued increase in funds following the Korean crisis. This period is marked by aggressive solicitations by national agencies in smaller communities leading to an increase in interdependency. In addition, smaller communities became aware of united giving because of its popularity among the larger cities. An examination of the *Annual Directory of Chests, United Funds and Councils* (UCFC) (1936 and 1956) shows that approximately one-third of the 429 community chests listed in 1936 were in towns of 25,000 or less population. In 1956, towns of this size represented better than half of the 1,182 community chests listed. Also see *United Giving in the Smaller Community* (New York, 1956).

[20] For details regarding the nonparticipation of national agencies, see *Organizing a United Fund* [1953] and *United We Stand* [1958] (New York, 1954, 1959); *1958 Experience in United Funds, 1957 Experience in United Funds,* and *United Giving in the Smaller Community* (New York, 1956); and F. Emerson Andrews, *Philanthropic Giving* (New York, 1950), pp. 152 ff., 156 ff.

the fluctuation of funds raised in community chest programs.

MULTIPLE DEPENDENCIES—DUAL CAMPAIGNS AND AGENCY EXCLUSIONS

Thus far the assumption has been that agencies are linked by one dependency relation, or if multiple dependencies exist they are consistent with each other. Where an agency has multiple relations with another and they are not consistent, i.e., some involve interdependency and some involve independence, then it will affiliate with coordinating agencies only on its own terms. This permits explanation of two classical problems in community chest programs—the exclusion of one agency by another and the running of dual campaigns.

For instance, Catholic agencies frequently insist that planned-parenthood agencies be excluded from community chest programs as a condition of their participation. What characterizes the Catholic agencies is mixed multiple dependencies with other agencies. Like the American Cancer Society, Catholic agencies in strong Catholic communities, have a fixed financial market. Unlike the American Cancer Society, the Catholic agencies perform services (family and recreational) that involve them in an interdependency relation with other agencies in the community. The American Cancer Society's chief service is research, which is equally valuable when done outside the confines of the community. Consequently, Catholic agencies have an incentive to join the local community chest while the Cancer Society does not. Yet, because of their financial independence, Catholic agencies can afford a policy of joining only where the situation is advantageous to them. If a Catholic agency is large, it can force the ouster of the smaller planned-parenthood organization, whose values are antithetical to theirs.

The concept of multiple and conflicting dependencies also explains why some organizations run dual campaigns. Thus Jewish agencies will frequently cooperate with the local community chest and in addition run a separate campaign. The Jewish agencies, like the Catholic agencies, may have a fixed financial market, but have local services which lead to interdependence with other agencies. In addition they have national services which are not dependent on local agencies, such as raising funds for Israel and for research on prejudice. Because of their dual service interests—local and national—their interests only partly overlap that of the local community chest. Because of their financial semi-independence they can enforce their demands for dual campaigns. Similarly, the Red Cross is also likely to run dual campaigns.

Where there are multiple dependencies, there are several possibilities which have different implications for affiliation with local coordination agencies. These are outlined in Table 1. Where all relations are independent of the local community, the organizations will refuse affiliation with local community chests (e.g., American Cancer Society). Where there are mixed dependencies, the organization is likely to enter the community chests only on its own terms (i.e., eliminate conflicting organizations or run dual campaigns). Where the organization has multiple dependencies and they mostly involve interdependence, there will be strong support of local coordinating organizations.

THE DECLINE OF SOCIAL SERVICE EXCHANGE

Since the 1940s there has been a steady decline in the number of social service exchanges from 320 exchanges in 1946 to 220 in 1956 to 175 in 1959.[21] If the hypothesis advanced here is correct, this decline should be a function of decreasing interdependence. To ascertain this relationship, it is necessary to know what the functions of the social service exchanges were. From the turn of the century up to the early 1930s one of the major services offered by private welfare agencies was direct material aid—money, clothing, housing, food, and the like. All agencies sought to maximize their services by providing the largest amount to the greatest number of needy. This made them interdependent, for if two agencies were both providing funds to the same individual without being aware of it, neither agency was maximizing its goals. The social service exchange served an important coordinating function, since any client coming to an agency could be checked through the exchange to see if he was receiving aid from another agency as well.

Two developments undermined the interdependence of the agencies and led to the decline of the social service exchange. First, the government in the middle 1930s took over most of the material assistance programs.

Secondly, the private agencies turned their attention to other services with a strong emphasis on psychiatric casework,[22] which did not necessitate communication between agencies. First, the client was unlikely to seek duplication of service as he might seek duplication of material benefits. Secondly, it was argued that all crucial information could be secured from the client;[23] consequently it was not necessary to have any record of prior counseling by some other agency. In addition, some theorists would argue that it would be unethical to secure information from outside sources without the client's knowledge or consent.[24] In other words, old services which were coordinated by the social service exchange have disappeared and the new services do not result in agency interdependence,[25] and the decline of social service exchanges can therefore be explained by the decreasing interdependence of the member agencies.

ADJUDICATORY FUNCTIONS AND TYPES OF INTERDEPENDENCY

Thus far the analysis has attempted to demonstrate that a series of seemingly diverse problems might all be related to the same underlying phenomenon. A simple derivative of the interdependency hypothesis might now be taken into account. If coordinating agencies develop when there is agency interdependency, the type of coordination should vary with type of dependency. Thomas points out

---

[21] Regarding the experiences of the exchange see *Summary Report of Research on the Social Service Exchange* (New York, 1959); *Social Work Yearbook 1957*, pp. 547 ff; Norton, *Cooperative Movement in Social Work*, pp. 22–24.

[22] See note 21 and *Budget $ in a Community Chest* (New York, 1953).
[23] See note 21.
[24] See note 21.
[25] More recent trends in treatment suggest that social service exchanges might be reorganized around different functions.

TABLE 1 MULTIPLE DEPENDENCIES AND AFFILIATIONS WITH COMMUNITY COORDINATING AGENCIES

Services	Financially Interdependent	Financially Independent (Fixed Markets)
Interdependent (local services)	Nondenominational family services generally have no fixed financial market and have local services which are interdependent with other agencies. They will affiliate most strongly.	Catholic family agencies in strong Catholic communities have a fixed market but are dependent for services. They will affiliate with coordinating agencies on their own terms, i.e., elimination of planned-parenthood groups.
Independent (national services)	National health organizations whose main activity is research but which have achieved no public acceptance of their importance will affiliate with community coordinating agencies.	National cancer associations have a fixed market (because of the public's fear of cancer) and have independence in services because these are mostly research. They will not affiliate with local community coordinating agencies.
Mixed interdependent and independent (both local and national services)	Agencies such as the Red Cross have both national and local services. They are becoming less independent because their tradition is fading. Therefore they enter into local community arrangements while insisting on maintaining their identity and the right to run national mass-media campaigns.	Jewish community councils in a strong Jewish community have a fixed market. At the same time they have both local services (family and recreation programs) and national services (i.e., research on anti-Semitism, aid to Israel, etc.). Hence they are likely to have dual campaigns.

that there is both a competitive and a noncompetitive form of interdependency.[26] In competitive interdependency an agency seeking to maximize its goal deprives another agency of doing likewise. Thus in a community chest where there is a limited amount of social welfare funds, the more one agency receives, the less another agency will receive. By contrast, the social service exchanges dealt with a noncompetitive facilitating interdependency, where maximal goal achievement by one agency was most likely when other agencies maximized their goals as well. Interdependency explains both the rise of the community chest and the decline of the social service agencies.

However, the competitive interdependency of community chests and the facilitating interdependency of social service agencies explains one of the basic differences between these agencies—the adjudicating functions of the community chest. Where a coordinating agency must deal with competitive interdependence, it must have some process for adjudicating the differences which must arise. Such agencies will therefore be characterized by some judicial processes. The budget committees of community chests are frequently the core committees whose major function is to hand down judgments by approving or disapproving budget requests of competing agencies. By contrast, the social service exchanges deal with situations where member agencies have no dispute but can only increase their goal achievement by communicating through the coordinating agencies. This explains why social service exchanges have minor adjudicatory functions.

[26] Thomas, *Human Relations*, 19.

GROWTH PATTERN OF COORDINATING AGENCIES AND SOME POLICY IMPLICATIONS

Our analysis suggests that where interdependency rests on some very stable set of social relations one can anticipate the growth of the coordinating agencies to be constant. Since financial support is one of the most stable social conditions in a money economy such as ours, there is good reason to predict the growth and continued existence of coordinating agencies such as the community chest. By contrast, interdependency based on services has no such stable support, for social services frequently rest on discoveries in the social sciences. For example, psychotherapy is constantly open to the changes of scientific progress,[27] and it would be hypothesized that coordinating agencies dealing with such services might have a much more uncertain future. One of the policy implications which follows is that such coordinating agencies must be given maximum discretion to alter their functions as necessitated by new scientific developments.

SELF-AWARENESS AND COORDINATING AGENCIES— THE FUTURE ROLE OF RESEARCH

Our hypothesis stated that in addition to dependency there must be self-awareness. In dealing with financial services there seems to be little problem in our moneyed economy of self-

[27] In this connection the tendency among some social workers and psychoanalysts to view principles of therapy as permanently fixed displays an attitude more akin to religious movements than to the spirit of scientific progress.

awareness. This in part explains the early emergence of the social service exchanges and the community chest. Interdependency based on services and resting on theories of social behavior might not be so easy to observe and, once observed, difficult to raise to agency self-awareness. To do this requires some publicly certified method such as scientific research. Thus it took a scientific survey such as Buell's[28] to raise to the agency policy level the fact that many agencies were treating different problems of the same families. By not being aware of this, the agencies frequently proposed programs of action to the client which were contradictory. As the social sciences develop, it is quite probable that agencies will increasingly turn to scientific research to see whether interdependence indeed exists.

Aside from the question of research, economic theorists suggest still another factor affecting public awareness of dependency. They point out that where there are many units in the field, e.g., farming, it is almost impossible to observe and communicate interdependency.[29] By contrast, where one has a few units, observability or interdependence is markedly increased. In the initial stages community welfare agencies were supported by a few wealthy individuals.[30] It was perhaps the small number of persons involved which contributed to their perception of the need for, and their ability to cooperate in, the development of community chest programs.[31] Whereas a

large number of agencies will make observability of interdependence difficult, a small number reduces the need for formal coordinating agencies, since coordination can be handled informally.

STANDARDIZATION OF COMMUNITY CHEST AND ENCROACHMENT ON WELFARE AGENCIES

This, in turn, points out the importance of the last term of the hypothesis—standardization of social action. In order for a coordinating agency to operate efficiently it must develop specialists. For such specialists to develop, however, the behavior to be coordinated has to be standard in character—continuing and repetitive over long periods. If, for instance, social workers in family agencies needed to consult with those in children's agencies, and each case was unique, there would be no real way of codifying this information or developing specialists in transmitting this information, and therefore no need for formal coordinating agencies. The most efficient way to handle this form of interdependence might be informal

---

[28] B. Buell, *et al., Community Planning for Human Services* (New York, 1952).
[29] Galbraith, *American Capitalism.* pp. 12–25, 33–53.
[30] See note 13.
[31] By contrast, current chest programs have

a large mass base. However, by 1959 close to 85 percent of the funds were collected under the aegis of business, and support for united fund drives comes from the managers of large organizations, who are relatively few in number. This estimate of 85 percent is rough and is based on the amount given directly by corporations and the amount collected at the place of work. See *Trends in Giving, 1958,* and F. Emerson Andrews, *Corporation Giving* (New York, 1952), pp. 156–58. Like the few wealthy individuals of the past, these managers are able to see the disruptive forces in having many diverse drives.

mechanisms of coordination—telephone conversations between workers, bringing in consultants, and the like.

In short, if one is to move from mechanisms of coordination to formal coordinating agencies, it is necessary to deal with standardized units of behavior. Conversely, to increase its efficiency, a coordinating agency must seek to standardize the behavior which makes up interagency dependency as much as possible. In this connection the growing detailed budgetary demands made by community chests on member agencies are most instructive. From the early times, where community chests asked for a rough estimate of the agencies' current budgetary needs, to the present time, where most elaborate forms are filled out for at least one year in advance, the pressure for standardization of budgetary requests has increased. The same process can be observed in social service exchanges where the drive for standardization has led to an increasingly detailed and complex categorizing of information.

However, the relationship between standardization and coordinating agencies is not monotonic. Thus where extreme standardization takes place, it is frequently possible to coordinate activities via rules or laws rather than community organization. This is ideally what the economists mean when they speak about automatic stabilizers.[32] A good illustration of how interaction between two organizations can be coordinated by rules is the escalator clauses in union-management contracts. It is

possible to have such rules because the computation of the living cost and wage payment is standardized—rules for computing them are readily made, publicly observable, and easily checked, and if done over and over again the same results would have a high probability of occurring.

MECHANISMS FOR PRESERVING CONFLICT

Thus far the analysis of coordinating mechanisms has with one exception centered on the element of cooperation or interdependence. If the interorganizational character is to be retained, there must also be some procedures for preserving autonomy and conflict. For instance, if the community chest were to concentrate just on the cooperative functions, there would be a tendency for organizational merger of member agencies or, as a minimum, the development of uniformity of services. Groups such as the community chest were originally organized around the goal of cooperation (i.e., fund raising and allocation). Group goals once set have a powerful socializing effect on members;[33] furthermore, the group tends to recruit only those who are sympathetic to its goals. Because these socialization and screening pressures for cooperation and merger have a group base, the counterpressures for preserving organizational autonomy

[32] E. Despres, M. Friedman, A. Hart, P. A. Samuelson, and D. H. Wallace, "The Problem of Economic Instability," *American Economic Review*, 40 (1950), 505–38.

[33] The socializing effects of the group on the individual have been thoroughly documented. For a recent summary see Eugene Litwak, "Some Policy Implications in Communications Theory with Emphasis on Group Factors," *Education for Social Work, Proceedings of the Seventh Annual Program Meeting* (New York, 1959), pp. 98–109.

and conflict must have an equally pervasive influence.

One type of group mechanism designated to preserve areas of autonomy and conflict is signaled by the phrase "conflict of interest." The mechanism is a law or a professional code of ethics which says that no individual can belong to two organizations which have legitimate areas of conflict. The incipient basis for this type of mechanism can be seen in the area of welfare fund raising as well. In contrast to the community chests, community councils have in recent years more and more taken the position of defending agency autonomy (i.e., arguing that the community chest does not have the right to make the decisions about the nature and quality of services). If this incipient division of labor crystallizes, then a code of ethics might eventuate in which a person will be said to have a conflict of interest if he sits on the budget committee of the community chest and is a member of the community council committee for preserving professional control of services.

Another possible procedure for maintaining legitimate areas of conflict is to have a division of labor *within* the coordinating agency, with one group dealing with areas of cooperation and the other with areas of conflict and autonomy.[34] Thus the budget committee of the community chest is frequently dominated by lay people who exercise considerable control over fund raising and allocation. Problems of fund allocations frequently lead to questions about the respective merits of various services, however, and the nonprofessional members may lean heavily on their staff experts. The professional members are frequently educated to accept the legitimacy of multiple and competing forms of service and act as a barrier to demands for merger or premature resolution of conflicts.

Still another mechanism for preserving conflict is the use of the ideology of "tradition" as a decision rule. Where there has been a profusion of services in the past, such a decision rule acts to maintain existing states of conflict.[35] This mechanism is generally vulnerable, however, because it does not provide for innovation in a society where change is a cultural characteristic. Therefore, if this mechanism is to survive in our society, it is likely to be used as the courts use the concept of "precedent." The fiction of tradition is maintained, although, *de facto*, much innovation is permitted. There are a variety of other mechanisms of equal merit[36] which will not be explored here.

It must be pointed out that, while interorganizational coordination requires both cooperation and conflict, at any given time emphasis might be on one or the other. Thus, since the middle eighteen-hundreds, the major

[34] For illustrations of a division of labor as a way for maintaining legitimized conflict see Blau, *Bureaucracy in Modern Society,* pp. 64–66; James D. Thompson and Arthur Tuden, "Strategies, Structures, and Processes of Organizational Decision," *In* James D. Thompson *et al.* (eds.), *Comparative Studies in Administration* (Pittsburgh, 1959), pp. 200–202.

[35] The ideology of progress rather than tradition might be used to provide for legitimate areas of conflict where the past has shown a monolithic uniformity.

[36] Mechanisms might be derived by analogy from a consideration of Robert K. Merton, "The Role-Set: Problems in Sociological Theory," *British Journal of Sociology,* 8 (June 1957), 106–20; and Eugene Litwak, "Models of Bureaucracy Which Permit Conflict," *American Journal of Sociology,* 47 (1961), 177–84.

problem in welfare fund raising has been to develop cooperation between competing agencies. It is only recently, when community chests have become exceedingly strong, that attention has shifted to the problem of agency antonomy and preserving legitimate areas of conflict. By contrast, in the business world since the middle eighteen-hundreds primary attention has been paid to preserving areas of conflict between concerns (antitrust laws) and only recently has more attention been paid to the need to maintain cooperation (fair price laws, farmer subsidies, and so on). The researcher must therefore keep in mind that despite the exigencies of any particular situation, interorganizational coordination is characterized by the need to maintain areas both of conflict and of coordination.

INTERACTION OF INTERDEPENDENCY, AWARENESS, AND STANDARDIZATION

Now that each variable has been discussed independently the full implications of our hypothesis can be spelled out by showing the simultaneous interaction of all three variables (interdependence, awareness, and standardization). The following rules should be kept in mind:

1. Standardization is curvilinearly related to coordinating agencies: too little leads to no coordination or *ad hoc* informal types of coordination, while too much means the use of rules or laws rather than coordinating agencies.
2. There is a monotonic relation between awareness and coordination, with low observability meaning little

coordination and high observability leading to high coordination.
3. There is a curvilinear relation between interdependence and coordinating agencies: high interdependency leads to the merger of organizations, with coordination taking place intra-organizationally, while low interdependence leads to no coordination rather than to coordinating agencies.

To these rules one will be added. Although the number of firms is related to awareness it also affects coordination independently. Thus in spite of awareness of interdependence, it is more difficult to develop coordinating agencies where there are a large number of organizations to coordinate (5,000). On the other hand, where there are only a few organizations (2–4) there is no need for coordinating agencies, since much of the coordination can be handled informally by telephone or a luncheon engagement. In short:

4. There is a curvilinear relation between number of organizations and the development of coordinating agencies.

Since in the present paper we are interested in interorganizational analysis, and in highlighting alternative forms of coordination between organizations, we will confine the discussion that follows to the situation where a moderate amount of interdependency occurs.

Table 2 is a scheme for presenting the alternative forms of coordination, given a moderate amount of interdependency. It can be seen that coordinating agencies will arise when there is a moderate amount of standardization, a high awareness, and a medium number of organizations to be coordinated (cell 5). This is a

TABLE 2 TYPES OF COORDINATING MECHANISMS RESULTING FROM THE INTERACTION BETWEEN AWARENESS, STANDARDIZATION, AND NUMBER OF AGENCIES UNDER THE CONDITION OF MODERATE INTERDEPENDENCE*

No. of Organizations	High Awareness			Low Awareness		
	HIGH STANDARDIZATION	MEDIUM STANDARDIZATION	LOW STANDARDIZATION	HIGH STANDARDIZATION	MEDIUM STANDARDIZATION	LOW STANDARDIZATION
Large (over 200)	1. Fair price laws, directories of agencies, etc.	2.	3. Permanent arbitrators for labor grievances	10. Adam Smith's "invisible hand" theory of "laissez faire," i.e., the price mechanism	11.	12. Little chance of coordination
Medium (10–200)	4.	5. Coordinating agencies-community chest	6.	13.	14. *Ad hoc* endorsement committees	15.
Small (2–9)	7. Dental care or unemployment information handled by family agency in small community by informal telephoning—no directories	8.	9. Case conferences or consultations between members of different organizations handled on an informal basis	16. Unstable situation leading to cell 7. Informal cooperation between members of different organizations handled as friendship favors	17.	18. Very poor coordination, handled by *ad hoc* rules and under guise of friendship favors

* Where there is great interdependence, the tendency will be towards organizational merger and the analysis will be intraorganizational mechanisms of coordination. Thus under conditions of great interdependence, high awareness, high standardization, and many people, there will be a tendency for Weber's model of bureaucracy to develop, while under the same conditions but little standardization there will be a tendency for professionalistic models (i.e., hospital) to develop, etc. Where no interdependence exists there is little concern for coordinating mechanisms.

precise statement of our hypothesis with regard to coordinating agencies. However, following rules 2–4 above allows us to develop other forms of coordination. For instance, where there are few organizations to be coordinated, awareness of interdependence on other agencies, and little standardization, the case conference between workers from the two agencies might be the form of coordination (cell 9). Because the worker has high awareness of dependence, she will seek aid; because the problems have not been standardized, there are no specialists who handle the matter of interagency communication; because there are few agencies involved, there is no need for formal organizational coordination. As a consequence, the case conference set up by the worker is likely to be the chief mechanism of coordination. Cell 7 would be slightly different. It has all of the features of cell 9 except that it deals with a highly standardized event. This might be illustrated by the case worker dealing with a client who needs dental care or employment. This is a recurrent problem and simple to describe. Rules in the form of directories are available and the social worker can look up her list and give the client an address or telephone number to call. The mechanism of coordination is a directory. Where there are few organizations involved, this directory will either be in the social worker's head or will be a fairly informal mimeographed sheet. By contrast, if one examines cell 1 which differs from cell 7 in only one regard—there are many organizations involved—one would expect that the directory would take the form of a fairly substantial printed volume. Cell 1 is also the ideal place for the economist's "automatic" stabilizers or the place where behavior between concerns is regulated by self-enforcing laws, e.g., escalator clauses, unemployment insurance. By contrast, cell 3, which differs from cell 1 in the degree of standardization, would have laws which embodied administrative commissions to make decisions. This is because the lack of standardization means that specific rules for each decision cannot be set up, and therefore a commission which understands the general intent of the law must be set up to judge each case as it comes up. The more fully developed the commission, the more likely it is to resemble a formal coordinating agency, as designated in cell 5. The more amorphous and *ad hoc* the commission, e.g., a one-man commission with little if any staff, the less likely it is to overlap with coordinating agencies.

All situations in cells 1–9 are characterized by high levels of awareness as contrasted with those in cells 10–18. Two generalizations can be made about these latter cells. Where they are characterized by high standardization and few organizations (cell 16) they are likely to be unstable (people will become aware), because it is hypothesized that these variables are partially correlated with awareness. Secondly, they are likely to lead to *ad hoc* solutions; where agencies are interdependent but not aware of it, they are likely to coordinate their behavior during periods of crisis and then permit it to lapse afterward.

Cell 14 would be represented by an *ad hoc* committee, such as the endorsement committees, which were the predecessors of the community chest organizations. These endorsement committees (usually set up by the Chamber of Commerce) would provide the stamp of legitimacy for the various drives by endorsing those they judged to be responsible. In effect they were performing a coordinating function. Because money raising was a fairly standardized procedure and because there were only a moderate number of drives, a formal group (a committee) could be set up. Because the awareness was limited, however, the formal group was *ad hoc*—attached to the Chamber of Commerce whose major function lay elsewhere. Furthermore, the committee was not completely formalized; i.e., it did not have the professional staff and fully developed adjudicating functions of later coordinating agencies.

Cell 10 would best be represented by Adam Smith's "invisible hand" theory of economic behavior, e.g., the wheat or cotton farmers before government subsidies. Cell 16 can be represented by friendship favors between workers in two different agencies. Because of standardization and high interdependence the workers are likely to have contact with each other regarding their cases; however, because they are not aware of the organizational interdependence, they might view their cooperation in terms of friendship favors. This state is likely to be unstable because the high standardization and the small number of agencies are both conducive toward the development of awareness and would lead to the behavior indicated in cell 7. By contrast, cell 18 is likely to exhibit the same behavior —the reliance on friendship favors— but because of the low standardization is likely to be highly stable. Cell 12 has low awareness, low standardization, and many agencies (e.g., "hard core" families in New York or Chicago) and is least likely to have any form of coordination.

From this brief analysis of Table 2, it can be seen in what sense the coordinating agency is only one form of interorganizational coordination and how a large variety of potential mechanisms can develop depending on the nature of interaction between interdependency, awareness, and standardization.

SUMMARY

This concludes the evidence for our hypothesis on coordinating agencies. Through a consideration of the concepts of interdependency, awareness, and standardization, one can show that a series of seemingly unrelated phenomena are actually closely related, e.g., the rise of community chests, the decline of social service exchanges, the reluctance of cancer agencies to join community chests, the exclusion of agencies such as planned-parenthood agencies from community chests, the increasing encroachment of community chests on welfare agency service, the fact that some coordinating agencies have adjudicatory functions while others do not, and the demands for coordination among the "hard core" families.

In addition, general rules are suggested for interrelating an entire series of coordinating mechanisms, e.g., committees, laws, directories, and friendship favors. This initial study does not exhaust the questions raised by the hypothesis; it is hoped that our consideration of the problem will stimulate further sociological inquiry into other aspects of interorganizational coordination.

11. ORGANIZATIONS AND INTERPROFESSIONAL COOPERATION

Louis Kriesberg

That professional activities are increasingly conducted within organizations is common knowledge. Social scientists have begun to investigate many aspects of the intraorganizational problems arising from the strains and contradictions between bureaucratic and professional requirements.[1,2] Much less is known about interprofessional relations as they are affected by organizations. Indeed, despite the growth in size and number of large-scale organizations, the many problems associated with their interrelations have barely been studied.[3]

[1] This paper is based upon a portion of the data presented in Louis Kriesberg, "Mental Health and Public Health Personnel and Programs: Their Relations in the Fifty States," University of Chicago, National Opinion Research Center, Report No. 83, January, 1962. The analysis has been developed further and placed in a somewhat different context in this paper than in the report.

The study upon which the report was based was prepared under a contract with the National Institute of Mental Health of the U. S. Public Health Service. The study was commissioned by the Professional Services Branch of the National Institute of Mental Health in order to aid the efforts of the Ad Hoc Committee on Mental Health Activities. Dr. Richard H. Williams, as Staff Coordinator of the Ad Hoc Committee, set the data collection objectives, conducted many interviews, and consulted at all stages of the work.

I am solely responsible for the analysis and interpretation presented.

[2] For example, see Everett C. Hughes, *Men and Their Work*, Glencoe, Ill.: Free Press, 1958, pp. 78–87, 116–30, 140–42; Theodore

Caplow and Reece J. McGee, *The Academic Marketplace*, New York: Basic Books, 1958; Erwin O. Smigel, *The Wall Street Lawyer: Professional Organization Man?* New York: The Free Press, 1964; Alvin W. Gouldner, "Cosmopolitans and Locals," *Administrative Science Quarterly,* 2 (Dec. 1957–Mar. 1958), pp. 281–306, 444–80; Peter M. Blau and W. Richard Scott, *Formal Organizations*, San Francisco: Chandler Publishing Co., 1962, pp. 60–64, 208–209, 244–47.

[3] Several studies and discussions, nevertheless, have been reported. See, for example, William R. Dill, "Environment as an Influence on Managerial Autonomy," *Administrative Science Quarterly,* 2 (Mar. 1958). pp. 409–43; Ray H. Elling and Sandor Halebsky, "Organizational Differentiation and Support: A Conceptual Framework," *Administrative Science Quarterly,* 6 (Sept. 1961), pp. 185–209; William M. Evan, "The Organization-Set: Toward a Theory of Interorganizational Relations," *In Approaches to Organizational Design,* James D. Thompson (ed.), Pittsburgh, Pa.: Univ. Pittsburgh Press, 1966, pp. 173–91; Louis Kriesberg, "Occupational Controls among Steel Distributors," *American Journal of Sociology,* LXI (Nov. 1955), pp. 203–12;

This paper is focused upon the co-operation between public health and mental health personnel in providing their services. I will examine the variations in the extent of such co-operation, particularly as related to differences in major organizational arrangements. Such cooperation is not always desirable and is not the only criterion for evaluation of different organizational arrangements. Both public and mental health personnel, however, think such cooperation is desirable and the developments in these professions and organizations impose pressure for cooperation as well as constraints against it. Whether or not different organizational arrangements affect cooperation and in what ways, therefore, is significant.

The findings reported in this paper are based upon information provided by personal interviews with 740 public health and mental health officials. Interviews were sought with the incumbents of certain key positions in the fifty states of the United States and in two or three communities, which had mental health programs, in each State.[4] Public health respondents

at the state level include heads of the overall public health programs, of public health nursing, of hospitals, and of community services. State mental health respondents are from community-based and hospital-based programs; they include heads of overall programs, of psychiatric nursing, psychiatric social work, psychological services, and of psychiatric services. In states in which there were alcoholism programs, the director of the program was also interviewed. At the local community level, heads of the public health programs, directors of mental health centers or clinics, heads of mental health bureaus or departments, and medical school associated persons who directed community mental health programs were interviewed. Officials were asked for their personal opinions on many matters and for information about themselves, as in any survey. They were also asked to provide information

---

Sol Levine and Paul E. White, "Exchange as a Conceptual Framework for the Study of Interorganizational Relationships," *Administrative Science Quarterly*, 5 (Mar. 1961), pp. 583–601; Eugene Litwak and Lydia F. Hylton, "Interorganizational Analysis: A Hypothesis on Co-ordinating Agencies," *Administrative Science Quarterly*, 6 (Mar. 1962), pp. 395–420; and Marshall E. Dimock, "Expanding Jurisdictions: A Case Study in Bureaucratic Conflict," *In* R. K. Merton, et al. (eds.), *Reader in Bureaucracy*, Glencoe, Ill.: Free Press, 1952, pp. 282–91.

[4] The list of respondents was prepared by the Professional Services Branch, National Institute of Mental Health. The Branch was assisted in the selection by the Community Services Branch and by the regional offices of the Public Health Service. Over

---

95 percent of the selected persons were interviewed. Two-thirds of the interviews were conducted by long distance telephone. All respondents were sent copies of the questionnaire in advance of the interview; 87 percent of the respondents used this opportunity to look through the interview schedule and 39 percent discussed the questions with their colleagues. The interviews lasted from about one hour to three hours and usually were between an hour and fifteen minutes to two hours.

The localities studied are not a sample of all localities in the United States, rather, they are a selection of cities and counties in which there is a mental health as well as a public health program. All the largest cities are represented; those with fewer than 25,000 persons are not included. Communities within three categories were selected: (1) medical school communities, (2) metropolitan communities (over 75,000 population and not a medical school community), and (3) smaller communities (with populations between 25,000 and 75,000 and not a medical school community).

about the organizational arrangements and interprofessional cooperation in their state or locality; they were informants about their own organization as well as respondents.

ISSUES AND HYPOTHESES

Several major changes in public health and mental health are relevant to the increasing cooperation between personnel in these and related fields.[5] First, mental health activities are expanding. The public demand for mental health services has increased. At the same time, more persons in a wider range of professions provide such services. Second, the activities of mental health personnel are changing. In the past, mental health activities were centered in psychiatry and dealt with the treatment of individuals, to a large extent, in institutions. At present, there is growing concern with preventive and social psychiatry. This is expressed by the development of integrated programs of care, treatment, and rehabilitation, by attempts at bridging the gap between hospital and community, by consultation and in-service training with other agencies which deal with people in trouble, and by at least some groping for methods of primary prevention. Third, the activities of

public health personnel are changing. Historically, the public health movement has been concerned with prevention of illness and the promotion of health as exemplified by public sanitation and control of communicable diseases. The related activities such as quarantine, case finding, licensing, and inspection are directed toward the total community. In recent years, public health persons have moved toward treatment and care and a concern with prevention and rehabilitation which is patient-centered. Thus, the fields of mental health and public health have converged in many areas.

Despite these convergences, the differences in training and work activities make it likely that the members of these two sets of professions view themselves as having distinct orientations.[6] The officials were asked:

Each profession and group of professions have their particular way of looking at matters related to their work. From your own experience and from what you have heard, what differences are there in approach between public health and mental health personnel that sometimes pose problems for cooperation between them?

Few respondents denied that there are problem-posing differences in ap-

---

[5] For descriptions and discussions of many of these issues, see Paul V. Lemkau, *Mental Hygiene in Public Health*, New York: McGraw-Hill Book Co., 1955; Richard J. Plunkett and John E. Gordon, *Epidemiology and Mental Illness*, New York: Basic Books, Inc., 1961; and the Report of the Surgeon General's Ad Hoc Committee on Mental Health Activities. *Mental Health and the Development of Comprehensive Health Programs in the Community*, Washington, D. C.: U.S. Government Printing Office, August, 1962.

[6] For a discussion of the peculiar position of psychiatry within the medical profession, see Harvey L. Smith, "Psychiatry in Medicine: Intra or Interprofessional Relationships?" *American Journal of Sociology*, LXIII (Nov. 1957), pp. 285–89. Smith writes, "The 'outsider' status of psychiatry in medicine has given the field an air of defensiveness. It is and it behaves like a minority group, constantly analyzing the sources of hostility, and preoccupied with 'selling' itself." p. 287.

proach between these two sets of professionals. Furthermore, both public and mental health officials generally agreed about what those differences were.

The most frequently mentioned specific difference in approach was that public health personnel are community or group oriented while mental health professionals are individually oriented. The head of the public health programs in one state replied to the question:

I would say public health personnel think in terms of groups of people for prevention and treatment. Mental health personnel, they think of health problems as they relate to an individual person and are unable to make use of public health's time-tested techniques; they are oriented toward treatment of disease.

This response also states the other relatively frequently mentioned specific difference in orientation: that public health personnel are preventively oriented while mental health personel are therapeutically oriented. Here is how the head of social services in a state mental health program expresses that idea:

Public health personnel are health oriented and mental health personnel are illness oriented. A public health person is relatively more interested in prevention; a mental health person is more interested in the clinical aspects. The basic difference is that between pathology and health. We tend to think in terms of direct services for their pathological conditions and they think of turning off the faucet. We live in different worlds. I've made it deliberately strong to highlight the differences.

In addition, respondents spoke of fears of domination by the other profession and of the failure of one or both professions to understand each other's problems or the nature of their work. The head of public health nursing services in one state observed:

The mental health people do not know enough about how the other disciplines work. They don't know enough about how the sanitarian has to work or what he's responsible for. And they don't know enough about the social workers. They do know something about nursing. They do not know administration. And above all, they do not know how to explain what they can do for somebody else because they don't know where they can fit in.

The public health people themselves don't have an understanding of how to use the mental health people. They do have an overall approach and they can't understand why this mental health person doesn't have an overall approach. "Why he's in the field of public health —he's working in the same agency— what did they hire him for at that fantastic salary if he doesn't know *ALL* like I know *ALL*."

Another important area is a resistance between the physician and another person who is not a physician. . . . This natural resistance isn't limited only to someone else being the top man to administer a program. . . . He's not going to cooperate with this mental health person and make things easier for him because if he does, and the mental health person gets too much power and starts too many programs and is in charge of too many areas, he will usurp the doctor as being the top man.

Clearly, public health and mental health officials are aware of many differences in approach and interest that sometimes cause problems in cooperation between them.

The officials, then, have differences in approach and of professional and organizational commitments which handicap cooperation.[7] These differences may even be large enough to be viewed as differences in interest which would make for opposition to cooperation, at least under certain organizational arrangements. On the other hand, the officials generally favor cooperation in principle.[8] The convergence of activities pushes them to it; their specialized and complementary skills attract them to it. They feel that their clients will be treated more effectively and comprehensively if they do cooperate. We will have to see how the interest in, and the concerns about, cooperation may affect the level of cooperation under different organizational arrangements.

The analysis here will focus upon several aspects of interprofessional cooperation. We will consider the extent to which (1) public health personnel are used in mental health programs, (2) mental health personnel participate in public health programs, and (3) mental health personnel are used in other related programs. In addition, I will discuss some varia-

tions in the nature of the cooperation in specific health activities.

The major variation in organizational arrangements which exist at the state and local level need to be described before we consider the possible consequences of different organizational arrangements upon interprofessional cooperation. The organizational arrangements will be described in terms of the operations used to assess them.[9] At the state level, a simple indicator of the overall organization is provided by the location of the "mental health authority." The 1946 National Mental Health Act authorized the Federal Government to allocate funds to the states, on a matching basis, for the support of community mental health programs. Each state designated one of its agencies or departments as the mental health authority with responsibility for receiving and allocating funds. The location of the authority in the states has often shifted. At the time of this study, twenty-five states had designated a public health department as the mental health authority; twelve states had designated a department of mental health or hygiene; and the remaining states had designated other departments: five a department of welfare, four a department of hospitals, three a department of health and welfare, and one a department of institutions.

The respondents were asked to characterize the actual organizational arrangements of mental health activities in their state or locality. These characterizations by officials in each state and locality were combined to yield an overall description of the organizational arrangements in each state and locality. Among the states,

---

[7] These differences are likely to affect the way and extent to which interprofessional cooperation occurs. Thus, when the members of the professions are asked to rank the relative priorities for the use of mental health personnel in public health programs, the professions are not in agreement. For example, mental health education for the public is ranked highest by public health personnel and lowest by mental health personnel. On the other hand, the respondents in mental health programs rank individual therapy highest and the public health officials rank it toward the bottom. Consultation with other public health or health-related agencies and counseling or guidance for people with emotional problems are ranked high by both public and mental health respondents (Louis Kriesberg, "Mental Health and Public Health Personnel and Programs. . . ." pp. 128–40).

[8] *Ibid.*, pp. 128–201.

[9] *Ibid.*, pp. 11–36, 82–127.

three different arrangements were distinguished: the mental health activities are autonomous, a division of public health, or dispersed.[10] Reports from three states were too discrepant to permit categorization. At the community level, the mental health activities were classified only as autonomous or not autonomous.

At the state level, it is possible to examine the relationship between the location of the mental health authority, the officials' characterization of the organization of mental health activities, and other aspects of the organization of mental health and public health programs. All states with the mental health authority formally located in a department of mental health or hygiene were also characterized by the officials as having an autonomously organized mental health program. States with the authority formally located in a department of public health were usually characterized as having the mental health activities organized as a division of public health (eighteen out of twenty-five). Among the states with the mental health authority formally located in another department or agency, most were characterized as having an autonomously organized mental health program (of the thirteen such states, eight were so characterized, four were designated as dispersed, and one as having mental health activities organized as a division of public health).

Mental institutions and community mental health programs are usually administered jointly in states with an autonomously organized mental health program; this is not likely where the mental health activities are a division of public health. States with an autonomous mental health program are slightly less likely to have close relations between the mental institutions and the public health department than are states in which the mental health programs are a division of public health.

At the local level, an autonomously organized mental health program does not necessarily mean that there is a government agency at an approximately equal level with a public health agency. In many cases it means that the community mental

[10] The respondents' characterizations of the organizational arrangements in their states or localities were made in response to a question in which alternative arrangements were presented. Each official was first asked to choose which statement came closest to his opinion about the best possible relationship and then to select the one which best described the actual situation. Any of the first three alternatives were considered to describe an autonomous arrangement, the fourth described an arrangement in which the mental health programs were part of public health, and the fifth or sixth alternatives described an arrangement in which the mental health programs were dispersed. The statements are:

1. Mental health activities are very distinctive and should be organized into separate programs.

2. Mental health activities should be separately and autonomously organized but have provision for consultation with other programs regarding special problems.

3. Mental health activities should be separately and autonomously organized but should have provision for regular and frequent liaison with other programs.

4. Mental health activities are a part of public health and should be a division in the department of public health.

5. There should be a distinct mental health unit within one of the (state) (local) agencies, with a small staff, and other mental health personnel should be assigned to other agencies for varying periods of time.

6. Mental health relates to all programs of health and welfare and mental health personnel should be dispersed among these various programs, with the provision that they meet for periodic conferences, perhaps with a chairman.

health program is nongovernmental or quasi-governmental.

The organizational arrangements at the state level seem to be largely determined by population characteristics of the states. Thus, the states with a relatively dense population generally have autonomously organized mental health programs and states with low density generally have such programs organized as a division of public health. At the local level, arrangements are greatly affected by the form of organization at the state level. Thus, in states with an autonomous mental health program, nearly all the localities have autonomously organized mental health programs; in states in which the public health programs are a division of public health, a majority of the localities have similarly organized mental health programs. It seems safe to regard the organizational arrangements as an independent variable, not determined by preferences regarding interprofessional cooperation.

Now we can consider the possible effects of such organizational variations upon interprofessional cooperation. First, consider the effects if we assume a simple mechanical model. Presumably, personnel in jointly administered programs will be more likely to cooperate than would those in separately administered programs. Assuming some general wish for cooperation, joint administration should facilitate its actualization. Administrative heads can order personnel from different programs to participate in each others' programs. The activities of each set of professions would be more visible to the personnel of the other than if the programs were administratively separate. Working in the same organization provides the

opportunity for shared experiences and common understandings which facilitate interprofessional cooperation. By this reasoning, we would expect that where the mental health programs are within a department of public health, mental health personnel would be extensively used in public health programs and the same would be true of public health personnel in mental health programs. The use of mental health personnel in other related, non-mental health programs would be highest where the mental health activities are conducted in other departments.

The implications of variations in organizational arrangements would be different if we assume a conflict model of organizations. We have observed that the personnel in this study have professional identities and organizational commitments which might make them reluctant to be subordinate to members of another profession. If we consider the relative power of the professions and the professional identity of heads of unified programs, the implications for interprofessional cooperation are somewhat different than if we assume a simple mechanical model.

If one professional is subordinate to another, each will have different interests regarding interprofessional cooperation. Thus, public health officials in states where the mental health programs are a division of public health are most likely to favor increased utilization of mental health personnel. On the other hand, mental health respondents in states in which the mental health programs are autonomously organized are most likely to favor increased utilization of mental health personnel in public health and other related programs. The very organizational arrangements, then, affect the desires for cooperation.[11] Furthermore, the arrangements may affect the relative power of different categories to implement their wishes: to force their own participation in the other's programs; to keep the others from participating in their own programs; or to coerce the others to participate in their own programs.

Taking into account these ways in which organizational arrangements affect wishes for cooperation and the balance of forces among the professions, we would expect that public health personnel uitlization in mental health programs would be greatest where the mental health programs are dispersed, and not a division of public health. This follows from several considerations. Mental health personnel in organizations in which they are subordinate to public health personnel would be reluctant to have public health personnel participate: they could not control their activities. They would be less reluctant in settings in which mental health programs are autonomous or even dispersed. The mental health professions would be least able to prevent public health personnel from participating in their programs when their activities are dispersed. The mental health professions would be most able to limit public health participation where their programs are autonomous but in those cases the public health personnel would be reluctant to participate. Consequently, public health personnel would be more extensively used in mental health programs where the programs are dispersed or in other departments and utilization would

be less extensive where the mental health programs are autonomously organized or in a department of mental health.

The conflict model should have more relevance at the state than at the local level. The feelings of professional and organizational identification are more strongly held by state than by community personnel.[12] Organizational arrangements in general may have more significance in the states than in the communities because organizational separation may be associated with greater physical distance between the programs within the state than within a locality. Furthermore, within the community informal, interpersonal processes can play a more important role than in the larger structures of the state.

This reminds us that interprofessional cooperation may be affected by many factors in addition to organizational arrangements. First of all, there are the inherent exigencies of the activities themselves. Cooperation will be concentrated in programs of greatest potential mutual benefit. Some programs, members of both professions agree, can benefit from the skills of both or need more common effort than other programs. For example, the officials generally believe that mental health personnel should be used in public health nursing programs and they agree that such personnel are less needed in environmental sanitation. And indeed, mental health personnel generally participate in public health nursing programs and not in environmental sanitation.

---

[11] Evidence in support of these statements may be found in Kriesberg, "Mental Health and Public Health Personnel . . . ," pp. 37–81.

[12] For evidence on this from the same study, see Louis Kriesberg, "Careers, Organization Size, and Succession," *American Journal of Sociology,* LXVIII (Nov. 1962) 355–59.

In addition, variations in the environments of the organizations may affect the degree of cooperation. Thus some states and localities differ in population size and density and ratio of different kinds of professionals to the population and to each other. These variations may affect the extent of interprofessional cooperation. Finally, one must allow for the idiosyncratic variations which may affect the way programs are administered and how members of particular professions work together.

THE FINDINGS

Public health and mental health personnel are visible and important to each other. At least at the level at which the respondents operate, some degree of contact between them is almost universal. The officials were asked if they had any dealings or interaction in the course of their professional work with personnel from the other profession. Among the respondents at the local community level, 86 percent of the public health officials said they had such contact with mental health personnel and 87 percent of the mental health respondents reported some interaction with public health officials. At the state level, 98 percent of the heads of public health programs and 91 percent of the other public health respondents reported that they interact with mental health personnel in the course of their professional work. Conversely, 94 percent of the state heads of mental health programs and 90 percent of the state mental health persons in community-based programs report interacting with public health personnel; the state mental health respondents in hospital-based programs are

relatively more isolated although even 80 percent of them report such interaction.

The respondents were also asked, "What is the purpose of the interaction?" Among respondents at the state level, the purpose most frequently mentioned is consultation concerning program planning or development; except that state mental health respondents in hospital-based programs are more likely to mention coordination of treatment or provision of services. Hospital-based mental health respondents are more isolated from public health personnel than are community-based mental health personnel. If they do interact with public health personnel, they are less likely than the community-based personnel to interact with the heads of the public health programs (19 percent compared to 32 percent). Related to this, hospital-based respondents are less likely than the community-based respondents to consult about program planning or development (26 percent compared to 49 percent).

At the local level, respondents mention referral of cases as the purpose of interaction somewhat more often than program planning. The local mental health respondents are most likely to mention case consultation as the purpose of their interaction with public health personnel.

The purpose of the interaction varies among respondents in different organization settings. Thus, if the mental health programs are part of public health or another department, officials tend to report interacting in the course of their regular administrative liaison activities. More significantly, where the mental health programs are part of another department, the respondents tend to report consultation about program planning and development; while if the mental health programs are autonomous, respondents are more likely to report interacting about particular, day-to-day activities, especially coordination of treatment or provision of other services.

A formally integrated organization relieves participants of the pressing need for day-to-day coordination—that kind of coordination is built into the formal procedures. Instead, they can engage in more general and broad coordination; indeed, they may be motivated to do so because it is required if the components' activities are to be sufficiently close to maintain the integrity of the formally unified department.[13]

Given the existence of independent mental health and public health agencies and some interdependence, a wide range of mechanisms could meet the needs for coordination. Since only a few organizations are involved, members are aware of the need for coordination, and the problems are varied and unstandardized, "case conferences or consultations between the members of different organizations handled on an informal basis" is the most likely form of coordinating mechanism.[14]

THE UTILIZATION OF PUBLIC HEALTH
PERSONNEL IN MENTAL HEALTH
PROGRAMS

In each locality, the respondents were asked to report whether or not

persons from certain public health departments were involved in various "direct" mental health programs. A definition of direct mental health programs that was to be used in answering the questions was provided:

By "direct" mental health programs are meant agency programs in which the *primary* responsibility is either: 1) care, treatment or rehabilitation, on an outpatient or in-patient basis, of persons whose primary disorder has been labeled as mental or emotional disorder; or (2) mental health education and promotion for the general public; or (3) some combination of the above two types of functions. (Thus, a vocational rehabilitation agency which concerns itself with the rehabilitation of some mental patients does not have that responsibility as its primary or major function, and would not be defined as a "direct" mental health program. If mental health personnel talk with parent-teacher groups on occasion, that would be defined as part of a "direct" mental health program, but if they consult, provide in-service training, or mental health education for the school or other agency program, that will be considered as the use of mental health personnel, with their concepts and techniques, in other health or health-related programs.)

The reports of the respondents were combined to yield a summary description. More often than not, if one person reported cooperation and the other did not, and we had no direct evidence to the contrary, cooperation in that program was considered to exist.

The reports from the 123 communities selected for study are presented in Table 1. Most localities utilize public health personnel in at least some mental health programs. Utilization is greatest in programs which can most readily benefit from

---

[13] This interpretation is consistent with the findings drawn from a wide range of organization studies; see Blau and Scott, *Formal Organizations*, esp. pp. 183–85.
[14] Litwak and Hylton, "Interorganizational Analysis," Table 2, p. 417.

TABLE 1 UTILIZATION OF PUBLIC HEALTH PERSONNEL IN DIRECT MENTAL HEALTH PROGRAMS, SUMMARY OF REPORTS FROM 123 LOCALITIES, IN PERCENTAGES

Mental Health Program	Public Health Division					No Such Personnel Used	No Such Local Program	No Information	Total Percent	Total Number of Localities
	Maternal and Child Health	Nursing	Health Education	Vital Statistics and Research	Hospital and Medical Facilities					
Diagnosis	33	36	10	12	33	29	3	4	160	123
Therapy	18	28	9	7	28	38	3	6	137	123
Supportive services for patients receiving therapy	27	69	9	8	25	15	2	4	159	123
Supportive services for families of patients	28	63	11	7	22	17	3	6	157	123
Services for patients leaving or formerly in mental hospitals	15	56	12	7	23	21	5	5	144	123
24-hour emergency service	1	6	–	2	23	31	33	10	106	123
Mental health education	33	52	42	8	18	20	5	6	184	123
Utilization of nursing homes, half-way houses, sheltered work shops, etc.	9	34	6	2	18	30	20	6	135	123

TABLE 2 UTILIZATION OF PUBLIC HEALTH PERSONNEL IN DIRECT MENTAL HEALTH PROGRAMS,
SUMMARY OF REPORTS FROM FIFTY STATES

Mental Health Program	Public Health Division						No Such Personnel Used	No Such State Program	No Information	Total Number of States
	Maternal and Child Health	Nursing	Health Education	Vital Statistics and Research	Hospital and Medical Facilities	Local Health				
Diagnosis	31	20	10	15	20	28	9	–	1	50
Therapy	20	22	10	10	21	20	13	–	1	50
Supportive services for patients receiving therapy	21	42	12	10	22	31	5	–	–	50
Supportive services for families of patients	22	42	13	10	18	32	2	–	–	50
Services for patients leaving or formerly in mental hospitals	12	41	7	9	22	34	2	1	–	50
24-hour emergency service	1	6	1	2	11	7	17	16	2	50
Mental health education	24	38	45	19	19	29	1	–	–	50
Utilization of nursing homes, half-way houses, sheltered work shops, etc.	7	22	9	7	28	21	5	6	1	50

the skills and activities of public health personnel. Thus, mental health education most frequently has some utilization of public health personnel, particularly from the nursing and health education divisions. Supportive services for patients receiving therapy and for families of patients also frequently involve public health personnel, usually from the nursing divisions. Diagnosis and services for patients leaving or formerly in mental hospitals have somewhat less frequent use of public health personnel, but more frequent than for other mental health programs.

Table 2 presents the findings for the states. In most states two or three officials, nearly always the heads of overall programs, provided the necessary information. Local health services are included among the public health divisions at the state level; but, since it is a state program, it is omitted from the localities. The data are presented in raw numbers and should be doubled to make them comparable with the percentages reported for the localities.

Clearly, cooperation is much more extensive at the state level than at the local level. The patterns of utilization, however, are essentially the same. For example, at the state level too, mental health education most frequently utilizes public health personnel. Public health personnel from the health education division, followed by nursing, are most frequently utilized.

The information summarized in Tables 1 and 2 also provides the basis for relating the extent of interprofessional cooperation with organizational arrangements. A summary score for each state and locality was derived by counting the number of public health divisions involved in each mental health program. The 24-hour emergency service program was omitted because so few states and localities had such a program. The resulting sum was divided by the highest possible sum.[15] The localities and the states were each ranked according to the resulting percentage scores. The variability was high. The localities and states were each divided into quartiles. Among the localities, the first quartile consists of communities with percentages of 28 or above; the second quartile are those with scores of 15–27; the third quartile are those with scores of 8–14; and the lowest quartile consists of localities with scores of 7 or less. Among the states the percentages are higher, reflecting the generally higher level of cooperation; the range in each quartile is: first quartile: 54 or above; second quartile: 40–52; third quartile: 30–38; and the lowest quartile: 26 or less.

Table 3 presents the association, among the localities, between the extent of utilization of public health personnel in mental health programs and the organization of mental health programs. Autonomously organized mental health programs are only slightly less likely than other programs to have very high utilization.

[15] In the localities, the highest possible score would be 35, since the local health division was not included; in the states the highest possible sum would be 42. The total score was divided by the highest possible score minus the number of programs for which information was missing times five in the states or five in the localities. The resulting percentage is not decreased by lack of information for a particular program, but it is reduced by the absence of any of the seven mental health programs used in the calculations. None are absent at the state level, only a few in the localities. See Tables 1 and 2.

TABLE 3 UTILIZATION OF LOCAL PUBLIC HEALTH PERSONNEL IN DIRECT
MENTAL HEALTH PROGRAMS BY CHARACTERIZATION OF LOCAL
MENTAL HEALTH ORGANIZATIONS, IN PERCENTAGES

Utilization of Public Health Personnel in Direct Mental Health Programs, Localities Ranked in Quartiles	Characterization of Local Mental Health Organization*	
	Autonomous	Not Autonomous
First quartile	21	32
Second quartile	26	20
Third quartile	23	34
Fourth quartile	30	14
Total percent	100	100
Number	(70)	(44)

* The organization of the mental health programs could not be characterized for nine localities.

TABLE 4 UTILIZATION OF LOCAL PUBLIC HEALTH PERSONNEL IN DIRECT
MENTAL HEALTH PROGRAMS BY ESTABLISHMENT OF A SEPARATE
GOVERNMENT AGENCY WHICH HAS PRIMARY RESPONSIBILITY FOR
COMMUNITY MENTAL HEALTH PROGRAMS, IN PERCENTAGES

Utilization of Public Health Personnel in Direct Mental Health Programs, Localities Ranked in Quartiles	Establishment of Separate Government Agency*		
	No Separate Agency	Established 1950 or Later	Established 1949 or Earlier
First quartile	20	25	39
Second quartile	30	18	17
Third quartile	24	32	22
Fourth quartile	26	25	22
Total percent	100	100	100
Number	(50)	(40)	(23)

* Information about the establishment of a separate government agency was unavailable for ten communities.

The direction of the relationship is as anticipated, but the degree of relationship is very low. Before attempting to interpret this finding, it is advisable to consider additional material.

Localities with long-established separate government agencies providing community mental health programs tend to have the most extensive utilization of public health personnel in mental health programs. (See Table 4). The relationship is not very strong, but it suggests that interprofessional cooperation, at least at the local level, depends upon informal understandings which take time to develop.

Community characteristics may also affect the level of cooperation independently of the organizational arrangements. Thus, in communities with personnel who are innovative and experimental, more extensive cooperation is likely. Localities with medical schools are particularly like-

TABLE 5 UTILIZATION OF STATE PUBLIC HEALTH PERSONNEL IN DIRECT
MENTAL HEALTH PROGRAMS AND ORGANIZATION OF
STATE MENTAL HEALTH PROGRAMS

Utilization of Public Health Personnel in Direct Mental Health Programs, States Ranked in Quartiles	*Characterization of State Mental Health Organization*			*Location of Mental Health Authority*		
	Autonomous	*Division of Public Health*	*Dispersed*	*Mental Health Dept.*	*Public Health Dept.*	*Other Dept., Agency*
First quartile	14	32	57	0	28	46
Second quartile	24	26	14	25	28	15
Third quartile	24	26	29	42	28	8
Fourth quartile	38	16	0	33	16	31
Total percent	100	100	100	100	100	100
Number	(21)	(19)	(7)	(12)	(25)	(13)

ly to have such personnel, followed by metropolitan communities, while small communities are least likely to have such personnel. This is indicated by the tendency for new developments in the use of mental health personnel outside of direct mental health programs being reported more often in medical school communities than in large metropolitan communities and least in small communities. Communities with medical schools are particularly likely to make extensive use of public health persons in mental health programs, the large metropolitan communities follow, and the lowest utilization is in the small communities. (The percent in the first quartile is: 37, 20, and 20 and in the second quartile: 24, 30, and 20, respectively.)

At the state level, organizational arrangements are markedly associated with the extent to which public health personnel are used in mental health programs (see Table 5). Utilization is much less extensive in states with autonomously organized mental health programs than in states in which the programs are a division of public health. This is consistent with the expectation that programs

which are administered together will have relatively high mutual participation by personnel from each program.

Utilization, however, is highest in states in which the mental health programs are dispersed. We must account for this higher utilization. The conflict model helps to do so. Consider how organizational arrangements affect the interests of each set of professions and the means of implementing their interests. Where the mental health programs are dispersed rather than a division of public health, mental health personnel would be more desirous of cooperation since the terms of cooperation would be less likely to be set by public health officials. Furthermore, cooperation with public health personnel may provide allies for the mental health personnel's efforts to maintain control over their own programs.

Organizational arrangements have more importance at the state than the local level because the professional and organizational identifications of the professionals are greater at the state level. Furthermore, the larger size and heterogeneity of the states compared to the localities means that idiosyncratic factors play a smaller role. Thus, states with long-established community mental health government agencies are no more likely than other states to have high utilization of public health personel in mental health programs. The number of psychiatrists per 100,000 population in each state is unrelated to the extent of utilization.[16] Population size and per capita income of the states are also unrelated to the extent to which public health personnel are utilized in mental health programs. There is a tendency for states with high densities to have relatively little utilization. High density, however, is strongly associated with mental health programs being organized autonomously. The relationship between population density and utilization, therefore, may be spurious.

THE UTILIZATION OF MENTAL HEALTH PERSONNEL IN PUBLIC HEALTH PROGRAMS

The heads of the mental health and public health programs in each state and each locality were asked to report the extent to which mental health personnel participated in various public health, welfare, and other programs. The respondents were given this definition of "mental health personnel":

By "mental health personnel" we mean a person who is employed in an *agency* (hospital or community, public or private) full- or part-time, and who has as least some professional training in one of the following fields: psychiatry,

clinical psychology, psychiatric social work, psychiatric or mental health nursing, or mental health education. "Mental health personnel" includes generic social workers if they have had some experience in a "direct" mental health program; it also includes social scientists if they have had some experience in a "direct" mental health program. (This definition excludes persons in private practice, unless they spend *some* of their time in work with an agency.)

The respondents reported the extent of utilization in the following terms: full-time person(s) employed, part-time person(s) employed, frequent consultation (at least once a week), occasional consultation, and in-service training. Employment meant that one or more persons gave full- or part-time services in the program being considered, regardless of who employed him. Of course, in a given state or locality, for a given program, mental health personnel might be used as occasional consultants and to provide in-service training; in that case, both kinds of utilization were indicated.

The reports from all the respondents in the same state or the same locality were combined. Information from other portions of the interviews and from published sources about the programs were used to help reconcile discrepancies. One public health program, "local health services," was not included among the localities, because it was only a state program.

Table 6 presents the utilization of mental health professionals in public health programs among the localities. Again, interprofessional cooperation is concentrated in public health programs which appear to be able to use mental health personnel most readily and, perhaps, with least threat. Utilization is highest in school health

[16] The information was for 1959; it was taken from Table 6 of *Fitfeen Indices: An Aid in Reviewing State and Local Mental Health and Hospital Programs,* Joint Information Service of the American Psychiatric Association and the National Association for Mental Health, Jan. 1960.

TABLE 6 EXTENT OF UTILIZATION OF MENTAL HEALTH PERSONNEL IN PUBLIC HEALTH PROGRAMS, SUMMARY OF REPORTS FROM 123 LOCALITIES, IN PERCENTAGES

Public Health Program	Extent of Utilization									
	Full-time Person Employed	Part-time Person Employed	Frequent Consultation	Occasional Consultation	In-Service Training	No Utilization	No Such Local Program	No Information	Total Percentage	Total Number of Localities
Communicable diseases	11	4	2	27	7	56	6	2	115	123
Chronic diseases	19	12	12	33	13	30	9	2	130	123
Aging	19	13	8	41	11	24	12	4	132	123
Dental health	6	2	2	5	3	67	17	2	104	123
Maternal and child health	24	17	27	30	24	24	2	3	151	123
Nursing	26	16	30	30	37	13	2	3	157	123
Environmental sanitation	4	2	1	11	4	67	11	5	105	123
Occupational health	2	2	2	18	2	54	19	3	102	123
Health education	19	15	18	41	18	19	2	5	137	123
Hospitals and medical facilities	36	15	15	24	13	22	7	3	135	123
Vital statistics and research	17	11	6	18	2	43	8	4	109	123
Drug addiction	16	9	5	19	2	33	28	3	115	123
Alcoholism	30	15	15	28	7	22	12	3	132	123
School health	37	20	40	23	15	13	2	2	152	123
Crippled children	18	11	15	34	8	27	10	3	126	123

Table 7 Extent of Utilization of Mental Health Personnel in Public Health Programs, Summary of Reports from Fifty States

Public Health Program	Full-time Person Employed	Part-time Person Employed	Extent of Utilization			No Utilization	No Such State Program	No Information	Total Number of States
			Frequent Consultation	Occasional Consultation	In-service Training				
Communicable diseases	9	4	4	17	3	21	–	–	50
Chronic diseases	15	5	9	21	10	10	–	–	50
Aging	20	10	11	26	12	4	–	–	50
Dental health	5	4	1	12	4	32	–	1	50
Maternal and child health	19	12	17	22	12	3	–	–	50
Nursing	31	7	24	13	20	1	–	–	50
Environmental sanitation	3	3	–	7	3	39	–	1	50
Occupational health	5	3	3	15	5	28	1	1	50
Health education	19	7	22	21	12	3	–	–	50
Hospitals and medical facilities	28	9	17	24	12	5	–	1	50
Vital statistics and research	21	11	9	15	8	16	–	–	50
Drug addiction	19	8	11	24	6	2	4	2	50
Alcoholism	28	16	16	21	10	3	1	–	50
School health	12	16	22	20	12	1	–	–	50
Crippled children	12	12	12	25	7	9	–	–	50
Local health services	16	15	20	23	11	4	–	–	50

and in nursing programs. It is also relatively common in health education, hospitals, and alcoholism programs. Where mental health personnel are used, it is typically as consultants and usually only occasionally. In-service training is not very widespread except in the nursing programs. Mental health personnel are used on a full-time basis most commonly in the school health and alcoholism programs.

The extent of utilization at the state level is presented in Table 7. As in the use of public health personnel in mental health programs, the states are much more likely than the localities to have extensive cooperation. The patterns of utilization among the states, however, are similar to those among the localities. Participation of mental health personnel is most extensive in the nursing, alcoholism, and hospitals and medical facilities programs. Utilization is also relatively extensive in the aging, maternal and child health, school health, local health services, and health education programs. Mental health personnel are used most frequently to provide occasional consultation. In-service training is most widely used in the nursing programs. Mental health persons are used on a full-time basis most commonly in the nursing, hospitals and medical facilities, and alcoholism programs.

In order to relate organizational arrangements with the utilization of mental health personnel in public health programs, a summary index of utilization for each state and locality was constructed. For each public health program, the use of full-time person(s) was weighted four; part-time person(s), three; frequent consultation, two; occasional consultation, one; and in-service training,

two. The sum for all the public health programs was divided by the highest possible score, minus twelve for any program about which we lacked information.[17] The states and the localities were ranked according to the resulting percentage scores and divided into quartiles.

Among the localities, as can be seen in Table 8, high utilization of mental health personnel in public health programs is slightly more like-

---

[17] The highest possible score for each program is twelve. For all sixteen state public health programs the highest possible sum would be 192. The utilization of mental health personnel was summed and divided by 192, minus twelve for any program about which we lacked information. For the localities, the local health services was omitted from the public health programs and the weighting method was slightly modified. The modification was adopted because of the possibility that a few respondents considered the various possible uses of mental health personnel as a scale rather than as independent of each other. Thus, they may have reported that some mental health persons worked full time in a particular utilization, but they may have felt it unnecessary to say that other mental health personnel were also used to provide occasional consultation in that program. On the other hand, a respondent may have said, "all uses" and every one of the kinds of uses would have been checked when that was an exaggeration. These problems are less significant for the state summaries because we usually had more than one and often more than two informants for each state. It was felt best, however, to make a slight modification in the case of the localities. The modification was as follows: If *only* "full-time person(s) employed" was reported for a given program, instead of getting a weight of four for that program, it was raised to six. If *only* a "part-time person(s) employed" was reported, then instead of a weight of three, a weight of four was given for that program. On the other hand, if each and every kind of use was given, instead of the total weight of twelve, a total weight of eleven was given.

TABLE 8 UTILIZATION OF LOCAL MENTAL HEALTH PERSONNEL IN PUBLIC
HEALTH PROGRAMS BY CHARACTERIZATION OF LOCAL MENTAL
HEALTH ORGANIZATIONS, IN PERCENTAGES

Utilization of Mental Health Personnel in Public Health Programs, Localities Ranked in Quartiles	Characterization of Local Mental Health Organization*	
	Autonomous	Not Autonomous
First quartile	19	30
Second quartile	26	27
Third quartile	24	23
Fourth quartile	31	20
Total percent	100	100
Number	(70)	(44)

* The organization of the mental health programs could not be characterized for nine localities.

ly where the mental health programs are not autonomously organized. This is consistent with the expectation that interprofessional cooperation will be higher where programs are administered together. The modifications of that model cannot be tested since we are not able to distinguish between mental health programs which are dispersed and those which are a division of public health.

The length of time that a separately organized government agency primarily responsible for community mental health activities has existed is positively, but not strongly related to the degree to which mental health personnel are used in public health programs. Thus, localities with longer established government agencies responsible for mental health programs are slightly more likely to have high utilization of mental health personnel in public health programs than are localities with no such agency (30 percent compared to 20 percent).

The type of community also has some effect upon the utilization of mental health personnel in public health programs, as shown in Table 9. Clearly, medical school commu-

nities are most likely to have relatively high utilization of persons in the mental health professions in public health programs; small communities are least likely. This may be due to greater experimentation in the use of mental health persons outside of mental health programs. Furthermore, there is more desire for interprofessional cooperation in medical school communities. Mental health personnel who are associated with medical schools are much more likely than other local mental health respondents to desire increased use of mental health personnel outside of mental health programs. In addition, the association may be due to the presence of larger numbers of mental health personnel per capita in the medical school communities and less personnel in the small communities.

Table 10 presents the relationship between the organization of mental health programs among the states and the utilization of mental health personnel in public health programs. In accord with the simple mechanical model, utilization is highest where the mental health programs are a division of public health. The tendency for utilization to be higher where the

TABLE 9   UTILIZATION OF LOCAL MENTAL HEALTH PERSONNEL IN PUBLIC
HEALTH PROGRAMS BY TYPE OF COMMUNITY, IN PERCENTAGES

Utilization of Mental Health Personnel in Public Health Programs, Localities Ranked in Quartiles	*Type of Community*		
	Medical School	*Metropolitan*	*Small*
First quartile	34	28	13
Second quartile	24	32	22
Third quartile	24	18	27
Fourth quartile	18	22	38
Total percent	100	100	100
Number	(38)	(40)	(45)

TABLE 10   UTILIZATION OF STATE MENTAL HEALTH PERSONNEL
IN PUBLIC HEALTH PROGRAMS AND ORGANIZATION
OF STATE MENTAL HEALTH PROGRAMS

Utilization of Mental Health Personnel in Public Health Programs, States Ranked in Quartiles	*Characterization of State Mental Health Organization*			*Location of Mental Health Authority*		
	Auto- nomous	*Division of Public Health*	*Dispersed*	*Mental Health Dept.*	*Public Health Dept.*	*Other Dept., Agency*
First quartile	24	32	14	17	24	31
Second quartile	14	37	14	17	32	15
Third quartile	33	21	29	42	24	15
Fourth quartile	29	10	43	25	20	39
Total percent	100	100	100	101	100	100
Number	(21)	(19)	(7)	(12)	(25)	(13)

mental health programs are autonomous rather than dispersed, however, is not accounted for by this model. To account for that finding, we must add the conflict model. Presumably, where the mental health programs are autonomously organized, mental health personnel are in a stronger position to arrange for cooperation. Since consultation is the most common form of cooperation, the secure base provided by autonomously organized programs facilitates such ventures. For mental health personnel in dispersed programs, the base for making such arrangements is weaker.

Now let us consider whether or not other state characteristics are associated with the extent to which persons in the mental health professions are used in public health programs. The number of years a separately organized government agency with primary responsibility for community mental health programs has been established is not related to this measure of cooperation. The number of psychiatrists per 100,000 population in the state is also not related. Among the population characteristics of the states, population density and per capita income are not related. Population size, however, is somewhat associated: states with larger populations tend to have more extensive utilization of mental health personnel in public health programs than do less populated states.

TABLE 11 EXTENT OF UTILIZATION OF MENTAL HEALTH PERSONNEL IN OTHER-RELATED PROGRAMS, SUMMARY OF REPORTS FROM FIFTY STATES

Other Programs	Extent of Utilization								
	Full-time Person Employed	Part-time Person Employed	Frequency Consultation	Occasional Consultation	In-service Training	No Utilization	No Such State Program	No Information	Total Number of States
Rehabilitation	24	9	17	17	9	5	–	–	50
Accident prevention	4	5	3	18	6	19	2	2	50
Juvenile delinquency	18	15	12	24	8	4	1	2	50
Family service	15	12	10	22	10	6	4	–	50
Mental health in education	22	15	16	20	13	–	–	1	50
Health and welfare council	8	4	8	24	4	10	2	1	50
Public assistance	3	2	14	24	7	12	–	1	50
Correctional and penal system	25	8	18	20	7	4	–	1	50

TABLE 12 UTILIZATION OF LOCAL MENTAL HEALTH PERSONNEL IN OTHER-RELATED PROGRAMS BY CHARACTERIZATION OF LOCAL MENTAL HEALTH ORGANIZATION, IN PERCENTAGES

Utilization of Mental Health Personnel in Other-Related Programs, Localities Ranked in Quartiles	Characterization of Local Mental Health Organization*	
	Autonomous	Not Autonomous
First quartile	28	23
Second quartile	19	32
Third quartile	26	20
Fourth quartile	27	25
Total percent	100	100
Number	(70)	(44)

*The organization of the mental health programs could not be characterized for nine localities.

THE UTILIZATION OF MENTAL HEALTH PERSONNEL IN OTHER-RELATED PROGRAMS

In addition to information about the activity of mental health personnel in public health programs, the respondents were asked to report about the extent of utilization of mental health personnel in the following programs: rehabilitation, accident prevention, juvenile delinquency, family service, mental health in education, health and welfare council, public assistance, and correctional and penal system. Note that several of these programs are large ones, more encompassing than some of the more specific programs considered part of the general public health service.

The state reports of the utilization of mental health persons in each of these other-related, but nondirect mental health programs are summarized in Table 11. Among these programs, several are reported to have about as extensive utilization as many of the public health programs. This is the case for the mental health in education, correctional and penal system, rehabilitation, and juvenile de-

linquency programs. In many states mental health personnel are employed on a full-time basis in these broad programs. On the other hand, little utilization is reported for accident prevention, and, significantly, for public assistance and health and welfare council programs.

In the local communities, again, there is less extensive utilization of mental health personnel than at the state level. The pattern of utilization is only a little different. Utilization is relatively high in juvenile delinquency, mental health in education, family service, and rehabilitation programs. Few localities report any utilization of mental health personnel in accident prevention programs.

Summary scores for the utilization of mental health personnel in these other programs were computed by the same weighting procedure used to summarize their utilization in public health programs. The states and localities were again divided into quartiles according to the resulting percentage scores.

As can be seen in Table 12, there is no relationship between the organization of mental health programs at the local level and the extent to which

TABLE 13 UTILIZATION OF STATE MENTAL HEALTH PERSONNEL
IN OTHER-RELATED PROGRAMS AND ORGANIZATION
OF STATE MENTAL HEALTH PROGRAMS

Utilization of Mental Health Personnel in Other-Related Programs, States Ranked in Quartiles	Characterization of State Mental Health Organization			Location of Mental Health Authority		
	Auto-nomous	Division of Public Health	Dispersed	Mental Health Dept.	Public Health Dept.	Other Dept., Agency
First quartile	19	32	29	25	24	23
Second quartile	29	21	29	17	24	39
Third quartile	14	37	29	8	36	15
Fourth quartile	38	10	14	50	16	23
Total percent	100	100	101	100	100	100
Number	(21)	(19)	(7)	(12)	(25)	(13)

mental health personnel participate in other-related programs. This is not inconsistent with the mechanical model. The mental health programs which are autonomously organized are not likely to be part of a welfare or other non-mental or non-public health program. Consequently, personnel in nonautonomous mental health programs are no more likely to be involved in other-related programs than are mental health personnel in autonomously organized programs.

The length of time a separate government agency has had responsibility for community mental health programs is also unrelated to the extent of utilization of mental health persons in other-related programs. The type of community, however, is clearly associated with the utilization of mental health personnel in these programs. Medical school communities and metropolitan communities are more likely to have extensive utilization than are the small communities. (The percent in the first quartile are 32, 25, and 20, respectively and 26, 35, and 36, respectively, in the second quartile.) The reasons for this are probably the same as those suggested to

explain the relationship between community type and the utilization of mental health personnel in public health programs: the relative per capita presence of mental health personnel, the relative tendency for innovation, and the greater desire of medical school associated mental health persons for personnel cooperation.

Among the states there appears to be a slight association between organizational arrangements and the utilization of mental health personnel in other-related programs (see Table 13). According to the simple, mechanical model, one would expect that mental health personnel would be most extensively employed in other-related programs where the mental health authority is in "other departments or agencies." There is only a slight indication of this, and only if high utilization is considered to be the upper two quartiles. The low degree of association may be due to the gross nature of the categories used. Perhaps where mental health programs are in a welfare department, utilization of mental health personnel in welfare programs is relatively high. Such relationships would be obscured by the heterogeneity of the organizational arrangement category, "other departments or agencies," and the heterogeneity of the index of other-related programs.

Utilization of mental health personnel in other-related programs may not be particularly high in states in which the mental health authority is located in "other departments or agencies," however, because of the considerations which are included in the conflict model. Mental health personnel presumably are reluctant to cooperate when they must do so on terms set by other professionals. Being administratively located within another agency often has this effect. Nevertheless, when so located, some cooperation may be induced. When the mental health authority is located in a mental health department, mental health personnel are most able to avoid cooperation on unsatisfactory terms, even if this means that cooperation is relatively low. Consequently, the use of mental health personnel in other-related programs would be low when the mental health authority is located in a mental health department and only moderately high if located elsewhere.

There is no relationship between the degree of utilization and (1) the length of time a separately organized government agency with responsibility for community mental health activities has been established, or (2) the population size, density, or per capita income of the state, or (3) the number of psychiatrists per 100,000 population of the state.

CONCLUSIONS

Interprofessional cooperation is based upon the inherent possibilities of mutual benefit from cooperation. Whether or not members of a given profession have skills or knowledge which members of another profession can utilize depends upon the state of the art in each and the kinds of material with which each is working. Cooperation of some sort may also be induced by the requirements arising from serving the same clients. Interprofessional cooperation, then, cannot be expanded indefinitely nor can it be completely prevented when it seems necessary or advisable to members of a profession.

Organizational arrangements affect interprofessional cooperation within the broad range set by the state of their professional skills and the commonality of their clients. The organizational structures within which professionals are employed can affect their awareness of other professions' activities and may increase or decrease the need for cooperative action in regard to clients. I began the analysis of possible organizational effects by presenting a simple mechanical model. Professions which are in the same organization are likely to cooperate with each other in their professional activities. Formal regulations and informal interactions would result in coordinated activities and awareness of the activities of other professionals in the organization. The potentialities of proliferating cooperation would thus tend to be realized.

The implications of a conflict model were also considered. Members of each profession develop particular ways of thinking about their work, what is important about their tasks, and what are their special contributions. Even in professions which have always existed within organizational settings, professionals do not want to give control of the use of their skills to persons outside of the field. Organizational arrangements vary in the extent to which members of a given profession retain control over their own professional activities. Consequently, members of a profession would be reluctant to cooperate with another profession insofar as that cooperation is conducted under terms set by the other profession. Furthermore, organizational arrangements vary in the extent to which one profession has the power to induce members of another profession to accept cooperation, to induce them to provide cooperation, or to prevent them from providing it. In short, organizational arrangements do not vary simply in the degree to which sets of professions within the organization are neutrally coordinated and brought into association. Arrangements vary in the relative power different professions within the organization have, and this affects the interests of the professions and their ability to implement those interests.

The findings support the simple mechanical model, with modifications drawn from the conflict model. Thus, we did find that public health participation in mental health programs was moderately high when the mental health programs were organized as a division of a public health department and the participation of mental health personnel in public health programs was greatest in such organizations. The findings, however, also indicate that modifications of the model must be made. Thus, the extent of interprofessional cooperation, by each measure, was relatively low when the mental health programs were organized autonomously. Presumably, under such arrangements, public health personnel would not be able to control their activities and therefore

would be reluctant to participate in mental health activities. Furthermore, mental health personnel would be reluctant to participate in non-mental health programs where their control over their own activities would be less than in their own organizations, and the authority of other professions to induce mental health personnel to participate in other programs would be less if mental health personnel had an autonomous structure. Thus, too, the participation of public health personnel in mental health programs was particularly high where the mental health programs were dispersed. Presumably, under such arrangements, public health personnel would not be reluctant to participate. Furthermore, the mental health personnel would not be resistant to the cooperation of public health personnel because the latter would not have the authority to dictate the terms of the exchange and may even be allies in dealings with other professions; perhaps, too, even if the mental health personnel are resistant, their ability to set limits to the participation of others is less than under other organizational arrangements.

Interprofessional cooperation is facilitated if the programs in which the professionals are working are administered together. Even with the divergencies of orientation and interest between the professions, joint administration facilitates cooperation. The findings also suggest that insofar as the joint administration entails subordination, the subordinated profession will be reluctant to cooperate.[18]

---

[18] It should be noted that interprofessional cooperation is not the only criterion for evaluating organizational arrangements. Even insofar as interprofessional coopera-

The effects of organizational arrangements upon interprofessional cooperation appear to be less at the local than at the state level. In part, this may be due to the lesser importance of organizational identification among public and mental health personnel at the local level. Unencumbered by organizational commitments, the personnel are freer to cooperate in terms of the inherent task requirements. In addition, at the local level, we are considering the relations between only a few agencies. Informal understandings developed over time and personal qualities and propensities of the heads of the agencies do not cancel each other out as is the case in a larger and necessarily more heterogenous unit such as a state. In short, within a given locality, the leaders and the rank-and-file professionals can reach understandings about cooperation—or fail to do so. Idiosyncratic characteristics of

the locality do affect the extent of interprofessional cooperation.

In essence, bringing members of possibly cooperating professions together under a common administrative head does not ensure the most extensive cooperation. Interprofessional relations have competitive and conflicting aspects as well as complementary and cooperative ones. Depending upon the balance of these aspects, varying combinations of the simple mechanical model and the conflict model would provide an adequate explanation for the extent of interprofessional cooperation. Similar studies of other professions in other organizations would be necessary to test this generalization further. The differences between the local and state levels provide some support for this interpretation. The differences also indicate some of the conditions which affect the importance of organizational arrangements in accounting for interprofessional cooperation. More detailed information about the form and nature of such cooperation would make it possible to further test the ideas presented. The collection and use of data from each state and from localities in every state necessitated using gross measures. We were thus able to examine fundamental variations in organizational arrangements under different conditions and for a relatively large number of cases.

---

tion is important, choices must be made about the professions between whom cooperation has special priority. All programs cannot be administered together at the same time. For example, at the state level, the joint administration of mental health and public health programs usually means the community mental health and the mental institutions are separately administered. This means that the cooperation between different mental health specialists in these two sets of programs is reduced.

12. ORGANIZATIONAL INTERDEPENDENCE
AND INTRA-ORGANIZATIONAL STRUCTURE

Michael Aiken and Jerald Hage

The major purpose of this paper is to explore some of the causes and consequences of organizational interdependence among health and welfare organizations.* The aspect of organizational interdependence that is examined here is the joint cooperative program with other organizations. In particular, we are interested in relating this aspect of the organization's relationships with its environment to internal organizational behavior.

Thus this paper explores one aspect of the general field of interorga-

Reprinted by permission of the American Sociological Association from *American Sociological Review*, 3, 6 (December 1968) 912–31.

* This is a revised version of a paper read at the annual meetings of the American Sociological Association, San Francisco, California, August 30, 1967. This investigation was supported in part by a research grant from the Vocational Rehabilitation Administration, Department of Health, Education, and Welfare, Washington D.C. We are grateful to Charles Perrow for helpful comments on an earlier version of this paper. In addition, we would like to acknowledge the cooperation and support of Harry Sharp and the Wisconsin Survey Laboratory during the interviewing phase of this project.

nizational análysis. The effect of the environment on organizational behavior as well as the nature of the interorganizational relationships in an organization's environment are topics that have received increasing attention from scholars in recent years. Among studies in the latter category, there are those that have attempted to describe the nature of organizational environments in terms of the degree of turbulence (Emery and Trist, 1965; cf. Terreberry, 1968) and in terms of organizational sets (Evan, 1966). Others have emphasized transactional interdependencies among organizations (Selznick, 1949; Ridgeway, 1957; Dill, 1962; Levine and White, 1961; Levine et al., 1963; Guetzkow, 1966; Litwak and Hylton, 1962; James Thompson, 1962; Elling and Halebsky, 1961; Reid, 1964.) Still others have emphasized the importance of an understanding of interorganizational relationships for such problem areas as education (Clark, 1965), medical care (Levine and White, 1963), rehabilitation and mental health (Black and Kase, 1963), delinquency prevention and control (Miller, 1958; Reid, 1964); services for the elderly (Morris and Randall, 1965); community action (Warren,

1967); and community response to disasters (Form and Nosow, 1958).

Few studies, however, have examined the impact of the environment on internal organizational processes. One such study by Thompson and McEwen (1958) showed how the organizational environment can affect goal-setting in organizations, while a study by Dill (1958) examined how environmental pressures affect the degree of managerial autonomy. Simpson and Gulley (1962) found that voluntary organizations with diffuse pressures from the environment were more likely to have decentralized structures, high internal communications, and high membership involvement, while those having more restricted pressures from the environment had the opposite characteristics. Terreberry (1968) has hypothesized that organizational change is largely induced by forces in the environment, and Yuchtman and Seashore (1967) have defined organizational effectiveness in terms of the organization's success in obtaining resources from the environment. Recently, James D. Thompson (1967) and Lawrence and Lorsch (1967) have suggested some ways in which elements in the environment can affect organizational behavior. There are also other studies which argue that another aspect of the environment—variations in cultural values and norms—may also affect the internal structure of organizations (Richardson, 1959; Harbison et al., 1963; Crozier, 1964). Each of these studies, then, suggests ways in which the organization's environment affects the internal nature of the organization. The purpose of this study is to show how one aspect of the organization's relationship with its environment, i.e., the interdependence that arises through joint cooperative programs with other organizations, is related to several intra-organizational characteristics. We shall do this by describing a theoretical framework about organizational interdependence and then by examining some results from an empirical study of organizational interdependence.

A second objective in calling attention to this relatively neglected area of organizational analysis is to suggest that the processes of both conflict and cooperation can be incorporated into the same model of organizational interdependence. The concept of interdependence helps us to focus on the problem of interorganizational exchanges. At the same time, the exchange of resources, another aspect of the relationships between organizations, is likely to involve an element of conflict. While Simmel has made the dialectic of cooperation and conflict a truism, as yet there has been little work that explains interorganizational cooperation and conflict. Caplow (1964) has suggested a model of conflict involving the variables of subjugation, insulation, violence, and attrition, but this model focuses neither on the particular internal conditions that give rise to interorganizational relationships nor on the consequences of them for organizational structure. These are key intellectual problems in attempting to understand exchanges among organizations.

The models of pluralistic societies described by Tocqueville (1945) and more recently by Kornhauser (1959) underscore the importance of autonomous and competing organizations for viable democratic processes. Such theoretical models assume that the processes of conflict as well as cooperation inhere in social reality. Recent American social theory has been criticized for its excessive emphasis on a static view of social processes and for failing to include conflict in its conceptual models (Dahrendorf, 1958; Coser, 1956; Wrong, 1961). The study of interorganizational relationships appears to be one area which can appropriately incorporate the processes of both conflict and cooperation. Therefore the concept of organizational interdependence becomes a critical analytical tool for understanding this process.

Most studies of organizational interdependence essentially conceive of the organization as an entity that needs inputs and provides outputs, linking together a number of organizations via the mechanisms of exchanges or transactions (cf. Ridgeway, 1957; Elling and Halebsky, 1961; Levine and White, 1961; Dill, 1962; James D. Thompson, 1962). Some types of organizational exchanges involve the sharing of clients, funds, and staff in order to perform activities for some common objective (Levine et al., 1963). The measure of the degree of organizational interdependence used here is the *number of joint programs* that a focal organization has with other organizations. The greater the number of joint programs, the more organizational decision-making is constrained through obligations, commitments, or contracts with other organizations, and the greater the degree of organizational interdependence (cf. Guetzkow, 1966). This type of interdependence among health and welfare organizations has variously been called "functional co-operation" by Black and Kase (1963), and "program co-ordination" by Reid (1964), and is considered a more binding form of interdependence and therefore a more interesting example of interorganizational cooperation. This

does not suggest that the cooperation that is involved in joint programs is easily achieved. On the contrary, there are a number of barriers to establishing such interdependencies among organizations (cf. Johns and de Marche, 1951), and the probability of conflict is quite high, as Miller (1958) and Barth (1963) point out.

The reader may wonder why the concept of the joint program is apparently such an important kind of interorganizational relationship. The answer is that, unlike exchanges of clients or funds (which may only imply the *purchase* of services) or other types of organizational cooperation, a joint program is often a relatively enduring relationship, thus indicating a high degree of organizational interdependence.

The *joint program* needs to be carefully distinguished from the *joint organization*. The latter refers to the situation in which two or more organizations create a separate organization for some common purpose. For example, the Community Chest has been created by health and welfare organizations for fund-raising purposes. Similarly, Harrison (1959) has noted that the Baptist Convention was created by the separate Baptist churches for more effective fund raising. Guetzkow (1950) has described interagency committees among federal agencies, representing a special case of the joint organization. Business firms have created joint organizations in order to provide service functions. These are clearly different from the joint program because these joint organizations have separate corporate identities and often their own staff, budget, and objectives.

Some examples of joint programs in organizations other than those in the health and welfare field are the student exchange programs in the Big Ten. Harvard, Columbia, Yale, and Cornell Universities are developing a common computerized medical library. Indeed, it is interesting to note how many universities use joint programs of one kind or another. We do not believe that this is an accident; rather, it flows from the characteristics of these organizations. In our study, which includes rehabilitation centers, we have observed the attempt by one organization to develop a number of joint programs for the mentally retarded. These efforts are being financed by the Department of Health, Education, and Welfare, and evidently reflect a governmental concern for creating more cooperative relationships among organizations. Even in the business world, where the pursuit of profit would seem to make the joint program an impossibility, there are examples of this phenomenon. Recently, Ford and Mobil Oil started a joint research project designed to develop a superior gasoline. This pattern is developing even across national boundaries in both the business and nonbusiness sectors.

It is this apparently increasing frequency of joint programs that makes this form of interdependence not only empirically relevant, but theoretically strategic. In so far as we can determine, organizational interdependence is increasingly more common (Terreberry, 1968), but the question of why remains to be answered.

THEORETICAL FRAMEWORK

The basic assumptions that are made about organizational behavior and the hypotheses of this study are shown in Figure 1. These assump-

FIG. 1　ASSUMPTIONS AND HYPOTHESES ABOUT ORGANIZATIONAL INTERDEPENDENCE

Assumptions:

I. Internal organizational diversity stimulates organizational innovation.

II. Organizational innovation increases the need for resources.

III. As the need for resources intensifies, organizations are more likely to develop greater interdependencies with other organizations, joint programs, in order to gain resources.

IV. Organizations attempt to maximize gains and minimize losses in attempting to obtain resources.

V. Heightened interdependence increases problems of internal control and coordination.

VI. Heightened interdependence increases the internal diversity of the organization.

Hypotheses:

1. A high degree of complexity varies directly with a high number of joint programs.

2. A high degree of program innovation varies directly with a number of joint programs.

3. A high rate of internal communication varies directly with a high number of joint programs.

4. A high degree of centralization varies inversely with a high number of joint programs.

5. A high degree of formalization varies inversely with a high number of joint programs.

tions provide the argument, or model, to use Willer's (1967) term, for the hypotheses to be tested below.

The first three assumptions deal with the basic problem of why organizations, at least health and welfare organizations, become involved in interdependent relationships with other units. The type of interdependency with which we are concerned here is the establishment of joint, cooperative activities with other organizations. If we accept Gouldner's (1959) premise that there is a strain toward organizations maximizing their autonomy, then the establishment of an interdependency with another organization would seem to be an undesirable course of action. It is the view here that organizations are "pushed" into such interdependencies because of their need for resources—not only money, but also resources such as specialized skills, access to particular kinds of markets, and the like (cf. Levine et al., 1963).

One source of the need for additional resources results from a heightened rate of innovation, which in turn is a function of internal organizational diversity. In several ways internal diversity creates a strain towards innovation and change. The conflict between different occupations and interest groups, or even different theoretical, philosophical, or other perspectives, results in new ways of looking at organizational problems. The likely result of this is a high rate of both proposals for program innovations as well as successful implementation of them (Hage and Aiken, 1967). But organizational diversity also implies a greater knowledge and awareness of the nature of and changes in the organizational environment, particularly when organizational diversity implies not only a spectrum of occupational roles in the organization, but also involvement in professional societies in the environment by the incumbents of those occupational roles, itself a type of organizational interdependency. Together the internal conflicts and awareness of the nature of the organization's environment create strains towards organizational change.

But innovation has its price. There is a need for more resources to pay the costs of implementing such innovations—not only money, but staff, space, and time. The greater the magnitude of the change or the number of changes within some specified period of time, the greater the amounts of resource that will be needed and the less likely that the normal sources will be sufficient. Some have called organizations that successfully accomplish this task effective ones (Yuchtman and Seashore, 1967). Thus, the leaders of innovating organizations must search for other possibilities, and the creation of a joint, cooperative project with another organization becomes one solution to this problem.

This mechanism for gaining resources, i.e., the establishment of a joint program, is best viewed as a type of organizational exchange. The leaders sacrifice a small amount of autonomy for gains in staff, funds, etc. While there are strong organizational imperatives against such exchanges, since they inevitably involve some loss of autonomy, as well as necessitate greater internal coordination, the increased intensification of needs for greater resources makes such an alternative increasingly attractive. Still another factor involved here is that some objectives can only be achieved through cooperation in some joint program. The goal may be so complicated or the distribution of risk so great that organizations are impelled to enter into some type of joint venture. Of course the creation of interdependencies with other organizations also has its costs. The organization must utilize some of its own resources in order to perform whatever coordination is necessary. Hence an organization with no surplus resources available could hardly afford a joint program. Thus there must be some slack in the resource base in the organization before any innovation or cooperative venture is likely.

This is not to argue for the perfect rationality of organizational leaders. Some decisions about change or the choice of a cooperative activity may be quite irrational, and perhaps non-logical (Wilensky, 1967). Indeed much of our argument about the conditions that lead to organizational innovation, i.e., conflict among different occupations, interest groups, or perspectives, is that this is hardly the most rational way to bring about change. Perhaps it is best to view the process as a series of circumstances that propel such events.

While we feel that this line of reasoning is a valid explanation of why organizations enter into interdependent relationships with other organizations via such mechanisms as the joint program, alternative explanations have been offered and must be considered. Lefton and Rosengren (1966) have suggested that the lateral and longitudinal dimensions of organizational commitment to clients are factors, at least in health and welfare organizations. These are probably not the primary factors in other types of organizations, such as economic ones. However, our concern has been to attempt to find the most general argument possible to explain organizational interdependence. At the same time we have left unanswered the question of why organizations become diverse in the first place, and their framework may provide one possible answer. Reid (1964) has indicated that complementary resources are also an important factor in understanding organizational interdependence. Without necessarily agreeing or disagreeing with these points of view, we do believe that the first three assumptions in Figure 1 represent *one* causal chain showing why organizations become involved in more enduring interorganizational relationships.

The next theoretical problem is what kind of organization is likely to be chosen as a partner in an interdependent relationship. Here we assume that organizations attempt to maximize their gains and minimize their losses. This is our fourth premise. That is, they want to lose as little power and autonomy as possible in their exchange for other resources. This suggests that they are most likely to choose organizations with complementary resources, as Reid (1967) has suggested, or partners with different goals, as Guetzkow (1966) has indicated. This reduces some of the problem of decreased autonomy, because the probability of conflict is reduced and cooperation facilitated in such symbiotic arrangements (cf. Hawley, 1951). This assumption also implies that other kinds of strategies might be used by the leaders of the organization once they have chosen the joint program as a mechanism of obtaining resources. Perhaps it is best to develop interdependent relationships with a number of organizations in order to obtain a given set of resources, thus reducing the degree of dependence on a given source. Again, we do not want to argue that organizational leaders will always choose the rational or logical alternative, but rather that they will simply *attempt* to minimize losses and maximize gains. Under circumstances of imperfect knowledge, some decisions will undoubtedly be irrational.

Our last theoretical problem is consideration of the consequences for the organization of establishing interdependent relationships as a means of gaining additional resources. Such joint activities will necessitate a set of arrangements between the participating organizations to carry out the program. This will mean commitments to the other organization, resulting in constraints on some aspects of organizational behavior. This in turn will mean an increase in problems of internal coordination, our fifth assumption. It is often difficult to work with outsiders, i.e., the partner in a joint activity. In this circumstance a number of mutual adaptations in a number of different areas will become necessary. One solution to this problem is the creation of extensive internal communication channels, such as a broad committee structure which meets frequently.

But perhaps a more interesting consequence of the joint program is that it can in turn contribute to organizational diversity. There is not only the likelihood of the addition of new staff from other organizations, but, more importantly, the creation of new communication links with other units in the organization's environment. New windows will have been opened into the organization, infusing new ideas and feeding the diversity of the organization, which means that the cycle of change, with all of its consequences, is likely to be regenerated.

In this way a never-ending cycle of diversity—innovation—need for resources—establishment of joint programs—is created. What may start as an interim solution to a problem can become a long-term organizational commitment which has a profound impact on the organization. In the long run, there is the tendency for units in an organizational set to become netted together in a web of interdependencies (cf. Terreberry, 1968).

With these six assumptions, a large number of testable hypotheses can be deduced. Indeed, this is one of the advantages of a general theoretical framework. Not only does it provide the rationale for the hypotheses being tested, but it can suggest additional ideas for future research. Since we are mainly concerned with the factors associated with high interdependency, and more particularly the number of joint programs, all of the hypotheses in Figure 1 are stated in terms of this variable.

Organizational diversity implies many different kinds of variables. We have examined three separate indicators of it: diversity in the number of occupations or the degree of complexity; diversity in the number of power groups or the degree of centralization; and diversity in the actual work experience or the degree of formalization. If assumptions I–III are correct, then the stimulation of change, and more particularly innovation brought about by each of these kinds of diversity, should be associated with a large number of programs. But this is not the only way in which these variables can be related; and that observation only emphasizes how the internal structure of the organization affects the extent of the enduring relationships with other organizations. The problems of internal coordination and the increased diversity, assumptions V and VI, are also related. Both mechanisms of coordination—communication and programming—are undoubtedly tried, but communication is probably preferred. This increases the advantages of diversity and also helps to bring about greater decentralization and less formalization. Similarly, the greater awareness of the environment, via the infusion of staff from other organizations, feeds this cycle of cause and effect relationships. Therefore, we have hypothesized that the number of joint programs varies directly with the degree of complexity (hypothesis 1) and inversely with the degree of centralization and formalization (hypotheses 4 and 5).

Since our arguments also involve statements about the stimulation of innovation, which in turn heightens the need for resources, it is clear that we would expect the degree of innovation to co-vary with the number of joint programs. This is hypothesis 2 of Figure 1. While program change is only one kind of organizational innovation, it is probably the most important, at least from the standpoint of generating needs for additional resources, and thus it goes to the heart of the argument presented in Figure 1. Program innovation in turn has consequences for the degree of centralization and formalization in the organization, but here we are mainly concerned about the relationship between the rate of organizational innovation as reflected in new programs and the number of joint programs, and not about these other mediating influences.

The degree of attempted internal coordination is measured by only one variable, namely the rate of communication, but again we feel that this is an important indication of this idea. Given the desire to minimize the loss of autonomy (assumption IV), organizational members must be particularly circumspect when dealing with staff and other kinds of resources from their organizational partners. This largely reduces the options about programming and encourages the elite to emphasize communication

rates. Probably special "boundary spanning" roles (Thompson, 1962) are created; these men negotiate the transactions with other organizations and in turn keep their organizational members informed. The problems of interpenetration by other organizational members will keep the communication channels open and filled with messages as internal adjustments are made. Thus this is the rationale for the third hypothesis.

STUDY DESIGN AND METHODOLOGY

The data upon which this study is based were gathered in sixteen social welfare and health organizations located in a large midwestern metropolis in 1967. The study is a replication of an earlier study conducted in 1964. Ten organizations were private; six were either public or branches of public agencies. These organizations were all the larger welfare organizations that provide rehabilitation, psychiatric services, and services for the mentally retarded, as defined by the directory of the Community Chest. The organizations vary in size from twenty-four to several hundred. Interviews were conducted with 520 staff members of these sixteen organizations. Respondents within each organization were selected by the following criteria: (a) all executive directors and department heads; (b) in departments of less than ten members, one-half of the staff was selected randomly; (c) in departments of more than ten members, one-third of the staff was selected randomly. Non-supervisory administrative and maintenance personnel were not interviewed.

AGGREGATION OF DATA

This sampling procedure divides the organization into levels and departments. Job occupants in the upper levels were selected because they are most likely to be key decision-makers and to determine organizational policy, whereas job occupants on the lower levels were selected randomly. The different ratios within departments ensured that smaller departments were adequately represented. Professionals, such as psychiatrists, social workers, and rehabilitation counselors, are included because they are intimately involved in the achievement of organizational goals and are likely to have organizational power. Non-professionals, such as attendants, janitors, and secretaries are excluded because they are less directly involved in the achievement of organizational objectives and have little or no power. The number of interviews varied from eleven in the smallest organization to sixty-two in one of the larger organizations.

It should be stressed that in this study the units of analysis are *organizations*, not individuals in the organizations. Information obtained from respondents was pooled to reflect properties of the sixteen organizations, and these properties were then related to one another. Aggregating individual data in this way presents methodological problems for which there are yet no satisfactory solutions. For example, if all respondents are equally weighted, undue weight is given to respondents lower in the hierarchy. Yet those higher in the chain of command, not the lower-status staff members, are the ones most likely to make the decisions which give an agency an ethos.[1]

We attempted to compensate for this by computing an organizational score from the means of social position within the agency. A social position is defined by the level or stratum in the organization and the department or type of professional activity. For example, if an agency's professional staff consists of psychiatrists and social workers, each divided into two hierarchical levels, the agency has four social positions: supervisory psychiatrists, psychiatrists, supervisory social workers, and social workers. A mean was then computed for each social position in the agency. The organizational score for a given variable was determined by computing the average of all social position means in the agency.[2]

The procedure for computing organizational scores parallels the method utilized in selecting respondents. It

---

[1] For a discussion of some of the basic differences between individual and collective properties, see Lazarsfeld and Menzel (1960) and Coleman (1964).

[2] One advantage of this procedure is that it allows for the cancellation of individual errors made by the job occupants of a particular position. It also allows for the elimination of certain idiosyncratic elements that result from the special privileges a particular occupant might have received as a consequence. An alternative procedure for computing organizational means is to weight all respondents equally. These two procedures yield strikingly similar results for the variables reported in this paper. The product-moment correlation coefficients between the scores based on these two computational procedures were as follows for the variables indicated:

Hierarchy of authority	0.93
Participation in decision making	0.85
Job codification	0.89
Rule observation	0.89
Index of specificity of jobs	0.93
Index of routinization of technology	0.94
Professional training	0.90
Professional activity	0.93

attempts to represent organizational life more accurately by not giving disproportionate weight to those social positions that have little power and that are little involved in the achievement of organizational goals.

Computation of means for each social position has the advantage of avoiding the potential problem created by the use of different sampling ratios. In effect, responses are standardized by organizational location—level and department—and then combined into an organizational score. Computation of means of social position also has a major theoretical advantage in that it focuses on the sociological perspective of organizational reality.

We make no assumption that the distribution of power, regulations, or rewards is random within any particular social position. Instead, each respondent is treated as if he provides a true estimate of the score for a given social position. There is likely to be some distortion due to personality differences or events unique in the history of the organization, but the computation of means for each social position hopefully eliminates or at least reduces the variation due to such factors. By obtaining measures from all levels and all departments, the total structure is portrayed and reflected in the organizational score.

THE MEASUREMENT OF
ORGANIZATIONAL INTERDEPENDENCE

The degree of organizational interdependence is measured by the number of joint programs with other organizations. There are several possible measures of the nature and degree of organizational interdependence among social welfare and health organizations. Among these are:

1. The number of cases, clients or patients referred or exchanged.
2. The number of personnel lent, borrowed, or exchanged.
3. The number, sources, and amounts of financial support.
4. The number of joint programs.

The first two of these were used in an earlier study of interorganizational relationships (Levine and White, 1961). In our research we found that organizations such as rehabilitation workshops and family agencies simply did not keep records of the number of walk-ins or calls referred by other organizations. Similar problems were encountered with exchanges of personnel. Thus, we found great difficulty in using these measures of interdependence. While the nature and amounts of financial support are interesting and important aspects of interorganizational analysis, they are not included in this study.

We asked the head of each organization to list every joint program in which his organization had been involved in the past ten years, whether terminated or not. A profile of each program was obtained, including the name of participating organizations, goals of the program, number and type of clients or patients involved, and source of financial and other resources for the program. Only existing programs and those involving the commitment of resources by all participating organizations—such as personnel, finances, space—were included in our analysis.

Since a number of our sixteen organizations had participated in joint programs with each other, it was possible to check the reliability of their responses. We did not find any difficulties of recall for this period of time. In part this is probably because most of the joint programs, once started, tended to continue over time. Some organizations had maintained their organizational relationships for as many as twenty years. Then too, the fact that the joint program is not a minor incident in the life of an organization also facilitates recall. We did discover that organizational leaders tended to think of the purchase of services as a joint program. To solve this problem we included in our interview schedule a series of follow-up questions about the amount of staff shared and the amount of funds contributed by each organization involved in the joint program.

Another problem of measurement centered on the difficulty of defining separate joint programs. For example, there was a tendency for an organization with a history of successful relationships (those that endured for more than two years) to develop a number of joint programs with the same organization. The relationships would grow in scope and depth in much the way that one would predict from Homans' (1950) hypotheses about the interaction between people. This raised the problem of whether joint programs with the same organization should be counted as separate programs. Our solution was to count

the program separately if it involved different activities. Thus a research program and an education program with the same organization, two common kinds of programs, would be counted as separate joint programs. The key in making this decision was the idea of separate activities. In fact, programs were usually developed at different dates, suggesting again that our solution was a correct one. At the same time, if an organization developed the same joint program with three organizations, this was counted only once. From a practical standpoint these attempts at refinement were not so important because it is clear that the differences in number of joint programs among the sixteen organizations in our study are so great that similar ranking would occur regardless of how one counted the programs.

The number of existing joint programs among these sixteen organizations ranged from none to 33. Rehabilitation centers had the highest average number of joint programs, although the range was quite extensive among some other kinds of organizations in our study (Table 1). The special education department and the hospitals had an intermediate range of programs. Social casework agencies and homes for the emotionally disturbed had the least

TABLE 1 AVERAGE NUMBER OF JOINT PROGRAMS BY TYPE OF ORGANIZATION

Type of Organization	Number of Organizations	Average Number of Joint Programs	Range
Rehabilitation Centers	3	20.7	8–33
Special Education Department —Public Schools	1	15.0	15
Hospitals	3	8.3	6–12
Homes for Emotionally Disturbed	3	2.3	1–3
Social Casework Agencies	6	1.2	0–4
All Organizations	16	7.3	0–33

number of joint programs. In every case, however, there was some variation within each organizational category.

FINDINGS

A strict interpretation of data would allow us to discuss only the consequences of interorganizational relationships on the internal structure and performance of an organization. This is true because the period of time during which measurement of the number of joint programs, our measure of organizational interdependence, was made occurred prior to most of our measures of structure and performance. Yet the reasoning in our theoretical framework suggests that these variables are both causes and effects in an on-going process. Strictly speaking, our data reflect the consequences of increased joint programs, but we shall still make some inferences about their causes.

1. Organizations with many joint programs are more complex organizations, that is, they are more highly professionalized and have more diversified occupational structures. By complexity we do not mean the same thing as Rushing's (1967) division of labor, a measure of the distribution of people among different occupations, but rather the diversity of activities. There are essentially two aspects of complexity as we have defined it: the degree to which there is a high number of different types of occupational activities in the organization; and the degree to which these diverse occupations are anchored in professional societies.[3] One of the

most startling findings in our study is the extremely high correlation between the number of different types of occupations in an organization and the number of joint programs (r = 0.87).

The relationship between the occupational diversity of the organization and the number of joint programs in 1967 is very high, whether we use the number of occupations in 1959 (r = 0.79), the number of occupations in 1964 (r = 0.83, or the number of occupations in 1967 (r = 0.87). While time sequence is not the same as causation, this does suggest that occupational diversity is not solely a function of new programs. Rather it suggests that organizations that have a high number of joint programs are organizations that have been occupationally diverse for a number of years.

The addition of joint programs evidently makes an organization aware of the need for still more specialties. One rehabilitation center used social workers in a joint program involving the mentally retarded with several other agencies. It then decided to add social workers to a number of its other programs. The addition of new specialties may also be necessary in order to help solve some of the problems of coordination created by the joint programs.

The dependent variable, number of joint programs, is quite dispersed

---

[3] It should be noted that our count of occupational specialties is not based on the number of specific job titles. Instead, each respondent was asked what he did and then this was coded according to the kind of professional activity and whether it was a specialty. This procedure was used for two reasons. First, it allows for comparability across organizations. Second, it avoids the problem of task specialization where one activity might be divided into many specific and separate tasks. (See Thompson, 1964.)

TABLE 2 RELATIONSHIPS BETWEEN THE NUMBER OF JOINT PROGRAMS
AND ORGANIZATIONAL CHARACTERISTICS

Organizational Characteristics	*Pearsonian Product-Moment Correlation Coefficients between Each Organizational Characteristic and the Number of Joint Programs*
1. Degree of Complexity	
Index of Professional Training	.15
Index of Professional Activity	.60**
Number of Occupations: 1967	.87****
2. Degree of Organizational Innovation: 1959–1966	
Number of New Programs (including new programs that are joint programs)	.71***
Number of New Programs (excluding new programs that are joint programs)	.74****
3. Internal Communication	
Number of Committees	.47*
Number of Committee Meetings per Month	.83****
4. Degree of Centralization	
Index of Participation in Decision-Making	.30
Index of Hierarchy of Authority	.33
5. Degree of Formalization	
Index of Job Codification	.13
Index of Rule Observation	−.06
Index of Specificity of Job	−.06

* P < .10.
** P < .05.
*** P < .01.
**** P < .001.

with a range from 0 to 33 and a mean of 7.3. It is entirely possible that the unusually high correlations for some variables in Table 2 are simply a function of a highly skewed distribution on this variable. Therefore, we computed two non-parametric measures of correlation, Spearman's rank order correlation coefficient (rho) and Kendall's rank correlation coefficient (tau) for the relationship between number of occupations in 1967 and the number of joint programs as shown in Table 3. The relationship between these two variables remains strong even when using the non-parametric statistics.

The objection could be raised that the very strong relationship between the very strong relationship between number of occupational specialties and the number of joint programs may also be a function of the type of organization. In Table 1, it was shown that rehabilitation centers had the most joint programs, followed by the special education department, hospitals, homes for the emotionally disturbed, and finally social casework agencies. The observation that there is a positive relationship between these two variables is valid within three of the four categories of organizations shown in Table 4. That is, within the categories of rehabilitation centers, mental hospitals, and homes for the emotionally disturbed the organizations having the highest number of occupations have the most

TABLE 3 COMPARISON OF PEARSONIAN CORRELATION COEFFICIENT (R), SPEARMAN'S RANK ORDER CORRELATION COEFFICIENT (RHO), AND KENDALL'S RANK CORRELATION COEFFICIENT (TAU) FOR THE FOUR LARGEST CORRELATIONS SHOWN IN TABLE 2

Organizational Characteristic	Correlation Coefficient between Number of Joint Programs and Organizational Characteristics		
	r	*rho*	*tau*
Number of Occupations: 1967	.87	.81	.74
Number of New Programs: 1959–1966 (including new programs that are joint programs)	.71	.84	.75
Number of New Programs: 1959–1966 (excluding new programs that are joint programs)	.74	.80	.70
Number of Committee Meetings per Month	.83	.61	.54

joint programs while those having the fewest occupational specialties have the smallest number of joint programs. Only among social casework agencies does the relationship not hold. It might be noted that only one social casework organization had more than one interorganizational tie.

The degree to which an organization is professionalized is also strongly related to the number of joint programs. We measured the degree of professionalism in organizations in two ways: first, the degree to which the organizational members received professional training; and second, the degree to which organizational members are currently active in professional activities, i.e., attending meetings, giving papers, or holding offices. The measure of current professional activity was also quite highly related to our measure of the number of joint programs (r = 0.60).[4] The degree of professional training had little relationship with the number of joint programs (r = 0.15).[5]

2. *Organizations with many joint programs are more innovative organizations.* The degree of organizational innovation is measured by the number of new programs that were successfully implemented in the organization during the eight-year period from 1959 to 1966. The correlation coefficient between joint programs and new programs is 0.71, as shown in Table 2. Of course, there is an element of spuriousness in this relationship, since some of the new programs

[4] The index of professional activity, which ranged from 0 to 3 points, was computed as follows: (a) 1 point for belonging to professional organization; (b) 1 point for attending at least two-thirds of the previous six meetings of any professional organization; (c) 1 point for the presentation of a paper or holding an office in any professional organization.

[5] The index was scored as follows: (a) high school graduates or less education, with no professional training, received a score of 0; (b) high school graduates or less education, with some professional training, received a score of 1; (c) staff members with a college degree or some college, but an absence of other professional training, received a score of 2; (d) staff members with a college degree or some college, and the presence of some other professional training, received a score of 3; (e) the presence of training beyond a college degree, and the absence of other professional training, received a score of 4; (f) the presence of training beyond a college degree, and the presence of other professional training, received a score of 5.

TABLE 4 NUMBER OF OCCUPATIONS IN 1967 AND NUMBER OF JOINT
PROGRAMS BY TYPE OF ORGANIZATION

	Number of Occupations 1967	*Number of Joint Programs*
Rehabilitation Centers		
Rehabilitation Center A	27	33
Rehabilitation Center B	24	21
Rehabilitation Center C	13	8
Department of Special Education		
Educational Organization D	19	15
Mental Hospitals		
Mental Hospital E	18	12
Mental Hospital F	18	7
Mental Hospital G	11	6
Homes for Emotionally Disturbed		
Home H	11	3
Home I	10	3
Home J	7	1
Social Casework Agencies		
Casework Agency K	7	1
Casework Agency L	6	0
Casework Agency M	5	1
Casework Agency N	5	1
Casework Agency O	4	4
Casework Agency P	1	0

are joint programs. If the correlation coefficient is recomputed, eliminating all new programs that are also joint programs, we find the same result ($r = 0.74$).

As in the case of number of occupational specialties in the organization, the finding based on non-parametric measures of association between each of these two measures of organizational innovation and the number of new programs is little different from the results based on the parametric statistical measure (See Table 3).

It could be that the above relationships between degree of organizational innovation and number of joint programs may simply be a function of complexity. We have argued that the degree of complexity gives rise not only to joint programs, but also to new programs. While there is

no relationship between professional training and the number of new programs ($r = -0.18$), there are relatively strong relationships between this variable and professional activity ($r = 0.74$) as well as occupational diversity ($r = 0.67$). When the relationships between the number of joint programs and the number of new programs (excluding new programs that are joint programs) are controlled for each of these three indicators separately, the relationship between these two variables remains relatively strong (see Table 5). This illustrates that the number of new programs is related to the number of joint programs independently of these various indicators of complexity.

The key idea in our interpretation is that it is the rate of organizational innovation that intensifies the need for new resources. The higher. this

TABLE 5 PARTIAL CORRELATION COEFFICIENTS BETWEEN NUMBER
OF JOINT PROGRAMS AND ORGANIZATIONAL INNOVATION,
CONTROLLING FOR INDICATORS OF COMPLEXITY

Control Variables	Partial Correlation between Number of Joint Programs and Number of New Programs 1959–1966 (Excluding New Programs that Are Joint Programs), Controlling for the Variable Indicated
Indicators of Complexity	
Index of Professional Training	.77
Index of Professional Activity	.55
Number of Occupations: 1967	.46

rate, the more likely organizations are to use the joint program as a mechanism for cost reduction in such activities. The fact that some new programs are joint programs only strengthens our argument that the joint program is a useful solution for the organization seeking to develop new programs.

This interplay between new programs and joint programs can be made clear with several examples from our study. One rehabilitation center with a high rate of new programs developed joint programs with several organizations that were primarily fund-raising organizations, as a solution for funding its growth. But in turn these organizations recognized new needs and asked the organization to develop still more new programs in areas for their clients. This particular agency is presently exploring the possibility of developing special toys for the mentally retarded because one of its joint programs is with an organization concerned with this type of client.

We may also re-examine the relationships between indicators of complexity and the number of joint programs. As shown in Table 6, only the relationship between the number of occupations and the number of joint programs remains strong when the number of new programs (excluding

new programs that are joint programs) is controlled (partial r = 0.75).

3. Organizations with many joint programs have more active internal communication channels. We measured the degree of internal communication in two ways. First, the number of committees in the organization and, second, the number of committee meetings per month. An active committee structure in an organization provides the potential for viable communication links in an organization. As shown in Table 2, there was a moderately strong relationship between the number of organizational committees and joint programs (r = 0.47) and a very strong relationship between the number of committee meetings per month and the number of joint programs (r = 0.83).

The relationship between the number of joint programs and the number of committee meetings per month remains moderately strong when the two non-parametric measures of association are computed. (See Table 3.)

Actually the system of communication for joint programs is even more complex than this. For example, one rehabilitation agency with the largest number of joint programs had a special board with the university with

TABLE 6 PARTIAL CORRELATION COEFFICIENTS BETWEEN NUMBER OF JOINT
PROGRAMS AND INDICATORS OF COMPLEXITY, CONTROLLING
FOR NUMBER OF NEW PROGRAMS
(EXCLUDING NEW PROGRAMS THAT ARE JOINT PROGRAMS)

Indicators of Complexity	*Partial Correlation between Number of Joint Programs and Indicators of Complexity, Controlling for Number of New Programs (Excluding New Programs that Are Joint Programs)*
Index of Professional Training	.32
Index of Professional Activity	.11
Number of Occupations: 1967	.75

which it had many joint programs and was in the process of establishing another joint board with a second university. Another rehabilitation agency created a special steering committee to suggest and supervise joint programs: the members of this committee were representatives from other organizations.

Controlling for the indicators of complexity and program change reduces the relationship between the number of committees and number of joint programs almost to zero in every case except that of professional training. Thus, the number of committees is evidently a function of these factors. On the other hand, the very strong relationship between the number of joint programs and the frequency of committee meetings is only moderately reduced when these controls are applied as shown in Table 7. This shows that the frequency of committee meetings is not simply a function of the complexity of the organization or the degree of organizational innovation, but has an independent relationship with the number of joint programs.

4. Organizations with many joint programs have slightly more decentralized decision-making structures. In our study, staff members were

asked how often they participated in organizational decisions about the hiring of personnel, the promotion of personnel, the adoption of new organizational policies, and the adoption of new programs or services. The organizational score was based on the degree of participation in these four areas of decision-making.[6] As shown in Table 2, there is a weak, positive relationship between the degree of participation in agency-wide decisions and the number of joint programs ($r = 0.30$). This appears to be measuring the way resources are controlled. A second kind of decision-making concerns the control of work. We measured the degree of decision-

[6] The index of actual participation in decision-making was based on the following four questions: (1) How frequently do you usually participate in the decision to hire new staff? (2) How frequently do you usually participate in the decisions on the promotion of any of the professional staff? (3) How frequently do you participate in decisions on the adoption of new policies? (4) How frequently do you participate in the decisions on the adoption of new programs? Respondents were assigned numerical scores from 1 (low participation) to 5 (high participation), depending on whether they answered "never," "sometimes," "often," or "always," respectively, to these questions. An average score on these questions was computed for each respondent, and then the data were aggregated into organizational scores as described above.

TABLE 7 PARTIAL CORRELATION COEFFICIENTS BETWEEN NUMBER OF JOINT
PROGRAMS AND INDICATORS OF INTERNAL COMMUNICATION,
CONTROLLING FOR INDICATORS OF COMPLEXITY AND INNOVATION

Control Variables	Partial Correlation between Number of Joint Programs and Number of Committees, Controlling for the Variable Indicated	Partial Correlation between Number of Joint Programs and Frequency of Committee Meetings, Controlling for the Variable Indicated
Indicators of Complexity		
Index of Professional Training	.45	.83
Index of Professional Activity	.13	.76
Number of Occupations: 1967	.11	.57
Indicator of Organizational Innovation		
Number of New Programs: 1959–1966 (excluding new programs that are joint programs)	.08	.64

making about work with a scale called the "hierarchy of authority."[7] This scale had a relationship with the number of joint programs in the opposite direction to our expectation (r = 0.33). While highly interdependent organizations have slightly more decentralization of decisions about organizational resources, there is slightly less control over work in such organizations. It is difficult to account for this other than that the

organizations with a high degree of program change during the period 1964–1966 had less control over work decisions in 1967 than in 1964. This suggests that the rate of change was so high in such organizations during this period that some more rigid mechanisms of social control were adopted in these organizations. Since the highly innovative organizations were also those with more joint programs, this helps to explain the reversal.

Partial correlations between the number of joint programs and the degree of participation in decision-making, controlling for each of the indicators of complexity, innovation, and internal communication, are shown in Table 8.

The relatively low relationship between these two variables is reduced, and in one case reversed, when these other factors are controlled by using partial correlations. Only in the case of frequency of committee meetings is the relationship strengthened. What this means is that the degree of participation in decision-making is largely a function of some of the

[7] The empirical indicators of these concepts were derived from two scales developed by Richard Hall (1963), namely, hierarchy of authority and rules. The index of hierarchy of authority was computed by first averaging the replies of individual respondents to each of the following five statements: (1) There can be little action taken here until a supervisor approves a decision. (2) A person who wants to make his own decisions would be quickly discouraged here. (3) Even small matters have to be referred to someone higher up for a final answer. (4) I have to ask my boss before I do almost anything. (5) Any decision I make has to have my boss's approval. Responses could vary from 1 (definitely false) to 4 (definitely true). The individual scores were then combined into an organizational score as described above.

TABLE 8 PARTIAL CORRELATION COEFFICIENTS BETWEEN NUMBER OF JOINT PROGRAMS AND INDICATORS OF CENTRALIZATION OF DECISION-MAKING, CONTROLLING FOR INDICATORS OF COMPLEXITY, INNOVATION, AND INTERNAL COMMUNICATION

Control Variables	Partial Correlations between Number of Joint Programs and Participation in Decision Making, Controlling for the Variable Indicated	Partial Correlations between Number of Joint Programs and Hierarchy of Authority, Controlling for the Variable Indicated
Indicators of Complexity		
Index of Professional Training	.27	.33
Index of Professional Activity	.01	.21
Number of Occupations: 1967	−.10	.31
Indicator of Organizational Innovation		
Number of New Programs: 1959–1966 (excluding new programs that are joint programs)	.20	−.28
Indicators of Internal Communication		
Number of Committees	.16	.17
Number of Committee Meetings per Month	.43	.22

previously discussed variables—professional activity, number of occupations, and number of committees. Thus, it has little independent relationship with the number of joint programs.

The relationship between hierarchy of authority and the number of joint programs is little affected by indicators of complexity, but somewhat more by the indicators of internal communication. (See Table 8.) On the other hand, the relationship between these two variables is reversed when the number of new programs is controlled, and the relationship is now in the expected direction, i.e., members of organizations with many joint programs having more control over individual work tasks. This finding buttresses our earlier interpretation that it was the dramatic increase of new programs that brought about less control over individual work decisions in organizations with many joint programs.

5. There is no relationship between formalization and the number of joint programs. Rules and regulations are important organizational mechanisms that are often used to insure the predictability of performance. There are several important aspects of rules as mechanisms of social control. One is the number of regulations specifying who is to do what, when, where, and why; this we call job codification.[8] A second is the diligency with which such rules are enforced; this we call rule obser-

[8] The index of job codification was based on responses to the following five statements: (1) A person can make his own decisions without checking with anybody else. (2) How things are done here is left up to the person doing the work. (3) People here are allowed to do almost as they please. (4) Most people here make their own rules on the job. Replies to these questions were scored from 1 (definitely true) to 4 (definitely false), and then each of the respondent's answers was averaged. Thus, a high score on this index means high job codification.

vation.[9] A third is the degree to which the procedures defining a job are spelled out; this we call the index of specificity of jobs.[10]

Two of these three indicators of formalization, the degree of rule observation and the degree of specificity of jobs, had very small inverse relationships with the number of joint programs (r = −0.06 in each case), but each of these is hardly different from zero. The index of job codification was directly related to the number of joint programs (r = 0.13), but it too is little different from zero, although it is in the opposite direction to our expectation.

We conclude from these findings that formalization is unrelated to the degree of organizational interdependence, suggesting that either this kind of internal diversity is not very important or that we do not have valid measures of this phenomenon. However, there is some problem of interpretation because there was also some movement of the highly innovative organizations toward greater formalization. For example, there is a negative partial correlation between the number of joint programs and each of the indicators of formalization, i.e., job codification (partial r = −0.11), rule observation (partial r = −0.37), and degree of specificity of jobs (partial r = −0.29), when the number of new programs during the period 1959–1966 is partialled out.

CONTROLS FOR SIZE, AUSPICES, AGE, AND TECHNOLOGY

The sixteen organizations included in this study are, from one point of view, relatively homogeneous. All of them provide either psychiatric, social, or rehabilitation services of one kind or another. In comparison to economic organizations, they are indeed homogeneous. In addition, they are all located in a single metropolitan area. The reader might wonder, therefore, how far we can generalize from our study to other kinds of organizations or to organizations in other communities.

There are several ways in which some estimate of the generality can be made. One approach would be to divide the organizations into different categories, as was done in Tables 1 and 4. Here we emphasized the differences among a set of organizations that, considering the range of all organizations, are relatively homogeneous. The difficulty with this approach is that we are making comparisons among so few cases in each category.

An alternative approach is to look

---

[9] The index of rule observation was computed by averaging the responses to each of the following two statements: (1) The employees are constantly being checked on for rule violations. (2) People here feel as though they are constantly being watched, to see that they obey all the rules. Respondents' answers were coded from 1 (definitely false) to 4 (definitely true), and then the average score of each respondent on these items was computed. Organizational scores were computed as previously described. On this index, a high score means a high degree of rule observation.

[10] The index of specificity of job was based on responses to the following six statements: (1) Whatever situation arises, we have procedures to follow in dealing with it. (2) Everyone has a specific job to do. (3) Going through the proper channels is constantly stressed. (4) The organization keeps a written record of everyone's job performance. (5) We are to follow strict operating procedures at all times. (6) Whenever we have a problem, we are supposed to go to the same person for an answer. Replies to these questions were scored from 1 (definitely false) to 4 (definitely true), and then the average score of each respondent on these items was computed as the other measures. A high score means a high degree of specificity of the job.

at some general variables that describe the conditions of all organizations. The size of the organization is one such variable. Similarly the auspices of the organization, i.e., whether private or public, is another. And the age of the organization may also be an important factor here. Perrow (1967) has recently suggested another variable, the degree of routinization of technology. Undoubtedly there are others, but these represent some of the variables that one is likely to encounter in the literature and, therefore, are a good starting place for controls.

Since there were such great differences in the size of organizations in the study, a rank ordering of size is used. The correlation coefficient between size and the number of joint programs is positive and moderate (r = 0.34), which means that larger organizations have slightly more joint programs.

The auspices of the organization is measured by a dummy variable of private (1) versus public (0). The correlation coefficient between auspices and number of joint programs is 0.20, meaning that private organizations have slightly more joint programs.

The age of the organization was measured by constructing a trichotomous variable: (0), the organization was started in the post-Depression years (1938 to present); (1), the organization was started in the years following World War I (1918–1923); and (2), the organization was started prior to 1900. The correlation coefficient between age of the organization and the number of joint programs is −0.15, indicating that the younger organizations have slightly more joint programs.

Finally we looked at the type of technology, measured by the degree of routineness of work activities. By routineness of work we mean the degree to which organizational members have non-uniform work activities (Perrow, 1967; Woodward, 1965).[11] The correlation coefficient between routineness of work and the number of joint programs is −0.24, meaning that organizations with many joint programs have less routine technologies.

None of these four variables has strong relationships with the number of joint programs. When each of the relationships between the number of joint programs and the indicators of complexity, organizational innovation, internal communication, centralization, and formalization are controlled by each of these four variables separately, the relationships shown in Table 2 are little affected. (See Table 9.) This means that the factors of organizational size, auspices, age, and technology (as we have measured them) have little or no effect on the findings of this study.

DISCUSSIONS AND CONCLUSIONS

We now return to the issues raised at the outset of this paper. How are organizational structure and interde-

[11] The index of routinization of technology was based on responses to the following five statements: (1) People here do the same job in the same way every day (reversed). (2) One thing people like around here is the variety of work. (3) Most jobs have something new happening every day. (4) There is something different to do every day. (5) Would you describe your job as being highly routine, somewhat routine, somewhat non-routine, or highly non-routine? The first four items were scored from 1 (definitely true) to 4 (definitely false). On the fifth item scores ranged from 1 (highly non-routine) to 4 (highly routine).

TABLE 9 PARTIAL CORRELATIONS BETWEEN THE NUMBER OF JOINT PROGRAMS
AND INDICATORS OF COMPLEXITY, INNOVATION, INTERNAL COMMUNICATION,
CENTRALIZATION, AND FORMALIZATION, CONTROLLING SEPARATELY
FOR ORGANIZATION SIZE, AUSPICES, AGE, AND TECHNOLOGY

	Partial Correlation Coefficient between Number of Joint Programs and the Organization Characteristic Indicated, Controlling for			
	Size	*Auspices*	*Age*	*Technology*
Complexity				
Index of Professional Training	.35	.14	.16	.02
Index of Professional Activity	.56	.61	.64	.60
Number of Occupations: 1967	.88	.86	.89	.86
Innovation				
Number of New Programs: 1959–1966 (excluding new programs that are joint programs)	.73	.76	.74	.75
Internal Communication				
Number of Committees	.41	.45	.48	.48
Number of Committee Meetings per Month	.81	.82	.82	.83
Centralization				
Index of Participation in Decision-Making	.25	.27	.40	.18
Index of Hierarchy of Authority	.38	.35	.29	.33
Formalization				
Index of Job Codification	.18	.12	.07	.19
Index of Rule Observation	−.27	.00	−.10	−.02
Index of Specificity of Job	−.19	.03	−.16	.12

pendence related? How can the study of an organization and its environment be combined? What kinds of organizations are more cooperative and integrated with other organizations?

We noted that there is a greater degree of complexity, i.e., more occupational diversity and greater professionalism of staff, in those organizations with the most joint programs. The participation in joint programs is evidently one mechanism for adding new occupational specialties to the organization at a reduced cost. By combining the resources of the focal organization with one or more others, there is the possibility of adding new occupational specializations to the organizational roster. This is especially true because joint programs are likely to be of a highly specialized nature, providing services and activities that the focal organization cannot support alone.

The involvement of staff in interorganizational relationships introduces them to new ideas, new perspectives, and new techniques for solving organizational problems. The establishment of collegial relationships with comparable staff members of other organizations provides them with a comparative framework for understanding their own organizations. This is likely to affect their professional activities—attendance at meetings of professional societies—as well as reinforce professional standards of excellence. In these ways the involvement of organizations in joint programs has the effect of increasing the complexity of these social and health welfare organizations.

The heightened interdependence has other important implications for the internal structure of organizations. The partial or total commitment of organizational resources to other organizations is likely to affect various departments and the business office as well as the central programs of such an organization. Problems of coordination are likely to become particularly acute under such circumstances. The organization is forced to overcome these problems by heightening the frequency of internal communication. A more diverse committee structure and more committee meetings are mechanisms for handling such problems.

We would have expected that the heightened rates of communication would have resulted in more decentralization than appears to be the case. It is entirely possible that the problems of internal coordination may be reflected in some attempts to tighten the power structure, thus leading to less movement towards decentralization than we had expected. Also, the problems of internal coordination may be reflected in greater programming of the organization, or at least attempts in that direction, and this may be the reason why there is a small relationship between heightened interdependency, as we have measured it, and the degree of centralization.

Diversity in occupations (the degree of complexity) and power groups (the degree of decentralization) are related to the number of joint programs, but diversity in work, as reflected in the absence of rules, is not related to this measure of interdependence. In part this may be a consequence of the sudden increase in the rate of program innovation. But it may also be that the degree of formalization is not a good measure of diversity. It is the diversity of occupations, including their perspectives and self-interests, along with the representation of these points of view in a decentralized structure, that allows for diversity with the most critical consequences.

Our assumptions help to explain the steadily increasing frequency of organizational interdependency, especially that involving joint programs. As education levels increase, the division of labor proceeds (stimulated by research and technology), and organizations become more complex. As they do, they also become more innovative. The search for resources needed to support such innovations requires interdependent relations with other organizations. At first, these interdependencies may be established with organizations with different goals and in areas that are more tangential to the organization. Over time, however, it may be that cooperation among organizations will multiply, involving interdependencies in more critical areas, and involve organizations having more similar goals. It is scarcity of resources that forces organizations to enter into more cooperative activities with other organizations, thus creating greater integration of the organizations in a community structure. The long range consequence of this process will probably be a gradually heightened coordination in communities.

REFERENCES

BARTH, ERNEST A. T. 1963. "The causes and consequences of interagency conflict." *Sociological Inquiry* 33 (Winter): 51–57.

BLACK, BERTRAM J. and HAROLD M. KASE. 1963. "Inter-agency cooperation in rehabilitation and mental health." *Social Service Review* 37 (Mar.): 26–32.

CAPLOW, THEODORE. 1964. *Principles of Organization.* New York: Harcourt, Brace & World, Inc.

CLARK, BURTON R. 1965. "Interorganizational patterns in education." *Administrative Science Quarterly* 10 (Sept.): 224–37.

COLEMAN, JAMES S. 1964. "Research chronicle: The Adolescent Society." Phillip Hammond (ed.), *Sociologists at Work.* New York: Basic Books.

COSER, LEWIS. 1956. *The Functions of Social Conflict.* Glencoe, Ill.: The Free Press of Glencoe.

CROZIER, MICHEL. 1964. *The Bureaucratic Phenomenon.* Chicago: The University of Chicago Press.

DAHRENDORF, RALF. 1958. "Out of Utopia: Toward a reorientation of sociological analysis." *American Journal of Sociology* 64 (Sept.): 115–27.

DILL, WILLIAM R. 1958. "Environment as an influence on managerial autonomy." *Administrative Science Quarterly* 2 (Mar.): 409–43; 1962. "The impact of environment on organizational development." *In* Sidney Mailick and Edward H. Van Ness (eds.), *Concepts and Issues in Administrative Behavior.* Englewood Cliffs, N. J.: Prentice-Hall, Inc. pp. 94–109.

ELLING, R. H. and S. HALEBSKY. 1961. "Organizational differentiation and support: a conceptual framework." *Administrative Science Quarterly* 6 (Sept.): 185–209.

EMERY, F. E. and E. L. TRIST. 1965. "The causal texture of organizational environments." *Human Relations* 18 (Feb.): 21–31.

EVAN, WILLIAM M. 1966. "The organization-set: toward a theory of interorganizational relations." *In* James D. Thompson (ed.), *Approaches to Organizational Design.* Pittsburgh, Pa.: University of Pittsburgh Press. pp. 173–91.

FORM, WILLIAM H. and SIGMUND NOSOW. 1958. *Community in Disaster.* New York: Harper and Row.

GOULDNER, ALVIN. 1959. "Reciprocity and autonomy in functional theory." *In* Llewellyn Gross (ed.), *Symposium on Sociological Theory.* New York: Harper and Row. pp. 241–70.

GUETZKOW, HAROLD. 1950. "Inter-agency committee usage." *Public Administration Review* 10 (Summer): 190–96; 1966. "Relations among organizations." *In* Raymond V. Bowers (ed.), *Studies on Behavior in Organizations.* Athens, Ga.: University of Georgia Press. pp. 13–44.

HAGE, JERALD and MICHAEL AIKEN. 1967. "Program change and organizational properties: a comparative analysis." *American Journal of Sociology* 72 (Mar.): 503–19.

HALL, RICHARD. 1963. "The concept of bureaucracy: an empirical assessment." *American Journal of Sociology* 69 (July): 32–40.

HARBISON, FREDERICK H., E. KOCHLING, F. H. CASSELL and H. C. RUEBMAN. 1955. "Steel management on two continents." *Management Science* 2:31–39.

HARRISON, PAUL M. 1959. *Authority and Power in the Free Church Tradition.* Princeton, N.J.: Princeton University Press.

HAWLEY, AMOS H. 1951. *Human Ecology.* New York: The Ronald Press.

HOMANS, GEORGE. 1950. *The Human Group.* New York: Harcourt, Brace and World, Inc.

JOHNS, RAY E. and DAVID F. DE MARCHE. 1951. *Community Organization and Agency Responsibility.* New York: Association Press.

KORNHAUSER, WILLIAM. 1959. *The Politics of Mass Society.* Glencoe, Ill.: The Free Press of Glencoe.

LAWRENCE, PAUL R. and JAY W. LORSCH. 1967. *Organization and Environment.* Boston: Graduate School of Business Administration, Harvard University.

LAZARSFELD, PAUL and HERBERT MENzel. 1960. "On the relation between individual and collective properties." *In* Amitai Etzioni (ed.), *Complex Organizations: A Sociological Reader.* New York: The Macmillan Company. pp. 422–40.

LEFTON, MARK and WILLIAM ROSENGREN. 1966. "Organizations and clients: lateral and longitudinal dimensions." *American Sociological Review* 31 (Dec.): 802–10.

LEVINE, SOL and PAUL E. WHITE. 1961. "Exchange as a conceptual framework for the study of interorganizational relationships." *Administrative Science Quarterly* 5 (Mar.): 583–61; 1963. "The community of health organizations." *In* Howard E. Freeman, S. E. Levine, and Leo G. Reeder (eds.), *Handbook of Medical Sociology.* Englewood Cliffs, N.J.: Prentice-Hall. pp. 321–47.

LEVINE, SOL, PAUL E. WHITE and BENJAMIN D. PAUL. 1963. "Community interorganizational problems in providing medical care and social services." *American Journal of Public Health* 53 (Aug.): 1183–95.

LITWAK, EUGENE. 1961. "Models of bureaucracy which permit conflict." *American Journal of Sociology* 67 (Sept.): 177–84.

LITWAK, EUGENE and LYDIA F. HYLTON. 1962. "Interorganizational analysis: A hypothesis on coordinating agencies." *Administrative Science Quarterly* 6 (Mar.): 395–426.

MILLER, WALTER B. 1958. "Inter-institutional conflict as a major impediment to delinquency prevention." *Human Organization* 17 (Fall): 20–23.

MORRIS, ROBERT and OLLIE A. RANDALL. 1965. "Planning and organization of community services for the elderly." *Social Work* 10 (Jan.): 96–102.

PERROW, CHARLES. 1967. "A framework for the comparative analysis of organizations." *American Sociological Review* 32 (Apr.): 194–208.

REID, WILLIAM. 1964. "Interagency coordination in delinquency prevention and control." *Social Service Review* 38 (Dec. 1964): 418–28.

RICHARDSON, STEPHEN A. 1959. "Organizational contrasts on British and American ships." *Administrative Science Quarterly* 1 (Sept.): 189–207.

RIDGEWAY, V. F. 1957. "Administration of manufacturer-dealer systems." *Administrative Science Quarterly* 1 (June): 464–83.

RUSHING, WILLIAM A. 1967. "The effects of industry size and division of labor on administration." *Administrative Science Quarterly* 12 (Sept.): 273–95.

SELZNICK, PHILIP. 1949. *TVA and the Grass Roots.* Berkeley, Cal.: University of California Press.

SIMPSON, RICHARD L. and WILLIAM H. GULLEY. 1962. "Goals, environmental pressures, and organizational characteristics." *American Sociological Review* 27 (June): 344–51.

TERREBERRY, SHIRLEY. 1968. "The evolution of organizational environments." *Administrative Science Quarterly* 12 (Mar.): 590–613.

THOMPSON, JAMES D. 1962. "Organizations and output transactions." *American Journal of Sociology* 68 (Nov.): 309–24; 1966. *Organizations in Action.* New York: McGraw-Hill.

THOMPSON, JAMES D. and WILLIAM J. McEWEN. 1958. "Organizational goals and environment: goal-setting as an interaction process." *American Sociological Review* 23 (Feb.): 23–31.

THOMPSON, VICTOR R. 1961. *Modern Organizations.* New York: Alfred A. Knopf, Inc.

TOCQUEVILLE, ALEXIS DE. 1945. *Democracy in America.* New York: Alfred A. Knopf, Inc.

WARREN, ROLAND L. 1965. "The impact of new designs of community organization." *Child Welfare* 44 (Nov.): 494–500; 1967. "The interorganizational field as a focus for investigation." *Administrative Science Quarterly* 12 (Dec.): 396–419.

WILENSKY, HAROLD L. 1967. *Organizational Intelligence.* New York: Basic Books, Inc.

WILLER, DAVID. 1967. *Scientific Sociology: Theory and Method.* Englewood Cliffs, New Jersey. Prentice-Hall.

WILSON, JAMES Q. 1966. "Innovation in organization: notes toward a theory." *In* James D. Thompson, ed., *Approaches to Organizational Design.* Pittsburgh, Pa.: University of Pittsburgh, Press. pp. 193–218.

WOODWARD, JOAN. 1965. *Industrial Organization.* London: Oxford University Press.

WRONG, DENNIS. 1961. "The oversocialized conception of man in modern society." *American Sociological Review* 26 (Apr.): 183–93.

YUCHTMAN, EPHRAIM and STANLEY E. SEASHORE. 1967. "A system resource approach to organizational effectiveness." *American Sociological Review* 32 (Dec.): 891–903.

13. TASK STRUCTURE AND INNOVATION IN PROFESSIONAL ORGANIZATIONS

Wolf V. Heydebrand and James J. Noell

This paper is concerned with certain neglected aspects of the structure of professional organizations, and more specifically with the structural elements conducive to innovativeness in such organizations. In the following, we will spell out our theoretical perspective, discuss the method and data on which our research is based, and present our findings and interpretations.

THEORETICAL PERSPECTIVE

The "professional organization" is a special type of organization, distinct from modern legal-rational bureaucracy as well as from traditional or charismatic forms of organization.[1] As an organization, by which we mean socially constructed forms and activities designed to accomplish specific tasks and to achieve definite goals, it must adequately resolve three central issues. First, there must be sufficient articulation and specification of the tasks and goals to be achieved. In a fundamental sense this issue concerns the "identity" of the

[1] Max Weber, *Economy and Society.* G. Roth and C. Wittich (eds.) (New York: Bedminster Press, 1968), Vol. 1, 215–83. Professional organizations are viewed here as work organizations rather than as professional (voluntary) associations, i.e., the organized interest groups of professional practitioners, scientists, or technicians.

organization. Identity is not established in isolation, but only in the interaction of the organization with its often "turbulent" environment. Obviously, the degree of complexity of the goal structure differs greatly among various organizations, depending in no small part on the degree of complexity of their environment.

A second problem is to develop adequate knowledge so that the "output" can be produced, the tasks and goals accomplished. Clearly, the nature and scope of knowledge will vary, depending on the tasks and goals to be accomplished, as well as on the variability or uncertainty of the environment in which they are to be realized. Of crucial importance here is the degree of rationalization or specification of an organization's knowledge base. Rationalization of knowledge implies not only standardization, formalization, codification, and systematization, but also accessibility and availability. Thus, the degree of rationalization of the knowledge base may vary from the "vision" of a political leader or religious prophet to the expert "judgment" of a doctor or lawyer to the technical "precision" of a machine or computerized information system.

The third problem concerns the amount of control over resources (means) necessary for the production of goods or services by those directly engaged in productive activities, i.e., control by workers as against control by management, a board of directors, or a state government. This factor has immediate and obvious implications for the tasks and goals an organization can accomplish as well as for the nature and rationalization of the knowledge base required.

All three of these basic organizational phenomena, then,—the complexity of the goal and task structure, the rationalization of the knowledge base, and the control over resources and means of production—may be said to be in a relation of dynamic tension or interaction.

Generally speaking, professional organizations are primarily characterized by the scope and complexity of their knowledge base. Professional knowledge is more highly rationalized than traditional or "sacred" knowledge, but less rationalized and specified than the technical knowledge involved in a mechanized production line or an automated information processing system. According to this criterion, professional organizations may be defined as work organizations in which the production of organizational output results from the activities of professionals. Professionals, in turn, may be defined as workers who are formally trained to produce, preserve, communicate, and apply specialized knowledge.[2]

An adequate definition of a professional organization, however, should take into account the complexity of the goal structure and the problem of control over resources.[3]

[2] Amitai Etzioni, *Modern Organizations.* (Englewood Cliffs: Prentice-Hall, 1964), pp. 77–78.

[3] In Weber's conception of organizations the problem of the knowledge base is no less important than the problem of control over the means of production. The problem of control, raised originally by Marx in terms of production, is obviously applicable, in general, to a variety of specific, modern occupational categories, including those of technicians, scientists, "new" professionals, etc.; cf Weber's brief discussion of the "expropriation of workers from the means of production," *Economy and Society*, pp. 137–40. The problem of the knowledge base is frequently treated only

While the goals are generally tied to socially defined values, e.g., health, justice, knowledge, creativity, salvation, welfare, survival, etc., professionals in such areas do not only have *license* to translate these goals into specific operational goals, objectives, tasks, and products, but they also tend to receive—collectively—a *mandate* (or community sanction) to define and specify the very nature of the goals.[4] The value-rational service-ideal and the collectivity-orientation

of professionals provide, in effect, a normative basis for their mandate.[5]

In sum, a professional organization may be defined as a generic type of work organization that is designed to achieve complex goals and in which professionals specify the goal and task structure, direct and carry out productive activities on the basis of special knowledge, and control the necessary resources.

A further aspect of professional organizations is the fact that *operative* (technical, functional, work-related) rules as well as *regulative* (coordinative, administrative) rules are internalized by the professional workers through formal education and the accompanying processes of socialization, thus eliminating or reducing the need for external supervision and control.

In bureaucratic organizations, on the other hand, the goal and task structure is determined and specified by the managerial or by extra-organizational control structures. Productive activities are directed by a nonprofessional—but nonetheless technically specialized and competent—administrative-managerial staff, and carried out according to an organizationally determined division of labor in which a high degree of job specialization typically corresponds to a low degree of person specialization. *Operative* rules are externalized, (e.g., as in blue prints and written procedural regulations concerning the operation of machines, assembly of products, etc.), a process which be-

---

in terms of functional rationality or technology, cf. J. D. Thompson, *Organizations in Action* (New York: McGraw-Hill, 1967), pp. 14–24; also Charles Perrow's synthetic task-structure-technology-variability conception, in his "A Framework for the Comparative Analysis of Organizations," *American Sociological Review* 32 (Apr. 1967), 194–208. Technology, however, especially machine technology, tends to fall only at the highly rationalized end of our underlying dimension of rationalization of the specialized knowledge base. Our conception, by contrast, is more encompassing and, at the same time, getting at more specific phenomena, including the residual category of "traditional" knowledge as well as affective, charismatic-personal knowledge, substantive or value-rationality, and functional (formal) or purposive rationality (cf. Weber, *Economy and Society*, pp. 24–26). For still another conception of the "specialized knowledge base," see Stinchcombe's notion of a "theory of how the activities can be organized to achieve the purpose of the organization," which stresses purposive rationality (the means-ends nexus) and partly overlaps with another of his organizational elements, the "authority system." Stinchcombe's last element, "resources," refers generally to the *availability* (scarcity) of resources, rather than to the more specific problem of *control* over resources as posed by Marx and Weber; Arthur L. Stinchcombe, "Formal Organizations," in N. Smelser (ed.), *Sociology.* (New York: John Wiley, 1967), pp. 156–72.
[4] E. C. Hughes, *Men and Their Work* (New York: Free Press, 1958), pp. 78–87.

[5] H. Wilensky, "The Professionalization of Everyone?" *American Journal of Sociology* 70 (1964), 137–58; Talcott Parsons, "The Professions and Social Structure," in *Essays in Sociological Theory* (New York: Free Press, 1949), pp. 185–99.

comes increasingly rationalized and routinized in mass production. *Regulative* rules emerge as a result of specialization, i.e., to deal with problems of coordination of specialized work activities and functions. Both operative and regulative rules, when externalized, require a supervisory staff for their enforcement and thus become a causal factor in the development of hierarchical levels, another factor being, of course, the bureaucratic control over resources. In technologically complex and highly mechanized or automated production processes, rules and regulations are built into the operational plans and into the technical process itself, so that supervision becomes more and more impersonal and ultimately gives way to mechanical modes of coordination and control, such as negative feedback systems in servo-mechanisms.[6]

[6] It should, therefore, not be surprising to find, empirically, negative relationships between (1) professionalization, (2) the extent of written rules, and (3) technical complexity, since all three variables represent different points on the continuum from medium to high rationalization of the specialized knowledge base. The more rationalized the knowledge base, the more will written rules supersede the internalized rules of professionals, and the more will technically rationalized and self-regulative forms of production supersede those which still require the supervisory-hierarchical enforcement of written operative and regulative rules. This replacement process, however, is probably not complete, as C. Wright Mills has pointed out: "As professional people of both old and new middle classes become attached to institutions, they acquire staffs of assistants who, in contrast to the old professional apprentices, are not . . . in training to become autonomous professionals themselves." "The bureaucratic manner has not replaced the entrepreneurial; rather, the professional strata today represent various combinations of the two: at the bottom extreme, the

Although the differences between professional and bureaucratic forms of organization are clear in contrast, the definition and meaning of "professional" itself is not agreed upon by all. Professionals, in the strict sense of the term, are persons who "profess" a certain type of specialized knowledge and praxis, that is they practice a profession. "The professions" are thus seen as ideal-typical occupations possessing certain characteristics. Vollmer and Mills, following Greenwood, describe professions as having "(1) a basis of systematic theory, (2) authority recognized by the clientele of the professional group, (3) broader community sanction and approval of this authority, (4) a code of ethics regulating relations of professional persons with clients and with colleagues, and (5) a professional culture sustained by formal professional associations."[7] However, these characteristics are more applicable to the "old" professions such as theology, law, and medicine rather than to the "new" professions such as engineering, teaching, nursing, and social work.[8]

In addition to the distinction between old and new professions there

---

staffs of lesser-skilled, newer members of the strata begin and remain bureaucratized; at the top the free and salaried professionals make their own curious adaptation to the new conditions prevailing in their work." C. Wright Mills, *White Collar.* (New York: Oxford University Press, 1956), pp. 114–15.

[7] Ernest Greenwood, "The Elements of Professionalization," in H. M. Vollmer and D. L. Mills (eds.), *Professionalization* (Englewood Cliffs: Prentice-Hall, 1966), p. 10.

[8] Harold Wilensky, "The Professionalization of Everyone?" pp. 137–58.

are others which are nevertheless frequently subsumed under the umbrella term "professional." Examples are the distinction between professionals who have clients and scientists who don't,[9] general practitioners and specialists, basic and applied scientists, and scientists and technicians. It is submitted here that all of these distinctions reflect differences in the degree to which the specialized knowledge base of a given "professional" group is rationalized, standardized, non-secret and accessible. Thus, for the pre-19th century forms of the "old" professions, the degree of secrecy of knowledge is relatively high, while the degree of rationalization is low. It borders on completely secret ("sacred"), inaccessible, personalized, charismatic knowledge in the case of pre-modern religious "professionals" such as magicians and of the members of secret societies.[10]

With increasing rationalization of the knowledge base, we move from the pre-modern professions to their newer science-based forms, from basic science to applied science, and from there to the new professions and to the technically skilled groups (technicians). The members of these

new occupational groups almost exclusively *apply* already available knowledge to routine situations and operate highly rationalized technologies. As the person specialization of professionals in organizations tends to decrease in this sequence, job specialization and the internal division of labor of organizations tend to increase.

The increasing rationalization of the knowledge base also has consequences for the relative accessibility of knowledge, and thus for the autonomy and relative status of professionals who work in organizations. For example, in universities, basic researchers tend to have more "charisma" and prestige than teachers, since the latter organize, rationalize, and preserve knowledge, while the former are seen as producing new knowledge. From this perspective, technicians are rationalized professionals who apply highly codified knowledge to fairly routine situations. To the extent that task complexity is reduced to the point of routinization, and knowledge is fully rationalized, old professionals (especially generalists) may be replaced by a series of specialists, new professionals, semi-professionals, and technicians who, in turn, may be replaced by machines and servo-mechanisms, e.g., computerized diagnostic and registration procedures, billing and tax assessment systems, teaching machines, automated laboratories and factories.

It seems obvious that such highly rationalized information and production systems lend themselves to impersonal, bureaucratic control in the sense of both specification of operational goals and procedures as well as control over resources, since the calculability of costs and outcomes is vastly increased. But it is also obvi-

---

[9] E. C. Hughes, *Men and Their Work* (New York: Free Press, 1958), pp. 78–87.

[10] The social functions and political influence of secret societies have been relatively well documented, given the nature of the subject; see, e.g., Charles W. Heckethorn, *The Secret Societies of All Ages and Countries*, 2 vols. (New York: University Books, Inc., Rev. Ed., 1965), and the classical discussion by Simmel, "Secrecy" and "The Secret Society," in Kurt H. Wolff (ed.), *The Sociology of Georg Simmel.* (New York: Free Press, 1950), pp. 330–78. For an excellent early sociological bibliography on secret societies, see Robert E. Park and Ernest W. Burgess, *Introduction to the Science of Sociology* (Chicago: University of Chicago Press, 1921), pp. 730–31.

ous that the technicians who operate such systems are not professionals in the sense of the general practitioner, but technical specialists for whom organizational and professional concerns tend to coincide.[11]

The less developed and rationalized the specialized knowledge base, as e.g., in the prescientific "old" professions, the greater the potential conflict between the practitioner and a bureaucratic system of control. One can probably argue that even *within* certain professions, e.g., medicine, much current conflict is generated by the increasing rationalization and routinization of the knowledge base, that is, by the fact that new medical technologies and their corresponding hierarchies of technical experts take an increasing number of diagnostic and therapeutic functions out of the hands of the already highly specialized medical professional practitioners who, moreover, become increasingly integrated into the internal division of labor of hospitals.

Similar conflicts can be identified in the field of social work, although they tend to be less pronounced than

[11] Much of the literature on "scientists in organizations" uses the term "professional" without making distinctions in terms of different degrees of rationalization of the knowledge base. But many studies show that the more scientists and technicians have "applied" and job-specialized characteristics, the less likely is there a conflict between the "professional" and the "bureaucratic" elements in their work situation; see, e.g., D. C. Pelz and F. M. Andrews, *Scientists in Organizations* (New York: John Wiley, 1966); W. Kornhauser, *Scientists in Industry* (Berkeley: University of California Press, 1963); S. Marcson, *The Scientist in American Industry* (Princeton: Princeton University Press, 1960); Mark Abrahamson, *The Professional in the Organization* (Chicago: Rand McNally, 1967); C. W. Mills, *White Collar*, pp. 77–141, 215–38.

in medicine since social work deals "only" with welfare rather than health and life. And since social work is a more recently established profession than medicine, it has, presumably, less autonomy to lose than medicine. The conflicts ensuing from the processes of rationalization and routinization are exacerbated by the fact that these processes often receive tacit and sometimes open support by highly bureaucratized agency administrations, external sources of funding (e.g., the United Fund), and government agencies providing resources, regulations, and controls. Many social work agencies view government contracts with a high degree of ambivalence. Private welfare agencies realize their desperate dependence on such external resources. But they also perceive government contracts, as well as Community Chests and Funds, as threats to their autonomy, particularly if they see themselves as doing professional rather than "efficient," depersonalized, in short, bureaucratic social work.

It follows from this explication of the underlying dimension involved here, viz., the degree of rationalization of the specialized knowledge base, that the new professions and technical specialities are *not* becoming more *professionalized*, but more *rationalized*, albeit not without a struggle. As socially involved interest groups, the new professions may strive to achieve the status, power, prestige, and privileges of the old professions, but that process needs to be distinguished from other developments. These are: (1) the de facto rationalization, codification, standardization, and broad accessibility of the specialized knowledge base; (2) the attendant increase in job specialization; (3) the integration of technical specialists into an organizational division of labor; (4) the involvement of new professionals and technical specialists in hierarchical authority relations in which they progressively lose not only the capacity to specify the goals and tasks defining their work activity which forms the basis of professional service, but also the control over resources. Professionalization, as the process of an occupation becoming like one of the old professions, thus becomes an exception rather than the rule. Among the new and applied fields of specialization that are based on new technologies and rationalized procedures, this process can only mean the development of protective associations, unions, political and economic countervailing power to defend the professionalizing occupation against the encroachment of bureaucratic controls and the erosion of jurisdictional and economic autonomy. Thus, the more professionalized the occupation, the greater the tendency that conflicts involve jurisdictional issues, i.e., issues involving goal-setting, control over work activities and self-regulation.

In effect, then, professionalization —as the process of becoming a profession—is clearly a retrogressive process insofar as it is motivated by self-interested considerations of achieving status, power, and autonomy, rather than by collectivity-oriented considerations of effectively dealing with social problems. It is at this point that the professions and the social structure come into fundamental contradiction, rather than being institutionally articulated with each other.[12]

[12] See, e.g., Talcott Parsons, "The Professions and Social Structure," in *Essays in Sociological Theory* (New York: Free Press,

In sum, the autonomy of professionals (and indirectly of professional organizations, too) may be reduced to the extent that 1) goals, objectives, tasks, products and service become specifiable and are specified by others and where task and environmental complexity and uncertainty become subject to manipulation; 2) the specialized knowledge base becomes increasingly rationalized, i.e., standardized and capable of routine application and thus more generally available and accessible to clients, audiences, markets, and future practitioners; and 3) control over resources is restricted, or is shifted to owners, managers, boards, or extra-organizational agencies. And to the extent that professionals and professional organizations derive wealth, power, prestige, and symbolic rewards from their monopoly on spe-

1949), pp. 185–99. The view of "professionalization" developed above follows, to some extent, that of Wilensky, "The Professionalization of Everyone?" and is in disagreement with the view of professionalization given in Vollmer and Mills, *Professionalization*. Moreover, what is called "professionalization" by virtue of the criterion that professional associations are formed can often be seen as a political attempt to retain or regain control over the specification of goals and the control over resources. These attempts lead to unionization and the formation of interest groups rather than to professionalization as such. But while Wilensky is quite sensitive to the problem of political control which the new professions encounter in their struggle for professionalization, he treats the questions of autonomy, definition and specification of goals (the "service ideal," i.e., value-rationality), and control over resources too much from the point of view of the ideal-type profession and the model of occupational specialization, rather than in terms of the separate effects of task complexity, knowledge base, and resource control on the realization of socially defined goals, as we are suggesting here.

cialized knowledge, they will resist attempts to have goals specified and operationalized, procedures prescribed and resources controlled by others. The defense and control of such values as academic freedom, privileged and secret communication between practitioner and client, objectivity of knowledge, quality of service, and "responsibility" for the consequences of expert judgment thus rank understandably high among professional practitioners and their collegial-professional associations.[13]

In this context the problems that typically accompany the process of innovation in a professional organization can be more fully understood. Innovation is, of course, central to the concerns of professionals, from basic research-oriented scientists to social workers concerned with community organization, insofar as it involves the creation of new knowledge or the application of specialized knowledge to new situations. But this is not to say that innovation is a static attribute of professional activity or of professional organizations, for this would ignore the structural context in which professionals must work, and especially those factors that threaten the power and autonomy of the professional. While, theoretically, innovation may be seen as a process of adaptation by which environmental uncertainty and task complexity are reduced, in the social structures where it must be implemented it involves a redefinition of the professional's rights and obligations, tasks and functions. Not only is the professional concerned

with the maintenance and extension of his autonomy in his relationships with the wider society, he is also involved in a constant struggle within the organizations in which he carries on his profession over the "objective" complexity of his tasks and who is to define them, over the applicability of his specialized knowledge, and over the control of the resources needed for his practice. When innovations are introduced, they disturb the compromises or exacerbate the conflicts that exist among the opposing interests involved, particularly between professionals and nonprofessionals, because they force a reconsideration of the arrangements and assumptions often only tacitly and reluctantly accepted.

An appreciation of the inherent conflict accompanying the process of innovation also serves to articulate the difference between types of innovations, the implications this distinction has for the behavior of professionals and nonprofessionals, and the relationships between them. The first basic type of innovation may be called the *rationalization* or *specification of knowledge*, a process similar to that of functional rationalization. In this process traditional tasks and goals are attacked in new ways through the generation of new methods, resulting in a technically more sophisticated specification of problems and solutions. A typical result is the simplification and serialization of the task, as, e.g., in the Planning-Programming-Budgeting system. Not infrequently improvements are registered in terms of economic and technological criteria, particularly in terms of efficiency and precision. The most obvious examples of this kind of innovation are to be found embodied in machine technology, and in new

---

[13] Wilensky found that, among professors, lawyers, and engineers, bureaucratic control threatens the service-ideal more than it threatens autonomy; "The Professionalization of Everyone?" p. 137.

methods of production and administration.

The other basic type of innovation
may be called the *extension of knowledge to new areas.* In the course of
this kind of innovation it is not the
generation of new methods or concepts that occurs so much as it is
the development of new products and
modes of application. While gains in
efficiency may be expected in terms
of the results of the application, those
who command the knowledge to
make the application enlarge upon
their sphere of competence. The development of experimental programs
and services is a ready example of
this type of innovation, as would be
the application of any general model
or procedure to a new field of inquiry,
administrative reorganization for purposes of diversification, i.e., the development of new products and markets, and various types of research
and demonstration projects.

Returning to the more specific
problem of innovation in professional
organizations, it is apparent that conflicts may develop within the organization between professionals and non-
professionals, especially bureaucrats
or managers, over what should be the
main foci of professional concern,
especially to the extent that this involves innovation. Professionals will
favor that type of innovation that
leads to the extension of their specialized knowledge base to new areas
in order to retain control over the
knowledge base and to expand their
domain. Such kinds of innovation as
research and demonstration (R & D)
projects, program expansion, and
adding new programs to existing
ones will find favor as they provide
areas for "personal growth" of professionals in terms of their knowledge,
as well as an increase in their pres-

tige and a reduction of their expend-
ability.[14] This process by which new
goals and tasks are incorporated
into the professional's mandate also
fundamentally means an increase in
the control they have over resources
at the operative level, as opposed to
that emanating from a higher organizational (bureaucratic) level. Expansion means an increase in professional
power.

By contrast, innovation as a process of rationalization and specification of knowledge resulting in the
incorporation of previously difficult
and complex tasks into simple routines will be favored by bureaucrats
and managers. Rationalizing innovations have several payoffs for the
organization as a whole, and for
bureaucrats in particular, since they
increase the capacity to control
production at higher organizational
levels, and at the same time decrease
the bureaucrats' dependence on professional experts as such innovations
tend to decrease the latters' autonomy (unless they retain explicit control over the new technology as, e.g.,
in radiology, pathology, anesthe-
siology).[15] In addition, rationalizing

[14] E.g., the development of mechanical engineering from craft to large-scale mechanization and mass production, where the
quality orientation of mechanical engineers
as craftsmen gave rise to a system of production which ultimately threatened and
subverted their own basis of autonomy and
prestige, thus leading eventually to the formation of engineering associations and
unions; cf. R. Heydebrand, *A Sociological
History of Engineering Education in the
United States,* unpubl. ms., 1970.

[15] It would be worth a systematic study to
find out whether physicians oppose the
introduction or adoption of new drugs, the
generic labeling of drugs on prescriptions,
or new medical technologies. The hypothesis would be that opposition arises because
all of these factors tend to rationalize the

innovations are designed to be "efficient," i.e., money-saving, or to provide more adequate services within given budgets. New programs and applications tend to increase costs and may require new resources from outside the organization, e.g., grants or contracts, thus increasing the organization's dependence on extraorganizational sources. Moreover, where task complexity and uncertainty are effectively reduced as a result of rationalizing innovations, the manipulation of uncertainty and complexity becomes manageable for the bureaucrats, and it may further increase the control over professionals and their new programs.

From this perspective, it is quite plausible to assume that the complexity of the situation, i.e., task complexity, uncertainty, seeing and creating problems, may be highly functional and profitable for both professionals and bureaucrats, albeit for opposite reasons. Complexity may be manipulated so as to increase one's ability to define the problem, to appeal to the need for secrecy or technically complex and thus cen-

tralized decision making, to cope with the problem in terms of one's own definition, to retain or increase control over resources and budgets, to increase costs artificially (appeal to "security," etc., costs before and after contract allocations, etc.), and to hide failures, inadequacies, and ineffectiveness.[16]

In this paper, only two relatively limited aspects of these theoretical considerations will be investigated empirically. First, we will focus on the interrelation between specialized knowledge base (professionalization), control over resources (bureaucratization), and the complexity of the task structure. Secondly, this set of relationships will be analyzed as to its effect on one type of innovativeness, viz., the extension and application of the specialized knowledge base to new areas in the form of research and demonstration projects. We will show that task complexity is a major determinant of this type of innovativeness, and that professionalization favors its occurrence, whereas bureaucratization does not.

DATA AND METHOD

The organizations on which this study is based are private welfare agencies, specifically neighborhood centers affiliated with the National Federation of Settlements and Neighborhood Centers. In 1964, a detailed

---

process of medical care, make it less secret and more accessible to patients and to semi-professional and technical personnel, and thus reduces the autonomy of physicians; for suggestive leads, see, e.g., Eliot Freidson, *Professional Dominance* (New York: Atherton, 1970), as well as his *The Profession of Medicine: A Sociological Analysis* (New York: Dodd, Mead, 1969), and "The Impurity of Professional Authority," in Howard S. Becker et al. (eds.), *Institutions and the Person: Papers Presented to Everett C. Hughes* (Chicago: Aldine, 1968), pp. 25–34; Elihu Katz, Herbert Menzel, and James Coleman, *Medical Innovation* (New York: Bobbs-Merrill, 1966); Oswald Hall, "The Informal Organization of the Medical Profession," *Canadian Journal of Economics and Political Science*, 12 (1946), 30–44.

[16] See, e.g., S. Warkov, "Irregular Discharge From V. A. Hospitals," unpublished Ph.D. dissertation, Department of Sociology, Yale University, 1959; and more generally S. Melman, *Pentagon Capitalism: The Political Economy of War* (New York: McGraw-Hill, 1970); H. Wilensky, *Organizational Intelligence* (New York: Basic Books, 1967); E. Shils, *The Torment of Secrecy* (New York: Free Press, 1956).

personnel questionnaire was sent out by the National Federation to all 270 member agencies and returned by 122 agencies, or about 45%.[17] The bias of selection operates against the smaller agencies.[18]

Settlements and neighborhood centers are private welfare agencies oriented toward social reform. Their objectives include the "improvement of living conditions" in urban neighborhoods, "strengthening family life," "creating a feeling of neighborliness by helping individuals and groups to relate to one another; developing indigenous leadership, and integrating a local neighborhood with its city, state, nation, and the world."[19] While the major thrust of early settlements, such as Hull House in Chicago under the leadership of Jane Addams, was directed at helping a neighborhood help itself and to work toward collective self-improvement through increasing initiative, local autonomy and self-sufficiency in community organization and control, the majority

of settlements today tend to be group work agencies. Only the larger and more complex agencies engage in multiple services, including case work, urban renewal programs, day care centers, clinics, and various aspects of community organization. Settlement houses are, on the average, about fifty years old, with the oldest settlements such as Hull House going back to the 1880s.

Current changes in the composition and structure of American cities, and the influx of federal funds through the "War on Poverty" in the 1960s have forced settlements into an increasingly serious self-evaluation of their programs, structure, and effectiveness. Local community chests and funds provide the bulk of support (about 70% of agency budgets for all agencies, and about 35% for the 122 agencies included in this study) and have been a potent force in bringing about mergers of smaller agencies as well as in the establishment of city-wide federations and associations.[20]

The data for this analysis are derived from the personnel questionnaires by constructing variables which are intended to measure general organizational characteristics of the agencies. In this way it is possible to compare the agencies on a relatively abstract level of analysis. More-

---

[17] We are indebted to Margaret Berry, executive director of the National Federation, for making available copies of the returned questionnaires for purposes of this analysis, and for providing many helpful suggestions for the interpretation of the meaning and limitations of these data.

[18] It should be noted that there are about 800 neighborhood centers in the United States, and that the 270 member agencies are themselves only a part of that larger spectrum reflecting the standards for program and personnel, conformity to which is a precondition for membership in the National Federation. See, e.g., National Federation of Settlements and Neighborhood Centers, *Standards for Neighborhood Centers* (New York, 1960).

[19] See Margaret Berry, "Settlements and Neighborhood Centers," *Social Work Year Book 1960* (National Association of Social Workers, New York); also National Federation of Settlements and Neighborhood Centers, *Neighborhood Goals in a Rapidly Changing World* (New York, 1958).

[20] See, e.g., *Neighborhood and City: New Designs for the Settlement Movement* (New York: National Federation of Settlements, 1965); for general historical accounts of the settlement movement in the context of the modern welfare state, see Berry, *Social Work Year Book 1960*; Clarke A. Chambers, *Seedtime of Reform* (Minneapolis: University of Minnesota Press, 1963); Philip Klein, *From Philanthropy to Social Welfare* (San Francisco: Jossey-Bass, 1968); H. L. Wilensky and C. N. Lebeaux, *Industrial Society and Social Welfare* (New York: Free Press, 1965).

over, the variables are quantified so as to be amenable to multivariate statistical analysis. While we are aware of the relative crudeness of such a procedure, especially as far as the interpretation of the empirical data is concerned, we feel that comparative-quantitative analysis of a relatively large number of organizations, based on general, theoretically relevant concepts and variables, remains an important way to advance and refine our theoretical understanding of the structure of organizations.

OPERATIONAL DEFINITIONS

In the following the structural variables used in this study will be operationally defined. Let us first look at the main defining characteristic of the organizations, namely "professionalization," and then take up the operational measures for the complexity of the task structure, bureaucratization, and innovation.

Professionalization. Settlement houses are governed by a board of directors and operated by a staff of professional social workers under the direction of an executive director. The executive director and the full-time professional staff typically have the MSW degree (Master of Social Work) or its equivalent, which is used here as the operational criterion for the term "professional."

In the context of this paper, social workers will be defined as *new* professionals, but as professionals nonetheless. The case of social work is somewhat ambiguous since it contains a strong "generalist" component, based on a value-rational commitment to social welfare and progress, as well as a "specialist" component, based on the behavioral sciences of sociology and psychol-ogy. Although the generalist element would seem to push social work toward the older professions, modern social work is sufficiently rationalized to qualify as a specialist form of professional practice, that is, as a new profession.[21]

To repeat, "professionalization," in this paper, will *not* be taken to refer to the process of an occupation becoming like a profession, but to the degree to which the organizational labor force consists of professionals, in this case, professional social workers with an MSW degree. The degree of professionalization of an agency is thus defined by the proportion of full-time equivalent personnel in social work functions who have the MSW degree, excluding managerial personnel, i.e., the executive director, his associate or assistant and, in large agencies, the director of group services (program director). While the range of this proportion varies considerably, depending on size and task complexity of the agency, the mean proportion of professionals for the 122 agencies investigated here is 32% (see Table 1).[22]

[21] Wilensky, too, argues that "in a sense social work has vacillated between the ministry (doctrine-oriented social reform) and medicine (science-oriented clinical practice) as models for the professional thrust." "The Professionalization of Everyone?" p. 140, fn. 5.

[22] Strictly speaking, a "professional organization" should approximate complete professionalization so that "professional" could be considered a constant characteristic of the organization. In practice, agencies have various programs auxiliary or subordinated to the services offered within the traditional social work categories of group work, case work, and neighborhood organization. For this reason, it is useful to consider professionalization as a variable in its own right, especially since the number of different programs is also used as a variable.

TABLE 1 MEANS, STANDARD DEVIATIONS, AND RANGE OF 7 VARIABLES

Variable	Mean	SD	Range
1. Complexity of Task Structure I: Geographical Dispersion (Number of Branches)	.5	1.2	0–10
2. Complexity of Task Structure II: Diversification (Number of Programs)	5.2	3.1	1–22
3. Complexity of Task Structure III: Size (Number of Personnel, Full-Time Equivalent)	14.5	12.3	4–75
4. Professionalization (% with MSW)	31.9	27.2	0–100
5. Bureaucratization I: Control Structure (Number of Levels in Hierarchy)	3.9	1.1	2–7
6. Bureaucratization II: Communications Structure (% Administrative-Clerical Staff)	30.4	8.3	20–45
7. Innovativeness (Number of R & D Projects)	.4	1.0	0–8

COMPLEXITY OF TASK STRUCTURE

The complexity of the task structure of settlements and neighborhood centers is operationalized here in terms of *three* dimensions, all of which are subject to considerable variation (see Table 1).

1. *Number of Branches.* First, the agencies may have up to ten branches at separate geographical locations, thus directly reflecting the varying degrees of the environmental complexity they have to deal with. However, the mean number of branches of the 122 agencies is less than one. This first measure of task complexity will be called *geographical dispersion.*

2. *Number of Programs.* Secondly, agencies vary in the degree to which their services are diversified. While the most complex of the 122 agencies had twenty-two separate regular programs in 1965, the average number for all agencies is about five programs. The existence of a program is operationally determined by the pre-

sence of at least one full-time worker responsible for a specialized activity carried out on a regular basis. Examples of such programs are day care centers, teen-age programs, adult or senior citizen programs, services to individuals and families, out-reach programs with delinquents, and various community organization programs. This second dimension of task complexity is, of course, closely related to such aspects of internal structural differentiation as departmentalization, functional-occupational specialization, and other aspects of the internal division of labor, aspects which are not separately investigated in this paper.

3. *Size.* A third aspect of task complexity is task volume or organizational size. For the purposes of this paper, size of the total organizational labor force is used, i.e., number of personnel, expressed in full-time equivalents. As can be seen from Table 1, the agencies under consideration are relatively small organi-

zations, ranging from 4–75, with a mean of about fifteen persons.

BUREAUCRATIZATION

The degree of bureaucratization is conceptualized in two ways.

1. *Number of levels.* First, the number of levels of the organizational hierarchy is determined by counting vertically differentiated job titles within the central division of the agency, usually group services or group work. Examples of typical levels are executive director, director of group services (program director), director (or supervisor) of a specific group work program, professional social worker, and group leader or assistant. The number of levels varies from two to seven, with a mean of about four levels. It should be noted here that the upper levels of the hierarchy are almost always staffed by professional social workers who thus *direct* and *carry out* the main productive activity of the organization. Professionals may have subprofessional or nonprofessional subordinates, but the authority relations are, as a rule, collegial rather than bureaucratic. Nevertheless, the fact that there are levels of super- and subordination—implying differential degrees of responsibility and discretion—clearly indicates the presence of a bureaucratic element.

While the executive director has control over the budget, i.e., over the available resources of the organization, two factors need to be considered which modify the ideal-typical bureaucratic character of the hierarchical control structure. One is the fact that for any level, except perhaps the lowest level, the next higher supervisory level is staffed by a professional. Second, the executive director is not completely autonomous with respect to resource control, since he is legally responsible to the governing board of the agency. Moreover, the majority of agencies are financially dependent on the local community fund or chest which thus becomes a powerful source of resource control as well as of control of program policies and personnel standards.[23]

In spite of these two modifying influences, especially the factor of professional supervision, it can be assumed that the further removed the executive from the operating level of the agency, the less does the production component control the available resources of the organization. It is in this sense that the number of levels in the hierarchy serves as a measure of bureaucratization and, specifically, of the distance between

[23] An attempt was made to examine the effect of the financial autonomy or dependence of agencies on their structural characteristics as well as on innovativeness in light of Zald's general proposition that "to the extent that board members control or represent salient external 'resources,' they are more powerful than if they do not control such resources," see Mayer Zald, "The Power and Functions of Boards of Directors: A Theoretical Synthesis," *American Journal of Sociology*, 75 (July 1969), 100. While Zald made no direct prediction as to the effect of board power on innovation, one could argue that a powerful, conservative board might block an organization's innovativeness, whereas a weak or progressive board might give the organization's executive more latitude to innovate. However, the relative dependence of the agencies on external resources (percent of budget received from the Community Fund) was not found to be related to innovativeness, although it was related negatively to size, budget, task complexity, number of hierarchical levels, and professionalization, and positively to administrative costs.

the locus of control over resources and the operating level.

2. *Administrative-clerical staff.* The second way in which bureaucratization is conceptualized refers to the presence and relative size of the administrative and clerical staff, i.e., the proportion of managerial and clerical personnel in the total personnel. The range of this percentage is between 20 and 45%, with a mean of 30.4% (see Table 1).[24]

INNOVATIVENESS

Innovativeness, the main dependent variable in this study, is defined by the number of "research and demonstration" (R & D) projects executed by an agency during the four-year period between 1961 and 1964.[25] The number of projects ranged from 0–8, with a mean of less than one (.4) (see Table 1).

The R & D projects used as the units of innovation in this study are of many different kinds, reflecting

essentially an intensification and extension of approaches and methods used in modern social work. Examples are "demonstration of the effectiveness of intervention by community organization methods in a neighborhood threatened with deterioration," a neighborhood organization project "to tackle problems of rehabilitation, illiteracy, school dropouts, juvenile delinquency," and techniques for "improving decision-making of young low-income couples." While these R & D projects vary both in cost and effectiveness, it is generally recognized within the social work field that they constitute a significant form of, or basis for, social service innovation.[26]

The raw data from the personnel questionnaire and from a separate comprehensive listing of R & D projects compiled in 1964 by the National Federation of Settlements were transformed into quantitative variables, punched on IBM cards, and analyzed by means of a stepwise multiple correlation and regression program.[27]

[24] It should be noted that this measure refers to the relative size of the *combined* managerial-clerical apparatus, i.e., the total managerial component, augmented by the relative size of the clerical staff of the agency. This measure corresponds, therefore, to the one used by Anderson and Warkov as well as by Heydebrand in their studies of hospitals; see selections 19 and 7 in this volume.

[25] The data for this study were collected during the last of the four years in which the R & D projects were implemented. While it would have been desirable also to obtain data on structural characteristics for the first year of this period or, even better, for every year, we feel that the relative lack of correspondence or of longitudinal data does not significantly alter our theoretical basis for making statements about causal direction. The reason for this assertion is that the settlements under consideration can be assumed to be structurally stable for the time period in question.

[26] See, e.g., Martin Rein and S. M. Miller, "The Demonstration Project as a Strategy of Change," in Mayer N. Zald (ed.), *Organizing for Community Welfare* (Chicago: Quadrangle Books, 1967), pp. 160–91; Morris H. Hansen and Genevieve W. Carter, "Assessing Effectiveness of Methods for Meeting Social and Economic Problems," in Leonard H. Goodman (ed.), *Economic Progress and Social Welfare* (New York: Columbia University Press, 1966), pp. 92–124; Eleanor B. Sheldon and Wilbert E. Moore, "Toward the Measurement of Social Change: Implications for Progress," in Goodman, *Economic Progress*, pp. 185–212.

[27] We hereby gratefully acknowledge support of this study by the Washington University Computation Center and its program for student and faculty research, under NSF Grant # G22296.

TABLE 2 INTERCORRELATIONS AMONG THE VARIABLES ($N = 122$)

Variables	1	2	3	4	5	6
1. Number of Branches	–					
2. Number of Programs	.46	–				
3. Size	.63	.75	–			
4. Professionalization	.20	.24	.28	–		
5. Number of Levels	.35	.51	.58	.17	–	
6. % Admin.-Cler. Staff	.04	−.15	−.22	.20	−.13	–
7. No. of R & D Projects	.48	.32	.32	.25	.11	.09

Insofar as we are dealing with a fairly generic type of professional organization, namely private welfare agencies where the bureaucratic control structure is staffed by professionals, we are generalizing to the type defined earlier as a professional organization. While professional organizations themselves are, of course, subject to a considerable amount of structural variation, for example, from the more 'autonomous' hospitals and universities to the more 'heteronomous' type including secondary schools and public welfare agencies, the structural patterns reported here are believed to be rather typical of all professional organizations.

THE BUREAUCRATIZATION OF PROFESSIONALS

The increasing rationalization of the specialized knowledge base makes professional knowledge more accessible and possibly less costly; but it also lends itself to increasing bureaucratic control over the specification of goals and resources. For the reasons outlined above, the conflict between professional autonomy and bureaucratic control should be less pronounced in private social work than in medicine, but more than in public social work, public administration, or engineering.

We would, therefore, expect to find neither a strongly negative nor a strongly positive relationship between the professional and bureaucratic elements in private welfare agencies. Our data show that there is, indeed, only a moderately positive correlation between professionalization and bureaucratization ($r = .17$ for number of levels, $r = .20$ for percent administrative-clerical staff) (see Table 2).[28]

Moreover, when size and task complexity are controlled, the relationship between professionalization and number of levels disappears, suggesting that professionalization and bureaucratization do not "militate" against each other, especially once the organizational context is taken into account. But they do not "favor" or reinforce each other either. A similar situation holds for the relation between professionalization and the relative size of the administrative-clerical staff, that is, it is reduced under the control of size and task complexity. But even if task complexity and size (or the task structure) provide a context for "accommodation" between professionalization and

[28] See W. Richard Scott, "Reactions to Supervision in a Heteronomous Professional Organization," *Administrative Science Quarterly*, 10 (June 1965), 67–68.

bureaucratization, it can be expected that the bureaucratic control structure is more strongly influenced by task structure variables than by professionalization.

This expectation is based not only on previous empirical research[29] but also on the simple reasoning that size and task differentiation tend to increase the bureaucratic control mechanisms, whereas professional activity is already part of the organizational division of labor: it intervenes between task structure and control structure, much like formal rules and technology as they represent different degrees of rationalization of the specialized knowledge base.[30] The correlations between task structure and professionalization and bureaucratization tend to bear out these expectations. Bureaucratization is more strongly influenced by task structure variables than professionalization. Thus, professionalization is only moderately positively related to the number of branches (r = .20), number of programs (r = .24) and size (r = .28), whereas the number of levels correlates more strongly with number of branches (r = .35), number of programs (r = .51), and size (r = .58) (see Table 2).

The pattern of relationships between administrative-clerical staff and task structure points in the opposite direction. Thus, the percentage of administrative-clerical staff is *not* related to number of branches (r = .04), and moderately negatively related to number of programs (r = −.15), and size (r = −.22).[31] The negative effect of size on the relative size of administrative-clerical staff confirms, of course, similar findings in the majority of studies concerned with this relationship, especially where the organizations investigated are work organizations rather than voluntary associations, such as churches and unions.[32]

What are the implications of these findings for the "bureaucratization of professionals," and for the presumed conflict between professional and bureaucratic elements in organizations?

The moderately positive zero-order relationship between professionalization and bureaucratization, and its disappearance under the control of size and task complexity, lends support to an obvious line of reasoning: in professional organizations, where the bureaucratic hierarchy is staffed by professionals, the contradiction or conflict between professional and bureaucratic elements is reduced or simply absent. In contrast, a strong negative relationship might be expected in bureaucratic organizations or possibly in heteronomous profes-

[29] W. Heydebrand, *Hospital Bureaucracy: A Comparative Study of Organizations* (New York: Dunellen-University Press of Cambridge, 1972).
[30] On the intervening effect of technology, see W. Heydebrand, P. Galloway, J. DeRoche and D. Magill, "Task Structure, Technological Complexity and Bureaucratic Organization." Paper presented at the Annual Meeting of the Canadian Sociological and Anthropological Association, Winnipeg, Canada, May, 1970.

[31] These weak and negative relationships can probably, in part, be attributed to the fact that we are dealing essentially with a managerial ratio where the total personnel constitutes the denominator. This interpretation is supported by the fact that the relation to number of levels is also negative (r = −.13).
[32] For a review of the most significant studies in this respect, see Pondy, 21, this volume; the "negative" cases of voluntary associations are provided, e.g., by Tsouderos, 15, also in this volume.

sional ones.[33] However, the agencies studied here are approaching the autonomous form of professional organization, even though they cannot be said to conform to a full-fledged autonomous type due to external private control and the presence of a bureaucratic element, viz., hierarchical differentiation.

We are suggesting, then, that the bureaucratization of professionals does not necessarily imply conflict between the professional and bureaucratic elements in professional organizations. Fundamentally, the problem is one of the degree of autonomy granted professional workers to specify and to define operationally the goals of the organizations as well as the nature of the task, to apply their specialized knowledge, and to control the available resources. Given these conditions, there should be little conflict between bureaucratic and professional elements, even where there is a hierarchy with top levels staffed by the same professionals as the production component, and where control over resources does not |reside in extraorganizational levels of public, governmental authority.[34]

[33] See, e.g., Scott, "Reactions to Supervision," and Stanley H. Udy, "Bureaucracy and Rationality in Weber's Theory," *American Sociological Review*, 24 (Dec. 19, 1959), 791–95.
[34] Weber has dealt with the phenomenon of hierarchy in an autonomous organization in terms of the concept of "autocephaly" which "means that the chief and his staff are selected according to the autonomous order of the organization itself, not, as in the case of heterocephaly, that they are appointed by outsiders." Moreover, ". . . it is possible for a heterocephalous group to be autonomous and an autocephalous group to be heteronomous; see Max Weber, *Economy and Society*. Vol. 1, p. 50. Historically there are many kinds of autonomous, autocephalous or-

Besides private welfare agencies where the executive is a professional social worker and relatively autonomous (in contrast to public welfare agencies which are subject to a

ganizations in which hierarchical differentiation and specialized knowledge are closely integrated. Examples of such generic professional organizations are the medieval craft shop under the direction of a "master," the pre-university organization of higher education under the direction of a "scholar," "sage," "rabbi," or "swami," the pre-hospital application of "medical" knowledge by a barber-surgeon or physician, or the pre-modern "school" of a master painter, sculptor, or musician. In each of these settings, more or less formal rank distinctions—e.g., as between master, apprentice, journeyman—reflected the degree to which the knowledge and skill necessary to master a given craft, trade, or profession had been acquired. The main point of this historical excursus is to assert that there is no necessary contradiction or opposition between authority of rank and authority based on competence.

However, there is a second consideration. Social situations characterized by a high degree of turbulence, uncertainty, and variability tend to give rise to "charismatic" authority of persons or offices who are able to provide leadership and certainty, and thus a reduction of the complexity of goals and tasks. The "knowledge" or "theory" which such figures possess is typically highly secret, if not sacred. Thus, magicians, shamans, and priests are charismatic professional practitioners insofar as their knowledge is "sacred." Politicians have charismatic qualities to the extent that they are imagined as having extraordinary visions, insights, and divine inspiration. Even the modern successful surgeon, psychiatrist, criminal defense lawyer, teacher, or administrator may acquire charismatic reputations due to their not quite explicable skill. The less accessible the specialized knowledge base, the more individualized the practice, the less it can be communicated, and the less does it lend itself to replication and application in an organizational context. It goes without saying that the knowledge base can be artificially protected, complicated and restricted so as to increase profit or power.

high degree of external bureaucrati-zation),[35] other modern examples of "low-conflict," hierarchical-profes-sional organizations could be cited.[36]

[35] See Carol H. Meyer, *Staff Development in Public Welfare Agencies* (New York: Columbia University Press, 1966) pp. 23, 38.
[36] As examples, consider the following:
1) Small private hospitals, especially com-munity general and psychiatric teaching hospitals; See, e.g., Perrow's physician-dominated second phase of hospital con-trol, Charles Perrow, "Goals and Power Structures: A Historical Case Study," in Eliot Freidson (ed.), *The Hospital in Mod-ern Society* (New York: Free Press, 1963), pp. 112–46; A. H. Stanton and M. S. Schwartz, *The Mental Hospital* (New York: Basic Books, 1954); O. Hall, "Some Prob-lems in the Provision of Medical Services," *Canadian Journal of Economics and Polit-ical Science*, 20 (1954), 456–66; W. Heyde-brand, *Hospital Bureaucracy*;
2) Research organizations where the execu-tive director is a professional; See, e.g., Peter H. Rossi, "Researcher, Scholars, and Policy-makers: The Politics of Large-Scale Research," *Daedalus*, 93 (1964), 1142–61; B. G. Glaser, *Organizational Scientists: Their Professional Careers* (Bobbs-Merrill, 1964);
3) Certain private colleges and universities where the faculty is very influential, or where the Chancellor is a professor; See, e.g., David Riesman and Christopher Jencks, *The Academic Revolution* (New York: Doubleday, 1968), pp. 266–67; N. J. Demerath, R. W. Stephens, and R. Robb Taylor, *Power, Presidents, and Professors* (New York: Basic Books, 1967), pp. 21–37;
4) Law firms in which professional success manifests itself by moving up through the ranks to partnership; See, e.g., Erwin O. Smigel, *The Wall Street Lawyer* (New York: Free Press, 1965);
5) Public personnel agencies and certain government agencies where the line struc-ture consists of civil service ranks, i.e., "specialists;" See, e.g., P. M. Blau, W. Heydebrand and R. Stauffer, "The Struc-ture of Small Bureaucracies," 27 in this volume;
6) Accounting firms which exhibit many similarities to the two preceding types of professional organizations; see, e.g., P.

By contrast, conflict between pro-fessional and bureaucratic elements in professional organizations will tend to occur where persons other than the professional workers specify and de-fine operationally the goals of the organization to the point of spelling out regulative rules and routinizing procedures, where the specialized knowledge base is rationalized by increasing codification of operative rules, job specialization, efficiency measures, mechanization and auto-mation,[37] and where control over re-sources is shifted to higher organiza-tional or extraorganizational levels of authority. Moreover, it should be obvious that a high degree of de facto control over resources at higher orga-nizational levels will tend to generate and promote all the other conditions described above, i.e., goal specifica-tion, rationalization, technological innovation, etc. In other words, in modern organizations, top level con-trol over resources will lead to an in-creasing rationalization of the knowl-edge base, to job specialization, to the prerogative of defining task com-plexity, "needs," services, and to a preference for efficiency and cost-benefit controls over quality of out-put or professional service.[38]

Montagna, "Professionalization and Bu-reaucratization," 28 in this volume; B. G. Glaser (ed.), *Organizational Careers: A Sourcebook for Theory* (Chicago: Aldine, 1968). In all these cases, and many others, a certain degree of bureaucratization of professionals occurs without producing the specific kind of conflict ascribed to the in-compatibility between professional and bureaucratic authority.
[37] See, e.g., P. M. Blau, "Hierarchy of Authority in Organizations," 29 in this volume.
[38] It is in this sense that Weber saw mod-ern bureaucracy itself as a form of innova-tion, based on technical knowledge and rationalized procedures; cf. Max Weber, *Economy and Society*, Vol. III, pp. 969–82.

In sum, the difference between the two sets of conditions determining the likelihood and nature of conflict appears to lie in the degree to which professional workers retain autonomy in the three areas outlined, viz., goal specification and task complexity, knowledge base, and resource control. The difference does not appear to lie in an a priori incompatibility between two normative principles or bases of legitimacy, resulting in an inherent conflict between professional and bureaucratic authority, but in the concrete social structures in which professionals and others must work. But it is precisely this presumed "normative" conflict which as been widely held to provide a rationale for the distinction, and which has been seen as pervading modern organizations insofar as they employ professionals.

It is submitted here that the issue is *not* conflict between two dualistically conceived normative principles, but the potential conflict over the *use and control of specialized knowledge by two or more opposed interests.* Where the interests of administrators and professionals are not opposed, as e.g., between civil service professionals and the government agencies in which they work, or in adequately funded and professionally directed hospitals or welfare agencies, such conflicts need not occur. The goals and skills of the professionals coincide with the goals and task structure of the organization. However, where interests based on considerations of profit or power are at stake, or are in collision with professional judgment based on technical expertise, the knowledge and autonomy of professionals will tend to be subordinated to bureaucratic authority. Professionals, in turn, will assert themselves by insisting either on the moral superiority of their position (the welfare of

the client, the public interest, i.e., service ideals or a collectivity orientation), or they will mobilize countervailing power by controlling access to knowledge.[39] In other words, professional-bureaucratic conflict manifests itself in the opposition of interests concerning the expansion, restriction, or application of resources and concerning jurisdictional powers over the domain of knowledge—over the right to define organizational realities. This perspective transcends the view of conflict as arising from the opposition between two dualistically conceived principles of legitimacy which threaten the unitary (monocratic) integration of the organization.

For Weber, this coexistence of bureaucratic-hierarchical control and technical expertise is not problematic; in fact, both complement each other in the modern organization. "Bureaucratic administration," Weber says at one point, "means fundamentally domination through knowledge."[40] The power position of bureaucracy derives from its control of special knowledge, and "every bureaucracy seeks further to increase this superiority of the professional insider through the means of keeping secret its knowledge and intentions."[41]

Legal-rational bureaucratic authority, then, is based on both rank differentiation and technical qualifications. The more rationalized the knowledge base, the more does the work activity lend itself to bureaucratization, i.e., to the a priori specification of procedures, to centralized control over resources, and to the reduction of the employment of professionals in favor

[39] Michel Crozier, *The Bureaucratic Phenomenon* (London: Tavistock, 1964), pp. 145–74.
[40] Weber, *Economy and Society*, Vol. I, p. 225.
[41] *Ibid.*, Vol. III, p. 992.

of technicians, subprofessionals, and workers with narrowly defined jurisdictions. But as long as professionals direct the work process and control resources themselves, bureaucratization need not generate conflict, although it is likely that the smaller the number of professionals, the more precarious is their position in the organizational division of labor.

Parsons was probably the first to allege a theoretical "tension" in Weber's conception of legal-rational bureaucracy, in general, and of technically competent managers and officials, in particular.[42] The problem, as raised, involves the incompatibility between rank authority as based on delegated powers and functional authority based on specialized knowledge. Parsons equates the competence of the technical specialists with that of the professional practitioner, in particular the general practitioner, and points out that hierarchical subordination to legally defined and legitimated "rank authority" violates the autonomy and legitimacy of professional authority. He defines the problem as one of contradiction between two normative principles or bases of legitimacy: knowledge (based on rational, cognitive criteria of validity) and institutional authority (based on moral, evaluative criteria of validity). The problem, however, does not at all lie in Weber's conception of legal-rational bureaucracy based on technical knowledge, but in Parsons' confusion of different degrees of rationalization of the specialized knowledge base, i.e., confusing the "generalist" professional practitioner with the technical

specialist. Thus, Parsons' critique is based on the concept of "expert" knowledge which he applies equally and indiscriminately to the generalist practitioner and to the modern civil service official, the modern basic and applied scientist, the technical expert and the technician. All of these latter categories of specialists, however, imply a *more rationalized knowledge base* than is the case with the general practitioner. Technically qualified workers in these occupational categories have, therefore, less "autonomy." They are more integrated into the organizational division of labor; they are more bureaucratized, and they tend to have both "professional" and organizational orientations, rather than exclusively professional, cosmopolitan, or peer-group orientations.[43] The more rationalized the knowledge base, the less applicable is a critique of Weber, predicated on the presumed opposition between bureaucracy and (functional) rationality. Parsons' mistaken criticism of Weber's concept of legal-rational bureaucracy has turned out to be very influential and has had a distinguished career having been quoted and elaborated by Gouldner, Blau, and many others.[44] While not abandoning the

[43] Louis C. Goldberg, Frank Baker and Albert H. Rubenstein, "Local-Cosmopolitan: Uni-Dimensional or Multi-Dimensional?," *American Journal of Sociology,* 70, 1965, 704–10; H. Wilensky, "The Professionalization of Everyone?"

[44] A. W. Gouldner, *Patterns of Industrial Bureaucracy* (New York: Free Press, 1954), p. 22. Gouldner, like Parsons, invokes the role of the physician to describe the prototypical "professional" expert; P. M. Blau and W. R. Scott, *Formal Organizations* (San Francisco: Chandler, 1962), pp. 35, 209; Blau, "Hierarchy of Authority," 29 in this volume; see also A. Etzioni, *Modern Organizations,* pp. 75–77; S. H. Udy, "Bureaucracy and Rationality"; W. R.

[42] Talcott Parsons, "Introduction" to Max Weber, *Theory of Social and Economic Organization* (New York: Oxford University Press, 1947), pp. 58–60, fn. 4.

assumption of a fundamental incompatibility between professional and bureaucratic elements, Scott has more recently broadened the framework of analysis by elaborating Weber's distinction between autonomous and heteronomous corporate groups, a distinction which provides for the covariation of knowledge base and locus of control.[45]

In sum, we find that due to the special character of private welfare agencies as professional organizations —autonomous in some respects, heteronomous in others,—there is no necessary conflict between professional and bureaucratic elements. The bureaucratic hierarchy is staffed by professional social workers, giving them a considerable amount of jurisdictional autonomy and, to a smaller extent, control over resources. Although social workers are professionals, they are less "professional" than the old professionals, especially with respect to the authority of their knowledge. Social work, like nursing and teaching, is therefore more amenable to rationalization, and to the consequent delegation of functions to subprofessionals. Social work agencies are therefore also more likely to become bureaucratized in terms of increasing numbers of hierarchical levels. As an occupational category, future social work can, for all these reasons, also be expected to become technically more specialized rather than more professionalized.

We have argued that the crucial determinants of conflict in these professional organizations are not normative incompatibility, but opposition between professional and managerial interests with respect to the specification of goals and tasks, the control over a specialized knowledge base, and control over available resources. In the next section we will show that these three factors also influence the likelihood of innovativeness in professional organizations.

THE INNOVATIVE CONSTELLATION[46]

Just as the nature and extent of conflict within the professional organization depends on its unique resolution of the basic organizational problems concerning its task and goal structure, its knowledge base and the degree of autonomy given its working members, so the innovativeness of the professional organization reflects its structural character, as well as the nature of the environment in which it functions. The central structural dimensions of the professional organization, as noted above, are its task and goal complexity, the extent of the "professionalization" of its staff, and the degree to which it has developed "bureaucratic" forms, specifically a hierarchy and an administrative staff. Our basic expectations concerning the extent of innovativeness—the frequency of innovation—

Scott, "Professionals in Bureaucracies— Areas of Conflict," in Vollmer and Mills, *Professionalization*, p. 273, fn. 26.

[45] W. R. Scott, "Reactions to Supervision"; see also R. H. Hall, "Professionalization and Bureaucratization," 25 in this volume. While Hall uses the distinction between autonomous and heteronomous professional organizations, he does not examine the correlations between professionalization and bureaucratization *within* each of these two settings.

[46] Portions of this section are based on James J. Noell, "Innovation in Professional Organizations," paper presented at the Annual Meetings of the Midwest Sociological Society, St. Louis, Mo., April, 1970.

are that it is more likely to occur in a professional organization the greater the complexity of its tasks and goals, the more developed its knowledge base, the more its resources are controlled by those who engage in the actual productive activities of the organization, and the greater the environmental uncertainty and variability it faces.[47]

In terms of the structural features of the professional organizations analyzed here, the hypotheses are that innovativeness (the number of R & D projects) will vary directly with the degree of complexity of the task structure (the number of branches and programs, and its size)[48] and with the degree of professionalization (proportion of social workers with professional qualifications, the MSW or its equivalent), but inversely with the degree of bureaucratic control (number of levels).

The hypothesis concerning bureaucratic control suggests that the less the organizational distance between those who control the resources (budget) and those who use the resources in the process of production, the greater the degree of innovativeness in the organization;[49] at the same

---

[47] These theoretical expectations apply, of course, mainly to one basic type of innovativeness, namely that involving the *extension of the knowledge base to new areas*, as in the R & D projects considered in this study. While innovativeness in professional organizations can be expected to be predominantly of this type, the other type, viz., *rationalizing innovations*, may, of course, also occur in professional organizations. Since we are not considering rationalizing innovations in this study, our generalizations are limited to innovativeness as represented by R & D projects. Theoretically, however, one might expect rationalizing innovations in professional organizations to vary *directly* with environmental and task complexity, and with the degree of bureaucratic control over resources, but *inversely* with the degree of rationalization of the knowledge base, assuming that a given knowledge base reflects the extent to which uncertainty and task complexity are reducible. In addition, rationalizing innovations—unlike the ones considered here—are likely to generate a considerable amount of bureaucratic-professional conflict, especially in such professional organizations as universities and research institutes. On the effect of rationalization on the reduction of uncertainty as well as on power relations, see Crozier, *Bureaucratic Phenomenon*, pp. 145–74, 195–98; see also Tom Burns and G. M. Stalker, *The Management of Innovation* (London: Tavistock, 1961), pp. 19–36, and Charles Perrow, *Organizational Analysis: A Sociological View* (Belmont, Calif.: Wadsworth Publishing Co., 1970), p. 47.

[48] Task complexity is described by Wilson as a factor which is positively related to the rate of innovative proposals, but inversely to the rate of actual adoptions of innovations; cf. James Q. Wilson, "Innovation in Organization: Notes Toward a Theory," in J. D. Thompson (ed.), *Approaches to Organizational Design* (Pittsburgh: University of Pittsburgh Press, 1966), pp. 193–218. Other studies relevant to the relationship between task complexity and innovation are Jerald Hage and Michael Aiken, "Program Change and Organizational Properties," *American Journal of Sociology* 72 (1967), 503–17 and V. Thompson, "Bureaucracy and Innovation," *Administrative Science Quarterly* 10 (1965), 1–20.

[49] Note that in this approach, control over available resources is considered more important than the relative availability or absolute size of resources. There is some empirical support for this assumption in that the correlation between size of budget and number of R & D projects is only $r = .17$, whereas it is $r = .62$ between budget size and number of regular programs. Although R & D projects are likely to be specially funded, the *impetus to innovation* is not so much a matter of budget size or organizational size, but rather of the complexity of the task structure and of the environment. While there is clearly a theoretical lower limit here in that production and innovation require certain minimum resources, we are emphatically rejecting the "scarcity" theory of organiza-

TABLE 3 THE EFFECTS OF TASK COMPLEXITY, PROFESSIONALIZATION, AND BUREAUCRATIZATION ON INNOVATIVENESS

Independent Variables	Zero-Order Correlation	Partial Correlation	Stand. Regr. Coeff. (b*)	Regression Error
1. Number of Branches	.48	.37	.45	.01
2. Number of Programs	.32	.16	.20	.01
3. Size	.32	−.05	−.08	.02
4. Professionalization	.25	.16	.15	.01
5. Number of Levels	.11	−.11	−.12	.01
6. % Admin.-Cler. Staff	.09	.04	.03	.01

Multiple R: .531   Coefficient of Determination (R^2): .282

time, the degree of professionalization of the organization may also be taken to refer at least indirectly to the amount of autonomy exercised by those who do the productive work. The complexity and variability of the environment in which these professional organizations operate have not been directly measured, but the number of branches (or the geographical dispersion) of the organization, that aspect of the task structure most closely integrated with the complexity of the environment, may be taken to be an indirect measure of it.

On the whole our data on these private welfare agencies are consistent with our theoretical expectations. The complexity of the task structure is positively related to the degree of innovativeness. Specifically, the geographical dispersion (or number of branches) of the agencies is moderately strongly related to innovative-

ness and remains so when the other structural variables are controlled (see Table 3). Similarly, the other two aspects of the complexity of the task structure, viz., the number of programs as well as size, are moderately positively related to innovativeness on the zero-order level. However, while the partial regression coefficient for the number of programs remains positive (although at a reduced level (b* = .20), the corresponding coefficient for size becomes negative (b* = −.08).

The virtual elimination of organizational size as a determinant of innovativeness, after task complexity is controlled, can be interpreted in the light of two considerations. First, the simple correlation of (r = .32) between size and innovativeness does not accurately portray the slightly curvilinear relationship between the two variables that indicates that R & D projects occur most frequently in moderately-sized agencies, rather than in very small or very large ones. Secondly, size is an important determinant of task complexity, that is, of the number of branches and the number of programs (see Table 2). The effect of size on innovativeness is, therefore, an indirect one since it is mediated by task structure vari-

---

tional structure in favor of asserting the critical importance of autonomy in budgetary decision making. From this perspective, Weber's distinction between autonomy and heteronomy is again much closer to accounting for both conflict and innovation in professional organizations than Parsons' postulated legitimacy difference between professional and bureaucratic authority.

TABLE 4 TASK COMPLEXITY (NUMBER OF BRANCHES) AND PROFESSIONALIZATION
AS MAJOR DETERMINANTS OF INNOVATIVENESS

Independent Variables	Zero-Order Correlation	Partial Correlation	Stand. Regr. Coeff. (b^*)	Regression Error
Number of Branches	.48	.45	.45	.01
Professionalization	.25	.18	.16	.01

Multiple R: .507   Coefficient of Determination (R^2): .257

ables. Once these variables are controlled, the effect of size disappears and becomes even slightly negative suggesting that large agencies are somewhat less likely to innovate than smaller and medium-sized agencies.

Considering the positive relationship between size and number of levels (r = .58), it is not surprising to find that the effect of number of levels, slightly positive on the zero-order level (r = .11), becomes negative ($b^* = -.12$) when size is controlled. Size and number of levels, holding other variables constant, thus contribute negatively to innovativeness. If we add to this the fact that the effect of the relative size of the administrative-clerical staff, already weak on the zero-order level, is further reduced on the partial level, it becomes clear that in professional organizations, bureaucratization does not favor innovativeness and may, in fact, hinder it. Professionalization, on the other hand, does have a positive effect (r = .25) which remains moderately positive ($b^* = .15$) when other structural variables are controlled.

The joint effect of the six structural variables on innovativeness ($R^2 = .282$) is not sufficiently strong to permit us to speak in terms of an "explanation" of innovativeness. However, the multivariate analysis presented in Table 3 makes it possible to show the *separate effects* of the task structure variables, professionalization, and bureaucratization on innovativeness. Moreover, by eliminating the weaker variables from the model by means of step-wise regression, it is possible to identify those factors which make the relatively strongest contribution to the dependent variable, while retaining roughly the same joint explanatory strength as the previous model. The results of this analysis are presented in Table 4. From the six structural variables considered in our analysis, number of branches and professionalization emerge as the two most important determinants of innovativeness, with the coefficient of determination having dropped only less than three percentage points to $R^2 = .257$. While the prevalence of innovative projects in private welfare agencies cannot be considered fully accounted for, we can conclude that the complexity of the task structure, especially geographical dispersion, as well as professionalization of the organizational labor force, are major determinants of innovativeness, and that bureaucratization is not a major determinant.

SUMMARY AND CONCLUSIONS

We have presented a theoretical perspective on organizational analysis that is both parsimonious and relatively broad in scope. It enables us to deal with certain types of structural change, conflict, and innovation in professional organizations. The core of this perspective is based on the conceptualization of three well-known organizational phenomena: (1) The complexity of the goal and task structure as mediating between external conditions and the complexity of internal organizational elements; (2) the rationalization of the specialized knowledge base, which ranges from primitive forms of specialized (secret) knowledge to professional practice to highly rationalized and specified technologies, and (3) the locus of control over resources, particularly the degree to which such control is exercised by the production component, in this case, by members of a central professional group. These concepts, we believe, help to clarify the relationships between rationalization, professionalization, and bureaucratization, and provide a basis for critically evaluating and challenging the widespread normative, rather than structural, definition of the professions first popularized by Parsons.

While the operational definitions of the three main concepts are relatively crude and leave much room for specification and refinement, we feel that they are adequate for purposes of interpreting the data on the 122 private welfare agencies used here to represent professional organizations. Thus, we have shown that the greater the complexity of the goal and task structure (especially the number of branches and the number of programs), the greater the innovativeness (the number of R & D programs) of the agencies. We have also shown that the greater the professionalization of an agency (proportion of non-managerial employees with an MSW), the more likely it will be innovative

on an ongoing basis. Size as well as bureaucratization (number of levels) have a slightly negative effect on innovativeness, and the relative size of the administrative-clerical staff does not appear to have any effect at all.

While the joint explanatory power of these variables is admittedly not very great, task structure variables, particularly an agency's geographical dispersion (number of branches) and professionalization, remain important determinants of innovativeness when other structural variables are controlled or eliminated.

The relationship between professionalization and bureaucratization has been explored conceptually and empirically. The result of the conceptual analysis was that professionalization is not necessarily in conflict with bureaucratization, especially in professional organizations where the bureaucratic-hierarchical control structure is staffed by the same professionals who also constitute the "production component" of the organization.

The results of the empirical analysis support the theoretical expectation that in private welfare agencies, professional and bureaucratic elements are moderately positively related or, controlling for size and complexity of task structure, simply coexist without conflict. Nevertheless, innovativeness is positively influenced by professionalization, but negatively by bureaucratization, i.e., by the organizational distance (in terms of number of levels) between the top executive and the "point of production."

We are suggesting certain theoretical generalizations which might fruitfully be investigated, explored, and tested by means of both detailed case analysis of conflict and innovation in other types of professional organizations,[50] as well as by broader, comparative studies of organizations in which the degree of rationalization of the specialized knowledge base, the control over resources, and the articulation between different spheres of complexity (environment, goals, task structure) is systematically controlled.

All three factors—task complexity, knowledge base, and resource control —may be used to generate *power* within and between organizations, and any one source of power may be used in order to restrict others or to enter into coalitions with any of the others. Workers may engage in various forms of sabotage to complicate the production process so as to gain control, time, leisure, and other benefits.[51] Professionals may represent a situation as "serious," "critical," "dangerous," "unsolvable" in order to increase their clients' dependence on them; they may even produce "fake" conditions for purposes of increasing profit (e.g., the notorious automobile or TV repair shops). Politicians or military professionals may describe a situation as problematic in order to increase budget appropriations as well as amount of discretion. Bureaucracies may limit access to information so as to control *both* the complexity of

the situation and the specialized knowledge necessary to deal with it. They may claim limited resources, external risks, increased responsibilities, etc., to justify controls. They may differentially allocate resources and priorities so as to enhance "desirable" services and to cut or eliminate "unnecessary" or "undesirable" ones, especially as far as the "unanticipated consequences" are concerned. Responsibility for both application of specialized knowledge and the need to balance budgets (or reduce spending) may thus serve as a justification for controlling the nature and direction of change and innovation. Such responsibility may also become an instrument of controlled and strategic conflict in situations of collective bargaining, the restriction of allocations for certain welfare services (e.g., the case of the Legal Aid Society), or military conflict (preventive or protective air strikes).

Clearly, just as innovativeness has been discussed in terms of the interrelation between task complexity, rationalization of the knowledge base, and resource control, so conflict can be expected to be maximized under certain conditions, minimized under others. First of all, the complexity of a given organizational environment, including turbulence, variability of supply/demand, uncertainty, etc., will by its very nature tend to generate different and possibly contradictory responses, a condition which gives rise to proposals and suggestions for alternative courses of action.[52] The lower the degree of rationalization and standardization of knowledge available to deal with such diversity and uncertainty, the

---

[50] See, e.g., Jay Schulman, *Remaking an Organization: Innovation in a Specialized Psychiatric Hospital* (Albany: State University of New York Press, 1969).

[51] See, e.g., W. P. Watson, "A Case Study in Industrial Sabotage," unpublished manuscript, Washington University, St. Louis, 1970; see also his "Counter-Planning on the Shop Floor," *Radical America*, 5, 3 (May–June 1971), 77–85; the classical general case is, of course, provided by Donald Roy, "Quota Restriction and Goldbricking in a Machine Shop," *American Journal of Sociology*, 57 (Mar. 1952), 427–42.

[52] cf. J. Q. Wilson, "Innovation in Organization."

greater the conflict among those who have access to—or claim possession of—special knowledge.[53]

Finally, the greater the distance between the locus of autonomy (including control over resources) and the point of actual production of the organization's output, the greater will be the jurisdictional conflict over goals and procedures, including conflict over the need to innovate and the nature of the innovation (e.g., increasing *rationalization* of the knowledge base as over against *extension* of that base). Conflict should, then, be highest in organizations where task complexity is high but where little or no rationalized knowledge (or Ellul's technique)[54] is as yet available, and where the locus of autonomy and the control over resources is far removed from those involved in the process of production. In such situations, hierarchical controls and commands must appear utterly irrational and unjustified, possibly generating open hostility and opposition rather than blind obedience. Even where professional knowledge is available, but professionals have little or no control over resources (e.g., physicians working with limited budgets in public hospitals; R & D departments being curtailed

in favor of stable production or increasing sales, etc.), conflict will be strong and endemic. However, where professional workers control the allocation of resources, conflict may be reduced and eliminated even in the face of a high degree of task complexity and uncertainty.

In general, it may be suggested that the problem of access to, and control of knowledge, while partly a function of its objective complexity, or rationalizability, is today increasingly determined by extraneous economic and political considerations. There are few widely accepted types of specialized knowledge which are *inherently* complex, supernatural, or otherwise inaccessible so as to require a high degree of "intelligence" or professional application, mediation or interpretation. Religion, physics, medicine, and law are cases in point, but business statistics, FBI files, or political and military decision-making are not. Information, knowledge, truth—the definition of reality—thus become commodities which can be manipulated to a large extent by organizational control of their complexity, validity (or "value"), accessibility and availability. Complex, dangerous, uncertain, or unpredictable situations or problems clearly tend to require a more professional, experienced, or even charismatic response for their solution than simple problems or predictable situations. Hence the high social premium on invention, innovation, new techniques and approaches, and, generally, creativity. However, it is also possible to create uncertainty, danger, and complexity (in part the mark of a good politician or charismatic leader), just as considerations of cost as well as order and stability may be used to stifle socially unacceptable forms of

---

[53] cf. also the "decision strategies" which Thompson and Tuden derived from the cross-tabulation of outcome preferences and beliefs about causation, i.e., ends and means, especially the "inspirational strategy" (charismatic leadership) where both dimensions are "uncertain;" the "judgmental strategy," characteristic of professional judgment; and the "computational strategy," characteristic of highly rationalized, routinized, bureaucratized tasks; in James D. Thompson, *Organizations in Action*, p. 134.

[54] cf. Jacques Ellul, *The Technological Society* (New York: Vintage, 1967).

creativity or to oppose boat-rocking innovations.

It seems that these considerations open up a wide field for comparative organizational research which, it is hoped, will go far beyond the range that could be covered empirically in this paper.

14. LOCATION OF NATIONAL HEADQUARTERS OF VOLUNTARY ASSOCIATIONS

Stanley Lieberson and Irving L. Allen, Jr.

The United States is often described as a nation of joiners. Although it is a moot question whether the population has an exceptionally high rate of participation compared to other Western nations, the importance of voluntary associations for the social order can hardly be overemphasized. Since urban Western communities are characterized by populations that are heterogeneous economically, socially, ideologically, and in other respects,[1] voluntary associations are a means of uniting both spatially distant individuals and individuals with some common goal or concern.[2] By uniting widely distributed populations, these organizations

Reprinted by permission from *Administrative Science Quarterly* (December 1962) pp. 317–38.

[1] A point well developed in Emile Durkheim, *The Division of Labor in Society* (Glencoe, Ill., 1949); Amos H. Hawley, *Human Ecology* (New York, 1950).

[2] See, for example, Arnold M. Rose, *Theory and Method in the Social Sciences* (Minneapolis, Minn., 1954), ch. 3; Herbert

serve to fill "gaps in the social structure, facilitating the operation of a subsystem, or integrating subsystems."[3] If we assume that headquarters of associations are generally the centers for administration and control of activities directed toward other segments of the society as well as coordinating the activities of members located at great distances from one another, then the examination of these national headquarters can contribute toward an understanding of the role of voluntary associations in the social system.[4] That is, the loca-

Goldhammer, "Voluntary Associations in the United States," in Paul K. Hatt and Albert J. Reiss, Jr., eds., *Cities and Society* (Glencoe, Ill., 1957), pp. 591–96; Sherwood Dean Fox, "Voluntary Associations and Social Structure," unpublished doctoral dissertation, Harvard University, 1952.

[3] Fox, *op. cit.*, p. 357.

[4] Richard L. Simpson and William H. Gulley, "Goals, Environmental Pressures, and Organizational Characteristics," *American Sociological Review*, 27 (1962), 344–51. See, however, David L. Sills, *The Volunteers—Means and Ends in a National Organization* (Glencoe, Ill., 1958).

tion of national headquarters may be viewed as partially delimited by the function of the organization and the geographic distribution of its members and therefore offers an opportunity to examine the central mechanisms by which national associations provide integrative functions that cannot be filled in a local community or through a political system based upon areal units. It is regrettable that much of the past research on voluntary associations has been confined to population differentials expressed as rates of participation within a community or city rather than exploring the broader problem of how associations link the membership to other segments of society.[5]

We would expect the location of national headquarters to be influenced by interaction between the functional and membership characteristics of each association and the variations among cities in their suitability as a locus for these characteristics. First, associations differ in the extent to which they perform "external" functions, i.e., functions directed towards other segments of the society on behalf of the membership; and "internal" functions, i.e., functions directed primarily towards their own members.[6] National college fraternities and many hobby associations illustrate organizations devoted primarily to internal services for their members, whereas the headquarters of many labor unions and business associations often deal with other seg-

ments of the society on behalf of their memberships.[7] Obviously, many associations—such as the American Medical Association and American Legion, which perform both external and internal functions—would be placed in a range intermediate between these two extremes.

Not only do the activities of associations vary, but the geographical distribution of their members also varies, and accordingly influences the location of associations. Compare, for example, the potential membership of a cotton growers' association with that of an association of skiing enthusiasts. Consequently, since metropolitan and other areas of the nation differ in both the social characteristics of their residents and the nature of their institutions, we would expect areas to vary greatly in their suitability as centers for the functions performed by associations.

In brief, an ecological perspective will be applied to the study of national voluntary associations through an exploration of the factors influencing the location of their national headquarters. After determining the areas that are the centers for national offices, we will use case studies to examine the significance of membership distribution, organizational functions, and urban specialization on their location. Finally, the impact of the growth of the federal government is considered through a longitudinal study of the interurban movement of headquarters from 1931 to 1959.[8]

[5] See, however, Murray Hausknecht, *The Joiners* (New York, 1962).

[6] See Rose, *Theory and Method* and his *Sociology: The Study of Human Relations* (New York, 1956), pp. 305–306; C. Wayne Gordon and Nicholas Babchuk, "A Typology of Voluntary Associations," *American Sociological Review*, 24 (1959), 22–29.

[7] See, for example, "Trade Association Survey," in Temporary National Economic Committee, *Investigation of Concentration of Economic Power*, Monograph no. 18 (Washington, D.C., 1941), pp. 373–74.

[8] This study was supported in part by a grant to the senior author from the Research Committee of the Graduate School, University of Wisconsin.

DATA AND METHODS

For information on the national headquarters of voluntary associations in the United States, circa 1959, we used the *Encyclopedia of American Associations*.[9] This directory provides data on the location, type, membership, staff size, and other characteristics of 6,341 national associations. As Table 1 shows, these associations are classified into nineteen interest groups.[10]

With several exceptions, our study includes all the associations listed within each category by the *Encyclopedia*. In the case of the category "Trade, Business, and Commercial Organization," which is the largest single group (with over 2,000 associations), we obtained a 25 percent sample ($N = 585$), which is accordingly inflated in our tables. "Chamber of Commerce" included a large subcategory of local chambers of commerce, which are omitted from our study because they are not national associations. Associations in a small category, "Received Too Late to Classify," were assigned to appropriate categories during the coding phase of the research.

Since the data source is not commonly used, we would like to point out some of its shortcomings. First, the classification of associations is at times arbitrary. Some ethnic associations, for example, are scattered in such categories as fraternal, educational, and cultural associations, as well as in their own categories. It is our impression, however, that most of the associations are correctly classified. In addition, we have evidence to indicate that in this type of study these errors, if they have any influence, work against our results.[11] Finally, although simple inspection of the *Encyclopedia* indicates that a large number of national associations are included, we do not know the sampling procedure used by the publisher or know of any systematic omissions.[12] We should note, however, that the total number of organizations examined compares very favorably with several earlier studies of national associations.[13]

FINDINGS

LOCATION OF VOLUNTARY ASSOCIATIONS

We classified each organization by the standard metropolitan statistical area (SMSA) or residual nonmetropolitan area in which it was located.[14] In general, there is a rough association between the size of a metropolis and its rank as a center for the headquarters of national associations. Of the 24 metropolises with more than

---

[9] (2d ed.; Detroit, 1959).

[10] Other typologies of associations are possible. See, for example, Gordon and Babchuk, "A Typology of Voluntary Associations"; Hausknecht, *The Joiners.*

[11] See, for example, Stanley Lieberson, "Ethnic Groups and the Practice of Medicine," *American Sociological Review*, 23 (1958), 543.

[12] According to a letter from the publishers, the data are based upon a much larger "master list" of organizations.

[13] See, for example, R. D. McKenzie, *The Metropolitan Community* (New York, 1933), p. 165; Fox, "Voluntary Associations," pp. 114–15; Noel P. Gist and L. A. Halbert, *Urban Society* (4th ed.; New York, 1956), pp. 379–80.

[14] We employed the classification scheme found in Bureau of the Budget, Office of Statistical Standards, *Standard Metropolitan Statistical Areas* (Washington, D.C., 1959). This scheme was modified slightly in later reports based on the 1960 Census of Population.

TABLE 1 DISTRIBUTION OF VOLUNTARY ASSOCIATIONS BY TYPE AND LOCATION*

| Type of Association | Standard Metropolitan Statistical Area | | | | Non-metropolitan | Total |
	New York %	Chicago %	Washington %	Other %	politan %	N
Business	38.1	17.3	14.7	26.9	2.9	2,340†
Agriculture	6.0	6.6	12.6	42.7	32.0	334
Government	18.9	20.1	36.6	20.0	4.2	164
Scientific	23.9	4.8	19.8	42.0	9.5	293
Education	32.2	7.5	22.5	28.5	9.1	583
Welfare	49.2	7.5	13.4	23.8	6.0	268
Health	30.6	14.6	8.2	35.9	10.3	437
Public affairs	53.5	3.1	26.0	16.6	0.8	127
Fraternal	9.2	11.8	5.9	65.2	7.6	119
Ethnic	59.9	5.4	6.3	25.1	3.2	222
Religious	51.5	9.7	10.0	26.1	2.7	299
Horticulture	11.5	1.1	5.7	60.5	20.7	87
War veteran	16.5	0.9	27.8	43.5	11.3	115
Hobby	27.0	3.0	5.0	45.0	20.0	100
Athletic	29.7	7.8	3.9	50.0	8.6	128
Labor	16.1	10.3	29.5	40.0	4.0	224
Chamber of commerce	49.2	1.5	2.3	24.4	22.7	132
College fraternal	10.4	7.5	3.9	53.6	24.4	307
Other	41.9	4.8	6.4	37.0	9.7	62
All associations	32.9	11.4	14.6	32.6	8.4	6,341

* Because of rounding off, the sum in some rows is not 100 percent.
† Inflated figure shown, based upon 25 percent sample.

one million inhabitants in 1960, all but 7 have at least thirty-five national headquarters.[15] Indianapolis, Indiana, and Columbus, Ohio, are the only metropolises of less than one million population that have at least thirty-five national headquarters.

Examination of the distribution of headquarters of all associations, shown in the last row of Table 1, discloses that New York, with 6 percent of the total U.S. population in 1960, has almost one-third of all headquarters of national voluntary associations.[16] Although distinctly subordinate to New York, the Washington

metropolitan area has 15 percent and the Chicago area has 11 percent of all national headquarters. Since Washington has slightly more than 1 percent and Chicago about 4 percent of the national population, all three metropolises are clearly centers for national headquarters far in excess of their proportion of the total population. Philadelphia, which is the fourth largest center for headquarters of voluntary associations, has only 3 percent of the national total. The nonmetropolitan area of the United States, with about 40 percent of the population, has only about 8 percent of all national headquarters.

In brief, nearly 60 percent of all headquarters of national organizations are located in three metropolitan areas: New York, Washington, and Chicago, a result in accord with

[15] These are: Atlanta, San Diego, Dallas, Seattle, Paterson-Clifton-Passaic, Houston, and Buffalo.
[16] The proportion would be even higher if we had used the broader unit, Standard Consolidated Area.

earlier studies. For example, using data compiled by R. D. McKenzie from a 1929 directory of commercial and industrial voluntary associations, we found that 65 percent were then located in these three cities.[17] Gist and Halbert, as well as Fox, report similar degrees of concentration in these areas for later years.[18] Since these results are based on different sources and may be confounded by variations in the criteria and types of associations included as well as the spatial units used, we later adopt a different procedure for examining changes in the positions of these centers with time.

Given this overall concentration, we are interested in the differences between types of associations in their location patterns. Referring to Table 1 again, we find that about half of the welfare, public affairs, ethnic and religious associations, and national chambers of commerce have headquarters in New York. By contrast, small proportions of the headquarters of agricultural, fraternal, college fraternal, and horticultural organizations are located there, although the nonmetropolitan segment of the nation, which is essentially underrepresented in terms of its total population, has a large proportion of some of these associations. Other metropolitan areas are similar in that the associations they attract vary greatly by type.

How do we account for these variations? Many of the differences between the groups are readily explained on an ad hoc basis. For example, we might interpret the differences in location between agricultural and industrial associations as due to the dissimilarity of the major

industrial and farming areas of the nation. Rather than attempt such interpretations for each unique distribution, we shall examine a limited number of specific types of associations and locations in terms of the implications of our basic thesis; first, that organizations differ in their functions and memberships and, second, that metropolitan areas vary in their suitability for national headquarters of voluntary associations.

LOBBYING

The interaction between the location of voluntary associations and the functions they perform is perhaps most readily determined for those organizations located in Washington, D.C. The national capital, with its singular economic base,[19] has neither a central location nor an exceptionally high population potential. Yet, of the leading metropolitan areas, Washington has the largest number of agriculture, government, war veteran, and labor union headquarters. It is also an important center for several other types of associations, although not the largest center (Table 2, col. 1). Presumably, Washington exerts a strong "pull" for voluntary associations that function on behalf of its members to represent their interests to the federal government.

In order to examine the influence of government on the variations between organizations in their propensities to locate in Washington, we used lobbying as an indicator of the degree to which associations attempt to act on behalf of their members in

[17] McKenzie, *Metropolitan Community.*
[18] N. P. Gist and L. A. Halbert, *Urban Society.*

[19] See, for example, Otis Dudley Duncan, W. Richard Scott, Stanley Lieberson, Beverly Duncan and Hal H. Winsborough, *Metropolis and Region* (Baltimore, 1960), pp. 518–20.

TABLE 2 TYPES OF VOLUNTARY ASSOCIATIONS AS RELATED TO LOBBYING
AND LOCATION IN WASHINGTON

Type of Association	Located in Washington %	National Total N	Associations with Lobbyists	
			No. in Sample	% (Col. 3/Col. 2)
Business	14.7	2,340	156	6.7
Agriculture	12.6	334	14	4.2
Government	36.6	164	5	3.0
Scientific	19.8	293	1	0.3
Education	22.5	583	4	0.7
Welfare	13.4	268	9	3.4
Health	8.2	437	14	3.2
Public affairs	26.0	127	7	5.5
Fraternal	5.9	119	1	0.8
Ethnic	6.3	222	1	0.5
Religious	10.0	299	2	0.7
Horticulture	5.7	87	1	1.1
War veteran	27.8	115	9	7.8
Hobby	5.0	100	0	–
Athletic	3.9	128	0	–
Labor	29.5	224	37	16.5
Chamber of commerce	2.3	132	2	1.5
College fraternal	3.9	307	0	–
Other	6.4	62	3	4.8

dealing with the federal government. From the list of all lobbying organizations reporting under the Federal Lobbying Act for the fourth quarter of 1960,[20] we found 266 associations that had one or more lobbyists and that were also listed in the *Encyclopedia*. It is therefore possible to infer the relative importance of government relations for each group of associations by examining the proportion having lobbyists during the sample period. There is much variation among the classes of associations in their use of lobbyists (Table 2, col. 4); for example, nearly 17 percent of the labor unions employed lobbyists during the sample period, whereas none of the hobby, athletic, or college fraternal associations reported lobbying during the same period. Organizations devoted to war veter-

ans, business, and public affairs also ranked high in their lobbying activities.

We find a positive correlation (*tau* = .45) between the measure of lobbying activity (col. 4) and the proportion of each organizational type with headquarters in the Washington metropolitan area (col. 1).[21] In other words, the types of associations particularly interested in governmental activities, as measured by their lobbying rates, are also the organizations most likely to locate their headquarters in close proximity to the federal government. There is no relationship, however, between these lobbying rates and the differences between organizations in their location in New York and Chicago (*tau* = .00 and .03, respectively).[22] Thus activity designed to influence the government affects

[20] *Congressional Record*, 107, no. 46 (1961), 3830–47; no. 98 (1961), 9463–67.

[21] p. < .05.

[22] p. > .05.

the proportion of each organizational type located in Washington, but is not related to the propensity of associations to locate in either of the other two leading centers.

Although Washington is the center for only 15 percent of all organizations, slightly more than half of the lobbying associations examined have headquarters in the capital (Table 3). Only 19 percent of lobbying organizations maintain their headquarters in New York and only 11 percent in Chicago. All other metropolitan and nonmetropolitan areas have the headquarters of about 17 percent of the associations employing lobbyists during the sample period. Thus New York and the residual areas are particularly underrepresented in lobbying associations compared with their overall positions as centers for voluntary organizations.

Since there is considerable variation between types of associations in both their degree of lobbying and in their location patterns, it is necessary to determine the "expected" distribution of lobbying associations in metropolitan areas based on the rates for each type of organization. For example, it is not clear whether New York's position as a center for lobbying organizations is due to its having those types of groups that have low lobbying rates in general, or whether among associations of a given type, New York is less apt to interest those that lobby. Applying the lobbying rates shown in column 4 of Table 2 to the numbers of each type of association located in an area, we are able to determine the number of lobbying associations expected in each area on the basis of the types of associations located there. For example, if two cities had an equal number of headquarters, but one had a large number

of labor unions and the other of fraternal associations, we would expect the first city to have a larger proportion of lobbying associations. Column 3 of Table 3 shows the distribution of lobbying organizations we would expect to find if voluntary associations of a given type were equally likely to lobby regardless of the location of their headquarters. Inspection of the differences between column 1, the "actual," and column 3, the "expected," percentage of lobbying organizations in each area, suggests that, in general, associations that lobby are far more likely to locate in Washington than are other associations of the same type.

Thus far, the relationship between function and location in Washington has been inferred on the basis of ecological correlations. If the likelihood of location in Washington is actually increased for associations that relate their membership to the federal government, then we would expect to find within each organizational category, e.g., labor unions, those specific associations with headquarters in Washington having higher lobbying rates than those organizations of the same type located outside of Washington. We have therefore examined two types of associations with a sufficiently large number of lobbyists to permit direct comparisons. With respect to business associations, columns 4 and 5 of Table 3 show that Washington is the headquarters of over half of all such associations reporting lobbyists, but is the headquarters of only 15 percent of business groups in the nation. By contrast, New York, Chicago, and the residual metropolitan areas have far greater proportions of business associations in general than of business organizations that lobby. Similarly,

TABLE 3 LOCATION OF ALL ASSOCIATIONS, LOBBYING ASSOCIATIONS,
AND EXPECTED DISTRIBUTIONS*

Area	Associations Lobbying (N = 266) %	All Associations (N = 6,341) %	Lobbying Associations: Expected Distribution† %	Business Associations		Labor Unions	
				Lobbying (N = 156) %	All (N = 2,340) %	Lobbying (N = 37) %	All (N = 224) %
New York	18.8	32.9	32.7	22.4	38.1	5.4	16.1
Chicago	11.3	11.4	13.8	9.6	17.3	8.1	10.3
Washington	52.6	14.6	17.2	53.8	14.7	56.8	29.5
Other SMSA‡	15.8	32.6	30.6	11.5	26.9	29.7	40.0
Nonmetro- politan	1.5	8.4	5.8	2.6	2.9	–	4.0

* Because of rounding off, the sum in some columns is not 100 percent.
† Based on lobbying rates for each association type applied to the distributions of associations among cities.
‡ Standard Metropolitan Statistical Area.

comparison between columns 6 and 7 indicates that lobbying labor unions are far more likely to establish headquarters in Washington than labor unions in general (respectively, 57 and 30 percent).

Since our lobbying data are based on a sample period, the variations in the proportions lobbying reflect the intensity or frequency of lobbying activities rather than the presence or absence of this function for a given class of voluntary associations. It appears reasonable to conclude that those types of associations most active in this function are more likely to locate their headquarters in Washington. Moreover, those associations for which government relations is a more important function—as measured by our lobbying index—tend to be centered in Washington to a far greater degree than other associations of the same type.

INDUSTRIAL ACTIVITY AND LOCATION
OF BUSINESS ASSOCIATIONS

If we hypothesize that the location of voluntary associations is also influenced by the areal distribution of its members, then we would expect the location of headquarters to reflect differences between organizations in the concentration of members—either actual or potential. If each person engaged in a given activity is viewed as equally likely to originate an association devoted to the activity, then areas with concentrations of such persons will have a higher probability of being the birthplace of the association. Also, after an association is established, we would expect that one of the "pulls" in determining the location of its headquarters would be the location of its members.

Since the industrial activities of cities vary greatly, the influence of these industrial differences on the locations of specific business associations provides us with one test of this membership hypothesis. A directory published in 1942, *Trade and Professional Associations of the United States*,[23] classifies the business and

[23] C. J. Judkins (Washington, D.C., 1942).

trade associations by the Standard Industrial Classification (SIC) scheme then in use. A more recent listing of associations classified by their precise industrial category is not available. Thus for the year 1942 we are able to determine the specific industry of each association as well as the city in which it was located. We restricted our study to the sixteen largest centers (those with 20 or more business and trade associations).

Our inferences about the economic activities of each city are based upon the 1940 Census of Population, which gives the industrial classification of the labor force of each city, using a 132-item condensation of the 1,411 industrial classes prepared by the Joint Committee on Occupational Classification. In order to obtain maximum comparability between our sources for associations and labor force, the labor force category was reduced to 65 categories of industrial activity, each comprising one or more two-digit classes.[24] Also, because the labor force data were available only for cities of at least 100,000, our analysis is based upon the associations located in central cities rather than reconstructed SMSA's.

Each of the cities is viewed as part of a closed system, and the proportion of the total labor force of all cities studied is compared with its proportion of the labor force in industries for which trade associations are located in the community. Column 1 of Table 4 shows the labor-force distribution of each urban center. For example, Denver has 1

percent of the 8.6 million employed in these sixteen cities, whereas New York's employed population has one-third of the total. If the trade associations locating their headquarters in a given city (numbers shown in column 2) were attracted to the community because it is a center for the industry, then we would expect employment in industries representing the city's trade associations to exceed its overall proportion of the total employed population. In fourteen of the sixteen cities, in fact, the trade associations are in industries in which employment exceeds the proportion of the total labor force found in the city (compare columns 3 and 1). To take a striking instance, Detroit has about 7 percent of the employed population of the cities specified in Table 4, but in those industries that have associations with their headquarters in Detroit, its average proportion of the labor force of the sixteen cities is nearly 25 percent. Several other cities are equally impressive in that their proportion of the total labor force engaged in industries with associations having headquarters in the city is more than double the city's percentage of the combined labor force of the sixteen centers. New York and Washington are the only exceptions to the general finding that business associations of a city tend to be in industries for which the city is particularly active.

Since the number of trade associations established for different industries varies greatly, some cities may have relatively large proportions of their labor force engaged in industries that tend to produce many associations, whereas the proportion of their labor force may be slight in those industries that have few trade associations. Consequently, the SIC dis-

[24] For a more detailed discussion of these classification schemes, see *Sixteenth Decennial Census: 1940, Population,* III, *The Labor Force* (Washington, D.C., 1943), 10; Judkins, *Trade and Professional Associations,* pp. 14, 225–26.

TABLE 4 INFLUENCE OF INDUSTRIAL COMPOSITION ON THE LOCATION OF
BUSINESS ASSOCIATIONS IN LEADING CITIES, CIRCA 1940

City	Distribution Employed, 1940* %	Headquarters in City 1942† N	Weighted‡ Mean Employed in Industries with Headquarters in:	
			Single City %	All Cities Specified %
Atlanta	1.48	18	1.64	1.27
Boston	3.16	64	3.50	2.89
Chicago	15.76	228§	19.93	18.80
Cleveland	3.73	50	8.93	4.54
Denver	1.36	18	2.29	1.27
Detroit	7.29	21	24.45	6.15
Los Angeles	6.84	20	18.08	7.02
Minneapolis	2.17	18	2.76	2.35
New Orleans	2.07	20	3.75	1.90
New York	33.09	787§	32.21	31.05
Philadelphia	8.20	49	9.48	8.78
Pittsburgh	2.60	30	5.98	2.87
St. Louis	3.77	25	4.45	4.47
San Francisco	3.16	46	4.20	3.01
Seattle	1.72	30	4.37	1.92
Washington	3.60	132§	1.78	1.71
Total	100.00	1,606	147.80	100.00

* Except on public emergency work.
† Excludes associations not categorized by standard industrial classification.
‡ Weighted by number of associations in each industrial class.
§ Inflated estimate based on random sample of 100 associations from total in city and rounded to nearest whole number.

tribution of trade associations for all sixteen cities was combined and applied to each city to determine the standardized percentage in the labor force expected if the trade associations in a city had the same SIC distribution as that for all cities investigated. In other words, column 4 of Table 4 gives the average labor-force employment in each city that would be expected on the basis of the sixteen-city industrial distribution of trade associations. Except in St. Louis, the labor force actually engaged in industries with associations located in each city exceeds the proportion expected if the industrial associations located in the city had the same SIC distribution as that of the sixteen combined cities (compare cols.

3 and 4). This further supports our general finding that the industrial activities of a city influence the kind of business associations located in the area.

INDUSTRIAL ASSOCIATIONS IN NEW YORK AND WASHINGTON

It is particularly important that we distinguish between the effects of comparing percentages and absolute numbers when considering New York City. Since the city has one-third of the total labor force employed in the sixteen cities studied, the largest single-city numerical concentration of employees in a given industry may be in New York but still comprise less than one-third of the total labor force

TABLE 5 LOCATION OF BUSINESS ASSOCIATIONS BY POSITION OF NEW YORK
IN THE INDUSTRY, CIRCA 1940

	Location of Largest Employment Center		
	New York City		
Industry Associations in New York	PERCENTAGE OF TOTAL LABOR FORCE ABOVE 33.09	PERCENTAGE OF TOTAL LABOR FORCE BELOW 33.09	All Other Cities
Percentage	54.5	45.8	44.2
Number*	663	534	409

* Total number of industrial associations in the sixteen cities specified in Table 4. Inflated figures rounded to nearest whole number.

engaged in the industry among the sixteen cities. Under such circumstances, New York may draw the associations of the industry, yet the city's average percentage of the labor force in industries with trade associations will be below its position with respect to the entire labor force.

Such a refinement does not go very far in explaining New York's position as a center for business associations. Table 5 shows that whether or not New York City is the largest single center of employment in an industry does not greatly influence the proportion of all national associations located there. The fourteen industries with the largest single numerical concentration of the labor force in one of the other fifteen cities still have roughly 44 percent of their industrial associations located in New York. When New York is the largest single center of an industry, yet has less than its total proportion of the labor force, it has slightly more of the associations (46 percent). Finally, when New York is both the largest single center and has a proportion of the industry's labor force in excess of 33 percent, then it has 55 percent of the associations of such industries. What is noteworthy here is not so much that the variations in the proportion

of associations in New York are in the expected direction, but rather that the city has nearly half of the organizations in industries for which it is not the largest single center.

Although the economic base of most cities influences the kind of associations that locate in them, it appears to have only a minor influence on the location of industrial associations in New York. For example, of approximately 400 associations in the fourteen industries for which New York is not the largest single center of employment, roughly 23 percent of the headquarters are in the leading city for such industrial employment.[25] By contrast, these cities have far smaller proportions of all associations covered in our industrial survey (Los Angeles, 1.25 percent; Detroit, 1.31 percent; Pittsburgh, 1.87 percent; Philadelphia, 3.05 percent; Chicago, 17.29 percent). This indicates that New York's drawing power for business associations, while not completely independent of the influence of its industrial activities, is still fairly independent of the forces that operate to distrib-

[25] In one industry, New York had more than 33 percent of the employment, but was not the largest single center.

ute these organizations among other cities. Examination of the relative significance of the concentration of company headquarters, the financial, advertising, and communications activities of the city, and the city's high population potential is beyond the purview of this study.

In view of our earlier discussion, Washington, the second exception to our general finding, requires less comment. The location of industrial associations there is probably due to the governmental setting and not to the concentration of an industry's labor force in the city, although for some industrial associations, the government's position as a consumer of industrial output undoubtedly has some influence. In the case of the aircraft industry, for example, sixteen of the twenty-seven trade associations are located in the capital, whereas the railroad industry locates only two of its thirty-five associations there.[26]

LOCATION OF ETHNIC ASSOCIATIONS

The implications of population distribution for the location of noneconomic associations can be examined for ethnic organizations. Here, our concern is with the influence that the distribution of each ethnic population exerts on the location of the headquarters of its ethnic associations. There is no single set of ethnic data adequate for approaching this problem. First, census data are at best generally available for only the first and second generations in the nation. Secondly, since nativity data are usually confined to specific countries of birth or descent, we cannot apply these data directly to associations

based on ethnic groups lacking a specific nation-state counterpart or comprising a limited segment of a foreign nation-state, for example, Jews, Armenians, and Slovenians. Consequently, our research procedure involves matching each ethnic association with an indicator of the population's distribution in the nation in 1930. Wherever possible, we employed country of birth and descent data for the foreign white stock. For white groups where this would be inappropriate, we used data on mother tongue. For some of the oriental ethnic associations, we used racial data given for so-called "minor" nonwhite racial groups. In all cases our analysis is based on data from the 1930 Census of Population, because an unusually detailed set of ethnic data is available for that year.[27] Finally, our comparisons are based upon the distribution of ethnic associations by metropolitan areas and the ethnic composition of the central cities of these areas. This is far less arbitrary than may appear, in view of the finding that foreign whites, particularly in earlier decades, were concentrated in the central cities of metropolitan areas.[28]

The overall results are shown in Table 6 for the leading centers of voluntary associations.[29] The proportion of each ethnic group's population located in a specific city was multiplied by the number of associations for that ethnic group found in the nation. The sum of cross products

[26] *Encyclopedia of American Associations,* pp. 18–20, 134–37.

[27] *Fifteenth Decennial Census: 1930, Population,* II, *General Report* (Washington, D.C., 1933).
[28] Stanley Lieberson, "Suburbs and Ethnic Residential Patterns," *American Journal of Sociology,* 67 (1962), 675–76.
[29] Areas with at least thirty-five headquarters of all types.

TABLE 6 INFLUENCE OF ETHNIC COMPOSITION ON THE LOCATION OF ETHNIC
ASSOCIATIONS IN LEADING METROPOLITAN AREAS, 1959

	Percentage of National Total	
Metropolitan Area	Standardized Ethnic Distribution	Weighted Mean for Ethnic Organizations in the Area
Baltimore	0.5	_*
Boston	1.3	1.9
Chicago	5.6	8.2
Cincinnati	0.2	–
Cleveland	1.9	·4.4
Columbus	0.3	–
Detroit	2.4	4.2
Indianapolis	0.1	–
Kansas City	0.2	–
Los Angeles	2.2	0.6
Milwaukee	0.6	1.9
Minneapolis–St. Paul	0.9	5.8
Newark	0.7	–
New York	14.8	17.0
Philadelphia	2.2	2.8
Pittsburgh	0.8	1.6
St. Louis	0.5	–
San Francisco–Oakland	3.7	7.4
Washington	0.2	0.4

* A dash indicates that no ethnic associations are listed with national headquarters in the metropolitan area.

divided by the total number of all ethnic associations in the country yields the standardized percentages shown in the first column. In other words, if there was no relationship between the ethnic associations located in Chicago and the ethnic concentrations of that city, then Chicago would have about 6 percent of the national population for the ethnic organizations found there. The second column of Table 6 gives the weighted average for only those ethnic groups actually locating their association's headquarters in the specified cities. With the exception of Los Angeles, the associations located in each city tend to be for those groups concentrated in the area; that is, in each city the weighted mean for ethnic groups with some associations exceeds the city's standardized ethnic

distribution. Further, we observe that several of the urban areas have no national headquarters of ethnic associations.[30] The average standardized ethnic proportion of these cities (0.4 percent) is much lower than the average standardized ethnic proportion for those centers (3.0 percent) that have ethnic headquarters.

These data for ethnic associations, like the results reported earlier for industrial organizations, tend to support the conclusion that differences between cities in their attraction to specific associations are influenced by the location of the relevant membership populations served by the associations.

[30] Our observations are restricted to those associations reported in the basic data source.

RECENT TRENDS

It is evident that in recent decades the activities of the federal government have expanded in both intensity and range. This raises a serious issue for the ecological framework with which we approach voluntary associations. If the location of headquarters is influenced by the interaction between the functions of associations and the areas most suitable for the performance of these functions, then we would expect a shift towards greater concentration of associations in Washington as the city becomes increasingly relevant to the activities of an expanding number of voluntary associations.

Our research design was simply to take a sample from the 2,634 interstate, national, and international associations listed in a 1931 directory of associations in the United States.[31] For each association in our sample, we endeavored to trace its location in 1959 through the use of the *Encyclopedia*. As might be expected, a large number of associations existing in 1931 did not survive until 1959. Doubtlessly some associations were lost because of changes in name that were not recorded in the 1959 source or simply because of errors of omission and differences in the process of selecting organizations for listing.[32] Our analysis is consequently restricted to a sample consisting of 190 national associations existing both in

[31] U.S. Department of Commerce, Bureau of Foreign and Domestic Commerce, *Commercial and Industrial Organizations of the United States* (rev. ed.; Washington, D.C., 1931).
[32] In the few cases where associations had merged, we compared the past location of the association drawn in the sample with the present location of the merged organizations.

1931 and in 1959 for which we obtained data on the location of their headquarters. Since a large proportiontion of these are business, trade, and commercial associations (if we use the 1959 source as a basis of classification), we analyzed them separately from a residual group composed of all other associations. Because of the sampling procedure used, it is not possible to infer from the ensuing discussion the spatial distribution of associations in either year.

Table 7 shows the location of business associations in 1931 and 1959. New York and Chicago were the two largest centers in 1931 with 33 and 22 percent respectively. Washington was the center for about 6 percent of these associations, and about one-third of all business associations were located in other metropolitan areas. The shift in the location of these associations between 1931 and 1959, involving about one-third of the business organizations (col. 5), is marked by a slight net loss for New York, and an exodus of nearly all of the small number of associations previously located in the nonmetropolitan areas to metropolitan centers (compare cols. 1 and 2). On the other hand, Washington, with slightly more than twice the surviving business associations in 1959 than it had in 1931 (12 and 6 percent, respectively), became a more important center for these associations.

A similar pattern unfolds when the net redistribution of organizations other than business associations is considered. Again we find that Washington gained an increasing proportion of associations between 1931 (20 percent) and 1959 (29 percent). New York again shows a net loss, Chicago a gain, other metropolitan areas

TABLE 7 CHANGES IN HEADQUARTERS OF VOLUNTARY ASSOCIATIONS
BETWEEN 1931 AND 1959*

	Distribution		Changes 1931–1959		
			No. Leaving Area	No. Entering Area	
Area	1931 %	1959 %			Stationary %
Business associations	$N = 121$	$N = 121$	$N = 39$	$N = 39$	$N = 82$
New York	33.1	29.8	8	4	80.0
Chicago	22.3	24.0	7	9	74.1
Washington	5.8	12.4	2	10	71.4
Other SMSA	33.1	33.1	16†	16†	60.0§
Not SMSA	5.8	0.8	6	0	14.3§
All places	100.0	100.0	–	–	67.8
Other associations	$N = 69$	$N = 69$	$N = 24$	$N = 24$	$N = 45$
New York	26.1	20.3	5	1	72.2
Chicago	11.6	15.9	1	4	87.5
Washington	20.3	29.0	1	7	92.9
Other SMSA	31.9	31.9	12‡	12‡	45.5§
Not SMSA	10.1	2.9	5	0	28.6§
All places	100.0	100.0	–	–	65.2

* Because of rounding off, the sum in some columns is not 100 percent.

† Includes six headquarters moving from one residual metropolitan area to another.

‡ Includes five headquarters moving from one residual metropolitan area to another.

§ Based on only those headquarters remaining in the same specific residual metropolitan area or specific nonmetropolitan area.

maintain their proportion, and the nonmetropolitan areas (cols. 6 and 7) again show a marked emigration of headquarters to metropolitan centers.

These data indicate that Washington has become important as a center for voluntary associations. If we look at the components of this movement, we find the city's improved position relative to New York is based on its success in attracting associations located elsewhere rather than being a movement from New York to Washington. New York actually had a larger proportion (80 percent) of business associations in 1959 than Washington (71 percent). While the pattern is less clear for other types of associations, New York retains a larger proportion of its associations (72 percent) than do all places considered (65 percent).

Our analysis does not indicate whether associations founded in recent decades are more likely to be located in Washington than associations established in earlier periods. One can attack this problem by comparing the present location of associations founded since 1950 with the location of those established prior to that date. In making this cross-sectional analysis we assume somewhat roughly that associations founded in 1950 or later had not moved by 1959, and thus compare the percentage of these associations located in Washington with the percentage of associations presently located in Washington but established before 1950. We find that 21 percent of business associations founded in the fifties, but only 14 percent of those founded before 1950 are located in Washington. Similarly, 18 percent of other associations founded since 1950 are located in Washington, whereas only 14 percent of such associations founded before 1950 are located in Washington in 1959.[33] Although our cross-sectional data could be interpreted in a very different way, it does lend itself to the position suggested earlier that Washington's role as a center for voluntary associations has grown in recent decades.

DISCUSSION

National voluntary associations have been examined from the perspective of the forces influencing the location of their headquarters. Applying admittedly rough indicators in some instances, we have explored the usefulness of an ecological approach to national voluntary associations. Based on a series of case studies, the location of headquarters is found to be related to the nature of the external and internal functions performed by the headquarters, the relative suitability of certain areas for carrying out such functions, and the spatial distribution of members. These findings have important implications for the study of social organization in general and administration in particular, insofar as the location of headquarters can be viewed in an ecological context. New York, Washington, and Chicago are the foci of the political, financial, industrial, communication, and transportation systems of the society. As a consequence, they tend to draw the administrative elements of those voluntary associations that serve to relate their members to these institutions. Those types of associations for which such external functions are less significant appear to have lower concentrations in these centers.

Although there is a general relationship between size and number of associations that have headquarters in a city, large urban centers differ from one another on the basis of more than size alone. Los Angeles, for example, is still not a major center for voluntary associations. The growth of Washington appears to be a reflection of the increasing role of the federal government and the increase in the range of institutions and activities affected by the government. Although New York remains the most important center of voluntary associations, there is evidence of some decrease in its importance.

Doubtlessly, there are additional factors that influence location; for example, the presence of other voluntary associations, the symbolic importance of the area, the population potential, the median transportation distance, and the concentration of members. Furthermore, it makes relatively little difference for some voluntary associations where their main offices are located. Although there are dimensions to the study of the headquarters of associations that require research designs other than the ecological one employed here,[34] the location of national offices provides us with a valuable indicator of metropolitan dominance and, moreover, an empirical approach to speculations about the role of voluntary associations in the nation's political, economic, and social system.

---

[33] Although these figures are lower than those reported for nonbusiness associations in Table 7, they are not directly comparable, since the data sources are different and the *Encyclopedia* includes a much wider range of nonbusiness groups.

[34] Simpson and Gulley, "Goals, Environmental Pressures, and Organizational Characteristics."

15. ORGANIZATIONAL CHANGE IN TERMS
OF A SERIES OF SELECTED VARIABLES

John E. Tsouderos

The study presented in this paper takes its point of departure from the working hypothesis that institutional and cultural change can be empirically observed through the growth of a number of selected variables.* In his writings F. Stuart Chapin has demonstrated the possibility of studying the successive values of certain strategic institutional variables over a period of time and establishing the "law of change" by the well-known statistical method of fitting a logistic curve to the time series.[1] Chapin has linked this time series analysis to one type of broad generalization on the cultural and social change in the

Reprinted by permission of the American Sociological Association from *American Sociological Review*, 20 (April 1955) 206–10.

* Paper read at the annual meeting of the American Sociological Society, September, 1954.
[1] F. Stuart Chapin, *Cultural Change,* New York: Appleton-Century Crofts, 1928, Ch. 11 and 12; and *Contemporary American Institutions,* New York: Harper, 1935, pp. 58–59 and pp. 296–99; see also S. A. Rice (Ed.), *Methods in Social Science,* Chicago: University of Chicago Press, 1931, pp. 307–52. Contributions have also been made to this general area by Hornell Hart and W. F. Ogburn.

social group which he calls the "cycle of the social process" or the "societal reaction pattern."

An attempt will be made in this paper to summarize some of the findings made in an empirical investigation of a number of quantitative variables related to the organizational growth of ten voluntary associations.[2] Theoretical considerations suggest that these variables are important in understanding the processes of organizational growth and formalization[3] which constitute the topic of this paper.

[2] The study was based on ten case histories which were written by the present author for the purpose, and as a part of, an intensive and extensive study of the formalization process in small groups. These ten associations were: The Minneapolis League of Women Voters; The Ancient Order of United Workmen of Minnesota; Minnesota Council of Churches; Minnesota Nurses' Association; Alano Society of Minneapolis; Minnesota Association of Cooperatives; Lutheran Welfare Society; Minnesota Division American Cancer Society; Hennepin County League of Planned Parenthood; and The International Institute.
[3] The process of formalization is defined as a sequential, stage-by-stage development of organizational activity over time; a *standardization* of social relationships and finally as an increasing bureaucratization of the organization. However, formaliza-

In the course of conducting the field work,[4] three sources of information were used: (1) the financial statements of the associations; (2) the membership lists and statistics; (3) service statistics mostly compiled by the administrative staffs on the volume of service activities discharged.

The variables subjected to time series analysis were: (1) total annual income; (2) total annual expenditures; (3) value of the property from year to year; (4) annual membership figures; and (5) the number of administrative employees from year to year.

---

tion can be defined operationally in terms of the changes discernible in the organizational variables over a period of time. This becomes implicit in the following discussion.

[4] The organizational histories of these associations were constructed from the documentary material taken from the files of the organization, i.e., minutes of board and committee meetings, pamphlets, publications, constitutions and by-laws, annual reports, letters and verbatim interviews with active key persons past and present. In gathering the data for these case histories an attempt was made to record as completely as possible all the successive changes in the manifest social structure of the association, such as formal membership criteria, specific functional positions of officers, the changes in board and committee structure, the changes in the administrative office procedure, the increases in physical property, personnel policies, size of paid regular staff workers, and the like. A consistent attempt was made to describe the life histories of the associations step by step in a temporal sequence. These ten associations were selected under the following conditions: (1) the officers of the association had to give approval to the research worker to have full access to all the records of the association; (2) the association had to have, for the purpose of this study, a fairly rich amount of documentary material; and (3) all ten belonged to a larger sample of voluntary associations (see footnote 6).

It was seen in the case histories that the initial acquisition of property takes place when an association furnishes a meeting place for the membership and provides equipment to facilitate the discharge of administrative tasks. As the membership increases, a larger home is required by the association; more furniture is needed; real estate becomes desirable. Simultaneously, the growth of the membership group is accompanied by an increase in the volume of administrative tasks and expenditures; more office equipment is needed, especially after the first administrative worker has been hired.[5]

Figure 1 is a graphic and composite representation of the relationship of these organizational variables, summarizing our findings.[6] The key points of the findings are formulated here as tentative generalizations. As can be seen from the graph there is a definite functional relationship between the growth in membership of an association and other variables such as income, administrative expenditures, property and staff workers; that is, when one of these variables is modified in time the other under-

---

[5] F. Stuart Chapin, "The Growth of Bureaucracy: An Hypothesis," *American Sociological Review*, 16 (December, 1951), pp. 835–36.

[6] The observations and interpretations made in this paper seem to be corroborated by a more inclusive and representative sample of voluntary associations which have been treated statistically by this author. A random sample was drawn from a list of 535 voluntary associations. The sample consisted of 119 associations, 91 of which responded to the request for interviews. The president and executive secretary of each association were interviewed with a schedule. For details statistical analysis see "Formalization Process of Voluntary Associations" Ph.D. thesis 1953 (University of Minnesota Library).

LEGEND

──────── Membership
──·── Income
■ ■ ■ ■ Administrative Expenditures
──────── Administrative Office Workers
── ── ── Property

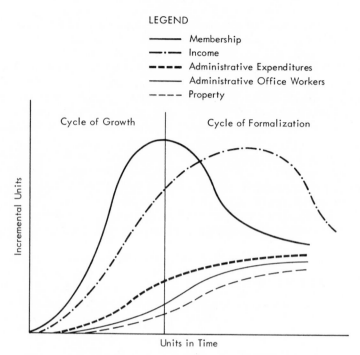

FIG. 1 GRAPHIC REPRESENTATION OF THE RELATIONSHIP
OF CERTAIN ORGANIZATIONAL VARIABLES

goes a corresponding modification. However, certain qualifications should be made in terms of a general growth pattern of the organizational development: (1) The membership growth precedes the growth of income. Even though we find a positive relationship between the increase of membership and growth of income this relationship does not seem to be continuous. With a decline of the membership in an organization there is no immediate or actual decline in income. (2) There is a positive relationship between the growth in total income of an organization and its administrative expenditures. However, the administrative expenditures have a much lower rate of growth than income. It can be noted then that the administrative expenditures increase rapidly after the peak of total income has been passed. (3) Property and administrative office workers continue to accumulate while membership and total income begin to shrink. However, property increases more rapidly in periods of rapid rise in income. We find also a close correspondence between the growth of administrative expenditures and increases in the property of the association.

In general, the above findings demonstrate that there is a certain tendency for the process of formalization to continue in the period when the social group contracts. Evidence shows[7]

[7] Note: These generalizations apply only to the ten case histories studied; this paper may be suggestive of an analytical approach to a method of studying the changing structure of a group.

that in this period of a contracting membership, the administrative staff expenditures, staff workers, and property, rise cyclically. The association which in the past has learned to cope effectively with its many problems by formalization and rationalization of its structure, attempts to survive by continuing the process of formalization.

The question arises as to why there is a functional relationship between the growth of membership, income, administrative expenditures, property, and staff workers. Why do voluntary associations have a tendency to increase their membership to a certain point and then reach a point of maximum growth? Furthermore, why does membership decline after a period of time? Why is it that with a decline in membership there is no immediate or actual decline in income, and, finally, why do property, administrative expenditures and office workers continue to accumulate while membership and total income begin to shrink? Before attempting to answer any of these questions we must clearly have in mind that the material presented above represents only an empirical study of a small selected group of voluntary associations and that the generalizations and interpretations might not fully conform to a more representative sample. It was attempted here merely to explore and suggest a possible method of observation, and, in addition, to present a set of hypotheses which would guide and offer some insight for further research in this field.

In general, then, the above can be conceived as an *ideal type construct* for use as a comparative guide in research on the manifest structural differentiation of small groups. With these limitations in mind let us try

to answer these questions in a series of interrelated and tentative propositions:

(1) The number of members and the continued growth of the membership group are the result of both the success of an association in coping with the internal functional problems posed by an expanding membership and the total adjustment or adaptation of an association as a functioning organizational unit to its social environment (including success in the enlistment of new members from this environment).

(2) The less specialized and segmental the role the members play in the association, the more pronounced is the tendency to regard participation in the association as an end in itself. This leads to a greater solidarity of the group and lessens the possibility of a decline in membership. The more specialized the role each member plays in the association, the more pronounced will be his tendency to regard participation as the means to an end. The loyalty of the members to their association can be stabilized when participation is regarded not merely as a means to the attainment of specified ends, but as the preservation of the association as an end in its own right. It is then to the advantage of the association to encourage primary group relations in the membership. However, a qualifying statement should be made here. We must not overlook on the other hand the stabilizing effect of the specialization and formalization of roles within an organization. That is to say, when the functional position or roles as such are abstracted from concrete persons and codified and defined by symbols, the organization acquires in general greater stability and flexibility than when it is under the personal

authority of one or more charismatic leaders. However, the problem of formalization versus lack of it is this: the members most affected by the specialization and formalization of roles are those "who run the show," i.e., are actively engaged as leaders of the organization, and they are less likely to withdraw their membership. The greatest turnover of the membership is observed in the passive membership *after formalization*, whose roles have been the least specialized. The passivity of this non-specialized group might be due to the disparity that exists between it and the highly formalized segment of the association. Thus, a balance between sociability and formalization must be attained to prevent the disintegration of the association.

(3) Certain associations may serve very specific interests and it is precisely for this reason that their appeal is limited to certain types of individuals. This imposes a maximum size on any one organization in any given area.

(4) With the increasing need of a service rendered by a voluntary association there is a corresponding increase of membership, and with the fulfillment or partial fulfillment of such a service there is a corresponding decrease in membership.

(5) With an increased membership, however, there is a corresponding increase in the heterogeneity of the group in terms of sentiments, interests, dedication to the "cause," etc., and a corresponding decline in a feeling of intimacy and frequency of interaction. More specifically, there is a decline of membership in meetings and volunteer work. As a consequence, the membership becomes extremely passive and increasingly removed from the leadership of the association. As the membership expands, the group as a whole is likely to lose its primary character. This is not to say, however, that the primary group disappears; certain clusters of individuals are found to interact with one another more frequently than they do with the rest of the membership. Sub-groups appear which retain the primary character previously extending over the entire membership. These sub-group clusters are integrated into the manifest social structure and the membership is organized in membership units. At the same time the need for control arises out of the fact that some of these membership units tend to become relatively autonomous from the rest of the organization. In varying degrees loyalty of the members is diverted from the association to the membership units so that the basis for a conflict with the organization has been laid.

(6) The loss of membership in the organization might be due then to several reasons, such as: increased secondary contacts, competing associations with similar functions, conflict within the association resulting from the heterogeneity of the group members, ineffectiveness of intracommunication, a decrease of the material or symbolic incentives offered by the association, a relative decrease in the need of a function or functions rendered by the association to its members or to the community and the extent to which the association is able to coordinate its formal and informal relationships.

(7) There is evidence that the formalization and contraction of the social group constitute a "vicious circle." In order to cope with its financial problems and declining membership, the association stream-

lines its structure and procedures according to modern organizational principles by introducing higher membership dues, professional help, and other means. These new organizational features alienate portions of the membership which had joined the association at an earlier and more informal stage, and lead to secession *en masse*. This mass separation creates even greater problems with which the association attempts to cope by formalizing its organization even more.

(8) With a declining membership, efforts are made to control the drop by introducing new incentives, added services, professional and administrative staff in order to discharge and supervise such services. Special communicative devices appear with the declining frequency of face-to-face interaction, preceded by the increasing structural differentiation and the separation of various functional activities. Furthermore, the association is confronted with the problem of enforcing the pertinent features of its program through a relatively expensive outlay. Thus with an increase of controls there is a corresponding increase of staff and administrative expenditures. This phenomenon of increased controls, efforts to improve communication, and the use of additional professional help can be found emerging not only when the membership declines, but also when the membership increases at a rapid rate.

(9) Increase of expenditures can also be explained in terms of increased capital outlay to improve facilities in order to maintain organizational prestige.

(10) With a decline in the membership of an organization, there is no immediate or actual decline in income. This phenomenon is due primarily to the greater efficiency of the organization in collecting dues and carrying out financial drives.

(11) Material property will increase over a period of time, and this increase is closely related to the expenditures for staff and upkeep. Unless the material property is withdrawn from use or permitted to deteriorate, these service expenditures cannot be reduced below a certain level.

16. ON THE GEOMETRY OF ORGANIZATIONS

W. H. McWhinney

THE "SHAPE" OF AN ORGANIZATION

In a widely cited article, Mason Haire[1] proposed, among other geometric models, that organizations might have bodily properties and growth characteristics typical of the biological world. He suggested that the relation of measures of the surface and the interior of an organization would be the same as the relation of the surface and interior of a compact solid. In the surface component (E) he classified all those whose job titles indicated they worked primarily with persons outside the organization. The interior component (I) included all those whose organizational life was spent primarily in contact with other members of the organization. Specifically he proposed that as the firm or organization grows, the ratio between the *square root* of the exterior component, and the *cube root* of the interior component, will remain nearly constant as given algebraically

Reprinted by permission from *Administrative Science Quarterly* (December 1965) pp. 347–62.

[1] Mason Haire (ed.), *Modern Organization Theory* (New York: John Wiley, 1959).

in equation (1) in the next·section. Haire tested the validity of his hypothesis with employment data from the history of four firms, going back as far as 35 years in one case. He conducted the tests in the following manner. First he divided the members of the organization into the two components according to their job description or department titles. This simple classification clearly introduced some error, particularly in dealing with the small firm, in which some individuals served more than one function, but it appears adequate for his intent. Next he transformed the data by taking the square root of the exterior count, and the cube root of the interior count; and finally he calculated the regression line for the least-square fit and tested the assumption of linearity by the significance of the correlation coefficients. In all four cases r equalled or exceeded 0.95. He noted that the slopes of the regression line were not 1.0, as would be consistent with the hypothesis, but 0.72, 0.51, 0.50, and 0.97. Furthermore, he noted that the intercept of the regression line was not at the origin. The high degree of correlation seemed to satisfy him as to the validity of the biological model; he reported slight

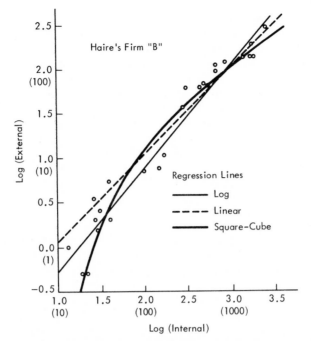

FIG. 1 EXTERNAL VS INTERNAL COMPONENTS OF THE FIRM: A COMPARISON
OF THE FITS TO LOGARITHMIC, LINEAR, AND SQUARE-CUBE MODELS

(The logarithmic representation was chosen over the linear display because of
the extreme range of the data. Figures in parentheses are numbers of employees.)

difficulty in developing an *ad hoc* explanation of the disconfirming aspect of the regression equations.

Since the appearance of Haire's article, two other empirical studies have been published that relate to this model.[2] The data from all three studies are treated in this paper.

ANALYSIS OF HAIRE'S DATA

Haire's proposition was reviewed by reanalyzing the internal-external

data of the four companies Haire treated as well as four others on which he had collected data and classified the employees. A general exponential model was used to retest the validity of the specific square-cube model. The same tests were also applied to the other two studies.[3]

Before Haire's central hypothesis was tested directly, the data were inspected for obvious contradictory evidence by plotting a scattergram of the raw data, and, as it seemed appropriate, running linear regression lines (see Fig. 1). Six of the eight companies, including all four of those companies appearing in the Haire article, displayed growth rates in the

[2] Seymour Levy and Gordon Donhowe, "Explorations of a Biological Model of Industrial Organization," *Journal of Business*, 35 (Oct. 1962), 335–42; Jean Draper and George Strother, "Testing a Model of Organizational Growth," *Human Organization*, 22 (1963), 180–94.

[3] Levy and Donhowe, "Explorations of a Biological Model"; Draper and Strother, "Testing a Model."

two components such as to produce very strong linear relations. Two firms, labeled E and F, showed remarkable linearity with correlation coefficients in excess of 0.95. Four others displayed similarly strong linearity when an occasional deviant point was ignored. The intercept of the regression line on the untransformed data for seven of the eight firms is within an insignificant distance of the origin, as is appropriate. The slope (E/I) of the regression lines varied from 0.08 to 0.59 for these seven firms.[4] Firm O presented no significant trend and showed a wide dispersion of ratios over the years. Even without further investigation, it is hard not to prefer, on ground of simplicity alone, the simpler hypothesis of proportionate growth to the biological square-cube relation. But a stronger argument against this biological analogy can be presented.

Formally Haire's hypothesized relation is expressed in the following equation:

$$E^{1/2} = a + b(I)^{1/3} \qquad (1)$$

where E = the number of external employees,

I = the number of internal employees,

b = the rate of change of one variable with the other, and

a = the intercept: the value of E when $I = 0$.

On common sense grounds, as Haire recognized, a must be zero, if sampling errors are ignored. For the biological model to be maintained, b must not differ significantly from

unity. Thus with a assumed and empirically noted to be zero, equation (1), with simplification and redefinition of the coefficient b, becomes

$$E = b(I)^{2/3} \qquad (2)$$

To allow testing of this hypothesis with the simple tools of linear regression, one can apply a logarithmic transformation to equation (2) and to the data. Thus equation (2) reads

$$\log E = \log b + c \log I \qquad (3)$$

and Haire's hypothesis is that the slope $c = 2/3$. The secondary hypothesis, that $\log b = 0$, need be tested only if the fundamental hypothesis holds.

The logarithmic transformation has a minor disadvantage, for it gives proportional weight to the small error-laden figures, whereas regression with the raw data minimizes the effect of these errors. But there is an advantage to using the logarithmic transformation, since it does not require the assumption of a particular proportional growth ratio. Rather it makes accessible an estimate of this growth parameter, which is useful in a more general growth model presented later.

A least-square regression equation was calculated for each of the eight companies and a two-tail Student's test was run to determine the likelihood that the sample growth parameter, c_i, could be from a population of organization characterized by $c = 0.667$. For seven of the eight companies, this hypothesis could not be maintained, as Table 1 shows in detail. Thus on the basis of Haire's longitudinal data, there appears to be *no evidence to support the square-cube biological-growth analogy.* The

[4] In the constant-ratio model, the slope defines the expected ratio between the number of external and internal employees. In the square-cube transformation, the slope is not so interpretable.

TABLE 1 REGRESSION EQUATIONS AND SIGNIFICANCE DATA
FOR MASON HAIRE'S FIRMS

Firm	Observation (Annual Where Available) N	Regression Equation (Log Transformation) E	r	Student's t*	Regression Equation for Principal Linear Trend† E
B	25	$0.032\,I^{1.19}$	0.95	4.90	$0.11\,I$
C	14	$0.048\,I^{1.68}$	0.97	8.48	$0.18\,I-3.$
E	32‡	$0.037\,I^{1.0}$	0.90	3.50	$0.41\,I$
F	17	$0.29\,I^{0.86}$	0.93	2.12	$0.11\,I+3.$
J	37	$0.37\,I^{0.94}$	0.96	6.37	$0.22\,I+3.$
K	40	$0.65\,I^{0.96}$	0.87	3.05	$0.59\,I$
M	15	$0.28\,I^{0.82}$	0.97	2.07	$0.08\,I$
O	43	$37\quad I^{-0.01}$	0.062	2.20	none

* Calculated against the hypothesis that $c = 0.667$. For all firms except M the likelihood of the firm being from a universe of $c = 2/3$ is less than 0.05 based on a two-tail test, d.f. $= n - 2$. For M, $p \cong 0.07$.

† Trend computed after off-trend observations were deleted by visual inspection. Only firm J had a significant number of deleted points—14. Of these, 10 are for the most recent years and form a second trend with zero slope.

‡ The first 5 of 37 observations were ignored as the classification placed all employees in interior of the firm.

aspect of the data which does nevertheless require some sort of explanation, is the constancy of the parameter c, or rather the high correlation, in seven of the eight firms. Discussion of this datum will be postponed until the remainder of the empirical data published on this model is reviewed in the discussions of generalized growth models.

THE LEVY-DONHOWE DATA

Following Haire's lead and method, Levy and Donhowe[5] presented a *cross-sectional* study of the internal-external makeup of 62 firms in eight manufacturing industries. Their data consisted of the component employment for each firm recorded at approximately the same time. Their analysis, while superficially similar to Haire's, introduced some additional

[5] S. Levy and G. Donhowe, "Explorations of a Biological Model."

problems in testing the model. They concurred with Haire's conclusion, saying the "Square-cube law is a reasonable and consistent description of the industrial organizational composition."

The present reanalysis began, as with the Haire data, by constructing scattergrams prior to introducing any statistical analysis. These graphs clearly suggest a constant ratio for all firms within each industry, with the exception of the aircraft and chemical groups, which show slight *increases* in the ratio E/I for the larger firms (20–70 thousand employees)—the direction opposite to the hypothesized change. In both the metal fabrication and machinery industries, the presence of a large sales-service oriented firm induces a best fit to a rising curve, but this tendency is clearly due to nonhomogeneity in the industrial samples.

A least-square regression equation was computed with the logarithmic

TABLE 2   LEVY-DONHOWE DATA

Industry	Mean Ratio of Employees in External and Internal Components	Mean Size of Firm
Drugs	.45	4,500
Food	.43	5,000
Metal fabrication	.29	4,000
Machinery	.23	7,000
Chemical	.19	8,000
Electrical	.18	7,000
Electronics	.13	9,000
Aircraft	.10	30,000

transformation on the complete sample. Here the best fit was found to be $E = 0.1 \ (I)^{0.81}$, compared to the hypothesized $E = I^{2/3}$. That the exponential is below 1.0 and close to the hypothesized value is an artifact of the sample selection.[6] Thus, in spite of their evaluation to the contrary *no evidence can be found in this cross-sectional selection of companies that will support the biological model.*

Levy and Donhowe's attempt to correlate various functional components such as research, administration, etc., with the internal-external ratio appears headed in a suggestive direction, though they are seriously hampered by retaining the odd-power transformation. Without referring to their full data, one can infer something about the internal makeup by establishing a simple rank ordering. With the assumption of a ratio independent of size, the (geometric) mean of the company ratios was com-

puted and the companies ranked by that mean ratio, as shown in Table 2. There is a clear trend from the customer-oriented food and drug companies through the heavy manufacturing component of the fabricating firms, to the increasingly important research and developmental organizations in the electronic and aircraft industries.

THE DRAPER AND STROTHER DATA

Draper and Strother[7] tested the various aspects of the Haire biological model by an analysis of the employment history of a single educational organization extending over 45 years. Besides examining Haire's analogies in a general way against the criteria of a good theory, they specifically examined the necessity of the square-cube law through a geometric exercise in which they compared the surface and volume of a great many archetypal solids. First they demonstrated that this square-cube relation is but a special case. Then they showed that for their data, a linear regression on the *raw* data produced nearly as good a fit as did a regression on the transformed data. With the location of a more parsimonious

[6] The selection of companies in this study produced a pairing of increasing total employment with decreasing external employees. This artifact of the study produces the *appearance* of a declining E/I ratio as a function of size for the total sample, in spite of the fact that each of the industries which makes up the sample has a near-constant or slightly rising ratio (see Table 2). Under such circumstances, testing for null hypothesis is meaningless.

[7] J. Draper and G. Strother, "Testing a Model."

TABLE 3 COMPARISON OF THE THREE METHODS OF FITTING THE DATA
REPORTED BY DRAPER AND STROTHER

| Method | Assumptions of Model | | | Estimating Equation | r | Unexplained Variance |
	Intercept	Slope	Power Ratio			
Square-cube	0	1	2/3	$E^{1/2} = 0.30 + 0.27(I)^{1/3}$	.99	790
Linear	0	–	1.0	$E = -26.65 + 0.51I$	.99	841
General—exponential	0	–	–	$E = 0.041(I)^{1.41}$	.99	697

model of equally good fit, they concluded that the square-cube law of organizational growth is at best superfluous. With this the writer concurs, but neither on parsimony nor on the other criteria Draper and Strother invoke is the linear hypothesis much superior. It is but one of the amazing variety of models with two free parameters, which can be fit to a nearly linear array of observations.

The general exponential model used for reanalysis of the other data is another of the two-parameter models. In this case it provides a better fit than the linear or square-cube model. It is also a more reasonable model, as it does not suppose an organization with an interior but no exterior or the converse, as is implied by a non-zero intercept in the linear model. A comparison of fitting methods is given in Table 3.

Note that both the intercept and the slope assumptions are neglected in the cube-square fit, and the intercept assumption is neglected in the linear fit. If the assumption of the zero intercept had been recognized at least by adding a first observation at (0,0), the correlation coefficients would have been markedly reduced in the first two cases. As performed, the first two regression analyses cannot be interpreted as tests of their models.

Although the Draper-Strother article casts strong doubt on the specific

model that Haire introduced, their devotion to the geometric and biological models seems almost to counterbalance the effect of their conclusion that *"the biological model does not seem to be valid* for describing or predicting the growth of organizations"* (italics added). Had they concentrated on demonstrating the lack of a homological basis, there would be little need for further discussion of geometric-biological models in the organizational context.

GENERALIZED GROWTH MODELS

The square-cube transformation applied to the internal-external data forces attention to one special case of the relation of the surface to volume. As Draper and Strother[8] illustrate, there is no *a priori* reason to suppose that organizations should usually have a form related to a special class of compact objects. They point out that the constant-growth ratio is a better representation of organizational geometry. And reanalysis of Haire's and Levy and Donhowe's data tends to support this tentative hypothesis. Yet the very concentration on the generalized geometric interpretation perpetuates a tradition that organizations can appropriately be described by archetypical objects in a three-dimensional

[8] *Ibid.*

space. In this concentration, these and other social scientists display a Pythagorean devotion to numbers, diverting their attention from the underlying processes either in the biological world they choose for illustrations or in the organizational world they describe.

The usefulness of making analogies is that it does produce processed data highlighting regularities which may stimulate the search for more relevant models.[9] In this instance, one striking regularity that is displayed in the longitudinal studies is the fact that a given parameter or pair of parameters can so well represent the growth patterns in the individual firm for periods as long as 45 years. One is inclined first to look for an explanation in the method of data preparation and analysis. Had the observed values of the growth ratio c been collected more markedly about unity, one would suspect a high degree of error and randomness in the assignment of employees to the two components. Variation in the assignment of given jobs over the sampled years would cause a regression of c toward 1.0. The wide variety of estimated growth parameters and the sharply differing ratios of the sizes of the two components as expressed in the (linear) slopes, however, tend to rule out the conclusion that the constancy is an artifact of the analysis. On the assumption that the constancy is not an artifact, two alternative explanations of the data are proposed.

1. *Factors of Growth.* Each of the functions (job titles) which Haire allots to the interior or exterior component of an organization can be characterized by its own economy of scale. While the notion of economy of scale is traditionally applied to productive functions, it is equally meaningful for other performances in the organizations. The detailed proportionality is recognized in practice in the manning tables of the military and the organization of a team to open a new branch store, to drill a well, or to install a computer. The economy of scale of two major components can be defined as the sum of the weighted indexes of each of the functions, departments, and so on, subsumed under each component. Thus, the growth parameter c is the ratio

$$\frac{dE}{dI} = \frac{\sum_{i} w_i \dfrac{de_i}{dN}}{\sum_{j} w_j \dfrac{di_j}{dN}}, \qquad (4)$$

where de_i/dN and di_j/dN are the growth rates of specific identifiable departments as a function of the total employment in the firm, and w_i, w_j are weight coefficients dependent on the technology of the industry and its capital deployment. At some base point in the history of the firm, they could be interpreted simply as a proportionality $w_i = n_j/N$.

Through aggregation, small variations in the component ratios over time are absorbed so that the overall organizational ratio may very well be a constant or a systematically changing ratio such as appeared in the majority of the firms and as was suggested by the cross-sectional data. Thus we can in fact use the geometry —as a way of representing the algebraic equations, as a predictive tool —as long as the technology remains significantly unchanged. The para-

[9] One doubts, however, that "the data themselves will suggest the model" as Draper and Strother ("Testing a Model," p. 46) forecast.

meter c is also associated with specific shapes, which in turn have come to be associated with the behavior of firms variously described as "production dominated," "sales dominated," or conforming to Parkinson's original law.

2. *Behavioral Regression.* Although one can expect a reasonable stability of the economy of scale functions in many parts of an organization, it is still surprising to find ratios as predictable as those that some of the sampled companies display. The relatively wide spread of values (of c) among the firms and within an industry suggests another "behavioral" source of stability. We can speculate that the stability arises from the backward-referenced planning conducted by the managers of the firms; that budgets for future growth are based largely on existing ratios and previous staffing decisions. In the absence of sufficient economic information for rational allocation of new budgetary employment, the least conflict-inducing method of distributing the new people is to maintain the existing ratios or the rate of change in those ratios. Change would be made in the allocation procedure only under extreme economic need or following the introduction of a significantly different technology.

And it may be that while the decision rules in current use are explicitly economic in theory, the ratios may be strongly conditioned by allocations and accounting conventions which can only be justified on traditional grounds. Thus, the two alternatives proposed may be behaviorally indistinguishable even though derived from quite different rationales.

Note that neither of these proposed alternatives to the biological model are either geometrically or biologically inspired, but are more nearly economic models. Furthermore, neither depends necessarily on dividing employees of the firm into an exterior and an interior component. *Any consistent classification scheme* would produce the same results: that is, a constant c and a constant b, though these parameters may take different values with each different classification pattern. The only link these explanations have with the geometric-biological world is through the common use of algebra as a mode of representation—hardly a sufficient base on which to claim anything approaching a homological identity.

CHAPIN'S FIBONACCI GROWTH MODEL

The frequency of making analogies without sufficient analysis of the underlying causal structure of the model and the process to be explained seems to increase with the number of isolated sets of data available to the social scientist and with his continuing adulation of the physical and biological sciences. A second (and earlier) example of this thinking in terms and analogies is provided by Chapin.[10] He attempted to find a rationale to associate some data[11] on the growth of a number of church congregations with their characteristics as viable and efficient organizations. His data consists primarily of (*1*) the sizes of the congregations in 1927 divided into the members (*M*) and those enrolled in

[10] F. Stuart Chapin, "The Optimum Size of Institutions: A Theory of the Large Group," *American Journal of Sociology*, 62 (March 1957), 449–60.
[11] Collected in Minneapolis by Wilbur C. Hallenbeck.

the Sunday School (*SS*)—mutually exclusive subsets, (*2*) the age of the churches, and (*3*) a measure of their institutional strength.

In trying to understand the relation of the figure of merit to the pattern of growth, Chapin speculated that since the Sunday School provided the source of new members, a healthy church would have the proportion of current membership to its recruiting subgroup in appropriate balance. He noted a formal and analogical similarity between the relation of the two components and the generation of the Fibonacci series, which generates a logarithmic curve that has been noted as producing geometric patterns akin to the growth in many sea shells and in plants such as the sunflower. Assuming these growth patterns to be representative of a homeostatic equilibrium, he proposed that organization displaying such a growth pattern in its components would be a strong one. The Fibonacci series is most simply generated by summing the latest two terms to form the new term. It can also be generated by augmenting the most recent term by the larger of the two components of which it is the sum. These are equivalent generators, but the second is more suggestive of the process with which Chapin was concerned. A sample of the series as it is generated is $1 + 1 = 2$; $1 + 2 = 3$; $2 + 3 = 5$; $3 + 5 = 8$; $5 + 8 = 13$; .... From the series we can construct a ratio

$$F = \frac{n_i}{n_{i-1} + n_{i-2}}$$

which rapidly converges as i increases to a value near 0.6180. If the organization is to grow according to this pattern, the components must be appropriately related, Chapin argued.

He expected to find that healthy organizations would more closely approximate this proportion than those which were less strong. He chose, therefore, to test the proposition that the organizational ratio, $F' = M (M + SS)$, should be clustered around the value of F, and that the variations should be correlated with the figure of merit for each church.

For the 80 churches in Chapin's sample, the mean of the ratio F' is 0.5850. He noted also the strong correlation of the individual church ratios with the age of the church and the measure of institutional strength. His Table 2 is reproduced in part as Table 4.

From this data, Chapin concluded that "the optimum [shape] of a church may occur when [F' approaches F]. This optimum ratio is the cluster of social traits—which yields the maximum degree of continuity of security for group members by achieving a moving equilibrium (social homeostasis) among conflicting social influences and yet is consistent with the preservation of group bonds."[12]

The basis on which he argues for a fundamental relation between the Fibonacci series and the growth dynamics of the human organization leads one to look for a less tenuous explanation of the concentration of F' near the value 0.6180 and of the correlation of the F' ratio with the measure of institutional strength. A most appropriate place to look is the source from which the church draws its members; that is, the population at large, and specifically the family group. The Minneapolis census for 1930 shows that the mean family size

[12] F. S. Chapin, "The Optimum Size of Institutions," p. 457.

TABLE 4 CHAPIN'S SUMMARY TABLE

Institutional Strength Rating	Mean Age of Churches	$F' = \dfrac{M}{M + SS}$	Deviation $F' - F$
Total	36.6	0.5850	−0.0330
A (highest)	47.5	0.6580	+0.0400
B + C	33.6	0.5566	−0.0614
D	18.0	0.5187	−0.0993
By Age			
Very old $(n = 8)$	75.3	0.6688	+0.0508
Very young $(n = 8)$	10.2	0.4056	−0.2124

was 3.78 persons, and that the ratio of adults (A) to children under 21 (C) in the total population was near $2:1$. The analogous F ratio for the population would be $F'' = A/(A + C)$. Thus the societal value of F'' for the relevant population lies between 0.53 and 0.67 (depending on how one treats adults not included in family units), a range which includes the mean F' and about 30 of the 80 churches in the sample. Chapin's *central statistic* can thus be obtained from the simple assumption that *the church population is a representative sample of the city population* on at least this dichotomous age classification.

The covariance of the F' ratio with the age of the church can be accounted for by a commonplace explanation based on two premises, the validity of which has not been checked in this case: (1) The population in older districts of the city has a higher portion of adults than the newer districts; and (2) older churches are found in older districts. Or a proposition might be deduced from this pair: newly formed churches (say, up to 20 years old) have members of a lower median age than older churches. Either basis leads to the prediction that there would be more children (the SS component) in the younger churches and

so to the prediction of the covariance of F' with age of the church. In turn, institutional strength appears to vary with the age of the churches utilized in the study (see Table 4). The general tendencies in the data are thus capable of being accounted for by simple *population statistics*. The normative property is reduced to the proposition that a "best" church is one which has a representative sample of age distribution in the congregation.

Here again, as in the case of Haire's proposition, there is a far simpler explanation than the biologically inspired geometric model. The two models discussed in this article appear to have a common weakness: in both cases, the biological analogy is superficially established. In the first case, it was based on a loose literary simile and permitted to persist by inappropriate analysis of data; in the second, a coincidence of two numerical values permitted a suggestive parallelism to be taken as a condition for organizational optimality. In spite of the fact that the explanations are belabored, there is some value in presenting these models if the data are presented in a form that others can also work with them. But this potential value can be heavily outweighed by the damage that can be caused by unskeptical acceptance. Haire's model is rapidly becoming part of the folklore of management theory, and now that it is embedded in textbooks as an empirical fact, it will take many years before the reverberations die down.

The use of analogies as an aid to constructing theories and models of social behavior has often proved fruitful; their very attractiveness makes it all the more important that care be used in their construction. The power of the imagery called up in such analogies as Social Darwinism goes well beyond the two examples given above, but it serves as a good example of how substantial normative force can be developed out of the biological analogies.

THE GEOMETRIC ANALOGY

In the main, this paper is an attempt to weaken the hold that models such as Haire's and Chapin's have apparently gained on the imagination of the students of organizations. This effort was aimed at the empirical basis supporting the plausibility of the models. A more general attempt is also needed to expose the groundlessness of analogies which depend on Euclidean geometry. Such an exposure would not, however, discredit the verbal similes associating spatial properties with groups and organization. It is generally understood, even if in a rather loose fashion, what is meant by a *compact* group, a person on the *fringe*, the *pyramid* of the organization, and so forth, but the Euclidean analogy can be put away with greater confidence if such loose analogies can be reestablished with another geometry more appropriate to the organizational world.

In order to maintain the existence of meaningful analogies of organiza-

tion to geometric shapes, a set of basic equivalences would have to be established. Those requisite are organizational equivalences to the *elements*, the *relations* among the elemental objects, and a *metric* to establish *shape*. If each could be established, it would be possible to invoke some of the propositions and theorems of geometry, and some from the physical and biological sciences as well. It is rather easy to propose various suggestive equivalences for elements and relations; the failure of the many analogies that have been tried lies in the inability to establish a suitable metric for the organizational space; the continued failure leads to the conclusion that if we are to obtain any approximation to a useful geometry, some non-Euclidean device should be introduced. One approach would be to substitute for the geometric point a distribution of possible locations representing the places at which a member might be located at a particular moment. Such looseness might not be tolerable for a high school geometry, but might be a rather useful construct in an organization theory. A second basis might be obtained by considering a human organization as converging through gradual adjustment toward a geometric Euclidean structure. Any actual organization operating in an unsettled environment with a continually changing set of employee members should not be expected to crystallize into a Euclidean solid.

A third variation on the geometric theme, based on the concept of individuals fulfilling roles in organizations, is one in which a complete fit to a geometric structure is obtained by introducing curved spaces which could be "deformed" to provide acceptance of a new role into the set of roles making up the extant organization. Deformation of the space could be seen as being caused by social, economic, and institutional forces. The introduction of shapes in curved spaces eliminates the possibility of translation and rotation essential to Euclidean geometry. Yet this aspect, inappropriate for the geometric analogy, fits common sense well; clearly an organization cannot be rotated or translated in a social space and be expected to retain its shape. Socialists and social reformers alike have run hard against this blunt fact.

Such analogies may provide some ideas on which a geometry of organizations might be constructed, but it is not at all certain that any of them would have value beyond serving as generators of ideas for the organizational theorists. The essential connection to the empirical world, an operational metric, is still missing. Possibly an economics of information will eventually provide an appropriate metric and the operations by which to establish empirical connections. If such a task is accomplished, geometry can enrich the science of administration as it has in the past aided mathematics, astronomy, physics, zoology, and other fields.

17. TOWARD A RATIONAL THEORY OF DECENTRALIZATION: SOME IMPLICATIONS OF A MATHEMATICAL APPROACH

Manfred Kochen and Karl W. Deutsch

This paper seeks to open for exploration the field of decentralization in politics and organizational design. As a first approach, it examines conditions under which decentralization is preferable from the viewpoint of rationality or cost-effectiveness. Our normative statements as to what would be best, or what should be

Reprinted by permission of The American Political Science Association from *American Political Science Review*, 63 (1969) 734–49.

done, are formulated first from the viewpoint of the subjects or clients, but they are expected to include the interest of the community in ensuring adequate service at low cost, and they also include the interest of the rulers, insofar as their power in the long run depends on their capacity to respond to the demands made upon them quickly enough and adequately enough to retain their political support.

The political theory underlying our study assumes that modern governments retain "their just powers by the consent of the governed," and hence that both their legitimacy and their power will depend at least in significant part on their ability to respond adequately to the popular demands made upon them. We do not deal in this study with other important criteria of preference, such as the psychological value which some of those who take the role of powerholders may put upon centralized control, or the contrary value which some of those who identify with their subjects may put upon power sharing and decentralization. We do hope to suggest, however, which side to the centralization-decentralization controversy is likely to be favored by the pressure of cost-effectiveness considerations, and under what conditions.

At this stage, we also assume ethnic, linguistic, cultural and social uniformity, as the conditions most likely to favor centralization. According to traditional theory, at least, strong centralization under non-uniform conditions usually would be more difficult.

We consider a situation where several identical and equally spaced facilities for decision making, information processing, or other operations perform services in response to requests from sources that are uniformly distributed in time and across varying distances. Such distances could be measured in terms of intervening decision points, switching points, waiting lines, or simple geographic space. As the simplest first approximation, we have analyzed this last type—service through communication and/or transport along a long thin spatial strip.

In the simplest models, the focus is on *costs*: the number of duplicated facilities is determined by setting the marginal increase in fixed costs equal to the marginal decrease in the costs of communication and transportation due to decentralization. In later models, the utility of *time* gained by more rapid service in response to requests is taken into account, and attention is given to the more dependable availability of service that comes with decentralization involving duplication of facilities. Throughout all these models the total *volume* of requests, and its ratio to the speed of communication and transport, turn out to be crucial.

As far as they go, the results of the present analysis suggest that the social, political and economic changes, which influence the rising volume of requests, may outweigh in many cases the effects of the technological changes that have speeded up communication and transport, and that societies which adopt the technological changes are likely to be societies that increase also—or even more—the volume of requests for service or responses. Where these conditions apply, current and future social, political and technical developments may increase, rather than decrease, conditions favoring decentralization.

More extended mathematical derivations and discussions are presented elsewhere.[1]

The present paper is the first of a projected series which is to investigate problems of centralization and decentralization by means of a series of models intended to be increasingly close to the actual variables and problems encountered in the practice of governments and other organizations. Problems of uneven distribu-

[1] M. Kochen and K. W. Deutsch, "A Mathematical Model for a Study of Political Decentralization," submitted to *Operations Research*, September 1968.

tions of messages or service requests, in space and time, questions of hierarchies among service or decision centers, and questions of lateral communications or interference among multiple facilities among several centers at the same level, will have to be investigated in such later papers.

DECENTRALIZATION AS A GENERAL PROBLEM

When the director of a research institute in which there are several independent investigators plans to provide computer-based information services, a choice presents itself. Should he provide each independent investigator with his own small computer? Should he install a large computer system everyone must share? Should he provide some mix of these two extremes?

When an architect plans a low-income housing project on a fixed budget, he faces a somewhat analogous choice. Should he provide one bathroom for each family but no swimming pool plus bathhouse for the project (assuming that the budget does not stretch to cover both) or should he provide 50% fewer bathrooms than families, thus making every two families share one, but providing a swimming pool plus bathhouse for use by all as well?

A university library system may comprise over a dozen branches plus departmental and special libraries. In planning the construction of new buildings and ordering library materials, should the university librarian favor the creation of branches and special libraries wherever they are wanted, supplying each with duplicate copies and each with a separate bibliographic control system? Or

should he favor the creation of a central custodial unit where responsibility for bibliographic control is concentrated?

A school system may concentrate most of the effective control in the hands of a single board of education for an entire metropolitan area with several million inhabitants, or it may decentralize much or most of this control down to about three dozen neighborhood school boards, each serving a community of between 100,000 and 200,000 people. Apart from group demands and local power contests, which arrangement would be more rational? In what respects and on what grounds?

To what extent should the commander-in-chief delegate various battlefield responsibilities to local commanders and platoon sergeants? What are the consequences of too much or too little autonomy for the junior managers and foremen of a 100,000-employee industrial organization, as distinct from rigid control by a strong chief executive?

Are the customers of an industry better served by a single firm, or a single decision-making unit within a firm, or by several firms or several decision-making units?

Is the population of a territory best served by a single nation-state or government or a single administrative center within a nation, or by several states, governments, or administrative centers?

All these questions have a common core. It is the concept of the "degree of decentralization" of an organization or institution and its relation to the "performance" of the latter. The performance of every human organization includes crucially its *responses* to information received from its environment. Service organizations, such as governmental housing or other public or private service agencies, health services, libraries, or computing centers, often appear passive in that they wait for requests from their potential clients or users, to which they then respond. Other public or private agencies appear more active in that they often initiate a sequence or transaction between themselves and some members of the public. Thus tax collection agencies, draft boards, truant officers, public health departments, and private sales organizations often take some initiative in this sense; and some organizations, such as legislatures, general administrative agencies, and police departments play a mixed role, initiating some transactions and also responding to messages from the outside.

Human organizations of all kinds, however, depend critically on the *feedback* of information from their environment in order to discover the results of their actions and to correct their errors.[2] It is in regard to this exchange of information, and often also of things and persons, with their environment, that the performance of more or less centralized or decentralized organizations is to be compared here, in a series of preliminary steps toward a theory of decentralization.

The approach proposed here would go somewhat deeper, therefore, than the familiar view that centralization is a matter of power—that the strong

tend to centralize in their own hands as much power as they can, and concede to the weak only as much decentralization as they must. It is quite true that a powerful person, group or office often can concentrate a great many flows of information and of decision making responsibilities in their own hands, but it does not necessarily follow that they will be able to use this information effectively to produce timely and adequate responses.

The relation between power and communication is thus not a one-way process. Power can command communication, but communication and information-processing capacity may increase power or reduce it to the point of paralysis. Where power originally produced centralization, delays or failures in information-processing or responsiveness may then tend to shift both loyalties and power away from the centralized but unresponsive offices or places of command. The operational effectiveness of centralized or decentralized information-processing or decision-making centers, governmental agencies, business organizations and service facilities, is thus in each case a question intellectually distinct from the question of power, and worth considering in its own right.

Much of the well-known political and social theory on centralization and decentralization implies that centralization is preferable on the grounds of efficiency, and that modern technology, with its jet aircraft and electronic communication, has increased the pressures toward centralization.[3] Some theories also assert,

---

[2] On the concept of feedback, see Norbert Wiener, *The Human Use of Human Beings,* (New York: Avon Books, 1967), ch. 1; K. W. Deutsch, *The Nerves of Government,* (2nd ed.; New York: Free Press, 1966), with references; and Robert A. Rosenthal and Robert S. Weiss, "Problems of Organizational Feedback Processes," *In Social Indicators,* Raymond A. Bauer (ed.), (Cambridge: M.I.T. Press, 1966), pp. 302–40.

[3] See, e.g., Herbert A. Simon, Donald W. Smithburg, and Victor A. Thompson, *Public Administration* (New York: Knopf,

however, that decentralization is better suited to protect the values of democracy, liberty, and popular participation in decision-making.[4] Some theorists point out that these different views balance to some extent, and that the optimal point on some more or less continuous centralization-decentralization scale must be discovered in each case; but they give little further indication as to how these discoveries are to be made.

For a start, we shall try to make explicit a few of the basic notions involved, leaving other aspects of the problem for later work. Thus we shall start from the feedbacks and transactions with the outside world, postponing for later analysis elsewhere the internal decision processes of organizations and their possible overloads which play such a large role in much of current organization theory.[5]

We stress in this paper the concern of the person with primary responsibility for the institutional organization rather than the concerns of the members of that organization. Further, we stress what he *should* be concerned with in terms of purposive rationality, rather than what may actually concern him most for personal, psychological, or sociological reasons. By "what he should be concerned with" we mean norms, related to the basic functions and the survival of the institution for which he is responsible; these norms are determined environmentally in terms of feedback processes that are decisive about the survival of the institution. Not that these neglected subjective aspects are unimportant. Far from it. They may well be the salient features of a viable theory of decentralization. So much more reason to treat them thoroughly, but separately, at a later stage.

There is surprisingly little published literature on which to base a formal explication of the decentralization concept.[6] Some of the opera-

1956), pp. 272–79. For a related argument in international relations, see Albert Wohlstetter, "Illusions of Distance," *Foreign Affairs*, 46 (Jan. 1968), p. 250.

[4] A qualified emphasis on decentralization is found in Joseph A. Litterer, *The Analysis of Organizations* (New York: John Wiley & Sons, 1965), pp. 378–93; and John M. Pfiffner and Frank P. Sherwood, *Administrative Organizations* (Englewood Cliffs, N.J.: Prentice-Hall, 1960), pp. 440–62.

[5] For some important general approaches, see Herbert Kaufman, "Organization Theory and Political Theory," *Amer. Pol. Sci. Rev.*, 58 (1964), 5–14, esp. 7–8, 13–14; Mason Haire, *Organization Theory in Industrial Practice* (New York: John Wiley & Sons, Inc., 1962), pp. 6–7; Albert H. Rubenstein and Chadwick J. Haberstroh, *Some Theories of Organization* (Homewood, Ill.: Irwin and Dorsey, 1966).

[6] For examples of discussions of the political and social aspects of decentralization and the size of political units or areas, see Bernard H. Baum, *Decentralization in a Democracy* (Englewood Cliffs, N.J.: Prentice-Hall, 1961); Robert A. Dahl, "The City in the Future of Democracy," *Amer. Pol. Sci. Rev.*, 61 (1967), 953–70; James W. Fesler, *Area and Administration* (University, Ala.: Univ. Ala. Press, 1942); S. W. Hess, *et al.*, "Non-Partisan Political Redistricting by Computer," *Operations Research*, 13 (1965), 998–1006; Philip Jacob and James V. Toscano (eds.), *The Integration of Political Communities* (Phila.: Lippincott, 1964); Arthur W. Macmahon, *Delegation and Autonomy* (New York: Asia Publications and Taplinger, 1967); E. A. G. Robinson (ed.), *Economic Consequences of the Size of Nations* (New York: St. Martins Press, 1963). General studies of decentralization are relatively rare in political science. *The Cumulative Index to the American Political Science Review* (1906–1963) (ed.), (Evanston, Ill.: Northwestern Univ. Press, 1964) lists only one article for the 57 years covered, S. G. Lowrie's "Centralization versus Decentralization (Federalism)", which appeared in the *Review* in

tions research literature dealing with warehouse allocation problems[7] is relevant, as is some of the applied mathematical statistics literature on problems for determining the optimum number of machines or service facilities.[8] Generally, however, customers are assumed to arrive at the

1922. During the same 57 years, three articles referring in their titles to the delegation of legislative powers appeared in 1908, 1926, and 1947, respectively.

[7] See Hess, *et al.,* "Non-Partisan Political Redistricting"; W. J. Baumol and P. Wolfe, "A Warehouse Location Problem," *Operations Research,* 6 (1958), 252–63; L. Hurwicz, *Decentralized Resource Allocation,* Cowles Commission Discussion Paper No. 2112, 1955; T. C. Koopmans and M. J. Beckmann, "Assignment Problems and the Location of Economic Activities," *Econometrica,* 25 (1957), 53–76; A. A. Kuehn and M. J. Hamburger, "A Heuristic Program for Locating Warehouses," *Management Science,* 9 (1963), 643–66; Alan S. Manne, "Plant Location under Economies-of-Scale—Decentralization and Computation," *Management Science,* 11 (1964), 213–35.

[8] J. P. Anderson, *et al.,* "D825—A Multiple Computer System for Command and Control," *In AFIPS Conference Proceedings,* Volume 22, (Washington, D.C.: Spartan Books, 1962), pp. 86–96; K. J. Arrow and L. Hurwicz, "Decentralization and Computation in Resource Allocation," in R. W. Pfouts (ed.), *Essays in Economics and Econometrics* (Chapel Hill: Univ. North Carolina Press, 1960), pp. 34–104; Information Dynamics Corporation, *A Methodology for the Analysis of Information Systems,* Final Report to the National Science Foundation, NSF-C-370, (1965); J. R. Jackson, "Networks of Waiting Lines," *Management Sciences Research Project Research Report No. 53* (Los Angeles: Univ. Calif., Mimeographed, 1957); Z. S. Wurtele, "A Criterion for Determining the Number of Identical Machines to be Installed at a Machine Center," *Management Sciences Research Project Discussion Paper No. 78* (Los Angeles: Univ. Calif., mimeographed, 1961); Edgar M. Hoover, *The Location of Economic Activity,* (New York: McGraw-Hill, 1948).

service facility, and the time for requests to pass from the customer's site to the facility and for responses to pass back to the customer is not taken into account. The conventional "warehouse-location" problem is to locate a specified number of warehouses and assign customers to each warehouse so that the sum of the squared distances between each customer and the warehouse closest to him is minimized. Actually, distance may not be best represented by its second power;[9] and the present paper will treat the best number of warehouses not as given but as to be computed. It is primarily in the analysis of information systems that such problems are encountered, and relatively little analytical study has been devoted to these.

In this paper we analyze the simplest of these mathematical problems which are, nonetheless, quite generic to a large class of situations in which centralization vs. decentralization is an issue.

MOVING PEOPLE, THINGS AND INFORMATION: THE LOGISTICS OF ORGANIZATION

Decentralization depends in large part on logistics, and all social organizations have problems of logistics. All of them must move messages from one place to another; many of them also must move people, such as field representatives, investigators, fire truck crews, riot squads, case workers or other agents of various kinds; and many must also move material objects, ranging from small

[9] K. W. Deutsch and W. Isard, "A Note on a Generalized Concept of Distance," *Behavioral Science,* 6 (1961), 308–11.

samples or mail order items to bulky goods in mass production. Yet some organizations mostly depend in their functioning on the inflow and outflow of messages, as do telephone exchanges, while others depend most critically on the movement of material goods, as do factories. Still other organizations depend primarily on receiving information, such as orders or requests, and on responding to these by moving material objects or people, as do mail order houses and at higher rates of speed also fire departments and ambulance services.

The agencies of government and politics overlap these various types. Public school systems depend upon the movement both of people and of information. The long-run recruitment and maintenance of an army depends upon the movement of persons and supplies, but the short-run intervention of some of its forces may occur in response to an order or message. A law court requires the physical presence of the parties or their representatives, and a prison insists on the physical presence of its in-

mates. Administrative decisions, on the other hand, often are sent out as control signals or messages in response to information that was received at some earlier stage. Legislation consists from this point of view in a special class of messages issued in response not only to earlier messages but also in response to the physical movement of various spokesmen for interest groups at formal hearings, or more informally of lobbyists, and to the bodily movement of legislators and constituents between their respective constituencies and the capital.

A simple overview of such organizations classified into basic logistic types is shown in Table 1.

Each entry in any cell in Table 1 refers to either a task to be performed ("medical examination and treatment") or to an institution which performs some task or tasks (e.g., "army," "hospital"). In some cases, such a task is performed only by relatively large institutions, while other tasks can be decentralized in their performance to the level of individual

TABLE 1 SOME EXAMPLES OF LOGISTIC TYPES OF ORGANIZATION

		OUTGOING	
		MATTER	INFORMATION
INCOMING	Matter*	Army Law Court Prison Repair Shop Hospital Medical Examination Factory or Plant Legitimate Theater	Quality Control Stations Analytical Laboratory Movie Studio Live Television Museum, Gallery, Archives
	Information	Military Task Force Police Fire Department Ambulance Relief Supplies Mail Order House	Decision-making and Control Centers (governmental and private) Telephone Switching Nets Data Centers Reference Services Computer Facilities

* Material objects and/or human bodies.

clients. Government and defense usually are concentrated in such larger institutions, but some physicians still visit patients in their homes. Even governments and armies, however, can decentralize their functions to a greater or lesser degree.

For a functional theory of decentralization, toward which the present paper is directed, the social tasks to be performed are more important than the historical institutions which currently happen to perform them. Though institutions have a great deal of persistence and tend to protect their own survival, they nonetheless do change. Some of these changes tend toward greater or lesser decentralization, and a functional analysis of the level of decentralization most appropriate to their chief task is essential in order to evaluate rationally the actual changes which occur in response to technological or political pressures.

We emphasize the distinction between the movement and storage of persons and materials on the one hand, and the transmission and storage of information on the other hand as most important from the viewpoint of logistics. Messages move more quickly by several orders of magnitude than do persons and materials, and unlike persons and materials they can be duplicated at low cost. All information, of course, depends on some material carrier or marker which bears it, much as a book depends on printer's ink and paper, but the ratio of amount of information to mass of carrier, say in bits per pound per hour, is very high and on a computer display terminal (e.g., teletypewriter or display screen), it is still higher. Our analysis will show that transmission speed is often critical for determining the optimum level of decentralization of a network of facilities and we may expect, therefore, to get different answers for systems depending primarily upon transport as against those depending primarily upon communication.

A simple exercise may illustrate these points. Here we idealize a special but prototypical problem to such an extent that we can analyze it mathematically. Our prototype model will deal with the supply of services from one or several storage facilities. This is not irrelevant. For politics and administration, government, administrative agencies, and law courts all can be thought of as storage places for memories, recorded in their files or carried in the minds of their specialized personnel, and as suppliers of decisions to their clients or constituents. The mathematical analysis of this simplified model may give us insights that a purely verbal analysis does not provide. Building on such a more precise and explicit foundation, we hope then to make some progress toward an edifice of theory that explicates the core problems and proves helpful in explaining the success of various organizations and possibly also in advising decision-makers.

A PROTOTYPE MODEL

Image an institution existing to supply objects of value, e.g., books or mail-order items, to customers located in an elongated region from Boston to San Francisco in which the north-south dimension is treated as negligible.

Let D be the east-west distance of this region in miles or in terms of relay stations, traffic intersections, intervening opportunities or other conditions affecting the probability and costs of transmission or transport (Definition 1). Let us make the further assumption that the demand for these valuable objects is spread uniformly over the length of this strip. For example, suppose that ten requests per month originate from each mile along the strip.

Let L denote the total load, in requests per month (Definition 2). The total load, L, resulting from this demand requiring service, then would be $L = 10D$ requests per month. Assume that we can control the way the institution is organized, and we wish to explore the consequences of various degrees of decentralization.

By the most centralized organization we mean a single service facility, say a warehouse, which maintains a large enough stock of the valuable objects to clear the demand at all times. (At this first stage of the analysis we assume that the time to forward and process requests is negligible.) It is obvious that the best

location for this warehouse is in the middle of our stretched-out region, as shown in Fig. 1.

The manager of the organization is uncertain about the exact distance x between the service facility and the site from which a request (for an object) originates at any moment. When such a request is made, the manager must find the wanted object in the warehouse and transport it to that location.

We assume having a transportation medium which transports at a uniform speed of v miles per hour (Definition 3).

Then the delivery time to a point at a distance of x from the warehouse is x/v. Because the sites of requests are assumed to be uniformly distributed over the length D, the average distance between the site of a randomly selected request and the warehouse at the midpoint is $D/4$. Hence, the average delivery time for a request is $D/4v$.

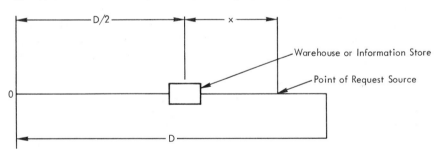

FIG. 1 A CENTRALIZED ORGANIZATION

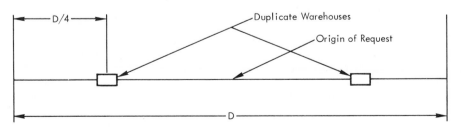

FIG. 2 A TWO-FACILITY ORGANIZATION

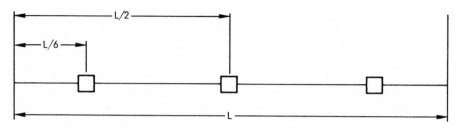

FIG. 3

By a slightly less centralized organization we mean two warehouses, with identical inventories (each containing a copy of each valuable object), located at the quarter points of our elongated region (see Figure 2). A request originating at any point is serviced by the warehouse nearest to it; requests from points equidistant from two facilities are serviced at random by either.

While for the single facility shown in Fig. 1, the delivery time, averaged over many randomly originating requests, was $D/4v$, it is half of that, or $D/8v$, for the two facilities shown in Fig. 2.

Let the dollar costs of operating a warehouse be $\$C$ per month (Definition 4).

Then the fixed cost of operating the single repository organization of Fig. 1 is C (including interest and amortization on its cost of installation) while that of the duplicated service in Fig. 1 is $2C$.

Let the dollar cost of delivering objects be c dollars per hour (Definition 5).

Then the total demand is L requests per month (with $L/2$ for each of the two warehouses in the organization of Fig. 2), and the average delivery cost is $cDL/4v$ dollars per month for Fig. 1 and $cDL/8v$ for Fig. 2.

If we used three warehouses, we would arrange them as shown in Fig. 3.

The most primitive index of decentralization is n, the number of duplicate warehouses (Definition 6).

We would, in the general case, place the left-most warehouse at distance $D/2n$ miles from the left, and space $n-1$ warehouses D/n miles apart, the right-most warehouse being $D/2n$ miles from the right end. Each warehouse meets requests issuing from a distance of D/n or fewer miles to its right or left. Since a request, on the average, should originate ½ $(D/2n)$ miles to the right or left of the warehouse, the average transport distance is $D/4n$. The average delivery time (in hours) is the average distance divided by transport speed (miles per hour) or $D/4vn$.

This first approximation neglects the internal cost of processing and servicing each request within each facility. It also neglects congestion effects and instead assumes *unobstructed* channels of transport and communication. That is, it assumes that the input load L, in requests per unit of time, has no effect on the transmission speed v, and that it has no effect on the throughput rate of the system.

The maximum throughput rate of the system is defined as its capacity, called here M for objects and B for information, respectively (Definition 7).

If the system were partially obstructed, the speed v of transport or transmission would decline with rising input loads; if the system were *overloaded*, its throughput rate would decline with increasing inputs, and it would fall increasingly below the system's capacities M or B. In reality, there often is an extended range of traffic loads L over which the speed v remains substantially unchanged. In the present prototype example, however, we are assuming that this range extends all the way to the maximum capacity point and beyond it, so that v is treated as independent from L at all times. More realistic congestion effects and other complicating possibilities must be left for later treatment.

Suppose time were of no value to users, and only costs mattered to them. Then it would pay to increase the number, n, of facilities until the marginal increase in fixed costs is equal to the marginal decrease in delivery costs.

Let C_n be the cost of operating an organization with n warehouses. Let us assume that $C_n = nC$, namely that it costs simply n times as much to operate an n-warehouse organization as it does to operate a single repository. That is, the marginal increase in fixed costs is $C_n + 1 - C_n$ or just $(n + 1 - n)C$; that is, it is simply equal to C and remains therefore constant.

We have shown earlier that the average delivery cost per month for a system of n facilities is $cDL/4vn$. An increase by 1 in the number of facilities reduces this cost to $cDL/4v$ $(n + 1)$, by a difference of

$$\frac{cDL}{4v}\left(\frac{1}{n} - \frac{1}{n+1}\right)$$

which is

$$\frac{cDL}{4v}\,\frac{1}{n(n+1)}.$$

There is a point, therefore, where the savings from lower delivery costs will be just equal to or less than C, the increase in capital costs, and where it will no longer pay to increase n, the number of facilities, any further. We set C equal to

$$\frac{cDL}{4v}\,\frac{1}{n(n+1)}$$

and solve for n. The best number n of decentralized facilities thus would be the integer just larger than:

$$\frac{1}{2}\left(\sqrt{1 + \frac{cDL}{Cv}} - 1\right) \qquad (1)$$

The average service cost per request, S, of this optimal service is given by:

$$s = \frac{nC}{L} + \frac{cD}{4nv} \qquad (2)$$

Even these simple formulas have some interesting implications. Let us suppose the following possibilities, as in Table 2:

This simple exercise demonstrates —as does, of course, the formula

$$\frac{1}{2}\left(\sqrt{1 + \frac{cDL}{Cv}} - 1\right)$$

given earlier—that this simple model is equally sensitive over a wide range to proportionate changes in c, D, L, C and v, but is more sensitive to changes in C and v where these values are very small. The table also shows that decentralization may decline as capital costs and/or delivery speeds increase, but that it may increase

TABLE 2 SOME EXAMPLES OF OPTIMAL DECENTRALIZATION LEVELS

	Low Load, Low Delivery Cost		High Load, High Delivery Cost	
	LOW CAPITAL COST, LOW SPEED	HIGH CAPITAL COST, MEDIUM SPEED	HIGH CAPITAL COST, HIGH SPEED	VERY HIGH CAPITAL COST, VERY HIGH SPEED
	A	B	C	D
1. Distance D (miles)	3,000	3,000	3×10^3	3×10^3
2. Load (requests per month) L	3×10^4	3×10^4	3×10^6	3×10^6
3. Costs of delivery c ($ per hour)	0.10	0.10	10.-	10.-
4. Capital cost C ($ per month)	10^2	10^4	10^4	10^5
5. Velocity of transport v (miles per hour)	10	10^2	10^3	10^4
cDL	9×10^6	9×10^6	9×10^{10}	9×10^{10}
Hence Cv	10^3	10^6	10^7	10^9
Then optimum number of facilities N	47	1	47	5
Distance among facilities	64	-	64	600
Cost of service, S, in dollars per request	.32	1.08	.32	.32

again at high levels of capital cost and delivery speeds, if the load of service requests and the costs of delivery have risen faster.

This result tends to modify the suggestion of Herbert Simon and his associates, that the introduction of long-distance or intercontinental telephones makes it "unnecessary" for governments "to allow (their) representatives much discretion in the choice of decisional premises." Generally, they stress that "improved methods of communication have made a much greater degree of centralization possible."[10] If we are to judge what is probable or rational,

in addition to what is merely possible, we now may consider that a society which produces telephones also produces higher request rates, service demands, and decision loads for public and private agencies, and that they may become more affluent in regard to capital costs, so that the optimum degree of decentralized facilities may increase.

The optimum level of decentralization emerges as a systems property in response to changes, not in one parameter, but in the configuration of several critical parameters. Such a configuration may favor the excellent telephone service and considerable political decentralization of present-day Switzerland rather than the slow messenger service and the much greater political centralization of ancient Egypt or Tokugawa Japan.[11]

[10] Simon, Smithburg, & Thompson, *Public Administration*, pp. 275, 279. Simon's thoughtful comments on the various tendencies making for actual, rather than merely possible, centralization are wholly compatible with our analysis. The latter merely adds some emphasis on several no less real tendencies which may work in the opposite direction.

[11] On centralization and communication at earlier levels of technology, Lewis Mumford comments: "Action at a distance,

Even under the simplified assumptions of our prototype model, growth of the capitalization and performance of service organizations of all kinds, including governments, may rationally lead to decentralization or to centralization, depending on which of the relevant parameters grow at a greater rate.

TRANSPORTATION VS. TRANSMISSION: THE BULK OF OBJECTS AND THE LENGTH OF MESSAGES

Whether or not to service requests with a centralized or decentralized deployment of facilities depends to some extent on what is being requested: materials or information. Both are transmitted through channels in which they would move at characteristic primary speeds if the channels were unobstructed. In each case, however, these channels have limited capacities. They can, and usually do, become overloaded and obstructed with a resulting decline in the effective rate of flow. Thus, congested roads may cut the effective speed of traffic flow from 60 to 15 miles per hour; congested airports may cut the effective speed of downtown-to-downtown jet air travel from 600 miles per hour to 300 miles per

hour for airport-to-airport speed and 100 m.p.h. for downtown-to-downtown speeds. Similarly, overloaded switchboards and relays reduce the effective speed of electronic transmission from the theoretical limit of the speed of light (186,000 miles per second, or over .67 billion miles per hour, making light from the sun take about nine minutes to reach the earth) to an average effective speed varying from 1,000 to 10,000 miles per hour. Even when delayed in this manner, however, electronically-optically transmitted information will tend to move on the average about 100 times as fast as would bulky material objects. Communication thus differs from transport by several orders of magnitude in regard to the degree of centralization or decentralization which it makes relatively optimal.

At this point it becomes desirable to consider the bulk or weight of objects, measured in pounds or tons, and the length of messages, measured in bits of information. (Actually, we shall be more concerned here with orders of magnitude than with precise measurements.) The cost variable previously introduced measured the cost of "delivering an object" in response to a request, in dollars per hour. But c depends not only on the speed but on the nature of the object as well. It costs more to deliver a massive object than a light one. It costs more to deliver a voluminous message that requires wider and costlier communication channels than to deliver a brief message.

As to the average volume of transmission per request, we shall call it m for material objects and measure it in pounds or tons; and we shall call it b when referring to the transmission of information, which is measured conventionally in "bits." (A bit

---

through scribes and swift messengers, was one of the identifying marks of the new megamachine (the centralized state)... 'The scribe, he directeth every work that is in this land,' an Egyptian New Kingdom composition tells us... They made possible the constant 'report to political headquarters' essential for a centralized organization": *The Myth of the Machine* (New York: Harcourt Brace, 1967), p. 192. Cf. also Harold A. Innis, *Empire and Communication* (Oxford: Oxford University Press, 1950).

Table 3 Summary of Key Variables

3a. Basic Variables

D = length of strip, in miles, typically 3,000 for a big country, 300 for little one

L = total load, in requests per month, about 30,000 for heavy demand, 3,000 for low demand

C = fixed cost for one facility, in dollars per month, about 10,000 for an expensive facility and 100 for a cheap one

v = average transport speed under actual traffic conditions, in miles per hour, about 1,000 for jet speeds and 10 to 100 for ground passenger speeds

m = mass or bulk of items to be transported in response to requests, in pounds, about 100 for massive objects to 1 for light ones

b = amount of information in an average message delivered in response to a request, in bits, from 10 megabits for a second's worth of TV to 10,000 for a printed page's worth

B' = rates of information transmission under channel conditions, in bits/second, from 10^7 for video to 2,000 for digital telephone

3b. Parameters	Unit Transport Cost	Average Cost to Service Request	Assumption
Simplest Model $(m = 0)$	c_v, dollars per hour, for transport at a speedcapacity of v miles per hour	$c_v \cdot \dfrac{D}{4nv}$	$v = V$
Bulk Taken into Account	c_{MV}', dollars per pound per hour, for transport characterized by speedbulk capacity of MV pound-miles per hour	$c_{MV}' \cdot m \dfrac{D}{4nv}$	$mv = MV$
Digital	c_B'', dollars per mile per hour, for communication characterized by a capacity of B bits per second	$c_B'' \dfrac{D}{4n} \dfrac{1}{3600} \cdot \dfrac{b}{B'}$	$B' = B$

is a single yes-or-no decision, such as the on-or-off position of a switch, or a dot or dash in the Morse code, or a black or white point on a television screen. A single digit number corresponds to about four bits, a teletype letter six bits, an average English word about thirty bits, a printed page in a book about 10,000 bits, a 300-page book three megabits, i.e., three million bits, and over twenty megabits for one second's picture on a normal television screen.) The capacity of a transportation channel then is the amount of mass M it can move times the velocity v (i.e., distance/time) at which it can do so under the best traffic conditions. The formula for this is Mv for the overall capacity of the channel and mv for its effective capacity in regard to the

size and speed of transmitting and/or servicing the average request. Both Mv and mv are formally analogous to the concept of momentum in mechanics. As it takes force to change momentum in mechanics, so it takes innovation—in the form of visible investment in capital equipment and/or invisible investment in new technology—to change capacity in a transport channel (e.g., to a supersonic transport aircraft). The change in capacity Mv is then a possible measure of the effect (or "force") of innovation in respect to the overall capacity of a channel, and the change in mv similarly would measure its effect in regard to the servicing of average sized requests.

Decentralization often depends critically on the effective service capacities of the available transport and communication channels, and changes in the optimum level of decentralization for a given organization, government or service.

The following table may clarify some of the relations between capacities, rates and the different conditions examined so far.

Actual rather than maximum transmission speeds, however, are very nearly the same for a person-to-person call over a distance of thirty miles and over a distance of 3,000 miles and what really counts is not the velocity in miles per hour but the capacity in bits per second. The value of v for telephone, telegraph, wireless via radio or television, etc., is substantially the same for local as for long-distance communication, though, of course, the cost differs. These channels differ mainly in their capacity, in how many bits, or bv, similar to v per second of information, mv for materials. In the communication processes, therefore, the number of duplicated facilities does not depend very much on geography with respect to saving message delivery time. The distribution of overall channel capacities, B (bits per second), and data transmission rates B', in place of bv (i.e., message speed times message length), plays a much more central role in this regard. A low value of B is about 2,000 bits per second for voice-grade telephone lines, and a high value about 200,000 bits per second for wireless transmission, such as radio telephony or telegraphy, and at least one hundred times this amount for television.

These considerations permit us to make our notion of current transport costs somewhat more realistic. Let us begin with the case of bulk movements, such as mail, freight, or personnel. We have previously considered c, or more precisely, c_V, as the transport cost in dollars per hour depending only on speed capacity, but regardless of the bulk to be moved. Now let us consider, instead, $c'MV$ as the transport cost in dollars per pound transported per hour for a carrier with capacity MV. Here it costs more to move the same bulk of freight more quickly, as airmail and airfreight cost more than do slower services, but it also still costs more to move a larger number of pounds at unchanged speeds. The average transport cost per request is simply $c'MV$ times m times D/v. The optimal number of facilities can therefore be calculated with these refined assumptions by the formula:

$$\frac{1}{2}\left(\sqrt{1 + \frac{c'_{MV}DLm}{Cv}} - 1\right) \qquad (3)$$

The average cost of service S' per request of average shipment weight m then becomes:

$$S' = \frac{nC}{L} + \frac{c'Dm}{4nv} \qquad (4)$$

and the total cost of service $S'' = S'L$ (Formula 4a).

In order to take into account in these formulas the weight of the average shipment, we had to replace c/C by c'/C and D/v by mD/v, while the total load of requests, L, has remained unchanged. If $c'_{MV} = m$, the cost of transporting the shipments of average weight m, equals c_V, the average transport cost of filling a request, then the weight of the average shipment would make no difference for the optimum level of decentralization, and the results of Table 2 would remain unchanged. If, however, an increase in the average weight of shipment would bring about an increase in the transport cost, then the optimum number of facilities would increase, in proportion to the square root of the change: a 100-fold increase in average shipment weight (and cost) would then require approximately a 10-fold increase in the most efficient number of facilities.

Let us assume that an administrative agency has to consult a file on each case on which it has to make a decision. Servicing a case would then require either transporting, on the average, one pound of documents from the repository to the site of the request, or else transmitting the information in those documents over a long distance computer channel. The file to be transmitted is assumed to contain the equivalent of a 200-page book, that is, about 4 million bits, or 4 megabits.[12] According to formula (3), the optimal number of facilities for electronic transmission under the above assumptions is now sixteen. This is more than three times as many as in the earlier case presented in column D of Table 2, where the transmission costs depended only on speeds and not on the amount of information being transmitted to service the average request.

Had we sent our four megabits by express messenger service at the rate of $c' = \$.04$ per pound-hour, then the optimal number of facilities, according to formula (2), would be three. In other words, *under the assumptions of our example, a slower service based on messengers or mail delivery could be much more highly centralized than a fast service based on a computer-based or satellite-based communication net.*

It might be interesting to compare the total costs for these two kinds of service. Let us recall that each of them would have to cope with 3 million requests per month, each request requiring transmission of four megabits. The cost of servicing requests by digital telephone—called "dataphone"—transmission would be $1.05 per request, compared with $.20 per request for service by mail or express messenger. *The five-fold increase in cost,* however, *here would buy a sixty-fold increase in speed.* The dataphone replies would be available within little more than half an hour, in contrast to the thirty hours response time required for the more highly centralized service based on messengers or mail.

The situation is similar in some respects to the transmission of messages through communication channels. Here c_B'' is the cost of transmission for a channel with a capacity (maximum rate) of B bits per second, in dollars per hour per mile. The average cost of servicing a request would then be $c_B''/3600 \cdot b/B \cdot D/4n$, because $D/4n$ is the average distance from a request to its nearest service facility when there are n such facilities. The actual cost of telephone transmission does not increase in *direct* proportion to distance; it increases by less for large distances than it does for small distances, but this will be neglected for the purpose of this paper. The cost c_B'' for long distance telephone is about $.02 per mile

[12] This calculation assumes roughly the usual average of 6 bits per character, 80 characters per line, and 42 lines per page. For further discussion, see Manfred Kochen (ed.), *The Growth of Knowledge* (New York: John Wiley, 1967); also Manfred Kochen, "Newer Techniques for Processing Bibliographic Information," *In* F. Kilgour (ed.), *Proceedings of the Symposium on Data Processing in University Libraries* (Phila.: Drexel Institute of Technology, 1968).

per hour for ordinary long-distance transmission. (This would amount to $3.00 for a three-minute business-hour call from Boston to San Francisco and $1.00 for a similar Boston-Chicago call.) Such a channel is characterized by a capacity of $B = 2000$ bits per second.

The formula for computing the optimal number of facilities in this case is therefore

$$\frac{1}{2}\left(\sqrt{1 + \frac{c_B{}''}{C} \cdot \frac{1}{3600} \cdot \frac{b}{B} \cdot D \cdot L} - 1\right). \quad (5)$$

Note that we have replaced c/C and D/v in formula (1), or c'/C and Dm/v in formula (2) by $c_B{}''/C$ and $1/3600 \cdot b/B$ respectively.

THE VALUE OF TIME: A FIRST APPROACH THROUGH OPTIMIZATION

In the primitive model treated so far, no value was assigned to time. Users were assumed not to care how long they had to wait for service. In fact, however, users find service with smaller delivery time more valuable than service with high delivery time. Similarly, clients or constituents of a governmental agency often request decisions which are to be acceptable to them in substance but which are valued more highly if they are prompt in time. In some other studies, the probability that a government, or a governmental agency, will produce within an acceptable time an acceptable response to the average demand upon it has been called the *responsiveness* of that agency.[13] Responsive-

ness and mean response time thus may be included among the highly relevant performance indicators of governments and their agencies. This section of our inquiry will attempt to make explicit some possible relationships between response time, the utility of time to the average user, and the degree of decentralization.

As a first step, let us assume a single "representative user" with the properties of both the average and the median users of the service, who are assumed to be identical. (We assume at this point uniform distribution of locations and utilities for all users).

The net worth, W, of the institution is its utility to the user minus the cost to operate it. Figure 4 shows a possible relation between utility and communication speed, compared with approximate current rates for sending a brief message across 1000 miles in the United States.

It is difficult to infer even very roughly the shape of the demand curve of the American people for speed of transmission of their messages. It is illuminating, however, to plot the rates for the transmission of messages by telephone, telegraph, and mail (air and regular). All these rates have been set by complex processes. These are at least partially responsive to the political demand generated by the population in their roles as interest groups and citizens. Since these rates have remained rela-

---

[13] On the concept of responsiveness, see K. W. Deutsch, S. A. Burrell, *et al.*, *Political Community and the North Atlantic Area* (Princeton: Princeton University Press, 1957, 1968), pp. 40–41, 199–200; Bruce M. Russett, *Community and Contention: Britain and America in the Twentieth Century* (Cambridge: M.I.T. Press, 1963), pp. 29–30; Dean Y. Pruitt, "Definition of the Situation as a Determinant of International Action," *In* Herbert C. Kelman (ed.), *International Behavior: A Social-Psychological Analysis* (New York: Holt, Rinehart and Winston, 1965), pp. 397–99.

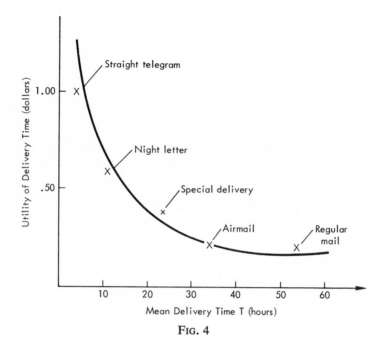

FIG. 4

tively stable and have not aroused intense opposition, they can serve as indicators of acceptability. Fitting a curve to these data suggests a monotonically decreasing function of rate versus delivery time such as shown in this figure.

Let us first consider the case of a society which can afford to back up its utilities completely with actual purchasing power representing all the required resources. Such a society might then consider increasing the number of decentralized facilities *n* so long as this increases the net worth to the society. It would stop increasing only when the marginal increase in net worth with *n* duplicated centers is zero. This enables us to derive a formula for *n*, which depends on the utility of time. The higher the utility of time, the more we shall be willing to pay for higher speeds of response or of service.

The utility of time will be large in a society that has urgent needs to save time or that puts great cultural value on speed (which some critics of contemporary Western culture might call impatience), or whose members have many attractive alternative opportunities for occupying, so that the opportunity cost of time to them is raised sometimes to an oppressive degree.[14] Our *R* may reflect a combination of all these pressures. The same cultural factors of urgency and impatience would be reflected to an even greater extent in the shape of a curve describing the variation of utility with response time. The greater

[14] On the general problem of the "quality of life," which is connected with our growing lack of and need for time, compare John Kenneth Galbraith, *The Affluent Society* (New York: Houghton-Mifflin, 1958) and *The New Industrial State* (New York: Houghton-Mifflin, 1967).

the society's concern with speed, the steeper the curve will be.

In the case just presented, the optimal degree of decentralization would be to make n as large as possible if the value of time is larger than the increase in total cost. If the opposite condition holds and increases in the speed of response on service are valued less highly than the increases in cost resulting from increases in decentralization, then the optimum number for n is 1; that is, complete centralization. A society as rich and as pressed for time, therefore, as we assumed it to be in this example would tend to go to one extreme or the other: complete centralization or decentralization. The tendencies toward substituting in many parts of the United States individual transportation by personal automobile instead of public transportation may resemble in some ways the second of these trends—up to the point, at least, where mutual interference among automobiles on congested streets and highways becomes critical.

MORE REFINED MODELS:
REDUNDANCY AND FLUCTUATIONS IN
DEMAND

Using multiple facilities for more dependable service. In the models analyzed so far, we assumed that if there are n duplicated facilities, any one of which could have serviced all the L requests per month, then each facility is used only $1/n$th of the time. Each is to some degree redundant, therefore, for each now services only L/n requests per month. For a decentralized organization, with large n, the utilization percentage is quite low and redundancy is high. If low response time has very high utility—i.e., the

value of R is high—and transmission costs are high but fixed costs are not too high, then such low utilization is tolerable. The unused portion of the time, however, has considerable potential value in:

(a) insurance against the effects of breakdown;
(b) smoothing losses due to fluctuating demands and busy local facilities;
(c) control of errors.

Clearly this average delivery time increases with the probability of breakdown in one particular facility, but in proportion to n. As we decentralize, we gain more side benefits in reduced mean time loss due to failure. The greater the transmission speed v, the greater the effect of this time saving. Technical progress may confront designers with a choice between increasing the speed or the reliability of their equipment. Decentralization and redundancy, at higher cost but at the same level of technology, may permit them to have both.

Total response time and fluctuations in demand. Instead of mean delivery time $\bar{T}_n$, it would be more realistic to consider the total response time Q_n. This is the total time lapse between the epoch the request originates and the epoch the information or item requested is received by the requestor at the site where it originated. It is this turn-around time which matters to the originator of a request. This is the sum of three terms:

$$Q_n = F_n + S_n + T_n \qquad (6)$$

Here F_n is the time to transmit and forward the request from its source to the nearest station able to service it.

It is the run-around time, which

the customer does not notice, apart from the turn-around time.

Next, we let Sn be the time it takes to service the request at that station, including the time at the other stations which had to decide whether to pass it on and to do so.

Finally, T_n is the time to transmit or transport the results back to the source, as defined before.

Since we can calculate $\bar{T}_n$, we can do likewise for $\bar{F}_n$ and $\bar{S}_n$. The latter term, the internal service time S_n, includes the time needed for decision-making and the possible delays resulting from the overloading of the decision-making capabilities of the service organization or bureaucratic agency. This aspect of the problem has received a good deal of attention in the literature of organization theory and management science.[15]

If the total demand is L' requests per hour, then each of n stations has to service L'/n requests per hour under the assumption of uniformity over length D of the strip. If we assume 10×30 or 300 hours per month, then $L = 300 \, L'$ where L is the load in requests per month, as previously defined. If one service could handle the total demand, its service time must be $S = 1/L'$ hours per request. Thus n replicated facilities offering this service could handle n times this total demand or each be utilized only a fraction $1/n$ of the time. On the other hand, slower services, with service time $S_n = n/L'$, could be used to handle the same demand, and these would be utilized one-hundred percent.

Of course, the cost of such a slower service with service time n/L' hours per request should not be C, the cost of a service with $S = 1/L'$ hours per

request; it should be lower. Since many identical such services are required, their fixed cost C_n might be lowered still further, at least in regard to those components that could be produced in quantity.

If the demand is not constant in time, but fluctuates randomly, and if the capacity of each facility is only equal to the average demand, then there will be times when a request cannot be serviced by the nearest server because it is busy. In that event, the request is forwarded according to the same pattern used for routing when the nearest server was down. If the request has to be rerouted several times, $\bar{F}_n$ becomes a "run-around time," comparable to the possibly longer or shorter waiting time in a queue or single centralized facility. In either case, the effective waiting time may exceed the waiting capacity or tolerance of the client, as in the case of emergency patients for hospitals, or of emergency responses in military or police systems, or in urgent local or national political decisions.

The formulas and calculations involved even in this simplified model would permit us to derive conditions on R and optimal n in many additional pages of more complex mathematics. For this reason, as well as for reason of the greater flexibility in modeling more realistic systems, it seems desirable for future work to obtain these quantities by computer, either by evaluating complex formulas or by Monte-Carlo simulation.

In this more realistic and complex analysis, we suppose that the service time, s, per server varies with the percentage u "he" is utilized. That is, u is the percentage of time a facility is utilized.

If u is small, $s(u)$ is high. He is slow because he is out of practice,

[15] See references in notes 2–6, above.

because start-up time causes delays, etc. If u is close to 100%, $s(u)$ is also high. He is slow again, this time because he is overloaded. Some services don't get done at all if the server is too overloaded, and this may be far more costly than under-utilizing him; this is especially true when the value of the service is high, as in cases where the server is a highly paid executive. For intermediate values of u, $s(u)$ is moderate. A curve like $s(u) = s_0 (u - u_0)^2 + s_{00}$ might represent the general shape of the curve.

SOME IMPLICATIONS FOR ORGANIZATION THEORY AND POLITICS: SOME SECULAR CHANGES IN KEY VARIABLES

Our crude models suggested that a greater number of multiple service facilities, n, and hence a higher degree of decentralization, becomes rational with an increase in the load or volume of services demanded. Also, a higher degree of decentralization becomes desirable with an increase in the value of time, and in those portions of service costs which are related to time and/or distance.

Our models further suggested that this optimal degree of decentralization increases with a decrease in the proportion of the fixed capital costs of the service among its total costs; and they suggest that the optimum degree of decentralization also increases with any decrease in the margins of error and of breakdown that are considered acceptable in the performance of the service.

All these decentralization-promoting conditions will tend to increase with economic growth and technological development. Let us first consider changes in direct costs. If other things remain equal, then the optimal number of decentralized facilities for a service increases in proportion to the square root of the ratio of its time-distance costs c to its capital costs C. Secular trends toward highly advanced levels of economic and technological development make human labor more expensive, and they make capital goods relatively cheaper. Thus they may tend to increase this ratio, and hence the desirable degree of decentralization. Some economic data suggest that this may have happened, both in Communist and non-Communist countries. An increase in real wages normally represents an increase in the price of labor relative to the price of goods, including capital goods, and hence also an increase in the c/C ratio. In many advanced countries of the world during recent decades, real wages have tended to grow on the average at about three percent per year, thus doubling every twenty-three years. If real wages should grow fourfold in the course of a half-century, while capital costs would not, then at the end of such a period the optimal number of decentralized facilities for a wide variety of services may well have as much as doubled during the same time. If capital costs should grow somewhat but less than real wages, there would still be a net tendency toward some decentralization, albeit to a lesser extent.

Demographic, economic and technological growth in many countries in recent decades, very roughly speaking, has proceeded at annual rates of about 2 percent and 3 percent, respectively, adding up to about annual 5 percent increase in the demands for many services, and doubling about every 14 years the load upon many of the public or private centers that have to supply them. Such increases in loads include the volume of demands for many political, administrative, judicial and quasi-judicial decisions and responses, as well as for many services and for the communication and transportation they imply.[16] Moreover, as technological

[16]In the 1950s, the average rate of per capita income growth in 68 countries, comprising 86 percent of the world's population, was about 3 percent, while the average rate of population growth in 111 countries, with 97 percent of mankind was 2.3 percent. (B. M. Russett, *et al., World Handbook of Political and Social Indicators,* New Haven: Yale University Press, 1964, pp. 46–48, 160–61.) More recently, in 1960–66, world population increased at an annual rate of 1.9 percent. During the last two decades, total GNP in many countries may have been rising, therefore, at about 5 percent per year, and thus doubling every 14 years. Request loads and service loads in many fields, including governments may have grown at about the same rate as GNP. *United Nations Demographic Yearbook,* 1966 (New York: 1967), p. 95. During the same years, 1960–66, the population of the United States increased at the rate of 1.4 percent, while its gross national product in constant 1958 prices grew at 4.8 percent. Murders and non-negligent homicides grew at 2.3 percent, all accidents at 2.8 percent, domestic mail at 3.5 percent, and daily telephone conversations at 5.0 percent, and automobile thefts at about 7 percent. In contrast to this, the average speed of motor vehicles increased only at 1.4 percent a year, and about the same low rate held for the 1945–66 period. The average speed of aircraft on scheduled domestic air carrier routes increased at about 3.5 percent for 1950–67 period, but rose more quickly, at 5.0 percent, during the years 1960–67, and the speed of aircraft on international flights in 1960–67 increased at about 7 percent per year. (Approximate rates, computed from data in the *Statistical Abstract of the United States 1967,* pp. 58, 86, 505, 508–509, 561 and 586; and *ibid.,* 1968, pp. 6, 550 and 573; and *Uniform Crime Reports for the United States,* 1960, p. 2, and *ibid.,*

progress speeds up transport and communication, it increases the opportunity cost of time, since more things now could be done or experienced in each unit of time than had been the case earlier. Finally, highly modernized and automated technologies may require higher levels of accuracy and reliability of service. Thus they may need more redundancy of facilities as an insurance against error and breakdown.

Perhaps most importantly, the growing need for greater precision and adaptability of responses to the increasingly complex, diverse and changing needs of people will require in many cases more frequent dialogs and feedback cycles of back-and-forth communication between service centers and customers, agencies and clients, administrators and constituents, the rulers and the ruled. This will multiply the effective distance D (regardless of whether it is measured in rules, switching points, or intervening obstacles or opportunities); it will multiply it by the average number of feedback cycles of communication, travel or transport required to ensure an acceptable fit between each specific demand and the particular response to it. The current demands for more popular partici-

1965, p. 3.) These figures exclude, however, the delays caused by getting to and from the airports, and the delays by traffic congestion on the ground, and in the air above many airports. If these delays are taken into account, it seems plausible that many activities, calling for public service, now may be growing faster than does our effective speed in moving persons and goods in daily practice. Something similar may apply to telephone communications: a telephone call from Washington to San Francisco during business hours does not get through much more quickly to the individual we want to reach in a busy office than it did in 1945.

pation, initiative and communication "from below," if heeded, would have similar effects: it would increase the average number of feedback cycles needed, and hence often the importance of distance and proximity. Each of these changes makes for an increase in the degree of desirable decentralization.

Under the assumptions of our models it seems quite possible, therefore, that many of the highly modernized and automated societies and nations which we may find by the end of this century will by then require a much greater degree of decentralization in public and private services than the one to which we are accustomed now. Doubtless some of these assumptions will have to be replaced by more realistic ones. In particular, refining our simple concept of decentralization, introducing the notion of hierarchies of facilities, and revising the assumption of uniform distribution of demand in space and time, all may well modify some of our findings. The present paper already may suggest, however, that the naive images of a future of ever increasing centralization in business organizations, public services, national governments, and the international political systems may have to be revised.

part three

SIZE, COMPLEXITY, AND ADMINISTRATION

INTRODUCTION

The relationship between organizational size, complexity, and administration has challenged students of organization since Weber and Durkheim. However, only recently a body of empirical research has emerged which has sought to deal with the question of why and to what extent organizations become more bureaucratized as they grow in size. Probably the best-known joke and the most widely shared stereotype pertaining to organizations and bureaucracy is the notion that work expands proportionally with the time available for its completion, and that organizations become inevitably more bureaucratized as they grow larger.[1]

Among sociologists dealing with this question systematically, Terrien and Mills were the first of a long line of researchers tackling the problem on an empirical basis. Using data on a total of 428 California school districts and grouping them by size, the authors find that the mean percentage of the administrative component increases with the size of the district. This finding, they conclude, indicates that organizational growth leads to an increase in administrative functions.

Anderson and Warkov use a simple and elegant design to test Terrien and Mills' hypothesis on the basis of data on forty-nine Veterans Administration TB and general hospitals. The findings reveal that the administrative component is negatively related to organizational size, but that it is positively related to "functional complexity," a concept comprising both the number of objectives and the extent of internal differentiation. Functional complexity is assumed to intervene between the effects of organizational size and the administrative component. In reinterpreting Terrien and Mills' findings in terms of the intervening effect of complexity, the authors suggest three new hypotheses: (1) the relative size of the administrative component decreases as the number

[1] C. Northcote Parkinson, *Parkinson's Law* (New York: Ballantine Books, 1964), pp. 15–27.

of persons performing identical tasks in the same place increases; (2) it increases as the number of places at which work is performed increases; and (3) it increases as the number of tasks performed at the same place increases. The authors thus suggest at least two aspects of the organizational task structure which are seen as affecting the relative size of the administrative apparatus, independently of size: functional complexity and the extent of geographical dispersion (e.g., number of locations).

Rushing's study of the relation between size, complexity, and administration in forty-one industries constitutes another test of the Anderson-Warkov hypothesis. Like these previous authors, Rushing finds that the administrative component is inversely related to size, but directly to complexity. Rushing, however, adds certain refinements to the analysis of these relationships. For example, he shows that size and complexity *interact* with each other in their effect on the relative size of the administrative component, a condition already suggested for hospitals (Heydebrand, 7 this volume). Furthermore, Rushing separates managerial from clerical personnel and other staff categories, thus specifying and elaborating the hypotheses suggested by Anderson and Warkov. It should be noted that Rushing is one of the first sociologists to use an adapted version of the Gibbs-Martin index of division of labor, thus providing a direct and quantitative measure of "complexity," similar to the adaptation of the Gibbs-Martin index and the Gini index used for measuring the division of labor in hospitals.[2]

Pondy, in developing a mathematical model of a manufacturing firm, provides both a critical reappraisal of previous research on the administrative component as well as new evidence, based on data from forty-five industries. Unlike Rushing, however, he uses a combined proportion of managerial, clerical and professional personnel, treating all three as constituent elements of his measure of "administrative intensity." Similarly to Kochen and Deutsch's concern with the cost-benefit ratio as a basis for administrative and economic rationality, Pondy assumes that the relative size of the administrative staff will reflect profit-maximizing behavior on the part of the top executive. Pondy finds that "administrative intensity" is inversely associated with size, but directly with functional complexity (using Rushing's adaptation of the Gibbs-Martin index). In addition, a most interesting finding is that administrative intensity increases with the separation of ownership and management, i.e., with the rationalization and differentiation of top managerial functions. Pondy thus adds an important aspect of the organizational control structure to the analysis, an aspect not unrelated to the dimension of organizational autonomy found to be so salient in the case of hospitals, other service organizations, and busi-

---

[2] For the original adaptation of the Gibbs-Martin index and its application to organizational analysis, see Wolf Heydebrand, "Differential Modes of Coordination in Formal Organizations," paper presented at the Annual Meetings of the American Sociological Association, Los Angeles, 1963; see also Heydebrand, selection 7 in this volume.

ness organizations (Elling and Halebsky, 6; Heydebrand, 7; Kriesberg, 11; Hall, 25, and Pugh et al., 2 and 23).

While a formal theory of organizations is beginning to emerge from these empirical studies—combining, as it does, technological and managerial determinants of structure—its formulation at this point would probably lead to hasty and premature conclusions. One reason is that such a formulation would be restricted to only a few variables such as size, division of labor, administrative staff, technology, and decision making; another reason is that it would be applicable only to a limited number of functional types of organizations.[3]

The last three studies in this section introduce as a separate dimension the aspect stressed by Pondy: discretion and decision making. Whereas Pondy had merely suggested the structural importance of managerial discretion and rationality by showing the relative fit between degree of incorporation of establishments (relative autonomy) and the profit and utility models, respectively, these other studies provide actual measures of power distribution, centralization, and other structural aspects of decision making.

Boland's study of 115 colleges and universities is published here for the first time. It focuses on two aspects of the organizational control structure: those specialized administrative functions concerned with "external relations"; and the distribution of power among different levels such as administration vs. faculty senate, on the one hand, and academic subject matter departments, on the other. The study is an extension and elaboration of the well-known earlier analysis, co-authored by Boland, of the relation between organizational size and the administrative component in colleges and universities.[4]

Boland shows that larger colleges and universities have a high external relations ratio, i.e., a specialized administrative subcomponent or "center" which mediates between organization and environment. The author also shows that larger institutions of higher learning have more powerful faculty governments, as well as more autonomous academic subject matter departments. The study thus provides further evidence which serves to qualify the popular stereotype of the positive effect of size on the centralization of administrative decision making. Clearly, in large educational institutions it is the professional staff—rather than the line structure which is perceived to have more power.[5] How-

---

[3] For two attempts in the direction of formalization, both involving the same data on government agencies, viz., employment security departments, see Sheila R. Klatzky, "Relationship of Organizational Size to Complexity and Coordination," *Administrative Science Quarterly*, 15 (Dec. 1970), 428–38; and Peter M. Blau, "A Formal Theory of Differentiation in Organizations," *American Sociological Review*, 35 (Apr. 1970), 201–18. The same analysis is reported in Peter M. Blau and Richard Schoenherr, *The Structure of Organizations* (New York: Basic Books, 1971).

[4] Amos H. Hawley, Walter Boland and Margaret Boland, "Population Size and Administration in Institutions of Higher Learning," *American Sociological Review*, 30 (Apr. 1965), 252–55.

[5] As Etzioni has pointed out, the staff-line relationship in professional organizations, such as universities, tends to be reversed compared to other functional types; see Amitai

ever, if one were to control for organizational autonomy (ownership and control), one might, in turn, be able to qualify these conclusions since, e.g., in large state universities the faculty may have less de facto power than in large private educational institutions.

Another interesting aspect of Boland's study is the use of a more differentiated concept of "administrative staff." Thus, Boland shows that certain specialized administrative functions—such as those pertaining to external relations —do increase with increasing organizational size whereas, in the original study by Hawley et al., the total administrative component was shown to decline with increasing size.

Pugh, Hickson, Hinings, and Turner provide a comprehensive scheme for defining and operationalizing certain central aspects of the internal structure of organizations. The authors derived a wealth of data from interviews with managers and department heads in fifty-two organizations in and around Birmingham, England. Of the fifty-two organizations, forty-six constitute a random sample stratified by size and product or purpose. The units of analysis are "employing units" of varying types of ownership and legal status, and include various manufacturing and service organizations. The results of this and the many other studies published by the authors can, therefore, be generalized to a large class of work organizations.

The present paper is mainly of a methodological nature. The authors start out with six basic concepts or "primary dimensions" of organization structure: (1) specialization, (2) standardization, (3) formalization, (4) centralization, (5) configuration, and (6) flexibility. These concepts are then operationalized in terms of sixty-four component variables, most of them scales constructed from the interviews and from other documentary materials. The third step involves a factor analysis of the scales, resulting in four main factors: structuring of activities, concentration of authority, line control of workflow, and size of the supportive component. The analysis of these four structural factors in terms of the organizational context is reported in another paper (Pugh et al., 2).

Etzioni, "Authority Structure and Organizational Effectiveness," *Administrative Science Quarterly*, 4 (June 1959), 43–67.

18. THE EFFECT OF CHANGING SIZE UPON THE INTERNAL STRUCTURE OF ORGANIZATIONS*

Frederic W. Terrien and Donald L. Mills

Ever since Plato observed that 5040 was a desirable number of people for a civic population, social thinkers have been speculating about the possible effect of the size of a social grouping upon the relations therein. Although few have developed their observations to the level of theory or have undertaken research in this area, a number of sociologists have made statements which are of interest. The effect of quantity is implicit in the *Gemeinschaft-Gesellschaft* formulation of Toennies, in the comments of Durkheim concerning his concept of *anomie*, and in the explorations of bureaucracy by Max Weber. Davis notes that "undoubtedly the character of the group tends to change with its size . . . ,"[1] and Williams says that "even in a structurally simple group . . . the addition of members rapidly produces changes in the internal organization."[2] It is the opinion of Bierstedt that "as social interaction is intensified by increase in size of population, so do the different kinds of relationships increase."[3] Coyle makes the specific statement that "structural form is itself affected by the number of those involved. The addition of new units in the process transforms it not only quantitatively, but also qualitatively."[4] These authors, along with Merton, Selznick, von Wiese, and others, have commented evocatively on the effect of group size upon internal relationships, but it is perhaps Simmel who has been most impressed

Reprinted by permission of the American Sociological Association from *American Sociological Review*, 20 (February 1955), 11–13.

* Paper read at the annual meeting of the American Sociological Society, August, 1953. The research reported here was supported by the Kellogg Foundation through its Cooperative Program in Educational Administration. The authors are indebted to Dr. Quinn McNemar and to Mr. Glenn Walker of Stanford University for their advice and assistance in processing the data.

[1] Kingsley Davis, *Human Society* (New York: The Macmillan Company, 1950), p. 293.

[2] Robin M. Williams, Jr., *American Society*. (New York: Alfred A. Knopf, 1951), p. 458 (footnote).

[3] Robert Bierstedt, "The Limitations of Anthropological Methods in Sociology," *The American Journal of Sociology*, 54 (July, 1948), 22–30.

[4] G. L. Coyle, *Social Processes in Organized Groups* (New York: Richard R. Smith, Inc., 1930), p. 89.

with the potentialities of size change. It was his belief that "when a change is directly required by a purely quantitative modification of the group, . . . the size immediately determines the form."[5]

Inasmuch as one of the most notable characteristics of the contemporary Western world appears to be a proliferation of formal organizations, the problem of the effects of size *per se* seems to be deserving of exploration. More specifically, a study of the size relationship of administrative components to their total containing organizations should yield some information about the effect of size upon the nature of intraorganizational structure.

Accordingly, the following hypothesis was formulated: The relationship between the size of an administrative component and the total size of its containing organization is such that the larger the size of the containing organization the greater will be the proportion given over to its administrative component.

Some guidance is available in sociological prototheory. Keller has written that "civilization is a function of numbers and the contact of numbers."[6] It is clear that an increase in the numbers of a group brings about an almost geometrical increase in the potential relationships therein. Bossard has noted that the relationship between even two persons increases in the order of triangular numbers as the group increases by simple whole numbers.[7] The total of all possible kinds of relationships is, of course, much higher. If the point be taken as axiomatic that the number of potential intragroup relationships increases at a greater rate than does the size of the group, then it would seem logical to suppose that those relationships would require at least a moderately increasing amount of supervision.

For the purpose of testing the hypothesis it was necessary to select a series of organizations which distributed themselves over a continuum of size and at the same time maintained a consistency of function. This objective was achieved in the selection of the school districts of one state—California. Here were a limited number of types of organized groupings, ranging in size from one to several thousand employees, performing the same general function and circumscribed by much the same legislation and directives.

The State of California contains 2081 school districts, divided into elementary, high school, unified and city, and junior college districts. Only the first three types were utilized in the test of the hypothesis because the junior college districts were too few in number. The sample was drawn in the following manner: The state's 58 counties were ranked and placed into eight strata according to the total yearly budget of districts in each county. Slightly less than half of the counties in each stratum were selected randomly, yielding a sample of 25 counties. The offices of the County Superintendents furnished job rosters of their systems for the school year

[5] Georg Simmel, "The Number of Members as Determining the Sociological Form of Groups," I and II, *The American Journal of Sociology*, 8 (1902– 3), 1–46, 158–96. See also, Kurt H. Wolff, *The Sociology of Georg Simmel* (Glencoe, Ill.: The Free Press, 1950).

[6] Albert G. Keller, *Societal Evolution* (New York: The Macmillan Company, 1931), p. 26.

[7] James H. S. Bossard, "The Law of Family Interaction," *The American Journal of Sociology*, 50 (Jan., 1945), pp. 292–94.

TABLE 1 ELEMENTARY SCHOOL DISTRICTS

Group Designation	Number in Group	Size Range	Administrative Component Mean Percentage	Standard Deviation
Small	178	10–49	9.5	4.1
Medium	60	50–149	12.6	3.2
Large	26	150–626	13.9	3.0

1951–52. However, an inspection of these data revealed relatively few districts with a large number of school system employees. The sample of school districts was therefore enlarged to include all districts having an average daily attendance of 2000 or more students, which were not already in the sample. This was done in order to yield a statistically more reliable picture of the larger sized organizations.

Next, criteria were established to allow a uniform distinction between administrative and non-administrative personnel in the few instances where the personnel rosters did not make this distinction. The administrative component of the school district included the superintendent, his assistants and immediate staff, principals, business managers and' the like. Persons in the non-administrative component were teachers, nurses, custodians, cafeteria workers and the like. Students were not included. Each of the three types of districts was divided into three groups—small, medium and large, and administrative sizes computed in terms of mean percentages of the total personnel involved therein.

Of the 1747 *elementary districts* in California, data were secured on 732. Because of the fact that in organizations of less than ten persons, one person does several jobs of both an administrative and non-administrative character, it seemed justifiable to remove from consideration those 468 elementary districts in which the total organization numbered less than ten. Hence, small districts were designated as those numbering from ten up to fifty; medium, as those from fifty up to 150; and large, as those of 150 and over. The mean percentage of each group which was administrative was 9.5, 12.6 and 13.9 respectively. Table 1 summarizes these findings. When the small group was compared with the large group, the difference between the means was 4.4, and the C.R. was 6.8, significant beyond the .001 level.

Of the 245 *high school districts*, data were secured on 100. Only four districts were less than ten persons in size, and these were removed from the small group. The designations, small, medium and large, were made on the same basis as those in the elementary districts. The mean percentage of each group which was administrative was 11.4, 12.3 and 17.6 respectively. Table 2 summarizes these findings. When the small group was compared with the large group, the difference between the means was 6.2, and the C.R. was 4.8, significant beyond the .001 level.

On the 69 *unified and city districts*, data were secured on 68. Because these districts tended to be larger, designations varied from those employed for the elementary and high school districts. Small districts were designated at those from ten up to

TABLE 2 HIGH SCHOOL DISTRICTS

Group Designation	Number in Group	Size Range	Administrative Component Mean Percentage	Standard Deviation
Small	55	10–49	11.4	4.0
Medium	25	50–149	12.3	4.4
Large	16	150–859	17.6	4.9

TABLE 3 UNIFIED AND CITY SCHOOL DISTRICTS

Group Designation	Number in Group	Size Range	Administrative Component Mean Percentage	Standard Deviation
Small	31	13–249	13.7	3.7
Medium	27	250–999	14.3	2.5
Large	10	1000–4624	15.6	1.7

250 persons. As the smallest unified district numbered thirteen employees, it was unnecessary to remove any districts from the small group. Medium districts were designated as those from 250 up to 1000; and large, as those of 1000 and over. The mean percentage of each group which was administrative was 13.7, 14.3 and 15.6 respectively. Table 3 summarizes these findings. When the small group was compared with the large group, the difference between means was 1.9, and the C.R. was 2.7, significant beyond the .01 level.

Thus, in all three types of districts the proportion of the organization which was administrative rose from small through medium to large sized districts, showing a significant difference between small and large groups in each case. For this sample of school districts in California during the school year 1951–52, the hypothesis was substantiated.

These findings indicate the administrative component mean percentage variability for school districts of various sizes and types, and they indicate that the school administrator may expect that the percentage of his organization which is devoted to administrative tasks may rise as his organization grows. There is undoubtedly a limit to which this may obtain—otherwise an organization would contain, as has been said of the Pentagon, "more chiefs than Indians." The implications of the findings as they stand, however, are suggestive for organizational planning, large-group dynamics and group theory. Further applications of the hypothesis to municipal, military and business organizations are planned.

19. ORGANIZATIONAL SIZE AND FUNCTIONAL COMPLEXITY: A STUDY OF ADMINISTRATION IN HOSPITALS

Theodore R. Anderson and Seymour Warkov

One of the important problems in any organization is the coordination of the various activities which occur within it. This coordination function is normally performed by the administrative component of the organization. The relative size of this component is an important dependent variable in much organization theory. In particular, the coordination of activities is alleged to become relatively more difficult (requiring a more than proportionately greater expenditure of time or energy or both) with an increased number of personnel and with a greater variety of role activities or tasks.

For example, Durkheim asserted that growing density of population in a society results in increasingly complex forms of organization.[1] Similarly, both Spencer and Simmel propose that an increase of size necessitates more complex forms of

Reprinted by permission of the American Sociological Association from *American Sociological Review*, 26 (February 1961) 23–28.

communication.[2] It is commonly claimed that, in addition to its effect on organizational complexity, growth also brings about a disproportionate increase in the size of the administrative component.[3] Finally, more and more complex tasks may require that the coordination of an organization's differentiated components be accomplished by an increasingly larger administration.[4]

Despite the apparently widespread interest in the concomitants of organizational size and complexity, few systematic researches have been undertaken to test the basic hypotheses. There are not many comparative

[1] Emile Durkheim, *On the Social Division of Labor in Society*, translated by George Simpson (New York: Macmillan, 1933), Part 2.

[2] Herbert Spencer, *Principles of Sociology* (New York: Appleton, 1898), Vol. I, pp. 525–28; Georg Simmel, "The Number of Members as Determining the Sociological Form of the Group," translated by A. W. Small, *American Journal of Sociology*, 8 (1902–1903), pp. 1–46.

[3] For a general discussion of this and other points relating to organizational size, and a review of the literature, see Theodore Caplow, "Organizational Size," *Administrative Science Quarterly*, I (Mar., 1957), pp. 484–505.

[4] See, e.g., Max Weber, *The Theory of Social and Economic Organization*, translated by A. M. Henderson and T. Parsons (New York: Oxford University Press, 1947), pp. 324–37.

studies of several large-scale organizations, presumably because of the expense of gathering data on such organizations. The tendency in research has been, instead, to focus attention upon one or at most a very few organizations. These studies present illustrative material and, at times, suggestive conclusions, but they do not represent tests of the hypotheses or conclusions.

Terrien and Mills provide one of the two systematic empirical studies in this general area. They make the Parkinsonian proposal that "the relationship between the size of the administrative component and the total size of its containing organization is such that the larger the size of the containing organization, the greater will be the proportion given over to its administrative component."[5] Data on school districts of California support this hypothesis in that the administrative component contained a higher mean percentage of the total staff in large than in small school districts. Bendix, in the other systematic study, presents evidence pointing in the opposite direction. Using data drawn from German industrial experience between 1907 and 1933, he shows that the percentage of administrative salary workers (of all employees) declines with increasing size of establishment for concerns with at least six employees. On the other hand, the percent of salaried technicians increases with growing size.[6] This paper presents further data bearing upon these contrasting hypotheses

and upon the hypothesis relating organizational complexity to the relative size of the administrative component.

DATA AND METHOD

Relevant data were secured for Veterans Administration hospitals in the United States for the year 1956. These data were derived from reports on the number of hospital personnel in various structural categories which are published monthly by the Central Office of the Veterans Administration.[7] Only hospitals discharging at least 40 tuberculous patients were included in the sample.[8] In 1956, there were 51 such hospitals; two were eliminated for technical reasons.[9] Thus 49 Veterans Administration hospitals, each with a substantial number of tuberculous patients, make up the final sample.

The dependent variable, the relative size of the administrative component, was measured by the percent of all employees classified in the category, "General Hospital Administration." This component includes

---

[5] F. W. Terrien and D. L. Mills, "The Effect of Changing Size Upon the Internal Structure of an Organization," *American Sociological Review*, 20 (Feb., 1955), p. 11.

[6] Reinhard Bendix, *Work and Authority in Industry* (New York: John Wiley, 1956), p. 222, Table 7.

[7] *Supplement, VA Statistical Summary* (Washington, D. C.: Central Office, Veterans Administration, January to December, 1956).

[8] These were originally assembled for the purpose of studying medically unsanctioned withdrawal from hospitals on the part of tuberculosis patients. See Seymour Warkov, *Irregular Discharge from Veterans Administration Tuberculosis Hospitals: A Problem of Organizational Effectiveness*, Ph.D. thesis, Yale University, 1959. The analysis reported in this paper, however, is not based upon this study.

[9] One hospital was eliminated because in fact it comprised two separate hospitals; the second because its administrative personnel were combined with those of another hospital in the statistical summary.

the Manager's Office, the Registrar's Office, and the Fiscal, Personnel, and Supply units.[10] The first independent variable, organizational size, was measured by the Annual Average Daily Patient Load (hereafter called ADPL) and was estimated for 1956 from the three months of February, May, and October. An alternative measure of organizational size is the total hospital labor force—that is, the denominator of the dependent variable. For the two groups of hospitals studied here (see below) these two measures of size are essentially equivalent. The correlations between these measures within each group of hospitals being .966 and .977, only one measure of size, namely, ADPL, was utilized in the main analysis.

The second independent variable, organizational complexity, was inferred from structural characteristics of the hospitals in the sample, which were divided into two distinct groups. Nineteen were classified as Tuberculosis Hospitals by the Veterans Administration. The percentages of the ADPL in these hospitals with pulmonary tuberculosis ranged from a low of 44 to a high of 100, with a median of 91.5 percent. The other 30 hospitals were classified as General Medicine and Surgery Hospitals (hereafter called GM&S). A wide range of diseases are regularly treated in these hospitals, including internal diseases and psychiatric illness as well as tuberculosis. The percentages of the ADPL with pulmonary tuberculosis in this second group ranged from a low of three to a high of 41, with a median of 16.5 percent. It is

assumed in this paper that the TB hospitals are less complex organizationally than are the GM&S hospitals in that fewer types of diseases are treated on a regular basis.

The concept of organizational complexity poses serious methodological and measurement problems. Udy's recent attempt to clarify the concept and to measure the degree of complexity suggests that it comprises three elements: the number of tasks performed, the maximum number of specialized operations ever performed at the same time, and the existence or non-existence of combined effort.[11] Using these criteria, it is reasonable to consider the GM&S hospitals as more complex because, not only are all tasks performed in the TB hospitals also carried out in the GM&S hospitals, but many other services that are regularly rendered in the GM&S hospitals are not provided in the TB hospitals. Of course, these two groups of hospitals also differ in many ways other than in complexity. For this reason, conclusions about complexity should be interpreted with caution.

It is important to note that the design used here permits the influence of size to be studied independently of the influence of complexity. All of the TB hospitals have about the same complexity. Furthermore, all of the GM&S hospitals have at least approximately the same degree of complexity, although some variation probably exists among them. Thus, within each category, complexity is sufficiently constant so that any relationship between size and proportion of per-

---

[10] The annual estimate for this component is based on the table reporting full-time equivalent hospital personnel employed in VA hospitals, *Supplement, VA Statistical Summary*, June, 1956.

[11] Stanley H. Udy, Jr., "The Structure of Authority in Non-Industrial Production Organizations," *American Journal of Sociology*, 64 (May, 1959), pp. 582–84.

sonnel in administration is not substantially influenced by complexity. Other hospitals were excluded from the analysis because their inclusion would tend to confound the effects of complexity and size. The size of the sample used here is sufficient to demonstrate statistically the impact of the data upon the hypotheses; it is believed that the avoidance of a confounding effect is more important for the purpose at hand than an increase in sample size.

RESULTS

The empirical results may be presented as replies to a series of questions. First, is there a relationship between type of hospital and organizational size? The data indicate that the GM&S hospitals are significantly and substantially larger than are the TB hospitals. In 1956, the mean ADPL (or size) of the GM&S hospitals was 770 and only 335 for the TB hospitals.

Second, do GM&S and TB hospitals differ with respect to the proportion of personnel in administration? The fact that about 12.5 percent of the employees were in administration in both types of hospitals is clearly inconsistent with previous research findings and speculations. According to existing theory, larger, more complex hospitals have a higher proportion of staff in administration. The interpretation of this contrary finding is deferred for the moment.

Third, is there a relationship between hospital size and percentage of personnel in administration? Since the GM&S hospitals were so much larger than the TB hospitals it seemed unreasonable to treat them as a single homogeneous group. Hence, this question was asked of each hospital type.

The TB hospitals were divided into three categories, with roughly one-third of them in each. The mean percent of employees in administration within each category is shown by the following figures:

	Size: Under 250	250–400	Above 400
No. of hospitals	5	8	6
Mean percent	15.6	12.0	10.7

It is clear that the larger the hospital the *smaller* the percent of all personnel in administration. An analysis of variance of these data indicates significance beyond the .01 level. Further, Eta^2 is .577, indicating that 58 percent of the variance in percentage of employees in administration can be accounted for by variations in size. Thus size is a powerful explanatory variable, although in a direction opposite to that expected.

That this result is not a peculiarity of TB hospitals is indicated by the results for the GM&S hospitals. Here, different size categories were used so as to place, as in the former case, approximately one-third of the hospitals in each, with the following results:

	Size: Under 600	600–900	Above 900
No. of hospitals	12	9	9
Mean percent	14.0	12.0	11.0

Again, the larger the hospital the *smaller* the percent of all personnel in administration. These results are also significant beyond the .01 level, and Eta^2 is .556, almost identical to the figure for the TB hospitals. This divergent finding, then, has some degree of generality, applying at least to two quite different types of Federal hospitals.[12]

Fourth, is the relationship between size of hospital and proportion of personnel in administration linear? The fact that within each type of hospital Eta[2] proved to be significantly greater than r[2] provides a negative answer. A scatter diagram of these data (not presented here) suggests that the slope of the regression line becomes more horizontal as size increases. It is possible that the slope might actually become positive with sufficiently large hospitals, but this is only a speculation, in view of the limitations of the present data.

Finally, if size is controlled or held constant, do the hospital types differ in percent of employees in administration? This is in fact the case, but the hospital types differ so much in size that all of the observations cannot be brought to bear upon the question (especially because the size regressions are not linear). In particular, only one size category (between 300 and 600) included an appreciable number of each type of hospital. Furthermore, within this reasonably narrow range, the GM&S and TB hospitals had roughly the same size distribution. In this range, the 11 TB hospitals averaged only 11.1 percent of personnel in administration; the corresponding figure is 14 percent for the 12 GM&S hospitals. This difference is significant at the .01 level. Thus, the earlier finding of no overall difference in the average percent of employees in administration appears to be entirely a function

of the size differential between the two types of hospitals. In general, if GM&S hospitals may be considered to be more complex than TB hospitals, then these data tend to confirm the hypothesis that organizational complexity and the relative size of the administrative component are positively related, as expected. However, the data refute, at least for these organizations, the hypothesis that organizational size and relative size of the administrative component are positively related; indeed they suggest perhaps the counter hypothesis.

DISCUSSION

On the surface, at least, the findings reported in this paper are in direct contradiction to those reported by Terrien and Mills. Moreover, these results are substantially at variance with what is apparently the common conception (among sociologists and others) of the relationship between organizational size and the relative size of the administrative component. There appear to be, in general, two ways to resolve these discrepancies. First, either or both sets of data may be inadequate in some way to test the hypothesis under discussion. Second, these two sets of data may not, in fact, be directly comparable. In the latter case, it should be possible to develop theoretical statements consistent with both sets of findings.

Both sets of data are derived from relatively straightforward enumeration procedures conducted by state and federal agencies. For fiscal and other reasons the accuracy of these data is important within the agencies concerned. There is no reason to

---

[12] It is important to emphasize the fact that an inverse relationship is not an artifact of the measure of size used here. Identical results were obtained using the labor force measure of size.

suspect that either set of basic data is in substantial error, certainly not to the degree necessary to eliminate the conclusion in contradiction to the earlier study.

Another possible explanation of this finding is that the administrative component was incorrectly identified or categorized in at least one of the two studies. There is no doubt that some administrative activities are performed by personnel who are not so classified. However, there is no reason to believe that the proportion of such personnel is substantially greater (or lesser) in large than in small organizations, which have a specialized, designated administrative component. Accordingly, it is reasonable to conclude that both the findings of Terrien and Mills and of the present investigation accurately reflect organizational processes which are (therefore) not directly comparable. If so, an explanation is called for which renders these findings mutually consistent.

The following propositions are offered as one possible resolution of the apparent discrepancy between the two sets of findings. The propositions are based upon the fact that some of the school districts studied by Terrien and Mills include more than one school and upon the assumption that the larger school districts incorporate more schools than do the smaller districts. In contrast, each of the organizations in the present study has a single location. Thus:

1. The relative size of the administrative component *decreases* as the number of persons performing identical tasks in the same place increases.[13]

---

[13] This proposition appears to be consistent with commonplace observations. For ex-

2. The relative size of the administrative component *increases* as the number of places at which work is performed increases.

3. The relative size of the administrative component *increases* as the number of tasks performed at the same place increases (or as roles become increasingly specialized and differentiated).

If these propositions are correct, then Terrien and Mills' findings may be interpreted as confirming the second proposition and *not* as nullifying the first proposition. Our findings, on the other hand, support the first and third propositions but do not bear upon the second one. Given this interpretation, the relative size of the administrative component in a single school should decline as school size increases, provided that the organizational complexity of the schools is held constant. In practice, it might prove difficult to devise an effective measure of organizational complexity within schools. These propositions are presented tentatively, of course, pending further investigation of these and other types of organizations.

At least one alternative means of rectifying the two sets of findings is available. The school districts and hospitals may differ in the extent to which they are subject to centralized authority. Where the central authority is powerful, special constraints may inhibit the emergence of the relation-

---

ample, as any teacher knows, administering a test in the same room to four times more students than usual does not require four times as many proctors. An alternative possibility is that the inverse relationship holds up to a point, and then becomes positive, thus producing an overall U-shape. Our data suggest that the curve flattens out eventually, but do not suggest the existence of an upturn.

ship between size and administration that would otherwise occur. In particular, some special bureaucratic constraint may operate within government hospitals which inhibits the "free" growth of the administrative component.

It is also important to recognize that these propositions, even if confirmed empirically, are not necessarily sufficient to explain all structural and temporal variations in the relative size of the administrative component. Specifically, the inclusion of a proposition concerning the routinization of roles would undoubtedly improve the general explanation of variations in the relative size of the administrative component. Routinization is not discussed in this paper because the apparent contradiction between the

two sets of findings could be resolved without taking it into account.

On the other hand, these propositions appear to explain adequately the apparent overall increase in the relative importance of administrative activities within organizations during the past several decades (as evidenced by the rapid rise in the percent employed in clerical occupations, for instance). It is often suggested that this increase in administration is a function of the sheer growth in organizational size. If our propositions are correct, however, the explanatory variable is organizational complexity rather than organizational size. Clearly, more systematic studies are required before any such conclusions can be considered to be substantially confirmed.

20. THE EFFECTS OF INDUSTRY SIZE AND DIVISION OF LABOR ON ADMINISTRATION

William A. Rushing

At least since Parkinson, students of organizations have been struck by the fact that the relative number of administrative personnel in some organizations and industries is greater than in others. In this paper an at-

Reprinted by permission from *Administrative Science Quarterly* (September 1967), pp. 267–95.

tempt is made to discover the extent to which variation in the relative number of administrative personnel in industry is associated with variation in either industry size or the division of labor (complexity). Although both variables have received considerable attention in efforts to account for the disproportionate increase in administrative personnel, very few definite conclusions can be made about either of them. Size has been investigated in a number of studies, but results show that, contrary to Parkinson and popular conceptions, increases in organization size apparently do not necessarily result in increases in the relative number of administrative personnel: only two studies report an increase, while six report a decrease and four report no change at all.[1] Concerning the

[1] Studies showing an increase in relative number of administrative personnel are: Frederic W. Terrien and Donald L. Mills, "The Effects of Changing Size upon the Internal Structure of an Organization," *American Sociological Review*, 20 (Feb., 1955), 11–14; and John E. Tsouderos, "Organizational Change in Terms of a Series of Selected Variables," *American Sociological Review*, 20 (Apr., 1955), 206–10.

Those showing a decrease in the relative number of administrative personnel are: Seymour Melman, "The Rise of Administrative Overhead in the Manufacturing Industries of the United States 1899–1947," *Oxford Economic Papers*, 3 (Feb., 1951), 62–112; Reinhard Bendix, *Work and Authority in Industry* (New York: Harper and Row, 1956), pp. 221–22; Theodore Anderson and Seymour Warkov, "Organizational Size and Functional Complexity: A Study of Administration in Hospitals," *American Sociological Review*, 26 (Feb., 1961), 23–28; Eugene Haas, Richard H. Hall, and Norman J. Johnson, "The Size of the Supportive Component in Organizations: A Multi-organizational Analysis," *Social Forces*, 43 (Oct., 1963), 9–17; Frederic W. Terrien, *The Effect of Changing Size Upon Organizations*. (San Francisco: Institute for Social Science Research, San Francisco State College, March 1963), pp. 2–4; and Amos H. Hawley, Walter Boland and Margaret Boland, "Population Size and Administration in Institutions of Higher Education," *American Sociological Review*, 30 (Apr., 1965), 252–55.

Those showing neither increase nor decrease are: Alan W. Baker and Ralph C. Davis, *Ratios of Staff to Line Employees and Stages of Differentiation of Staff Functions* (Columbus, Ohio: Bureau of Business

division of labor, despite the general belief that it is positively associated with the relative size of administration, no empirical investigations have been made of this relationship. The present paper reports the results of the first such study.[2]

THE HYPOTHESIS

The general hypothesis to be investigated, first explicitly formulated by Anderson and Warkov,[3] is that the number of administrative personnel increases disproportionately as organizations become increasingly complex. Here it will be referred to as the "complexity-administrative growth hypothesis." The hypothesis is a straightforward deduction from two assumptions: (*1*) that increases in the division of labor lead to increases in problems of coordination,[4]

Research, Ohio State University, 1954); Mason Haire (ed.), *Modern Organization Theory* (New York: John Wiley, 1959), pp. 272–306; Jean Draper and George B. Strother, "Testing a Model for Organizational Growth," *Human Organization*, 22 (Fall 1963), 180–94; and Terrien, *op. cit.,* 5–6.

[2] Although Anderson and Warkov hypothesize that increases in the division of labor cause disproportionate growth in administrative personnel, actual measures of the division of labor are not provided. Hawley, Boland, and Boland are also concerned with the complexity-administrative growth relationship, but the measure of complexity employed is really a measure of *structural differentiation* rather than the division of labor. The nature and relevance of the distinction between these two terms is discussed in the section on division of labor.

[3] Anderson and Warkov. See also Peter M. Blau and W. Richard Scott, *Formal Organizations* (San Francisco: Chandler, 1962), p. 227.

[4] This assumption goes back at least as far as Durkheim, who wrote, "the more complex an organization is [i.e., the greater its

and (2) that administrative personnel, rather than production personnel, are the ones primarily concerned with problems of coordination.[5]

Proponents of this hypothesis emphasize that the significant factor in the disproportionate growth of administrative personnel is the increase in complexity rather than the increase in number of personnel. The relative number of administrative personnel[6]

is not necessarily related to the total number of personnel, because increases in the number of personnel do not necessarily increase problems of coordination. As a result, complexity and relative number of administrative personnel are directly related, regardless of the total number of personnel; but the total number of personnel and the relative number of administrative personnel are directly related only where the increase in personnel is positively related to complexity. Where the number of personnel and complexity are not related, no relationship, or even a negative relationship, between number of administrative personnel and total personnel may be expected.[7] Thus, the complexity-administrative growth hypothesis actually consists of two hypotheses:

Hypothesis 1. The division of labor and the relative number of administrative personnel are directly related, and this relationship is not affected by variation in the total number of personnel.

Hypothesis 2. The total number of personnel[8] and the relative number of administrative personnel may or may not be directly related; but when the effects of the division of labor are controlled, the two variables are either inversely related or not related at all.

Neither hypothesis has actually been subjected to empirical test.

---

division of labor], the more is the need for extensive regulation felt." Cf. George Simpson (trans.), Emile Durkheim, *The Division of Labor in Society* (Glencoe, Ill.: The Free Press, 1949), p. 367.

[5] The assumption that administrative personnel are concerned primarily with a coordinative function is not an uncommon one. It is involved in the conceptions found in the following works: Anderson and Warkov, "Organizational Size and Functional Complexity"; P. G. Herbst, "Measurement of Behavior Structures by Means of Input-Output Data," *Human Relations*, 10 (1957), 341; Bernard P. Indik, "Some Effects of Organization Size on Member Attitudes and Behavior," *Human Relations*, 4 (1965), 378; William H. Starbuck, "Organization Growth and Development," *In* James G. March (ed.), *Handbook of Organizations* (Chicago, Ill.: Rand McNally, 1965), pp. 499–511. Also, Haire, *Modern Organization Theory*, p. 303, implies the same definition for "staff" personnel. This is not to say, of course, that studies of administrative personnel have generally employed operational definitions that are consistent with the conceptual definition that such personnel perform coordinative functions. Considering the heterogenous character of the occupations that have been included in the administrative category in some of the studies, no such claim is justified. See William A. Rushing, "Organization Size and Administration: The Problems of Causal Homogeneity and a Heterogeneous Category," *Pacific Sociological Review*, 9 (Fall 1966), 100–108.

[6] In this paper, relative number of administrative personnel refers to the ratio between the number of administrative personnel and the number of production personnel. This is discussed in the section on data and measurement of variables.

[7] Blau and Scott, *Formal Organizations*, p. 227.

[8] To be consistent with the statements of proponents of the "complexity-administrative growth hypothesis," reference in both hypotheses is to *total* number of personnel. However, as will be indicated in the section on data and measurement of variables, measures in this paper are based on total *production* personnel.

However, if it assumed that the division of labor and difficulties of coordination are directly related, the first hypothesis is plausible.[9] And although much of the evidence cited is consistent with the second hypothesis, there is no explanation for why the number of administrative personnel and the total number of personnel may be negatively related. While it is understandable that there may be no relationship when complexity is held constant, why there should be a negative relationship is not clear. Therefore, in addition to testing both hypotheses for entire industries, an effort is made to provide an explanation for the second one. In addition, an analysis is made of the interaction between the effects of size and complexity, and of the relationship of these to different groups of administrative personnel.

Although industries cannot be directly compared to organizations, there is nothing in the logic of the complexity-administrative growth hypothesis that would prevent its application to entire industries. As the division of labor in an industry increases, problems of coordination should increase, and with this the relative number of industry-wide administrative personnel should increase.

INDUSTRY SIZE, DIVISION OF LABOR, AND INTERACTION EFFECTS

The effects of a variable are not always additive. For example, the relationship between the division of labor and the number of administrative personnel may be stronger for large industries than it is for small industries. This would mean that the effects of division of labor vary depending upon the value of another variable, in this instance, industry size; in which case, the division of labor and size would be said to interact.

The complexity — administrative growth hypothesis states nothing explicitly about interaction effects; but since it predicts that relative number of administrative personnel is directly related to division of labor and negatively related to size, the hypothesis suggests that the (positive) effects of division of labor are strongest in small industries, where the (negative) effects of size are weakest; and that the effects of size are strongest in industries where the effects of the division of labor are weakest. To determine whether these relationships exist, the relationship between each independent variable and administrative personnel is computed while minimizing the effects of the other. If interactive effects other than those mentioned are found, the hypothesis will have to be extended or modified.[10]

ADMINISTRATIVE GROUPS

A recent analysis suggests that the different groups of administrative personnel may be differentially related to

---

[9] However, the findings on structural differentiation by Hawley, Boland and Boland, "Population Size and Administration," are consistent with this hypothesis, and suggestive evidence is reported by Anderson and Warkov, "Organizational Size and Functional Complexity."

[10] For a discussion of the use of interaction effects in theory building, see Hubert M. Blalock, Jr., "Theory Building and the Concept of Interaction," *American Sociological Review*, 30 (June 1965), 374–80. Not only can interactive effects be the basis for building theory, they can lead to the clarification and modification of existing theory.

organization size.[11] It is possible that they are also differentially related to industry size and industry complexity. Three administrative groups are considered: managerial personnel, clerical personnel, and professional personnel. Division of labor and industry size are investigated not only in relation to total administrative personnel, but also in relation to each of the three administrative groups.

The different groups would appear to be involved in the administrative and coordination process in different ways. Managerial personnel represent coordination through *managerial hierarchy*. Since the managerial hierarchy exerts its coordinative functions primarily through hierarchical authority and supervision, the relative number of managerial personnel in an industry indicates the extent to which coordination is achieved through these mechanisms. For professional personnel the primary coordinative mechanism is *professional authority*. The relative number of professional personnel reveals the extent to which status and authority are legitimated on the basis of knowledge and technical skills. An increase in professional personnel represents an elaboration and development of the staff or advisory functions in industry, and an increase in direction and coordination of production activities based on technical knowledge and expertise. Clerical personnel are concerned with paper work and communication. The relative number of this group is indicative, therefore, of the development of files and the degree to which production activities are regularized and standardized through formal written *specifications*

and *communications*, which can be transmitted simultaneously through formal channels to many individuals in various positions, thus facilitating coordination.[12]

DATA AND MEASUREMENT OF VARIABLES

The source of data is the *Occupation by Industry* subject report of the 1960 United States Census, which gives the number of persons for each of 279 detailed U.S. Census occupations, by industry, in 12 major occupational categories,[13] of which six are used in this paper: (*1*) managers, officials, and proprietors (referred to hereafter as managerial personnel), (*2*) professional personnel, (*3*) clerical personnel, (*4*) craftsmen, (*5*) operatives, and (*6*) laborers. The first three categories are classified as administrative personnel, while the last three are classified as production personnel.[14]

[11] Rushing, "Organization Size and Administration."

[12] See Peter M. Blau, Wolf V. Heydebrand, and Robert E. Stauffer, "The Structure of Small Bureaucracies," *American Sociological Review*, 31 (April 1966), 179–91, esp. 184–85 for measures of managerial, clerical, and professional personnel in their study of small bureaucracies, and their comments on the coordinative functions performed by each.

[13] These occupations are derived from the 494 occupations that constitute the detailed occupational classification system of the U.S. Census. Not all 494 are included in *Occupation by Industry*; 197 occupations, which derive from industry subgroups (e.g., "laborers, furniture and fixtures"), are eliminated, as are several others because certain combinations are made. As a result, the total number of specific occupations is reduced to 279. See *Occupation by Industry*. U.S. Department of Commerce, Bureau of the Census, 1960, p. viii.

[14] The distinction corresponds to distinctions others have made between produc-

The measures of industry size and the division of labor are based on production personnel *only*. Industry size refers to the number of production personnel in each industry, while the division of labor measure is based on how evenly production personnel are distributed throughout the total number of production occupations. Measures of administration are based on the *ratio* of administrative personnel to production personnel.

INDUSTRY SIZE

Since the complexity-administrative growth hypothesis posits that administrative personnel exist to solve problems of coordination among production personnel, the appropriate measure of industry size is obviously the total number of craftsmen, operatives, and laborers in each industry. Therefore in the discussion that follows, overall industry size refers to production personnel (PP), not to total personnel.

RELATIVE NUMBER OF
ADMINISTRATIVE PERSONNEL

The measure of administrative personnel is the ratio of the total number of administrative personnel to production personnel (A/PP), and thus refers to the ratio between the

total number of managerial, clerical, and professional personnel and the total number of craftsmen, operatives, and laborers.[15] Ratios for managerial personnel (MGR/PP), clerical personnel (CLER/PP), and professional personnel (PRO/PP) are used as measures of managerial hierarchy, formal communication, and professional authority, respectively.

In some industries, one or more of the three administrative categories are typically involved in production operations; e.g., "newspaper publishing and printing," where the relative number of both clerical and professional positions is high. Consequently, industries were eliminated in which the ratio of either managerial, clerical, or professional personnel is .33 or above.[16] In addition, several industry categories were eliminated because of their ambiguous or heterogeneous characteristics; e.g., "not specified metal industries," "miscellaneous food production and kindred products," etc. Therefore, although 60 manufacturing categories are listed in *Occupation by Industry*, only 41 are included in the present analysis.

---

tion, direct, or line personnel; and administrative, indirect, or staff personnel. As one example, Stinchcombe employs the same census categories to investigate different administrative systems in industry. See Arthur L. Stinchcombe, "Bureaucratic and Craft Administration of Production: A Comparative Study," *Administrative Science Quarterly*, 4 (Sept., 1959), 168–87; also "Social Structure and Organization," in James G. March, *Handbook of Organizations*. p. 256.

[15] Use of A/PP ratios as a measure of relative number of administrative personnel was first used in Seymour Melman's study, "The Rise of Administrative Overhead," of organization size and administration in manufacturing industries.

[16] The cutting point of .33 is based on the frequency distribution of the ratio values. The minimum ratio value for any of the three categories of administrative personnel is .008, with gradual increases up to .326. There is a perceptible break at this point, the next ratio value being .416. So while the decision to eliminate all industries in which any of the three ratios is above .33 is to some degree arbitrary, it has an empirical basis in that it corresponds to a natural break in the data.

TABLE 1 ILLUSTRATIONS OF THE MEASUREMENT OF THE DIVISION
OF LABOR IN FOUR HYPOTHETICAL INDUSTRIES

Occupation	Industry A	Industry B	Industry C	Industry D
Cabinetmaker	1,000	100	300	100
Carpenter	–	100	100	100
Electrician	–	100	50	100
Machinist	–	100	25	100
Plasterer	–	100	25	100
Upholsterer	–	–	–	100
Dyer	–	–	–	100
Milliner	–	–	–	100
Welder	–	–	–	100
Plumber	–	–	–	100
$\sum x$*	1,000	500	500	1,000
$\sum x^2$	1,000,000	50,000	103,750	100,000
$1 - [\sum x^2/(\sum x)^2]$	.0000	.8000	.5850	.9000

* x is number of persons in an occupation.

DIVISION OF LABOR

It is necessary to distinguish division of labor from the related term, "structural differentiation." Structural differentiation means the number of structural parts, e.g., departments, levels in the hierarchy, or occupations, which exist in a society, organization, or industry. Division of labor, on the other hand, refers to the *distribution of individuals* among the structural parts. The number of parts is an inaccurate measure of the division of labor, since it does not take into account the distribution of individuals throughout the parts.[17] For example, an industry with 10 occupations may have 90 percent of all its personnel in only one occupation, whereas in another industry personnel may be equally distributed throughout the same number of occupations.

In this paper, the measure for the division of labor is based on the formula developed by Gibbs and Martin,[18]

$$D = 1 - \frac{\sum X^2}{(\sum X)^2}$$

where D is the division of labor and X the number of persons in an occupation. Although this measure has been used only to study the division of labor in societies,[19] it is conveniently adaptable for studying the division of labor in industries.

Table 1 presents illustrations of the measure for four hypothetical industries. As can be seen, there is no division of labor in industry A because

[17] See Sanford I. Labovitz and Jack P. Gibbs, "Urbanization, Technology, and the Division of Labor: Further Evidence," *Pacific Sociological Review*, 7 (Fall 1964), 5–6.

[18] Jack P. Gibbs and Walter T. Martin, "Urbanization, Technology, and the Division of Labor: International Patterns," *American Sociological Review*, 27 (Oct., 1962), 669.

[19] *Ibid.* 667–77; Labovitz and Gibbs, "Urbanization, Technology and Division of Labor," 3–9; and Jack P. Gibbs and Harley L. Browning, "The Division of Labor, Technology, and the Organization of Production in Twelve Countries," *American Sociological Review*, 31 (Feb., 1966), 81–92.

all employees are in the same occupation, so that the value of D is zero. In industry B, individuals are equally dispersed throughout five occupations, and the value of D for an industry with five occupations is maximum. The value of D for industry C is less than for industry B, but it is still considerably above zero. In industry D, personnel are evenly dispersed throughout 10 occupations and the value of D is maximum. Note, however, that although the division of labor is maximum in both industry B and industry D, its value is higher in industry D, because D_{max}, the maximum value possible for D, is a function of the total number of occupations (N) in the industry. (D_{max} is computed from the formula, $D_{max} = 1 - 1/N$). Note also that D_{max} can never be 1.00, although it can approximate this value when N is large.

Since N will vary from industry to industry, it is clear that variation in D values by industry may reflect variation in structural differentiation (N) as well as variation in the division of labor. As N becomes large, however, the extent to which D_{max} can vary with variation in N decreases quite rapidly, as the following figures show:

N	5	10	15
D_{max}	.8000	.9000	.9333
N	20	25	30
D_{max}	.9500	.9600	.9670

The effect of N on D_{max} is very slight when the number of occupations increases beyond 30. In the present group of industries the number of production occupations per industry[20]

[20] Although the total number of occupations listed in *Occupation by Industry* under the three categories of production personnel is 123, in no industry are persons employed in all 123 occupations. It was

varies between 27 and 89, so that range in D_{max} values is only from .9630 to .9888; furthermore, in only 13 industries is D_{max} less than .9800, and in only one instance is it below .9700. Thus variation in D values due to variation in the total number of occupations per industry is negligible. Nevertheless, D values obtained with the formula are "adjusted" for the total number of occupations by dividing each D by D_{max}.[21] Consequently, D/D_{max} rather than D is the actual measure used, the formula being,

$$\frac{D}{D_{max}} = 1 - \frac{\sum X^2/(\sum X)^2}{1 - 1/N}.$$

The D/D_{max} values for the 41 industries are listed in column 2 of Table 2.

FINDINGS AND INTERPRETATIONS

Although it is generally assumed that size and the division of labor are directly related, there is little actual evidence for this.[22] In the present

decided that any occupation with at least one member should be included in the division of labor measure for an industry; however, the lowest number for any of the production occupations for any of the 41 industries was 18.

[21] To say that D is adjusted for the total number of occupations when it is divided by D_{max} only means that it is possible for an industry to have a division of labor value of 1.00. As is illustrated in Table 1, D_{max} is .8000 and .9000 for industries with 5 and 10 occupations respectively, even when industry personnel are evenly distributed throughout the total number of occupations. Although D does not yield a value of 1.00 under this condition, D/D_{max} does (e.g., $.9000/.9000 = 1.00$).

[22] There is no evidence from studies of either organizations or entire industries that the two variables are associated. However, three studies have reported findings that

TABLE 2 MEASURES OF INDUSTRY SIZE, DIVISION OF LABOR, RELATIVE NUMBER OF ADMINISTRATIVE PERSONNEL AND PROPORTION OF ADMINISTRATIVE PERSONNEL WHO ARE PROFESSIONAL AND CLERICAL, FOR 41 INDUSTRIES, 1960*

	Industry Size (Total Number Production Personnel)	Division of Labor (D/D_{max})	Administrative Personnel (A/PP)	Managerial Personnel (MGR/PP)	Professional Personnel (PRO/PP)	Clerical Personnel ($CLER/PP$)	PRO/PP $MGR/PP+ PRO/PP$	CLER/PP $MGR/PP+ CLER/PP$
			Ratio of Different Groups of Administrative Personnel to Production Personnel					
Apparel and accessories	850,256	.6025	.140	.044	.013	.083	.228	.654
Electrical machinery, equipment, and supplies	839,268	.7881	.554	.069	.248	.237	.782	.775
Motor vehicles and motor vehicle equipment	588,536	.8840	.271	.034	.090	.147	.726	.812
Yarn, thread, and fabric mills	491,368	.7445	.131	.029	.023	.079	.442	.731
Blast furnaces, steelworks, and rolling and finishing mills	441,580	.8866	.228	.023	.070	.135	.753	.854
Sawmills, planing mills, and mill work	319,501	.8170	.150	.071	.016	.063	.184	.470
Furniture and fixtures	271,981	.8451	.212	.069	.025	.118	.266	.631
Bakery products	244,586	.8110	.211	.085	.008	.118	.086	.581
Meat products	224,765	.6700	.225	.075	.024	.126	.242	.627
Fabricated structural metal products	210,157	.8820	.389	.110	.114	.165	.509	.600
Dairy products	204,895	.7650	.319	.121	.036	.162	.229	.572
Pulp, paper, and paperboard mills	203,192	.7130	.260	.049	.083	.128	.629	.723
Footwear, except rubber	202,155	.5271	.150	.033	.008	.109	.195	.768

* U.S. Bureau of the Census, U.S. Census of Population: 1960. Subject Reports. Occupation by Industry (Washington, D.C.: U.S. Government Printing Office, 1963).

TABLE 2 (CONTINUED)

	Industry Size (Total Number Production Personnel)	Division of Labor (D/D_{max})	Administrative Personnel (A/PP)	Managerial Personnel (MGR/PP)	Professional Personnel (PRO/PP)	Clerical Personnel ($CLER/PP$)	PRO/PP $MGR/PP +$ PRO/PP	$CLER/PP$ $MGR/PP +$ $CLER/PP$
Primary nonferrous industries	201,430	.8306	.324	.059	.103	.162	.636	.733
Ship and boat building and repairing	181,725	.9430	.249	.038	.084	.127	.689	.770
Rubber products	174,619	.6370	.323	.063	.085	.175	.574	.735
Knitting mills	161,035	.7876	.128	.036	.010	.082	.217	.695
Logging	145,132	.4511	.087	.066	.010	.011	.132	.143
Canning and preserving	139,230	.7430	.277	.087	.045	.145	.341	.625
Professional equipment and supplies	133,642	.8550	.736	.098	.321	.317	.766	.764
Beverage industries	129,660	.8451	.337	.136	.042	.159	.236	.538
Petroleum refining	125,536	.8570	.718	.106	.289	.323	.732	.753
Cement, concrete, gypsum, and plaster products	125,139	.8200	.300	.127	.054	.119	.298	.484
Glass and glass products	119,016	.7798	.251	.048	.072	.131	.600	.732
Paperboard boxes and containers	114,250	.6540	.272	.065	.052	.155	.444	.705
Cutlery, hand tools, and other hardware	88,123	.8481	.295	.063	.053	.179	.457	.740
Grain mill products	87,761	.8449	.423	.158	.072	.193	.313	.550
Office computing and accounting machines	84,559	.8477	.740	.101	.326	.313	.763	.756

TABLE 2 (CONTINUED)

| | Industry Size (Total Number Production Personnel) | Division of Labor (D/D_{max}) | Ratio of Different Groups of Administrative Personnel to Production Personnel | | | | PRO/PP | CLER/PP |
			Administrative Personnel (A/PP)	Managerial Personnel (MGR/PP)	Professional Personnel (PRO/PP)	Clerical Personnel (CLER/PP)	MGR/PP+ PRO/PP	MGR/PP+ CLER/PP
Farm machinery and equipment	80,627	.8910	.408	.077	.104	.227	.575	.747
Plastic products	78,453	.6180	.331	.095	.073	.163	.434	.632
Tobacco manufactures	61,150	.6630	.183	.053	.028	.102	.346	.658
Structural clay products	59,706	.7630	.190	.064	.040	.086	.385	.573
Confectionery and related products	49,212	.6992	.283	.088	.022	.173	.200	.663
Dyeing and finishing textiles except wool and knit goods	43,394	.6797	.239	.035	.037	.167	.516	.827
Leather products, except footwear	41,922	.5600	.216	.080	.017	.119	.175	.598
Synthetic fibers	36,838	.6587	.278	.022	.156	.100	.876	.820
Photographic equipment and supplies	33,258	.8580	.658	.081	.268	.309	.768	.792
Pottery and related products	32,677	.6070	.209	.044	.056	.109	.560	.712
Leather products: tanned, curried, and finished	26,775	.5540	.170	.063	.018	.089	.222	.586
Floor coverings, except hard surface	24,116	.7640	.264	.065	.041	.158	.387	.709
Watches, clocks, and clock-operated devices	17,877	.7660	.356	.083	.068	.205	.450	.712

case, the Spearman rank correlation (ρ) is only .24. Thus, although the two variables are related for entire industries, the relationship is not very strong.

TESTS OF THE HYPOTHESES

As can be seen from row 1 of Table 3, the division of labor has a moderately strong effect on the relative size of the total number of administrative personnel ($\rho = .51$), as hypothesis 1 predicts. To minimize the effects of industry size, the 41 industries were divided into the 20 largest industries and the 21 smallest industries, and the relationship between the division of labor and the relative number of administrative personnel was computed for each group. The results indicate that the effects of the division of labor are independent of industry size inasmuch as ρ for both groups is positive and moderate to high in magnitude (.40 and .76). But the fact that ρ for smaller industries is considerably higher than ρ for larger industries reveals that the effects of the division of labor are influenced by industry size.

The results are also consistent with hypothesis 2, since industry size and relative number of administrative personnel are inversely related (see Table 3, row 5), not only for all 41 industries, but for the 20 industries with

the highest division of labor and the 21 industries with the lowest division of labor. Analysis further reveals that for each of the two groups, ρ is smaller than for the whole group (−.49 and −.27 versus −.20), indicating that division of labor may depress the effects of size. This also reveals, however, that the effects of industry size are to some degree independent of division of labor. At the same time, the differences in the magnitudes of ρ indicate that the effects of size vary, depending upon the division of labor.

As noted, the complexity-administrative growth hypothesis does not provide an explanation for the negative effects of size on administration. One interpretation might be that size and complexity are inversely related, so that large industries require proportionately fewer administrative personnel. However, common sense and the findings of a positive (if small) correlation between size of production personnel and division of labor indicate that size and complexity are probably directly related. Still, if the assumption that number of administrative personnel increase in response to problems of coordination is valid, the findings appear to suggest that coordinative difficulties decrease with industry size. It is not likely, however, that larger industries have fewer coordination difficulties than smaller ones. What may occur is that coordination problems resulting from increased size are qualitatively different from those resulting from increased division of labor. In itself, an increase in number of personnel leads to more production personnel and activities of the type that already exist. Although this may require that additional orders, instructions, information, and communication which

suggest that organizational size and *structural differentiation* may be related. See Hawley, Boland, and Boland, "Population Size and Administration," 253; Blau, Heydebrand, and Stauffer, "Structure of Small Bureaucracies," Table 4, 186; and Richard H. Hall, Eugene Haas, and Norman J. Johnson, "Organization Size and Organization Structure," paper read at the meeting of the American Sociological Association, Chicago, Ill., 1965.

TABLE 3 SPEARMAN RANK CORRELATIONS BETWEEN RELATIVE NUMBER OF
ADMINISTRATIVE PERSONNEL AND (1) NUMBER OF PRODUCTION
PERSONNEL AND (2) DIVISION OF LABOR

	Size of Production Personnel			Division of Labor		
Administrative Component	*All Indus- tries (N = 41)*	*High Division of Labor* (N = 20)	*Low Division of Labor†* (N = 21)	*All Indus- tries (N = 41)*	*Large Indus- tries§ (N = 20)*	*Small Indus- tries‡ (N = 21)*
Total administration (A/PP)	−.20	−.49	−.27	.51	.40	.76
Managerial hierarchy (MGR/PP)	−.15	−.44	−.07	.26	.00	.47
Formal communication structure (CLER/PP)	−.21	−.45	−.25	.48	.36	.71
Professional authority (PRO/PP)	−.12	−.29	−.28	.53	.54	.56

* Industries where the division of labor is .7798 or above.
† Industries where the division of labor is less than .7798.
§ Industries with more than 130,000 production personnel.
‡ Industries with less than 130,000 production personnel.

originate with administrative personnel be made available to more production personnel, administrative personnel may perform essentially the same activities, utilize the same techniques, and transmit identical communications. Since the *type* of coordination problems may not increase, the existing administrative personnel may need only apply what they already do to a larger number of activities and persons. An increase in administrative personnel may not be necessary. Increases in the division of labor, however, may generate problems which require a corresponding increase in administrative personnel. When new production roles are introduced, new problems of coordination may arise, and additional knowledge, techniques, and therefore personnel may be required to solve them. Industry size and the division of labor may have opposite effects on the relative number of administrative personnel precisely because

the coordination difficulties associated with each of them may be different.

As noted, the specific roles performed by the different administrative groups and the mechanisms employed by each group may be different. If increases in size and complexity have different effects on the different roles and mechanisms, the relationship between the three groups and each of the independent variables should be different.

In general, however, findings for the three groups are consistent with those for total administrative personnel, as Table 3 shows. First, the effects of division of labor on the administrative groups are consistently positive, while the effects of size are consistently negative (see columns 1 and 4). The general effects of each of these two variables are not modified even when the effects of the other are minimized: five of six correlations involving the division of labor for large and for small industries are positive, while for industry size all six correlations for industries with low and with high division of labor are negative. These findings are consistent with the complexity-administrative growth hypothesis and the interpretation that the coordination difficulties associated with industry size and the division of labor are qualitatively different.[23]

The finding that all six correlations between industry size and relative size of administrative groups are higher before the effects of the division of labor are minimized, reveals once more that the positive effects of the division of labor may counteract and depress the negative effects of the division of labor. The data thus show that the effects of the two variables are independent, since in most in-

stances controlling for one does not result in the disappearance or even reduction in the correlations between the other and the relative size of any of the three administrative groups. Finally, differences in the magnitude of ρ indicate that the two variables also interact.

INTERACTIVE EFFECTS

As previously noted, the complexity-administrative growth hypothesis suggests that the effects of the division of labor would be greatest in smaller industries where the effects of size are weakest; whereas the effects of industry size would be greatest in industries where the division of labor is low. Results in Table 3 are consistent with the first prediction, but they contradict the second—the negative relationship between industry size and administration tends to be higher in industries where the division of labor is highest. Although this finding is inconsistent with the prediction of the complexity-administrative growth hypothesis, it can nevertheless be explained by a straightforward extension of it and the assumption that coordination problems associated with size and the division of labor are qualitatively different. Since the number of administrative personnel is disproportionately high in industries where the division of labor is high, coordination problems stemming from the addition of more production personnel may be readily solved without an increase in administrative personnel. Administration may remain stable and grow at a disproportionately slow pace, so that the negative correlation between industry size and relative number of administrative personnel is generally higher

---

[23] In the case of professional personnel, and perhaps also clerical personnel, another possible explanation should be mentioned. It might be argued that the correlation between the division of labor and the relative size of the professional group is due to the fact that an increase in professional personnel is one aspect of the general increase in the division of labor, so that the division of labor and PRO/PP measures are not independent. They must, therefore, be correlated because a variable is always correlated with itself. However, since PRO/PP is a measure of the relative number of professional personnel, this explanation is not consistent with the finding of a very small correlation ($\rho = .24$) between the division of labor among production personnel and the number of production personnel. There is even less reason to expect a built-in correlation between the division of labor among production personnel and the number of nonproduction personnel, such as professional personnel. Even if one did exist, the findings for industry size are still left unexplained. Furthermore, the interactive effects between size and complexity would be left unexplained.

in industries where the effects of the division of labor are stronger.

Any interpretation of these interaction effects must be tentatively accepted, however. For one thing, the procedures through which statistical controls are exerted are quite crude, so that the effects of size and division of labor are only partially controlled.

The interaction effects vary among the different administrative components. They appear to be stronger for managerial personnel, although they are noticeably strong for clerical personnel as well. In the case of professional personnel, however, interaction effects appear not to exist. Thus, professional authority may be a less variable coordination mechanism than managerial authority and formal communication.

RELATIVE INCREASE IN ADMINISTRATIVE GROUPS

The analysis of interaction effects allows an assessment of the relative stability of the relationships between the administrative groups and industry size and complexity, but it does not provide a basis by which the rate of change among the three administrative groups may be compared. It is possible, however, that the three administrative groups do not increase at the same rate as industry size and/or complexity increase. Indeed, evidence in Table 3 suggests that the managerial hierarchy grows less rapidly with increases in the division of labor than the other two groups; the ρ coefficient for division of labor and MGR/PP ($\rho = .26$) is only about half as high as for the other two groups ($\rho = .48$ and $.53$). This suggests that with increases in the division of labor, managerial activities

may be increasingly supplemented with the activities of clerical and professional personnel. Thus, relative to managerial authority and supervision, formal communication and professional authority may become increasingly important in coordination as industries become increasingly complex. Decisions may be made and coordination may be effected less and less on the basis of direct observation of the work process by the managerial hierarchy and more and more indirectly on the basis of information processed by professional and clerical personnel. This *interpretation* implies, then, that increases in formal communication structures and professional authority may be functional substitutes for increases in the managerial hierarchy as the division of labor increases.

In any case, the data are consistent with such an interpretation. In Table 2, column 7, the proportion of managerial and professional personnel who occupy positions requiring professional and technical skills are given, and the last column gives the proportion of managerial and clerical personnel who are in positions that call for clerical skills. The relationship between each of these and industry size and the division of labor is shown in Table 4. As can be seen, ρ between the division of labor and the two ratios is moderately high and in the expected direction. Thus while the relative size of all administrative groups increases as industry-wide division of labor increases, clerical and professional personnel seem to increase at a faster rate. The advisory or staff role of professional positions and the communication role of clerical positions as supplements to or functional substitutes for managerial roles appear to increase as the divi-

TABLE 4 SPEARMAN RANK CORRELATIONS BETWEEN RATIO OF CLERICAL AND
PROFESSIONAL PERSONNEL TO MANAGERIAL PERSONNEL AND (1) NUMBER
OF PRODUCTION PERSONNEL AND (2) DIVISION OF LABOR

	Size of Production Personnel			Division of Labor		
Ratio	*All Industries* (N = 41)	*High Division of Labor** (N = 20)	*Low Division of Labor†* (N = 21)	*All Industries* (N = 41)	*Large Industries§* (N = 20)	*Small Industries‡* (N = 21)
$\dfrac{\text{CLER/PP}^{\parallel}}{\text{MGR/PP} + \text{CLER/PP}}$	−.01	−.09	−.09	.27	.36	.28
$\dfrac{\text{PRO/PP}^{**}}{\text{MGR/PP} + \text{PRO/PP}}$	−.06	−.07	−.18	.46	.45	.37

* Industries where the division of labor is .7798 or above.
† Industries where the division of labor is less than .7798.
§ Industries with more than 130,000 production personnel.
‡ Industries with less than 130,000 production personnel.
∥ See Table 2, column 7.
** See Table 2, column 8.

sion of labor increases. Since correlations are about as high in large industries as they are in small industries, industry size and the division of labor do not appear to interact in so far as this process is concerned; as a matter of fact, industry size appears not to be related to this at all, since ρ's between the two ratios and industry size are quite small, although they are consistently negative.

SUMMARY AND CONCLUSIONS

The effects of the division of labor and industry size on the relative number of administrative personnel are complex. They are opposite, independent, and they interact. The findings may be summarized as follows:

1. The relative number of administrative personnel is directly related to the division of labor among production personnel, but inversely related to the total number of production personnel. This is true for all administrative groups.

2. Controlling for the effects of size and division of labor does not usually cause the relationship between the other variable and the relative size of the administrative groups to disappear. In fact, control for the division of labor increases the relationship between industry size and administration. To this extent, the effects of the two variables are independent.

3. At the same time, however, the variables interact. The effects of the division of labor are greater in smaller industries, while the effects of industry size are greater in industries where the division of labor is high. This finding, however, is not true for the relative number of professional personnel.

4. Finally, the ratio of clerical and professional personnel to managerial personnel increases as the division of labor increases.

These data are generally consistent with the complexity-administrative growth hypothesis, which states that coordinative difficulties increase with the division of labor and that the major function of administrative personnel is to resolve these difficulties. Nevertheless, this hypothesis does not provide an explanation for the negative effects of industry size, nor does it explicitly account for the interactive effects. These findings can be explained, however, by an extension of this hypothesis, and the interpretation that the coordinative difficulties generated by size and the division of labor are qualitatively different. However, the finding that the relative number of clerical and professional personnel increases at a faster rate than managerial personnel as the division of labor increases suggests the additional hypothesis that as the division of labor increases, clerical and professional personnel become functional substitutes for managerial personnel.

Perhaps the most important point to be made is that any theory of the effects of size and the division of labor on the relative number of administrative personnel must be complex, because the effects themselves are complex. The issue concerning the effects of division of labor and size is not so much the relative importance of each (although in terms of the growth of clerical and professional personnel relative to managerial personnel, the division of labor is clearly more important), but rather, the fact that the effects of the two variables are independent, opposite, and interactive. Probably no single hypothesis can account for all of the relationships found.

It should be noted again that the findings are based on data for industries, not organizations. Whether similar results would be obtained for organizations cannot be answered with the data at hand.

21. EFFECTS OF SIZE, COMPLEXITY, AND OWNERSHIP ON ADMINISTRATIVE INTENSITY

Louis R. Pondy

For a sample of 45 manufacturing industries, the number of administrative personnel per 100 production workers varies from 8.7 for the logging industry to 131.1 for the drug

Reprinted by permission from *Administrative Science Quarterly* (March 1969), pp. 47–61.

industry, with a mean of 37.7 and a standard deviation of 28.8. This is a wide variation in an important structural characteristic of formal organizations. A theory of organization structure ought to explain why the relative size of the administrative component varies so widely across organizations in different industries, and should also have something to say about the *optimum* administrative intensity for a given industry or organization; i.e., optimum in terms of maximum efficiency or profit for a given level of operation. The purpose of this paper is to present such a theory as applied to manufacturing firms and to report the results of testing it against available census data.[1]

MANAGERIAL DISCRETION VERSUS TECHNOLOGICAL DETERMINISM

The central idea of the theory is that the number of administrative personnel employed in an organization is *chosen* so as to maximize the achievement of goals of the dominant management coalition. For example, for the classical owner-managed firm, it is assumed that the size of the administrative component is increased as long as the marginal return exceeds the marginal cost of additional administrative personnel. (The decision rule is slightly more complex for the firm managed by nonowners, who do not have a direct stake in the profitability of the firm.) Thus the relative size of the administrative component of an organization is treated as a vari-

able *subject to managerial discretion* (Williamson, 1964).

This treatment is in contrast to most analyses, which assume administrative intensity to be *technologically* determined by the task of the organization or by other situational or structural characteristics. For example, it has been argued that:

1. Task complexity and division of labor create problems of coordination, which in turn require administrative personnel to perform coordination functions (Blau and Scott, 1962: 227).
2. With spatial dispersion of organization members, and multiple departments in an organization, coordination is more difficult and requires more administrators than with spatially concentrated members (Anderson and Warkov, 1961).
3. Variability and heterogeneity of the task environment require large numbers of administrators to standardize, stabilize, and regulate input and output transactions, so that the core technology of the organization can operate in an environment of technical rationality (Thompson, 1967).

Hypotheses deriving from these arguments have been subjected to a large amount of more or less rigorous empirical testing. Data from numerous studies consistently support the first argument (Anderson and Warkov, 1961; Bell, 1967; Campbell and Akers, 1968; Chester, 1961; Heydebrand, 1967; Lindsay, 1968; Pugh *et al.*, 1968; Raphael, 1967; Woodward, 1965). As Starbuck (1965) warns, however, one should be wary of accepting the consistency of these results too eagerly, because of the great variations across studies in defining and measuring both complexity and administrative intensity. This comment, of course, applies to the other two hypotheses as well.

[1] A number of persons provided helpful comments and criticisms on an early draft of this paper. The author wishes to express his thanks to John O. Blackburn, Peter Clark, David G. Davies, Louis D. Volpp, and especially to Louis DeAlessi, William H. Starbuck, and Oliver E. Williamson. Starbuck's comments were particularly helpful in treating the problem of bias in estimates resulting from using data on plant size, and Williamson's comments were most helpful in understanding the factors related to variations in the $1-(U_2/U_1)$ variable. The author, of course, accepts final responsibility for any errors.

The second argument is weakly supported by data on tax-supported colleges and universities (Hawley, *et al.*, 1965) and by data on public schools, provided size is controlled (Lindenfeld, 1961). However, data collected by Raphael (1967) on local labor unions strongly contradict the hypothesis.

The third argument is generally consistent with Chandler's (1962, esp. ch. 7) longitudinal and cross-sectional analysis of the administrative structure of American corporations. Recent research by Harvey (1968) and by Lawrence and Lorsch (1967: 17–18), however, suggests that administrative intensity is *lower,* i.e., larger span of control, fewer hierarchical levels) in those organizations or organizational subunits facing changeable or unpredictable environments and technologies (e.g., basic and applied research divisions) than in those facing relatively stable or predictable environments and technologies (e.g., sales and production divisions).

The implicit assumption common to all of these assertions, hypotheses, and empirical studies is that the task, design, and environment of the organization *determine* an administrative component of uniquely appropriate size. However, the deterministic approach fails to consider the contribution of administrative personnel to the goals of management; and it fails to take account of the costs (or other consequences) of under-coordination or over-coordination. In doing so, it ignores the developments of the last two decades in the theory of organizational decision making (Cyert and March, 1963; Feldman and Kanter, 1965). Empirical studies of administrative structure, lacking the integrating principle of rational, goal-seeking behavior, have too often consisted

of a search for empirical regularities with no consistent theoretical basis. And hypotheses have amounted to little more than *ad hoc* statements about empirical regularities, rather than being shown to be isomorphic to propositions rigorously derived from more fundamental postulates.

The relationship between administrative intensity and organization size provides an example. Graicunas (1933) argued that administrative intensity would increase with the size (number of members) of an organization because the number of relationships to be coordinated increases faster than the number of persons being coordinated. Some research workers have since conjectured that if the complexity of the relationships among people (i.e., "interconnectedness") were controlled, the positive correlation between administrative intensity and organization size might disappear or even become negative (e.g., Blau and Scott, 1962: 227). In fact, as is indicated in the results section of this paper, some empirical evidence bears out this conjecture. However, no one has explained why it might be *rational* (relative to the goals of the organization) for administrative intensity to decrease with organization size. The usual explanation (Rushing, 1967: 288–89) is that as an organization grows without increasing in complexity (i.e., by merely adding activities of a type that already exist), administrators perform essentially the same analyses but merely transmit them to more people. Thus, it is argued, the administrative component may grow, but at a slower rate than the rest of the organization. But this explanation, besides not being derived from the more fundamental postulate of rational goal-seeking, does not and cannot predict how the

412   *Size, Complexity, and Administration*

rate of decrease of administrative intensity with size might itself vary with complexity or other factors.

One of the objectives of the theory to be presented is to provide this missing rational basis for explaining empirical regularities associated with variations in administrative intensity.

PROPOSED MODEL

In the present formulation, administrative personnel are treated as one of the factors of production, along with the more traditional input factors of labor and capital. As with labor and capital, the marginal productivity of administrative personnel is assumed to be positive but decreasing. For a manufacturing organization, the total physical output of the organization is assumed to be given by the following production function, which is merely an expansion of the well-known Cobb-Douglas production function (Douglas, 1948):[2]

$$(1) \quad Q = \Theta A^\alpha K^\beta X^\gamma, \quad 0 < \alpha, \beta, \gamma < 1$$

where, $Q =$ total output in number of physical units
    $A =$ number of administrative personnel
    $K =$ total productive capital of the organization
    $X =$ number of production personnel
    $\Theta =$ productivity scale factor
  $\alpha, \beta, \gamma =$ marginal relative productivities of administration, capital and labor, respectively.

[2] It is assumed that this production function is descriptive only of organizations large enough to realize the principal economies that size affords. It is further assumed that it is descriptive of the actual production function in the relevant range, though perhaps not for all ranges of the variables.

If there are constant returns to scale, then the production function is homogeneous and of the first order, and

$$(2) \quad \alpha + \beta + \gamma = 1.$$

However, Tullock (1965), Williamson (1967) and Downs (1967: 112–43) argue that there are increasing cumulative control losses across hierarchical levels, which result in decreasing returns to scale, in which case it would be expected that,

$$(3) \quad \alpha + \beta + \gamma = 1 - \lambda, \quad 0 < \lambda < 1,$$

where λ is the control loss parameter. Furthermore, if

$k = K/X =$ capital intensity per worker
$A/X =$ administrative intensity per worker

then the production function can be written

$$(4) \quad Q = \Theta(A/X)^\alpha k^\beta X^{1-\lambda}.$$

Finally, it is assumed that productivity is directly related to the degree of occupational specialization; that is,

$$(5) \quad \Theta = \Theta_0 S^\sigma, \quad 0 < \sigma < 1,$$

where $S =$ number of distinct occupational specialties represented in the labor force of the organization
    $\sigma =$ marginal relative productivity of specialization
    $\Theta_0 =$ productivity scale factor.

This merely asserts that a worker's productivity increases as he becomes more specialized. The variable S is used both as a measure of worker specialization and as a measure of the functional complexity of the organization (i.e., number of distinct occupational specialties represented in the labor force). The requirement that $0 < \sigma < 1$ means simply that there are positive but decreasing returns to specialization. Doubling the number of occupational specialties for a given organization task will increase productivity, but is not likely to increase it by as much as a factor of two. Thus, the final form of the production function is given by

$$(6) \qquad Q = \Theta_0 S^\sigma (A/X)^\alpha k^\beta X^{1-\lambda}.$$

Suppose now that a profit-maximizing motive is imputed to the management of the organization. The device of motivating management is the means by which the model is made *discretionary* rather than deterministic. Profit and cost are given by

profit = revenue − costs
cost = variable nonwage costs + labor costs + administrative costs + fixed costs

therefore

$$(7) \qquad \pi = pQ - rQ - W_0 X - W_1 A - FC,$$

where π = profit
p = market price of product per unit
r = variable nonwage product costs per unit
W_0 = average wage per production worker
W_1 = average salary per administrative worker
FC = fixed costs.

Assuming now that the organization has already made its decisions regarding capital intensity, degree of specialization, and number of production workers, it is further assumed that it will set the administrative in-

tensity to maximize profits. To find this point equation (7) is differentiated with respect to A/X and the derivative is set equal to zero; that is

$$(8) \quad \frac{d\pi}{d(A/X)} = \alpha\Theta_0(p - r)(A/X)^{\alpha-1}$$
$$\times k^\beta S^\sigma X^{1-\lambda} - W_1 X = 0.$$

Solving for the optimum administrative intensity gives

$$(9) \quad (A/X)^* = [\alpha\Theta_0(p - r)/W_1]^{1/(1-\alpha)}$$
$$\times k^{\beta/(1-\alpha)} S^{\sigma/(1-\alpha)}$$
$$\times X^{-\lambda/(1-\alpha)},$$

where the asterisk denotes an optimum. That is, if it is assumed that organizations choose an administrative intensity to maximize profits, then the model predicts that administrative intensity should be positively correlated with the ratio of net price to administrative salary, with capital intensity, and with degree of specialization (functional complexity), and negatively correlated with organization size, as measured by the number of production personnel. Note that the negative relationship between administrative intensity and organization size is due to the existence of control losses across hierarchical levels. This is discussed further in the section on size effects in the Discussion (see especially equations 27, 28, and 29).

UTILITY-MAXIMIZING VERSION OF THE MODEL

With the separation of ownership and management, management's motivations may not be strictly oriented toward profit maximization. Management may be motivated to increase administrative personnel beyond the optimum profit point. After all, non-owner managers do not share directly in increased profits, although they may share more directly by spending those profits on subordinate administrative personnel to enhance their prestige, to make their jobs easier, and so on; that is, they value hierarchical expense *per se*, as well as profitability. Or management may attach a *negative* "expense preference" to administrative personnel (Williamson, 1964). Owner-managers, for example, may not wish to weaken control of the organization by bringing into the administrative structure persons outside of their families. They may even be willing to accept a lower profit as a result of being underadministered, in exchange for maintaining close personal or family control of the organization. The dominant managers' utility function is defined to include both profit and hierarchical expense (following Williamson, 1964, 1967); that is

(10) $\quad U = U(\pi_0 - H, H)$,

where U = utility function of dominant management coalition

π_0 = profit exclusive of administrative costs

$H = W_1 A$ = hierarchical expense (administrative costs)

Since both π_0 and H can be expressed in terms of number of administrative personnel, A, then it is only necessary to differentiate U with respect to A, set the derivative equal to zero, and solve for the administrative intensity which maximizes managerial utility; that is,

(11) $\quad \dfrac{dU}{dA} = U_1 \left(\dfrac{d\pi_0}{dA} - \dfrac{dH}{dA} \right)$

$\qquad + U_2 \dfrac{dH}{dA} = 0$,

where U_1 and U_2 are the partial derivatives of U with respect to the first and second arguments. But

(12) $\quad \dfrac{d\pi_0}{dA} = \dfrac{dR}{dA}$

$\qquad$ = marginal net revenue,

where R = net revenue = $(p - r)Q$.

Since A does not enter either labor costs or fixed costs, and since

(13) $\quad dH/dA = W_1$

$\qquad$ = marginal cost of one

additional administrative worker, the maximum condition can be restated as,

(14) $\quad \dfrac{dR}{dA} = W_1 \left(1 - \dfrac{U_2}{U_1} \right)$

That is, if the management of the organization values administrative overhead *per se* (i.e., $U_2 > 0$), administrative intensity will be expanded even beyond the point where marginal revenue equals marginal cost. We would expect this condition to increase as ownership and management became more and more separated. Alternatively, if administrative overhead is *negatively* valued (i.e., $U_2 < 0$), administrative intensity will be maintained below the point of maximum profit. The optimum administrative intensity for maximum utility is given by

(15) $\quad (A/X)^* = [\alpha\theta_0(p - r)/W_1]^{1/(1-\alpha)}$
$\qquad \times k^{\beta/(1-\alpha)} S^{\sigma/(1-\alpha)} X^{-\lambda/(1-\alpha)}$
$\qquad \times [1 - (U_2/U_1)]^{-1/(1-\alpha)}$,

which differs from the maximum profit optimum only by the presence of the $[1 - (U_2/U_1)]^{-1/(1-\alpha)}$ term. If the manager does not value administrative overhead, then $U_2 = 0$, and equation (15) reduces to that given by the profit-maximizing model in equation (9).

Under what conditions might U_2/U_1 be expected to increase or decrease? It has already been argued that as the manager's *personal* stake in the profitability of the organization decreases, his relative preference for hierarchical expenses *per se* will increase. This is likely to be the case when ownership and management are separated; i.e., when the active top management of the organization is made up of professional, nonowner managers. Stock-option and other incentive plans for upper management are, of course, intended to make managers' utility functions more nearly coincident with the profit-oriented goals of the stockholders. Such incentive schemes are likely to produce a depressing effect on U_2/U_1. Even in the absence of such incentives, managers cannot afford to ignore profit goals altogether, lest they be dismissed or lose their promotions and salary increases. The extent to which the stockholders can effectively enforce their goals on management is a function primarily of how closely or widely the stock is held and whether the board of directors is an inside board made up of active members of management, or an outside board made up of elected representatives of the stockholders not within the organization. Like incentive schemes, closely held stock and an outside board are likely to depress U_2/U_1.

The U_2/U_1 preference ratio may also be affected by the opportunity set; that is, the more profit an organization is *already* making, the less its managers will value *additional* profit. Thus, U_1, the marginal utility of profit, will decrease as total profit increases, and, *ceteris paribus*, $U_2/$ U_1 will increase. This is likely to be the case when large profits accrue to organizations as a result of monopolistic or oligopolistic market structure, barriers to entry, patent protection, and the like. Thus, in large organizations, the downward pressure on administrative intensity resulting from control losses may be offset by the upward pressure of larger profits made possible by its ability to control its market and technological environment. As U_2/U_1 increases, $[1 - (U_2/U_1)]^{-1/(1-a)}$ also increases, and the model predicts a positive correlation between administrative intensity and those factors which exert upward pressure on U_2/U_1 (e.g., ownership-management separation, and conditions favorable to excess profits). An empirical test of the ownership aspect of this prediction, together with the earlier predictions, follows.

EMPIRICAL TEST OF THE MODEL

The equation to be tested is of the form,

$$(16) \quad A/X = a_0[(p - r)/W_1]^{a_1}k^{a_2}S^{a_3}X^{a_4} \times [1 - (U_2/U_1)]^{a_5}$$

a_0, a_1, a_2, a_3, a_4, and a_5 are parameters to be estimated from the data, and are assumed to be constant across organizations. It has been predicted that $a_1 > 0$, $a_2 > 0$, $a_3 > 0$, $a_4 < 0$, $a_5 < 0$.

In order to transform this model into a form suitable for using techniques of linear regression analysis to estimate the parameters, it is necessary to take natural logarithms of both sides of the equation, with the result that

(17) $\ln(A/X) = \ln a_0$
$\qquad + a_1 \ln[(p-r)/W_1]$
$\qquad + a_2 \ln k + a_3 \ln S$
$\qquad + a_4 \ln X$
$\qquad + a_5 \ln[1 - (U_2/U_1)].$

DATA

This model has been tested using census data from a sample of 45 manufacturing industries (Bureau of the Census, 1958, 1960). Of 62 manufacturing industries for which data are available in the *Occupation by Industry* census, 17 were eliminated because they represented miscellaneous or heterogeneous categories. This is a similar sample to that used by Rushing (1967) in a recent study, except that it includes five industries not included by Rushing, and excludes one industry that he included. Rushing included data from the "miscellaneous plastic products" category because it is the only industry classification for plastics. In this analysis, this industry as well as the other sixteen miscellaneous groups were excluded. Rushing also eliminated data from five industries in which "one or more of the three administrative categories are typically involved in production operations." While this justification applies more or less to two of the industries eliminated (drugs and newspaper publishing) it is less convincing for the other three (paints, aircraft, and printing). All five of these industries are included here and only the 17 "miscellaneous" and "not specified" industry classifications are excluded. Rushing excluded some of the most interesting data points from his sample in the five included in this analysis. (The statistical analysis is not markedly changed when the drug and newspaper publishing industries are removed from the sample.)

Although it would have been desirable to test this model on data by *organization*, this type of information is not available in the published census data. Therefore industry averages have had to be used to represent the "typical" organization in each industry. Since industry averages are weighted by size of organization, the data represent primarily characteristics of large organizations in each industry. Furthermore, because size and the other variables covary across industries, data on industry averages create more multicollinearity problems than would occur with raw data. Efforts are being made to secure other data by organization, in order to subject the model to a more rigorous test.

There is one further problem with the census data, though only a minor one. Data on the total number of personnel and the occupational breakdown are drawn from the *Occupation by Industry* subject report (Bureau of the Census, 1960), and data on the other variables are drawn from the *Census of Manufactures* (Bureau of the Census, 1958). The *Occupation by Industry* subject report uses an industrial classification system that is not the same as the Standard Industrial Classification (SIC) used in the *Census of Manufactures*; however, it provides the SIC codes for industries listed that correspond to the industries in the *Census of Manufactures*.

MEASURES

A description of the measure used for each of the variables follows:

Administrative intensity. This is the number of administrative personnel per 100 production workers in a given industry. "Administrative personnel" is defined to include all those in the standard occupational census categories of "managerial," "professional," and "clerical" personnel. "Production workers" comprise all those in the "craftsman," "operative," and "laborer" categories. This definition is identical to that used by Rushing (1967) and Stinchcombe (1959). Defined in this way, "administrative personnel" includes those employed by the central headquarters staff as well as those located at operating plants.

Market price net of variable nonwage costs, p − r. This is roughly equivalent to value added per unit of output. The census defines "value added" as the dollar value of shipments, plus receipts for services rendered, plus value added by merchandising operations, plus net change in finished goods and work-in-process inventories, minus cost of materials, supplies, containers, fuel, purchased electrical energy, and contract work (Bureau of the Census, 1958: 13). Since the definition of a unit of output is arbitrary, an attempt has been made to obtain a standardized measure of $p − r$ by dividing the total value added for an industry by the total number of production workers.

Average administrative salary. This is total administrative payroll expenses divided by the total number of administrative personnel.

Capital intensity. This is the total undepreciated fixed assets per production worker.

Functional complexity. This is closely related to Rushing's measure, "division of labor." If all occupational specialties in an industry are equally populated, then only the number of occupational specialties needs to be counted to get a measure

of functional complexity. However, the effective number of occupational specialties will be somewhat less than this, if the workers are concentrated in a few of the categories. Rushing's measure of division of labor for a specific industry is given by

$$D = 1 - [\sum X_i^2/(\sum X_i)^2],$$

where X_i is the number of workers in the ith occupational grouping. This reduces to $D = 1 - (1/N)$, when all groupings are equally populated, where N is the total actual number of specialties. Calculating D as Rushing did, $S = 1/(1 - D)$ is defined to be the *effective* number of occupational specialties, or functional complexity.

Number of production personnel per organization. Ideally, to determine the average size of an organization in a given industry, one need only divide the total number of production personnel in the industry by the number of organizations in the industry. Unfortunately, manufacturing census data are collected by "establishment" (roughly equivalent to a plant), not by organizations, partly to conceal the identity of large organizations. The number of organizations in an industry is given in only 10 out of the 45 cases. The rank order correlation between average organization size and average plant size is +.988 for these ten cases, so that average size of plant has been used instead of average size of organization. However, this procedure will tend to bias estimates of the regression coefficients. Another procedure might be to use data only from the ten industries for which information on the average size of organizations is available. But with only four degrees of freedom, estimates of regression coefficients are likely to be statistically insignificant. This problem is discussed in more detail in the section on results.

Separation of ownership and management. As already discussed, the U_2/U_1 ratio may vary because of market structure, availability of stock option plans, etc., as well as because active managers are not also owners. In this paper, only the ownership aspect of variations in U_2/U_1 are investigated; the effects of market structure, etc., are left to future research. The ratio U_2/U_1 reflects the degree to which the management of a firm is willing to trade profit for administrative expense. The percentage of managers in the industry who are owner-managers is used as a very rough measurement of $1 - (U_2/U_1)$ for a given industry. As the percentage of owner-managers increases, one would expect the aggregate managerial preference for administration expense to decrease and $1 - (U_2/U_1)$ to increase. Another possible substitute measure of owner-management separation is the percentage of establishments in an industry that belong to corporations, as opposed to proprietorships or partnerships. This measure was also used in the regression analyses, and the results were qualitatively the same, although slightly less significant than those with the owner-manager measure. This is the least satisfactory measure of the six variables. In particular, there is some concern whether any variations in the percentage of owner-managers would remain, once small organizations were omitted from the sample. If differences were to remain, the same results might not be obtained. At this stage of the research, this problem has not been resolved. More work simply needs to be done.

RESULTS OF REGRESSION ANALYSIS

The coefficients of the relevant variables were estimated using equation (17) as the regression model. All coefficients except that for capital intensity were in the expected direction and statistically significant. The coefficient of determination, adjusted for degrees of freedom, was $R^2 = .57$; that is, it explained 57 percent of the variance in administrative intensity. This appears to be especially satisfactory for the very rough type of data being used. The intercorrelations among the variables are shown in Table 1, the results for the utility-maximizing model in Table 2, and those for the profit-maximizing model in Table 3.

The finding that administrative intensity is negatively correlated with organization size is consistent with those of others (Anderson and Warkov, 1961; Bendix, 1956; Blau et al., 1966; Campbell and Akers, 1968; Chester, 1961; Haas et al., 1963; Haire, 1959; Hawley et al., 1965; Heydebrand, 1967; Indik, 1964; Lindenfeld, 1961; Lindsay, 1968; and Melman, 1951). (The finding by Blau et al. on small bureaucracies is particularly interesting in view of Starbuck's (1965: 499–501) suggestion that administrative intensity is probably an increasing function of organization size for organizations of fewer than 100 employees.) However, a few other studies have produced positive correlations between size and administrative intensity (Raphael, 1967; Tsouderous, 1955).

As Raphael, demonstrates in her study, one must exercise extreme caution in interpreting zero first-order

TABLE 1 MEANS, STANDARD DEVIATIONS AND LOG-LOG INTERCORRELATIONS
FOR ALL VARIABLES

Variables	$(p-r)/W_1$	k	S	X	$1-(U_2/U_1)$	A/X
k	.62					
S	.23	.27				
X	−.07	.31	.20			
$1-(U_2/U_1)$	−.32	−.56	−.24	−.74		
A/X	.61	.46	.48	.03	−.45	
Mean	2.07	11.4*	5.36	128.2	.177†	37.7‡
Standard deviation	.99	10.8	3.08	234.0	.145	28.8

* Thousands of dollars.
† Proportion of managers self-employed.
‡ Number of administrators per 100 workers

TABLE 2 RESULTS OF REGRESSION ANALYSIS OF ADMINISTRATIVE INTENSITY
FOR 45 MANUFACTURING INDUSTRIES BASED ON
UTILITY-MAXIMIZING MODEL

Model: $(A/X)^* = a_0(p-r/w_1)^{a_1}k^{a_2}S^{a_3}X^{a_4}(1-U_2/U_1)^{a_5}$

$R^2 = .57,$ $F = 12.5,$ $df = (5, 39),$ $p < .0005$

Variables	Parameter	Estimate of Parameter	Standard Error of Coefficient	t	Level of Significance
Constant	a_0	15.3	–	–	–
Net price–salary	a_1	0.462	0.201	2.304	<.025
Capital intensity	a_2	−0.047	0.111	−0.425	n.s.
Functional complexity	a_3	0.437	0.130	3.372	<.005
Organization size	a_4	−0.266	0.093	−2.731	<.005
Proportion of owner-managers	a_5	−0.453	0.129	−3.505	<.005

TABLE 3 RESULTS OF REGRESSION ANALYSIS OF ADMINISTRATIVE INTENSITY
FOR 45 MANUFACTURING INDUSTRIES BASED ON
PROFIT-MAXIMIZING MODEL

Model: $(A/X)^* = a_0(p-r/W_1)^{a_1}k^{a_2}S^{a_3}X^{a_4}$

$R^2 = .44,$ $F = 9.76,$ $df = (4, 40),$ $p < .0005$

Variables	Parameter	Estimate of Parameter	Standard Error of Coefficient	t	Level of Significance
Constant	a_0	9.8	–	–	–
Net price/salary	a_1	0.678	0.127	3.315	<.005
Capital intensity	a_2	0.047	0.122	0.385	n.s.
Functional complexity	a_3	0.433	0.147	2.952	<.005
Organization size	a_4	−0.012	0.074	−0.159	n.s.

correlations between size and administrative intensity. The positive correlation appeared in her case only when a third variable, spatial dispersion of members, was controlled. It is important to note that, for the sample in this study, the *first-order* log correlation is 0.03—essentially zero. It is only *when a measure of ownership-management separation is introduced that the partial regression coefficient of size becomes significantly negative.* When the percentage of owner-managers is omitted from the regression; i.e., when the profit-maximizing model is used, the value of R^2 drops significantly, and the regression coefficient of the size variable becomes insignificant (see Tables 2 and 3). The coefficient associated with functional complexity is surprisingly stable (0.437 versus 0.433), but that associated with net price to salary ratio changes markedly (from 0.462 to 0.678). The instability of coefficient estimates is due in large part to the multicollinearity associated with the owner-manager variable. (The first-order log correlations of the percentage of owner-managers with net price to salary ratio and organization size are -0.32 and -0.74, respectively. This is roughly analogous in experimental design to having variables confounded, so that their effects cannot be separated. The major effect of multicollinearity among the independent variables is that regression estimates are biased, and explanatory power tends to be arbitrarily allocated among the independent variables. With Farrar and Glaubner's (1967) "diagnostics," the owner-manager variable has been demonstrated to be the dominant source of multicollinearity in the analysis. This, of course, does not solve the problems associated with multicollinearity. As suggested earlier, changing the data base from industry averages to data on individual organizations may help somewhat.

There are two possible explanations for the lack of significance of the coefficient of capital intensity. First, the capital stock measure—

undepreciated fixed assets—may be inappropriate. It appears now that a measure more closely related to *productive* capital (e.g., depreciated plant and equipment) might have yielded the expected result, but this was not tried. Second, if productive capital takes the form of mechanized or automated equipment, some of the coordinative functions may be performed by the machinery itself. This would tend to reduce the requirements for administrative personnel and counteract the marginal return to administration resulting from higher capital intensity (Blau and Scott, 1962:176–83).

BIAS RESULTING FROM USE OF PLANT SIZE DATA

As suggested earlier, the use of data on average *plant* size rather than average *organization* size tends to bias *all* of the regression coefficient estimates. This can be illustrated as follows. Suppose *plant* size, X, is a function of *organization* size, Y, as well as the other independent variables; then

$$(18) \quad \ln X = b_0 + b_1 \ln [(p - r)/W_1] \\ + b_2 \ln k + b_3 \ln S + b_4 \ln Y \\ + b_5 \ln [1 - (U_2/U_1)].$$

Substituting this expression for ln X in equation (17), gives

$$(19) \quad \ln (A/X) = a_0 + b_0 a_4 + (a_1 + b_1 a_4) \\ \times \ln [(p - r)/W_1] \\ + (a_2 + b_2 a_4) \ln k \\ + (a_3 + b_3 a_4) \ln S \\ + b_4 a_4 \ln Y \\ + (a_5 + b_5 a_4) \\ \times \ln [1 - (U_2/U_1)].$$

The estimates in equation (19) thus include bias corrections in *all* coefficients as a result of the use of plant-size data. The parameters in equation

(18) were estimated using data on the subsample of ten industries for which organization data were available, with the following results:

(20) $\ln X = 0.845 - 0.525$
$\qquad$ (.101)
$\qquad \times \ln [(p - r)/W_1]$
$\qquad - 0.012 \ln k + 0.004 \ln S$
$\qquad$ (.040) $\qquad$ (.039)
$\qquad + 0.713 \ln Y - 0.315$
$\qquad$ (.028) $\qquad$ (.046)
$\qquad \times \ln [1 - (U_2/U_1)],$
$\qquad R^2 = 0.999.$

The standard errors of the coefficients are given in the parentheses below each coefficient. Thus, by using plant-size data, relatively little bias was introduced into estimates of the coefficients of the capital-intensity and functional-complexity variables, but the results given in Table 2 tend to *understate* the magnitude of the effect of "net price to salary" ratio, and *overstate* the effects of size and ownership. If the estimates in equation (20) are assumed to be descriptive of the entire 45-industry sample, the corrected estimates for the administrative intensity expression would be

(21) $\ln (A/X) = 12.4 + 0.602$
$\qquad \times \ln [(p - r)/W_1]$
$\qquad - 0.044 \ln k + 0.436$
$\qquad \times \ln S - 0.190 \ln Y$
$\qquad - 0.369$
$\qquad \times \ln [1 - (U_2/U_1)],$

where Y denotes *organization* size rather than plant size. These estimates should be compared with those in Table 2.

To illustrate the effects of bias further, the coefficients in equations (17) and (19) were estimated directly from data on the subsample of ten industries. Because of the small sample size, the standard errors of the

coefficients are large, and none of the estimates are statistically significant. However, the adjusted R^2 is still 0.57 in both cases, as for the full sample. The results, using average plant size are:

(22) $\ln A/X = 17.2 + 0.806$
$\qquad$ (1.280)
$\qquad \times \ln [(p - r)/W_1]$
$\qquad + 0.139 \ln k + 0.345 \ln S$
$\qquad$ (.426) $\qquad$ (.364)
$\qquad - 0.535 \ln X - 0.689$
$\qquad$ (.534) $\qquad$ (.619)
$\qquad \times \ln [1 - (U_2/U_1)].$

Using average organization size they are:

(23) $\ln (A/X) = 10.8 + 1.081$
$\qquad$ (1.108)
$\qquad \times \ln [(p - r)/W_1]$
$\qquad + 0.147 \ln k + 0.342$
$\qquad$ (.428) $\qquad$ (.364)
$\qquad \times \ln S - 0.383 \ln Y$
$\qquad$ (.301)
$\qquad - 0.533$
$\qquad$ (.507)
$\qquad \times \ln [1 - (U_2/U_1)]$

The direction of bias, as shown in equations (22) and (23), is consistent with the earlier analysis of the tendencies toward overstatement or understatement. The estimates in equation (22) are, of course, slightly different from those in Table 2, because the characteristics of the industries in the ten-industry subsample are somewhat different from those in the full sample. The industries in the subsample, relative to those in the full sample, are higher on the measures of administrative intensity, net price to salary ratio, capital intensity, and average plant size, and lower on functional complexity and proportion of owner-managers.

These difficulties point up again the need to test the model using organization-by-organization data rather than just industry averages.

DISCUSSION

Despite the statistical difficulties, it is possible to have confidence in the finding that administrative intensity is positively related to functional complexity. This finding is consistent with the prediction and interpretation of the technological determinists; that is, that functional complexity leads to coordination problems, which require more administrative personnel. However this finding is interpreted differently here: As functional complexity increases, the marginal productivity of administrative personnel also increases, and it therefore becomes *more profitable* at the margin to employ administrators. From equation (6),

$$(24) \qquad Q = \Theta_0 S^\sigma A^\alpha k^\beta X^{1-\lambda-\alpha}.$$

Marginal productivity of administration is given by

$$(25) \qquad \partial Q / \partial A = \alpha \Theta_0 S^\sigma A^{\alpha-1} k^\beta X^{1-\lambda-\alpha}$$

and

$$(26) \qquad \frac{\partial}{\partial S} \left(\frac{\partial Q}{\partial A} \right) > 0;$$

that is, marginal productivity of administration, and thus the optimal number of administrators, increases with functional complexity.

One can also be confident that if type of ownership is held constant, administrative intensity will decrease with increasing size of organization. (It is important to note that this is a statement about cross-sectional effects, not longitudinal ones!) This is

consistent with the common allegation that there are administrative economies of scale; that is, if the size of the labor force increases by some percentage y, then the number of administrative personnel *needs* to increase only by some percentage $z < y$. This again is an argument following from technological determinism. However, the present managerial discretion model suggests an entirely different interpretation, as a result of the phenomenon of control loss. If the parameter λ equals zero (i.e., if there are no labor diseconomies of scale resulting from control loss), then the model implies that administrative intensity should be constant with respect to organization size (see equation 9). However, if $\lambda > 0$, as seems likely, and a given administrative intensity is maintained, then the marginal productivity of administration *decreases* with size. Technological requirements aside, it simply is not *profitable* to maintain or increase administrative intensity as the size of the organization increases. This can be seen by rearranging the term on the right-hand side of equation (25), giving

$$(27) \qquad \partial Q / \partial A = \alpha \Theta_0 S^\sigma (A/X)^{\alpha-1} k^\beta X^{-\lambda};$$

then

$$(28) \qquad \frac{\partial}{\partial X} \left(\frac{\partial Q}{\partial A} \right) < 0,$$
$$\text{for } A/X = \text{constant.}$$

This effect can be explained solely with reference to the phenomenon of control loss across hierarchical levels. One of the implications of this result is that one would expect a weaker negative correlation between size and administrative intensity among those organizations that have minimized control losses. Such organizations might be those with highly developed bureaucratic controls, those with a high level of goal similarity among members, etc. Under such conditions, the marginal productivity of administration would not decrease as markedly with organization size.

However, the preceding analysis assumes that functional complexity, S, and capital intensity, k, are constant and do not vary with size, but as can be seen from Table 1, both S and k are positively correlated with size for the sample studied. If variations in S and k with size are taken into account, then it can be shown that, for constant A/X

$$(29) \quad \frac{d}{dX}\left(\frac{\partial Q}{\partial A}\right) = \left(\frac{\partial Q}{\partial A}\right)\left[\frac{\sigma}{S}\left(\frac{dS}{dX}\right) + \frac{\beta}{k}\left(\frac{dk}{dX}\right) - \frac{\lambda}{X}\right].$$

That is, assuming $dS/dX > 0$ and $dk/dX > 0$, if X is sufficiently large and S and k are sufficiently small, then it is possible that $d/dX\,(\partial Q/\partial A) > 0$. Under these conditions, the marginal productivity of administration and therefore administrative intensity would *increase* with size of organization! At least relative to manufacturing organizations, labor unions might be expected to have a lower functional complexity and a lower capital intensity. It is interesting, therefore, that Raphael's (1967) study of labor unions is one of the few that show a positive partial correlation between size of organization and relative size of the administrative component. The same result might be expected in other large, relatively unspecialized, labor-intensive organizations, such as church hierarchies, government agencies, and professional associations. Thus Parkinson's

famous dictum—that administrative staff increases faster than the rest of the organization—may be true only for a certain class of organizations. Furthermore, because of the indirect effects of size on complexity and capital intensity, it may be that for some organizations, a more than proportional increase in administrative staff may very well be rational, relative to organizational criteria of efficiency.

The most important finding of this research is the negative relationship between administrative intensity and the proportion of owner-managers, or conversely, the positive relationship between size of administration and ownership-management separation. As already indicated, the same relationship holds although somewhat less strongly, for percentage of corporations in an industry (as opposed to proprietorships or partnerships) as a measure of ownership-management separation. It is argued here that this is because professional managers have a stronger preference for hierarchical expense *per se* than owner-managers, but there are three other explanations for this finding:

(1) Professional administrative personnel are more efficient than owner-managers and their families; their marginal productivity is higher; therefore it is profitable to employ more of them. However, their salaries tend to be higher, so that this partly counteracts their higher productivity.

(2) Owner-managers and employed relatives are willing to work longer hours than professionals; therefore fewer are needed to get the administrative work done. Analysis of the *components* of administration makes this explanation questionable. The *managerial* component is essentially not correlated with measures

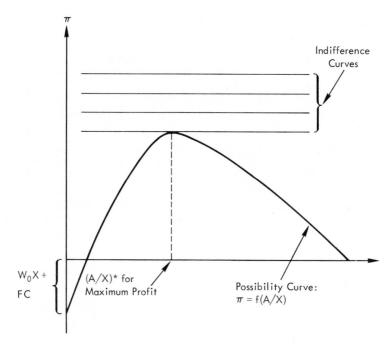

FIG. 1 POSSIBILITY CURVE AND INDIFFERENCE MAP
FOR CLASSICAL OWNER-MANAGER

of ownership-management separation. The positive correlation between administrative intensity and ownership-management separation is due almost solely to the professional-technical and clerical components.

(3) Owner-managers are unwilling to dilute their personal power and control over the organization by adding professional, nonfamily personnel, even if it means accepting a lower profit. This is the most convincing of the alternative explanations. It is also not inconsistent with the basic notion that variability in administrative intensity is partly due to differing utility functions of top management.

To illustrate the effect of different utility functions more explicitly, equation (7) is treated following Williamson (1964), as a "possibility curve" that relates administrative

intensity to profitability for a given level of operation. This is shown in Fig. 1 as a curve which rises as long as the marginal return to administration exceeds W_1, the marginal cost of administration, and falls when the marginal return is less than W_1. Also shown in Fig. 1 are several indifference curves for the classical owner-manager who values only profitability. The point of tangency indicates the administrative ratio that yields maximum profit. Figure 2 shows the same possibility curve, but a new set of indifference curves appropriate for the professional, nonowner managers who value hierarchical expense *per se*, as well as profitability. In the extreme, the professional manager's indifference curves would all be vertical, and he would expand the administrative component until the organization reached the point at

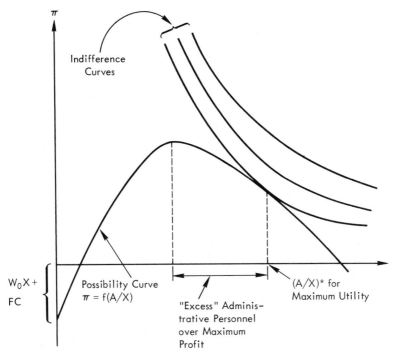

FIG. 2 POSSIBILITY CURVE AND INDIFFERENCE MAP
FOR PROFESSIONAL, NONOWNER MANAGER

which profitability equalled the minimum profit acceptable to the stockholders. The "excess" administrative expense over that appropriate for maximum profit would be a measure of the organizational slack absorbed by management (Cyert and March, 1963).

As suggested, the owner-manager may actually attach a negative preference to administrative staff, thus sacrificing some profitability in return for avoiding dilution of control. In this case, his indifference curves would slant upwards from left to right, in the opposite direction from those shown in Fig. 2, and his maximum utility point for administrative intensity would occur to the left of that appropriate for maximum profit. In such a case, one would expect the profit-maximizing version of the

model to provide a poor fit to such organizations, but the utility-maximizing version to provide a good fit.

As a rough test of this idea, the full sample of 45 industries was divided into three subsamples: one with a low, one with a medium, and one with a high percentage of incorporation of establishments. Both the profit-maximizing and utility-maximizing models were tested on data from each subsample. The results are shown in Table 4.

As can be seen, data from the owner-managed industries (low degree of incorporation) provide a singularly poor fit to the profit model, but an excellent fit to the utility model. At the other extreme, data on professionally managed industries (high degree of incorporation) fit the profit model extremely well, and the

TABLE 4 COMPARATIVE GOODNESS OF FIT OF THE PROFIT-MAXIMIZING AND
UTILITY-MAXIMIZING MODELS FOR INDUSTRIES WITH HIGH,
MEDIUM, AND LOW DEGREE OF INCORPORATION

Degree of Incorporation	Percent of Plants Incorporated	n	R^2 (Adjusted)	
			Profit Model	Utility Model
High	77–100%	15	.80	.88
Medium	61–74	16	.44	.40
Low	4–58	14	.09	.85

fit is improved only slightly by including $1 - (U_2/U_1)$ term (i.e., the utility-maximizing model). For industries with a medium degree of incorporation, the adjusted R^2 actually drops from the profit model to the utility model (because one additional degree of freedom is used up without any improvement in fit). Although this analysis is highly tentative, one might wish to draw the inference that proprietorships and partnerships tend to be underadministered relative to a profit criterion. Furthermore, industries with a high degree of incorporation appear to have an administrative intensity consistent with profit-maximizing motives, with possibly only a moderate amount of "excess" administration. The data seem to suggest that "expense preference" (Williamson, 1964) for administrative staff shifts from a negative to a positive preference as one moves from owner-managed to professionally managed organizations.

In conclusion, it is argued that administrative intensity in organizations is a function of both economic and technological variables, but is also strongly influenced by managerial motivations and patterns of ownership. If the analysis of the data has not "proved" the theory, it has at least given it plausibility. Furthermore, formalizing the theory as a mathematical model has made it possible to derive testable conjectures which were neither obvious in the present data nor yet systematically investigated by others.

REFERENCES

ANDERSON, THEODORE and SEYMOUR WARKOV. 1961. "Organization size and functional complexity: a study of administration in hospitals." *American Sociological Review*, 26: 23–28.

BELL, GERALD D. 1967. "Determinants of span of control." *American Journal of Sociology*, 73: 100–109.

BENDIX, REINHARD. 1956. *Work and Authority in Industry*. New York: John Wiley.

BLAU, PETER M., W. V. HEYDEBRAND and R. E. STAUFFER. 1966. "The structure of small bureaucracies." *American Sociological Review*, 31: 179–91.

BLAU, PETER M. and W. RICHARD SCOTT. 1962. *Formal Organizations*. San Francisco: Chandler.

BUREAU OF THE CENSUS. 1958. *Census of Manufactures, Summary Statistics*. Washington: U. S. Department of Commerce.

BUREAU OF THE CENSUS. 1960. "Occupation by industry." *Subject Report* 7C, *U. S. Population Census*. Washington: U. S. Department of Commerce.

CAMPBELL, FREDERICK L. and RONALD L. AKERS. 1968. "Organizational growth and structural changes in occupational associations." Unpublished paper presented at annual meeting of American Sociological Association. Boston.

CHANDLER, ALFRED D. 1962. *Strategy and Structure: Chapters in the History of Industrial Enterprise.* Cambridge, Massachusetts: M. I. T. Press.

CHESTER, T. E. 1961. *A Study of Post-War Growth in Management Organizations.* Project 347. Paris: European Productivity Agency.

CYERT, RICHARD M. and JAMES G. MARCH. 1963. *A Behavioral Theory of the Firm.* Englewood Cliffs, N. J.: Prentice-Hall.

DOUGLAS, PAUL H. 1948. "Are there laws of production?" *American Economic Review,* 38: 1–41.

DOWNS, ANTHONY. 1967. *Inside Bureaucracy.* Boston: Little, Brown.

FARRAR, DONALD E. and ROBERT R. GLAUBNER. 1967. "Multi-collinearity in regression analysis: the problem revisited." *The Review of Economics and Statistics,* 49: 92–107.

FELDMAN, JULIAN and HERSCHEL E. KANTER. 1965. "Organizational decision making." *In* James G. March (ed.), *Handbook of Organizations.* pp. 614–49. Chicago: Rand-McNally.

GRAICUNAS, V. A. 1933. "Relationship in organization." *Bulletin of the International Management Institute,* 7: 39–42.

HAAS, EUGENE, R. H. HALL and N. J. JOHNSON. 1963. "The size of the supportive component in organizations: a multi-organizational analysis." *Social Forces,* 43: 9–17.

HAIRE, MASON. 1959. "Biological models and empirical histories of the growth of organizations." *In* Mason Haire (ed.), *Modern Organization Theory.* pp. 272–306. New York: John Wiley.

HARVEY, EDWARD. 1968. "Technology and the structure of organizations." *American Sociological Review.* 33: 247–59.

HAWLEY, A. W., W. BOLAND and M. BOLAND. 1965. "Population size and administration in institutions of higher education." *American Sociological Review,* 30: 252–55.

HEYDEBRAND, WOLF V. 1967. "Division of labor and coordination in organizations: a comparative study." Unpublished manuscript. Chicago: Department of Sociology, University of Chicago.

INDIK, BERNARD P. 1964. "The relationship between organization size and supervision ratio." *Administrative Science Quarterly,* 9: 301–12.

LAWRENCE, PAUL R. and JAY W. LORSCH. 1967. "Differentiation and integration in complex organization." *Administrative Science Quarterly,* 12: 1–47.

LINDENFELD, FRANK. 1961. "Does administrative staff grow as fast as organization?" *School Life,* 43: 20–23.

LINDSAY, PHILIP D. 1968. "Administrative staff size in national labor unions." Unpublished manuscript. Pittsburgh: Graduate School of Business. University of Pittsburgh.

MELMAN, SEYMOUR. 1951. "The rise of administrative overhead in the manufacturing industries of the United States: 1899–1947." *Oxford Economic Papers,* 3: 62–112.

PUGH, D. S., D. J. HICKSON, C. R. HININGS and C. TURNER. 1968. "Dimensions of organization structure." *Administrative Science Quarterly,* 13: 65–105.

RAPHAEL, EDNA A. 1967. "The Anderson-Warkov hypotheses in local unions: a comparative study." *American Sociological Review,* 32: 768–76.

RUSHING, WILLIAM A. 1967. "The effects of industry size and division of labor on administration." *Administrative Science Quarterly,* 12: 273–95.

STARBUCK, WILLIAM H. 1965. "Organizational growth and development." *In* James G. March (ed.), *Handbook of Organizations.* pp. 451–533. Chicago: Rand-McNally.

STINCHCOMBE, ARTHUR L. 1959. "Bureaucratic and craft administration of production: a comparative study." *Administrative Science Quarterly,* 4: 168–87.

THOMPSON, JAMES D. 1967. *Organizations in Action.* New York: McGraw-Hill.

TSOUDEROUS, JOHN E. 1955. "Organization change in terms of a series of selected variables." *American Sociological Review*, 20: 206–10.

TULLOCK, GORDON. 1965. *The Politics of Bureaucracy*. Washington: Public Affairs Press.

WILLIAMSON, OLIVER E. 1964. *The Economics of Discretionary Behavior: Managerial Objectives in a Theory of the Firm*. Englewood Cliffs, N. J.: Prentice-Hall.

WILLIAMSON, OLIVER E. 1967. "Hierarchical control and optimum firm size." *Journal of Political Economy*, 75: 123–38.

WOODWARD, JOAN. 1965. *Industrial Organization: Theory and Practice*. London: Oxford University Press.

22. SIZE, EXTERNAL RELATIONS, AND THE DISTRIBUTION OF POWER: A STUDY OF COLLEGES AND UNIVERSITIES

Walter R. Boland

There has been considerable discussion and controversy over the influence of size on the structure of formal organizations.[1] Recent comment and research indicates that increasing size is relatively unimportant when compared to the much greater impact of two factors: (1) the type of technology (i.e., long-linked, "people-changing," etc.,) characterizing the organization; and (2) the nature of the organization's environment (i.e.,

This study has been supported, in part, by a faculty research grant from the University of Connecticut Research Foundation 217-038.

[1] This discussion has been centered on the nature of the relationship between increasing size and the development of "bureaucratic" structures and processes. Gouldner (1955), for example, has attacked the pessimism of Weber (1947) and Michels (1949) who view increasing size as being inevitably associated with the development of "bureaucratic" and "oligarchical" systems, respectively. Gouldner's position has been supported by the work of Hall, et al. (1967), which found little or no relationship between size and the degree of functional complexity and formalization. The conclusion of Hall, et al. (1967:912), however, which states that "These findings suggest that size may be irrelevant as a factor in determining organizational structure . . ." is misleading given the faulty sampling procedures employed. Blau, et al. (1966), on the other hand, find a relatively strong relation between size and structural differentiation. In a related fashion, the findings of Hawley, et al. (1965) conflict with those of Anderson and Warkov (1961) and Raphael (1967) on the relationship between size and the proportion of administrators. The latter claim that this proportion is a result of the organization's functional complexity rather than size. (See Starbuck (1965) for a review of the literature on the implications of organizational growth.)

its heterogeneity and instability, hostility, etc.). With regard to the former, Perrow (1967), Victor Thompson (1961), and James Thompson (1967) assume that technological differences among organizations take precedence over size considerations in understanding the degree to which decision-making power is centralized, the functional complexity of the system, the degree of autonomy enjoyed by the lower hierarchical levels, and the type of control which is used—whether by means of programs or feedback control mechanisms. Their position has been supported by the empirical studies of Woodward (1965) and Harvey (1968) which indicate that the technology—structural variation relation—remains considerable even with organizational size controlled. Similarly, while the study of the relationship between the organization's environment and its internal structure and processes has been neglected, the theories of Lawrence and Lorsch (1967), Thompson (1967), and the findings of Aiken and Hage (1968) indicate that this factor has a significance which is quite independent of size considerations.[2] The assumption made in the present study, on the other hand, is that there is still reason to believe that size makes a difference in the ways in which formal organizations are structured to handle their technical and environmental affairs. To find out if this is indeed the case, this investigation focuses on the rela-

tionship between size and the centralization of decision-making power associated with two aspects of the structure of formal organizations. These two aspects are (1) those having to do with *internal* or technical affairs, and (2) those concerned with certain crucial *external* relations. To provide a reasonable "test" of this notion it is necessary to limit the types of organizations studied to those with similar technologies and substantively similar environments. The assumption is examined, therefore, within one class of formal organization—namely institutions of higher learning.

While there have been a number of suggestions by Kerr (1963), Ridgeway (1968), Wilson (1942) and others as to how institutions of higher learning are structured to handle these matters, there has been little systematic effort to "explain" the particular forms that have been described. With this in mind, it seems reasonable to argue that the demands of numbers "force" these institutions to make use of an organizational model which is quite different from that used in smaller institutions.[3] Where this model is found, furthermore, the faculty has considerable power to influence the institution's educational policy as well as matters of particular interest to each group of academic professionals through the faculty's governmental system and autonomous subject-matter departments. Power over these internal or technical affairs is, therefore, decen-

[2] Many students of organization have examined the nature and significance of organizational differences in technology and environmental settings. (See Perrow (1967), James Thompson (1967) and Aiken and Hage (1968) for recent reviews of this literature.) The present study limits itself to considering only those contributions which are concerned with the relative significance of organizational size in understanding organizational structures and processes.

[3] As was mentioned in an earlier article (Hawley, et al., 1965:255) ". . . the determinants of institutional structure come to reside in a parent system, so that functions of all kinds tend to be shaped and adapted to a standard institutional structure." Which model is used, however, tends to reflect size considerations.

tralized. The independence of the faculty is, however, never complete. Rather, it is dependent on the continued integrity and viability of the model.[4] The latter is assured through organizational mechanisms devoted to the maintenance and development of institutional legitimacy and material support. Control over these activities, on the other hand,—that is, those having to do with crucial external relations—is centralized at the highest level. At a somewhat higher level of abstraction, the model defines an umbrella structure in which the topmost levels exert rather limited control over the institution's faculty, mainly through their concern with matters pertaining to the maintenance of the system. In fact, the power of decision over the latter occurs at the "expense of" their control over the institution's internal or technical affairs. In any case, where this model is not employed—in the smaller institutions—it follows that such a loosely integrated federation of administrative and faculty subunits will be absent. Increasing size is treated, therefore, as a necessary condition for the realization of some of the important aspects of faculty self-government and collegial authority. This seems paradoxical when compared to the writings of Weber, Michels, and others who have assumed an inevitable relation between size and a "bureaucratic" and oligarchical character of organizations.

HYPOTHESES AND MEASURES

The following hypotheses are examined in the present study. They are rather straightforward derivations from the foregoing discussion of the relationship between size and the type of model employed by institutions of higher learning. To insure clarity, the measures of both the independent and dependent variables are included in this section of the paper.

1. *As institutional size increases,[5] a "center" becomes apparent which is specialized in mediating those external relations which are crucial to the maintenance and development of institutional legitimacy and material support.* The center is made up of "the representative" of the institution —the president—and a variety of "mediating roles" staffed by individuals skilled in persuasion, the manipulation of public opinion, and "money-management." By implication, the development of such a mechanism highlights the increasing concern of presidents with matters of "public" relations and financial affairs and a less pressing concern with the more mundane matters associated with the coordination and/or direction of the other administrative officials and the institution's subject matter departments. The relative distinctiveness of the center is suggested by the frequency and directness of communication between these mediating roles—that is, those roles with supervisory responsibility for public relations, "image" producing publications, alumni relations and "money-

---

[4] It would be expected that the power to "apply" these standards would be delegated to a middle level of administrative officials.

[5] A full-time equivalent measure of faculty size is used to measure institutional size. This measure assured some independence of variation relative to the dependent variables and is comparable to measures of size used in other studies. This measure has the further advantage of being highly correlated with the size of the student body and seemed, therefore, more than adequate for the purposes of this study.

management"[6]—and the president. To measure the frequency and directness of communication, a ratio was devised indicating the percentage of externally oriented administrative functions whose supervisors report directly to the president to the percentage of all administrative functions[7] which have direct access to the president. A ratio of relatively great magnitude would describe a situation in which there was a centralization of control over the mediation function. Although it is a rather crude measure of this form of development, the ratio does allow a reasonable test of the hypothesis. In fact, given the relatively narrow range of variation allowable by such a measure, it would seem a rather severe test. For convenience, this ratio will hereafter be referred to as the "External Relations" ratio.[8]

[6] The latter includes the management of endowments, bequests and other investment funds, the dividends from which are used for either special or general institutional purposes.

[7] Eighteen selected administrative functions were examined in a rather detailed fashion. They were Official Publications, Investments, Alumni Relations, Public Relations, Scholarly Publications, Student Publications, Accounting, Staff Benefits, Institutional Development, Personnel—Nonacademic, Admissions, Student Health, Religious Affairs, Student Loans, Scholarship Funds, Counseling-Academic, Counseling-Discipline, and Libraries. The first four functions were designated as externally oriented and were elements of the center. It will be noted that although admissions is an externally oriented function it is not included as one of the elements of the center. This exclusion was based on the fact that this function has only indirectly to do with matters of legitimacy and material support and is mainly concerned with the routine and technical matters of processing student applications.

[8] The "External Relations" ratio has a mean size of 1.66, standard deviation of 1.00, and range of 0 to 6.50.

2. *As institutional size increases, institutions of higher learning are characterized by an increasingly powerful faculty "Senate" or governing body and a greater autonomy of subject matter departments over matters of particular concern to them.* The contention of the faculty and administration over these matters is well expressed by Burton Clark (1962: 156–57):

... the long-term trend in American higher education has been for authority to move from external to internal sources with faculties contending with the administration about who has authority over what. The faculties march under the banner of self-government and academic freedom, emphasizing the equality of relations among colleagues and de-emphasizing administrative hierarchy. The administrations move forward under the banner of increased efficiency, united effort, public relations—and the reducing of chaos to mere confusion.

While this contention is found in varying degrees in all colleges and universities, it is expected that the conditions favoring significant faculty self-government will be contingent on size considerations.[9]

The measurement of the autonomy and decision-making power of the Senate and the subject matter departments is rather straightforward. First of all, the power of the Senate is suggested by its ability to influence the policy decisions of the administrative officials on academic policy, appointments to official positions, etc. Moreover, the "role" of the Senate—that

[9] Gross (1968) shows, however, that the goals of the administration and the faculty are remarkably alike. If this is the case, it would imply a good deal less contention than might be supposed.

is, whether it is concerned primarily with the formulation of educational policy, information dissemination or the approval of recommendations from above—is examined. The reasoning behind this analysis is clear. If the Senate is mainly concerned with information dissemination, etc., then its power over educational goals through the formulation of policy would necessarily be restricted.[10] Secondly, the degree of autonomy associated with the institution's subject matter departments is measured by whether or not the decision on the addition of new or the withdrawal of old courses from the department's offerings, promotions and merit increases for departmental faculty, recommendations for new appointments and the termination of old appointments, and the determination of the need for new personnel is made within or outside the department in question. The latter measures are supplemented through an analysis of the role of the department chairman. This analysis centers its attention on the time the chairman spends on teaching, administration, research, etc. While this measure provides less detail than the other measures of

autonomy, it does suggest whether or not a department is a self-administered unit. This would be the case, of course, if the chairman spends considerable portions of his time on administrative duties. Related to this, the level at which departmental decisions are reviewed by administrative officials is examined. It is expected that this authority will be delegated to the academic vice president or to the dean of the college in the larger institutions. Their concern would be centered, therefore, on evaluating the degree to which a particular subject matter department meets a set of system-wide standards. Such a review would assure the integrity of the structural model employed, while allowing for a considerable degree of variability of organizational styles and patterns within the institution.

DATA COLLECTION

The data for the present study were secured through two questionnaires. One was addressed to the presidents of publicly supported colleges and universities.[11] Data pertaining to "administrative matters"[12] were provided by the one hundred and fifteen institutions which returned this questionnaire. A second questionnaire, pertaining to faculty matters—including the power of the Senate and the autonomy of subject matter depart-

[10] Two questions which were answered by department chairmen were used to infer this concern and power. First, the chairman's perception of the role of the Senate was assessed. Whether, that is, it is a body concerned with the formulation of educational policy or not. Second, the chairman's perception of whether or not the faculty body has sufficient power to influence the policy decisions of the administrative officials, especially on academic policy, was determined. It was felt that the chairman could answer these questions in a more perceptive manner than others. His role as a mediator between the administration and a group of faculty members provides him with insight into both academic and administrative activities.

[11] The universe was all tax-supported institutions of higher education having, in 1961, four-year undergraduate degree granting programs.

[12] Some data pertaining to the faculty such as its size, its rate of growth, its quality, and data on the complexity of the academic component were also provided by this questionnaire. It was lengthy (49 pages) and covered many aspects of administration.

TABLE 1 STUDENT ENROLLMENT IN UNIVERSE AND SAMPLE,
INSTITUTIONS OF HIGHER EDUCATION

	Number of Institutions in		*Percent Sample is of Universe*
Student Enrollment	*Universe*	*Sample*	
Under 1,000	62	20	321
1,000–2,499	112	28	25
2,500–4,999	86	26	30
5,000–9,999	49	23	47
10,000 and over	47	18	38
Total	356	115	Average 32

ments—was addressed to departmental chairmen within the one hundred and fifteen institutions in the sample. Seven hundred and twenty of these questionnaires were completed and returned. As can be seen from an examination of Table 1, the sample institutions are spread adequately through the range of student sizes, and each size category is well represented.

While the present study focuses on the effects of size, other variables may be as important in affecting the dependent variables. A variable that seems likely to be of particular importance is the degree of organizational complexity.[13] Both organizational complexity and the development of such a strategic "center," a powerful faculty government, and autonomous subject matter departments represent aspects of organizational diversity and can be expected to vary together. For this reason, the effect of complexity

is examined and controlled. Other control variables are the rate of institutional growth over a five-year period,[14] and institutional quality.[15] It seems reasonable to expect a "lag" in organizational development to be associated with a high rate of growth. Lastly, it is assumed that structural differences, as well as the differences in organizational goals found by Gross (1968), will be associated with institutional quality. It seems likely that the higher quality institutions will have faculties with greater influence over educational policy through their faculty government and greater control over those matters of particular concern to their subject matter departments. This may be nothing more than a "professorial bias," however.

[13] Organizational complexity is measured by the number of subject matter departments and non-departmentalized schools. As was mentioned elsewhere (Hawley, et al., 1965), this measure has certain disadvantages. That is, it does not adequately express the total range of diverse activities present or potentially present in a modern university. For the purposes of this study, however, such an approximation seemed adequate.

[14] The rate of institutional growth was measured by the rate of growth in the student body over a five-year period.
[15] Institutional quality was measured by the proportion of undergraduates of an institution who later became scholars. The output of students who later received Ph.D. degrees in a twenty-one year period, 1936–1956, is divided by the student size of each institution for a representative year (1949) to provide a ratio of scholars produced per student enrolled. The data were acquired from *Doctorate Production in the United States Universities, 1936–1956, with Baccalaureate Origins of Doctorates in Sciences, Arts, and Humanities* (1958).

FINDINGS

SIZE AND EXTERNAL RELATIONS RATIO

The beta weights presented in Table 2 indicate the relatively strong association between size and the External Relations ratio when the other variables are controlled. A standardized increase in faculty size is most highly associated with the ratio when organizational complexity is controlled. Although organizational complexity is related in the predicted direction to the dependent variable, the direction and magnitude of the relationship is altered when institutional size is held constant. The rate of institutional growth is also related in the predicted direction to the ratio. Its influence, however, appears negligible when the effects of size are removed.[16] The same is true in the case of institutional quality. These results seem to attest to the relatively strong influence of size. To allow a more detailed analysis of this hypothesis, and to clarify this relationship more fully, a tabular presentation of the joint distribution of institutional size, organizational complexity, and the ratio is presented in Table 3. The choice of organizational complexity was made because of its relatively strong relationship to the ratio and the "causal" priority given it by some investigators in regard to other aspects of administrative organization.

Table 3 provides a rather interesting bit of additional information bearing on the hypothesis that as institutional size increases a center

becomes apparent which is specialized in mediating certain crucial external relations. That is, a "threshold" is apparent in the relationship between institutional size and the centralization of those activities and decisions concerning institutional legitimacy and material support. The relatively large beta weights and coefficients describing this relationship are due to the effect of the larger institutions. Moreover, when the interior cells of the table are examined, additional support is given to the validity of the hypothesis. Thus, when the effects of increasing organizational complexity are examined within categories of size (i.e., when size is controlled) the ratio is reduced in all cells except one.[17] On the other hand, when complexity is controlled, increasing size is positively associated with the magnitude of the ratio. The results lend considerable support to the notion that size has a strong effect both on the degree of centralization of control over strategic institutional relations and on organizational complexity.[18] It is apparent, therefore, that institutional size makes a significant difference in the way in which institutions of higher learning structure themselves to handle their environmental affairs.

SIZE AND THE DECISION-MAKING POWER AND AUTONOMY OF THE FACULTY

The analyses of the relationship between size and the manner in which colleges and universities structure themselves to handle their "technical" or internal academic affairs is pre-

---

[16] Tabular analysis indicates that the negative relationship between the External Relations ratio and the rate of institutional growth is due to the negative relationship between institutional size and the rate of growth.

[17] Cells with less than two cases are not considered in this analysis.

[18] The size-organizational complexity relationship is relatively strong ($r = .840$).

TABLE 2 BETA WEIGHTS AMONG INSTITUTIONAL SIZE, ORGANIZATIONAL
COMPLEXITY, RATE OF INSTITUTIONAL GROWTH, INSTITUTIONAL
QUALITY AND THE EXTERNAL RELATIONS RATIO

Institutional Size and the Control Variables	Zero-Order Correlations Y*	Beta Weights			
		1	2	3	4
1. Institutional Size	.495	–	.665	.527	.450
2. Organizational Complexity	.395	–.201	–	.382	.289
3. Rate of Institutional Growth	–.304	.106	.072	–	–.001
4. Institutional Quality	.301	.094	.218	.311	–

* Y represents the External Relations ratio.

TABLE 3 THE RELATIONSHIP BETWEEN INSTITUTIONAL SIZE, COMPLEXITY,
AND THE EXTERNAL RELATIONS RATIO

Number of Subject-Matter Departments	Institutional Size				
	0–85	86–155	156–325	326+	Total
0–12	1.29 (15)	1.57 (5)	1.18 (1)	– (0)	1.35 (21)
13–20	1.24 (3)	1.24 (12)	1.44 (10)	– (0)	1.32 (25)
21–45	1.12 (1)	1.13 (3)	1.39 (11)	2.16 (7)	1.59 (22)
46+	– (0)	.54 (1)	4.00 (1)	2.72 (15)	2.67 (17)
Total	1.27 (19)	1.27 (21)	1.51 (23)	2.54 (22)	1.66 (85)*

* Only 85 institutions provided information on institutional size, organizational complexity, and the External Relations ratio.

TABLE 4 THE RELATIONSHIP BETWEEN INSTITUTIONAL SIZE AND WHETHER
THE INSTITUTION'S ACADEMIC GOVERNMENT HAS SUFFICIENT POWER TO
INFLUENCE THE POLICY DECISIONS OF ADMINISTRATIVE OFFICIALS

Sufficient Power	Institutional Size			
	–145	146–315	316+	Total
Yes	35%*(57)	51% (94)	73% (219)	370
Yes and No	15 (25)	13 (23)	12 (37)	85
No	50 (80)	36 (66)	15 (45)	191
Total	162	183	301	646

* Many of the percentages have been rounded.

sented below. As was discussed in the foregoing, the primary concern is to isolate and identify the influence of size on (1) the power of the faculty government; and (2) the degree of autonomy associated with the subject matter departments.

The results presented in Table 4 indicate that the relationship between institutional size and the power of the faculty government to influence policy decisions is rather strong.[19] In fact,

[19] The results are based on the perceptions of the department chairmen. The chairmen were asked the following question: "Generally, do you feel that your institution's academic government (faculty body) has sufficient power to influence the policy

TABLE 5 THE RELATIONSHIP BETWEEN INSTITUTIONAL SIZE AND THE
AUTONOMY OF THE SUBJECT MATTER DEPARTMENTS OVER THE
ADDITION OF NEW OR THE WITHDRAWAL OF OLD COURSES

The Level at which	*Institutional Size*			
the Decision is Made	*–145*	*146–315*	*316+*	*Total*
Department	67% (91)	76% (126)	88% (249)	466
Outside the Department	33 (45)	24 (40)	12 (34)	119
Total	136	166	283	585

TABLE 6 THE RELATIONSHIP BETWEEN INSTITUTIONAL SIZE AND THE
AUTONOMY OF THE SUBJECT MATTER DEPARTMENTS OVER
PROMOTIONS AND MERIT INCREASES

The Level at which	*Institutional Size*			
the Decision is Made	*–145*	*146–315*	*316+*	*Total*
Department	45% (71)	68% (126)	83% (251)	448
Outside the Department	54 (85)	31 (58)	17 (51)	194
Total	156	184	302	642

surprisingly so.[20] The faculty in the larger institutions are much more likely to develop a strong faculty government. Those in the smaller institutions, on the other hand, are more often subject to the decrees of administrative officials. In the latter, it is likely that the "role" of the faculty government would be restricted to that of a body within which information is disseminated. This is the case in fifty percent of the smallest institutions.[21] In contrast, thirty-five per-

cent of the largest institutions have a faculty "Senate" which is mainly concerned with the formulation of educational policy. The analysis of the power and the role of the faculty government indicates, therefore, that the degree of centralization of control over educational policy is much less in the larger than in the smaller institutions.

When the relationship between size and the degree of autonomy associated with the subject matter departments is examined in Tables 5–8, the results indicate quite clearly that the larger institutions are much more likely to have these decisions made within the department. The only exception is noted in the rather weak relationship between size and control over curriculum. It seems that professional prerogative rather than size considerations takes precedence here. The results reported in these tables, furthermore, are not affected appreciably when the relationships are examined within categories of

---

decisions of the administrative officials (especially on academic policy, appointment to official positions such as President, Dean, etc.)? Comment."

[20] When this relationship is examined within categories of the control variables, the effects of size are not reduced appreciably.

[21] The chairmen were asked to comment on the role of this group. Their answers were distributed over four categories: (1) policy-making, (2) discussion and taking limited action, (3) making recommendations and giving approval to administrative suggestions, and (4) acting as a body in which information is disseminated.

TABLE 7 THE RELATIONSHIP BETWEEN INSTITUTIONAL SIZE AND THE AUTONOMY OF SUBJECT MATTER DEPARTMENTS OVER RECOMMENDATIONS FOR NEW APPOINTMENTS AND THE TERMINATION OF OLD APPOINTMENTS

The Level at which the Decision is Made	Institutional Size			
	–145	*146–315*	*316+*	*Total*
Department	28% (46)	48% (87)	72% (221)	354
Outside the Department	72 (119)	52 (95)	28 (86)	300
Total	165	182	307	654

TABLE 8 THE RELATIONSHIP BETWEEN INSTITUTIONAL SIZE AND THE AUTONOMY OF THE SUBJECT MATTER DEPARTMENTS OVER THE DETERMINATION OF NEED FOR NEW PERSONNEL

The Level at which the Decision is Made	Institutional Size			
	–145	*146–315*	*316+*	*Total*
Department	25% (42)	42% (78)	67% (204)	324
Outside the Department	74 (123)	58 (106)	33 (100)	329
Total	165	184	304	653

TABLE 9 THE RELATIONSHIP BETWEEN INSTITUTIONAL SIZE AND THE PERCENTAGE OF TIME DEPARTMENT CHAIRMEN SPEND ON DEPARTMENTAL ADMINISTRATION, TEACHING, AND RESEARCH

Percentage of Chairman's Time	Institutional Size			
	–145	*146–315*	*316+*	
Administration—40%+	26%	44%	60%	
Teaching—50%+	58	30	10	
Research—10%+	30	46	59	
Total	157	179	291	627

the control variables—organizational complexity, rate of institutional growth and institutional quality.[22] It seems reasonable to conclude, therefore, that the larger institutions place a greater emphasis on the expertise of their faculties and this is indicated by the power of the faculty government to influence educational policy or the power of the various groups of academic professionals over their particular subject matter departments.

It is apparent from an inspection of Table 9 that the largest institutions are most likely to have self-administering subject matter departments. That is, the results indicate that the department chairmen in these institutions are much more likely than those in the smaller to spend a considerable portion of their time on

[22] The only exception is when organizational complexity is controlled. In this case the relationship is reduced. This is due, however, to the strong relationship between size and complexity. When, on the other hand, the complexity-autonomy of subject matter departments relationship is examined within categories of institutional size, the relationship is almost completely eliminated.

TABLE 10 THE RELATIONSHIP BETWEEN THE EXTERNAL RELATIONS RATIO
AND WHETHER THE INSTITUTION'S ACADEMIC GOVERNMENT HAS
SUFFICIENT POWER TO INFLUENCE THE POLICY DECISIONS
OF ADMINISTRATIVE OFFICIALS

Sufficient Power	External Relations Ratio			Total
	0.0–1.0	*1.1–2.5*	*2.6–6.5*	
Yes	51% (120)	49% (170)	74% (78)	368
Yes and No	15 (35)	12 (43)	12 (13)	91
No	34 (78)	39 (134)	13 (14)	226
Total	233	347	105	685

TABLE 11 THE RELATIONSHIP BETWEEN THE EXTERNAL RELATIONS RATIO
AND THE AUTONOMY OF SUBJECT MATTER DEPARTMENTS OVER
RECOMMENDATIONS FOR NEW APPOINTMENTS AND THE
TERMINATION OF OLD APPOINTMENTS

The Level at which the Decision is Made	External Relations Ratio			Total
	0.0–1.0	*1.1–2.5*	*2.6–6.5*	
Department	46% (108)	49% (174)	72% (77)	359
Outside the Department	54 (125)	51 (181)	28 (30)	336
Total	233	355	107	695

the administration of departmental affairs. It seems reasonable to conclude, therefore, that the relatively autonomous and self-administered departments found in the larger institutions have the wherewithal to fashion their own way of doing things.[23] The chairmen of departments in the smaller institutions, on the other hand, are seemingly delegated little administrative authority by the institutions' administrative officials. Rather, they spend a considerable portion of their time teaching.

The findings suggest that the larger schools are much more likely to delegate the authority to review those decisions made within subject matter departments. There is a very noticeable tendency for either lower ranking administrative officials (i.e., academic

vice presidents, deans of the colleges) or faculty committees to evaluate the decisions in relation to an array of system-wide standards.[24] This finding complements the others reported in this section of the paper.[25]

[23] This diversity in organizational style found in universities is the subject of another investigation.

[24] The coding procedure in this case was not ideal for the purpose of this analysis. The instructions asked the coder to code only the highest official mentioned who reviewed these departmental decisions. As a result, the influence of size is not as clear as might be expected. However, forty to fifty percent of the chairmen in the largest schools mentioned the academic vice president or the dean of the college as the highest official while only ten to fifteen percent did so in the smallest. In the latter, the president is invariably involved.

[25] There is also a considerable delegation of specialized administrative services in the larger institutions. The administrative subunits charged with these services are, in the largest institutions, quite remote from the presidents. These "staff" functions merely "serve" the faculty and have no formal authority over them.

Lastly, the data of the present study allow an examination of the degree to which the centralization of control over the mediation of strategic relations occurs at the "expense of" power over the technical or internal affairs of the institution. The findings in Tables 10 and 11 indicate that this may indeed be the case. The relationships between the External Relations ratio and the faculty's power over educational policy and matters of particular concern to the academic departments are relatively small in size but are in the predicted direction.[26] This would provide additional support for the appropriateness of the model described. This model, it will be remembered, defined an umbrella structure in the largest institutions.

SUMMARY AND CONCLUSIONS

This study examined the relationship between institutional size and the manner in which colleges and universities structure themselves to handle their technical and environmental affairs. It was shown that increasing institutional size was strongly associated with the development of (1) a "center" at the highest organizational level which mediates those external relations which are crucial to the maintenance and development of institutional legitimacy and material support, and (2) a considerable power on the part of the faculty to influence the institution's educational policy as well as matters of particular interest to each group of academic professionals through the faculty's gov-

ernmental system and autonomous subject matter departments. The results suggest that while the independence of the faculty in the larger universities is never complete, it is considerable indeed. It seems reasonable, moreover, to characterize these institutions as loosely integrated federations of administrative and faculty subunits. This is in contrast to the corporate structures characteristic of the smaller colleges. That these relationships were found within formal organizations with similar technologies and substantively similar environments highlights the considerable importance of numbers in understanding these matters.[27]

It seems reasonable to argue that the demands of numbers force these organizations to make use of a model which is different from that found in the smaller institutions. The model itself is, no doubt, a more effective technique of handling the system's technical and environmental affairs than Weber's "bureaucracy."[28] In fact, the model eliminates many of the contradictions found in Weber's conception.[29] The larger universities, while allowing the faculty a considerable degree of decision-making power and autonomy, exert a limited control through the development of structures and procedures which maintain the integrity of the model. The "cen-

---

[26] Because of space considerations, only one measure of departmental autonomy is used. Other measures show a similar relationship to the External Relations ratio.

[27] It certainly leads one to question the assumptions of Perrow (1967), Thompson (1967), and others.

[28] See Ellul's 1964 interesting discussion of technique.

[29] Both Gouldner (1959) and Thompson (1961) have criticized Weber for failing to see the possible source of conflict within an organization composed of experts where behavior is controlled by general rules and commands from above. Rules may be a source of rigidity, hierarchy a source of status-seeking, etc.

ter" is one such structure. Through its actions in mediating those relations which are crucial to maintaining and developing institutional legitimacy and material support, the university is prevented from becoming something created by "market" demands. Thus, departments of classics and romance languages survive and take their place beside those, such as physics and chemistry, which are granted liberal support by a variety of external sources. Finally, the nature of the system of control and the autonomy of subject matter departments within the larger universities suggest that the success of academic subunits is measured in terms of results. There are, of course, any number of ways of accomplishing these tasks. The university becomes, therefore, an umbrella structure which accommodates itself to any number of differing styles of organization associated with the various schools and departments.

REFERENCES

AIKEN, MICHAEL and JERALD HAGE. 1968. "Organizational Interdependence and Intra-organizational Structure." *American Sociological Review* 33:912–30.

ANDERSON, THEODORE and SEYMOUR WARKOV. 1961. "Organizational Size and Functional Complexity: A Study of Administration in Hospitals." *American Sociological Review* 26: 23–28.

BLAU, PETER M., WOLF V. HEYDEBRAND and ROBERT E. STAUFFER. 1966. "The Structure of Small Bureaucracies." *American Sociological Review* 31:179–91.

CLARK, BURTON R. 1962. *Educating the Expert Society.* San Francisco: Chandler.

Doctorate Production in the United States Universities, 1936–1956, with Baccalaureate Origins of Doctorates in Sciences, Arts, and Humanities. 1958. Washington, D. C.: National Academy of Sciences–National Research Council.

ELLUL, JACQUES. 1964. *The Technological Society.* New York: Alfred A. Knopf, Inc.

GOULDNER, ALVIN W. 1955. "Metaphysical Pathos and the Theory of Bureaucracy." *American Political Science Review* 49:496–507.

GOULDNER, A. W. 1959. "Organizational Analysis." *In* R. K. Merton, L. Bloom and L. S. Cottrell, Jr. (eds.), *Sociology Today.* New York: Basic Books Inc. pp. 400–28.

GROSS, EDWARD. 1968. "Universities as Organizations: A Research Approach." *American Sociological Review* 33:518–44.

HALL, RICHARD H., J. EUGENE HAAS and NORMAN J. JOHNSON. 1967. "Organizational Size, Complexity, and Formalization." *American Sociological Review* 32:903–12.

HARVEY, EDWARD. 1968. "Technology and the Structure of Organizations." *American Sociological Review* 33: 247–59.

HAWLEY, AMOS H., WALTER BOLAND, and MARGARET BOLAND. 1965. "Population Size and Administration in Institutions of Higher Learning." *American Sociological Review* 30: 252–55.

KERR, CLARK. 1963. *The Uses of the University.* Cambridge: Harvard University Press.

LAWRENCE, PAUL R. and JAY W. LORSCH. 1967. *Organization and Environment.* Boston: Graduate School of Business Administration, Harvard University.

MICHELS, ROBERT. 1949. *Political Parties.* Glencoe, Ill.: Free Press.

PERROW, CHARLES. 1967. "A Framework for the Comparative Analysis of Organizations." *American Sociological Review* 32:194–208.

RIDGEWAY, JAMES. 1968. *The Closed Corporation.* New York: Random House.

STARBUCK, WILLIAM H. 1965. "Organizational Growth and Development," *In* James G. G. March (ed.), *Handbook of Organizations.* Chicago: Rand McNally and Company. pp. 451–533.

THOMPSON, JAMES D. 1967. *Organizations in Action.* New York: McGraw-Hill.

THOMPSON, VICTOR R. 1961. *Modern Organizations.* New York: Alfred A. Knopf, Inc.

WEBER, MAX. 1947. *The Theory of Social and Economic Organization.* Glencoe, Ill.: Free Press.

WILSON, LOGAN. 1942. *The Academic Man: Sociology of a Profession.* London: Oxford University Press.

WOODWARD, JOAN. 1965. *Industrial Organization.* London: Oxford University Press.

23. DIMENSIONS OF ORGANIZATION STRUCTURE

D. S. Pugh, D. J. Hickson, C. R. Hinings, and C. Turner

A major task of contemporary organization theory is the development of more sophisticated conceptual and methodological tools, particularly for dealing systematically with variations between organizations. Udy,[1] for example, feels that "comparative analysis is an appropriate initial, boundary-setting approach to general organizational theory." Without it, case studies remain haphazard and generalizations remain dubious. Mayntz[2] is of the same mind, but she fears that to regard all organizations as comparable systems is so abstract that "propositions which hold for such diverse phenomena as an army, a trade union, and an university, must necessarily be either so trivial or so abstract as to tell hardly anything about concrete reality." There is as yet insufficient evidence to support or refute this view.

This paper reports attempts to investigate and measure structural differences systematically across a large number of diverse work organiza-

Reprinted by permission from *Administrative Science Quarterly* (June 1968), pp. 65–106.

[1] S. H. Udy, Jr., "The Comparative Analysis of Organization," in J. G. March (ed.), *Handbook of Organizations* (Chicago: Rand McNally, 1965).

[2] Renate Mayntz, "The Study of Organizations: a Trend Report and Bibliography," *Current Sociology*, 13 (1964), 3.

tions, using scalable variables for multidimensional analysis. A previous paper[3] described the conceptual framework upon which the present studies are based, which accords closely with that which Evan[4] has advocated, and with concepts from which Hage[5] derives his axiomatic theory.

From an examination of the literature on organizations, six primary dimensions of organization structure were defined: (1) specialization, (2) standardization, (3) formalization, (4) centralization, (5) configuration, (6) flexibility. These "constitutive" definitions, as Kerlinger[6] has termed them, were then translated into operational definitions, and scales constructed. Scales were also constructed for aspects of organizational context, and these were used as independent variables in a multivariate analysis to predict structural forms. The present paper describes the methods and results of scaling the structural variables.

[3] The authors are members of the Industrial Administration Research Unit, at the University of Aston in Birmingham, England. Research conducted by the Unit is jointly supported by the Social Science Research Council and the University. D. S. Pugh, D. J. Hickson, C. R. Hinings, K. M. Macdonald, C. Turner and T. Lupton, "A Conceptual Scheme for Organizational Analysis," *Administrative Science Quarterly*, 8 (December 1963), 289–315.
[4] W. M. Evan, "Indices of the Hierarchical Structure of Industrial Organizations," *Management Science*, 9 (April 1963), 468–77.
[5] J. Hage, "An Axiomatic Theory of Organizations," *Administrative Science Quarterly*, 10 (December 1965), 289–320.
[6] F. Kerlinger, *Foundations of Behavioral Research* (New York: Holt, Rinehart and Winston, 1964).

SAMPLE

Data were collected on 52 organizations in the Birmingham area. Of these, 46 were a random sample stratified by size and product or purpose, according to the Standard Industrial Classification of the British Ministry of Labour. They include firms making motor cars and chocolate bars, municipal departments repairing roads and teaching arithmetic, large retail stores, small insurance companies, and so on. These 46 organizations were distributed as shown in Table 1 (three organizations of the original sample felt unable to cooperate and were replaced in the present sample). Data were also available for the other six organizations. The information on the 52 organizations was used in the construction of scales, since the analysis was for internal consistency and scalability and because it formed a larger pool of data. For all analyses relating scales to each other or relating structural variables to contextual ones, only data on the 46-organization sample were used.

The sample of organizations was drawn from the 293 employing units in the area, which had more than 250 employees. Each was a unit listed as an employer by the British Ministry of Labour, irrespective of ownership, so that the sample includes several units that belong to the same industrial group or to the same local government. In ownership, the sample ranged from independent family-dominated firms to companies owned by private shareholders, a cooperative, branch factories of large organizations, municipal departments, and national organizations. Since these employing units are work organiza-

TABLE 1 SAMPLE: ORGANIZATIONS STUDIED ($n = 46$)

Number of Employees		
251–500	*501–2,000*	*2,001+*
Metal manufacture and metal goods		
Components	Metal goods	Nonferrous
Components	Metal goods	Metal automobile components
Research division	Metal goods	
Components	Domestic appliances	
Manufacture of engineering and electrical goods, vehicles		
Components	Engineering tools	Automobile components
Vehicles		
Components	Repairs for government department	Commercial vehicles
Components		Vehicles
	Automobile components	Carriages
	Engineering components	
Foods and chemicals, general manufacturing, construction		
Food	Civil engineering	Confectionery
Paper	Glass	Public civil engineering department
Toys	Printer	
Abrasives	Food	Brewery
		Automobile tires
Services: public, distributive, professional		
Government inspection department	Public water department	Public education department
	Department store	Public transport department
Public local savings bank	Chain of retail stores	Bus company
Public baths department	Chain of shoe repair stores	Cooperative chain of retail stores
Insurance company		

tions and pay their members, voluntary organizations were excluded.

METHOD

Organizations were first contacted by a letter addressed to the chief executive of the Birmingham organizational unit, who might be a works manager, an area superintendent, a chairman, or some other administrator. Field work began with interviewing him at length. There followed a series of interviews with department heads of varying status, as many as were necessary to obtain the information required. Interviews were conducted with standard schedules listing the data desired. Since these data were descriptive and about structure, not personal data about the respondent, no attempt was made to standardize interview procedure. Wherever possible, documentary evidence was sought to substantiate verbal accounts. Interviews took place between mid-1962 and mid-1964.

As the method used was that of wide-ranging interviews within a comparatively short time—from a few days to several weeks spent in an organization—it was not possible to obtain adequate data on the sixth variable, flexibility, which involves changes in structure and requires a more detailed study over a longer period of time.

It is the strength and the weakness of this project that no items were used unless they are applicable to *all* work organizations, whatever they did; several possible items of information had to be sacrificed to this end. Since the research strategy was to undertake a wide survey to set the guidelines, the result was superficiality and generality in the data. The project deals with what is officially expected *should* be done, and what is in practice *allowed* to be done; it does not include what is *actually* done, that is, what "really" happens in the sense of behavior beyond that instituted in organizational forms.

It also avoids, or at least attempts to minimize, the employees' perceptions of their organizations. This is in contrast to the kind of data reported by Hall[7] on hierarchy of authority, division of labor, rules and procedures, impersonal relations, and selection by competence; and by Aiken and Hage[8] on centralization, both hierarchy of authority and participation, and formalization, which approximates the definition of standardization on this project. Both use scores from forced-choice responses of employees to subjective statements about work practices.

The data collected were analyzed under the headings of the conceptual scheme. Scales were constructed to define the variables operationally. These measured the degree of a particular characteristic present by linking together a large number of items that could show this characteristic. The basic methodological problem to be faced was whether the results on single items could be added up to form, if not an equal interval dimension (such as height or weight), at least a stable ordered scale (such as intelligence or neuroticism) to represent the characteristic.[9] Such scales make it possible to undertake correlational analyses with subsequent multivariate prediction. The example of intelligence is apposite, since the procedures for statistical analysis have drawn primarily upon the methods of psychological test construction.

This problem was approached by carrying out item analysis of the data on a particular variable, using the Brogden-Clemans coefficient[10] to test whether the items scaled and could therefore be regarded as representing a dimension. The advantage of using this relatively little-known coefficient as an index of item-total correlation is that no assumption is required about the underlying score distribution, as would be the case for other indices.[11] Indeed, as Lord has shown, even when a distributional assumption can be made, this coefficient gives a

[7] R. H. Hall, "The Concept of Bureaucracy: an Empirical Assessment," *American Journal of Sociology*, 69 (July 1963), 32–40; also "Intraorganizational Structural Variation," *Administrative Science Quarterly*, 7 (December 1962), 295–308.

[8] M. Aiken and J. Hage, "Organizational Alienation: a Comparative Analysis," *American Sociological Review*, 31 (August 1966), 497–507.

[9] C. H. Coombs, *A Theory of Data* (New York: John Wiley, 1964).

[10] H. E. Brogden, "A New Coefficient: Applications to Biserial Correlation and to Estimation of Selective Efficiency," *Psychometrica*, 14 (1949), 169–82.

[11] We are grateful to Dr. P. M. Levy, Visiting Research Fellow, for bringing this statistic to our notice, and for much other statistical advice and encouragement.

TABLE 2 DIMENSIONS AND SCALES

Scale Number of Dimension	*Scale Title*
Specialization	
51.01	Functional specialization
51.02–51.17	Specializations no. 1/16 (see Appendix A)
51.18	Qualifications
51.19	Overall role specialization (51.02–51.15, and 51.17)
Standardization	
52.00	Overall standardization
52.01	Procedures defining task and image
52.02	Procedures controlling selection, advancement, etc.
Formalization	
53.00	Overall formalization
53.01	Role definition
53.02	Information passing
53.03	Recording of role performance
Centralization	
54.00	Overall centralization of decisions
	Criteria to evaluate performance:
54.01	Finance
54.02	Costs
54.03	Time
54.04	Quality
54.05	Labor relations
54.06	Output volume
54.07	Decisions affecting whole organization
54.08	Decisions affecting subunits of organization
54.09	Decisions affecting individual
54.10	Autonomy of organization to make decisions
Configuration	
55.08	Chief executive's span of control
55.09	Subordinate ratio
55.42	Status of specializations
55.43	Vertical span (height) of workflow hierarchy
55.44	Direct workers (%)
55.46	Female direct workers (%)
55.47	Workflow superordinates (%)
55.48	Non-workflow personnel (%)
55.49	Clerks (%)
55.50–55.65	Size of specializations (%, see Appendix A)
Traditionalism	
56.00	

better estimate of correlation than does an index that makes such an assumption.[12] The item analysis values show the extent to which the actual distribution of a particular item corresponds to the distribution, assuming that all the items formed a perfect scale in terms of cumulative scaling procedures. An item analysis value of 1.00 would indicate that the actual and perfect distributions are the same. This is seldom obtained with the data discussed here. A judg-

[12] F. M. Lord, "Biserial Estimation of Correlation," *Psychometrica*, 28 (1963), 81–85.

ment has to be made as to whether a variable can be represented by a score on a scale, taking into account the size of the item analysis values, the number of items going into the scale, and the further analysis to which the scale is subjected. Multivariate procedures combining several scales, to form profiles for example, make lower mean item analysis values acceptable. Principal-components analysis[13] can then be used in the identification of underlying factors and, in many cases, these can be conceptualized as variables summarizing a number of scales in the original list.

This procedure was followed in constructing 64 scales. Some of these were major dimensions, such as overall formalization or centralization; some were subscales concerned with only parts of a major variable, such as formalization of role definition, centralization of decisions affecting the whole organization; some were summary scales extracted by principal-components analysis to summarize a whole dimension, as with overall role specialization; or certain aspects of it, as with standardization of procedures defining task and image. The scales comprising configuration, the "shape" of the organization's role structure, were concerned with totals and percentages, which present no problems of scaling. The scales are listed in Table 2.

The objective was to assemble items that were as representative as possible of the potential population of such items in a work organization. For example, if specialization scales are to measure the specialization of functions and roles in an organiza-

tion, then the activities included as items in the scales must represent fully all activities engaged in by an organization; standardization scales must include a representative sample of the procedures that could feasibly be used; and so on. The generalized description of the activities of organizations given by Bakke[14] was used to guide the search for items, for although very abstract, it does point to every range of activities. For example, the danger that standardization is measured only with items on procedures regulating *workflow* activities (such as procedures regulating production work) is avoided if attention is drawn also to *perpetuation* procedures (such as those about buying materials or engaging employees) and to *control* procedures (quality inspection, budgeting, etc.). Bakke's concepts also have the merit of being applicable to every work organization, whether industrial, commercial, retail, or otherwise.

By this means a list of items pertinent to each variable was prepared. The method was then to ask each organization whether it had a specialized role for each of the potentially specializable functions, or a standardized procedure for each of the standardizable routines, and so on. Since the potential population of such items is not known, strictly speaking no claim can be made as to the representativeness of the scales; but the fact that there are internal consistencies among widely ranging items that make it possible to construct scales, supports the view that stable characteristics of the kinds conceptualized are being measured.

[13] H. H. Harmon, *Modern Factor Analysis* (Chicago: University of Chicago, 1960).

[14] E. Wight Bakke, "Concept of the Social Organization," in M. Haire (ed.), *Modern Organization Theory* (New York: John Wiley, 1959).

PRIMARY DIMENSIONS OF STRUCTURE

SPECIALIZATION

Specialization[15] is concerned with the division of labor within the organization, the distribution of official duties among a number of positions.[16] Analysis of data from a pilot survey of organizations in terms of the Bakke activity variables made it possible to construct a list of sixteen activities (see Appendix A) that are assumed to be present in *all* work organizations, and on which any work organization may therefore be compared with any other. These activities or functions exclude the workflow activities of organization, and so are not concerned with operatives in manufacturing, sales clerks in retailing, and similar activities. Thus it can be seen whether an activity is specialized in an organization; that is, performed by someone with that function and no other, who is not in the workflow superordinate hierarchy (line chain of command). An endorsement of a specialization in this scale by an organization means only that the particular specialization is performed by one or more persons full time. No account is taken here of the *number* of specialists (this is an aspect of configuration, as discussed below) or of their status. Furthermore, only functions carried out by the organization itself are included in this scale: use of specialists from other organizations, for example, consultants, ser-vice agencies, experts from the head office, is considered to be an aspect of the organization's interdependence with its context.

Item analysis carried out using the Brogden-Clemans coefficient gave a mean item analysis of 0.76, which seems satisfactory for a first attempt. It was thus meaningful to talk of a scale of Functional Specialization and of an organization's score on it. The organizations ranged from those in which all these sixteen activities were performed by nonspecialists, to those in which they were all performed by specialists working in a functional relationship to the workflow management.

A second aspect of specialization is the extent to which specialist roles exist within each of the sixteen functional specializations, that is, role specialization. In those organizations with *functional specialization*, data were collected on the distribution of subtasks, and by using the Brogden-Clemans coefficient, a subscale covering each specialization was developed. These are listed in Table A.2 of Appendix A.

A further development of this analysis was to examine the relationship among all the role specializations. A principal-components analysis of all sixteen role-specialization scales extracted a first factor accounting for 65 percent of the variance, which is heavily loaded (range of 0.59 to 0.88) on all except one of the scales—legal specialization (scale no. 51.16) being the exception. On this basis, a scale of Overall Role Specialization (scale no. 51.19) was formed by summing the scores on the remaining fifteen scales. An organization could now be meaningfully characterized by its degree of specialization of role on a scale ranging from 0, for a govern-

[15] A preliminary discussion of this variable is given in C. R. Hinings, D. S. Pugh, D. J. Hickson and C. Turner, "An Approach to the Study of Bureaucracy," *Sociology*, 1 (January 1967), 61–72.

[16] Pugh *et al.*, "A Conceptual Scheme for Organizational Analysis."

ment inspection agency in which no specializations, as defined here, were found; to 87, representing the highest degree of role specialization occurring in the sample, for a large confectionery manufacturing company. This is a much wider range of scores and therefore gives much finer discrimination than the original sixteen-point functional specialization scale, and in a single scale operationalizes the constitutive concept of specialization.

STANDARDIZATION

Standardization of procedures is a basic aspect of organizational structure, and in Weber's terms would distinguish bureaucratic and traditional organizations from charismatic ones. The operational problems here revolve around defining a procedure and specifying which procedures in an organization are to be investigated. A procedure is taken to be an event that has regularity of occurrence and is legitimized by the organization. There are rules or definitions that purport to cover all circumstances and that apply invariably.[17] The score is obtained by a count of the number of such procedures available to an organization from those in a given list (Appendix B). No assumption is made as to the use of procedures. Scores obtained ranged from 30, by a chain of retail stores, to 131, by a metals processing plant. This scale has a relatively low mean item analysis value of 0.41, partly because of the large number (157) of heterogeneous items used. However, when a principal-components analysis of scores on the items was carried out, it produced two meaningful factors. One factor, accounting for 27 percent of the variance (after correcting for

negative roots) was defined as Procedures Defining Task and Image. The 33 items with a loading of 0.5 and above on this factor were collected into a scale (scale no. 52.01 in Appendix B) giving a mean item analysis value of 0.65. The second factor, accounting for 13.5 percent of the variance, was a bipolar one. The positive end of the factor was concerned with the standardization of Procedures Controlling Personnel Selection and Advancement, and so on; the negative end of the factor was nonstandardization of workflow control. A scale formed from the items with a loading of 0.5 and over on the second factor (reversing the scores where the loading was negative), that is, scale no. 52.02 in Appendix B, gave a mean item analysis value of 0.62. A high score on this scale therefore means not only that the organization *does* standardize its procedures for selection and advancement, and so on, but also that it *does not* standardize its procedures for workflow control.

FORMALIZATION

Formalization denotes the extent to which rules, procedures, instructions, and communications are written.[18] Definitions of 38 documents were assembled, each of which could be used by any known work organization. Adding an assessment of the range of personnel to whom a document applied, gave a total of 55 items and subitems. These are listed in Appendix C. A *document* is at least a single sheet of paper; therefore several copies of the same sheet of paper may each score as separate documents if used for separate purposes. For example, organization *A* may

---

[17] *Ibid.*

[18] *Ibid.*

score 3 for unrelated pieces of paper, while organization *B* may score 3 for a set of carbon copies, each of which is detached for a different purpose. The problem of a single sheet of paper serving separate purposes did not arise. The mean item analysis value of the 55-item scale was 0.63. Scores ranged from 4, for a single-product food-stuffs factory, to 49, for the same metals-processing plant that headed the standardization scores.

A principal-components analysis of all the items gave a first factor, taking out 34 percent of the variance, but not extracting any factors meaningfully distinctive from overall formalization. Nevertheless, it was felt to be conceptually desirable to make some distinctions within the overall scale, which was split into three subscales concerned with Formalization of Role Definition, Information Passing, and Recording of Role Performance. The documents grouped together to constitute items on the subscale of formalization of role definition were all those designed primarily as prescriptions of behavior; for example, written terms of reference, job descriptions, and manuals of procedures. Information-passing documents were those intended to pass from hand to hand; for example, memo forms, and house journals. Role-performance records notified or authorized in writing the accomplishment of some part of a role; for example, records of the carrying out of inspection, or of maintenance of equipment.

The items going into these subscales (see Appendix C) gave mean item analysis values of 0.74, for Role Definition, 0.68 for Information Passing, and 0.67 for Recording of Role Performance. Unlike subscales formed to represent orthogonal factors (for example, see standardiza-tion), these subscales are highly inter-correlated, correlations ranging from 0.55 to 0.81.

Although filing is characteristic of a bureaucracy, an attempt to discriminate between organizations in this respect failed. Once a document is in existence, copies of it appear to be filed for a very long time.

CENTRALIZATION

Centralization has to do with the locus of authority to make decisions affecting the organization.[19] Authority to make decisions was defined and ascertained by asking, "Who is the last person whose assent must be obtained before *legitimate action* is taken—even if others have subsequently to confirm the decision?" This identified the level in the hierarchy where executive action could be authorized, even if this remained subject to a routine confirmation later, for example by a chairman or a committee. A standard list of 37 recurrent decisions was prepared covering a range of organizational activities (see Appendix D). For each organization, the lowest level in the hierarchy with the formal authority to make each decision was determined. Table 3 gives a generalized paradigm, which makes it possible to compare the levels across organizations. This overcomes the problem of deciding whether a foreman in factory *A* is at the same level as a shop-buyer in retail store *B* or a head clerk in commercial office *C*. Levels were equated in terms of the scope of the segment of workflow (that is, the proportion of the production activities) that they control. Where authority does not ultimately reside in the workflow hierarchy (line

[19] *Ibid.*

TABLE 3   CENTRALIZATION: LEVELS IN THE HIERARCHY

| | | | Examples | |
Score	Level	Metal Manufacturer	Chain of Retail Shoe Repair Shops	Local Education Department
5	Above chief executive	Board of group	–	City council
4	Whole organization	Managing director	Chairman	Chief education officer
3	All workflow activities	Production manager	Sales manager	Assistant education officer
2	Workflow subunit	Plant manager	Area manager	Headmaster
1	Supervisory	Foreman	Shop manager	Head of department
0	Operating	Direct worker	Repairer	Teacher

management) but in a staff or service department, a judgement has to be made approximating this to the equivalent level in the hierarchy, but there are comparatively few instances of this. An organization may have more than one managerial grade at a given comparative level; or it may not have a grade corresponding to a particular level.

The 37 decisions generated 148 biserial items. Eliminating items with poor discrimination gave a scale of 128 biserial items, which has a mean item analysis value of 0.40. Scores were obtained by scoring a decision taken outside the unit of organization (for example, at the head office) as 5, a decision taken at the chief executive level as 4, and so on to 0 for a decision at the operating level. Thus a high score means highly centralized, the maximum possible score being 128. The scores range from the most decentralized organization with a score of 51, an independent manufacturer of transporting equipment, to an extremely centralized organization with a score of 116, a branch factory where most of the decisions were taken right at the top or above the chief executive.

A further analysis of centralization scores indicated the degree of auton-

omy of the particular organizational unit. How many decisions did it have to refer to a headquarters or to a parent organization? This varied from independent companies, where the owner-managers had complete control over all the operations of the enterprise, to a government agency, where a considerable number of decisions had to be referred upwards to higher authority. A scale was constructed by selecting from the 37 decisions of the main centralization scale those 23 decisions that showed the greatest discrimination between organizations as to whether the decisions were taken inside or outside the organization (see Appendix D). The total score of an organization was the number of the 23 decisions that lay within its jurisdiction. A high score means great autonomy, and the range was found to be from 1 to 23. The mean item analysis value of the scale is 0.74.

CONFIGURATION

Configuration is the "shape" of the role structure.[20] Its data would be contained in a comprehensive and detailed organization chart that included

[20] *Ibid.*

literally every role in the organization. The assessment of the configuration of this hypothetical chart requires the use of a combination of selected dimensions, each of which provides a measure of the development of a particular aspect of the structure.

The vertical span of control (or height) of the workflow superordinate hierarchy (line chain of command) was measured by a count of the number of job positions between the chief executive and the employees directly working on the output. Lateral "widths" could include the chief executive's span of control, the ratio of subordinates to first workflow superordinates (first-line supervisors), and the percentage of total employees that were direct-output employees. Note that in a savings bank, the cashiers are direct-output employees, as are drivers in a bus company, and so on. The total workflow employees, that is, those directly responsible for the output (including management), could be compared with the number of those engaged in other activities, functional specialists, or staff departments. Totals of employees in each of the sixteen specializations could be calculated and related. Here the number of those engaged in a specialization was taken account of, apart from their specialization, which was measured with the specialization scale.

For example, a symptom of bureaucratization may be the number of clerks. A clerical job is defined as one where the main prescribed task is writing and recording, but where there is no supervisory responsibility for subordinates other than typists. This definition excludes office managers with authority over other clerks, but would include both a clerk and his typist. For the 52 organizations, the percentage of clerks ranged from 2 percent in small manufacturing firms to 29 percent in a commercial office. Appendix E lists some of the principal data obtained. Since these are concerned with totals and percentages, considerations of scalability do not arise.

TRADITIONALISM

An ideal standardization scale would be composed of items adequately representing a potential population of *customs* in organizations (a custom is an implicitly legitimized verbally transmitted procedure) and a potential population of *bureaucratic procedures*, being those explicitly legitimized by commitment to written form in rules, instructions, and other forms. Such a scale would indicate the extent to which an organization was standardized by customs or by rules. If rules were the means of standardization used, the formalization scores of the organization would be far higher than those of an *equally* standardized organization where the customs prevailed, since the rules would be embodied in documents. The relation between standardization scores and formalization scores could therefore be held to illustrate the Weberian distinction between traditional and bureaucratic types.

Because of the comparatively brief acquaintance of the research workers with the organizations studied in this project, the scores on the standardization scales reported here are thought to represent the rules and instructions of bureaucracy rather than procedures of customs. Nevertheless, ten items in the standardization scales were selected, which roughly corresponded to document items in formalization scales; for example, comparing routine frequency of inspection with documents recording the inspection, and central interviewing procedure with employment application forms. The reliability of field-work methods was supported when it was confirmed that organizations scored higher on the ten standardization items than on the equivalent ten formalization items: the reverse would have purported to show documents but not the procedures whose prescription or operation the documents recorded. The assumption was then made that if an organization had a procedure but did not have a corresponding document, then the procedure was more customary than bureaucratic. The hypothesis was that the degree to which an organization's standardization score on these items exceeded its formalization score reflected in a crude way its Traditionalism. An index was constructed, which ordered organizations on this discrepancy in scores (see Appendix F).

The highest score was obtained by an old, established, small, branch factory, while the lowest point on the scale included a number of large manufacturers, a research organization, and an omnibus company. The association with the patriarchal-traditional type is direct, even though a question must remain about the adequacy of this simple scale as a measure of the type.

INTERCORRELATION OF STRUCTURAL VARIABLES

STANDARD SCORES

The measures described afford comparisons between organizations on any one scale but not on scales of different variables, such as a comparison of an organization's standardization score with its centralization score. Comparability is obtained by converting raw scores into standard scores with a common mean of 50 and standard deviation of 15. This makes it possible to set the many scores of an organization side by side as a *profile* of its structure. Figure 1 shows the profile of a number of organizations.[21]

INTERCORRELATIONS OF STRUCTURAL SCALES

With scales to represent the postulated primary dimensions of structure, one can explore the relationship between the dimensions and search for underlying similarities.

Intercorrelating the 64 scales of structural variables produces a large matrix of 2,016 coefficients. Selecting the scales that most fully represent the variables and that were most distinctive gave the small matrix in Table 4. It is evident that many of the measures of structure are highly intercorrelated. For example, Overall Role Specialization (scale no. 51.19) has a correlation of 0.80 with Overall Standardization (scale no. 52.00), of 0.68 with Overall Formalization (scale no. 53.00), of 0.66 with Configuration, Vertical Span (scale no. 55.43); and 0.56 with Configuration, Percentage Non-Workflow Personnel (scale no. 55.48). In other words, an organization with many specialists tends also to have more standard routines, more documentation, and a larger supportive hierarchy. A hypothesis on this process is that as specialists increase in number, they

---

[21] A full report of the relationship between context and structure will be given in a later paper.

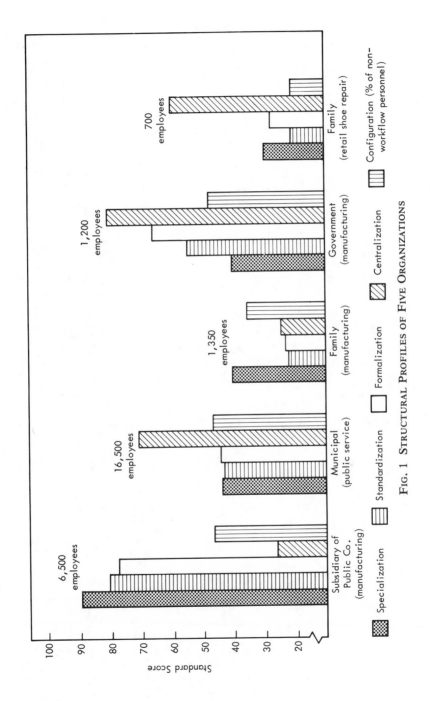

FIG. 1 STRUCTURAL PROFILES OF FIVE ORGANIZATIONS

453

TABLE 4 PROycT-MOMENT CORRELATION BETWEEN SELECTED SCALES OF STRUCTURE ($n = 46$)

No.	Title	Functional Specialization	Legal Specialization	Overall Role Specialization	Overall Standardization	Standardization—Selection, etc.	Overall Formalization	Recording of Role Performance	Overall Centralization	Autonomy of Organization	Chief Executive's Span	Subordinate Ratio	Vertical Span (Height)	Workflow Superordinates (%)	Non-Workflow Personnel (%)	Clerks (%)	Traditionalism
51.01	Functional specialization	—															
51.16	Legal specialization	0.32	—														
51.19	Overall role specialization	0.87	0.34	—													
52.00	Overall standardization	0.76	0.27	0.80	—												
52.02	Standardization—selection, etc.	−0.15	0.47	0.09	0.23	—											
53.00	Overall formalization	0.57	0.26	0.68	0.83	0.38	—										
53.03	Recording of role performance	0.66	0.11	0.54	0.72	−0.12	0.75	—									
54.00	Overall centralization	−0.64	−0.04	−0.53	−0.27	0.30	−0.20	−0.27	—								
54.10	Autonomy of organization	0.50	−0.15	0.40	0.06	−0.52	−0.02	0.10	−0.79	—							
55.08	Chief executive's span	0.22	0.15	0.34	0.28	0.04	0.32	0.32	0.10	0.02	—						
55.09	Subordinate ratio	0.25	−0.14	0.05	0.13	−0.46	0.04	0.39	−0.14	−0.14	−0.16	—					
55.43	Vertical span (height)	0.57	0.48	0.66	0.57	0.23	0.48	0.33	−0.28	−0.06	0.24	−0.05	—				
55.47	Workflow superordinates (%)	−0.53	0.21	−0.38	−0.37	0.39	−0.24	−0.52	0.52	0.47	0.12	−0.50	−0.01	—			
55.48	Non-workflow personnel (%)	0.58	0.11	0.56	0.51	−0.02	0.46	0.43	−0.40	−0.32	0.10	0.01	0.21	−0.43	—		
55.49	Clerks (%)	0.17	0.12	0.29	0.31	0.31	0.29	0.08	−0.04	−0.05	0.12	−0.24	−0.01	−0.05	0.46	—	
56.00	Traditionalism	−0.36	−0.13	−0.26	−0.24	0.06	−0.47	−0.54	0.39	0.30	−0.22	−0.17	−0.14	0.19	−0.26	−0.08	—

introduce procedures to regulate the activities for which they are responsible—the personnel specialist his selection procedure, the inspector his quality control—resulting in documentation—the application forms for vacancies and the inspection reports. A tall hierarchy results to encompass the specialists and the large number of non-workflow jobs.

This intercorrelation of these five scales contrasts markedly with the correlations between Centralization (scale no. 54.00) and these scales, which are all *negative*, and much smaller. This appears to disprove the hypothesis,[22] drawn from the Weberian tradition and the notion that bureaucracies pass decisions to upper levels, that specialization, formalization, and centralization would be highly positively correlated. Hage too, incorporates in his axiomatic theory the proposition that "the higher the centralization, the higher the formalization" (standardization).[23] On the other hand, the correlations support his proposition summarizing Thompson, Gouldner, and Blau and Scott: "The higher the complexity, the lower the centralization,"[24] "complexity" for Hage being specialization of tasks plus the length of training required for the task.

Standardization of Selection Procedures (scale no. 52.02) is even more interesting. First, it breaks the pattern of a strong positive relationship within specialization, standardization, formalization, and many configuration variables, correlating only 0.09 with Overall Role Specialization (scale no. 51.19) and 0.37 with Overall Formalization (scale no. 53.00). The low correlation of scale no. 52.02 with the other standardization scales would be anticipated, because it is constructed to represent an independent standardization factor, and it therefore suggests a structure of a different kind. Second, all its correlations with centralization are *positive*, the only scale of specialization, standardization, and formalization where this is so. In this the hypothesis of a positive relationship between standardization and centralization *is* supported, but applies to this aspect of standardization only.

The meaning of patterns of structural scores should be kept in mind when interpreting these correlations. An organization that scores high on specialization, standardization, and formalization (which is probable in view of the intercorrelations among these variables) would have gone a long way in the regulation of the work of its employees. As an organization, it would have gone a long way in *structuring* its activities; that is, the intended behavior of employees has been structured by the specification of their specialized roles, the procedures they are to follow in carrying out those roles, and the documentation of what they have to do. In short, what these three associated variables are exploring is the range and pattern of *structuring*.

The scales of centralization cannot be regarded as measures of structuring in this way. To assess structuring in terms of centralization would require measurement of how specific the loci of authority are; that is, how definite it is that authority for decision X rests in role Y. But the centralization scales treat this as a constant and measure only the vertical distribution of authority over the hier-

[22] Pugh *et al.*, "A Conceptual Scheme for Organizational Analysis."
[23] Hage, "An Axiomatic Theory of Organizations."
[24] *Ibid.*

TABLE 5 PRINCIPAL-COMPONENTS ANALYSIS OF SELECTED SCALES OF STRUCTURE AFTER GRAPHIC ROTATION

No.	Scale Title	Factor I Structuring of Activities	Factor II Concentration of Authority	Factor III Line Control of Workflow	Factor IV Relative Size of Supportive Component
52.00	Standardization	0.89*	−0.01	−0.21	0.10
51.19	Role specialization	0.87*	−0.33	0.01	−0.13
53.00	Formalization	0.87*	0.14	−0.21	0.17
56.00	Traditionalism	−0.41‡	0.18	0.32	−0.02
55.08	Chief executive's span	0.42‡	0.23	−0.07	−0.03
55.01	Functional specialization	0.78*	−0.47‡	−0.21	−0.17
55.48	Non-workflow personnel (%)	0.58†	−0.43‡	0.06	0.41‡
51.16	Legal specialization	0.51†	0.25	0.31	−0.43‡
55.43	Vertical span	0.69*	0.03	0.08	−0.54†
55.49	Clerks (%)	0.40‡	−0.09	0.42‡	0.67*
53.03	Recording of role performance	0.69*	−0.05	−0.64*	0.13
55.09	Subordinate ratio	−0.05	−0.19	−0.80*	−0.06
52.02	Standardization—selection, etc.	0.40‡	0.59†	0.50†	0.09
55.47	Workflow superordinates (%)	−0.23	0.60*	0.50†	−0.22
54.00	Centralization	−0.33	0.83*	0.01	0.21
54.10	Autonomy of the organization	0.10	−0.92*	0.00	−0.13
	Variance (%)	33.06	18.47	12.96	8.20

* Weightings > 0.06
† Weightings > 0.5
‡ Weightings > 0.4

archy. That one organization scores as centralized, whereas another scores as decentralized, does not necessarily bear any relationship to how specific the allocation of authority is within the two. Basing the measures of centralization upon a conceptual basis different from the rest of the structural variables has a very important effect upon the results.

UNDERLYING DIMENSIONS OF STRUCTURE

The intercorrelations suggested that the interpretation would be improved by a search for basic dimensions of organizational structure by the method of factor analysis. Principal-components analysis was applied to the matrix given in Table 4, and four factors were extracted, accounting in turn for 33, 19, 14, and 8 percent of

the variance after rotation. These factors are orthogonal to one another, that is, mutually independent. The loadings of the variables on the factors are given in Table 5.

The meaning of the factors is readily apparent. Factor I can be seen to be most highly loaded on the variables of standardization, specialization, and formalization, as would be expected from the pattern in Table 4. This dimension therefore is called *structuring of activities*. The concept of the structuring of organizational activities has the advantage of applying to any or all parts of the organization; whereas it is a question whether the Weberian concept of bureaucracy can or cannot be applied outside the administrative hierarchy to the workflow operatives. Both clerical activities and shop floor activities can be more or less structured; whether they can both be bureaucratized is open to question.[25] Structuring therefore includes and goes beyond the usage of the term bureaucracy. It has the further advantage of being conceived and defined as an operationalized dimension, and not as an abstract type.

This usage accords with Etzioni,[26] who prefers to avoid terms such as bureaucracy, formal organization, and institution in favor of using the term organization "to refer to planned units, deliberately structured." Etzioni does not go on to use this definition to examine organization theory from the standpoint of variations in *structuring*, but this approach follows from Hickson's[27] argument that a common thread of this kind runs through the subject, which he calls the varying "specificity of role prescription." Specificity has a very close affinity to structuring. Thus standardization may be considered as the specificity of procedures to cases, specialization as the specificity of tasks to roles, and so on. Hickson's linking of the approaches of twenty-two organization theorists by the concept of specificity also suggests that measures of structuring are prerequisite to further development in the subject.

Factor II is marked by the opposition of centralization and autonomy and is thus concerned with *concentration of authority*. Specialization is in the direction of dispersed authority, as would be expected; with more

specialization, authority is likely to be distributed to the specialists. "Non-workflow personnel" also has a definite weighting toward dispersed authority, but the percentage of workflow superordinates is firmly weighted in the direction of concentrated authority. Thus the greater the percentage of the line hierarchy, the more concentrated is the authority, and the less decentralized are the decisions down the line. Standardization of selection procedures is also positively loaded on this factor, as would be anticipated from its correlation with centralization.

In factors III and IV, variables of configuration predominate. The third factor is characterized by the heavy positive loading of Percentage of Workflow Superordinates and negative loading of Subordinate Ratio, and is concerned with the line hierarchy. Formalization of role performance records has a high negative loading, and inspection of the items of this scale (for example, record of work, record of time, record of maintenance) indicates that these records are those prepared on the workflow personnel for control purposes. The factor may thus be considered as that of *line control of workflow* (rather than impersonal control). This characterization is supported by the significant positive loading of the scale, standardization of procedures for selection, advancement, and so on (scale no. 52.02), the bipolar scale, and a high score on it means not only that there *are* procedures for selection, and so on, but also that there are *not* procedures for controlling the workflow. Thus control would be expected to rest in the hands of the workflow personnel themselves and their line superordinates.

Factor IV has its high loadings on

---

[25] For example, T. Caplow, *Principles of Organization.* (New York: Harcourt, Brace, 1964), p. 287.
[26] A. Etzioni, *Modern Organizations* (Englewood Cliffs, N. J.: Prentice-Hall, 1964), p. 4.
[27] D. J. Hickson, "A Convergence in Organization Theory," *Administrative Science Quarterly*, 11 (September 1966), 225–37.

percentage of clerks and percentage of non-workflow personnel. The factor is thus concerned with the amount of activity auxiliary to the main workflow of the organization. Following Haas *et al.*,[28] the term *supportive component* is used in relation to these activities. This factor is distinguished from Factor III, which was concerned with the *control* of *workflow* activities, whereas Factor IV is concerned with the *amount* of *auxiliary* activities of a noncontrol kind (all the structuring and authority variables are negligibly loaded). There are many noncontrol supportive activities, such as clerical, transport, catering, and others.

Thus it must be presumed that there are a number of distinctive underlying dimensions of structure—this particular trial produces four. Since these are mutually independent, an organization's structure may display all these characteristics to a pronounced degree, or virtually none at all, or display some but not others. In so far as the original primary dimensions of structure, specialization, standardization, formalization, centralization, and configuration were drawn from a literature saturated with the Weberian view of bureaucracy, this multifactor result has immediate implications for what we have elsewhere called the Weberian stereotype.[29] It is demonstrated here that bureaucracy is *not* unitary, but that organizations may be bureaucratic in any of a number of ways. The force of Blau's criticism of the "ideal type" can now be appreciated:

"If we modify the type in accordance with the empirical reality, it is no longer a pure type; and if we do not, it would become a meaningless construct."[30] The concept of *the* bureaucratic type is no longer useful.

SUMMARY AND DISCUSSION

From an examination of the literature of organization theory, six primary dimensions of organization structure were postulated: specialization, standardization, formalization, centralization, configuration, and flexibility. The first five of these concepts were then operationalized by generating 64 component scales to measure various aspects of the primary dimensions.

Some of these component scales were primary dimensions themselves, such as Overall Formalization; some were subscales concerned with only parts of a major variable, such as Autonomy of the Organization—an aspect of centralization, Percentage of Non-Workflow Personnel—an aspect of configuration, and so on. Some were summary scales extracted by principal-components analysis to summarize a whole dimension, as with Overall Role Specialization, or certain aspects of it, as with Standardization of Procedures for Selection and Advancement.

Comparative data across 52 different work organizations made it possible to test the internal consistency of these 64 scales and to examine the intercorrelations between them. A principal-components analysis of 16 of the 64 scales, which most fully

[28] E. Haas, R. H. Hall and N. J. Johnson, "The Size of the Supportive Component in Organizations," *Social Forces*, 42 (1963), 9–17.

[29] Hinings *et al.*, "Approach to Study of Bureaucracy."

[30] P. M. Blau, "Critical Remarks on Weber's Theory of Authority," *American Political Science Review*, 57 (June 1963), 305–16.

represented the primary dimensions, yielded four empirically established underlying dimensions of organization structure: *structuring of activities*, encompassing Standardization, Formalization, Specialization, and Vertical Span; *concentration of authority*, encompassing Organizational Autonomy, Centralization, Percentage of Workflow Superordinates, and Standardization of Procedures for Selection and Advancement, *line control of workflow*, encompassing Subordinate Ratio, Formalization of Role Performance Recording, Percentage of Workflow Superordinates, and Standardization of Procedures for Selection and Advancement; and *Relative Size of Supportive Component*, encompassing Percentage of Clerks, Vertical Span, and Percentage of Non-Workflow Personnel.

The establishment of these scales and dimensions makes it possible to compile profiles characteristic of particular organizations, and examples of these are given. As a result of this dimensional analysis, it is clear that to talk in terms of the bureaucratic ideal type is not adequate, since the structure of an organization may vary along any of these four empirical dimensions. Figure 2 gives the profiles of the five organizations shown in Fig. 1, but using the factor dimensions. It will be seen that these profiles pinpoint more sharply the structural differences between these organizations. Thus the subsidiary manufacturing organization is distinctively high on Factor I, Structuring of Activities. The municipal public service is high on Factors II, Concentration of Authority, and III, Line Control of Workflow; the family manufacturing is low on all factors; the government manufacturing is high on Factors I, Structuring of Activities, and II, Con-

centration of Authority; and the family retailing is distinctively high on Factor III, Line Control of Workflow.

The dimensional approach described here has immediate implications for further work. By making it possible to pinpoint structural differences between organizations, it makes it possible to conduct more systematic and rigorous studies of group composition and interaction, comparative role analysis of conflict and performance, and individual personality and behavior, since the effects of structural aspects of the organizations can be controlled.

The second major gain from establishing dimensions is that it makes possible a multivariate approach to causality. If similar scales can be developed for aspects of an organization's context, then the relationships between dimensions of context and dimensions of structure can be examined using correlational and multivariate techniques. This obviates the need to select a particular aspect of context *a priori* as the determining variable for structure. For example, both the variables of size and technology have been presented as *the* determining ones for structure, but the relative importance of these two factors has still to be demonstrated. A multivariate dimensional approach could attempt this.

The relative status of the primary conceptual variables, the subscales, and the empirically established underlying dimensions of structure have become clear. The conceptual dimensions and subscales have been demonstrated to be empirically meaningful, and hypotheses can be set up and investigated relating these aspects of structure to other aspects of the organization's context and functioning.

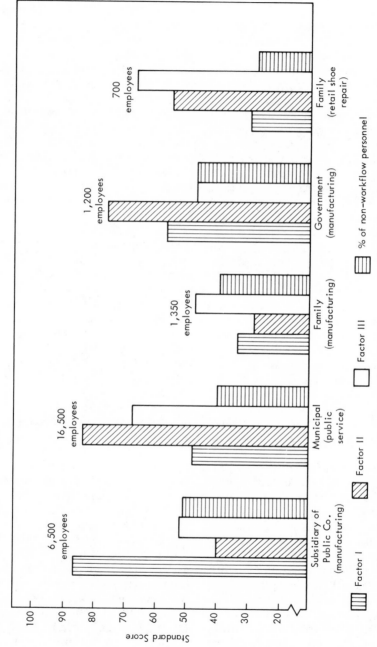

FIG. 2 UNDERLYING DIMENSIONS OF STRUCTURE IN THE FIVE ORGANIZATIONS IN FIG. 1

TABLE A.1 ANALYSIS OF FUNCTIONAL SPECIALIZATION
($n = 52$, SCALE NO. 51.01)

Specialization			*No. of Organizations*	*Item Analysis Value*
No.	*Example of Title*	*Activities*		
1	Public relations and advertising	Develop, legitimize, and symbolize the organization's charter	17	0.82
2	Sales and service	Dispose of, distribute, and service the output	37	0.74
3	Transport	Carry outputs and resources from place to place	47	0.38
4	Employment	Acquire and allocate human resources	36	0.87
5	Training	Develop and transform human resources	21	0.81
6	Welfare and security	Maintain human resources and promote their identification with the organization	40	0.59
7	Buying and stock control	Obtain and control materials and equipment	50	1.00
8	Maintenance	Maintain and erect buildings and equipment	49	0.83
9	Accounts	Record and control financial resources	49	0.70
10	Production control	Control workflow	38	0.79
11	Inspection	Control quality of materials and equipment and outputs	40	0.87
12	Methods	Assess and devise ways of producing output	25	0.82
13	Design and development	Devise new outputs, equipment, and processes	36	0.87
14	Organization and methods	Develop and carry out administrative procedures	22	0.73
15	Legal	Deal with legal and insurance requirements	12	0.49
16	Market research	Acquire information on operational field	11	0.86
Mean item analysis value				0.76

Range obtained = 0–16; Mean = 10.19; S.D. = 5.19.

The underlying dimensions have been shown empirically to be a parsimonious method of summarizing an organization's structure, and more suitable for many purposes of prediction and statistical control. In particular, the development of a taxonomic classification could be expected to be founded more stably on the underlying dimensions. Accepting that there are a number of component dimensions in structure, four of which are (*1*) structuring of activities, (*2*) concentration of authority, (*3*) line control of workflow, and (*4*) relative size of supportive component, gives an empirical basis for a taxonomy of organization structures.

APPENDIX A. SPECIALIZATION

This appendix demonstrates the extent to which scales of role specialization can be produced, and indicates the nature of the items making up the scales. The item analysis value shows the extent to which the actual distribution of that particular item corresponds to the distribution, assuming that all the items formed a perfect scale (in terms of cumulative scaling procedures). Thus a value of 1.00 means that the "actual" and "perfect" distributions are the same. The items are formulated in the language of manufacturing industry, since this is most readily recogniz-

TABLE A.2 ANALYSIS OF ROLE SPECIALIZATION

Specialization and Items	No. of Organi- zations	Item Analysis Value	Specialization and Items	No. of Organi- zations	Item Analysis Value
Specialization no. 1 (n = 17, scale no. 51.02)			Specialization no. 2 (n = 37, scale no. 51.03)		
Publicity staff	16	1.00	Sales or service	36	0.57
Public relations	8	1.00	Pricing and orders	28	0.94
Customer relations	8	0.75	Sales by customer or product	26	0.89
Display	8	0.58	Sales records	17	0.76
Publicity by product	4	0.80	Export sales	10	0.76
Overseas relations	3	1.00	Service by customer or product	6	0.67
Mean item analysis value	–	0.86	Mean item analysis value	–	0.77
Range obtained = 1–6 Mean = 2.76 S.D. = 1.63			Range obtained = 1–6 Mean = 3.32 S.D. = 2.13		
Specialization no. 3 (n = 47, scale no. 51.04)			Specialization no. 4 (n = 36, scale no. 51.05)		
Drivers	44	0.59	Role specialized for part of organization	36	1.00
Dispatchers	35	0.78	Role specialized for whole of organization	31	1.00
Administration and planning	17	0.83	Role specialized by type of employee or process	11	0.85
Drivers by vehicle or product	16	0.83	Administration/records	10	1.00
Dispatch specialized by product	6	1.00	Interviewers	3	1.00
Travel and excursions	2	1.00	Role specialized by type of employee and process	2	0.83
Planning and adminis- tration specialized by product	2	1.00			
Mean item analysis value	–	0.86	Mean item analysis value	–	0.95
Range obtained = 1–7 Mean = 2.60 S.D. = 1.57			Range obtained = 1–6 Mean = 2.58 S.D. = 1.12		
Specialization no. 5 (n = 21, scale no. 51.06)			Specialization no. 6 (n = 40, scale no. 51.07)		
Operative training	15	0.81	Security staff	29	0.77
Apprentice training	8	0.51	Nurses	27	0.79
General education	4	0.61	Canteen staff	26	0.87
Clerical training	4	0.86	Welfare officer	12	0.86
Management training	4	0.46	Safety officer	11	0.83
Sales training	3	0.53	Fire service	8	0.81
Mean item analysis value	–	0.63	Sports and social	7	0.91
Range obtained = 1–5 Mean = 1.85 S.D. = 2.34			Other medical	6	0.97
			Magazine editor	6	0.94
			Suggestions officer	2	1.00
			Mean item analysis value	–	0.87
			Range obtained = 1–10 Mean = 3.35 S.D. = 3.17		

TABLE A.2 (CONTINUED)

Specialization and Items	No. of Organizations	Item Analysis Value	Specialization and Items	No. of Organizations	Item Analysis Value
Specialization no. 7 (n = 50, scale no. 51.08)			**Specialization no. 8** (n = 49, scale no. 51.09)		
Storekeeper	49	1.00	Engineer	49	1.00
Buyers	43	0.74	Machine maintenance	49	1.00
Storekeepers specialized by product, material, or process	33	0.97	Building maintenance	34	0.86
Stock control	31	0.91	Electrical maintenance	24	0.84
Buyers specialized by product or material	22	0.88	Machine maintenance specialized by process, etc.	24	0.95
Stock controllers specialized by product, material, or process	11	0.93	New works force	12	0.88
Administrator	10	0.93	Surveyor or architect	10	0.83
Administrator specialized by particular material, etc.	3	1.00	Instrument maintenance	3	0.85
			Research into maintenance	3	0.92
Mean item analysis value	–	0.92	Electrical maintenance specialized by process, etc.	2	1.00
Range obtained = 1–8 Mean = 4.04 S.D. = 1.98			Mean item analysis value	–	0.91
			Range obtained = 2–10 Mean = 4.29 S.D. = 1.89		
Specialization no. 9 (n = 49, scale no. 51.10)			**Specialization no. 10** (n = 38, scale no. 51.11)		
Wages clerk	48	1.00	Processing	33	0.48
Costs clerk	38	0.69	Planning and scheduling	29	0.83
Ledgers clerk	34	0.82	Processing specialized by process, etc.	16	0.79
Cashier	31	0.75	Scheduling specialized by process, etc.	15	0.89
Financial accounting	20	0.79	Machine loading	4	0.74
Costing specialized by product, factory, etc.	11	0.97	Mean item analysis value	–	0.74
Financial data processing	11	0.86	Range obtained = 1–5 Mean = 2.55 S.D. = 1.57		
Salaries payment	10	0.86			
Auditing	9	0.81			
Budgeting	6	0.91			
Cost follow up	3	0.55			
Mean item analysis value	–	0.82			
Range obtained = 1–10 Mean = 4.51 S.D. = 2.45					
Specialization no. 11 (n = 40, scale no. 51.12)			**Specialization no. 12** (n = 25, scale no. 51.13)		
Product inspection	40	1.00	Work study	25	1.00
Product inspection specialized by stages	34	1.00	Work study specialized by process	13	0.95
Raw material control	20	1.00	Methods	10	0.95

TABLE A.2 (CONTINUED)

Specialization and Items	No. of Organi- zations	Item Analysis Value	Specialization and Items	No. of Organi- zations	Item Analysis Value
Specialization no. 11 (cont.)			*Specialization no. 12 (cont.)*		
Laboratory test of product	9	0.87	Policy and administration	9	1.00
Division of raw material	8	0.96	Process planning	5	1.00
Inspection standards	6	0.85	Production engineering	4	0.88
Policy and administration of inspection	6	1.00	Layout	3	1.00
			Draftsmen	2	1.00
Mean item analysis value	–	0.95	Mean item analysis value	–	0.95
Range obtained = 1–7 Mean = 3.07 S.D. = 1.92			Range obtained = 1–8 Mean = 2.84 S.D. = 2.89		
Specialization no. 13 (n = 36, scale no. 51.14)			*Specialization no. 14 (n = 22, scale no. 51.15)*		
New product research	35	0.50	Statistics clerks	18	0.57
Drawing office	28	1.00	Organization and methods	11	0.60
Process and equipment research	16	0.87	Subdivision of statistics	9	0.78
New product research by product	14	0.91	Filing and post	7	1.00
Division into mechanical and electrical	10	0.91	Committees and policies	3	1.00
Pure research	3	1.00	Mean item analysis value	–	0.68
Administration of research	2	1.00	Range obtained = 1–5 Mean = 2.18 S.D. = 1.96		
Mean item analysis value	–	0.88			
Range obtained = 1–7 Mean = 3.00 S.D. = 1.78					
Specialization no. 15 (n = 12, scale no. 51.16)			*Specialization no. 16 (n = 11, scale no. 51.17)*		
Legal or insurance	11	1.00	Market research	11	1.00
Share registrar	3	0.66	Market research specialized by product	3	1.00
Legal section subdivision	2	0.62	Economic analysis	1	1.00
Legal inquiries	1	1.00			
Mean item analysis value	–	0.86	Mean item analysis value	–	1.00
Range obtained = 1–3 Mean = 1.73 S.D. = 2.05			Range obtained = 1–3 Mean = 1.36 S.D. = 2.34		

Overall role specialization* (n = 52, scale no. 51.19)
Range obtained = 0–87
Mean = 31.77
S.D. = 19.90

* Scores formed by summing the total scores on each of scale nos. 51.02 to 51.15 inclusive, and scale no. 51.17. (Organizations without a specialization given a score of 0.)

able, but they are applicable to all organizations.

APPENDIX B.
STANDARDIZATION

This appendix gives a list of possible procedures, each rated for their degree of standardization. A high score means highly standardized and a low score less standardized. All multiple-answer questions have been converted into biserial items.[31]

INSPECTION

Frequency* (*0*—none, *1*—haphazard, *2*—random sample, *3*—100%) (Negative on scale no. 52.02)

Range (*0*—none, *1*—some, *2*—all new, *3*—all)

Method* (*0*—none, *1*—visual, *2*—attributes, *3*—measurement) (Negative on scale no. 52.02)

Type† (*0*—none, *1*—one of raw materials, process, or final inspection, *2*—process+final inspection, *3*—raw materials+process+final inspection)

Special inspection process, e.g., statistical quality control†

STOCK CONTROL

Stock taking (*0*—never taken, *1*—yearly, *2*—semiannually, *3*—quarterly, *4*—monthly, *5*—weekly, *6*—daily)

OPERATIONAL CONTROL

Firm plans (*0*—1 day, *1*—week, *2*—month, *3*—quarter, *4*—year, *5*—over one year, *6*—permanent)

Scheduling* (*0*—as needed, *1*—monthly, *2*—weekly, *3*—daily, *4*—continuous) (Negative on scale no. 52.02)

Progress checking*† (*0*—none, *1*—irre-

gular, *2*—regular) (Negative on scale nos. 52.01 and 52.02)

Maintenance (*0*—no procedure, *1*—breakdown procedure, *2*—mixed, *3*—planned maintenance, *4*—programmed replacements)

FINANCIAL CONTROL

Type (*1*—whole firm, historical, *2*—job costing, *3*—budgeting, *4*—standard costs, *5*—marginal costs)

Range (*1*—whole firm, *2*—one product, *3*—some products, *4*—all products, *5*—all activities)

Comparison with budgets† (*0*—none, *1*—yearly, *2*—half-yearly, *3*—quarterly, *4*—monthly, *5*—weekly, *6*—continually)

PEOPLE: CONTROL

Definition of operative's task*† (*1*—custom, *2*—apprenticeship or profession, *3*—manuals, *4*—rate fixing, *5*—time study, *6*—work study, *7*—work study and task description) (Negative on scale no. 52.02)

Work study*† (*0*—none, *1*—some direct workers, *2*—all direct workers, *3*—all direct workers+operatives, e.g., maintenance, etc., *4*—all direct workers+operatives+clerks) (Negative on scale no. 52.02)

Job evaluation†

Discipline* (set offenses)

Discipline* (set penalties)

Discipline* (procedure for dismissing staff)

Salary and wage review

Personal reports by superiors†

Staff establishment†

Labor budgets*†

COMMUNICATION

Decision seeking*† (*0*—as needed, *1*—semistandardized, *2*—standardized, *3*—project justification)

---

[31] See Brogden, "A New Coefficient."
* Also incorporated in scale no. 52.02.
† Also incorporated in scale no. 52.01.

* Also incorporated in scale no. 52.02.
† Also incorporated in scale no. 52.01.

Decision conveying* (*0*—as needed, *1*—semistandardized, *2*—standardized)

Research and development† (*0*—none, *1*—development as needed, *2*—development department, *3*—development program, *4*—research and development department, *5*—research and development program)

Obtaining ideas† (*0, 1, 2, 3, 4, 5*—number of the following that the organization does: conference attending, conference reporting, periodicals circulation, periodicals reporting, suggestion scheme)

Ordering procedures*† (*0*—as needed, *1*—production plans, *2*—datum stocks) (Negative on scale no. 52.02)

Buyer's authority over what to buy (limited)

Buyer's authority over whom to buy from (limited)

Buyer's authority over how much to buy (limited)

Procedure for buying nonstandard items

Procedure for notifying head office of purchases, etc.

Bidding procedure

Contracts procedure

Promotion procedure* (*1*—as needed, *2*—grade+qualification, *3*—internal advertisement and selection)

Selection of operative† (*1*—interview by superior, *2*—interview by personnel officer, *3*—grading system or interview board, *4*—testing procedure, *5*—outside appointer)

Selection of foremen*† (as for selection of operatives)

Selection of executives* (*1*—interview by superior, *2*—interview by personnel officer, *3*—grading system or selection board, *4*—outside appointer)

Recruitment policy

Central recruiting procedure*†

Central interviewing procedure*†

Standard procedure for getting increases in staff

Standard procedure for getting increases in works

Apprenticeships†

Day release (that is, operators and managers allowed to attend courses at a technical college for one day in each week)

Operator training†

Evening classes encouraged

Courses arranged for management†

Courses arranged for supervision†

Management trainees†

Graduate apprentices†

Block release† (that is, managers allowed to attend courses outside the organization for a specified period, full time)

House journals† (*0*—none, *1*—irregular, *2*—regular)

Ceremonies† (*0*—none, *1*—irregular, *2*—regular)

Trademarks

Sports and social activities† (*0*—none, *1*—irregular, *2*—regular)

Participation in displays and exhibitions† (*0*—none, *1*—irregular, *2*—regular)

Conference attendance† (*0*—none, *1*—irregular, *2*—regular)

Induction courses† (*0*—no employees, *1*—few, *2*—many, *3*—all)

Handbooks provided for employees† (*0*—for none, *1*—for few, *2*—for many, *3*—for all)

Uniforms provided for employees (*0*—for none, *1*—for few, *2*—for many, *3*—for all)

TABLE B.1 STANDARDIZATION ($n = 52$)

Scale		Mean Item Analysis Value	Range Obtained	Mean	S.D.
No.	*Title*				
52.00	Overall	0.41	30–131	83.88	22.71
52.01	Procedures defining task and image	0.65	3–31	17.44	7.91
52.02	Procedures controlling selection, advancement, etc.	0.62	0–18	8.79	4.54

SALES

Catalog (*0*—none, *1*—giving products, *2*—as in *1*+giving prices of standard products, *3*—as in *2*+subject to regular review, *4*—as in *3*+giving price of nonstandard products, *5*—as in *4* +giving delivery times)

Sales policy (*1*—general aims, *2*—some specific aims, *3*—sales policy)

Market research† (*0*—contacts with existing customers, *1*—circularizing existing customers, *2*—circularizing potential customers, *3*—systematic market research or market intelligence, *4*—market research involving highly specific assessment of customers)

MISCELLANEOUS

Personnel reports and statistics† (*0, 1, 2, 3, 4, 5*—number of areas covered from among sickness, timekeeping, absence, labor turnover, accidents)

Operations research

Central discipline procedure

APPENDIX C. FORMALIZATION

ITEMS INCORPORATED IN SCALE NO. 53.01: ROLE DEFINITION

Who has written contracts of employment (includes legal contract, formal letter of appointment, and terms of engagement or rules signed by employee)

† Also incorporated in scale no. 52.01.

Proportion of employees who have handbooks

Number of handbooks

Organization chart

Written operating instructions available to direct worker

Written terms of reference or job descriptions

Manual of procedures or standing orders

Written policies (excluding minutes of governing bodies)

Workflow ("production") schedules or programs

Research programs or reports

ITEMS INCORPORATED IN SCALE NO. 53.02: INFORMATION PASSING

Management approval in writing required for certain decisions

Suggestion scheme

Memo forms

Notification of engagement of direct workers

Minutes for senior executive meeting (i.e., centralization level 2, personnel)

Conference reports

Agenda for senior executive meeting (i.e., centralization level 2, personnel)

Agenda for workflow (production) meeting

Minutes for workflow (production) meeting

Written reports submitted for workflow (production) meeting

Welfare documents for direct workers on engagement

Dismissal form or report recording or communicating the dismissal

House journal

TABLE C.1 ANALYSIS OF FORMALIZATION ($n = 52$)

Scale		*Mean Item Analysis Value*	*Range Obtained*	*Mean*	*S.D.*
No.	*Title*				
53.00	Overall*	0.63	4–49	27.17	11.66
53.01	Role definition	0.74	0–20	9.17	5.65
53.02	Information passing	0.68	0–15	7.00	3.84
53.03	Recording of role performance	0.67	2–11	7.87	2.64

* Includes all items.

ITEMS INCORPORATED IN SCALE NO. 53.03: RECORDING OF ROLE PERFORMANCE

Record of inspection performed (e.g., report, certificate, quality card, etc., recording *both* positive and negative results, not merely a rejection slip)

Work assessment record (work study)

Record of maintenance performed on workflow (production) equipment

Record of direct worker's work

Record of direct worker's time

Document stating tasks done or to be done on unit of output (e.g., batch dockets, route tickets, etc.)

Petty cash voucher, authorizing and/or recording petty expenditure

Written application for, or sanction against, spending £1,000

Requisition for engagement of direct worker

Application or engagement form for direct worker

Frequency of records of direct worker's work

ITEMS NOT INCORPORATED IN SCALE NOS. 53.01, 53.02, AND 53.03

Appeal form against dismissal

Document identifying units of output (e.g., batch cards, work tickets, sales checks or tickets in a retail store, insurance policies in an insurance office)

Dispatch note communicating dispatch of unit of output

Written trade union procedures for negotiation, raising grievances, etc.

Written history of the organization

APPENDIX D. CENTRALIZATION

The responses to the questions in terms of the six hierarchical levels have been converted into biserial items.[32]

ITEMS USED FOR SCALE ON CENTRALIZATION

Labor force requirements

Appointments to direct worker jobs

Promotion of direct workers

Representing the organization in labor disputes

Number of supervisors*

Appointment of supervisory staff from outside the organization*

Promotion of supervisory staff*

Salaries of supervisory staff*

Spending of unbudgeted or unallocated money on capital items*

Spending of unbudgeted or unallocated money on revenue items*

Selection of type or brand for new equipment*

Overtime to be worked

Delivery dates or priority of orders

New product or service*

Marketing territories to be covered*

[32] See Brogden.

* Incorporated in scale no. 54.10.

Extent and class of market (operational field) to be aimed for*

Costing; i.e., to what costing system, if any, will be applied*

Inspection; i.e., to what items, processes, etc. the inspection system, if any, will be applied*

Operations that will have work studies made of them*

Plans to be worked on

Outputs to be scheduled against given plans

Dismissal of operative

Dismissal of supervisor*

Methods of personnel selection

Training methods*

Buying procedures*

Suppliers of materials to be used*

Methods of work to be used (not involving expenditure); i.e., how a job is to be done

Machinery or equipment to be used for a job

Allocation of work among available workers

Welfare facilities to be provided*

Price of the output*

Altering responsibilities or areas of work of functional specialist departments*

Altering responsibilities or areas of work of line department*

Creation of a new department (functional specilist or line)*

Creation of a new job (functional specialist or line, of any status, probably signified by a new job title)*

Who takes over in the chief executive's absence

TABLE D.1   ANALYSIS OF CENTRALIZATION ($n = 52$)

Scale		Mean Item Analysis Value	Range Obtained	Mean	S.D.
No.	Title				
54.00	Overall*	0.40	51–116	77.48	13.47
54.10	Autonomy of organizations	0.74	1–23	15.00	6.04

* 11 items omitted.

APPENDIX E. CONFIGURATION

TABLE E.1   DEFINITIONS USED IN CONFIGURATION SCALES

Scale No.	Definitions
55.08	*Chief executive's span.* Number of subordinates who report directly to chief executive with no intervening level, irrespective of the status of the subordinates.
55.09	*Subordinate ratio.* Number of workflow subordinates (direct workers) per first-line supervisor (i.e., the lowest job that does not include prescribed direct work).
55.43	*Height.* Number of jobs in the longest "line" between direct worker and chief executive (inclusive of both), excluding assistants *to*, and secretaries.
55.47	*Workflow superordinates.* All employees in supervisory or managerial jobs responsible for work on outputs, with assistants and deputies, but excluding supervisors whose jobs include prescribed direct work.
55.48	*Non-workflow personnel.* All employees with no direct or supervisory responsibility for work on the outputs.
55.49	*Clerks.* Employees whose main prescribed task is writing and recording (including records in other than written form), and who have no subordinates other than typists.

* Incorporated in scale no. 54.10.

TABLE E.2 ANALYSIS OF CONFIGURATION ($n = 52$)

Scale				
No.	*Title*	*Range*	*Mean*	*S.D.*
55.08	Chief executive's span of control	2–14	6.08	3.08
55.09	Subordinate ratio	3–123	31.67	23.90
55.43	Vertical span (height)	4–11	6.71	1.42
55.47	Workflow superordinates (%)	0.4–29.0	5.64	6.58
55.48	Non-workflow personnel (%)	5.6–89.1	34.39	17.85
55.49	Clerks (%)	1.7–29.4	8.57	5.62

APPENDIX F. TRADITIONALISM

Scale no. 56.00, traditionalism, incorporates items from scale no. 52.00, overall standardization, and scale no. 53.00, overall formalization. Each item is scored 1 for all scores of 1 or above on the original scales. Scores are calculated by the following formula:

$$\frac{\text{score on standardization items} - \text{score on formalization items} \times 100}{\text{score on formalization items}}$$

Analysis showed:
Range = 0–800
Mean = 53.35
S.D. = 122.08

TABLE F.1 STANDARDIZATION AND FORMALIZATION ITEMS USED

Items from Scale No. 52.00, Overall Standardization	*Items from Scale No. 53.00, Overall Formalization*
Inspection frequency	Record of inspection performed
Workflow scheduling	Workflow (production) schedules or programs
Maintenance	Record of maintenance performed on workflow (production) equipment
Definition of operative's task	Written operating instructions available to direct workers
Work study	Work assessment record (work study)
Discipline: procedure for dismissing staff	Dismissal form or report recording or notifying dismissal
Decision conveying	Management approval in writing
Research and development	Research programs or reports
Central recruiting procedure	Requisition for engagement of direct worker
Central interviewing procedure	Application or engagement form for job as direct worker

part four

PROFESSIONALIZATION
AND BUREAUCRATIZATION

INTRODUCTION

This last section deals with the bureaucratic and nonbureaucratic dimensions of the organizational control structure. The professionalization of the organizational labor force represents, of course, an aspect of the skill structure. Yet its consequences for coordination and, specifically, for the degree of externality of rules, the nature of supervision, and the problem of hierarchy are so pervasive that it is useful to conceptualize professionalization as a nonbureaucratic form of coordination. As such, professionalization has been used as a structural variable by studies already included in preceding sections.[1]

Similarly, bureaucratization, particularly "internal bureaucratization" in the form of the A/P ratio has been dealt with in the previous section.[2] But there are other aspects of bureaucratization that need to be considered, e.g., hierarchical differentiation, the supervision ratio, the span of control, and the problem of centralization of authority.

The studies included in this section, then, are concerned with the determinants of various modes of coordination, and specifically with the relationship between bureaucratization and professionalization.

Stinchcombe's analysis provides a framework for dealing with bureaucratic as against nonbureaucratic modes of coordination. Starting with Weber's conception of rational administration, Stinchcombe conceptualizes bureaucratic and craft (or professional) administration as subtypes of rational administration. Moreover, bureaucratic and craft administration are seen as alternative modes of coordination such that as one increases, the other decreases. Based on a comparative analysis of 1950 census data on mass production industries

[1] See, e.g., Heydebrand, 7; Kriesberg, 9 and 11; Heydebrand and Noell, 13; Rushing, 21; and Pugh et al., 25 this volume.
[2] Among the first studies to make use of the A/P ratio are, of course, Seymour Melman, "The Rise of Administrative Overhead in the Manufacturing Industries of the United States, 1899–1947," *Oxford Economic Papers*, 3 (February 1951), 62–112, and Reinhard Bendix, *Work and Authority in Industry*. New York: Harper and Row, 1956, pp. 221–22.

and the construction industry, Stinchcombe shows that the proportion of clerical as well as professional personnel within administration is significantly smaller in the craft-dominated construction industry. Due to the special nature of work organization in terms of subcontractors (relative autonomy) and the variability of the task structure (economic instability and seasonal variation), the construction industry is seen as functionally decentralized such that technical and economic decisions are made at the work level, rather than in central headquarters or specialized staff departments.

Stinchcombe makes the important distinction between *goal setting* and *supervision*, the former being tied to the locus and nature of decision making, the latter to hierarchical differentiation, the supervision ratio, and the span of control. Thus, while the goals of craft subcontractors are defined for them, the procedures of goal attainment are not, resulting in the reduction or elimination of regulative rules, of the bureaucratic enforcement of conformity to rules and, therefore, of external supervision and hierarchical differentiation.

Hall's study approaches the relation between professionalization and bureaucratization from a somewhat different perspective, although he arrives at the same general conclusion namely, that both are inversely related. Hall distinguishes between structural and attitudinal aspects of professionalization. The structural aspects are measured in terms of Wilensky's criteria for occupations that pass through certain stages in becoming a profession, e.g., creation of a full-time occupation, establishment of training schools, formation of professional associations, and formation of a code of ethics. The attitudinal aspects are measured by such characteristics as reference group orientation, service ideal, dedication, self-regulation, and autonomy.

Based on an analysis of eleven types of occupations in twenty-seven different organizational settings, Hall finds that the structural and attitudinal aspects of professionalization do not necessarily vary together. A particularly interesting dimension of his analysis is the grouping of organizational settings in terms of organizational autonomy. The settings vary from a high degree of autonomy (and a low degree of bureaucratization) in clinical settings, law firms, and public accounting firms, to an intermediate degree of autonomy (heteronomy) in social work agencies and schools, to a relatively low degree of autonomy represented by departments in larger organizations. The thrust of Hall's analysis is in the direction of showing the interpenetration of professional and bureaucratic characteristics of organizations.

Indik's study of the effect of size on the supervision ratio in five different sets of organizations represents one of the earliest examples of an empirical analysis of this particular relationship. The study has several important and noteworthy features. First, supervision ratio is defined as the ratio of supervisors to total personnel, *excluding* from the numerator all clerical personnel. Second, he uses a logarithmic transformation of size in order to correct for the curvilinear nature of the relationship between the raw variables. Third, he analyzes data from a total of 116 organizations, representing five different organizational settings. The study has, consequently, a simple but relatively powerful design. Indik shows that the relation between size and supervision ratio has a logarithmic form and is negative. The latter finding especially has generally been confirmed in most subsequent studies of work organizations which use the supervision ratio as a variable.

The study of 156 public personnel agencies by Blau, Heydebrand and Stauffer is one of the first analyses to come out of the Comparative Organization Research Program initiated in 1964 at the University of Chicago.[3] The study focuses on the effects of internal division of labor (functional specialization) and professionalization on the supervision ratio and on the relative size of the clerical staff, holding size constant. Furthermore, variations in the cost ratio, i.e., the relative level of operating costs, are analyzed in the light of these structural variables. The relative level of operating costs is defined by the ratio of an agency's salary expenditures to the total payroll of civil service personnel administered by the agency.

Increasing internal division of labor is shown to produce a smaller supervision ratio, but only at low levels of professionalization. This relationship is interpreted as indicating that a central authority structure is well suited for the coordination of functions differentiated into simple routines, but not for that of professional specialties. Moreover, internal structural differentiation is shown to impede economies of scale (cost reduction due to size). However, a relatively larger clerical staff appears to contribute to balancing the direct and indirect negative effects of size and differentiation on operating costs.

The findings of this study are, on the whole, consistent with those applying to other professional organizations (Heydebrand, 7, Heydebrand and Noell, 13, and Montagna, 28, this volume). Some differences in interpretation derive from the fact that in the present study, a small supervision ratio is defined in terms of centralization without taking into account the number of hierarchical levels involved, nor the actual decision-making structure of agencies. Furthermore, the managerial staff belongs to the same category of professionals as the operating staff, a fact which makes agencies in this respect quite similar to autonomous professional organizations, rather than to government agencies, and explains the positive relation between professionalization and supervision ratio ("centralization"). However, actual variations in autonomy, in the complexity of the task structure, and in the *nature* of professionalization (as over against its *extent*) are not considered in this study.

Montagna's study of eight large and four medium-sized public accounting firms constitutes a serendipitous replication of many aspects of the study of public personnel agencies described above. Based on self-administered questionnaires and interviews, Montagna was able to develop a model of the basic structural pattern characteristic of "professional bureaucracies." He shows that professionalization is positively related to centralization and to the relative size

---

[3] For a description of this program, see Heydebrand, 1 this volume.

of the administrative staff. In large firms, high levels of professionalization and centralization coexist with a relatively small administrative component, whereas in smaller (medium-sized) firms professionalization and centralization are inversely related, regardless of the relative size of the administrative staff. In Montagna's study, the key independent variables are professionalization and size. Technical complexity, specialization, and differentiation are conceptually subsumed under professionalization and size, but not measured separately.

Two aspects of Montagna's study are of particular interest since they are often noted but seldom documented. First, the accounting firms studied here were found to contain three separate hierarchies: certified public accountants, experts in "management services," and nonprofessional supporting staff. While this dimension of the complexity of the task structure is, in the present study, a constant characteristic rather than a variable, its existence suggests parallels with other complex professional organizations, e.g., hospitals (Heydebrand, 7). Second, one of Montagna's generalizations is that the process of professional development may involve "the simultaneous occurrence of rationalization of one body of knowledge and the development of another." Both types of innovative development, viz., the *rationalization of the knowledge base* and the *extension of knowledge to new areas,* have been stressed as crucial, though contradictory, aspects of organizational change in still other professional organizations, e.g., private welfare agencies (Heydebrand and Noell, 13).

The next study by Peter Blau represents an analysis of state and local finance departments. Like the study of public personnel agencies, the finance agency project was part of the Comparative Organization Research Program.

Blau's paper represents an attempt to bring certain conclusions from the earlier analysis of the public personnel agencies in line with those emerging from the analysis of the 254 finance departments. In this re-interpretation, however, the public personnel agencies are still defined as "government agencies" rather than professional organizations, just as the presumed conflict between professional and bureaucratic authority is attributed to the alleged normative incompatibility between competence and rank differentiation first noted by Parsons.[4]

For the finance agencies, professionalization is measured by the proportion of staff *required* to have (rather than actually possessing) the B.A. degree. These training requirements are shown to be positively associated with the overall supervision ratio, the number of levels, the average span of control of middle managers, and decentralization of decision making in matters of budgeting, accounting, and personnel decisions. The number of hierarchical levels, in turn, is negatively related to the number of subunits, but positively related to size, span of control of middle managers, the existence of certain rules and regulations, and decentralization in decision making relevant to the promotion

---

[4] For a critique of this argument, see Heydebrand and Noell, 13 this volume; see also Eliot Freidson, *Professional Dominance: The Social Structure of Medical Care.* New York: Atherton, 1970.

of personnel. The number of levels is also positively related to automation (presence of computers), a relationship elaborated by Meyer.[5] Blau also gives certain initial findings from the analysis of employment security departments, another project of the Comparative Organization Research Program.[6]

Bell's study of thirty different departments in a community general hospital focuses exclusively on various determinants of the supervisory span of control. Based on informal observations, interviews, and questionnaires, Bell ascertains the existence and variation of such factors as job complexity of supervisors and subordinates, respectively, as well as closeness of supervision. Job complexity is measured by an index composed of four elements: the degree of predictability of work demands, amount of discretion exercised, extent of responsibility, and number of different tasks performed. The analysis shows that span of control decreases with the increasing complexity of the jobs of both supervisors and subordinates. Moreover, job complexity of supervisors is correlated with that of subordinates. Closeness of supervision, however, is not related to the supervisor's span of control.

Bell concludes that technological aspects of work organization such as job complexity are key determinants of the span of control such that, in general, the greater the degree of job complexity, the smaller the span of control. Unfortunately, size is not systematically measured so as to provide a test of Indik's prediction that, holding job complexity constant, increasing size will lead to an *increase* in the supervision ratio, i.e., a decrease in the span of control.

Since the concept of job complexity includes certain dimensions characteristic of professional work, it seems that Bell's conclusions can be interpreted as generally supporting the hypothesis that professionalization is inversely related to bureaucratization. This is true especially if a small span of control, (i.e., a large supervision ratio) is interpreted in terms of a high degree of control, an interpretation which Bell's data appear to negate. It is, therefore, more plausible to argue that the complexity of tasks—unless broken down into functionally specialized fragments—gives rise to discretion and autonomy at the work level, and therefore to relatively smaller spans of control.

---

[5] Meyer's study of the 254 finance departments focuses on the direct and indirect effects of computerized data-processing facilities on bureaucratic structure. (Marshall Meyer, "Automation and Bureaucratic Structure," *American Journal of Sociology*, 74 [November 1968], 256–264.) The analysis shows that there is a significant negative relationship between automation and training requirements. Such a relationship is, of course, to be expected when automation is interpreted as an advanced form of rationalization of the specialized knowledge base, thus coming into conflict with less rationalized forms such as professional work; cf. Heydebrand and Noell, 13. Moreover, Meyer's analysis shows that automation leads to bureaucratization by encouraging the development of hierarchical levels. However, automation has a differential effect on the span of control, the average span being smaller at upper levels, but larger at lower levels of the hierarchy. Meyer concludes that human relations problems are created not so much by the direct effects of automation, but indirectly by the effects of automation on organizational structure.

[6] See Peter M. Blau and Richard Schoenherr, *The Structure of Organizations*, New York: Basic Books, 1971.

24. BUREAUCRATIC AND CRAFT ADMINISTRATION OF PRODUCTION: A COMPARATIVE STUDY

Arthur L. Stinchcombe

Administration in the construction industry depends upon a highly professionalized manual labor force.[1] The thesis of this paper is that the professionalization of the labor force in the construction industry serves the same functions as bureaucratic administration in mass production industries and is more rational than bureaucratic administration in the face of economic and technical constraints on construction projects.

Specifically we maintain that the main alternative to professional socialization of workers is communicating work decisions and standards through an administrative apparatus. But such an apparatus requires stable and finely adjusted communications channels. It is dependent on the continuous functioning of administrators in official statuses. Such continuous functioning is uneconomical in construction work because of the instability in the volume and product mix and of the geographical distribution of the work. Consequently the control of pace, manual skill, and effective operative decision (the essential components of industrial discipline) is more economical if left to professionally maintained occupational standards.

After presenting evidence and argument for these assertions, we will try to show why work on large-scale tract construction of houses continues to be administered on a nonbureaucratic, craft basis. Tract housing turns out to be a major revision in the *marketing* of construction products, rather than a revision in the *administration of work*.

Reprinted by permission from *Administrative Science Quarterly* (September 1959), pp. 168–87.

[1] "Professionalized" here means that workers get technical socialization to achieve a publicly recognized occupational competence. "Public recognition" involves preferential hiring (ideally to the point of excluding all others) of workers who have proved their competence to an agency external to the hiring firm or consumer. Often this agency is a professional association composed exclusively of qualified persons and more or less exhaustive of the occupation. This professional association itself often enforces preferential hiring rights of its members. The professional's *permanent labor market status* is not to be confused with permanent firm status (preferential hiring or continued employment of the current employees of a firm). This definition, therefore, differs somewhat from that of Nelson Foote in "The Professionalization of Labor in Detroit," *American Journal of Sociology*, 58 (1953), 371–80.

Our method will be to reanalyze certain published demographic and economic data for their administrative implications. Since the data were collected for other purposes, they fit the requirements of our problem only roughly. The gaps in the information and the gross character of the categories make it necessary, therefore, to use very rough statistical procedures and to limit the data to a suggestive role.

On the basis of the empirical findings, we will re-examine Max Weber's model of bureaucracy, showing that some elements of that model are not correlated with other elements. This will provide a basis for constructing a model of bureaucracy as a subtype of rational administration, with professionalization another main subtype. A general model of rational administration will be built out of the common elements of these subtypes.

BUREAUCRATIC ADMINISTRATION AND CRAFT ADMINISTRATION

Craft institutions in construction are more than craft trade unions; they are also a method of administering work. They include special devices of legitimate communications to workers, special authority relations, and special principles of division of work, the "jurisdictions" which form the areas of work defining labor market statuses. The distinctive features of craft administration may be outlined by contrasting it with mass production manufacturing administration.[2] The object of this section is to show that craft institutions provide a functional equivalent of bureaucracy.

Mass production may be defined by the criterion that *both* the product *and* the work process are planned in advance *by persons not on the work crew*. Among the elements of the work process planned are: (1) the location at which a particular task will be done, (2) the movement of tools, of materials, and of workers to this work place, and the most efficient arrangement of these work-place characteristics, (3) sometimes the particular movements to be performed in getting the task done, (4) the schedules and time allotments for particular operations, and (5) inspection criteria for particular operations (as opposed to inspection criteria for final products).

In construction all these characteristics of the work process are governed by the worker in accordance with the empirical lore that makes up craft principles. These principles are the content of workers' socialization and apply to the jobs for which they have preferential hiring rights.

This concentration of the planning of work in manual roles in construction results in a considerably simplified communications system in the industry; but the simplification does not markedly reduce the number of people in administrative statuses. Administrative statuses are roughly equivalent to occupations in census categories: proprietors, managers, and officials; professional, technical, and kindred workers; and clerical and kindred workers.

The proportion of administrative

---

[2] This account of mass production institutions is derived from Peter Drucker, *The New Society* (New York, 1950), and his *The Practice of Management* (New York, 1954), along with the work of David Granick, *Management of the Industrial Firm in the U.S.S.R.* (New York, 1954).

personnel in the labor force in various fabricating industries does not vary widely. In construction the proportion of the labor force in the three administrative occupations is 15.5 percent; in manufacturing as a whole it is 20.6 percent; in iron and steel primary extraction, 15.5 percent; motor vehicles and motor vehicle equipment, 17.6 percent; in chemicals and allied industries, 33.4 percent.[3] But these rough similarities in proportion of administrative personnel conceal wide differences in the internal structure of the communications system.

To provide a rough index of one of these differences in the internal structure of the authority systems, we have computed the proportion of clerical positions in the administration. This should provide an index of the proportion of people in administration who do not legitimate by their status the communications they process (e.g., typists, filing clerks, bookkeepers). They file the communications; they do not initiate them. Authority structures with special communications-processing positions may be called "bureaucratic" structures.[4] They provide for close control of the work process farther up the administrative hierarchy, and hence facilitate the control and planning of the work process in large enterprises. They decrease the dependence of the

enterprise on empirical lore and self-discipline at the work level and allow technical and economic decisions to be concentrated. Finally, they allow the processing of information and communications from distant markets, enabling the enterprise to be less dependent on the geographical location of clients.

The proportion of administrative personnel who are clerks in various fabricating industries is presented in Table 1.

Clearly the proportion of all administrative personnel who are clerks is considerably greater in manufacturing generally than it is in construction, and the typical mass production industries tend to have even greater development of specialized communications processing structures. The centralized planning of work is associated with this development of filed communications, with specialized personnel processing them.

Another type of internal differentiation of authority structures (systems of originating and processing communications legitimately directing workers) concerns the status and training of the originators. In some authority structures in fabricating industries, people in authority are largely defined by ownership and contract institutions, while in others their status derives from professional institutions. That is, communications from a position in the authority system may be considered legitimate because of the special competence of the originator, a professional; or they may be legitimate because of the special responsibility of the originator, as owner or official, for economic decisions.

We may contrast administrations by the proportion of people in authority whose status derives from

---

[3] *Characteristics of the Population.* Part 1 (U.S. Summary) (*Census of the Population,* 2 [1950]), Table 134, pp. 290–91.

[4] This takes one of Weber's criteria of bureaucratization as an empirical indicator, namely administration on the basis of files. I believe some of the other characteristics of bureaucracy named by Weber can be derived from this one, while some cannot. See Max Weber, *From Max Weber: Essays in Sociology,* tr. by H. H. Gerth and C. W. Mills (New York, 1946), pp. 196–98.

TABLE 1 THE PROPORTION OF ADMINISTRATIVE PERSONNEL* WHO ARE CLERKS
IN SELECTED FABRICATING INDUSTRIES, U.S., 1950

Industry or Industry Group	Administrators' Clerks
Manufacturing	53%
Motor vehicles and accessories	63%
Iron and steel primary extraction	60%
Chemicals and allied	45%
Construction	20%

* Proprietors, managers, and officials; professional, technical, and kindred workers.
Characteristics of the Population, Part 1, pp. 290–91.

TABLE 2 THE PROPORTION OF TOP ADMINISTRATORS* WHO ARE
PROFESSIONALS IN VARIOUS INDUSTRIES, U.S., 1950

Industry or Industry Group	Professional Authority Positions
Manufacturing	50%
Motor vehicles and accessories	63%
Iron and steel primary extraction	64%
Chemicals and allied	65%
Construction	31%

* Proprietors, managers, and officials; and professional, technical and kindred workers.
Characteristics of the Population, Part 1, pp. 290–91.

special education. This may be denoted as "the professionalization of authority." The proportion of all "top" administrative personnel (proprietors, managers, and officials; *and* professionals) who are professionals in the selected industries is presented in Table 2.

The contrast in the degree of professionalization of authority between manufacturing and construction, and more especially between mass production and construction, is just as clear as was the case with bureaucratization.

The engineering of work processes and the evaluation of work by economic and technical standards take place in mass production in specialized staff departments, far removed from the work crew in the communications system. In the construction industry these functions are decentralized to the work level, where entrepreneurs, foremen, and craftsmen carry the burden of technical and economic decision.

This decentralization of functions of the firm to the work level in construction, and the relative lack of information about and professional analysis of work processes at administrative centers, is accompanied by a difference in the types of legitimate communication.

In the construction industry, authoritative communications from administrative centers carry only specifications of the product desired and prices (and sometimes rough schedules). These two elements of the communication are contained in the contract; first, the contract between the client (with the advice of architects or engineers) and the general contractor,[5] and, second, between the

---

[5] This step is omitted in the case of operative builders, but otherwise the authority structure is similar.

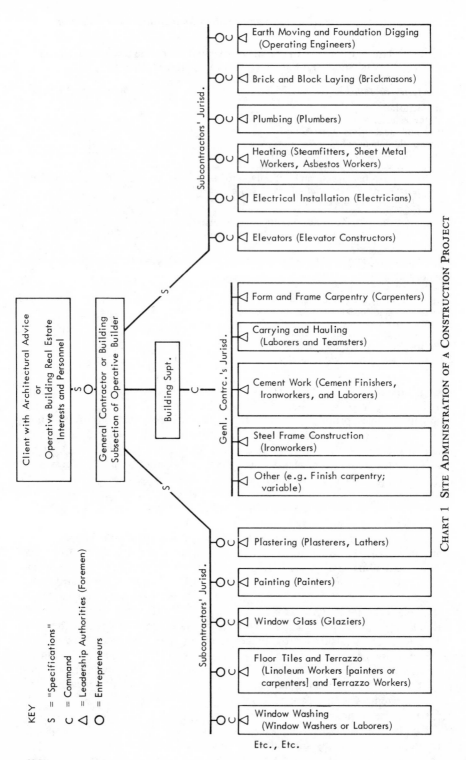

KEY

S = "Specifications"

C = Command

◁ = Leadership Authorities (Foremen)

○ = Entrepreneurs

CHART 1 SITE ADMINISTRATION OF A CONSTRUCTION PROJECT

Client with Architectural Advice or Operative Building Real Estate Interests and Personnel

General Contractor or Building Subsection of Operative Builder

Building Supt.

Subcontractors' Jurisd.

- ○ ○ ◁ Earth Moving and Foundation Digging (Operating Engineers)
- ○ ○ ◁ Brick and Block Laying (Brickmasons)
- ○ ○ ◁ Plumbing (Plumbers)
- ○ ○ ◁ Heating (Steamfitters, Sheet Metal Workers, Asbestos Workers)
- ○ ○ ◁ Electrical Installation (Electricians)
- ○ ○ ◁ Elevators (Elevator Constructors)

Genl. Contrc.'s Jurisd.

- ◁ Form and Frame Carpentry (Carpenters)
- ◁ Carrying and Hauling (Laborers and Teamsters)
- ◁ Cement Work (Cement Finishers, Ironworkers, and Laborers)
- ◁ Steel Frame Construction (Ironworkers)
- ◁ Other (e.g. Finish carpentry; variable)

Subcontractors' Jurisd.

- ○ ○ ◁ Plastering (Plasterers, Lathers)
- ○ ○ ◁ Painting (Painters)
- ○ ○ ◁ Window Glass (Glaziers)
- ○ ○ ◁ Floor Tiles and Terrazzo (Linoleum Workers [painters or carpenters] and Terrazzo Workers)
- ○ ○ ◁ Window Washing (Window Washers or Laborers)

Etc., Etc.

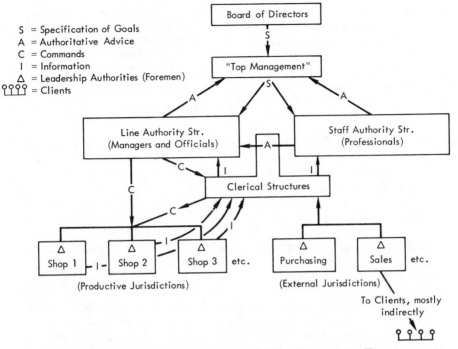

S = Specification of Goals
A = Authoritative Advice
C = Commands
I = Information
Δ = Leadership Authorities (Foremen)
ϙϙϙϙ = Clients

CHART 2 ADMINISTRATION OF A MASS PRODUCTION FIRM

general contractor and subcontractors. Subcontractors do the work falling within the "jurisdiction" of the trade they specialize in.

In mass production, where both the product and the work process are centrally planned, we find a system of legitimated advice on work and legitimate commands from line officials to foremen and workers to do particular work in particular ways. This more finely adjusted communications system depends on the development of specialized communications positions (clerks) and staff advice departments (professionals). These differences in administration are shown in Charts 1 and 2.

Craft administration, then, differs from bureaucratic administration by substituting professional training of manual workers for detailed central-

ized planning of work. This is reflected in the lack of clerical workers processing communications to administrative centers and less complex staffs of professionals planning work. It is also reflected in the simplification of authoritative communications from administrative centers.

VARIABILITY AND BUREAUCRATIZATION

In this section we try to demonstrate that professionalization of manual labor is more efficient in construction because bureaucratic administration is dependent on stability of work flow and income, and the construction industry is economically unstable.

Bureaucratization of administration may be defined as a relatively permanent structuring of communications channels between continuously functioning officials. This permanent structuring of channels of legitimate communications, channels defined by the permanent official status of the originator of the communication and of its receiver, permits the development of routine methods of processing information upward and authoritative communication downward. That is, it permits administration on the basis of files and the economical employment of clerical workers.

Routine processing of administrative communications and information is economical only when the overhead cost of specialized information-processing structures is highly productive; this productivity will be high only if rules concerning the route of communication can be taught to clerks. Otherwise, if it is necessary to use discretion in the choice of the receiver of a communication, it is cheaper to rely on visual supervision and executive or professional discretion.

THE CASE OF MASS PRODUCTION

Bureaucratization of administration depends therefore on the long-term stability of the administration. Of bureaucratic industrial administrations Peter Drucker says,

The central fact of industrial economics is not "profit" but "loss"—not the expectation of ending up with a surplus . . . but the inevitable and real risk of ending up with an impoverishing deficit, and the need, the absolute need, to avoid this loss by providing against the risks. . . . The economic activity of an industrial economy is not "trade" taking place in the almost timeless instant of exchange, but production over a very long period. *Neither the organization* (the human resources) nor the capital investment (the material resources) *are productive in the "here and now" of the present.* It will be years before the organization or the investment will begin to produce, and many more years before they will have paid for themselves.[6]

It is clear that he cannot be talking about construction organizations, which have to be productive "here and now."

This association between orientation to stability and large-scale bureaucratized firms reflects the social requirements of complex communications systems between designated officials. Administrations faced with critical problems of instability and flexibility, such as those in the construction industry, will not find it economical to teach clerks rules for channeling communications. For it is impossible to hire a clerk on the labor market who will know the firm's communications channels, so clerks have to be kept on even when they are not productive.[7] And it is difficult

[6] *The New Society*, p. 52 (our italics). Veblen said the same thing in a different moral vocabulary: "Under the changed circumstance [the replacement of the 'captain of industry'] the spirit of venturesome enterprise is more than likely to foot up as a hunting of trouble, and wisdom in business enterprise has more and more settled down to the wisdom of 'watchful waiting.' Doubtless this form of words, 'watchful waiting,' will have been employed in the first instance to describe the frame of mind of a toad who had reached years of discretion . . . but by an easy turn of speech it has also been found suitable to describe the safe and sane strategy of that mature order of captains of industry who are governed by sound business principles" (Thorstein Veblen, *The Portable Veblen* [New York, 1950], pp. 385–86).

[7] Also the class position of clerks makes it more difficult to hire temporary clerks.

TABLE 3 THE RELATIONSHIP BETWEEN MEAN SIZE OF FIRMS, SEASONALITY OF
EMPLOYMENT, AND THE PERCENTAGE OF THE LABOR FORCE CLERKS,
FOR BRANCHES OF THE CONSTRUCTION INDUSTRY*

Type of Contractor	Mean Size of Firms (1939)	Index of Seasonality of Employment (1926–1936)†	Percent of Clerks in Labor Force‡ (1939)
More than 8 employees per contractor			
Street, road, and sewer	12.3	73	4.8
Sand, gravel, excavation	9.9	43	7.6
Ventilating and heating	8.2	29	11.7
4–8 employees per contractor			
Brick, stone, and cement	5.5	47	3.3
General contracting	6.9	43	5.2
Sheet metal and roofing	4.9	29	11.7
Plumbing	5.1	20	10.9
Electrical	6.3	13	12.5
Less than 4 employees per contractor			
Painting and decorating	2.5	59	3.9

* Taken from Viva Boothe and Sam Arnold, *Seasonal Employment in Ohio* (Columbus: Ohio State University, 1944), Table 19, pp. 82–87. Plasterers are omitted from this table, because the number employed was not large enough to give a reliable figure on seasonality of clerks' work, the original purpose of the publication. There were less than 50 clerks in plastering enterprises in the state. Consequently the needed figure was not reported in the source. Plasterers' employment is very unstable, so the omission itself supports the trend.

† See footnote 8.

‡ Excluding sales clerks.

to specify rules for channeling communications in advance when volume, product mix, and work-force composition change rapidly, as they do in construction.

THE CASE OF CONSTRUCTION

The variability of the construction industry, its intimate dependence on variations in local markets, makes the development of bureaucracy uneconomical. Table 3 shows the relationship between one type of variability and the employment of clerks.

Data are for some types of construction firms, for all firms in Ohio large enough to have to report to the State Employment Office (those normally employing 3 or more persons). In the first column the mean size of firms in the branch is reported (computed here), and the branches are classified by mean size. In the second column is an index of seasonality of employment for the years 1926–1936 (computed in the source[8]). In the last column the average proportion of the labor force who were clerks in 1939 is reported (computed here).

[8] The index of seasonality was computed in the source in the following way: The monthly index of employment in firms reporting was computed for each year of the ten-year period, to the base of the mean employment of that year. Then the ten indices (one index for each of the ten years) for each month were arrayed, and the median taken. The 12 monthly medians give an overall picture of seasonality for the category for the ten years. Scatter diagrams of these monthly indices, standardized for the general level of employment during the year as outlined above, are presented in Viva Boothe and Sam Arnold, *Seasonal Employment in Ohio*.

The relationship between the development of clerical statuses in administration and the stability of the work flow is clear from Table 3. The strength of the relationship within the industry can give us confidence in asserting that instability decreases bureaucratization. There are only two inversions, and these are of insignificant size: sheet metal and roofing should have been less bureaucratized than plumbing; and painters should have been less than brick, stone, and cement firms. This is a strong support for the hypothesis that the lack of bureaucratization in the construction industry is due to general instability.

We do not have space to document adequately the sources of variability in the work flow of construction administrations. The main elements may be outlined as follows:

1. Variations in the volume of work and in product mix in the course of the business cycle.[9]
2. Seasonal variations in both volume and product mix.[10]
3. The limitation of most construction administrations, especially in the specialty trades, to a small geographical radius. This smaller market magnifies the variability facing particular firms according to well-known statistical principles (individual projects can form a large part of a local market).[11]
4. The organization of work at a particular site into stages (building "from the ground up"), with the resulting variability in the productive purpose of any particular site administration.[12]

SUMMARY OF EMPIRICAL PROPOSITIONS

It now seems wise to review the argument thus far. We are trying to show that the professionalization of the manual work force persists partly because it is a cheaper form of administration for construction enterprises than the bureaucratic form.

First we argued that bureaucracy and professionalized work force were

---

(Columbus, 1944), Chart 16, pp. 83–86. Graphs of seasonality are presented by drawing lines through the median monthly indices. This procedure eliminates between-years (presumably cyclical) variations in employment level.

After this array of 12 monthly indices is found, the index of seasonality reported in Table 3 is computed by the formula: $\frac{\text{maximum} - \text{minimum}}{\text{maximum}} \times 100$, where the maximum is the largest median monthly index, and minimum the smallest. This gives an index ranging from zero (no seasonality) to 100, which would be the result of no employment at all in the minimum month. From the scatter diagrams, this might result in an under-estimation of the short-time instability only for electrical contracting firms. But other evidence indicates that electrical construction firms have very stable employment. See W. Haber and H. Levinson, *Labor Relations and Productivity in the Building Trades* (Ann Arbor, 1956), p. 54. They rank construction occupations by percentage working a full year. Electricians work less than proprietors but more than any other occupation, including "foremen, all trades."

[9] Miles L. Colean and Robinson Newcomb, *Stabilizing Construction* (New York, 1952), pp. 18–20, 49–50, and Appendix N, pp. 219–42. Also Clarence Long, *Building Cycles and the Theory of Investment.* (Princeton, 1940).
[10] The data reported from Boothe and Arnold show both great seasonality and differential seasonality by trade. Their data show construction to be one of the most seasonal industries (*Seasonal Employment in Ohio*, pp. 23–27).
[11] *Cf.* Colean and Newcomb, *Stabilizing Construction*, pp. 250–51, for the ecological limitations on administrative scope. For data on variations in volume in local areas, see U.S. Bureau of Labor Statistics, *Construction during Five Decades* (Bulletin no. 1146 [July 1, 1953]), pp. 22–25.
[12] *Cf.* Gordon W. Bertran and Sherman J. Maisel, *Industrial Relations in the Construction Industry* (Berkeley, 1955), pp. 3–5.

real alternatives, that: (a) decisions, which in mass production were made outside the work milieu and communicated bureaucratically, in construction work were actually part of the craftsman's culture and socialization, and were made at the level of the work crew, (b) the administrative status structure of construction showed signs of this difference in the communications structure by relative lack of clerks and professionals, and (c) the legitimate communications in construction (contracts and subcontracts) showed the expected differences in content from the orders and advice in a bureaucracy. Contracts contained specifications of the goals of work and prices; they did not contain the actual directives of work, which, it seemed to us, did not have to be there because they were already incorporated in the professionalized culture of the workers.

Secondly, we argued that the bureaucratic alternative was too expensive and inefficient in construction because such administration requires continuous functioning in organizational statuses. But continuous functioning is prevented by the requirement that construction administrations adapt to variability in both volume and product mix. Using the employment of clerks as an index of bureaucratization, a close relation was found between seasonality in branches of construction and bureaucratization. This strong relationship was combined with knowledge of the general instability of construction to support the contention that bureaucracy was inefficient in construction.

THE IMPLICATIONS OF MARKETING REFORM

There is a good deal of careless talk about the bureaucratization of construction and the introduction of mass production by operative building of tract homes. The central innovation of operative building is in the field of marketing and finance rather than in the administration of production. The similarity of productive administration in operative building and in other large-scale building is well summarized by Sherman Maisel:

Many popular assumptions about subcontracting—that it lowers efficiency, raises costs, and leads to instability—are contradicted by our study in the Bay area of the reasons for subcontracting and its efficiency relative to its alternatives. Building appears to be one of the many industries where vertical disintegration increases efficiency and lowers costs without lessening stability. The fact that most large [operative housebuilding] firms have tried integrating various of the processes normally subcontracted but have usually returned to subcontracting them, is of great importance because it shows that the present prevalence of subcontracting is the result of a policy deliberately adopted by builders after testing alternative possibilities. . . .

The logic of trade contracting has developed as follows: (1) Efficiency reaches its maximum effectiveness under specialized labor. (2) Specialized labor reaches its maximum effectiveness when applied regularly on many units. . . . (3) The problem of sustaining specialized jobs as well as the coordination of the movement of men among them requires special supervision, usually performed by trade contractors. . . .

Given a need for specialized mechanisms, the builder gains greater flexibility and a decrease in the problems of supervision through subcontracting.[13]

The central limitation on supervision is the increase in overhead

---

[13] *Housebuilding in Transition* (Berkeley and Los Angeles, 1953), pp. 231–32.

when mediated communication is introduced. "A disproportionate increase takes place [in overhead in the largest construction firms] because production has spread beyond the area of simple visual control by the owners or owners [of the firm]."[14]

In fact, the characteristic of mass production administration, increasing specialization of tools and other facilities at a planned work place, does not take place with increasing size. Most machinery added in large firms consists of hand power tools and materials-handling machinery.[15]

The low development of distinctively bureaucratic production-control mechanisms, such as cost accounting, detailed scheduling, regularized reporting of work progress, and standardized inspection of specific operations, is outlined by Maisel.[16] What happens instead of centralized planning and bureaucratic control of work is an increase in the fineness of stages on which crews of workers are put. This results in the development of more efficient but still quite diversified skills. And most important, these skills still form a component of a labor market rather than an organizational status system.

Operative decisions are still very important at the work level, rather than being concentrated in production engineering and cost-accounting departments. Modification of tools for special purposes is done by workers (e.g., the making of templates which provide guides for standardized cutting operations, or the construction of special scaffolds for the crew.) There is no large element in

the administration with the specialized task of planning technological innovation in the work process. And stable communications between work crews and decision centers are poorly developed.

The central consideration is that variability of work load for the administration is not very much reduced, if at all, by operative building. And it is not necessarily economical to take advantage of what reduction there is, when the subcontracting system and structured labor market are already in existence.

What is changed, what makes the economies possible, is the place of the goal-setting function. The productive goals in the past were set by clients with architectural advice, who quite naturally did not set goals in such a way as to maximize productive efficiency. In operative building productive goals are set autonomously by the administration. This means that they can choose, among the products they might produce, those which are technically easier. The main reduction of costs, of course, comes from the planning of the construction site so as to minimize transportation and set-up costs. Sites next to each other minimize costs of moving men, materials, and equipment to the site. Warehousing of materials can be planned to fit the individual site, rather than burdening builders' supply places. Uniformity of design reduces the complexity of materials distribution, reduces design costs, and so forth.

The main innovation, then, is the planning of the *product* for ease of production, rather than in the planning of the *productive process*. This is the introduction of the conceptions of Eli Whitney of *standardized parts* into construction, rather than of

[14] *Ibid.*, p. 102.
[15] S. Maisel, *Housebuilding in Transition*, p. 103.
[16] *Ibid.*, pp. 123–30.

Henry Ford's innovation of *standardized tasks.*

RATIONAL ADMINISTRATION AND BUREAUCRACY

Since Weber, there has been a tendency to regard rational administration as identical with bureaucratic administration. This tendency has been especially strong among sociologists. We have chosen to define bureaucracy as a special type of rational administration and to discuss the social sources of an alternative method of institutionalizing rationality, namely, professionalization.

The central point of this analysis is that the components of Weber's ideal type do not form an inherently connected set of variables. Some of the components of the ideal type are relatively uncorrelated with others, while some are highly correlated.

We have called craft production unbureaucratized, although it does involve "the principle of fixed and official jurisdictional areas, which are generally ordered by rules."[17] The rules in this case are to be found in the jurisdictional provisions of trade unions, in the introductory sections of collective contracts, and in state licensing laws for contractors. The duties in construction are "distributed in a fixed way as official duties"[18] through legally binding contracts. "The authority to give the commands required for the discharge of these duties is distributed in a stable way."[19] The sanctions, especially firing, are stably allocated to contrac-

tors and subcontractors on the particular project.

The principal difference comes in the criterion: "Methodical provision is made for the *regular and continuous* fulfillment of these duties and for the execution of the corresponding rights."[20] It is not the rules governing jurisdiction and authority which we take to be characteristic of bureaucracy, but the regularity and continuity of work and status within an administrative system. We have shown that regularity and continuity are in fact correlated with our operational criterion of bureaucratization, the proportion of clerks among administrators.

Secondly, we have argued that "the principles of office hierarchy ... in which there is supervision of the lower offices by the higher ones,"[21] is dependent on stable communications structures, provided we differentiate *goal setting* from *supervision.* In construction there is no possibility of "appealing the decision of a lower office [subcontractor] to its higher authority [the general contractor or client]."[22] The goals of subcontractors are set by "higher authorities." But their work is not supervised, nor are their decisions appealable. Office hierarchy in the command-advice sense, then, is correlated with regularity and continuity in official statuses. Goal-setting arrangements can be changed drastically (e.g., from the client to the operative building corporation) without changing the administration of work in a bureaucratic direction.

The other main criterion Weber proposes concerns the stable structuring of communication (files), which we have taken as the empirical indi-

---

[17] Max Weber, *Essays in Sociology*, p. 196.
[18] *Ibid.*
[19] *Ibid.*

[20] *Ibid.* (our italics).
[21] *Ibid.*, p. 197.
[22] *Ibid.*

cator of stable, rule-governed communication channels among official statuses.

These last three elements of Weber's ideal type (continuity, hierarchy, and files), then, are functionally interrelated; they are found together in mass-production administration but are absent in construction administration. But the first three elements (stable jurisdictions, official duties, and authority) are found in both construction and mass production, so they cannot be highly correlated with the elements of continuity, hierarchy, and files.

Weber draws from his ideal type certain implications concerning the position of the official. Some of these are derived from distinctive characteristics of bureaucracy as we have defined it, and some are derived from general requirements of rationality. Characteristics common to bureaucracies *and* nonbureaucratic rational administrations include:

1. Positions in the organization are separated from the household. Positions in construction as workers, foremen, and entrepreneurs involve the separation of work from home life, firm accounts from household accounts, firm and trade promotions from family ties.[23]
2. Rational administration requires the allocation of work to those who are competent. This often involves hiring on the basis of formal training, cer-

tification, and examination. Not only civil servants, but also craftsmen, and private legal and medical practitioners, have to pass examinations or possess certificates of formal training. The main difference is that professional examinations allocate work throughout a labor market, while civil service examinations recruit only to organizational statuses.
3. To a large extent pecuniary compensation, regulated by the status of the worker, characterizes rational administration, as well as bureaucracy. At least, wage rates for each occupational status in construction are negotiated.

A characteristic of bureaucratic officials not found in construction is permanent appointment. Authorities on a construction project are appointed by subcontracts only for the duration of the project. The basis of responsibility for leadership duties is the contract for specific work (and the contractors' reputations) rather than generalized loyalty to the administration. Payment to authorities is not salary determined by the status of the official but payment for performance set by competitive bidding. Finally the career of the worker in construction is structured not by administrative regulation but by status in a structured labor market. These differences also distinguish private professional practice from bureaucratic administration.

We would construct an ideal type of functionally interrelated characteristics of bureaucracy as follows: The defining criterion would be stable, rule-ordered communications channels from and to continuously occupied statuses. This criterion implies: (1) development of files and employment of clerks, (2) hierarchical command-advice authority structures, and (3) career commit-

[23] Not that being a contractor's son doesn't give a competitive advantage; it is only that positions are not inherited, but awarded on a competitive basis. A contractor's son still has to meet occupational standards. On the advantage of sons of *Handwerker* in various trades in Germany, see Heinz Lamprecht, Über die soziale Herkunft der Handwerker, *Soziale Welt*, 3 (Oct., 1951), 42, 52.

ment to an *organizational* rather than a labor market or *occupational* status system.

Bureaucracy thus defined is a subtype of rational administration. Rational administration requires the government of work activity by economic and technical standards and hence requires:

1. Differentiation of the work role from home life (and other deep interpersonal commitments).
2. The organization of work statuses into some sort of career, in which future rights and duties depend on present performance according to specified standards.
3. A stable allocation of work to persons formally identified as able and willing to work and subject to discipline by understood work standards, and payment by the administration only when such workers are "productive."
4. A stable legitimate way of communicating at least the goals to be reached by subordinates and of seeing that these goals are accomplished.

This means that we take Weber's observations on the "Presuppositions and Causes of Bureaucracy"[24] to be mainly about the presuppositions and causes of any kind of rational administration. The presuppositions of bureaucracy are conditions facilitating continuous operation of an organizational status system, either continuity of work load and returns or institutionalized legitimacy of the status system itself (e.g., the military).

Continuity in status in a labor market, instead of an organization, we take to be the defining characteristic of professional institutions. Both the traditional professions and crafts in construction have profes-

[24] Weber, M., *Essays in Sociology*, pp. 204–209.

sional institutions in this sense. These are characterized by (roughly) occupationally homogeneous organizations seeking control of the rights and duties associated with doing work within a defined jurisdiction. By this control they assure competence, discipline. Both professions and crafts, then, guarantee labor market rights and enforce labor market duties which make up a professional status.

CONCLUSION

Concepts in organizational theory, such as bureaucracy, tend to take on a nebulous character because research in this area has consisted largely of case studies of particular organizations. An industrial firm engaged in mass production may certainly be bureaucratic, but not all the characteristics of the organization are distinctive of bureaucracy. Case studies cannot, ordinarily, sort out the inherent from the ephemeral connections among organizational characteristics. Systematic comparisons of different types of organizations, which we have attempted here, can refine our conceptual apparatus by defining complex concepts comprised of elements that hang together empirically.

The concept of bureaucracy developed here is not merely a descriptive one; it contains propositions about the connection between its elements. Such a concept can be refined either by proving new elements to be necessarily connected to those already incorporated or by disproving the hypothesized connection between elements. Similar definition is needed for other complex concepts in the social sciences: the city, sovereignty, the firm.

A definition of the firm, for example, should include those characteristics inevitably found in social units producing goods for markets. Such a definition of the firm would be not merely a category to put concrete organizations into, but a set of propositions about the relations between markets and social groups. Such propositional definitions can be best derived from the systematic comparative study of organizations.

25. PROFESSIONALIZATION AND BUREAUCRATIZATION

Richard H. Hall

Two related but often noncomplementary phenomena are affecting the social structure of Western societies today. The first of these is the increasing professionalization of the labor force. Occupational groups that have held the status of "marginal professions" are intensifying their efforts to be acknowledged as full-fledged professions. Occupations that have emerged rather recently, and some that have not previously been thought of as professions, are also attempting to professionalize. At the same time, work in general is increasingly becoming organizationally based. This is true among both the established professions and the professionalizing occupations. The intent of this paper is to examine the professionalization process in the context of the organizational structures in which professional or professionalizing workers are found, in order to determine how these phenomena affect and are affected by each other. Data from a variety of occupational groups found in a variety of organizational settings will be used in this analysis.*

BACKGROUND

Discussions about the nature of professions typically revolve around the professional model. This professional model consists of a series of attributes which are important in distinguishing professions from other occupations. Movement toward correspondence with the professional model is the process of professional-

Reprinted by permission of the American Sociological Association from *American Sociological Review*, 33 (February 1968), 92–104.

* Grateful acknowledgement is given to Grant GS 882 from the National Science Foundation which provided support for the project from which this report is taken.

ization.[1] The attributes of the model are of two basic types. First are those characteristics which are part of the structure of the occupation, including such things as formal educational and entrance requirements. The second aspect is attitudinal, including the sense of calling of the person to the field and the extent to which he uses colleagues as his major work reference.

The structural side of the professional model has been intensively examined by Wilensky, who noted that occupations pass through a rather consistent sequence of stages on their way to becoming professions[2] Wilensky includes the following attributes in his discussion:

1. Creation of a full-time occupation— this involves the performance of functions which may have been performed previously, as well as new functions, and can be viewed as a reaction to needs in the social structure.
2. The establishment of a training school—this reflects both the knowledge base of a profession and the efforts of early leaders to improve the lot of the occupation. In the more established professions, the move is then followed by affiliation of the training school with established universities. In the newer professions, university affiliation is concurrent with the establishment of training schools.
3. Formation of professional associations—the formation of such associations often is accompanied by a

change in the occupational title, attempts to define more clearly the exact nature of the professional tasks, and efforts to eliminate practitioners who are deemed incompetent by the emergent professionals. Local associations unite into national associations after a period of some political manipulations. As stronger associations are formed, political agitation in the form of attempts to secure licensing laws and protection from competing occupations becomes an important function.
4. Formation of a code of ethics—these ethical codes are concerned with both internal (colleague) and external (clients and public) relations. They are designed to be enforced by the professional associations themselves and, ideally, are given legal support.[3]

A professional attribute that is both structural and attitudinal is the presence of professional autonomy.[4] While the structural aspect of autonomy is indirectly subsumed under the efforts of professional associations to exclude the unqualified and to provide for the legal right to practice, autonomy is also part of the work setting wherein the professional is expected to utilize his judgment and will expect that only other professionals will be competent to question this judgment. The autonomy attribute also contains an attitudinal dimension: the belief of the professional that he is

[1] See Howard M. Vollmer and Donald L. Mills (eds.), *Professionalization* (Englewood Cliffs, N.J., Prentice-Hall, 1966), for a clear distinction between the terms profession, professionalization, and professionalism (pp. vii–viii). Their distinctions will be followed in this paper.
[2] Harold L. Wilensky, "The Professionalization of Everyone?" *American Journal of Sociology*, Vol. LXX, September, 1964, 137–58.

[3] Theodore Caplow uses a slightly altered formulation in his "Sequential Steps in Professionalization." *In* Vollmer and Mills, *Professionalization.*, pp. 20–21. Both Wilensky and Caplow include the same general variables, with Wilensky's appearing to be more descriptively accurate.
[4] For discussions of the importance of autonomy see William Kornhauser, *Scientists in Industry.* Berkeley, University of California Press, 1963 and Simon Marcson, *The Scientist in American Industry.* New York: Harper Bros., 1960.

free to exercise this type of judgment and decision making.

The attitudinal attributes of professionalism reflect the manner in which the practitioners view their work. The assumption here is that there is some correspondence between attitudes and behavior. If this assumption is correct, then the attitudes comprise an important part of the work of the professional. If he or his occupation has met the structural prerequisites of professionalism, the approach taken in practice becomes the important consideration. The attitudinal attributes to be considered here are:

1. The use of the professional organization as a major reference—this involves both the formal organization and informal colleague groupings as the major source of ideas and judgments for the professional in his work.[5]
2. A belief in service to the public—this component includes the idea of indispensability of the profession and the view that the work performed benefits both the public and the practitioner.[6]
3. Belief in self-regulation—this involves the belief that the person best qualified to judge the work of a professional is a fellow professional, and the view that such a practice is desirable and practical. It is a belief in colleague control.[7]
4. A sense of calling to the field—this

reflects the dedication of the professional to his work and the feeling that he would probably want to do the work even if fewer extrinsic rewards were available.[8]
5. Autonomy—this involves the feeling that the practitioner ought to be able to make his own decisions without external pressures from clients, those who are not members of his profession, or from his employing organization.[9]

The combination of the structural and the attitudinal aspects serves as the basis for the professional model. It is generally assumed that both aspects are present to a great degree in highly professionalized occupations, while they are present to lesser degrees in the less professionalized occupations. Whether or not this is the case will be examined in this research. It may be, for example, that occupations which are attempting to become professions may be able to instill in their members strong professional attitudes, while the more established professions may contain less idealistic members.

Variations from the professional model occur in two ways. In the first place, occupations vary in the degree to which they are professionalized. The established professions, such as medicine or law, appear to fit the professional model in most ways, although the attitudinal attributes may or may not adhere to this pattern. The newer emerging professions do not appear to be as profes-

[5] See William J. Goode, "Community Within a Community: The Professions," *American Sociological Review*, Vol. 22, April, 1957, 194; and Ernest Greenwood, "The Elements of Professionalization," in Vollmer and Mills, *Professionalization*, pp. 9-19.
[6] See Edward A. Gross, *Work and Society*. New York: Thomas Y. Crowell, 1958, pp. 77–82; and Talcott Parsons, "The Professions and Social Structure," *Social Forces* 17 (May 1939), 457–67.
[7] See Greenwood, *op. cit.*, and Goode, *Amer. Sociol. Rev.*, 22.

[8] See Gross, *Work and Society*.
[9] Richard Scott distinguishes between autonomous and heteronomous professional organizations while, at the same time, stressing the importance of autonomy for the professional in "Reactions to Supervision in a Heteronomous Professional Organization," *Administrative Science Quarterly*, Vol. 10, June, 1965, 65–81.

sionalized on the various attributes. If each attribute is treated as a separate continuum, multiple variations are possible in terms of the degree to which occupations are professionalized.

The second form of variation is intraoccupational. Even among the established professions, members vary in their conformity to the professional model in both the structural and attitudinal attributes.[10] Both interoccupational and intraoccupational variations appear to be based on three factors. First is the general social structure which, at the abstract level, may or may not need the services performed by the occupation and, at the more pragmatic level, may not give the occupation the legal and behavioral sanctions to perform its functions. The second factor lies within the organization of the occupation itself. Here, for example, the presence of multiple and competing professional organizations may be divisive and thus inhibit professionalization through multiple standards for entrance and through varied regulative norms. The third source of variation is the setting in which the occupation is performed. The work situation may have an impact on the degree to which the profession can be self-regulative and autonomous.

Professionals work in four distinct types of settings. Many members of established professions are found in individual private practice. This set-

ting for professional work appears to be diminishing in importance as organizationally based professional practice increases, and it will not be considered in this analysis. Lawyers are increasingly found in law firms or in legal departments of larger departments of larger organizations, and medical doctors are increasingly working in group or clinic practices. Among the professionalizing groups, almost all are coming from an organizational base such as the social work agency or the business firm.[11]

These organizational bases for professional occupations are of three types. Following Scott's useful distinction, the first type is the *autonomous* professional organization exemplified by the medical clinic or the law firm.[12] Here the work of the professional is subject to his own, rather than to external or administrative jurisdiction. The professionals themselves are the major determiners of the organizational structure, since they are the dominant source of authority. The second type is the *heteronomous* professional organization in which the professional employees are subordinated to an externally derived system. Examples are public schools, libraries, and social work agencies, all of which are affected by externally (often legislatively) based structuring. Scott suggests that the level of professional autonomy is correspondingly lessened in such a setting, a point which will be examined in this research. The third organizational setting is the professional *department* which is part

[10] Bucher and Strauss, in "Professions in Process," *American Journal of Sociology,* Vol. LXVI, January, 1961, 325–34 discuss this type of variation as do Jack Ladinsky and Joel B. Grossman in "Organizational Consequences of Professional Consensus: Lawyers and Selection of Judges," *Administrative Science Quarterly*, Vol. 11, June, 1966, 79–106.

[11] Brandeis recognized the trend toward professionalization among businessmen as early as 1925 in Louis D. Brandeis, *Business—A Profession*. Boston: Small, Maynard, 1925.

[12] Richard Scott, *Admin. Sci. Quart.,* 10, 65–81.

of a larger organization. Examples of this are the legal or research departments of many organizations. In this kind of situation, the professionals employed are part of a larger organization and may or may not be able to affect the manner in which their own work is structured. It is this setting which has served as the basis for many discussions of professional-organizational conflict.

One way of analyzing these three types of settings is to determine the nature of the organizational structures found in the different organizational bases. In order to do this, the degree of bureaucratization within each type will be examined with a dimensional approach to the concept of bureaucracy.[13] This allows determination of the degree of bureaucratization of an organization, or a segment thereof, in terms of the degree of bureaucratization on *each* dimension.

The dimensions utilized are:

1. The hierarchy of authority—the extent to which the locus of decision making is prestructured by the organization.
2. Division of labor—the extent to which work tasks are subdivided by functional specialization decided by the organization.
3. Presence of rules—the degree to which the behavior of organizational members is subject to organizational control.
4. Procedural specifications—the extent to which organizational members must follow organizationally defined techniques in dealing with situations which they encounter.
5. Impersonality—the extent to which both organizational members and outsiders are treated without regard to individual qualities.
6. Technical competence—the extent to which organizationally defined "universalistic" standards are utilized in the personal selection and advancement process.

Each of these dimensions is treated as a separate continuum. Previous research has indicated that these continua do not necessarily vary together.[14] It is generally assumed that there is an inverse relationship between professionalization and bureaucratization.[15] In this study the relationship will be examined without making that assumption. Instead, it is anticipated that the empirical findings will show that on some dimensions of bureaucracy, there is a positive relationship with professionalization. For example, a highly developed division of labor might well be related to a high degree of professionalization on all attributes, since professionals are specialists. By the same token, a high emphasis on technical competence as the basis for hiring and advancement would also appear to have a logical relationship with professionalization. On the other hand, a rigid hierarchy of authority

[13] See Stanley H. Udy, Jr., "Bureaucracy and Rationality in Weber's Theory," *American Sociological Review*, Vol. 24, December, 1959, 791–95, and Richard H. Hall, "The Concept of Bureaucracy: An Empirical Assessment," *American Journal of Sociology*, Vol. LXIX, July, 1963, 32–40. The discussions are primarily based, of course, on Weber's original discussion of bureaucracy in Max Weber, *The Theory of Economic and Social Organization* (trans. A. M. Henderson and Talcott Parsons), New York: Oxford University Press, 1947.

[14] Hall, *Amer. J. Sociol.*, 69.
[15] Peter M. Blau, Wolf V. Heydebrand and Robert E. Stauffer in "The Structure of Small Bureaucracies," *American Sociological Review*, Vol. 31, April, 1966, 179–91 began with this assumption which was later modified.

seems incompatible with a high level of professionalism, especially in terms of the attributes of autonomy and colleague control. The presence of extensive organizationally based rules and procedures likewise appears to be negatively associated with a high level of professionalization. Thus, findings of a mixed nature are anticipated on this basis.

METHODOLOGY

Measurement of the degree of professionalization is accomplished in two basic ways. The structural attributes of the several occupations included in the study will be examined using the method followed by Wilensky.[16] Personnel managers and stockbrokers, occupations not included in his study, are examined here using the Wilensky format. The use of this approach not only allows comparison with the Wilensky work, but also will permit categorization of the occupations by length of time the professional attributes have been met by the occupation and the order in which the occupation has proceeded in its attempt to professionalize. According to Wilensky, the closer the occupation follows a given sequence of professionalization steps, the more likely it is to be more professionalized. In this case, the two additional occupations would fall in the "doubtful professional" category, since some of the structural criteria are not met.[17]

The attitudinal attributes, including use of the professional organization as a major reference, a belief in service to the public, belief in self-regulation, a sense of calling to the field, and a feeling of autonomy in work are measured by standard attitude scales. The scales were developed by use of the Likert technique.[18] This technique was chosen not only because of its relevance for the kinds of attitudes being measured, but also because the question format is the same as that for the measurement of the degree of bureaucratization.[19]

Each of the bureaucratic dimensions was measured by means of a series of items which form a scale for the dimension.[20] The subjects in each organization responded to the items according to the degree to which the statement corresponded to their own perception of the organization. An ordinal scaling of each dimension was thus obtained. For both the professional attitude scales and the bureaucracy scales, the mean score for

[16] Wilensky, *Amer. J. Sociol.*, 70.

[17] William M. Evan discusses some of the barriers to the professionalization of stockbrokers in "Status-Set and Role-Set Conflicts of the Stockbroker: A Problem in the Sociology of Law," *Social Forces*, Vol. 45, September, 1966, 80–82.

[18] The advantages of this form of scaling are discussed in John E. Barclay and Herbert B. Weaver, "Comparative Reliabilities and Ease of Construction of Thurstone and Likert Attitude Scales," *Journal of Social Psychology*, Vol. 58, 1962, 109–20 and Charles R. Tittle, "Attitude Measurement and Prediction of Behavior: An Evaluation of Five Measuring Techniques," unpublished Ph.D. Thesis, University of Texas, 1965.

[19] Each scale attained a reliability of .80 or higher using the split-half method with the Spearman-Brown correction formula. Pretest data also suggested that the scales were valid. Physicians, nurses, teachers, and accountants comprised the pretest group. A complete discussion of the procedures followed is contained in Richard H. Hall, *Professionalization and Bureaucratization*, unpublished manuscript, Indiana University, 1966.

[20] Hall, *Amer. J. Sociol.*, 69, contains a discussion of the development of these scales.

TABLE 1 RESPONDENT DISTRIBUTION BY OCCUPATION, TYPE OF ORGANIZATION,
NUMBER DISTRIBUTED, AND RATE OF RETURN

Occupation	Type of Organization	N Distributed	N Returned	%
Physician	University Health	17	10	59
	Government Hospital	18	11	61
Nurse	University Student Health	15	8	53
	General Hospital	50	26	52
Accountant	University Department	3	2	67
	Manufacturing Firm	20	14	70
	CPA Firm 1	40	15	38
	CPA Firm 2	30	13	43
Teacher	High School	40	29	73
	Elementary School	14	12	86
Lawyer	Law Firm 1	18	9	50
	Law Firm 2	25	13	52
	Law Firm 3	13	9	69
	Legal Department 1	6	4	67
	Legal Department 2	17	11	65
	Legal Department 3	10	6	60
Social Worker	Private Agency 1	8	7	88
	Private Agency 2	17	11	65
	Public Agency	20	14	70
Stock Broker	Brokerage Firm 1	10	8	80
	Brokerage Firm 2	20	8	40
Librarian	Public Library	60	44	73
Engineer	Manufacturing Firm	20	15	75
Personnel Management	Manufacturing Firm 1	10	7	70
	Manufatcuring Firm 2	25	14	56
Advertising	Advertising Firm 1	10	4	40
	Advertising Firm 2	6	4	67
Total		542	328	61

each set of respondents was utilized as the measure for the group involved.

At the outset of the research, it was decided to try to obtain a wide selection of occupations and employing organizations. The purpose of the research called for inclusion of occupations which are acknowledged professions in addition to those which are aspiring to become professions. At the same time, a variety of organizational settings was desired for the analysis of this variable. With these considerations in mind, organizations were contacted to determine if they were interested in cooperating in the research. The selection of organizations was based on at least some knowledge of their size and functioning. Those selected do not represent a sample of the universe of organizations, but they do appear to be representative of organizations of similar types. After the initial contact was made, personal interviews with officials in each organization were held and cooperation was solicited. Three organizations declined participation. Table 1 indicates the kinds of organizations included in the study, as well as the number of questionnaires distributed and returned. In all cases, all of the professional personnel were asked to complete the questionnaire.

The lawyers in the study represent three medium-sized law firms, two legal departments of private corporations, and part of a department of the federal government. The physicians are members of a medical department in a large government hospital and of a university student health service. The nurses work in a private general hospital and in the same university health service. Both of the Certified Public Accountant groups are part of large national CPA firms, while the accounting departments are part of larger organizations. The teachers are in the same school system at the levels indicated. The social workers represent two private agencies and a social work department of a school system. The stockbrokers are part of large national brokerage firms, while the advertising agencies are both small, regional concerns. The engineering department and the personnel departments are part of large national manufacturing firms. The library is the public library in a large metropolitan area.

FINDINGS

Evidence from the behavior of the respondents provides strong support for the validity of two of the professionalism scales and also suggests that the attitudes measured are quite strongly associated with behavior. Background information regarding the frequency of attendance at professional meetings and membership in professional organizations was cross-tabulated with the attitude scale which measures the strength of the professional organization as a reference group. The behavioral data support the validity of the scales and also

suggest that the respondents practice what they verbalize. Similarly, the scale measuring belief in self regulation is strongly associated with the actual presence of licenses or certification as reported in the background questions.[21]

The results on the attitude scales reveal some interesting and somewhat surprising patterns. On the belief in service to the public and sense of calling to the field attributes, both of which are related to a sense of dedication to the profession, the teachers, social workers, and nurses emerge as strongly professionalized. This may be related to the relatively low financial compensation which these fields receive since dedication seems necessary if one is to continue in the field. An interesting exception is that the teachers are somewhat weaker on the sense of calling to the field variable. An important factor appears to be the entry of many women into teaching because it is a "safe" women's occupation rather than because of any real dedication. The established professions are relatively weak on these variables.

Among the lawyers, the results indicate that on all but one attribute a legal department is more professionalized than the law firms. This suggests that professionals working in large organizations are not, by definition, confronted with situations which reduce the level of professionalization. The variations among the lawyers also suggest that the conditions

[21] Those who strongly believed in using the professional organization as a reference group also belonged to and attended the meetings of professional organizations ($p <$ .001). Similarly, belief in self-regulation is associated with the presence of licensing and certification ($p < .001$).

TABLE 2 RANKS ON PROFESSIONALISM SCALES BY OCCUPATIONAL GROUP

	Scale				
Occupational Group	(A) Professional Organization as Reference	(B) Belief in Service to Public	(C) Belief in Self Regulation	(D) Sense of Calling to Field	(E) Feeling of Autonomy
Accounting					
CPA Firm 1	12	18	15	18.5	19
CPA Firm 2	16	10	20	10.5	6
Acct. Dept. 1	2.5	6	24.5	4	3
Acct. Dept. 2	1	1	2.5	1	1
Advertising					
Ad. Agency 1	8	4	9	15	20
Ad. Agency 2	20	23	7	20	23
Engineering					
Engineering Dept.	4	9	2.5	5	11
Lawyer					
Law Firm 1	22	16	19	10.5	14
Law Firm 2	13	14	22	7	22
Law Firm 3	23	12.5	18	13	15
Legal Dept. 1	26	11	23	8.5	10
Legal Dept. 2	99	24	14	2.5	25
Legal Dept. 3	11	5	4	2.5	26
Librarian					
Public Library	21	15	11	25	4.5
Nurse					
Nursing Division 1	10	20.5	16	18.5	4.5
Nursing Division 2	14	19	27	24	2
Personnel Mgmt.					
Per. Dept. 1	7	2	5.5	8.5	7.5
Per. Dept. 2	5.5	7.5	9	22	13
Physician					
Med. Dept. 1	19	3	17	21	21
Med. Dept. 2	5.5	7.5	9	16	12
Social Worker					
Private Agency 1	17	17	12	17	9
Private Agency 2	18	22	21	27	16
Public Agency	25	20.5	5.5	26	17
Stock Broker					
Firm 1	2.5	12.5	24.5	6	24
Firm 2	27	25	26	23	27
Teacher					
Elem. School	24	26	13	14	7.5
High School	15	27	1	12	18

NOTE: Lower rank indicates lower degree of professionalization.

of employment may play a dominant role in the development of professional attitudes. The lawyers in this study have quite common backgrounds in terms of their legal education and bar organizational memberships. Thus it appears that these attitudinal variations should probably be attributed to the organizational "climate" in which they work.[22]

[22] Jerome E. Carlin suggests that law firms vary in the degree to which ethical norms are enforced. Jerome E. Carlin, *Lawyers Ethics.* New York: Russell Sage Foundation, 1966, pp. 96–103. The climate should also affect other professional attitudes.

TABLE 3 RANKS ON BUREAUCRACY SCALES BY OCCUPATIONAL GROUP

Occupational Group	I Hierarchy of Authority	II Division of Labor	III Rules	IV Procedures	V Impersonality	VI Technical Competence
Accounting						
CPA Firm 1	3	5	5	6	9	16
CPA Firm 2	11	4	7	9	15.5	25
Acct. Dept. 1	19	25	21	26	24	2
Acct. Dept. 2	27	27	27	27	27	1
Advertising						
Ad. Agency 1	9.5	3	9	12	1	20.5
Ad. Agency 2	2	10.5	1	3	3	4
Engineering						
Engineering Dept.	17	18	17	19.5	11	3
Lawyer						
Law Firm 1	1	2	2	1	7	24
Law Firm 2	4.5	8	3	4	12	18
Law Firm 3	6	6	6	2	13	20.5
Legal Dept. 1	21	15.5	8	7	4	13.5
Legal Dept. 2	4.5	1	4	8	10	19
Legal Dept. 3	9.5	17	11	10	19.5	5
Librarian						
Public Library	25	19.5	26	24	14	23
Nurse						
Nursing Division 1	24	21	25	23	21.5	10
Nursing Division 2	26	23	24	25	25	15
Personnel Mgmt.						
Per. Dept. 1	18	26	15.5	19.5	26	8.5
Per. Dept. 2	22	13	18	18	6	12
Physician						
Med. Dept. 1	12	12	12	5	5	7
Med. Dept. 2	23	22	21	21	17	17
Social Worker						
Private Agency 1	16	10.5	13	13	21.5	22
Private Agency 2	14	15.5	14	16	8	26
Public Agency	13	9	10	14	2	13.5
Stock Broker						
Firm 1	7	14	22	22	18	6
Firm 2	8	7	15.5	11	15.5	27
Teacher						
Elem. School	20	19.5	23	17	19.5	11
High School	15	24	20	15	23	8.5

NOTE: Lower rank indicates lower degree of bureaucratization.

Table 3 indicates the ranks for each occupational group on each of the bureaucratic dimensions. There are rather wide variations in degree of bureaucratization both among and within occupational groups. There are also rather strong interrelationships among the dimensions, as Table 4 indicates, except in the case of the technical competence dimension, where the relationship is reversed. Apparently these organizations, unlike more broadly based samples of organizations, are rather internally consistent in their degree of bureaucratization. It should be noted that these results represent both the total organization (in the cases of the

TABLE 4 SPEARMAN RANK ORDER CORRELATION COEFFICIENTS
BETWEEN BUREAUCRATIC DIMENSIONS

	Hierarchy of Authority	Division of Labor	Rules	Pro-cedures	Imper-sonality	Technical Competence
Hierarchy of Authority	....	.791	.821	.737	.477	−.242
Division of Labor	....	....	.796	.782	.682	−.573
Rules	....	....	....	.898	.641	−.272
Procedures	....	....	....	....	.618	−.342
Impersonality	....	....	....	....	....	−.270

autonomous and heteronomous professional organizations) and organizational segments (in the cases of professional departments). Whether or not such internal consistency exists throughout the larger organizations involved in the latter case is subject to further investigation. It seems doubtful in view of the wider variations in task which would be found in the organizations as a whole. For example, while an engineering department might exhibit essentially the same degree of bureaucratization on the various dimensions, the sales department of the same organization might not.

The distribution of the groups into the autonomous, heteronomous, and departmental categories was relatively simple, using Scott's criteria. In the autonomous category are found the physicians (who, even though they are part of larger organizations, autonomously determine their own work structures), the law firms, the CPA firms, and the advertising agencies. The latter were included in this category because of their direct relationships with clients and the fee basis of their financing. Also, both agencies had been established by persons who had been in the advertising business with larger firms and had later established their own organizations without external administrative constraints.[23]

Similarly, the heteronomous organizations were rather easy to classify using Scott's criteria. The social work agencies, the library, and the two schools were placed in this category. Two other occupational groups also were placed in this category on the basis of their degree of self-determination of structure and policy. Neither is considered by Scott in his development of this category, but both appear to fit. First are the nurses. As a professional group, nurses are subject to both the administrative and policy practices of the medical staff. Nursing services must, therefore, adjudicate between the policies of the medical staff and their own professional codes. Stockbrokers also were placed in this category. This occupational grouping, which appears to operate quite autonomously within each regional office, nevertheless is subject to rather extensive external policies. The rules of the various stock and commodity exchanges, the Securities and Exchange Commission and the particular company policies themselves appear to make placement in the heteronomous category most appropriate. Brokers do have individual clients and

[23] See Scott, *Admin. Sci. Quart.*, 10.

TABLE 5 AVERAGE RANKS AND ONE WAY ANALYSIS OF VARIANCE (H)
ON DEGREE OF BUREAUCRATIZATION IN THESE TYPES
OF PROFESSIONAL SETTINGS

	Autonomy (Average Rank)	Heteronomous (Average Rank)	Department (Average Rank)	H Value (2 df)
Hierarchy of Authority	8.0	16.8	17.4	6.96*
Division of Labor	8.1	16.3	17.9	7.31*
Rules	7.3	19.2	13.7	14.70***
Procedures	7.0	18.0	17.0	9.80**
Impersonality	9.2	16.8	15.9	4.29
Technical Competence	16.9	16.2	8.0	5.11*

* = $p < .05$.
** = $p < .01$.
*** = $p < .001$.

operate on a fee basis as do members of the autonomous category, but placement in this category appears unwarranted because of the factors noted above. The departmental category is comprised of the three legal departments, the engineering department, the personnel departments, and the accounting departments.

The data were analyzed by means of the Kruskal-Wallis one-way analysis of variance (H).[24] This technique allows the determination of whether or not the differences in the ranks of the various categories are due to chance or to real differences in the populations studied.

On the hierarchy of authority dimension, the autonomous organizations are significantly less bureaucratic than the other two types of occupational groupings, as Table 5 indicates. There is relatively little variation among the ranks in this category, while more variation exists within the heteronomous and departmental categories. This is consistent with Scott's suggestions in this regard.

[24] For a discussion of this technique, see Sidney Siegel, *Non-Parametric Statistics for the Behavioral Sciences.* New York: McGraw-Hill, 1956, pp. 184–93.

At the same time, the variations within the latter two categories are sufficient to suggest that neither category is inherently more rigid in its hierarchy of authority. With the exception of one legal department, (see Table 3), the various settings in which lawyers work are essentially the same on this dimension. This suggests that work in the larger organization does not, by definition, impose a more rigid hierarchy on the practitioner. Nevertheless, the term "autonomous professional organization" appears to be relevant since these organizations do, in fact, exhibit less bureaucratization on this dimension.

On the division of labor dimension, the autonomous organizations are again much less bureaucratic, while the heteronomous organizations and departments are essentially similar. The autonomous organizations examined apparently have not begun the more intensive division of labor that Smigel found among larger New York law firms. On this dimension, also, the law firms and the legal departments do not vary widely among themselves. While the division of labor is more intense in the other two categories, again there is rather extensive variation in these categories. Obviously, the extent of the division of labor is dependent upon the tasks being performed rather than on the level of professionalization or the externally imposed administrative structure.

Findings on the presence of rules dimension are somewhat consistent with those already discussed. The autonomous organizations are characterized by much less bureaucratization on this dimension. In this case, however, the professional departments are less bureaucratic than the heteronomous organizations. This is consistent with Scott's discussion, but at the same time suggests that professional departments in larger organizations are not inherently more bureaucratic than professional organizations. The case of the lawyers in the two settings provides evidence for this position. These results raise an important issue in regard to professional-organizational relationships. The data suggest that the occupational base of an organization (or an organizational segment) may have a real impact on the structure which the organization itself takes.[25] In this case, the professional's self-regulatory patterns may reduce the need for and utility of organizational rule systems. It might be hypothesized that the more developed the normative system of the occupations in an organization, the less need for a highly bureaucratized organizational system.

Findings on the procedural specifications dimension of bureaucracy

[25] Blau, *et al., Amer. Sociol. Rev.*, 31, and D. S. Pugh, D. J. Hickson, *et al.*, "A Scheme for Organizational Analysis," *Administrative Science Quarterly*, Vol. 8, December, 1963, 289–315 make this suggestion, also.

are quite similar to those discussed above. The autonomous organizations are characterized by quite a low level of bureaucratization, while the heteronomous organizations are the most bureaucratic and the professional departments are slightly less bureaucratic.

On the impersonality dimension, the same general pattern emerges, although not to the same degree. Autonomous organizations are the least bureaucratic, while the other two types exhibit more impersonality. The higher level of impersonality found in the latter two categories may be an aspect of the "bureaucratic personality" which has been discussed as a characteristic of organizations such as social work agencies. The aloofness and detachment which may inhibit the effectiveness of these groups appears to be due partially to the fact that the professions in the heteronomous category must deal with relatively large client populations. Those in the autonomous category have smaller such populations, and professions in the departmental category usually do not have individual clients. While the number of clients may contribute to impersonality, a high level of impersonality may itself inhibit the occupation in its drive toward professionalization. If public acceptance as a profession is a component of professionalism, then this higher level of impersonality may partially block further professionalization. The question remains whether or not this higher level of impersonality is a result of organizationally generated norms or of standards imposed upon the organization by the professions themselves.

The findings in regard to the last dimension, technical competence as

TABLE 6 RANK ORDER CORRELATION COEFFICIENTS BETWEEN
PROFESSIONALISM SCALES AND BUREAUCRACY SCALES

	Professional Organization Reference	Belief in Service to Public	Belief in Self-Regulation	Sense of Calling to Field	Feeling of Autonomy
Hierarchy of Authority	−.029	−.262	−.149	.148	−.767**
Division of Labor	−.236	−.260	−.234	−.115	−.575**
Rules	−.144	−.121	−.107	.113	−.554
Procedures	−.360**	−.212	−.096	.000	−.603**
Impersonality	−.256	−.099	−.018	−.343*	−.489**
Technical Competence	.593**	.332*	.420**	.440**	.121

$* = p < .05.$
$** = p < .01.$

the basis for hiring and advancement, are reversed from those previously discussed. On this dimension, the autonomous and heteronomous organizations are relatively bureaucratic, while the professional departments are relatively non-bureaucratic. Here it appears that a higher level of bureaucratization or more emphasis on technical competence is quite compatible with professional standards in that the practitioner is selected for employment and advancement on the basis of ability. In this case, a real source of conflict for persons employed in a professional department is evident if criteria other than performance are utilized in the personnel policies.[26]

The relationships between professionalization and bureaucratization are examined from two perspectives. First is an analysis of the relationships between the attitudinal variables and the bureaucratic dimensions, as

[26] Marcson has noted the frustrations felt by scientists when the reward system is blocked if they follow a strictly research route in their careers. The higher rewards come from joining the administrative structure, which is a contradiction of their professional standards. Simon Marcson, *The Scientist in American Industry*. New York: Harper Bros., 1960, pp. 66–71.

indicated in Table 6. The generally negative relationships indicate that higher levels of professionalization are related to lower levels of bureaucratization, and vice versa.

When each of the professional variables is examined, some interesting patterns emerge. First, in the case of the professional organization as a reference group, there is a relatively small negative relationship between this variable and the presence of a rigid hierarchy of authority. It appears to make little difference if there is extensive reliance upon such a hierarchy in professionalized organizations. This conclusion is supported by the findings of Blau, et al., who suggest that the presence of such a hierarchy may facilitate the work of professionals if they serve coordination and communication functions.[27] This is particularly so when the hierarchy is recognized as legitimate. The professional may thus recognize and essentially approve of the fact that certain decisions must be made by people in the hierarchy.

A stronger negative relationship is found on the division of labor dimension. If a division of labor is very

[27] Blau, *et al.*, *Amer. Sociol. Rev.*, 31.

intense, it may force a professional person away from his broader professional ties. This interpretation recognizes specialization within the professions, but the question here is the level of organizationally based division of labor. At the same time, strong professional identification may impede intensive specialization on the part of organizations. A weaker relationship is found on the presence of rules dimension. Organizationally developed rules governing the behavior of members appear not to intrude strongly on this or on other professional attitudes.

There is a strong negative relationship between professional attitude and the procedural specifications dimension. This is predictable since strong professional orientations appear to be in basic conflict with organizationally developed techniques of dealing with work situations. As more procedures are developed by the organization, they may become more burdensome for the professional.

The previously discussed relationship between the level of professionalization and the degree to which impersonality is stressed is borne out by the findings here in regard to the impersonality dimension. That is, the more professional the attitude on this variable, the less impersonality is stressed. The more professional groups apparently do not need to utilize impersonality in their organizational arrangements.

The strong positive relationship between this professional variable and the organizational emphasis on technical competence is not unexpected. Since this bureaucratic dimension is so strongly related to most of the professional attitudes, it might serve as an informal indicator of the level of professionalism in organizations if other indicators are not available.

The findings on the belief in service to the public, belief in self-regulation, and sense of calling to the field variables are essentially similar to those just discussed. The areas of congruence and conflict which might emerge also are similar.

Strong negative relationships exist between the autonomy variable and the first five bureaucratic dimensions. This suggests that increased bureaucratization threatens professional autonomy. It is in these relationships that a potential source of conflict between the professional and the organization can be found. The strong drive for autonomy on the part of a professional may come into direct conflict with organizationally based job requirements. At the same time, the organization may be threatened by strong professional desires on the part of at least some of its members. Future research should delineate both the extent of the conflict and its sources and the extent to which it is felt by and threatens both the professional(s) and the organization.

When the structural aspect of professionalization is considered, essentially the same findings emerge. As Table 7 suggests, the more professionalized groups are found in settings which are less bureaucratic. The more professionalized groups, that is, those with more self-regulation and longer socialization in preparation for the field, perhaps do not "need" the same kinds of organizational controls as less professionalized groups in dealing with problems and decisions. At the same time, the presence of more bureaucratic systems for the less professionalized groups may serve as

TABLE 7 AVERAGE RANKS AND ONE-WAY ANALYSIS OF VARIANCE (H)
ON DEGREE OF BUREAUCRATIZATION OF THE WORK
SETTINGS OF THREE TYPES OF PROFESSIONALS

	Established (Average Rank)	Process (Average Rank)	Doubtful (Average Rank)	H Value (2 df)
Hierarchy of Authority	9.5	18.9	14.1	6.14*
Division of Labor	9.2	17.8	15.7	5.57
Rules	7.9	19.1	15.9	9.65**
Procedures	7.3	18.5	17.3	10.96**
Impersonality	11.2	16.2	15.1	1.65
Technical Competence	16.5	14.7	10.2	2.02

* $= p < .05$.
** $= p < .001$.

an inhibitor to their further professionalization.

SUMMARY AND CONCLUSIONS

Among the major findings of this research is the fact that the structural and the attitudinal aspects of professionalization do not necessarily vary together. Some "established" professions have rather weakly developed professional attitudes, while some of the less professionalized groups have very strong attitudes in this regard. The strength of these attitudes appears to be based on the kind of socialization which has taken place both in the profession's training program and in the work itself. An additional factor is the place of the occupation in the wider social structure. If the occupation receives relatively few rewards in a material sense, the level of dedication is likely to be higher. If the occupation is allowed to be self-regulating, it will tend to believe quite strongly in this. Therefore, changes in the social structure may bring about corresponding attitudinal adjustments.

The organizations in which professionals work vary rather widely in their degree of bureaucratization. The variation is not based on the distinction between professional departments and professional organizations, since some professional departments are less bureaucratic than some professional organizations, and vice versa. There is, however, a general tendency for the autonomous professional organization to be less bureaucratic than either the heteronomous organization or the professional department. This suggests that the nature of the occupational groups in an organization affects the organizational structure. The workers (professionals) *import* standards into the organization to which the organization must adjust. In the development of a new organization, this importation would probably occur without any conflict. In an established organization, the importation, either by an entire department or by new employees within a professional department, might be a real source of conflict if the professional and organizational standards do not coincide.

With the exception of the technical competence dimension, a generally inverse relationship exists between the levels of bureaucratization and professionalization. Autonomy, as an important professional attribute, is most strongly inversely related to bureaucratization. The other variables are not as inversely related. This suggests that increased bureaucratization and professionalization might lead to conflict in either the professional organization or department, but that this conflict is not inherent, given the relative weakness of most of the relationships found. Conflict occurs within a professional group or within an organization only to the degree that specific aspects of bureaucratization or professionalization vary enough to conflict with other specific aspects. Stated in another way, the implication is that in some cases an equilibrium may exist between the levels of professionalization and bureaucratization in the sense that a particular level of professionalization may require a certain level of bureaucratization to maintain social control. Too little bureaucratization may lead to too many undefined operational areas if the profession itself has not developed operational standards for these areas. By the same token, conflict may ensue if the equilibrium is upset.

An assumption of inherent conflict between the professional or the professional group and the employing organization appears to be unwarranted. If it is present, the bases of conflict in terms of professional attitudes and/or organizational structure should be made explicit. After this is done, the analysis of conflicts based upon specific issues such as resistance to non-professional supervision, can proceed. After any particular conflict situation, changes in either the profesional orientations or the organizational structure should be noted so that the essentially stable conditions from which conflicts emerge can be established. Since conflicts probably create changes, any conflicts which follow would necessarily emerge from a different setting than that originally noted. These changes must be noted in any longitudinal analyses of professional-organizational relations.

26. THE RELATIONSHIP BETWEEN ORGANIZATION SIZE AND SUPERVISION RATIO

Bernard P. Indik

The structure of organizations has long been of interest to students of administration. Parkinson's observation[1] of the disproportionate increase of "chiefs" to "Indians," as organizations increase in size, is not supported by the data presented in this paper.[2] We have found in the five sets of organizations studied here that the relationship between organization unit size and supervision ratio is logarithmic in form and negative in slope. Several reasons for this finding are suggested and explored; no rationale, however, has yet been experimentally proven.

Organizational unit size and ratio of supervision are variables which are relatively easy to measure. Though there has been considerable literature (both classical[3] and recent[4]) built up in both sociology and administration on the relationship between these variables, few conclusions have been systematically derived from examination of the empirical data available.[5] In this paper we intend to

Reprinted by permission from *Administrative Science Quarterly* (December 1964), pp. 301–12.

[1] C. N. Parkinson, *Parkinson's Law and Other Studies in Administration.* (Boston, 1957).

[2] The data to be reported were collected with the cooperation of the Survey Research Center, University of Michigan; the Research Program of the Institute of Management and Labor Relations, Rutgers; The State University, and the Psychology Department, Rutgers; The State University, New Brunswick, N. J., with the support of Navy Contract Nonr-404(10), Group Psychology Branch, Office of Naval Research.

[3] I. Hamilton, *The Soul and Body of an Army.* (London, 1921), p. 229; L. Urwick, "Organization as a Technical Problem." *In* L. Gulick and L. Urwick (eds.), *Papers on the Science of Administration.* (Institute of Public Administration, New York, 1937).

[4] F. W. Terrien, *The Effect of Changing Size upon Organizations.* (First Annual Report of the Institute for Social Science Research, San Francisco, 1963); M. Haire, "Biological Models and Empirical Histories of the Growth of Organizations." *In* Mason Haire (ed.), *Modern Organization Theory.* (New York, 1959); S. Melman, "The Rise of Administrative Overhead in the Manufacturing Industries of the United States, 1899–1947," *Oxford Economic Papers*, 3 (1951), 64–66, 89.

[5] E. Dale, *Planning and Developing the Company Organization Structure.* (American Management Association Research Report No. 20; New York, 1952), pp. 57–59; Doris R. Entwisle and J. Walton, "Observations on the Span of Control," *Administrative Science Quarterly*, 5 (1961), 522–33; P. Blau and W. R. Scott, *Formal Organizations.* (San Francisco, 1962), pp. 225–27; R. Bendix, *Work and Authority in Industry.* (New York, 1956), pp. 221–22.

explore empirical data and theoretical explanations to find out which possible interpretations agree with the data. Since very different kinds of organizations are to be discussed here, several definitions are necessary before we can continue.

An *organizational* unit is defined as a system containing two or more members who share the over-all purpose or purposes of the system and who are related to each other in a prescribed manner within the boundary of the system. For the specific requirements of this set of studies only organizational units whose sites were geographically separated from each other were considered. To avoid the confounding effect of other structural variables, only organizational units consisting of three-level authority hierarchies were considered.

Supervision ratio is defined as the ratio of the number of supervisors to the total number of members; applying this definition to the different organizational units, however, raised a rather difficult problem. What is a supervisor? For our purposes this category included those individuals whose functional role involved mainly direct interpersonal supervision or key organizational administrative decision making. This definition excluded those non-rank-and-file personnel higher in the organization who were serving mainly clerical functions.

Two alternative hypotheses suggest themselves. The first is that as the size of the organizational unit *increases,* the ratio of supervision will tend to *increase.* This expectation is based on Parkinson's Law and on the mathematical specifications of Kephart,[6] which show that there is

some pressure and necessity to increase supervision at a faster rate than that by which the organization increases. The alternative hypothesis of this set of studies is that as the size of the organizational unit *increases,* the ratio of supervision will tend to *decrease.* A qualification should be added that we expect this to be true so long as the role of the lower-level individuals in the local units remains the same, that is, if the complexity of task of lower-level individuals in the system increases as size increases, then the supervision ratio may *increase* with size.

We speculate further that the relationship of size to supervision ratio will be curvilinear (logarithmic), since less interpersonal supervision per member is necessary as members are added, and since alternative forms of control (bureaucratic control and role prescriptions) may tend to appear as organization size increases. The placement of the curve indicates to an essential degree a characteristic related to the amount of interpersonal control potentially exercised by supervision in the set of organizations.

As an ancillary part of several studies of organizations, data were accumulated on organizational unit size and on the ratio of supervisors to organizational members.

Five sets of data are available. The five sets of organizations were selected in order to obtain a range (though not systematic in a sampling sense) of data including two sets of business organizations and three sets of voluntary organizations. Each set of organizations studied will be described in detail below.

---

[6] C. N. Parkinson, *Parkinson's Law;* W. M. Kephart, "A Quantitative Analysis of Intragroup Relationships," *American Journal of Sociology,* 55 (1950), 544–49.

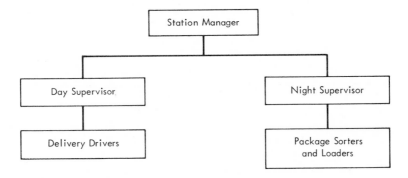

FIG. 1 STRUCTURE OF A TYPICAL DELIVERY ORGANIZATION

ORGANIZATIONS STUDIED

A. PACKAGE DELIVERY STATIONS (N = 32)

The organizations included in this part of our study consisted of 32 package delivery organizations located in metropolitan areas. The typical organizational form is shown in Fig. 1. The organization structure had three levels, and the major structural variation was the number of members in each of the organizations. The size of the 32 units varied from 15 to 61 members. Each unit was subject to and functioned within the policies of the parent firm. The common objective was the delivery of packages to customers at the lowest possible cost per package to the delivery organization. The lower-level members were markedly controlled in their behavior by sets of time-study standards against which each person's performance was compared. This was an all-male organization.

B. AUTOMOBILE SALES DEALERSHIPS (N = 36)

The organizations included in this part of the study consisted of 36 automobile dealership organizations located in or adjacent to metropolitan areas. The typical organizational form is shown in Fig. 2. The basic hierarchical structure showed three levels, and the major structural source of variation was the number of members in each of the organizations. The various dealerships differed in respect to having combined or separated departments for new and used automobile sales, but this appeared to be irrelevant for our purposes since the number of supervisors per salesman did not covary with this characteristic for dealerships of the same size. The total size of the 36 units varied from 25 to 132 members. Each unit, though independently owned, functioned within certain common policies of the supplying firm toward the basic objective of profitable sales and servicing of automobiles and automobile parts.

The behavior of lower-level employees in this situation was partially controlled by quotas which they were assigned both in sales and other

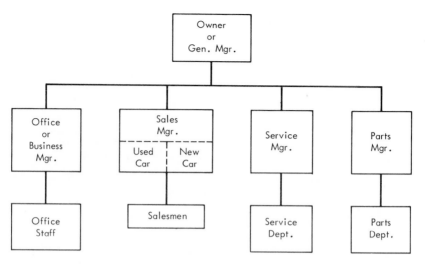

Fig. 2 Structure of a Typical Automobile Sales Dealership Organization

measurable performances. However, the amount of time controlled by these quotas was not nearly as stringent as in the case of the package delivery stations. The men controlled a good portion of their own time, especially that period of time when they were off the sales floor (about four hours a day). The amount of necessary supervisory control was moderate.

C. VOLUNTEER FIRE COMPANIES ($N = 12$)

Twelve volunteer fire companies belonging to the same state volunteer fire company association were studied. They were located in smaller communities adjacent to a large metropolitan area. The local units of this parent organization had a dual organizational structure. The fire-fighting structure included a chief, his officers, and the rank and file. This organization overlapped with the companies' other functional organization that handled social events. The "social events" organization included the president, his officers, and the rank and file. There is some overlap in the officers in both structures. This too was an all-male organization.

D. INDUSTRIAL LABOR UNION LOCALS ($N = 8$)

Eight labor union locals located in an eastern metropolitan state allowed us to obtain data. These locals were members of the same district of a large international union. The local unions were basically structured into three-level hierarchies. These included the decision makers (the president, business agents, or executive boards), the other officers (stewards), and the rank and file. The need for supervisory control was intermittent in these locals. Members of these organizational units were both males and females.

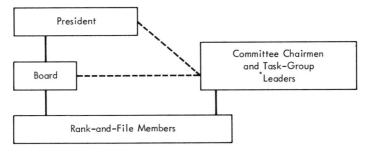

FIG. 3 TYPICAL STRUCTURE OF VOLUNTARY ASSOCIATIONS

E. NONPARTISAN POLITICAL
ORGANIZATION CHAPTERS
(*N* = 28)

The organizations included in this part of the study were 28 local associations affiliated with the same national organization. Each of the units was located in a metropolitan area. The typical voluntary association unit had the organizational structure shown in Fig. 3. The basic hierarchical structure showed three levels, and the major structural source of variation was the number of members in each of the organizational units. The president and board members were locally elected for limited tenure. The size of the units varied from 101 to 2,983 members. Each unit functioned within the policies of the parent national organization toward the objective of increasing citizen participation in political activities. The organization operated basically through the skills and supervisory activities of its leaders, who attempted relatively little control over member behavior. Its members were all females.

RESULTS

The results of the data collections in each case can be seen in Fig. 4. In each instance where higher-level *clerical* personnel were present, they have been eliminated from consideration as supervisors. In each of the sets of organizations there is a significant negative slope to the curves: as size of the local organizational unit increases, the supervision ratio declines. The relationship is logarithmic, curvilinear, and asymptotic to the axis. The curves are therefore plotted on semilogarithmic scales. There is a striking similarity in the slope of the curves. In all five cases, the data became surprisingly linear when plotted on semilogarithmic scales, and in four of these five cases the slope of the lines is remarkably alike (the exception is the slope for the eight local unions). The similar slopes are sharp and decline at much the same rate (Fig. 4 and Table 1). Not only do sizable increases in the number of lower-level members take place before any increase at all takes place in the number of supervisors, but as the size of the organizations increases, the organizations seem to take in more and more lower-level members before adding new supervisors.

From Table 1 we can see that the general equation of the fit of the logarithmic curve is of the form $x = e^{a+by}$ where the sign of the b coefficient in all five cases is negative, indicating a negative slope. The pro-

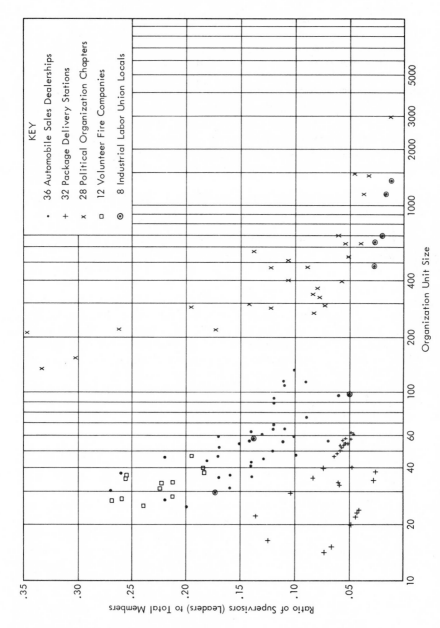

FIG. 4 COVARIATION OF ORGANIZATIONAL UNIT SIZE AND SUPERVISION RATIO FOR FIVE SETS OF ORGANIZATIONS

TABLE 1 ORGANIZATION SIZE AND SUPERVISION RATIO FITTING
A LINEAR LOGARITHMIC CURVE*

Set of Organizations	N	$x = e^{a+by}$	Pearson r Correlation Coefficients
Package delivery stations	32	$x = e^{4.08-7.48y}$	$-.375$ $(p < .05)$
Automobile sales dealerships	36	$x = e^{4.79-5.45y}$	$-.514$ $(p < .01)$
Volunteer fire companies	12	$x = e^{4.35-3.83y}$	$-.644$ $(p < .02)$
Industrial labor union locals	8	$x = e^{6.91-21.60y}$	$-.925$ $(p < .001)$
Nonpartisan political organization chapters	28	$x = e^{6.84-6.25y}$	$-.821$ $(p < .001)$

* $x =$ organization size; $y =$ supervision ratio.

posed curves fit the data quite well as is shown in Table 1 by the correlation coefficients for each set of data.[7] The curve for the package delivery stations fits least well, but all of the five correlation coefficients are statistically significantly different from zero at less than the p .05 level of significance.

For the purpose of this analysis we have considered x to be the natural logarithm of organization size and y to be the supervision ratio. This was done rather than having $y = e^{a+bx}$ where y would equal the natural logarithm of the supervision ratio and x would equal organization size, because the former curve gave a better fit to the five sets of data. It should also be noted that the fit of the present curves is not adequate for each set of data for extremely large organizations and that at extremely small sizes the other hypothetical curves would not adequately fit the data.

We may assume that the initiating point of each set of data is close to the smallest viable form of that organization. If we take a dynamic view, the structure of the local unit is set early, and as size increases there is a decline in supervision ratio. Addi-

tions to the supervision component come as size increases occur but not at a sufficient rate to maintain the earlier level of supervision ratio.

DISCUSSION

Clearly the data support the second of the two suggested hypotheses. This second hypothesis, then, needs to be explored in detail. Let us first approach the problem of how widespread are the findings reported here. We do have five sets of data, but we have *not* sampled all organizations; further, Terrien and Mills have reported, contrary to the present findings, that in school districts as size increases the ratio of administrative personnel to total members increases.[8] The discrepancy between these, the present data, and the Terrien and Mills' data, may be the latter's inclusion of staff nonsupervisory personnel in their administrative component; recently Terrien has found evidence in agreement with the present findings when this factor was considered.[9] Secondly, the phenomena we have re-

[7] I would like to thank S. A. Foote for advice on curve fitting.

[8] F. W. Terrien and D. L. Mills, "The Effects of Changing Size upon the Internal Structure of Organization," *American Sociological Review*, 20 (1955), 11–13.

[9] F. W. Terrien, Inst. Soc. Sci. Res.

ported may be limited to local units at the lower levels of multiunit organizations. There are, however, indications that size of company and span of control are positively correlated at the top of organizations as well as at the bottom local unit level.[10]

Anderson and Warkov suggest that if functional complexity stays the same, size and supervision ratio are negatively correlated.[11] This is directionally consistent with our findings, since within each of the five sets of organizations each of the local units serves the same function.

Two related questions present themselves. Why does a set show a particular curve? What makes a set of organizational units a set? Let us consider these questions jointly. It is from Fig. 4 and Table 1 that we can see that each set of data has its negatively sloped curve of fairly similar form. If one looked at the data irrespective of the set of organizations considered, little of a systematic nature could be concluded except that very large units tend to have relatively small supervision ratios. However, considering the points from each set of organizations as a set, the data are then organized into more interpretable form. Plotting on semilog grids straightens out the curves. This kind of presentation of the data shows that small units show higher supervision ratios than middle-size units, which in turn show higher supervision ratios than large units when each set of data is considered separately. This conclusion is supported for all five

sets of data, but it is least supported for the volunteer fire companies. The reason in the latter case may be that the size range is not sufficient to allow us to explore this proposition adequately.

With the findings in mind what can we say about a set? Within each set of organizations studied there is a group of persons who share the overall purpose, a common set of policies, and a common three-level hierarchical structure. These essential facts might lead to the results shown, but the reason they would is as yet unclear.

A possibility may be that the top management of each of these organizational sets feels that one of the benefits of large size is that less supervision per member is necessary due to the similarity of tasks of the added members. However, in three of the sets of organizations studied (those where the necessary data were available), increased size was associated with increased task specialization[12] implying the need for more supervision per member—so that this explanation is not especially tenable.

However, it might also be that the placement of each of these curves reflects at its origin (the *a* coefficient) the initial size of a viable organizational form given the purposes and policies of the set of organizations, and that the placement of the curve reflects the degree of interpersonal control over the members of the respective sets necessary for viable maintenance of the organizational units. The data available here on the relationship of organization

[10] E. Dale, *AMA Res. Rpt.* 20, and Doris R. Entwisle and J. Walton, *Admin. Sci. Quart.*, 5.

[11] J. R. Anderson and S. Warkov, "Organization Size and Functional Complexity: A Study of Administration in Hospitals," *American Sociological Review*, 26 (1961), 23–28.

[12] B. P. Indik, "Organization Size and Member Participation: Some Empirical Tests of Alternative Explanations," *Human Relations*, 17 (1964).

size to other forms of control are not clear.

It may be that a combination of the amount of behavior to be controlled per member per day, and the restriction to specific behaviors required by the organization involved, sets the placement of the curve. To be more specific, of all sets of organizations the delivery-service organizations require both the largest amount of behavior control per member (eight hours per day) and the most delimiting controls of member behavior, since each member must conform (within narrow limits) to standard behavior requirements as set by time-studied rates of performance. At the other extreme, the political organization chapters have the least necessity for interpersonal control or, for that matter, control of any kind over their members. Most members may be contacted only once or more a month while relatively few members spend any portion of their time constrained by organizational requirements that control their behavior.

The three sets of organizations whose curves fall between these two extreme curves might be there for a combination of reasons compatible with the present explanation. (It should be remembered that this is *post hoc* conjecture and needs to be explored in detail in future studies.) The automobile dealerships directly constrain the behavior of their salesmen to four hours per day on the sales floor and allow the rest of the sales time of salesmen to be allocated by themselves so long as sales quotas are maintained; specific behavior of the salesmen is not rigidly controlled. The members of the volunteer fire companies are less controlled in terms of time by their supervisors than are the members of the delivery-service organizations and the automobile sales dealerships; however, they are more constrained to specific risky behavior when they are fulfilling their organizational roles. They are certainly more frequently controlled by organizational constraints than are the members of the voluntary political organizations.

The industrial labor union locals also fit this pattern; they function very much like the volunteer fire companies when they are small and somewhat like the voluntary political organizations when they are large. To be more specific, when the local union is small, a core of leaders and cadre are more constrained and controlled when emergencies arise, but the time constraints are not nearly as severe as they are for the members of the delivery organizations, nor are they as minimally controlled as the voluntary political organization members. However, as the size of the local increases, the per-member constraints on behavior and the concomitant interpersonal (supervisory) control necessary for the local's viability decline, and then approach the functional level of the voluntary political organizations.

Further, the levels of the b coefficient for each set of organizations seem to be characteristic of each particular set of data and may reflect the differential need for interpersonal supervisory control for each kind of organization. Both of these explanations support the structure-function position in that from structural characteristics of a system, the functional properties and processes flow. In this case, from a simply obtained bivariate structural relationship one may infer significant functional characteristics of an organization.

27. THE STRUCTURE OF SMALL BUREAUCRACIES

Peter M. Blau, Wolf V. Heydebrand and Robert E. Stauffer

Why does Weber's analysis of bureaucratic structure continue to be regarded as the classic on the subject half a century after it was written, despite the many, often justified, criticisms that have been directed against it? Does this merely reflect a romantic regard for one of the great old men of social theory? We think not. Weber's great contribution is that he provided a framework for a systematic theory of formal organization; the fact that his analysis has certain limitations does not detract from this important achievement.

A theory of bureaucratic structure should meet two basic requirements.* Above all, it must be concerned with the interdependence among structural attributes of complex organizations and not take these characteristics of the structure as given and merely examine the decisions or behavior of

individuals in the context of complex organizations. The focus of Weber's theory is precisely on this interdependence among various characteristics of the organizations themselves. In addition, a theory of bureaucracy should account for the connections between organizational attributes by analyzing the social processes that have produced these connections. It is not enough, for example, to indicate, as Weber did, that impersonal authority in which personnel can readily be replaced and the use of formalized procedures tend to occur together in bureaucracies; we would also like to know what processes are responsible for this joint occurrence. Gouldner's analysis of managerial succession, though based on a single case, vividly shows how the exigencies of the role of a new manager constrain him to resort to formalized procedures, thereby helping to explain why recurrent replacement of personnel tends to be associated with formalized methods of operation.[1]

Generally the numerous case studies of organizations that have been

Reprinted by permission of the American Sociological Association from *American Sociological Review*, 31 (April 1966), 179–91.

* We gratefully acknowledge grant GS-553 from the National Science Foundation. This is the first report of the Comparative Organization Research Program which it supports.

[1] Alvin W. Gouldner, *Patterns of Industrial Bureaucracy*. Glencoe: Free Press, 1954, pp. 45–101.

carried out in recent decades have complemented Weber's analysis by investigating the social processes within bureaucracies, particularly the informal processes and their significance for the formal organization. At the same time, however, the focus of these studies on informal relations and practices in *one* organization has had the result that investigators lost sight of the central problem of bureaucratic theory, namely, what the interrelations between various structural attributes of formal organizations are. This problem can only be studied by comparing different organizations and not through the intensive analysis of a single case.

At the core of Weber's theory, in contrast, are the structural attributes of bureaucracy and their relationships, in the narrow sense of "structural" as referring to the differentiation of social positions along various lines. At the outset, Weber stresses that responsibilities in a bureaucracy "are distributed in a fixed way as official duties,"[2] elaborating later that this involves a systematic division of labor and often a high degree of specialization. Complementing this specialization is the requirement of "thorough and expert training,"[3] which means that many positions in the organization are occupied by professionally or technically qualified specialists. The formal status hierarchy is a third fundamental characteristic of bureaucracy: "The principle of hierarchical office authority is found in all bureaucratic structures."[4] Finally, the emphasis upon written communication and official

documents in bureaucracies makes the employment of many clerks necessary, "a staff of subaltern officials and scribes of all sorts."[5]

We propose to return to Weber's approach in this paper and to analyze the interrelations among these four structural attributes of bureaucracy and their implications for operations —the division of labor, professionalization, the hierarchy of authority, and the administrative staff of clerks. To be sure, Weber's analysis is not confined to these four but encompasses other formal characteristics of organizations that are not structural in the narrow sense of referring to aspects of status differentiation,[6] such as the rules governing operations, the stable careers of officials, and the impersonal orientation that prevails in bureaucratic relations. In this study, however, attention is restricted to the four organizational attributes indicated, and two others—size and an effect criterion. The investigation is based on data from about 150 public personnel agencies, which represent most of the larger organizations of this type in North America.

METHOD

The systematic study of bureaucratic structure necessitates a method of inquiry adapted to the purpose as well as an appropriate theoretical approach. The variables under investigation must be structural characteristics *of* the bureaucracies themselves, such as a status distribution in the

---

[2] *From Max Weber: Essays in Sociology.* New York: Oxford University Press, 1946, p. 196.
[3] Weber, *Essays in Sociology*, p. 198.
[4] *Ibid.*, p. 197.

[5] *Ibid.*
[6] The term "status" is used here in its broader sense as complementary to role and synonymous with social position, not in the narrower sense that restricts it to hierarchical distinctions in social position.

organization, rather than merely attitudes or behaviors of the individuals *in* these bureaucracies. Moreover, the research design must involve the systematic comparison of a fairly large number of organizations, and not just a few cases assumed to be typical, in order to determine how variations in some characteristics affect variations in others. The important point is that such large-scale comparisons are required not only to test theoretical propositions once they have been formulated but also initially to formulate and refine the theory.

When Weber portrayed a typical bureaucracy in bold strokes, on the basis of comparative analysis on a wide historical scale, he surely did not intend to suggest, as a simplistic interpretation sometimes assumes, that all the characteristics he outlined are highly correlated under all conditions. On the contrary, the complex interdependencies he traces clearly imply that the relationships between any two characteristics of bureaucracies often depend on and are modified by a third factor or even by a combination of several others. Our empirical data strongly confirm this crucial insight that the various aspects of bureaucratic structure interact in their effects on each other. In other words, it is usually not possible to state simply what the relationship between two organizational attributes is, because it depends on one or more other attributes. We suspect that such higher-order interaction effects are a fundamental characteristic of social structures. In any case, given these complex interrelations in bureaucracies, the next step in refining the theory of formal organization is to specify the conditions under which different relationships hold. Such specification requires the

quantitative analysis of concomitant variations in a fairly large number of cases.

The organizations selected for the study are public personnel agencies, which are the executive agencies of the civil service commissions that administer the personnel policies of state and local governments. The sample consists of all members of the Public Personnel Association who returned a questionnaire about their agency in a survey administered by the Association in 1958.[7] Returns were received from nearly one half of the member agencies (252 of 528). Although the sample is not representative, it includes most of the larger public personnel agencies in the United States and some in Canada,[8] with the bias of self-selection working against smaller agencies and those least identified with the merit principles of civil service. All but seven of the 50 state agencies are in the sample, as are most of the agencies of the largest American cities, some of counties, and a few miscellaneous agencies, such as that of the TVA.

Public personnel agencies are small bureaucracies. Nearly two-fifths of the 252 organizations represented had a total staff of fewer than five persons. These were excluded from

[7] These data were kindly made available to us for statistical analysis by Messrs. Kenneth O. Warner and Keith Ocheltree, to whom we are indebted not only for doing so but also for helpful advice.

[8] There are only 14 Canadian cases, 4 provincial and 10 city agencies. Since tabulations showed that these do not essentially differ from the corresponding agencies in the United States, they have not been eliminated from the analysis in order to maximize the number of cases. The U.S. Civil Service Commission and its Canadian counterpart were excluded.

the investigation, since the status distribution measures used have little validity if constructed on such a small base. This leaves 156 cases for analysis, with a slightly lower total in most tables because of no answers. Even after these tiny bureaucracies have been eliminated, the median staff of the rest is only between 16 and 17 persons, and a mere 17 agencies have a staff of more than 100. Agencies are divided into small ones with a staff of less than 20 (but at least 5) and larger ones with a staff of 20 or more. This division close to the median separates agencies all of whose members can easily have frequent face-to-face contact from those whose somewhat larger size makes it unlikely that every member knows all others well.[9]

The six variables under consideration are size, four attributes of internal structure, and a weighted measure of operating cost. The internal structure can be considered to have two major dimensions: specialization, which is a mechanism to deal with task complexity; and bureaucratic coordination, which is a mechanism to deal with the organizational complexity introduced by specialization. Specialization can be subdivided into the division of labor in the organization and the degree of professionalization of its staff. Two mechanisms of bureaucratic coordination are the hierarchy of managerial authority and the administrative apparatus.

The following are the operational measures for these four structural attributes—two aspects of specialization and two kinds of coordinating mechanism:

1. *Division of Labor:* the number of distinct occupational titles pertaining to the nonclerical staff, not counting those indicative of status differences within a specialty rather than different specialties.[10] Dichotomized between three and four specialties.[11]
2. *Professionalization:* the proportion of the operating staff (excluding managers as well as clerks) who are required to have, at least, a college degree with a specified major. Dichotomized at 50 percent.[12]

[9] Theodore Caplow specifies 20 members as the upper limit of a primary group, "in which each member interacts with every other member"; "Organizational Size," *Administrative Science Quarterly*, 1 (1957), 486.

[10] Thus, "Personnel Technician I" and "Personnel Technician II" were counted as one specialty. Since the absolute number of occupational titles is closely related to size, the question arises whether a relative index of the division of labor would not be preferable to an absolute one. But such a relative index—the ratio of occupational positions to size of staff—is just as much negatively associated with size as the absolute index is positively associated with it.

[11] In this case, the basic procedure for determining the cutting points of the dichotomies was modified for substantive reasons. The basic criterion for dichotomizing was to come as close to the median as the initial categories on the IBM cards permitted. Since the middle category was sometimes fairly large, and since elimination of the agencies with a staff of under 5 changed the proportions, the numbers of cases in the two classes of the dichotomy are often not the same. Two exceptions to the use of this criterion were made for conceptual reasons. Division of labor was dichotomized between three and four to avoid calling agencies with only three different positions highly differentiated, as would be required if the median were used, and professionalization was dichotomized above the median lest agencies with a single professional on the operating staff be defined as highly professionalized. These decisions about cutting points were made before the substantive analysis of cross-tabulations was carried out.

[12] Although agencies were divided on the basis of whether less than 50, or 50 percent or more, of the operating staff are re-

3. *Managerial Hierarchy:* the ratio of men in managerial to those in nonsupervisory positions among the nonclerical staff, excluding those for whom neither alternative was indicated.[13] Dichotomized at one to three.[14]

4. *Administrative Apparatus:* the proportion of clerks among the total staff.[15] Dichotomized at 60 percent.

A weighted measure of cost is employed to investigate one of the implications of the various aspects of administrative structure for opera-

---

quired to have the specified professional qualifications, the differences are actually more extreme—since the distribution is bimodal. In more than four-fifths of the less professionalized agencies there are no professional requirements for any position, and in more than three-quarters of the professionalized ones professional qualifications are required of the entire staff. The reason for excluding managerial personnel from this index is to assure that no relationship between professionalization and management hierarchy can be due to lack of independence of the two measures. Managers in professionalized agencies generally are also required to meet professional qualifications.

[13] Actually, the nonclerical personnel had been classified by respondents into four categories—deputy directors, heads of major divisions, journeymen, and apprentices. The index is the ratio of the first two to the last two. Positions that were not classified by respondents might be staff consultants or ambiguous cases.

[14] Since this excludes clerks, it corresponds to considerably more than three subordinates per manager—probably about seven.

[15] This is the only index that uses total staff in the denominator. The index provides a narrow operational definition of administrative staff; a wider one would include other positions responsible for maintaining the organization, such as bookkeepers, but there are advantages in restricting it to clerical personnel, since they are the ones most directly concerned with communication.

tions. The index of operating costs is the ratio of the salary budget of the personnel agency itself to the total payroll for the entire civil service personnel under its jurisdiction —specifically, whether this ratio exceeds one-half of one percent or not. This measure adjusts cost not only to the magnitude of the agency's operations but also to regional variations in standard of living. It even takes into account, to some extent, that it is more difficult to administer highly qualified than unskilled personnel, since such differences are reflected in the denominator. While this is an adjusted measure of operating costs, it is not a reliable measure of efficiency, inasmuch as it does not take into account either the scope of personnel services provided or the quality of performance.

Although the organizations under investigation are not a representative sample of a larger universe, statistical tests have been performed to furnish an external criterion for deciding whether or not to place some confidence in the complex relationships observed.[16] The use of these tests rests on the assumption that a given pattern of differences observed would be unlikely to occur by chance in a sample drawn from a hypothetical universe of similar organizations.

[16] The statistic developed by Leo A. Goodman has been used; "Modifications of the Dorn-Stouffer-Tibbits Method for 'Testing the Significance of Comparisons in Sociological Data'," *American Journal of Sociology*, 66 (1961), 355–63. In a few cases, the criterion for the assumption of a normal distribution that each cell contain at least 5 observations was not met; interpretation there should proceed with caution. We gratefully acknowledge John Wiorkowski's assistance in performing the statistical tests, and Leo Goodman's advice.

PROFESSIONALIZATION AND MANAGERIAL AUTHORITY

Professional qualifications undoubtedly lessen the need for close supervision, other things being equal. We had expected therefore that the ratio of managers to operating officials would not be as high in organizations with a professional staff as in those where most of the staff is not required to meet professional qualifications. The reasoning was that a high managerial ratio implies a narrow span of control, with few subordinates per manager, and such a narrow span of control is often assumed to be associated with close supervision. Contrary to expectations, however, professionalized public personnel agencies are more likely to have a high ratio of managers than other agencies under most conditions, though not under all. Unless one is willing to believe that professionals are being more closely supervised than employees with less training, which seems improbable, this finding calls for a reappraisal of the significance of the managerial ratio. Instead of making a priori assumptions about closeness of supervision, let us start with the attributes of bureaucratic structure this ratio directly reflects, and proceed with the analysis before drawing inferences that are consistent with the data.

The managerial ratio indicates whether the administrative authority rooted in formal status in the hierarchy is centralized in the hands of relatively few officials or distributed among a larger number. To be sure, how centralized actual decision making is in the organization depends not only on the degree of centralization in the formal hierarchy but also on other conditions, such as the delegation of responsibilities by superiors to subordinates. No information is available on these conditions, nor on closeness of supervision. The ratio singles out for attention an attribute of the formal status structure, not an aspect of operations, specifically, the extent to which authority positions are centralized rather than being more widely dispersed in an organization.[17]

A centralized hierarchy of managerial authority is least likely to develop in small professionalized organizations, as Table 1 shows. In small agencies with a professional staff, in other words, the probability of a high ratio of managers to subordinates is greatest. Only 16 percent of these agencies have a centralized management (low ratio), whereas about two-fifths of the less-professionalized small and of either kind of larger agencies do. Professionalization and centralization of authority are inversely related in smaller agencies but not in larger ones. Further analysis reveals, however, that these two factors are also inversely related in larger agencies provided that certain conditions are met.

Table 2 indicates that a centralized hierarchy of official authority is less prevalent in professional than in other

---

[17] The span of control is also indicative of the formal status hierarchy, and not of supervisory practice. The average span of control depends on the number of levels in the hierarchy as well as on the ratio of managers. No data on the number of levels are available. Though the ratio is not equivalent to the average span of control, the two are undoubtedly highly correlated, because variations in number of levels cannot be very large among organizations few of which have a staff of more than 100.

TABLE 1   PERCENT WITH CENTRALIZED HIERARCHY*
BY SIZE AND PROFESSIONALIZATION

Professionalization***	Small Agencies	Large Agencies**
Low	38 (61)	41 (32)
High	16 (31)	43 (28)

NOTE: The difference in the left column is significant (at the 0.05 level).

* The managerial hierarchy is *centralized* when the ratio of non-clerical personnel in managerial positions to non-clerical personnel in non-supervisory positions, excluding those listed as neither, is less than one to three; it is *dispersed* when the ratio is one to three or more.

** *Small agencies* have a total staff of less than 20 (but five or more); *large agencies* have a total staff of 20 or more.

*** Professionlization is *low* when the proportion of the operating staff (excluding managers as well as clerks) who are required to have, at least, a college degree with a specified major, is less than 50 percent; *high* when it is 50 percent or more.

TABLE 2   PERCENT WITH CENTRALIZED HIERARCHY BY SIZE,
PROFESSIONALIZATION, AND ADMINISTRATIVE APPARATUS

	Small Agencies		Large Agencies	
Profession-alization	Administrative Apparatus* Low	High	Administrative Apparatus* Low	High
Low	35 (31)	40 (30)	29 (17)	53 (15)
High	11 (19)	25 (12)	47 (15)	38 (13)
Difference	−24	−15	+18	−15

NOTE: The difference between differences in cols. 1 and 3 is significant (at the 0.05 level); that between cols. 2 and 4 is not.

* The administrative apparatus ratio is *low* when the proportion of clerks among the total staff is less than 60 percent; *high* when it is 60 percent or more.

organizations in three of the four comparisons, the only exception being those larger agencies that have a low ratio of administrative personnel. Professionalization reduces the likelihood of centralization of authority not only in smaller agencies, whatever the administrative ratio (−24, −15), but also in larger ones if the administrative ratio is high (−15), though not if it is low (+18). The sharpest contrast is between the 19 smaller professionalized agencies with a low administrative ratio, a mere 11 percent of which have a centralized hierarchy, and the 15 larger professionalized agencies with a high administrative ratio, 53 percent of which do. The two ques-

tions to be answered are, first, why the negative relationship prevails in most situations and, second, what accounts for the deviant case. The answers suggested are admittedly *post hoc* interpretations.

Professional training may be assumed to make a man more self-directing in his work. It was on the basis of this assumption that we had expected—incorrectly, as it turned out—that agencies with a professional staff would have a low ratio of managers. Identification with professional standards, however, tends to make a man working in an organization not only less dependent on direct supervision but also more aware of the broader implications of his job and more interested in seeing to it that agency policies and operations do not violate professional principles. Such a man is likely to detect problems that escape the notice of one without professional qualifications and to want to have administrative procedures modified to remedy these problems. The professional's informed concern with helping shape agency procedures and policies is at the root of the recurrent conflict between professionals and administrators, but it is simultaneously a resource available to the organization for improving operations.

Management cannot give professionals free rein, since there is often a genuine conflict between professional and administrative considerations. Yet if management seriously frustrates professionals in the exercise of their responsibilities, it not only courts the danger of dissatisfactions and defections from the organization but also fails to take advantage of an important resource at its disposal, which includes the professional's interest in perfecting operations as well as his expert knowledge. For management to channel the initiative of professionals into administrative improvements instead of stifling it requires frequent contact and close collaboration between managers and professionals. Though conflicts between professional and administrative concerns are inevitable, the best chance for advantageous compromise is probably provided by extensive communication between the officials responsible for professional and those responsible for administrative decisions. The higher the ratio of managers, with few subordinates for each, the greater are the opportunities for frequent discussions in which prob-

lems can be explored, dissatisfactions expressed, and conflicts reconciled.

A high managerial ratio, which implies a dispersed management, promotes extensive vertical communication in the hierarchy of authority. It facilitates downward communication, which makes it easier for superiors to direct the work of subordinates and check up on them. But it also facilitates upward communication, which makes it easier for subordinates to convey information to superiors and to influence administrative decisions. Our original expectation had exclusively focused on the significance of a high managerial ratio for downward communication, whereas the data suggest that its significance for upward communication is the more crucial here. To encourage upward communication by appointing a high proportion of managers is particularly important for organizations with a professional staff, because only by doing so can they take full advantage of the contributions professionals are capable of making.

Professionalization and centralization of authority appear to be alternative methods for organizing responsibilities. Since professional qualifications enhance a man's ability to see the implication of his work and place it into a wider context, professionals can contribute to coordination in an organization; the task of management is to draw upon these contributions and fit them into the administrative framework. This requires a sufficient number of managers to work in close collaboration with the professional staff. If the staff lacks professional training, on the other hand, it can make only limited contributions to coordination, and the task of management is, consequently, to effect coordination largely on its own rather than to collaborate with operating officials for this purpose. A hierarchy in which authority is concentrated in the hands of relatively few managers serves distinctive functions in such a situation, because it makes it possible to achieve coordination through centralized planning by a small headquarters group and then issuing pertinent directives to the staff. The limitations on discretion centralized planning and direction impose upon the staff are undoubtedly more objectionable to professionals than to men whose lack of expertness would make it hard for them to exercise much discretion. To be sure, a centralized structure makes it more difficult for the relatively few managers to keep in close touch with operating officials and supervise them closely. But modern administration has devised substitute methods for obtaining information on operations and checking on the work of subordinates that do not require frequent direct contact, such as detailed statistical records of performance.[18]

In the absence of a professionally trained staff, according to these considerations, a centralized hierarchy of authority has important advantages for an organization and comparatively few disadvantages. Its major advantage is that it can meet the need

for coordination through centralized planning. In a relatively large organization, however, this requires an adequate administrative apparatus of clerks to maintain the channels of communication that are essential for coordination from a central headquarters. This interpretation brings us back to the findings in Table 2, because it suggests why a centralized hierarchy is more likely to develop in agencies that are not professionalized than in professionalized ones if they are small or if they are larger and have a high administrative ratio, and why this is not the case for larger agencies with a low administrative ratio. Professionalization as well as centralization, in turn, depend on the division of labor.

STRUCTURAL DIFFERENTIATION

Expansion in size has a pronounced impact on the structural differentiation of functional specialties within the organization. An advanced division of labor with four or more occupational specialties is found in only 14 percent of the 92 small public personnel agencies but in 66 percent of the 62 larger ones. A minimum size is virtually required for the development of several distinct functional positions in an organization.[19] In contrast to this strong influence on the division of labor, size exerts little influence on the three other bureaucratic attributes under investigation. Thus, a high administrative ratio is as likely

[18] One might even speculate whether the very fact that a low ratio of managers facilitates close supervision does not make it particularly *inappropriate* for a nonprofessional staff. The experienced manager in charge of a nonprofessional staff is more likely to be tempted to supervise too closely if conditions permit than is the manager in charge of expert professionals. Since a low ratio facilitates close supervision (indicated by research to be detrimental to performance), and since the inclination to resort to close supervision is greatest if the staff is not highly skilled, a low ratio of managers may be most dysfunctional for operations with an unskilled staff.

[19] In the extreme case, such a relationship is a mathematical necessity—agencies of less than four persons could not possibly have four or more positions—but none of the agencies had a staff of less than five.

to be found in larger agencies as in small ones.[20] There is no significant difference between larger and small agencies, moreover, either in the likelihood that their staff is professionalized or in the likelihood that their authority structure is centralized. Although size has no direct effect on these factors, it has distinct indirect effects that modify their interrelations and condition their significance for operations.

Structural differentiation, which is typically a consequence of expanding size, in turn affects other characteristics of the organization. It has implications for professionalization and for centralization: the pattern revealed by the resulting relationships supports the previous conclusion that professionalization and centralization are alternative modes of organization, the existence of one being somewhat incompatible with that of the other. The division of labor promotes either professionalization or centralization but not both, and whether it promotes the one depends on the absence of the other. Thus, the chances that

the hierarchy of authority becomes centralized increase with advances in the division of labor only if the staff is not professional, and not at all if it is professional, as Table 3 shows. About one-third of the agencies with a rudimentary division of labor have a centralized structure, whatever the degree of professionalization, and even slightly fewer of the more differentiated agencies that are professionalized, compared to one-half of the more differentiated agencies that are not professionalized.[21] In brief, task differentiation seems to further the development of a centralized hierarchy of authority unless the organization is professionalized.

The conclusion that the influence of the division of labor on the management hierarchy depends on professionalization is, however, suspect. The relationship in Table 3 is not significant, and size has not been controlled, although it is known to have a strong impact on the division of labor and some bearing on the two other variables. But controlling for size does not destroy the pattern observed; on the contrary, it accentuates it. In both smaller and larger agencies, as Table 4 indicates, an intensification of the division of labor raises the likelihood of the emergence of a centralized hierarchy if the staff is not professionalized, but it actually lessens this likelihood if it is professionalized; these differences are statistically significant. When the staff lacks professional qualifications, the proportion of centralized hierarchies

[20] Whereas other studies of organizations found that the administrative ratio declines with size, this is the case only after a certain size has been reached. This is probably the reason for the difference in findings—since our data are primarily based on fairly small organizations. See Seymour Melman, "The Rise of Administrative Overhead in the Manufacturing Industries of the United States, 1899–1947," *Oxford Economic Papers*, 3 (1951), 89–90; Reinhard Bendix, *Work and Authority in Industry*. New York: John Wiley, 1956, pp. 221–22; Theodore R. Anderson and Seymour Warkov, "Organizational Size and Functional Complexity," *American Sociological Review*, 26 (1961), 23–28; and Wolf V. Heydebrand, "Bureaucracy in Hospitals; An Analysis of Complexity and Coordination in Formal Organizations," unpublished Ph.D. dissertation, Department of Sociology, University of Chicago, 1965.

[21] The pattern is complementary when percentages for the data in Table 3 are computed with professionalization as the dependent variable. Differentiation tends to promote professionalization in the absence of centralization but not when it is present.

TABLE 3 PERCENT WITH CENTRALIZED HIERARCHY BY PROFESSIONALIZATION
AND DIVISION OF LABOR

Division of Labor	Professionalization	
	Low	High
Rudimentary	33 (64)	31 (36)
Advanced	50 (28)	26 (23)

NOTE: The difference in the left column is not significant at the 0.05 level.

*The division of labor is *advanced* when the non-clerical staff represents four or more occupational specialties; *rudimentary* when it represents less than four.

TABLE 4 PERCENT WITH CENTRALIZED HIERARCHY BY SIZE,
DIVISION OF LABOR, AND PROFESSIONALIZATION

	Small Agencies		Large Agencies	
	Professionalization		Professionalization	
Division of Labor	Low	High	Low	High
Rudimentary	36 (53)	19 (26)	18 (11)	60 (10)
Advanced	50 (8)	0 (5)	50 (20)	33 (18)
Difference	+14	−19	+32	−27

NOTE: The difference between the pooled differences in columns 1 and 3 and those in columns 2 and 4 is significant at the 0.05 level. (One-half observation, or ten percent, was substituted for the zero cell, because variance cannot be estimated, by the method used, for cells with zero observations.)

increases with growing task differentiation in smaller agencies (+14) as well as in larger ones (+32). When the staff meets professional requirements, in contrast, the proportion of centralized hierarchies *decreases* with growing task differentiation in both smaller (−19) and larger (−27) agencies. Holding size constant magnifies the interaction effect of differentiation and professionalization on centralization. This confirms the conclusion that structural differentiation promotes the emergence of a centralized hierarchy only in the absence of professionalization; in its presence, it does not and may even have the opposite result.

The division of labor in an organization can take two entirely different forms. On the one hand, it may involve the subdivision of the overall task of the organization into specialized responsibilities that permit, and indeed require, greater utilization of expert specialists. This development is illustrated by the difference between a hospital medical staff consisting of general practitioners and one composed primarily of specialists. On the other hand, the division of labor may entail the fragmentation of responsibilities into simple assignments with routine duties that require minimal skills. The assembly line factory is an extreme example of this tendency. Since many professionals are essential in the one case while few are needed in the other, the extent of professionalization in a public personnel agency indicates which one of these two forms the division of labor has taken. Specialized differentiation of tasks (an advanced division of labor in combination with professionalization) and routinized differentiation of tasks (an advanced division of labor in the absence of professionalization) pose different administrative problems.

Routinized differentiation, which minimizes the need for professional experts, maximizes the need for managerial coordination. Centralized planning and direction are effective means for coordinating fragmented duties performed by a relatively untrained staff. Routinized differentiation accordingly enhances the likelihood of the development of a centralized authority structure.[22] Specialized differentiation does not pose the same problem of coordination for management as routinized differentiation does, because tasks are not as fragmented, because professionals are qualified to assume wider responsibilities, and because management gains advantages from eliciting their contributions to coordination instead of imposing directives from a central headquarters on them. A centralized management has great disadvantages in a professionalized organization, as has been noted. Hence, specialized differentiation does not enhance the likelihood of the development of a centralized hierarchy.

[22] The conclusion that routinized differentiation creates a need for centralization, and the earlier conclusion that centralization in larger agencies depends on an adequate administrative staff, together imply that routinized differentiation should lead to the expansion of the administrative apparatus. The data give some support to this inference. The proportion of agencies with a high administrative ratio increases with growing differentiation neither in small agencies nor in larger professionalized ones but only in larger agencies lacking professionalization, from 18 percent of 11 cases to 60 percent of 20. This difference barely fails to reach the conventional level of statistical significance, being significant at the 0.07 level.

In sum, structural differentiation in public personnel agencies sometimes is accompanied by greater professionalization and sometimes by greater centralization of authority, and whether it leads to the elaboration of one of these depends in part on the absence of the other of these two alternative modes of organizing responsibilities. An advancing division of labor that is associated with professionalization raises entirely different administrative problems from one that is not. The former makes adequate *upward* communication especially important, without which management is deprived of some of the contributions the professional staff can make. To encourage upward communication requires a high ratio of managers dispersed throughout the organization. The subdivision of labor among a staff lacking professional qualifications, in contrast, makes adequate *downward* communication particularly important, without which the coordination of diverse simple routines cannot be accomplished. A centralized hierarchy of authority facilitates such coordination, provided that it is complemented in organizations beyond a minimum size by a sufficient administrative staff of clerks to maintain the essential lines of communication. These considerations suggest that, in an organization, a high ratio of managers is of special importance for upward communication and a high ratio of clerks for downward communication.

IMPLICATIONS FOR OPERATING COSTS

How do various conditions in the bureaucratic structure affect operating costs? To be sure, it would be of great interest to examine the significance of differences in the administrative structure for other aspects of operations as well as cost, but the data necessary for this purpose are not available. There is no denying the importance of budgetary considerations in government agencies and most other formal organizations; the study of operating costs is consequently a good starting point for clarifying the implications of bureaucratic attributes for operations. The weighted measure of operating costs, to repeat, is whether or not the salary budget of the public personnel agency exceeds one-half of one percent of the total salary budget for the civil servants under its jurisdiction.

Structural differentiation, on the whole, lowers operating costs. Whereas exactly one-half of the 98 agencies with a rudimentary division of labor operate at relatively high costs, 35 percent of the 54 with an advanced division of labor do. Since larger agencies also operate on the average at lower costs than smaller ones, and since size and the division of labor are strongly related, the question arises whether task differentiation or operating on a large scale actually produces these cost reductions. The answer is that both lead to economies, as Table 5 reveals, but their effects are not cumulative. Small undifferentiated agencies are most likely to operate at high costs. Either an increase in differentiation or an increase in size tends to reduce operating costs, but the occurrence of both does not reduce them further. Although task differentiation, which usually accompanies growth, effects economies, it simultaneously destroys the economic advantage that operating on a large scale otherwise has

(the right-hand value is the lower one in the first but not in the second row of the table).

The significance of professionalization for operating costs closely parallels that of the division of labor. Table 6 shows that operations are most likely to be costly in small agencies with few professionals. Professionalization greatly lessens the likelihood of high costs in small organizations (from 60 to 31 percent), though only there, just as is the case for differentiation. The finding that professionals, despite the higher salaries they command, lower the cost of operations in small agencies implies that they make contributions to administrative efficiency—apart from those their expert skills make to performance quality, which are not reflected in the cost measure. Operating on a larger scale without professionals, however, also lessens the likelihood of high costs (from 60 to 28 percent), and professionalization in large organizations has, if anything, a detrimental effect on operating economy, in sharp contrast to its beneficial effect in small organizations. These data suggest that professionalization, as well as differentiation, has two contradictory implications for operations.

Differentiation and professionalization influence operations directly, and they also produce changes in the organizational structure that have indirect repercussions for operations. The direct effects are most evident in smaller organizations, and the indirect ones, which have opposite implications for operations, in larger organizations. Task differentiation has the manifest purpose of raising efficiency, and it achieves this purpose in small agencies. At the same time, however, differentiation increases the internal complexity of the

TABLE 5 PERCENT WITE HIGH COSTS* BY SIZE AND DIVISION OF LABOR

Division of Labor	Small Agencies	Large Agencies
Rudimentary	55 (77)	33 (21)
Advanced	23 (13)	39 (41)

NOTE: The difference in the left columns is significant at the 0.05 level.

* Agencies in which the salary budget of the agency itself is 0.5 percent or more of the total payroll for the entire civil service personnel the agency administers.

TABLE 6 PERCENT WITH HIGH COSTS BY SIZE AND PROFESSIONALIZATION

Professionalization	Small Agencies	Large Agencies
Low	60 (61)	28 (32)
High	31 (29)	43 (28)

NOTE: The difference in the left column is significant at the 0.05 level.

organizational structure. While the immediate purpose of professionalization is to improve performance quality, the findings indicate that it also raises efficiency in small agencies. The reason may be that the ability of professionals to fit their own tasks into a wider framework contributes to the overall coordination in organizations sufficiently small to permit regular face-to-face contacts among the entire staff, but much less so in larger organizations with several departments. Separate departmental groups of professional specialists increase the structural complexity of an organization, just as does the division of labor. Internal complexity gives rise to problems, which are reflected in operating costs, as can be seen most clearly when complexity is viewed as a condition that modifies the basic influence of size on operating costs.

Simple agencies exhibit an economy of scale, whereas complex ones do not. Whether the division of labor or professionalization is taken as the indication of structural complexity, larger organizations tend to operate at lower costs than smaller ones if their structure is simple, but not if it is complex (see Tables 5 and 6). Internal complexity nullifies the economic advantage operations on a large scale have in its absence, because it gives rise to problems of communication and coordination in larger organizations. While this is self-evident in the case of the division of labor, it requires explanation in the case of professionals—whose coordinating ability has been noted. Professionals who are "locals" and identify themselves with the organization in which they work have been distinguished from "cosmopolitans," who are primarily oriented to the wider group of professional colleagues anywhere.[23] It seems reasonable to assume that locals predominate in smaller organizations and cosmopolitans in larger ones. The broader context into which professionals tend to fit their own tasks is the work of the organization, for locals, but the work of fellow specialists outside, for cosmopolitans. The very identification of professionals with their responsibil-

[23] Alvin W. Gouldner, "Cosmopolitans and Locals," *Administrative Science Quarterly,* 2 (1957/58), 281–306, 444–80.

TABLE 7 PERCENT WITH HIGH COSTS BY SIZE, DIVISION OF LABOR,
AND ADMINISTRATIVE APPARATUS

Division of Labor and Administrative Apparatus	*Small Agencies*	*Large Agencies*	*Difference*
Rudimentary:			
Low Administrative Ratio	51 (41)	36 (14)	−15
High Administrative Ratio	58 (36)	29 (7)	−29
Advanced:			
Low Administrative Ratio	12 (8)	50 (20)	+38
High Administrative Ratio	40 (5)	25 (20)	−15

NOTE: The difference between the differences in rows 1 and 3 is significant at the 0.05 level; that between rows 2 and 4 is not (0.63).

TABLE 8 PERCENT WITH HIGH COSTS BY SIZE, PROFESSIONALIZATION,
AND ADMINISTRATIVE APPARATUS

Professionalization and Administrative Apparatus	*Small Agencies*	*Large Agencies*	*Difference*
Low:			
Low Administrative Ratio	55 (31)	24 (17)	−31
High Administrative Ratio	63 (30)	33 (15)	−30
High:			
Low Administrative Ratio	28 (18)	60 (15)	+32
High Administrative Ratio	36 (11)	23 (13)	−13

NOTE: The difference between the differences in rows 1 and 3 is significant at the 0.05 level; that between rows 2 and 4 is not.

ities that leads the locals in an organization to converge in their orientations leads the cosmopolitans to diverge. Professionals in larger organizations, often working in diverse departments and oriented to different professions outside, consequently intensify problems of communication. The interpretation suggested is that the problems of communication produced by professionalization as well as by differentiation in larger agencies account for the adverse effects of these structural complexities on operations. This interpretation implies that complexity no longer has adverse effects once mechanisms to deal with problems of communication have been developed. The data support this inference.

Organizational complexities destroy the economy of scale that is otherwise observable, but appropriate bureaucratic mechanisms for coping with the problems posed by these complexities restore the economy of scale. Table 7 reveals that, among simple organizations with a rudimentary division of labor, a larger scale of operations tends to reduce costs, whether the administrative ratio is low (−15) or high (−29). Among complex organizations with an advanced division of labor, however, a larger size tends to raise costs if the administrative ratio is low (+38) and reduce them only if it is high (−15). The same pattern appears when professionalization is substituted for the division of labor, as shown in Table 8. In the absence of professionalization, an increase in size lessens the likelihood of high costs, whatever the administrative

TABLE 9 PERCENT WITH HIGH COSTS BY SIZE, DIVISION OF LABOR, AND MANAGERIAL HIERARCHY

Division of Labor and Managerial Hierarchy	Small Agencies	Large Agencies	Difference
Rudimentary:			
Dispersed Hierarchy	50 (54)	23 (13)	−27
Centralized Hierarchy	65 (50)	50 (8)	−15
Advanced:			
Dispersed Hierarchy	11 (9)	39 (23)	+28
Centralized Hierarchy	50 (4)	39 (18)	−11

NOTE: The difference between the differences in rows 1 and 3 is significant at the 0.05 level; that between rows 2 and 4 is not.

ratio (−31, −30), but in professionalized agencies, an increase in size raises the likelihood of high costs (+32) unless the administrative ratio is high (−13).

An adequate administrative apparatus to maintain channels of communication can meet the problems created by structural complexity in organizations beyond a minimum size; thereby it reinstates under complex conditions the economy that accrues to large-scale operations under simple conditions without it. A centralized authority structure serves equivalent functions, although only for task differentiation and not for professionalization. If the division of labor is rudimentary, as Table 9 indicates, operating costs tend to decline with expanding size regardless of the management hierarchy (−27, −15) but if the division of labor is advanced, costs tend to rise with expanding size (+28) unless the hierarchy is centralized (−11). Centralization of formal authority facilitates the coordination of diverse tasks—a major problem in differentiated larger organizations. The pattern of findings in Table 9 corresponds closely with those in Tables 7 and 8. Since centralization and administrative apparatus are not significantly related, and neither are division of labor and pro-

fessionalization, the three sets of findings are not redundant but actual replications. The combined influence of professionalization and centralization does not, however, reveal the same pattern. This is hardly surprising in the light of the earlier indications that a centralized hierarchy is not a suitable coordinating mechanism for a professional staff.

In short, procedures instituted to meet some problems often have repercussions in the organizational structure that create new problems. These conflicting influences had to be inferred from the analysis. Thus, both the division of labor and professionalization lower operating costs, as manifest in the data from small agencies, but they simultaneously increase the structural complexity of the organization. Operating on a larger scale also lowers operating costs, as revealed by the data from simple agencies, though not by those from complex ones (because of the disturbing influence of complexity). Structural complexity raises problems of communication in larger organizations which, if unresolved, impede effective operations, as implied by the findings that complexity eliminates the economic advantage of larger agencies but administrative mechanisms that meet problems of communication re-establish this advantage.

CONCLUSIONS

The interrelations among four bureaucratic attributes in American public personnel agencies have been analyzed—task differentiation, professionalization, the management hierarchy, and the administrative apparatus. It is noteworthy that all six zero-order relationships between any two of these four organizational attributes are insignificantly small, not one making a difference of as much as 12 percent. Even when size is controlled only one of the six reveals a significant difference (that between professionalization and centralization). It is primarily in the higher-order interactions that distinct relationships become apparent. This creates methodological difficulties, since many more than the 150 cases of organizations here available would be needed to explore adequately the intricate interrelations. But it is also of substantive significance, for these higher-order interactions reflect and provide empirical validation for the theoretical conception of social structure, which implies a complex interdependence between elements rather than correlations between pairs of attributes unaffected by other conditions.[24]

Professionalization plays a dual role in the bureaucratic structure, being in some respects the counterpart of the division of labor, and in

others that of the authority hierarchy. Just as does an advanced division of labor, professionalization lowers costs, engenders structural complexities that produce communication problems, and requires the assistance of an administrative staff. On the other hand, it seems to be an alternative to a centralized authority structure. Whereas the analysis of operating costs implies that professionalization increases problems of coordination and communication, its inverse relationship to centralization suggests that it helps meet problems of coordination, but only if complemented by a dispersed management. Although these findings appear contradictory, they can readily be reconciled. The inverse relationship between professionalization and centralization means, after all, nothing else than that a professional staff is usually accompanied by a large and dispersed managerial component; this does not in the least conflict with the interpretation that professionalization intensifies problems of communication. To be sure, professionals also make some contributions to coordination, particularly by detecting problems and proposing knowledgeable solutions for them. For these contributions to be realized in effective coordination, however, an adequate staff of managers is essential to work in close contact with professionals, and to implement their proposals as well as solicit them. The effectiveness of a professional staff, in sum, depends on its being complemented by an adequate managerial component and in larger organizations also by an adequate administrative component. These are required to meet the problems of coordination and communication professionalization raises, notwithstanding the

---

[24] Hubert M. Blalock, Jr., stresses the importance of taking explicitly into account such higher-order interactions in sociological theory; "Theory Building and the Statistical Concept of Interaction," *American Sociological Review*, 30 (1965), 374–80.

ability of professionals to help solve these problems.

A systematic analysis of bureaucratic structure, like the one attempted here, seeks to discover the consistent interrelations among organizational attributes. Consistent patterns cannot be found in all the data; those that can are singled out for attention. While such selectivity is inevitable in exploratory research, it creates the danger of conveying an impression of greater functional integration in the structure than actually exists. It should be mentioned as a *caveat,* therefore, that functional relationships, though often implicit in the analysis, by no means prevail throughout the bureaucratic structure. There are numerous elements that reveal no positive feedback from their consequences to make them functional for operations. To cite only one example: an increase in size promotes task differentiation but not the expansion of the administrative staff. This is a dysfunctional consequence, since task differentiation lowers operating costs only in small agencies but raises them in larger ones unless supplemented by an adequate administrative staff.

The general conclusion suggested by the analysis is that the complex interrelations and higher-order interactions observed in the organizational structure are more likely to be functionally adapted by feedback than the separate attributes themselves. Feedback processes seem to produce not so much the elimination of dysfunctional elements as a greater functional interdependence among them in the bureaucratic structure. A refined conception of functional interdependence is implicit here, which would neither simply mean that the elements in a social structure are interrelated nor assume that each one of them serves important functions, but which would refer specifically to the fact that the complex, higher-order relationships among elements in the structure have been adapted by feedback to minimize dysfunctions. The interdependence is functional, although the specific factors may not be. External circumstances and vested powers often impose conditions on organizations that are dysfunctional for operations; feedback processes can at best minimize dysfunctions within this framework beyond their control.

28. PROFESSIONALIZATION AND BUREAUCRATIZATION IN LARGE PROFESSIONAL ORGANIZATIONS

Paul D. Montagna[1]

In recent years, several sociologists have emphasized the professionalization of modern industrial society.[2] Professionalization is seen as the newest major process that is an "effect" of technological change on the occupational structure of the community, the other processes being industrialization, urbanization, and bureaucratization.[3] As the number

and types of professionals in the work organization have increased, their conflict with the bureaucratic process has generally deepened.[4] However, it has been shown that a reconciliation can be achieved between the two,[5] that, in fact, the professionalization

Reprinted by permission of the publisher, University of Chicago Press, from *American Journal of Sociology*, 74 (September 1968), 138–45.

[1] This study was supported by National Science Foundation grant GS-804 and by a New York University fellowship. I wish to thank Harry Gracey, Marvin Koenigsberg, and Erwin O. Smigel for their comments and advice on earlier drafts of this paper.

[2] Nelson N. Foote, "The Professionalization of Labor in Detroit," *American Journal of Sociology*, LVIII (January, 1953), 371–80; Howard M. Vollmer and Donald L. Mills, "Nuclear Technology and the Professionalization of Labor," *American Journal of Sociology*, LXVII (May, 1962), 690–96; Harold L. Wilensky, "The Professionalization of Everyone?" *American Journal of Sociology*, LXX (September, 1964), 137–58; William A. Faunce and Donald A. Clelland, "Professionalization and Stratification Patterns in an Industrial Community," *American Journal of Sociology*, LXXII (January, 1967), 341–50.
[3] Faunce and Clelland, "Professionalization

and Stratification Patterns." The authors acknowledge the classification of the latter three processes by Maurice Stein, *The Eclipse of Community* (Princeton, N.J.: Princeton University Press, 1960).
[4] Among the earlier examinations of this development are: Logan Wilson, *The Academic Man* (New York: Oxford University Press, 1942); Peter M. Blau, *The Dynamics of Bureaucracy* (Chicago: University of Chicago Press, 1955); Roy G. Francis and Robert C. Stone, *Service and Procedure in Bureaucracy* (Minneapolis: University of Minnesota Press, 1956); Harold L. Wilensky, *Intellectuals in Labor Unions: Organizational Pressures on Professional Roles* (New York: Free Press, 1956); Alvin W. Gouldner, "Cosmopolitans and Locals: Toward an Analysis of Latent Social Roles —Parts I and II," *Administrative Science Quarterly*, II (1957, 1958), 281–306, 444–80.
[5] For example, Mary E. W. Goss, "Influence and Authority among Physicians in an Outpatient Clinic," *American Sociological Review*, XXVI (February, 1961), 39–50; Ronald G. Corwin, "The Professional Employee: A Study of Conflict in Nursing Roles," *American Journal of Sociology*, LXVI (May, 1961), 604–15; Howard M.

and bureaucratization processes are of necessity interdependent in bureaucratic organizations.[6]

For professional organizations[7] a similar interdependence has been suggested by Litwak, which he calls *professional bureaucracy,* a third model of organization which is, in effect, a synthesis of professional and bureaucratic models.[8] Upon examin-

ing large law firms, Smigel uncovered a pattern of bureaucracy which also is given the name of "professional bureaucracy."[9]

In an analysis of the largest professional organizations extant, the "Big Eight" public accounting firms, I inquired into the relationship among the aforementioned processes. A form of professional bureaucracy was found which combined elements of the perspectives of both Litwak and Smigel, thereby indicating their complementarity, and which disclosed changes in the relationship as measured by organizational variables of size, centralization, and size of administrative component.

BACKGROUND AND PROCEDURE

The Big Eight are international public accounting firms[10] founded

---

Vollmer, "Entrepreneurship and Professional Productivity among Research Scientists," *In* Howard M. Vollmer and Donald L. Mills (eds.), *Professionalization* (Englewood Cliffs, N.J.: Prentice-Hall, Inc., 1966), pp. 276–82; Richard H. Hall, "Some Organizational Considerations in the Professional-Organizational Relationship," *Administrative Science Quarterly,* XII (December, 1967), 461–78.

[6] William Kornhauser, *Scientists in Industry: Conflict and Accommodation* (Berkeley: University of California Press, 1962), p. 197; Blau, *The Dynamics of Bureaucracy* (rev. ed.; Chicago: University of Chicago Press, 1963), p. 9, describes an interdependence maintained in an environment of continual change.

[7] A professional organization is here defined as an organization in which: (1) members of one or more professional groups define and achieve the primary organizational goals (as compared with a professional association—a group organized to initiate and promote general professional objectives of the entire profession or segments thereof); (2) the majority of the people in the organization are professionals; (3) the administrative hierarchy of authority lies within the firm, whereas authority in professional matters is placed in the hands of the professional associations; (4) the profession promotes norms of personal autonomy and altruistic action in all matters relating to use of the body of knowledge.

[8] Eugene Litwak, "Models of Bureaucracy Which Permit Conflict," *American Journal of Sociology,* LXVII (September, 1961), 182. The author does not use the term "professional organization," but the examples he gives—a large hospital, a graduate school, a research organization—fit the definition (see fn. 7, above). The third

model is a "co-ordination" of the unlike efficiencies of the first two: the Weberian (bureaucratic) model of recurrent events and traditional knowledge and the human relations (professional) model of uncertainty situations—ever developing, nonrecurring events involving new knowledge.

[9] Erwin O. Smigel, *The Wall Street Lawyer: Professional Organization Man?* (New York: Free Press, 1964), pp. 275–86: Utilizing Gouldner's rules criterion for distinguishing three patterns of bureaucracy (Alvin W. Gouldner, *Patterns of Industrial Bureaucracy* [New York: Free Press, 1954], pp. 216–17), Smigel depicts a fourth pattern, professional bureaucracy, which is composed of a system of rules external to the organization, is devised by professional associations and the government, and which conditions the behavior of the lawyer through a long socialization process.

[10] The eight firms, alphabetically, are: Arthur Andersen & Co.; Ernst & Ernst; Haskins & Sells; Lybrand, Ross Bros. & Montgomery; Peat, Marwick, Mitchell & Co.; Price Waterhouse & Co.; Touche, Ross, Bailey & Smart; Arthur Young & Co.

around the turn of the century as small, local partnerships to manage the bookkeeping and accounting of corporations. With the growth of these clients over the succeeding decades and with the federal requirements of taxation and annual audit set up in the 1930s, the firms expanded their auditing services. Each firm presently has an average of eighty offices located in forty foreign countries and fifty offices located in the major cities of the United States. Offices of the largest American cities contain upward of fifty, and in a few instances more than 1,000, public accountants. The average size of a firm, including all offices, is 5,500.

The focus for this study is the largest offices of the Big Eight, located in New York City.[11] Each office, averaging 1,500 personnel contains three separate hierarchies: one of public accountants, one of non-accounting "management services" experts, and a non-professional supporting staff. The largest group, the public accountants, number about 1,000, of whom approximately half are in the beginning position of "junior." Another 300 are seniors, 100 are managers, and the 100 top positions are filled by partners. The average size of the management services hierarchy is 200. Slightly more than half of these are "associates," another quarter are at the next higher level of supervisor, and the remaining 15 percent are at the highest level of "principal." The clerical staff of 300 constitutes the third major group

of the firm, with a system of ordered positions similar to the clerical arrangement found in large bureaucratic departments.

Each firm is also stratified according to four major areas of work. The largest area, auditing, is the primary function of the firm—examining the financial structure and processes of the client. The tax area includes tasks ranging from preparation of corporate and individual tax returns to tax advice on mergers, reorganizations, liquidations, estate planning, and special surveys. The accounting personnel perform the duties of these two areas.[12] In the third area, management services, are located most of the non-accounting specialists (engineers, mathematicians, social scientists), who inform and advise clients on data processing, operations research, general management, personnel, organizational structure, marketing, and other economic considerations. The fourth area, firm administration, is shared by partners and some managers. It consists mostly of recruitment of personnel and their assignment and of periodic meetings on serious client matters.

The work of these firms is extremely important to the financial and investment communities. Collectively, these eight firms audit nearly half the total corporate wealth of the United States. They audit 94 percent of the 500 largest industrial corporations

[11] The national and international executive quarters for these firms are, with two exceptions, located in New York City. This policy-making group functions independently of the operating or "line" offices in New York City, but is usually housed in the same building.

[12] Within each of these work areas there is further specialization by the CPA. Although a partner has a specialty within an area, e.g., corporate reorganizations or tax planning, he assumes responsibility for the entire audit of each of his approximately thirty-five clients. As a result, specialization is limited to that amount of time remaining after his examination and analysis of all financial and related aspects of the client organization.

and the same percentage of the fifty largest merchandising firms, the fifty largest transportation companies, and the fifty largest utility companies.[13] The smaller organizations are not excluded; nor are those which are not required by law to be audited.[14] The average number of clients for a Big Eight firm is 10,000.

Initially, a pilot study was carried out at each firm. On the basis of these broad reviews, a self-administered questionnaire was developed, pretested, and mailed to a systematic random sample of the New York City offices of three Big Eight firms. The sample was stratified first on the basis of the four major work areas and then within each area by position in firm. A highly satisfactory return was received on the first mailing for a total number of 111.[15] From purposive samples constructed based on position in firm, fifty-one standardized interviews were conducted at six of the

eight firms.[16] At one of these six firms, observation was conducted of the entire work process at a client's offices and of the firm's recruitment procedures.

ORGANIZATIONAL SIZE, CENTRALIZATION, AND ADMINISTRATION

From the pilot studies it was obvious that the first task of the research was to detect how professional organizations of such large size manage to remain relatively free from increasing bureaucratization.[17] First, examination of apportionment of work time showed that total time of all professionals in firm administration averaged 12 percent of total professional work time. This administrative work is spread among 40 percent of the professional staff, and only 4 percent

---

[13] This amounts to $300 billion + in total sales and net revenues and $400 billion + in total assets, based on the lists in *The Fortune Directory* (1965) (as compared with mention of auditors in the 1965 series of Moody's industrial, public utility, and transportation manuals and *Poor's Register of Corporations, Directors and Executives* [1965]), and personal telephone calls. These percentages are relatively stable over the span of a few years, because clients rarely change their auditors, and rarely do they fall from their top listing during that time.

[14] One Big Eight firm alone audits more than 1,000 banks, 700 savings and loan associations, 700 insurance companies, and 1,200 non-profit institutions, including universities, hospitals, and local, state, and federal governmental bodies; from T. A. Wise, "The Very Private World of Peat, Marwick, Mitchell," *Fortune,* LXXIV (July 1, 1966), 91.

[15] The total return was 92, 85, and 66 percent for the three firms. Homogeneity and, in some cases, size of the thirteen subsamples limited the disproportionateness of the stratification.

[16] For a total sample number of 162 for the eight firms. Thirty-nine interviews contained a majority of the items appearing on the questionnaire. The remaining twelve focused on areas of special knowledge of those interviewees in positions of senior partner, management services director, and executive partner. Two firms granted only a single lengthy interview and no questionnaires. Enough material was gathered on size and work apportionment to include it in the analysis. In these two cases, the problems of professional conservatism and secrecy outweighed the interest to participate any further. These problems of gaining access I have examined in my Ph.D. thesis, "Bureaucracy and Change in Large Professional Organizations: A Functional Analysis of Large Public Accounting Firms" (unpublished, New York University, 1967), pp. 36–46.

[17] Bureaucracy is in this instance defined as the process of rationalized efficiency, according to Weber's characteristics; H. H. Gerth and C. Wright Mills (eds.), *From Max Weber: Essays in Sociology* (New York: Oxford University Press, 1946), pp. 196–98.

spend the majority of their time in it. Clerical staff comprise 20 percent of the firm. This produces a grand total of 32 percent spent in non-professional work.

Second, the formal managerial decision-making structure of a Big Eight firm is highly centralized, with a senior partner as "president" of the firm and chairman of the executive or managing committee. The committee is composed of partner-directors for each of the firm's major areas of specialization, with lines of authority within each area and for each region of the country. Even though every partner is given personal responsibility over his audit for the client, the system of checks on his work, along with the formal structure, allows the firms to be classified as highly centralized. One executive partner succinctly stated: "'The audit partner calls the signals on the job. He can consult on his problems with any specialists in the firm. One partner reviews all opinions [final report on the client], but this comes after the fact, after the opinion is issued. The partner is responsible to the partnership for his work, but he has complete autonomy within the firm."

How is it, then, that these firms spend so little of their professional man-hours in administration? First, administrative authority is located at the very top. General firm policy is decided by the executive committee. Other administrative tasks such as recruitment and assignment are shared by the partnership as equally as possible. In two of the firms, personnel department positions are filled by a system of rotating partners every few years. As already evidenced, nearly all partners and professional employees remain active in client work. Otherwise, they feel the stigma

of being known as a "kept accountant." Second, the public accountant's work is conducted at the client's offices in small groups of three to ten persons, thereby spreading lower-echelon administration throughout the organization. Informality within the work groups is the norm. For each client, the partner selects a work team of managers, seniors, and juniors on the basis of their technical background and their ability to work smoothly with both client and partner. These employees move from one work team to another and from one partner to another several times a year. Centralization therefore is compatible with these professionalized firms.

The comparison of the relation of size to administrative component and to degree of centralization for these firms can be made to only one other study without becoming methodologically inconsistent.[18] This is the analysis of professional organizations of public personnel agencies.[19] The relationship, according to size, is similar in both studies. Using the

[18] William A. Rushing, "Organizational Size and Administration: The Problems of Causal Homogeneity and a Heterogeneous Category," *Pacific Sociological Review*, IX (Fall, 1966), 100–108, emphasizes that the many studies dealing with the relationship between organizational size and relative size of administrative component have reached inconsistent results because total administrative component is a heterogeneous category with respect to types of occupations; therefore, it is not significant as a single total measure. Rather, classes of personnel must be related. In the case of the studies under consideration, only one class is dealt with—large-firm professionals, social agency and public accounting.

[19] Peter M. Blau, Wolf V. Heydebrand, and Robert E. Stauffer, "The Structure of Small Bureaucracies," *American Sociological Review*, XXXI (April, 1966), 179–91; see especially Table 2, p. 183.

measurement bases for the agencies,[20] the largest personnel agencies and the largest accounting firms display a high degree of professionalization, high centralization, and a small administrative component. And the changed relationship for medium-sized agencies (approximately 200 personnel) and medium-sized accounting firms[21] remains alike: a high degree of professionalization and low centralization, whatever the administrative ratio. All twelve accounting firms, the eight large and four medium-sized, follow the pattern of the majority of personnel agencies of like size. More important, the eight largest firms show a much higher measurement on these three variables than do the personnel agencies. Further investigation uncovered factors that indicate the determining variable to be professionalization.[22]

---

[20] *Ibid.*, p. 183: "The administrative apparatus ratio is *low* when the proportion of clerks among the total staff is less than 60 percent; *high* when it is 60 percent or more.

"The managerial hierarchy is *centralized* when the ratio of non-clerical personnel in managerial positions to non-clerical personnel in non-supervisory positions, excluding those listed as neither, is less than one to three; it is *dispersed* when the ratio is one to three or more.

"Professionalization is *low* when the proportion of the operating staff (excluding managers as well as clerks) who are required to have, at least, a college degree with a specified major, is less than 50 percent; *high* when it is 50 percent or more."

[21] For purposes of comparison by size, four medium-sized accounting firms (average size 200 personnel) were extensively interviewed: The hierarchy of job titles and occupational specialties is basically the same as that of the large firms, except that the Big Eight afford greater specialization in each work area.

[22] All of the Big Eight have an administrative ratio of less than 30 percent, are centralized at a ratio of less than one to six if all partners are included as managerial

PROFESSIONALIZATION VS. BUREAUCRATIZATION: CONFLICT AND INTERDEPENDENCE

Blau feels that the unusual combination of centralization and professionalization is possible because there are "substitute methods of modern administration," such as detailed statistical records of performance, which check on the work of subordinates and obtain information on operations without frequent direct supervision.[23] In the highly professionalized accounting firms, besides the annual opinions and other performance reports, additional substitute methods of administration are the rules and procedures external to the organizations. These are the responsibility of the professional association of CPA's, the American Institute of Certified Public Accountants. These external

---

personnel, and are 100 percent professionalized (using Blau's bases for measurement—see n. 20, above). It is obvious that for highly professionalized organizations more sensitive measures must be developed. For the accounting firms, professionalization is given a wider definition, which includes the attributes of: a body of knowledge with a developed intellectual technique, supported by a formalized educational process with standardized testing and licensing, a code of ethics governing relations with colleagues, clients, and other external organizations, and a professional association to facilitate the maintenance and development of all of the former. Attempts to empirically measure these and other ideal type attributes are found in Richard M. Lynch, "Professional Standards for Management Consulting in the United States" (unpublished Ph.D. thesis, Graduate School of Business Administration, Harvard University, 1959), pp. 30–31, 138–39; Montagna, *op. cit.* (see n. 16, above), chap. iv.

[23] Blau, *The Dynamics of Bureaucracy* (rev. ed.), chap. iii; Blau, Heydebrand, and Stauffer, "The Structure of Small Bureaucracies."

rules include an elaborate and much revised code of ethics, a newly codified volume of principles of accounting, and revised auditing standards and procedures. They are constructed and revised by Institute committees in which the views of the large firms are well represented. These rules serve as a foundation for the firms' more specific internal rules, a few of which are more stringent, others of which merely expand on the external rules. Nearly to a man, the total sample agreed that compared with internal rules, the external rules were the more important rules for their firms and for the profession as a whole. For the firms, the number of problems inherent in constructing and enforcing these professional standards are greatly reduced. And changes are made without an opposing vested interest—there are virtually no full-time administrators whose jobs depend on an elaborate bureaucratic system of one specified routine based on the affected rules.

In the case of these organizations, then, bureaucratization, in the pejorative sense of dysfunction, that is, routine, rigidity, overconformity, is limited by the external rules and by personal autonomy. However, because of the tremendous increase in the number, extent, and specificity of these rules, CPA's fear a severe limitation on the scope of their professional judgment. What was once unwritten rule or mystique is now rationalized; in the process of formalizing its rules, the profession transforms that knowledge from an intellectual to a mechanical technique. As one senior partner put it, "The client asks not what to do but how to do it, as the body of knowledge becomes detailed and easier to interpret." The power of the expert

disappears as soon as the area of uncertainty (professional judgment) can be translated into rules and programs.[24] As one partner concluded, "We could audit IBM [the ninth largest corporation in America] in almost one day with very little risk because their internal systems of control are so tight." Partly because of rule making, partly because of computerization, the traditional annual audit, required by federal law, is becoming what one executive partner termed "the annual nuisance." The CPA finds he must submit to detailed professional requirements when constructing reports and opinions for his client. Yet, he should be free of such encumbrances to properly exercise his professional judgment.

The public accountant's response to this threat has been to expand into new areas of uncertainty, especially management services[25] and taxes.

[24] Michel Crozier, *The Bureaucratic Phenomenon* (Chicago: University of Chicago Press, 1964), p. 299: "The elimination of the 'bureaucratic systems of organization' in the dysfunctional sense is the condition for the growth of 'bureaucratization' in the Weberian sense." Also, Michel Crozier, "Crise et renouveau dans l'administration française," *Sociologie du travail,* VIII (July–September, 1966), 327; Peter M. Blau and W. Richard Scott, *Formal Organizations* (San Francisco: Chandler Publishing Co., 1962), pp. 240–42; Victor A. Thompson, "Bureaucracy and Innovation," *Administrative Science Quarterly,* X (June, 1965), 4; James D. Thompson, *Organizations in Action* (New York: McGraw-Hill, 1967). The writings of a leading public-accounting spokesman reflect this thinking: John L. Carey, *The CPA Plans for the Future* (New York: American Institute of Certified Public Accountants, 1965), pp. 191–92, 227. A theoretical perspective of uncertainty is given by Ralf Dahrendorf, *Essays in the Theory of Society* (Stanford, Calif.: Stanford University Press, 1968).

[25] More recently, there has been experimentation with the management attest, an

Presently, each of these areas accounts for 20 percent of the professional man-hours in a Big Eight firm. Many CPA's contend that, like taxes, management services were always an integral part of the audit process, and indeed there is very little that cannot be classified within the broad definition of "internal control" (an audit term). Regardless, new developments in management services, such as computerization, offer CPA's the ability to integrate the planning, measuring, attesting, and communicating of the total information system of an economic organization.[26] Thirty-five percent of the total sample voluntarily suggested this area (called "operations auditing") to be the only one where judgment and creativity are found to a significant degree. It is the person who is familiar with the computer process who *composes* an "automated audit."

The movement into management services provides the profession with new non-rationalized intellectual techniques. But at the same time, this knowledge is not integrated within the profession and has proved to be

dysfunctional to the firms. If the management services' work for a client is coordinated with the partner's audit, some administrative authority will tend to be legitimated in terms of incumbency of office. In this situation, obedience is stressed as an end in itself because the CPA as administrator is not able to judge the non-accountant expert on the basis of that expert's knowledge. Rules are initiated by one party (a CPA)—characteristic of "punishment centered" bureaucracy.[27] Added to this is the task of each firm having to organize independently and enforce a new code of ethics and procedures for this technical field until, in time, the professional organization takes over this function.

In sum, the move into areas of uncertainty provides an important basis for continued professionalization—an expanded body of knowledge which supports an intellectual technique and requisite judgment.[28] However, because of this, new bureaucratic

audit conducted for stockholders and other interested third parties to determine management's compliance with certain of its own prearranged standards for information collection, decisioning, and control processes, but not of the results of these processes. Some in the profession are now suggesting that the CPA should begin to think about prearranging the standards for management.

[26] These functions of the economic organization are defined by leaders in the profession. For example Herman W. Bevis, "The Accounting Function in Economic Progress," *Journal of Accountancy*, CVI (August, 1958), 27–34; John L. Carey (ed.), *The Accounting Profession: Where Is It Headed?* (New York: American Institute of Certified Public Accountants, 1962), p. 11.

[27] Alvin W. Gouldner, "Organizational Analysis," *In* Robert K. Merton, Leonard Broom, and Leonard S. Cottrell, Jr. (eds.), *Sociology Today: Problems and Prospects* (New York: Basic Books, 1959), p. 403. See also a summary discussion by Louis R. Pondy, "Organizational Conflict: Concepts and Models," *Administrative Science Quarterly*, XII (September, 1967), 314–17.

[28] This move takes place because of the rationalization of CPA knowledge in external rules. As Faunce and Clelland ("Professionalization and Stratification Patterns," p. 342) point out: "While industrialization, urbanization, bureaucratization, and professionalization may occur *simultaneously*, they do not ordinarily develop at the same rate. More typically, they form a *sequence* with a high level of development of one acting as a spur to development of the next. Increased professionalization is, *in part*, an outgrowth of the bureaucratic emphasis upon expertise and rationalism" (emphasis my own, P. D. M.).

problems rapidly emerge. The process can be examined beginning at any stage of its development. External rules form a *pattern* (to use Smigel's term) for professional bureaucracy. They inject uniformity into the social system. But the danger of uniformity and the normal rate of technological development spur the search for new areas of professional control. At any one time in the organizational process, there is a conflicting yet interdependent mixture of uniform and non-uniform events, of rationalization and uncertainty (to use Litwak's description).

CONCLUSIONS

On the basis of the analysis, three generalizations can be drawn concerning large professional organizations: (1) The more highly professionalized the organization, the more highly centralized it is and the smaller its administrative component. (2) As organizations become larger and more complex, technically, strong patterns of punishment-centered bureaucracy may form which are not found in smaller organizations.[29] (3) The collection, analysis, classification, standardization, and enforcement of external rules carried out by the professional association may involve the simultaneous occurrence of rationalization of one body of knowledge and the development of another. With regard to (3), both occur-

rences tend to create dysfunctions. Even though the process of professional bureaucracy allows for change, there is concern that the change may be too rapid or far reaching, as well as too precise or narrow.[30] Also, with rapid innovation, the firms must solve the immediate problems of administration until the slower-moving professional association develops profession-wide norms and laws. The rate of change must somehow be regulated, or the process will be disrupted.

Ultimately of more concern is the problem caused by increased size in (2). If these largest firms are the prototype for the future organization,[31] the serious problems of bureaucracy may not be so easily overcome in a future accelerated process of professional bureaucracy generated by more rapid social and technological change.[32]

[29] This pattern was not a significant one in the twenty largest law firms in the United States (Smigel, *Wall Street Lawyer.* p. 279), which are, on the average, only one-tenth the size of the large public accounting firms.

[30] Wilensky, "The Professionalization of Everyone?" (see n. 2, above), pp. 148–49, defines the problem as knowledge being too vague (e.g., social work) or too precise and that there may be an optimal base for professional practice.

[31] Warren G. Bennis, *Changing Organizations.* (New York: McGraw-Hill 1966), chap. i. Bennis forecasts "on thin empirical ice" that the work organizations of the future will contain adaptive, rapidly changing, temporary systems of diverse professionals operating in complex and creative environments and will displace bureaucracy as the primary form of organizational structure. Also, Harold L. Wilensky, *Organizational Intelligence: Knowledge and Policy in Government and Industry.* (New York: Basic Books, 1967), pp. 46–47. Galbraith's "technostructure" agrees with this description; John Kenneth Galbraith, *The New Industrial State* (Boston: Houghton Mifflin Co., 1967), pp. 57–71, 168–75.

[32] See Litwak's explanation for his assumption that "non-uniform events will constitute a major factor in organizational analysis in the foreseeable future" (Litwak, "Models of Bureaucracy," p. 181).

29. THE HIERARCHY OF AUTHORITY
IN ORGANIZATIONS

Advances in the social sciences do not occur in straight lines of uniform progress, as the recurrent rediscoveries of half-forgotten classics indicate, be it Simmel's analysis of conflict or Durkheim's of the division of labor, the insights of Karl Marx, Adam Smith, or even Plato. But neither does the development of sociology move in circles or simply fluctuate between alternative theoretical approaches. There is some continuity, and there is some progress. The analysis of pattern variables by Parsons and Shils surely is a refinement of Toennies' concepts of *Gemeinschaft* and *Gesellschaft*, for example, and the research of Lipset, Trow, and Coleman clearly advances our knowledge of union democracy far beyond Michels' theory of oligarchy which inspired it. The pattern of scientific development may be described as dialectical. Mounting criticisms of one approach lead to concentration on another designed to overcome the first's shortcomings; yet the second approach is likely, in due

time, to reveal limitations of its own that encourage still other lines of scientific attack; but slowly some progress is made.[1]

The study of formal organizations is a case in point. Weber's theoretical analysis, which has long dominated the field, was increasingly criticized for presenting an idealized conception of bureaucracy and for examining only its formal characteristics and ignoring the informal modifications that occur in actual practice. In response to this criticism, research on organizations concentrated on informal relations and unofficial practices, the attitudes of individual members and their observable behavior. The resulting studies of the informal or-

Reprinted by permission of the publisher, University of Chicago Press, from American Journal of Sociology, *73 (January 1968), 453–67.*

[1] This paper is the sixth report of the Comparative Organization Research Program, supported by grant GS-553 from the National Science Foundation, which is gratefully acknowledged. I also want to thank Marshall W. Meyer for his excellent comments on an earlier draft of this paper as well as for his assistance in the collection and analysis of the data, and Charles Perrow for his helpful criticisms. The staff of the National Opinion Research Center did an outstanding job in conducting a rather unusual survey of organizations and obtaining the required data from virtually all finance departments selected.

ganization of work groups and the actual performance of duties in bureaucracies have undoubtedly contributed much to our understanding of these complex structures. While complementing Weber's approach, however, the new focus neglected the basic theoretical problem to which he addressed himself. One question a student of organizations may ask is how the existing conditions in a bureaucracy affect attitudes and conduct, for instance, why bureaucratic conditions stifle initiative and what the processes involved are.[2] But there is another question that can be asked, namely, why certain conditions emerge in organizations in the first place, for example, what determines the development and the characteristics of the authority structure. Weber was concerned with the second problem—explaining the configurations of bureaucratic conditions —whereas recent research focused on the first—investigating their consequences for individuals and groups— to the virtual exclusion of the second, in part because the case study method usually employed is not suitable for answering the second question.

A theory of formal organization, as distinguished from a theory of group life in a bureaucratic context, seeks to explain why organizations develop various characteristics, such as a multilevel hierarchy or decentralized authority. To furnish these explanations requires that the characteristics of organizations are not taken as given but the conditions that produce them are investigated. Thus one may ask how the qualifications of an organization's staff influence the structure of authority in it, or generally what conditions affect the shape of the hierarchy, which are the two problems posed in this paper. In order to answer this kind of question, it is necessary to compare different organizations and not merely to study the influence exerted on behavior by the conditions found in a single case. The method of comparison might involve analyzing bureaucracies in different historical periods, which was Weber's approach; or intensive examination of two contrasting forms of organization, as in Stinchombe's study cited below; or quantitative comparisons of many organizations and multivariate analysis of their characteristics. The last procedure is adopted here.

The assumption made in choosing this procedure is that the analysis of the interdependence between organizational attributes based on systematic comparisons of large numbers of organizations promises to contribute most to organizational theory. If the ultimate aim of this theory is to derive general principles that explain the emergence of structures with various characteristics, the first step must be to advance more limited generalizations that specify the conditions that affect the development of different characteristics, and quantitative comparisons permit such specification. The analysis of the authority structure to be presented is based on data collected from several hundred government agencies. Only agencies of a specific type are directly compared, to eliminate the disturbing influence of differences between types; but the results of one such study are confronted with those of another, to discern whether conclusions are confined to a single type. The inquiry is restricted to the formal attributes

[2] See Robert K. Merton, *Social Theory and Social Structure* (2d ed.; New York: Free Press, 1957), pp. 195–206.

of organizations, since it was not possible to collect data on informal patterns and individual attitudes in hundreds of government agencies. This limitation of the approach to organizational research here adopted may well give rise in the future to different approaches not similarly limited to easily accessible data. But the prospect of a possible counter-trend in the future should not deter us now from exploiting the scientific contribution that systematic comparisons of even relatively simple organizational traits can make at the present stage of knowledge.

The exposition is deliberately designed to call attention to continuities in bureaucratic theory and research, and the paper also seeks to reveal the role that theoretical speculations which go beyond the empirical evidence play in establishing continuities between different investigations. The research reported is conceived within the framework of Weber's theoretical tradition; it follows his approach of studying the interrelations between formal conditions in bureaucratic structures, rather than the individuals and human relations within them, and it deals with two substantive issues his theory poses—the relationship between expertness and authority, and the significance of the formal hierarchy of offices. Moreover, the continuities from one empirical investigation to another are indicated as the tentative interpretations of earlier findings are tested and refined in a subsequent study. I shall try to illustrate that advancing highly speculative generalizations in interpreting empirical findings serves important scientific functions, for such inferential conjectures are the basis for the cumulation of scientific knowledge, provided that they are followed up by further research. The only connection between different empirical investigations, and hence the only source of cumulation, is the generalizations derived from each that go beyond its limited evidence.

PROFESSIONAL AND BUREAUCRATIC AUTHORITY

The relationship between the expert qualifications of a professional staff and the bureaucratic authority vested in a hierarchy of offices poses an interesting theoretical issue. Professionalism and bureaucracy have much in common, such as impersonal detachment, specialized technical expertness, and rational decision making based on universalistic standards. There are also divergent elements, however, and professional principles often come into conflict with the requirements of bureaucratic authority. Weber implied that the professional authority rooted in expert technical knowledge and the bureaucratic authority rooted in a hierarchy of offices with legitimate claims to disciplined compliance tend to occur together, both being distinctive characteristics of complex rational organizations. "The role of technical qualifications in bureaucratic organizations is continually increasing."[3] But, in addition, "each lower office is under the control and supervision of a higher one."[4] The assumption that professional expertness and bureaucratic discipline are simply two aspects of the rational organization of large-scale tasks not

---

[3] Max Weber, *The Theory of Social and Economic Organization* (New York: Oxford University Press, 1947), p. 335.
[4] *Ibid.*, p. 331.

only conflicts with the prevailing impression that professional work suffers if subjected to bureaucratic discipline but also has been questioned on both systematic theoretical and empirical grounds.

In a well-known footnote, Parsons criticizes Weber for confounding two analytically distinct types of authority.[5] Professional authority rests on the certified superior competence of the expert, which prompts others voluntarily to follow his directives because they consider doing so to be in their own interest. Bureaucratic authority, in contrast, rests on the legitimate power of command vested in an official position, which obligates subordinates to follow directives under the threat of sanctions. Superior knowledge is not required for bureaucratic authority (expert knowledge is not what authorizes the policeman to direct traffic, for example, or what induces us to obey his signals), whereas it is essential for professional control, and mandatory compliance is enforced by coercive sanctions in the bureaucratic but not in the professional case. Gouldner similarly stresses the difference between the influence exerted on the basis of technical competence and the compelling authority in a bureaucratic hierarchy, and he derives from this distinction two contrasting forms of bureaucracy—"representative" and "punishment-centered."[6]

Research results also challenge Weber's assumption that technical expertness and hierarchically enforced discipline typically occur together. Stinchcombe's comparison of two industries suggests, for example, that the technical skills of construction workers, which contrast with the low level of skill in mass production, promote rational performance and therefore serve as a substitute for the bureaucratic hierarchy through which the work in mass production is rationally organized.[7] Thus technical expertness and hierarchical authority seem to be alternatives, not complementary. Udy's research on the organization of production in 150 non-industrial societies arrives at parallel results.[8] He finds that several bureaucratic characteristics, including a hierarchical authority structure, are directly correlated with one another but not, even inversely, with several rational characteristics, including specialization, which may be considered a primitive forerunner of technical expertness, and so may rational work procedures in general. Udy concludes: "Bureaucracy and rationality tend to be mutually inconsistent in the same formal organization."[9] It is noteworthy that both of these studies do not deal with advanced levels of professionalization but with rather rudimentary forms of expert qualifications.

The various components of professionalism must be distinguished in analyzing its implications for hierarchical authority in organizations. Full-fledged professionalization entails not only expert skills but also a body of abstract knowledge underlying them, a self-governing association

---

[5] Talcott Parsons, "Introduction," *ibid.*, pp. 58–60.

[6] Alvin W. Gouldner, *Patterns of Industrial Bureaucracy* (Glencoe, Ill.: Free Press, 1954), esp. pp. 21–24.

[7] Arthur L. Stinchcombe, "Bureaucratic and Craft Administration of Production," *Administrative Science Quarterly*, IV (1959), 168–87.

[8] Stanley H. Udy, Jr., " 'Bureaucracy' and 'Rationality' in Weber's Organization Theory," *American Sociological Review*, XXIV (1959), 791–95.

[9] *Ibid.*, p. 794.

of professional peers, professional standards of workmanship and ethical conduct, and an orientation toward service. Some of these factors may easily come into conflict with the discipline required by bureaucratic authority. Research indicates that a professional orientation toward service and a bureaucratic orientation toward disciplined compliance with procedures are opposite approaches toward work and often create conflict in organizations.[10] Besides, the identification of professionals with an external reference group may well lessen their loyalty to the organization.[11] It is also reasonable to expect that conflicts arise as decisions made strictly on the basis of professional standards are recurrently set aside for the sake of administrative considerations by bureaucratic authorities. All these conflicts refer to fairly advanced aspects of professionalization. But Weber's concern was not so much with these components of professionalism as with technical expertness, which he held to be an integral part of hierarchically organized bureaucracies. The findings of Stinchcombe and Udy imply, however, that even a moderate degree of technical expertness conflicts with bureaucratic authority.

Yet there can be no question that hierarchically organized bureaucracies do employ personnel with expert training and qualifications. As a matter of fact, formal organizations typically *require* their staff to meet certain educational or technical qualifications, and these requirements indicate that a minimum of expertness is indeed an integral part of the bureaucratic structure. If expertness itself is, nevertheless, incompatible with some elements of strict bureaucratic authority, as the findings cited suggest, the question is how it modifies the structure of authority in organizations. The present paper addresses itself first to this problem of how variations in the qualifications of the personnel affect the authority structure in formal organizations, and it then turns to the question of how other conditions affect the hierarchy of authority.

A simple working hypothesis for investigating the first problem can be derived from a few plausible considerations. Entrance requirements that assure that the agency staff (meaning all personnel, in line as well as "staff" positions) has relatively high minimum qualifications might be expected to lessen the need for guidance and close supervision. The implication is that such expert requirements widen the span of control of managers, increasing the number of subordinates under each,[12] and therefore reduce the proportion of managerial person-

[10] See, e.g., Roy G. Francies and Robert C. Stone, *Service and Procedure in Bureaucracy* (Minneapolis: University of Minnesota Press, 1956).

[11] See Alvin W. Gouldner, "Cosmopolitans and Locals," *Administrative Science Quarterly*, II (1957–58), 281–306, 444–80; Theodore Caplow and Reece J. McGee, *The Academic Marketplace* (New York: Basic Books, 1958), esp. p. 85; Everett C. Hughes, *Men and Their Work* (Glencoe, Ill.: Free Press, 1958), esp. p. 137; and Peter M. Blau and W. Richard Scott, *Formal Organizations* (San Francisco: Chandler Publishing Co., 1962), pp. 64–74.

[12] The assumption that less close supervision widens the span of control is made explicit by A. Janger, among others: "If the manager practices close supervision, . . . then he is decreasing the number of people he can supervise. He broadens his span by granting them more authority." See "Analyzing the Span of Control," *Management Record*, XXII (July–August, 1960), 9.

nel in the organization, because each superior can supervise more subordinates if they are experts than if their lower skills necessitate much guidance and checking. These inferences, which appear straightforward and perhaps even self-evident, suggest as an initial hypothesis that expert requirements decrease the ratio of managerial to non-supervisory personnel in organizations, which widens the average span of control.

STUDY OF PUBLIC PERSONNEL AGENCIES

This hypothesis was tested as part of a previously published study of 156 public personnel agencies,[13] and a brief summary of the pertinent results suffices to introduce the problems investigated in subsequent research. The data were collected by the Public Personnel Association through questionnaires to its members. They pertain to the executive agencies of the civil service commissions of most state and major local American governments, with the bias of selection favoring larger agencies and those identified with merit principles. These agencies are small bureaucracies, with a median staff of not quite seventeen (even after the ninety-six with a staff of less than five were eliminated from the analysis). The measure of expertness is whether the operating staff, excluding both managerial and clerical personnel, is required to have a college degree with a specified job-related

major.[14] The only available information on the hierarchy of authority is the ratio of managers to non-supervisory officials.[15]

The employment of experts with stipulated educational qualifications does not reduce the proportionate size of the managerial staff in public personnel agencies. On the contrary, under most conditions, though not under all, agencies that require their employees to meet relatively high qualifications are more likely than others to have a high ratio of managers. Expertness, moreover, . seems to prevent other conditions from reducing the proportion of managers. An increase in the division of labor tends to decrease the managerial ratio in the absence of expert requirements but increase it in their presence. The hypothesis that the expertness of the operating staff widens the span of supervisory control and consequently is reflected in a low ratio of managers is clearly negated by these results.

In the light of these negative findings we reconceptualized the meaning attributed to the managerial ratio. Since it does not appear reasonable that better-trained personnel officers are more closely supervised than those lacking similar qualifications, the initial assumption that a higher ratio of managers is indicative of

---

[13] For a full discussion, see Peter M. Blau, Wolf V. Heydebrand, and Robert E. Stauffer, "The Structure of Small Bureaucracies," *American Sociological Review*, XXXI (1966), 179–91.

[14] The measure was dichotomized in contingencies tables on the basis of whether at least half of the operating staff has to meet this requirement, but the actual distribution is bimodal, and in most organizations either all of the staff or none of it has to meet this educational requirement.

[15] The criterion of manager was being head of a division rather than a journeyman or apprentice, which probably includes most supervisory personnel in these small agencies, though some chiefs of small sections may have been excluded, particularly in the few large agencies (only seventeen have a staff of more than one hundred).

closer supervision must be questioned. An alternative interpretation of the significance of this measure, which is compatible with the findings, is that a low ratio of managers implies a centralized authority structure, with managerial authority concentrated in the hands of comparatively few officials. When administrative authority is centralized in few positions, management presumably is carried out largely by a central headquarters that issues directives to the operating staff, whereas management in a structure with a large proportion of authority positions probably entails more reciprocal adjustments as the result of the greater opportunities for communication between managerial and operating personnel.

The difference in assumptions between the original and the revised interpretations of the managerial ratio should be made explicit. The initial formulation assumed that few managers indicate a wide span of control, hence less close supervision, which permits subordinates to exercise more autonomy in their work. The reconceptualization assumes that few managers imply a centralized authority structure, which encourages management through one-sided directives with little feedback from operating levels, thus reducing the autonomy of subordinates. The empirical data, though they were the basis for the revision are not adequate to validate either set of assumptions. However, the reconceptualization permits some suggestive conjectures.

Appointing employees with expert qualifications and instituting a centralized authority structure appear to be alternative modes of organization, which are somewhat incompatible. This conclusion is in broad agreement with the one reached by both Stinchcombe and Udy in their empirical studies, as well as with the theoretical distinction Parsons makes between professional and bureaucratic authority. But our research specifies the source of the incompatibility. What is inappropriate for an organization staffed by experts is a hierarchy in which official authority is centralized in the hands of few managers. It seems paradoxical that more managers are required to direct employees with superior qualifications than those less well trained. The explanation lies in the implications of a low ratio of managers already adumbrated and in the implications of expert qualifications.

Expert training may be expected to make a man not only more independent in the performance of his duties but also more aware of the broader implications of his work and more capable of detecting operating problems and finding solutions for them than is an untrained person. Experts are more likely to resent having their discretion limited by managerial directives than employees whose lesser skills make them welcome some guidance. In addition, experts can make greater contributions to the improvement of operating procedures than men without specialized training. Hence, feedback communication from the operating staff is especially valuable for management if this staff consists of experts. To take full advantage of the contributions experts can make to operations, management must facilitate the flow of upward communication. A low ratio of managers tends to discourage upward communication, however, inasmuch as a small contingent of managers can most easily direct operations by issuing orders from a central headquarters to the staff. A high ratio of managers increases opportunities for communication between officials responsible for administrative and those responsible for operating decisions. Such extensive two-way communication is of special importance if the personnel has expert qualifications, not alone because experts tend to be more alienated by one-sided directives but particularly because they make greater contributions through feedback than persons with poorer qualifications.

In short, the interpretation suggested is that the added significance the expertness of the staff lends to the free flow of upward communication in organizations accounts for the association between expert requirements and a high ratio of managers. We were able to muster a bit of indirect evidence in support of this interpretation in the study of public personnel agencies. An expert staff improves operating economy in very small agencies, with a personnel of less than twenty, but it impedes economy in larger agencies unless the clerical staff is relatively large. In agencies of sufficient size to make communication a serious problem, the absence of an adequate clerical apparatus to maintain channels of communication has an adverse effect on operating economy if and only if the staff consists of experts.[16] This finding implies that expert qualifications of operating officials enhance the importance of communication, indirectly supporting our interpretation.

[16] Blau *et al.*, "Structure of Small Bureaucracies," p. 189, Table 8. Among larger agencies *with* an expert staff, 60 percent of those with a low but only 23 percent of those with a high clerical ratio operate at high cost; whereas in larger agencies *without* an expert staff, high cost is as unlikely with a low (24 percent) as with a high clerical ratio (33 percent).

Nevertheless, the generalizations we advanced rest on shaky grounds. They are based on data from only one kind of organization, a specific type of government agency. Besides, public personnel agencies are very small, while bureaucratic theory presumably deals with large organizations. (It should be noted, however, that the stereotype of the huge government bureaucracy with a staff of thousands is misleading as far as particular agencies of state and local governments are concerned, among which a personnel of one hundred is undoubtedly much above the average.) Moreover, the only measure of the hierarchy of authority available, the proportion of managers, is clearly insufficient to analyze this complex institution. Finally, the inference that expertness promotes a decentralized authority structure is highly speculative, since the implication is that decision making is decentralized, but a large proportion of managers is not necessarily indicative of decentralization of *decision making*. One might even argue that, on the contrary, the *smaller* the proportion of managers, the more likely will they be to delegate responsibilities to subordinates in order to lighten the burden of their duties.

STUDY OF GOVERNMENT FINANCE DEPARTMENTS

A study of 254 finance departments of state and local governments made it possible to test the hypothesis that staff expertness leads to decentralization of responsibilities, and further to explore the conditions that influence the structure of authority in organizations. Original data were collected for the purpose of this study by N.O.R.C. interviewers from informants (senior managers) in the major finance department of each government. The universe consists of the departments in all states, all counties with a population of more than 100,000, and all cities with a population of more than 50,000, in the United States, except those with a staff of fewer than twenty or with no subdivision of responsibilities into two or more units.[17] The sample comprises the entire universe, and information was obtained from 96.6 percent of these organizations. Although responsibilities vary, nearly all departments maintain financial records and preaudit disbursements, and the majority are also responsible for postauditing other departments, investment management, and fixed-asset accounting. The median department' has a staff of sixty, six major subdivisions, and four hierarchical levels.

A number of the questions raised by the conclusions of the earlier study can be answered by this research. Another type of government agency has now been investigated, making it possible to check whether the previous findings merely reflect some special conditions in personnel work. The organizations under examination are larger, with a minimum size of twenty instead of five and a median of sixty instead of seventeen, and a larger number of cases is available for analysis, increasing the reliability of findings. Of greatest importance is the fact that a variety of measures of the structure of authority were deliberately designed to permit refinement of the earlier inferences. Information was obtained on the proportion of managerial personnel, specifically defined as all officials with

supervisory duties; the number of levels in the hierarchy (the mean for the various divisions); the average span of control—number of subordinates—of first-line supervisors and that of middle managers; the proportion of their time managers spend on supervision; and the hierarchical level on which various specified decisions are made, furnishing direct indications of delegation of responsibilities and decentralization of authority. The index of expert requirements is the proportion of the staff expected to have a college degree, roughly parallel to the index used in the other study,[18] and departments are dichotomized on the basis of whether at least one-fifth of the total personnel (which is about two-fifths of the non-clerical personnel) is expected to meet the requirement of college graduation.

The basic finding reported from the study of public personnel agencies is confirmed by this research on another type of government agency; a high ratio of managerial personnel is more often found in finance departments with a large proportion of college-trained experts than in those with comparatively few employees so qualified (Table 1, row 1).[19] The

---

[17] Data on these smaller departments were also obtained, in this case by mail questionnaire, but they are not included in the present analysis.

[18] Although the number required to have a college degree in accounting was ascertained as well, which would furnish an index exactly parallel to that used in the previous study, this number was so low (an average of one-tenth of the staff) that the less stringent requirement—college degree whatever the major—is considered to be the preferable index of staff expertness.

[19] The implicit assumption that proportion of managers is inversely associated with span of control over the operating level is strongly supported by the data. The proportion of departments in which first-line supervisors average six or more subordinates is 72 percent in the 151 with a managerial ratio of less than one-quarter and 20 percent in the 102 with a higher managerial ratio.

TABLE 1 TRAINING REQUIREMENTS AND AUTHORITY STRUCTURE

| *Percentage of Finance Departments (In Cols. [1] and [2]) in Which:* | *Proportion of Staff Required to Have B.A.** | | *Yule's Q (Gamma)* |
	Low (1)	*High* (2)	(3)
1. The proportion of managers exceeds one-quarter of the total personnel	35 (147)	48 (106)	.27
2. The number of levels is four or more	36 (148)	51 (106)	.29
3. The mean span of control of first-line supervisors is six or more	56 (147)	44 (106)	−.23†
4. The mean span of control of middle managers is 1.6 or more	38 (135)	54 (100)	.32
5. The average manager spends more than two-fifths of his time supervising	52 (145)	38 (106)	−.29
6. Division heads make budgeting or accounting decisions	40 (122)	54 (86)	.26†
7. An official below the director recommends promotions and dismissals	30 (147)	45 (104)	.32

* Since this variable is not associated with size, it is not necessary to control size.

† All relationships are significant below the .05 level except these two, which are significant on the .08 and .06 levels, respectively.

more extensive data of the second study make it possible to stipulate the structural implications of the higher ratio of managers in organizations with many experts. The employment of an expert staff seems to give rise to vertical differentiation, increasing the number of managerial levels in the organization. The number of hierarchical levels tends to be larger in departments requiring of its personnel relatively high educational qualifications than in those with lower requirements (row 2). The span of control of first-line supervisors is, on the average, somewhat narrower if the staff has superior qualifications than if it does not (row 3).[20] The span of control of middle managers (those between the top executive and first-line supervisors) is, by contrast, wider in agencies with well-trained personnel than in others (row 4). But these middle managers have many fewer subordinates in any case, averaging less than two, than first-line supervisors, whose median is six subordinates. Managers have typically broader responsibilities than operating officials, and very few managers report to a single superior; expert qualifications presumably broaden the responsibilities of operating employees, which is reflected in a parallel reduction in the number reporting to a single supervisor. This consistent inverse association between scope of responsibilities and width of span of control clearly indicates that a narrow span of control must not be assumed to be indicative of closeness of supervision.[21]

The utilization of employees with superior qualifications raises the pro-

[20] A parallel result, showing complexity of task to be inversely related to width of span of control, is presented in Gerald D. Bell, "Determinants of Span of Control," *American Journal of Sociology,* LXXIII (1967), 100–109.

[21] Bell has some direct evidence on closeness of supervision, which shows it to be unrelated to span of control (*ibid.,* p. 106).

portion of managers in an organization, apparently because it tends to increase the number of managerial levels and decrease the span of control of first-line supervisors without decreasing that of higher managers. The question arises how the extra managerial manpower is utilized in departments with a highly qualified staff. The time estimates of informants permit tentative answers to this question. If much of the staff is college trained, managers are less likely to spend most of their time in actual supervision than if it is not (Table 1, row 5, based on the mean for all managers), and this is the case for first-line supervisors as well as higher managers. The finding that superiors of experts devote comparatively little time to actually supervising them helps to explain why their narrow span of control does not imply close supervision. Managers in departments with highly qualified personnel seem to spend more time than other managers on professional work of their own which keeps them in touch with the problems encountered by the operating level.[22] Such greater involvement in actual operations on the part of managers of an expert staff, compared to other managers, may well improve their qualifications to discuss technical problems of the work with their subordinates and thus to take full advantage of the greater opportunities for communication that

the smaller numbers of subordinates per superior create.

The question of prime interest is whether the hypothesis that expertness promotes decentralization, which rested merely on inferential conjecture, is confirmed by the directly pertinent data from finance departments. This is in fact the case. Responsibilities of various kinds tend to be delegated by management to lower levels in agencies where the staff has relatively high qualifications. Thus budgeting and accounting decisions are more likely to be made by division heads rather than the department director himself if the staff includes many college-trained men than if it includes few (Table 1, row 6). The likelihood that an official below the top executive recommends promotions and dismissals is also greater in agencies with many experts than in others (row 7). Parallel relationships with expertness, though they are somewhat less pronounced, are revealed by other indications of decentralization of responsibilities, such as the top executive's policy to let his division heads make most decisions, and the fact that first-line supervisors, not higher officials, formally evaluate the performance of non-supervisory employees. In sum, managerial authority over decision making appears indeed to be more decentralized in organizations with large proportions of trained experts than in others.

[22] One might think that the finding could also be interpreted to show that departments with many experts have more complex responsibilities and their managers devote more time to planning and administration, but the instructions were that such activities be included under supervision, and virtually the only activity excluded, except for top executives, would be work of one's own.

MULTILEVEL HIERARCHIES

The finding that superior qualifications of the personnel in government agencies encourage delegation of responsibilities is not surprising. But what is unexpected is that such superior qualifications are also associated with vertical differentiation into multilevel hierarchies. It is generally assumed that the proliferation of hierarchical levels in organizations is a sign of over-bureaucratization and an impediment to rational operations, and the results of Udy's study of primitive production organizations point to this conclusion,[23] whereas the opposite is implied by the association obtained here between levels and training requirements, since superior training undoubtedly entails more rational decision making. The question arises of what conditions in contemporary American agencies promote hierarchical differentiation.

A multilevel hierarchy is associated with several basic characteristics of finance departments. (1) The number of levels increases with increasing size, that is, the number of employees (Pearsonian zero-order correlations .51[24]). (2) Although the zero-order correlation between number of levels and number of major subdivisions[25] is virtually zero ($-.05$), there is an inverse association between the two when size is controlled ($-.34$). (3) The wider the average span of control of middle managers, the larger is the number of levels in the hierarchy (.27). (4) Automation in the form of computers is associated with multiple levels (.34). (5) Explicit written promotion regulations encourage hierarchical differentiation

[23] Udy, " 'Bureaucracy' and 'Rationality'."
[24] Regression analysis is used here, partly because the number of levels is a genuine continuous variable and so are most independent variables, and particularly because this procedure makes it possible to examine partial associations while holding all seven other correlates constant.
[25] The criterion of "major subdivision" is a division whose head reports directly to the department director (or his deputy, if he has a single deputy).

(.22). (6) The number of levels increases the more weight written examinations have for promotions (.24), and it decreases the more weight seniority ($-.22$) and supervisory evaluations ($-.16$) have for promotions.[26] (7) Decentralization of responsibility for promotions and dismissals is correlated with multiple levels (.18). (8) The larger the proportion of employees required to have college degrees, finally, the larger the number of levels (.16).

Since so many factors are associated with hierarchical levels, partial correlations were computed between each of the eight and number of levels holding constant the other seven. The results of this analysis, which provide the basis for the further discussion, are presented in Table 2. The multiple correlation between all eight factors and levels is .65. These characteristics of finance departments explain 43 percent of the variance in hierarchical levels, with most of the difference being due to three factors—size, divisions, and automation.

Some reflections on the considerations that probably influence the decision to add new levels in the hierarchy can serve as a starting point for interpreting these associations. As an organization expands in size and complexity, it is likely that additional major divisions are established, which increases the number of officials directly responsible to the department director and overburdens him with supervisory responsibilities. To lighten this administrative load of the top executive and free him to devote more time to his primary executive

[26] Only the weight of written promotion examinations is considered in the subsequent analysis, since the two other factors are complementary to it.

TABLE 2 CORRELATIONS WITH NUMBER OF LEVELS IN THE HIERARCHY

Independent Variable	Zero-Order Correlation	Partial Correlation	Standardized B*	Regression Error	Data on Employment Agencies: Zero-Order Correlation
1. Number of employees	.51	.50	.53	.06	.60
2. Number of major divisions	−.05	−.32	−.30	.06	.19
3. Span of control of middle managers	.27	.11	.09	.05	.31
4. Automation (computers)[a]	.34	.23	.19	.05	.53
5. Explicit promotion regulations[a]	.22	.04	−.03	.06	.33
6. Weight of examinations in promotions	.24	.13	.12	.06	[b]
7. Decentralization of promotion decisions[a]	.18	.12	.09	.05	.19
8. Proportion of staff required to have B.A.	.16	.03	.02	.05	−.00

[a] These three factors are dichotomous and were used as dummy variables in the regression analysis. All others are continuous variables except weight of examinations, which was coded in four categories.

[b] No corresponding variable is available for the employment security study.

functions, a few assistant directors may be installed on a new level to whom the division directors report and who in turn report to the director, just as the creation of the U.S. Secretary of Health, Education, and Welfare constituted an intermediate level between the President and officials who formerly reported directly to him. The introduction of such a new level of assistant directors would account for the inverse association observed between levels and major subdivisions because the few "superdivisions" headed by the assistant directors, not the former divisions, would now be defined as the "major subdivisions" by the criterion used. This change would also help to explain why number of levels and span of control of middle managers, which includes assistant directors, are correlated without controls (.27) but are no longer significantly related once size, subdivisions, and other conditions are controlled (.11). The assumptions here are that the assistant directors, whose establishment increases levels, have a particularly wide span of control—hence the zero-order correlation—but that the introduction of this new level occurs usually in large agencies and reduces the number of major subdivisions—hence the considerably lower correlation under these controls.

Differentiation into a multilevel hierarchy has evident advantages for expanding organizations, according to these conjectures. In fact the number of levels in finance departments increases with increasing size, as previously noted; so does the number of major subdivisions, however (the zero-order correlation between size and subdivisions being .43, nearly as large as that between size and levels, .51). Not all large agencies have many levels and few major divisions. The inverse association between levels and subdivisions when size is controlled implies the existence of two contrasting departmental structures, one that is primarily differentiated horizontally into many major divisions and one that is primarily differentiated vertically into many levels. The question is what conditions discourage horizontal differentiation—which places an excessive administrative burden on top management—and encourage vertical differentiation instead.

The clue for answering this question is provided by the other major correlate of number of levels, namely, automation, which reveals a substantial association with it (.34) that persists when other conditions are controlled (.23). Although extending the hierarchy has administrative advantages for the top executive of a large organization, it also removes him increasingly from the operating level and makes it difficult for him directly to control operations and keep tight reins on them. This loss of close contact with the operating level is a serious disadvantage for a director who relies largely on direct supervision for control, but it is not such a disadvantage if top management has instituted indirect mechanisms of control and can exercise with their aid sufficient influence on operations by setting policies and formulating programs. The automation of accounting procedures through computers is just such an impersonal mechanism of control in finance departments. It places much controlling influence over operations into the hands of the top executives whose decisions determine the over-all setup of the automated facilities and the nature of the computer programs, thereby obviating the need for much direct supervision. The assembly line serves similar functions in factories.[27]

Since automation serves as a control mechanism that greatly reduces the main disadvantage of multilevel hierarchies, it furthers their development.[28]

The general principle suggested is that conditions in organizations that make the reliable performance of duties relatively independent of direct intervention by top management further the development of multilevel hierarchies. Advanced technological equipment, inasmuch as it mechanizes operations and makes them to some degree self-regulating, often serves this function. The mechanization of facilities is not the only condition that affects the reliability of performance, however. Regardless of how automated operations are, top management must rely on its managerial staff to implement its objectives and administer its policies. Herein lies the significance of promotion procedures for the hierarchy. Explicit promotion regulations furnish uniform standards that all higher officials must have met. But these standards assure top management that higher officials will have adequate qualifications for their responsibilities only if they stipulate that promotions be based primarily on examinations designed to test these qualifications rather than on seniority or the possibly idiosyncratic evaluations of supervisors. A significant correlation between the weight of written examinations in promotions and number of levels remains when other conditions are controlled (.13), but the correlation between the exist-

[27] Blau and Scott, *Formal Organizations,* pp. 176–78.

[28] It is also possible that the causal direction is the opposite from that assumed above, which would mean that agencies with multiple levels are more likely than others to introduce automation, quite possibly because they benefit particularly from its function as a control mechanism.

ence of promotion regulations and levels disappears when the weight of examinations and other conditions are controlled (.04). The reason probably is that only promotion regulations that give merit examinations much weight guarantee that all managerial officials have certain minimum qualifications and thus reduce top management's reluctance to lose direct contact with the operating level by establishing intervening layers in the hierarchy.

The more top management trusts the middle managers who constitute its administrative arm to discharge their responsibilities in accordance with its guidelines and directives, the more inclined it will be in all likelihood to delegate responsibilities to them. The implication is that the degree of confidence top executives place in their managerial assistance will promote decentralization of authority as well as multilevel hierarchies. If this surmise is correct it could explain why the zero-order correlation between number of levels and decentralization (.18) is reduced to a point that falls just short of significance at .05 when other conditions that affect management's trust are controlled (.12).

Entrance requirements that demand comparatively high qualifications of employees undoubtedly improve their abilities to perform their duties without close supervision. The interpretation advanced implies, therefore, that the proportion of the agency personnel expected to have college degrees and the number of levels in the hierarchy are positively related. As a matter of fact, such a positive zero-order correlation has been observed (.16), but controlling other conditions reduces this correlation to the vanishing point (.03). The

proportion of employees with college training is not strongly associated with any of the other control variables under consideration, but it is somewhat correlated with four of them (between .12 and .14), its most pronounced zero-order correlation being that with decentralization (.14). A plausible explanation of this pattern of findings can be derived if expert qualifications are viewed as simply one element in a configuration of conditions indicative of operations that are relatively self-regulating and independent of direct intervention by management. As part of this configuration, the qualifications of employees are associated with the development of multilevel hierarchies. But once the other factors that manifest independence of managerial intervention are controlled, including those to which expert qualifications directly contribute, such as decentralization, the entire significance of qualifications for the hierarchy has been taken into account, and they are no longer associated with the number of levels.

TWO CONTRASTING TYPES

In conclusion, some inferences about two contrasting types of formal organization will be drawn from the associations with multilevel hierarchy observed. One of these types may be considered the modern organization governed by universalistic standards; the other represents the old-fashioned bureaucracy.

A fundamental issue confronting the executives of organizations is whether to manage primarily by means of direct or indirect controls. Management through direct controls entails keeping in close touch with operations and issuing corrective orders whenever necessary. Management through indirect controls involves devising impersonal control mechanisms that constrain operations to follow automatically the policies and programs specified by top executives. The substitution of indirect mechanisms of control for direct control requires that an orientation to abstract universalistic standards replace reliance on personal judgments. The development of these impersonal control mechanisms is most likely if technical considerations and effective performance are supreme values, whereas ideological commitments and particularistic solidarities have little significance.[29]

Today the prototype of an impersonal control mechanism is the computer, which dramatically illustrates how technological facilities automate operations and simultaneously give top management—whose decisions govern the basic computer setup—much control over them without requiring frequent direct intervention. Not only the operations themselves but also the recruitment of employees and that of the managerial staff tend to become standardized in the modern organization in terms of universalistic principles of effective performance. Explicit personnel regulations stipulate merit criteria for employment and for advancement to managerial positions, relieving top management of administrative tasks, lessening the influence of personal bias and variations in judgment over personnel decisions, and assuring minimum qualifications. Both the

automation of the work process and the merit standards that the managerial and operating staff must meet contribute to the reliable performance of duties and help to make operations comparatively self-regulating within the framework of the organization's objectives and management's policies. These conditions reduce management's need to keep close direct control over operations and, consequently, often give rise to major changes in the hierarchy. To wit, vertical differentiation creates a multilevel hierarchy, which usually decreases the number of major divisions whose heads report to the agency director and increases the span of control of these division heads, and responsibilities become decentralized. The strongest pressure to institute impersonal mechanisms of control, and thus the conditions that facilitate these structural changes, comes from the expanding size of organizations.

In short, the modern organization is characterized by a tall, slim hierarchy with decentralized authority. The opposite type, which may be called an old-fashioned bureaucracy, has a squat hierarchy with authority centralized at the top. In this case, which is most prevalent in smaller organizations, the top executive maintains tight control over operations by directly supervising many division heads, assigning each of them only few subordinates, refraining from introducing intermediate levels that would increase his distance from the operating personnel, and delegating few responsibilities. The lesser interest in impersonal mechanisms of control under these circumstances is reflected in the rare instances of automation and in the nature of the personnel policies. Explicit regulations that specify personnel qualifica-

[29] It is evident that this orientation is inappropriate for certain kinds of organizations, such as religious congregations or ideological political parties.

tions are infrequent; promotions are largely left under the discretion of management; and insofar as promotion standards do exist, they tend to give weight to seniority and personal judgments of superiors rather than objective merit criteria, thus implicitly placing the importance of loyalty above that of technical competence.

A final question to be raised is whether these conclusions concerning two contrasting types of formal structure apply to all work organizations (those employing people to perform tasks), or only to government agencies, or perhaps only to government finance departments. The methodological point made in the introduction bears repeating in this connection: generalizing beyond the data is necessary for scientific cumulation because such generalizing supplies the sole connection between different empirical studies. The finding that multilevel finance departments in the United States have fewer major divisions than others of the same size, for example, can neither be negated nor confirmed by research on other organizations, for the association between levels and divisions in another type of agency simply has no direct bearing on it. Only if the investigator is willing to advance generalizations that refer to broader concepts than his empirical data—all work organizations or vertical differentiation of any kind—is it possible to replicate or refute his conclusions and ultimately to develop a scientific theory.

Hence the empirical findings from the study of finance departments are deliberately used to suggest tentative principles about work organizations in general, to be tested and appropriately modified in future research, just as the inferences drawn in our earlier study were tested and refined this one. Some indication that the conclusions about hierarchical structure are at least not restricted to finance departments is provided by a preliminary analysis of data on quite another type of government agency. The state employment security agencies in this country are large roof organizations, each consisting of a state headquarters and an average of forty local offices dispersed throughout the state, and their median size is more than ten times that of finance departments. Despite these differences, most of the factors associated with multiple levels in finance departments reveal similar zero-order correlations in state employment agencies, even though several of the measures are far from identical (compare the last with the first column in Table 2). Controlling size tends to increase the similarity; for instance, number of divisions and number of levels are inversely correlated when size (after logarithmic transformation) is controlled in employment security agencies ($-.37$), as they are in finance departments ($-.34$).

These parallels lend some credibility to the claim that the propositions about hierarchical differentiation suggested in this paper are fairly general principles about work organizations, or in any case about the government agencies among them, though further research will undoubtedly call for revisions and refinements. The tentative conclusion is that impersonal mechanisms of control, such as automation and merit personnel standards, help transform flat structures in which the chief executive exercises much personal control into multilevel hierarchies with decentralized authority.

30. DETERMINANTS OF SPAN OF CONTROL

Gerald D. Bell[1]

Even though the magic range of five to seven is repeatedly cited as an ideal size for administrators' spans of control, there are many cases reported in which effective spans have ranged from one up to thirty.[2] One might ask, then, what are the determinants of variations in size of span of control?

Perspectives on this subject have been taken primarily from the super-visor's position, and many investigations have been directed toward determining psychological and group properties which affect supervisory control.[3] There is an absence of concern with limitations placed upon span of control which stem from technological demands of the productive processes.[4]

Pertinent literature concerning characteristics of productive activities suggests three main factors which affect span of control. These are: (1) the complexity of the tasks performed by subordinates, (2) the extent to which administrators closely supervise their charges, and, finally, (3) the complexity of supervisors' jobs. The aim of this paper is to explore the associations between the above three factors and span of control.

Span of control refers to the number of workers directly supervised by an administrator. Job complexity indicates the qualitative difficulty of an

Reprinted by permission of the publisher, University of Chicago Press, from *American Journal of Sociology,* 73 (July 1967) 100–109.

[1] The author is greatly indebted to Stanley H. Udy, Jr., Elton F. Jackson, and Chris Argyris, who provided keen critiques of several of the ideas presented in this paper. Part of the research is based on the author's dissertation, "Formality Versus Flexibility in Complex Organizations: A Comparative Investigation Within a Hospital" (unpublished Ph.D. dissertation, Yale University, 1965). The research was conducted while the author held a United States Public Health Training Fellowship. Revision of a paper presented at the American Sociological Association's Sixty-First Annual Meeting, Miami Beach, Florida, September, 1966.

[2] Doris R. Entwisle and John Walton, "Observations on the Span of Control," *Administrative Science Quarterly,* V (Mar. 1961), 522–34.

[3] For a review of these investigations, see Peter M. Blau and W. Richard Scott, *Formal Organizations* (San Francisco: Chandler Publishing Co., 1962), pp. 140–83.

[4] For an exception, see Stanley H. Udy, Jr., "Technical and Institutional Factors in Production Organization: A Preliminary Model," *American Journal of Sociology,* LXVII (Nov. 1961), 251.

TABLE 1 DEPARTMENTS AND THEIR ATTRIBUTES

Departments	Size*	Average Span of Control	Average Subordi- nates' Job Complexity	Average Supervisors' Job Complexity	Average Closeness of Supervision
Administration	5	L	H	H	L
Business Office	9	L	H	H	L
Admitting Office	5	H	M	L	M
Purchasing	4	M	L	H	M
Dietary	19	M	M	H	M
Housekeeping	10	H	L	L	H
Laundry	11	H	L	L	H
Maintenance	9	M	H	L	L
Nursing Adm.	6	M	H	H	L
Nursing Dept. 1	6	M	M	H	L
Pediatrics	6	M	M	M	M
Maternity	6	H	M	H	L
Nursing Dept. 2	5	M	M	M	L
Surgery 2	5	H	M	H	L
Nursing Dept. 3	7	H	M	M	M
Surgery 3	4	M	L	M	L
Self-care Unit	4	M	L	L	M
Medical Records	6	M	L	M	H
Operating Room	9	M	M	L	L
Delivery Room	8	H	L	H	L
Anesthesia	5	L	H	H	L
Radiology	9	L	M	H	H
Laboratories	10	L	H	H	M
Central Supply	8	H	L	L	M
Pharmacy	4	L	L	H	H
Emergency Room	6	H	H	M	L
Psychiatric Clinic	5	L	H	H	H
Health Clinic	4	L	H	L	M
Physical Therapy	5	H	L	L	H
Recovery Room	4	M	L	L	M

* Full-time, day-shift employees.

individual's job, while closeness of supervision is defined by the degree to which a supervisor observes and regulates his subordinates' activities.

RESEARCH DESIGN

Data were gathered for this investigation in the Griffin Community Hospital which is located in Derby, a small city near New Haven, Connecticut. The sample selected for study within the hospital was composed of the 204 full-time, day-shift employees. These day-shift workers were distributed throughout thirty-three departments in the hospital. Three of these departments, however, consisted of only two employees each and thus they were dropped from the study.[5] The departments included in the sample and their scores on the main variables listed above appear in Table 1.

[5] The small size of the departments, of course, sets limits upon any generalizations from this study. However, the processes involved would seem to be applicable to large organizations. See, e.g., Peter M. Blau, Wolf V. Heydebrand, and Robert E. Stauffer, "The Structure of Small Bureaucracies," *American Sociological Review*, XXXI (April, 1966), 179–92.

The data were collected by two methods. First, informal observations and interviews were conducted from January through June, 1963. Second, a questionnaire was used which was pretested at Grace New Haven Hospital, revised, and pretested again at the same institution. They were then distributed in Griffin Community Hospital in mid-May, and final follow-ups were completed in the second week of June, 1963. An 84 percent return was obtained.

A relatively high proportion of respondents were (*a*) Catholics (62 percent), (*b*) nurses (30 percent), (*c*) over forty years of age (61 percent), (*d*) married (57 percent), and (e) had completed high school (54 percent). No significant differences were found between non-respondents and respondents as far as age, length of employment, marital status, religion, department of employment, and education. However, a disproportionate number (56 percent) of non-respondents were nurses. This factor merits special comment.[6]

Shortly after the research was begun there was a change in nursing administration which caused tension and suspicion among the nurses. As a result of the change from a "motherly" to a more "task oriented" administrator, the researcher was faced with problems of convincing the nurses that he was not connected with management or the new nursing administrator. In spite of intensive attempts to remove this false perception, it appeared that the thirteen nurses who did not complete the questionnaire were quite insecure and anxious about their positions. Therefore, our findings might be biased to

some extent by the self-elimination of insecure respondents.

DEFINITIONS AND MAJOR CONCEPTS

Span of control was measured by simply counting the number of subordinates under the control of each supervisor. The spans of control were relatively small due to the minute size of the departments within the organization. We computed the average span of control for each department by summing the spans of management for each supervisor within a given department and then dividing this total by the number of supervisors in that unit. Supervisors who had five or more subordinates were placed in the high span of control category, those with three or four subordinates in the medium group, and those with one or two subordinates in the low span of control category.

To develop an individual level analysis it would have been necessary to know the exact subordinates each supervisor controlled and then to have ascertained the average complexity of the tasks these subordinates carried out. Data were collected on the task complexity for each subordinate; however, names of subordinates over which a supervisor was in charge were not ascertained. The variations in spans of control within departments, however, were quite small. Thus, by taking the departmental average we are not distorting the individual level of analysis to a great extent; for supervisors' spans of control differed within only eight of the thirty departments, and in only two of these units did supervisors' spans vary by two ranks.

---

[6] Approximately 30 percent of the employees in the hospital were nurses.

Thus, even though the departmental indexes are crude in the sense that they do away with some individual differences within each supervisory level in the departments, and they may suffer from problems of ecological correlation, they allow us to provide tentative evidence concerning the hypotheses.

The index of the *complexity of subordinates' and supervisors' jobs* was composed of four factors: (1) degree of predictability of work demands, (2) amount of discretion they exercise, (3) extent of responsibility they have, and (4) number of different tasks they perform. *Predictability* was established by asking respondents two questions. First, they were asked, "If you wrote a list of the exact work demands which you expect to confront you on an average workday, what percent of these do you think would be interrupted by unexpected events?" The second question was, "Every job is composed of certain routine and repetitive activities. What percent of the *work demands* connected with your job would you consider to be of a routine nature?" There were five possible answers to these two questions, ranging from "0 to 20 percent of my activities" to "80 to 100 percent."[7]

Discretion was measured by asking respondents three questions. They were first asked (1) to list the main tasks they performed during a typical workweek and then to indicate for *which* of these tasks they used their own judgment concerning whether or not to actually perform them. In the second question we asked (2) for

which of the tasks they performed did they exercise their own judgment in determining *how* they performed them. In the final question, respondents were asked (3) for which of the tasks they performed did they make decisions in determining *in what order* the tasks were carried out. The scores were summed, and then respondents were ranked according to the total percent of decisions they made.[8]

Responsibility was established by asking supervisors to estimate and then give examples of (*a*) the average length of time in the future for which their decisions committed the hospital, and (*b*) the average length of time which elapsed after they made decisions before someone checked up on their judgment.[9]

Finally, to measure *the number of different tasks* which individuals performed, the researcher held lengthy discussions with each respondent. Respondents were asked in a personal interview what were the main activities they performed on a typical workday. They were asked to list these tasks beginning with the first ones performed in the morning and progressing to a listing of the tasks they performed up to the end of the workday. A janitor, for example, would say something like the following:

I just start out in the morning by picking up my supplies—brooms, mops, cloths, buckets—and I carry these to the first floor over on the West Wing. I go up and down the halls sweeping the floors for about fifteen minutes there, then I clean the trays and dust in the halls. After that I go into each room

---

[7] The Kendall's T rank-order correlation between these two questions is $r_c = .52$, $P < .001$, and thus lends some credence to the assumption that these two indicators are representing the same concept.

[8] These three questions were all intercorrelated above $r_c = .78$, $P < .001$.

[9] See Elliot Jaques, *The Measurement of Responsibility* (Cambridge, Mass.: Harvard University Press, 1956).

and empty the trash first, then sweep, dust, mop and so on. . . .

By the end of the day the janitor has performed approximately thirty to thirty-five different tasks. Many of these tasks are repeated quite frequently. Picking up supplies was counted as one task, carrying these to an assignment was a second, sweeping floors a third, and so forth.

In contrast, a department head would state something like:

I start out in the morning by (1) asking the night-shift supervisor about each patient. (2) I keep notes on each patient, then (3) make a plan for the day for each one, (4) decide what should be done with each one, (5) who should do it, (6) talk with others about their ideas in regard to the above, (7) then assign jobs to each person in our department, (8) call admissions to find how many new patients we have coming in during the day, (9) plan how to handle these newcomers. (10) I then go around and check to make sure all the assignments are being carried out, and so forth.

A typical department head performs about 180 to 200 different tasks on an average workday. The tasks differ in content and quality, of course, from those of the janitor. However, for the present we are concerned only with the number of different tasks.

It is assumed that when an individual is confronted by many *unexpected events* the decisions he makes will be more difficult since there will be many alternatives to consider, and the alternatives themselves will be of a diverse nature. Consequently, *decision-making* efforts will be more perplexing and time-consuming. Correspondingly, the more *different tasks* he has of the above nature the more complex his job will be. And, finally,

the more *responsibility* he has the more important the consequences of his decisions will be, and therefore the more attention he will devote to trying to make good decisions. Thus, when these four factors are present, employees' jobs are considered to be highly complex.[10]

An index of *closeness of supervision* was established by asking respondents two questions. First, they were asked, "How often does your supervisor keep a close check on what you are doing and closely observe your work?" There were five possible responses to this question, ranging from "very often" to "seldom." Second, they were asked, "To what extent does your immediate supervisor influence what you do in a typical workweek?" Again there were five possible responses, ranging from "0 to 20 percent of my activities" to "80 to 100 percent of my activities." Respondents' scores on these two questions were added, and workers were ranked into nine categories of closeness of supervision. The data indicate that these two indexes are moderately associated, and, thus, the relationship is consistent with the assumption that we are measuring the same underlying variable—which we have labeled closeness of supervision. (Kendall's T rank-order correlation between these two questions is $r_c = .54$, $P < .001$.)

Since this measure of closeness of supervision involves the workers' perceptions of how closely they are supervised, it is possible that their estimates could be biased by many personality and social-background factors. Holding the extent of the

[10] For another measure of job complexity, see Udy, "Technical and Institutional Factors," (n. 4).

"real closeness of supervision" constant, for example, a highly-authoritarian worker might believe he is not closely supervised, while a non-authoritarian individual might feel that he is very closely controlled. With this limitation in mind, we attempted to control for, at least partially, possible selective perception biases by asking supervisors how closely they controlled their subordinates. Then supervisors' scores on closeness of supervision in each of the departments were correlated with the average closeness of supervision scores as determined by the subordinates' estimates. The supervisors' estimates, of course, are subject to the same type of perception biases; however, the likelihood of both the subordinate and the supervisor in the same department having biased estimates is probably small.

The relationship between these two factors was both positive and significant at the .01 level, and thus lends some support to our measure of closeness of supervision. (Kendall's T $r_c = .63$, $P < .01$.) This support is only partial, however, since we had to consider departments as the unit of analysis, and thus we did not have the supervisors' corroborating estimates of closeness of control for each subordinate. This latter estimate would appear to be a more valid index upon which future research might be based.

THE FINDINGS

SUBORDINATES' TASK COMPLEXITY AND SPAN OF CONTROL

When subordinates' jobs are highly complex it is very difficult for supervisors to control more than a few employees. When subordinates are continually performing a variety of novel activities, when their decisions have many diverse alternatives to be considered, supervisors will spend much time and energy with each subordinate in controlling his work. The subordinates' problems will be difficult to solve and thus will require much attention from the supervisor.

Consistent with the above interpretation is Richardson and Walker's finding that in an automated plant, as jobs were enlarged, that is, as the workers performed more different tasks and had more discretion and responsibility, the supervisors' spans of control were delimited.[11] And in a study of a cabinet factory, Miles, Eyre, and Bennett indicate that the types of skills needed to perform cabinet work involved much discretion and the performance of many different tasks on the part of subordinates; and, correspondingly, the supervisors had narrow spans of control.[12] Blau and Scott also report findings which are consistent with the above notions.[13]

We have hypothesized, then, that *the more complex the subordinates' tasks the lower the supervisors' spans of control.*

The rank-order correlation between these two variables indicates that they are negatively and significantly related (Table 2). The more complex subordinates' tasks the narrower the

[11] Frederick L. Richardson and Charles R. Walker, *Human Relations in an Expanding Company* (New Haven, Conn.: Labor and Management Center, Yale University, 1948), p. 27.

[12] G. H. Miles, A. B. Eyre, and H. P. Bennett, "An Investigation in a Cabinet Factory," *Occupational Psychology* (April, 1923), p. 223.

[13] Blau and Scott, *Formal Organizations* (n. 3), pp. 160–61.

TABLE 2 RELATIONSHIPS BETWEEN COMPLEXITY OF SUBORDINATES'
TASKS AND SPAN OF CONTROL

	Subordinates' Task Complexity*				
	Low		Medium		High
Span of Control	1	2	3	4	5
Low	0	1	1	3	3
Medium	1	5	5	0	2
High	3	2	4	1	0

* $r_c = -.47$, $P < .01$.

supervisors' spans of control. On the other hand, when subordinates have relatively straight-forward jobs, their supervisors are able to control a larger number of employees. Furthermore, when the size of departments is controlled the above relationship remains both statistically significant, although it is decreased, and negative in direction. Similarly, there was no meaningful modification of the relationship when controlling for closeness of supervision and supervisory job complexity.[14] Thus, we can tentatively conclude that the greater the complexity of tasks which one's subordinates perform the fewer individuals a supervisor can control.

SPAN OF CONTROL AND
CLOSENESS OF SUPERVISION

Previous research suggests that closeness of supervision indirectly affects the job complexity of subordinates.[15] When supervisors closely regulate subordinates' activities, the latter's discretion is restricted and their responsibility delimited. Conse-

quently, closeness of supervision is an indirect cause of supervisors' span of control. For the closer the supervision the less complex the subordinates' jobs; and when job complexity is low, supervisors are able to control a larger number of subordinates. Thus, closeness of supervision indirectly increases span of control.[16]

In addition to this indirect effect, it is also interesting to note that closeness of supervision appears to have a direct negative effect upon supervisors' spans of control. Simply stated, we might theorize that the closer an administrator supervises his subordinates the fewer subordinates he could control. The more closely he attends to his subordinates the more time and energy he will have to spend with each worker. On the contrary, when a supervisor is keeping a distant relationship with his charges, we would expect him to be able to control a larger number. Following this reasoning we have hypothesized that *the closer the supervision the narrower the span of control.* An interesting point now arises in connection with the above hypothesis. That is, if the above postulate is valid, then we have a case in which the indirect and the direct effect of closeness of supervision are producing opposite results upon span of control. The

[14] For small departments $r_c = -.42$, $P < .01$; for large departments $r_c = -.35$, $P < .01$; for close supervision $r_c = -.51$, $P < .01$; for distant supervision $r_c = -.48$, $P < .01$; for high supervisory task complexity $r_c = -.62$, $P < .01$; for low supervisory task complexity $r_c = -.37$, $P < .01$.

[15] Bell, "Formality vs. Flexibility" (n. 1).

[16] *Ibid.*

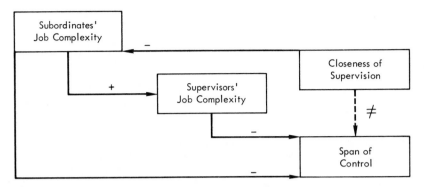

Fig. 1 Causal Relationships.

(*Arrows* indicate the direction of the associations, while *plus* and *minus* *signs* suggest positive and negative relationships, respectively.)

Table 3 Relationship between Closeness of Supervision and Span of Control

| | Closeness of Supervision* | | | | |
| | High | | | | Low |
Span of Control	1	2	3	4	5
Low	3	1	1	2	1
Medium	1	5	4	1	1
High	3	3	2	2	0

* $r_c = .09$, $P < .01$.

indirect effect of closeness of supervision causes low discretion, which, in turn, causes subordinates to perform few different tasks, which finally encourages supervisors to have large spans of control. Thus, in the indirect causal network, closeness of supervision is a positive determinant, producing large spans of control (Fig. 1).

On the contrary, the direct effect of closeness of supervision upon span of control is a negative one. That is, we would expect that the more closely one supervised his subordinates the narrower would be his span of control. Let us turn, then, to an analysis of how this potential dilemma is accommodated within the organization by considering the hypothesis

that *the closer the supervision the supervision the narrower the span of control.*[17]

When span of control and closeness of supervision are correlated, the data indicate that the hypothesis is not supported (Table 3). Although this relationship is what one would

[17] It should be pointed out that several investigations have posited an opposite causal direction between these two factors. However, in this organization it appeared that there were few formal procedures established for creating or maintaining given levels of span of control. Rather, it appeared that span of control was determined by other factors such as are examined here. See, for instance, George Strauss and Leonard R. Sayles, *Personnel* (Englewood Cliffs, N.J.: Prentice-Hall, Inc., 1963), p. 379.

expect when the independent variable has both a positive (although indirect) and a negative effect upon the dependent variable, when controls were made in the attempt to limit the indirect effect there was still no association between closeness of supervision and span of control. This non-relationship was maintained when controlling for supervisors' and subordinates' job complexity within departments. Similarly, there appeared to be few, if any, structural effects between these variables.[18]

One possible explanation for this finding, other than the fact that the hypothesis is actually not tenable or that we were unable to control the indirect effect of closeness of supervision, might stem from the relationship between rule usage and closeness of supervision.

Previous research indicates that one of the means by which administrators attempt to control their subordinates is through the utilization of rules and regulations.[19] And if management utilizes rules as a substitute for personally supervising their subordinates, then their control efforts would not be as time-consuming as would be their attempts at personally supervising subordinates. Consequently, management control via rules would not directly affect span of control. And, thus, the direct effect of closeness of supervision upon span of control might be reduced.

If the above notions are valid, then the utilization of rules in regulating workers' behavior might partially explain the lack of a significant relationship between closeness of supervision and span of control. The inter-relationships between the above variables would, nevertheless, seem to merit attention in future research.

SUPERVISORS' JOB COMPLEXITY IN RELATION TO SPAN OF CONTROL

The third element which has an important influence upon span of control is the supervisors' job complexity. Supervisors' job complexity influences span of control primarily by an ecological type of relationship. When supervisors are performing complex tasks, they are able to devote less time to controlling subordinates. Furthermore, in this case the duties of the supervisor probably are co-ordinating tasks, rather than direct, personal supervision of task performance. The activities he performs are highly diverse and involved, especially in decision-making pursuits.

On the other hand, when supervisors have relatively simple jobs, their decision-making efforts are less complex and they are able to devote a much greater proportion of their time to supervising subordinates. Consequently, they tend to have more subordinates or greater spans of control.

Stinchcombe reports, for instance, that in mass-production industries supervisors have fairly simple jobs and at the same time have wide spans of control. However, in construction firms he found that supervisors had quite diverse activities and narrow spans of control.[20] Evidently, in these different organizations the ability of supervisors, who had unique tasks, to control subordinates was curtailed by their expenditure of both time and

---

[18] For measurements of structural effects we drew rough scattergrams.
[19] Strauss and Sayles, *Personnel* (n. 17).

[20] Arthur L. Stinchcombe, "Bureaucratic and Craft Administration of Production: A Comparative Study," *Administrative Science Quarterly,* IV (1959), 173.

TABLE 4 RELATIONSHIP BETWEEN SUPERVISORS' TASK COMPLEXITY
AND SPAN OF CONTROL

| | Supervisors' Task Complexity* | | | | |
| | Low | | | | High |
Span of Control	1	2	3	4	5
Low	0	1	0	5	2
Medium	0	4	4	2	2
High	2	3	2	2	1

* $r_c = -.38$, $P < .01$.

TABLE 5 RELATIONSHIP BETWEEN SUBORDINATES' AND
SUPERVISORS' TASK COMPLEXITY

| | Supervisors' Task Complexity* | | | | |
| Subordinates' | Low | | | | High |
Task Complexity	1	2	3	4	5
Low— 1	2	1	1	0	0
2	0	3	1	3	0
3	0	2	3	2	3
4	0	1	1	2	0
High—5	0	1	0	2	2

* $r_c = .37$, $P < .01$.

effort in performing many varied activities.

We have theorized, then, that *the more complex the supervisors' tasks the narrower the span of control.*

THE FINDINGS

The findings indicate that our hypothesis is moderately supported (Table 4).

The more complex the tasks of administrators are the fewer the number of subordinates they control. Furthermore, this relationship was unaltered when controlling for subordinates' job complexity, closeness of supervision, and size of department.[21] Also, controls for possible

structural effects indicate that these variables seem to be related only on an individual level.

SUBORDINATES' AND SUPERVISORS' TASK COMPLEXITY

It should be noted that both subordinates' and supervisors' task complexity tend to decrease spans of control. These two factors appear to have an additive effect because the more complex are subordinates' activities the more their supervisors' jobs are unpredictable, which in turn encourages them to exert much discretion and a large number of different tasks (Table 5). These latter three factors combine to increase the complexity of supervisors' jobs. Thus, when subordinates' jobs are highly complex, the complexity makes it

[21] For high subordinates' job complexity $r_c = -.59$, $P < .01$; for low $r_c = -.39$, $P < .01$; for close supervision $r_c = -.28$, $P < .01$; for distant supervision $r_c = -.33$, $P < .01$; for small departments $r_c = -.31$,

$P < .01$; for large departments $r_c = -.38$, $P < .01$.

difficult for supervisors to keep up with the subordinates' activities. Therefore, they can regulate only a few subordinates, and their span of control is curtailed. At the same time, when subordinates have simple jobs the repetitiveness and predictability of the tasks produce more simplicity in work demands for supervisors. In this manner, the subordinates' activities are technological determinants of supervisors' jobs.[22] And these technological demands influence the complexity of administrators' jobs, which in turn affects their spans of control.

CONCLUSIONS

Our efforts have been directed toward an analysis of three determinants of span of control. Data were collected from 186 employees in a small community hospital. Findings suggest that the more complex the tasks subordinates perform the smaller will be administrators' spans of control. The data further indicate that closeness of supervision is unrelated to span of control. Evidently, even though an administrator is keeping a close rein over his subordinates, this does not restrict the number of employees he can oversee, and/or when supervisors control only a few subordinates they will not necessarily do so in a close manner. It is also possible that this lack of association could be due to the fact that administrators who desire to closely regulate their charges might do so, to a large extent, by using rules and regulations. If this is the case, then supervisors could control many subordinates with rules and not have their time consumed by supervisory efforts, and could then control more subordinates.

The final relationship suggested by the data is that the more complex the administrators' tasks the fewer are the subordinates they regulate. These findings raise some rather intriguing questions. For example, if job expansion produces small spans of control, are skill levels, motivation, and efficiency, at the same time, increased? As the spans of control are delimited, are the number of levels of authority increased? If the latter proposition is true, then what happens to communication, coordination, and, finally, motivation and efficiency?[23]

Further relationships between job complexity and factors, such as degree of coordination required for the efficient completion of subordinates' duties, geographical contiguity of employees, workers' competence, and number of supervisory assistants which are assigned to an administrator, should be examined in order that we might establish a systematic framework upon which appropriate levels of span of control might be based in order to maximize organizational efficiency. If such a framework were to be developed, it would be possible to weigh the variables according to their contribution to span of control and thereby to formulate a "span of control index" for adminis-

---

[22] There was little association between supervisors' task complexity and closeness of supervision. (Kendall's T rank-order correlation is $r_c = -.19$, $P < .21$.) Evidently, administrators, if so inclined, can closely supervise their subordinates regardless of the complexity of their tasks.

[23] See Paul R. Lawrence and Jay W. Lorsch, *Differentiation and Integration in Complex Organizations* (Cambridge, Mass.: Division of Research, Harvard Business School, forthcoming).

trative positions within organizations. We would assume that an appropriate matching of given levels of span of control to the situational and technological demands would produce optional levels of efficiency of operations, holding other factors constant.[24]

[24] See Harold Stieglitz, "Optimizing Span of Control," *Management Record*, XXIV (Sept. 1962), 121–29.